# SAT DIGITAL

# READING AND

# WRITING POWER

Unlock Proven Techniques and In-Depth

Practice for SAT Reading and Writing with Over

1025 Questions and 2 Full Tests

MR COMPANY

# SUMMARY

Chapter 1: Understanding the Digital SAT ................................................................ 12

1.1 What is the Digital SAT? ...................................................................................... 12

Overview of the format ............................................................................................. 12

Key Differences from the Paper-Based SAT ............................................................ 14

Digital Interface and Tools ...................................................................................... 16

1.2 How the Adaptive Testing Works ....................................................................... 18

Benefits and Challenges .......................................................................................... 20

1.3 SAT Reading & Writing Sections ........................................................................ 23

Breakdown of the Writing Section .......................................................................... 24

Chapter 2: Proven Techniques for SAT Reading ...................................................... 27

2.1 Mastering Passage Reading ................................................................................. 27

Active Reading Strategies ........................................................................................ 27

Identifying Main Ideas and Themes ....................................................................... 29

2.2 Question Types and How to Approach Them ...................................................... 31

Inference Questions ................................................................................................. 31

Evidence-Based Questions ....................................................................................... 31

Big Picture Questions .............................................................................................. 32

Strategies for Success .............................................................................................. 32

Strategies for "Function" and "Tone" Questions ..................................................... 33

Function Questions ................................................................................................. 34

Tone Questions ........................................................................................................ 35

Integrating Function and Tone ............................................................................... 36

2.3 Time Management Optimizing Time per Question .............................................. 37

Optimizing time per question .................................................................................. 37

Understanding Time Limits ..................................................................................... 37

Categorizing Questions by Difficulty ...................................................................... 37

Skipping and Returning to Questions ..................................................................... 38

Practice the 30-Second Rule .................................................................................... 38

Pacing Yourself Throughout the Section ................................................................. 38

Efficient Reading Strategies .................................................................................... 38

Handling Complex Questions .................................................................................. 39

Using Time Wisely on Writing Questions ............................................................... 39

Practice Under Timed Conditions ........................................................................... 40

When to Skip and Guess ..................................................................................... 40

Understanding the Guessing Strategy ................................................................. 40

Recognizing When to Skip .................................................................................. 40

Using the Process of Elimination ....................................................................... 41

Guessing with Confidence .................................................................................. 42

When Guessing Should Be Your Go-To ............................................................ 42

Returning to Skipped Questions ........................................................................ 42

Practice Makes Perfect ....................................................................................... 43

Chapter 3: Proven Techniques for SAT Writing ............................................... 44

3.1 Mastering Grammar Rules ........................................................................... 44

Key grammar topics tested ................................................................................. 44

Sentence Structure and Parallelism .................................................................... 47

3.2 Effective Editing and Revising ..................................................................... 51

Tips for Clarity and Conciseness ....................................................................... 51

Avoiding Common Writing Errors ..................................................................... 55

3.3 Punctuation and Style .................................................................................. 59

Using Commas, Semicolons, and Colons Correctly .......................................... 59

Commas: Clarifying Ideas and Creating Flow ................................................... 59

Semicolons: Linking Closely Related Ideas ....................................................... 60

Colons: Introducing Information ....................................................................... 61

Common Mistakes to Avoid .............................................................................. 62

Developing a Consistent Style ............................................................................ 63

Understanding SAT Writing Style Expectations ............................................... 63

Clarity and Precision .......................................................................................... 63

Formal Tone ....................................................................................................... 64

Logical Flow and Coherence .............................................................................. 64

Effective Argumentation .................................................................................... 65

Varied Sentence Structure .................................................................................. 66

Conciseness and Avoiding Redundancy ............................................................. 66

Chapter 4: Test-Taking Strategies and Mindset ................................................ 68

4.1 Building Confidence ..................................................................................... 68

Understanding Test Anxiety ............................................................................... 68

Preparation: The Antidote to Anxiety ............................................................... 69

The Power of Positive Self-Talk ......................................................................... 69

Developing a Pre-Test Routine ................................................................................................ 70

Managing Anxiety During the Test ........................................................................................ 70

Post-Test Anxiety Management ............................................................................................. 71

4.2 Strategy for Answer Elimination ..................................................................................... 74

Eliminating Wrong Answers Effectively .............................................................................. 77

4.3 Balancing Speed and Accuracy ....................................................................................... 80

Double-checking work without wasting time ...................................................................... 82

Chapter 5: Practice Reading Exercises .................................................................................. 86

5.1 Comprehension Exercises ................................................................................................ 86

Examples of question types: ................................................................................................. 86

250 Practice Questions ........................................................................................................... 88

Section 1: Narrative Passage Comprehension ..................................................................... 88

Narrative Passage 1: General understanding of plot, character development, and relationships ............. 88

Narrative Passage 2: Key themes and implicit meanings .................................................... 90

Narrative Passage 3: Interpretation of tone, mood, and author's voice ............................. 92

Narrative Passage 4: Analysis of setting and historical context ........................................ 95

Section 2: Social Science Passage Comprehension ............................................................. 97

Social Science Passage 1: Identifying Main Ideas and Details ........................................... 97

Social Science Passage 2: Evaluating Evidence and Argumentation .................................. 99

Social Science Passage 3: Synthesizing Information from Multiple Sources ................... 101

Social Science Passage 4: Interpretation of Data and Graphs .......................................... 103

Section 3: Natural Science Passage Comprehension ......................................................... 106

Natural Science Passage 1: Understanding Scientific Concepts and Research Findings ............ 106

Natural Science Passage 2: Assessing Scientific Hypotheses and Conclusions ............... 108

Natural Science Passage 3: Interpreting Technical Terms and Complex Data ................ 110

Natural Science Passage 4: Relationship Between Text and Graphs or Tables ................ 112

Section 4: Historical Documents Passage Comprehension ............................................... 115

Historical Document 1: Analysis of Political Speeches or Official Statements ................ 115

Historical Document 2: Comparison of Two Historical Texts .......................................... 118

Historical Document 3: Understanding Historical Nuances and Author Perspectives ............ 121

Historical Document 4: Critical Analysis and Evaluation of Historical Arguments ............ 123

Variety of Topics: Humanities, Science, History ............................................................... 126

Passage 1: Humanities – Exploration of Artistic Movements ........................................... 126

Passage 2: Science – The Ethical Implications of Gene Editing ....................................... 126

Passage 3: History – The Formation of the United Nations ................................................ 127

Passage 4: Philosophy – The Debate Between Free Will and Determinism .......................... 127

Passage 5: Environmental Science – Climate Change and Global Policy ............................ 128

5.2: Inference and Analysis Exercises ............................................................................... 128

    Introduction ................................................................................................................ 128

Practice Exercises: 125 Questions Divided into Groups of 15-20 Questions ..................... 129

Section 1: Direct Logical Inferences ................................................................................. 129

Section 2: Context-Based Inferences ................................................................................ 134

Section 3: Inferences About Author's Opinions and Attitudes ......................................... 138

Section 4: Inferences on Missing or Implied Details ........................................................ 143

Section 5: Inferences on the Interrelation of Concepts ..................................................... 147

Section 6: Inferences on Tone and Language ................................................................... 150

Section 7: Multiple Inferences from Multiple Sources ...................................................... 154

Conclusion Practice: Managing Inference Questions in the SAT ...................................... 159

5.3 Tone and Perspective Interpretation ........................................................................... 159

    Introduction ................................................................................................................ 159

Practice Exercises: 75 Questions Divided into Groups of 15-20 Questions ....................... 160

Section 1: Identifying Author's Tone ................................................................................ 160

Section 2: Recognizing Shifts in Tone .............................................................................. 164

Section 3: Author's Perspective and Bias ......................................................................... 167

Section 4: Comparing Perspectives in Two Texts ............................................................. 170

Section 5: Analyzing Author's Intent and Purpose ........................................................... 174

Conclusion Practice: Tone and Perspective Interpretation ............................................... 176

5.4 Context Meaning Questions ...................................................................................... 176

    Introduction ................................................................................................................ 176

Practice Exercises: 50 Questions Divided into Groups of 10-15 Questions ....................... 177

Section 1: Understanding Word Meaning Through Context .............................................. 177

Section 2: Identifying the Function of Words in Sentences ............................................... 179

Section 3: Using Surrounding Sentences to Clarify Meaning ........................................... 180

Section 4: Interpreting Figurative Language in Context .................................................... 182

Section 5: Recognizing Multiple Meanings of Words ....................................................... 184

Conclusion Practice ........................................................................................................ 185

Chapter 6: Practice Writing Exercises .............................................................................. 187

6.1 Sentence Correction and Grammar ............................................................................ 187

Practice Exercises: 225 Questions Divided into Groups of 15-25 Questions.................................187

Section 1: Sentence Structure and Syntax................................................................................187

    Practice Questions..................................................................................................................187

Section 2: Verb Tense and Agreement.....................................................................................190

Section 3: Pronouns and Antecedents......................................................................................193

Section 4: Punctuation and Capitalization................................................................................197

Section 5: Parallelism..............................................................................................................200

Section 6: Modifiers and Word Placement................................................................................203

Section 7: Word Choice and Precision.....................................................................................206

Section 8: Subject-Verb Agreement and Consistency.................................................................209

Section 9: Redundancy and Wordiness.....................................................................................212

Section 10: Idiomatic Expressions and Prepositions..................................................................215

Section 11: Combining Sentences............................................................................................218

Section 12: Consistency in Tense and Tone..............................................................................221

Conclusion Practice:...............................................................................................................223

6.2 Practice Exercises: 125 Questions Divided into Groups of 20-25 Questions...........................224

Section 1: Improving Sentence Clarity.....................................................................................224

Section 2: Logical Flow Between Sentences...............................................................................228

Section 3: Paragraph Coherence..............................................................................................231

Section 4: Eliminating Redundant or Irrelevant Information.......................................................234

Section 5: Correcting Ambiguous Pronouns and References.......................................................238

Section 6: Combining Ideas for Clarity....................................................................................241

Section 7: Enhancing Sentence Variety for Better Flo................................................................245

Section 8: Maintaining Consistent Tone and Style....................................................................249

Conclusion Practice:...............................................................................................................253

6.3 Text Revision Questions.....................................................................................................253

    Introduction..........................................................................................................................253

Practice Exercises: 100 Questions Divided into Groups of 10-20 Questions.................................254

Section 1: Clarifying Ambiguous Sentences..............................................................................254

Section 2: Enhancing Logical Flow Between Sentences..............................................................258

Section 3: Combining and Restructuring Sentences for Coherence..............................................261

Section 4: Eliminating Redundancies and Wordiness.................................................................263

Section 5: Improving Paragraph Coherence..............................................................................266

Section 6: Correcting Punctuation and Grammar Errors............................................................269

Section 7: Replacing Vague Words with Specific Language ........................................ 271

Conclusion Practice ........................................................................................ 273

Chapter 7: Full-Length Practice Tests ................................................................ 275

7.1 Two Full-Length Practice Tests with Detailed Solutions ................................ 275

Test 1: 108 Questions ..................................................................................... 275

Narrative Passage: 12 Questions ...................................................................... 276

Social Science Passage: 14 Questions ............................................................... 277

Natural Science Passage: 14 Questions ............................................................. 279

Historical Document Passage: 14 Questions ...................................................... 281

Section 2: Writing and Language ...................................................................... 283

Grammar and Sentence Structure (15 Questions) ............................................... 284

Section: Punctuation and Capitalization (15 Questions) ...................................... 286

Section: Logical Flow and Coherence (12 Questions) .......................................... 288

Section: Sentence Clarity and Precision (12 Questions) ....................................... 290

Test 2: 108 Questions ..................................................................................... 293

Section 1: Reading Comprehension ................................................................... 293

Narrative Passage (12 Questions) ..................................................................... 293

Social Science Passage (14 Questions) .............................................................. 295

Natural Science Passage (14 Questions) ............................................................ 298

Historical Document Passage (14 Questions) ..................................................... 301

Section 2: Writing and Language ...................................................................... 304

Grammar and Sentence Structure (15 Questions) ............................................... 304

Punctuation and Capitalization (15 Questions) .................................................. 306

Logical Flow and Coherence (12 Questions) ...................................................... 308

Sentence Clarity and Precision (12 Questions) ................................................... 310

Time Management Instructions ........................................................................ 313

TEST 1 SOLUTIONS ...................................................................................... 314

3. Detailed Solutions with Explanations for Every Answer ................................. 314

Overview ...................................................................................................... 314

Narrative Passage Solutions ............................................................................ 315

Social Science Passage Solutions ..................................................................... 318

Natural Science Passage Solutions ................................................................... 322

Historical Document Passage Solutions ............................................................ 326

Section 2: Writing and Language ...................................................................... 330

Grammar and Sentence Structure Solutions.................................................................330

Punctuation and Capitalization Solutions .................................................................334

Logical Flow and Coherence.......................................................................................336

Sentence Clarity and Precision Solutions ..................................................................338

Test 2 Solutions:.............................................................................................................339

Reading Comprehension (Narrative Passage) Solutions ...........................................339

Social Science Passage Solutions ...............................................................................341

Natural Science Passage Solutions ............................................................................343

Historical Document Passage Solutions.....................................................................345

Writing and Language ................................................................................................347

Grammar and Sentence Structure Solutions..............................................................347

Logical Flow and Coherence Solutions .....................................................................349

Sentence Clarity and Precision Solutions ..................................................................351

Development Approach for Test Sections ...................................................................353

Question Development ...........................................................................................353

Detailed Solutions..................................................................................................353

Test Experience Simulation ...................................................................................353

Chapter 8: Answer Keys and Explanations for All Exercises .........................................354

Section 1: Narrative Passage Comprehension ...........................................................354

Narrative Passage 1: General understanding of plot, character development, and relationships ............354

Narrative Passage 2: Key Themes and Implicit Meanings.........................................355

Narrative Passage 3: Interpretation of Tone, Mood, and Author's Voice ..................357

Narrative Passage 4: Analysis of Setting and Historical Context..............................359

Section 2: Social Science Passage Comprehension ...................................................361

Social Science Passage 1: Identifying Main Ideas and Details.................................361

Social Science Passage 2: Evaluating Evidence and Argumentation.........................363

Social Science Passage 3: Synthesizing Information from Multiple Sources .............365

Social Science Passage 4: Interpretation of Data and Graphs...................................367

Section 3: Natural Science Passage Comprehension .................................................369

Natural Science Passage 1: Understanding Scientific Concepts and Research Findings...........................369

Natural Science Passage 2: Assessing Scientific Hypotheses and Conclusions .........371

Natural Science Passage 3: Interpreting Technical Terms and Complex Data ..........373

Natural Science Passage 4: Relationship Between Text and Graphs or Tables...........375

Section 4: Historical Documents Passage Comprehension.........................................377

Historical Document 1: Analysis of Political Speeches or Official Statements ............................ 377

Historical Document 2: Comparison of Two Historical Texts ............................................. 379

Historical Document 3: Understanding Historical Nuances and Author Perspectives ......................... 382

Historical Document 4: Critical Analysis and Evaluation of Historical Arguments ....................... 384

Variety of Topics: Humanities, Science, History ........................................................ 386

Passage 1: Humanities – Exploration of Artistic Movements .............................................. 386

Passage 2: Science – The Ethical Implications of Gene Editing .......................................... 386

Passage 3: History – The Formation of the United Nations .............................................. 387

Passage 4: Philosophy – The Debate Between Free Will and Determinism ................................... 387

Passage 5: Environmental Science – Climate Change and Global Policy .................................... 388

Inference and Analysis Exercises ....................................................................... 389

Section 1: Direct Logical Inferences ................................................................... 389

Section 2: Context-Based Inferences .................................................................... 391

Section 3: Inferences About Author's Opinions and Attitudes ............................................ 394

Section 4: Inferences on Missing or Implied Details .................................................... 396

Section 5: Inferences on the Interrelation of Concepts ................................................. 398

Section 6: Inferences on Tone and Language ............................................................. 400

Section 7: Multiple Inferences from Multiple Sources ................................................... 402

Tone and Perspective Interpretation .................................................................... 404

Section 1: Identifying Author's Tone ................................................................... 404

Section 2: Recognizing Shifts in Tone .................................................................. 406

Section 3: Author's Perspective and Bias ............................................................... 408

Section 4: Comparing Perspectives in Two Texts ......................................................... 410

Section 5: Analyzing Author's Intent and Purpose ....................................................... 412

Context Meaning Questions .............................................................................. 413

Section 1: Understanding Word Meaning Through Context ................................................... 413

Section 2: Identifying the Function of Words in Sentences .............................................. 415

Section 3: Using Surrounding Sentences to Clarify Meaning .............................................. 416

Section 4: Interpreting Figurative Language in Context ................................................. 417

Section 5: Recognizing Multiple Meanings of Words ...................................................... 418

Sentence Correction and Grammar ........................................................................ 419

Section 1: Sentence Structure and Syntax ............................................................... 419

Section 2: Verb Tense and Agreement .................................................................... 421

Section 3: Pronouns and Antecedents .................................................................... 423

Section 4: Punctuation and Capitalization...................................................................425

Section 5: Parallelism...................................................................................................426

Section 6: Modifiers and Word Placement..................................................................429

Section 7: Word Choice and Precision.........................................................................431

Section 8: Subject-Verb Agreement and Consistency.................................................433

Section 9: Redundancy and Wordiness........................................................................435

Section 10: Idiomatic Expressions and Prepositions..................................................437

Section 11: Combining Sentences................................................................................439

Section 12: Consistency in Tense and Tone................................................................441

Section 1: Improving Sentence Clarity........................................................................442

Section 2: Logical Flow Between Sentences................................................................444

Section 3: Paragraph Coherence..................................................................................445

Section 4: Eliminating Redundant or Irrelevant Information.....................................447

Section 5: Correcting Ambiguous Pronouns and References.....................................448

Section 6: Combining Ideas for Clarity.......................................................................449

Section 7: Enhancing Sentence Variety for Better Flow.............................................451

Section 8: Maintaining Consistent Tone and Style.....................................................454

Section 1: Clarifying Ambiguous Sentences................................................................456

Section 2: Enhancing Logical Flow Between Sentences.............................................458

Section 3: Combining and Restructuring Sentences for Coherence..........................460

Section 4: Eliminating Redundancies and Wordiness.................................................462

Section 5: Improving Paragraph Coherence................................................................463

Section 6: Correcting Punctuation and Grammar Errors...........................................465

Section 7: Replacing Vague Words with Specific Language........................................466

Time Management Instructions:..................................................................................467

# CHAPTER 1: UNDERSTANDING THE DIGITAL SAT

## 1.1 What is the Digital SAT?

### Overview of the format

The Digital SAT marks a significant shift from the traditional paper-based exam, reflecting a broader trend toward digitization in education. This new format has been carefully designed to offer a more streamlined and efficient testing experience, reducing logistical challenges and offering flexibility. With this change, it's crucial for students to understand not only how the test works but also how to prepare for it effectively, as it differs from the familiar pen-and-paper method many students are accustomed to.

The Digital SAT is administered entirely on a computer or tablet, making it accessible via any device approved by the testing organization. This means students can take the test in a designated testing center or, in certain circumstances, at home, under monitored conditions. The interface is designed to be user-friendly, with features such as a built-in calculator, note-taking tools, and easy navigation between questions, ensuring that students can focus on the content rather than the logistics of the test itself.

One of the most important aspects of the Digital SAT is its adaptive nature. The exam is divided into two modules per section—one for Reading and Writing and another for Math. In each module, the questions adapt to the student's performance. For example, if a student performs well in the first set of questions, the subsequent questions will increase in difficulty. Conversely, if a student struggles, the difficulty level will adjust downward to better match their performance level. This adaptability allows for a more personalized assessment of each student's abilities, as it tailors the test to their strengths and weaknesses.

The scoring system for the Digital SAT remains consistent with the traditional format. Scores are still measured on a scale from 400 to 1600, combining the results from the Reading and Writing section (scored from 200 to 800) and the Math section (also scored from 200 to 800). However, the adaptive format provides a more accurate reflection of the student's proficiency across these areas by adjusting the difficulty of the questions in real time.

One of the key advantages of the Digital SAT is the streamlined process for delivering results. Since the exam is administered electronically, the scoring is completed more quickly, with results typically delivered within days rather than weeks. This rapid turnaround allows students to review their performance and make timely decisions about college applications, scholarship opportunities, or retaking the test if necessary.

The test's content remains focused on core academic skills. The Reading and Writing section combines comprehension and grammar, requiring students to analyze texts, identify the main ideas, and apply grammatical rules in context. Meanwhile, the Math section covers algebra, problem-solving, data analysis, and advanced math topics such as geometry and trigonometry. Despite the shift to a digital platform, the types of questions students will encounter are familiar and consistent with the traditional SAT format. This continuity ensures that the test remains a rigorous and reliable measure of college readiness.

With the Digital SAT, the College Board has also implemented several features to enhance accessibility. Students with disabilities can take advantage of accommodations such as extended time, screen readers, and magnification tools, all integrated seamlessly into the digital platform. This focus on accessibility aims to create a more inclusive testing environment, allowing all students to demonstrate their abilities without the limitations posed by traditional paper-based testing.

The digital platform also includes tools to help manage time during the test. A visible timer in the corner of the screen helps students keep track of how much time they have left for each section. There is also the option to flag questions and return to them later, which can be particularly useful in managing difficult or time-consuming questions. This allows students to pace themselves more effectively and ensures they can focus on maximizing their score potential.

One potential concern for students unfamiliar with digital testing is the possibility of technical difficulties. To mitigate this, the College Board has put systems in place to ensure that any technical issues are addressed quickly. For instance, the test automatically saves answers in real-time, so even if a student's device experiences a power failure or loss of internet connection, their progress is not lost. Test administrators are also trained to assist with troubleshooting any technical problems that may arise during the exam.

Another important feature of the Digital SAT is the built-in calculator. For the Math section, students can access an on-screen calculator for the entire duration of the test, rather than just a portion of it. This is a significant shift from the traditional SAT, where calculator usage was restricted to specific sections. The calculator feature makes the test more accessible for students who may feel less confident with mental math or complex calculations.

In addition to these practical changes, the Digital SAT also offers benefits in terms of environmental sustainability. The transition to a digital format reduces the need for paper, printing, and physical shipping of test materials, making the test more environmentally friendly. This shift aligns with broader trends in education toward more sustainable practices, which is increasingly important to both institutions and students alike.

Understanding the new format of the Digital SAT is essential for success. The transition to digital testing has streamlined many aspects of the exam, offering a more efficient and adaptable way to assess students' readiness for college. However, this shift also brings new challenges, and it is crucial for students to familiarize themselves with the format, the tools available, and the adaptive nature of the test to fully take advantage of the benefits the digital platform offers.

## Key Differences from the Paper-Based SAT

The transition from the traditional paper-based SAT to the Digital SAT represents a significant change in how the exam is structured and administered. These differences not only affect the format of the test but also impact how students prepare and approach each section. Understanding these key distinctions is essential for students aiming to maximize their performance on the Digital SAT.

One of the most noticeable differences between the two formats is the method of delivery. The paper-based SAT required students to fill in answer bubbles on a physical answer sheet using a pencil. In contrast, the Digital SAT is entirely computer-based, meaning students complete the exam on an electronic device. This shift eliminates the possibility of errors like incomplete bubble filling or stray marks, which could negatively affect a student's score on the paper version. Instead, students interact with an intuitive interface designed to make navigation between questions easy and seamless. This is a major change, as students no longer have to flip back and forth through paper pages to review previous questions.

The adaptive nature of the Digital SAT is another significant departure from the static paper-based exam. The paper-based SAT presented all students with the same set of questions, regardless of their ability level. The Digital SAT, however, uses a multistage adaptive approach, meaning that the difficulty of the questions presented in each module adjusts based on the student's performance. This adaptation happens after the first set of questions in each section, allowing the second module to better align with the student's proficiency. For high-performing students, this can result in more challenging questions, while students who struggle with the initial module will see questions better suited to their skill level.

Timing on the Digital SAT also presents a key difference. While the overall time allocated for each section remains similar, the Digital SAT provides students with an on-screen timer that makes it easier to track how much time is left in each section. This replaces the need for frequent manual time checks during the paper-based test. Students can also flag questions they want to return to later, a feature that was present in the paper format but now enhanced by the digital system's fluid navigation.

The way students interact with the Math section has also been revised in the digital format. One of the most notable changes is that the digital version provides a built-in on-screen calculator for use throughout the entire Math section. This is a major shift from the paper-based test, where calculator use was limited to only one part of the Math section. This change means students must now balance mental calculations with calculator use throughout the section, which may influence how they approach certain types of problems.

The Reading and Writing section of the Digital SAT has also undergone structural changes. In the paper-based SAT, the Reading and Writing sections were split into two distinct parts. In the Digital SAT, these sections are combined into a single Reading and Writing section, with a variety of question types integrated throughout. The questions in this section are shorter and often more focused, with many being centered around single sentences or paragraphs rather than lengthy passages. This makes the test feel less like an endurance test of reading large blocks of text and more of an analytical challenge, focusing on specific comprehension and grammar skills.

Scoring between the paper-based and Digital SAT remains on the same 400-1600 scale, but the adaptive nature of the Digital SAT results in a more tailored assessment of a student's abilities. While both formats aim to evaluate the same core skills in math, reading, and writing, the digital version's adaptive questioning ensures that students are tested at the appropriate level of difficulty based on their performance in real-time, rather than being faced with the same standardized questions as everyone else. This change can result in a more accurate reflection of a student's knowledge and abilities.

The test-day experience has also changed significantly. With the paper-based SAT, students were required to bring their own pencils, calculators, and identification to the testing center. The Digital SAT, however, is taken on an electronic device provided by the test center, or in some cases, students may use their own approved devices. This eliminates the need to carry physical materials and reduces the logistical challenges associated with administering the test. Additionally, because the test is digital, it can be offered more frequently and in a greater variety of locations, providing students with more flexibility in scheduling their exams.

One of the major advantages of the Digital SAT is the quicker score reporting. While the paper-based SAT required several weeks for scores to be processed and reported, the digital version allows for faster processing of results, often within days. This can be especially beneficial for students applying to colleges with tight application deadlines, as they can receive their scores more quickly and make informed decisions about retaking the test if necessary.

Another key difference is how students practice for the test. While both formats allow for practice tests and preparation materials, the Digital SAT has introduced new online tools and resources that mirror the actual test environment more closely than traditional paper-based practice exams. These digital resources give students a more realistic practice experience, helping them become familiar with the interface, the adaptive question style, and the digital tools they will use during the actual test. These tools include on-screen calculators, note-taking features, and a digital timer—all of which are available during the real exam.

For students with disabilities, the Digital SAT offers enhanced accommodations that are seamlessly integrated into the digital platform. Features such as screen readers, magnification tools, and extended time are easier to implement and manage in the digital format compared to the paper-based test. These accommodations are designed to create a more inclusive testing environment, ensuring that all students have the opportunity to perform to the best of their abilities.

The environmental impact of the Digital SAT is another notable shift. By eliminating the need for paper, ink, and physical transportation of testing materials, the digital format is a more sustainable option. This move aligns with broader societal goals of reducing waste and conserving resources. For institutions and students who are increasingly conscious of environmental issues, this shift may be viewed as a positive development.

Overall, the Digital SAT represents a modernized approach to standardized testing. The move from paper to digital not only changes the mechanics of how students interact with the test but also provides a more personalized and efficient way to measure academic readiness. By embracing these key differences, students can approach the Digital SAT with confidence, knowing that they are being tested in a format designed to be more reflective of their abilities and more attuned to the demands of a digital world.

## Digital Interface and Tools

The digital interface of the SAT is designed to streamline the test-taking experience, offering a user-friendly platform that integrates various tools to assist students as they navigate through the exam. Understanding how these digital tools work and how to use them efficiently is key to maximizing performance.

The main component of the digital interface is the layout of the exam screen. The screen is divided into two primary sections: the question display on one side and the passage or problem (depending on the section) on the other. This layout is specifically designed to minimize distractions and allow students to focus on the task at hand. Questions are presented clearly, and the passages or math problems are displayed in a separate, easy-to-read column. This prevents the need for excessive scrolling or switching between pages, a feature that was more cumbersome in the paper-based version.

One of the most useful features of the digital interface is the flagging tool. This allows students to mark questions they wish to revisit later. In a timed exam like the SAT, this is particularly helpful for managing time effectively. If a student encounters a difficult question, they can flag it and move on, ensuring they don't waste valuable time. Once they've completed the section, they can easily return to the flagged questions with a simple click, making the test navigation more efficient and less stressful.

The on-screen calculator is another integral tool of the digital SAT. Available for the entire Math section, this calculator can be accessed at any time with just a click. The built-in calculator ensures students have immediate access to calculations without needing to juggle a physical calculator. It provides the basic functions needed for most SAT math problems, as well as more advanced options like square roots and exponents. Familiarity with this calculator before test day is essential, as it operates slightly differently from a standard calculator. Students can practice using this tool in official SAT practice exams to ensure they are comfortable with its functions.

Alongside the calculator, the digital notepad is another important tool that allows students to take notes directly on the screen during the test. This can be used for working through math problems or jotting down important points while reading passages. The notepad can be particularly useful in complex problem-solving scenarios where writing out steps can help clarify thoughts and avoid mistakes. Unlike paper notes, the digital notepad ensures that all notes are in one place and easily accessible throughout the test, eliminating the need for scratch paper.

The annotation tool is another feature designed to enhance the reading and writing experience. In the Reading and Writing sections, students can highlight important portions of the text directly in the passage. This can be useful for marking key details, identifying areas of confusion, or emphasizing information that is directly tied to the questions. Highlighting sections can help students keep track of important elements in longer passages, reducing the need to re-read large portions of text and helping focus attention on specific areas relevant to the questions. This tool is particularly valuable in identifying shifts in tone or structure, which are commonly tested in the Writing section.

The ability to cross out answer choices directly on the screen is another feature that enhances efficiency during the test. When faced with multiple-choice questions, students can eliminate options they know are incorrect by digitally crossing them out. This helps narrow down the choices and reduces confusion, allowing students to focus on the most likely answers. This process mimics the natural test-taking strategy used in the paper-based exam, but the digital format makes it even quicker and cleaner, with a simple click to remove wrong answers from view.

The on-screen timer is an essential part of the digital interface. It keeps track of the time remaining for each section and is constantly visible, allowing students to pace themselves throughout the exam. Unlike in the paper-based version, where students had to rely on wall clocks or personal watches, the digital timer ensures that everyone has equal access to a precise countdown. If desired, students can hide the timer to reduce anxiety and then check it periodically. This flexibility helps test-takers manage their time more effectively, making it easier to allocate time based on question difficulty and section length.

For students with specific accommodations, such as extended time or screen readers, the digital SAT provides customizable features to ensure that these accommodations are seamlessly integrated. The interface can be adjusted to meet individual needs, ensuring that all students have a fair testing environment that aligns with their specific requirements. These features are built into the test platform, making the administration of accommodations more efficient and standardized across all test centers.

The review screen is another valuable aspect of the digital interface. At the end of each section, students are presented with a summary screen that shows all the questions in the section. This screen highlights any questions that were left unanswered or flagged for review, ensuring that students have one last opportunity to check their work before moving on to the next section. This review process is simplified compared to the paper-based test, where students had to flip through pages manually. The digital format ensures that no question is overlooked, and students can quickly navigate back to any flagged or unanswered question with just a click.

How to use the interface and the available tools effectively is key to navigating the Digital SAT smoothly.

## 1.2 How the Adaptive Testing Works

Adaptive testing is one of the key features of the digital SAT, offering a tailored approach to assessing students' abilities. Unlike the traditional paper-based SAT, where all students receive the same set of questions, adaptive testing adjusts the difficulty level of questions based on the student's performance in real-time. This format is designed to provide a more precise measure of a student's skills while enhancing the efficiency of the testing process.

The digital SAT is structured in two modules for each section—Reading and Writing, and Math. When students begin the first module of a section, they receive a set of questions that vary in difficulty, covering a broad range of topics. The student's performance in the first module directly influences the difficulty level of the second module. If a student performs well in the first set, the second module will present more challenging questions. Conversely, if the performance in the first module is lower, the second module will include easier questions. This dynamic adjustment helps to gauge the student's ability more accurately than a fixed set of questions could.

Each module consists of a combination of easy, medium, and difficult questions. The adaptive nature of the test ensures that students are challenged but not overwhelmed. This design allows for a more personalized testing experience. It also helps alleviate test anxiety by preventing students from facing an entire section filled with questions that are too difficult for their skill level. The adaptive model offers a more balanced distribution of question difficulties, reducing the chances of a student being stuck on too many hard questions in a row.

In adaptive testing, the scoring algorithm is designed to consider both the number of correct answers and the difficulty level of the questions answered. Students who answer more difficult questions correctly will receive a higher score than those who answer easier questions correctly, even if the total number of correct answers is the same. This means that simply getting more questions right isn't always the key to a high score—students must also be able to tackle higher-level problems when presented with them.

A key advantage of adaptive testing is its ability to streamline the exam process. By focusing on questions that are most appropriate for each student's ability level, the test can more efficiently assess the full range of skills in less time. This eliminates the need for excessive repetition of questions that are too easy or too hard for the individual student. For instance, students who demonstrate high proficiency in the first module will not be required to answer numerous basic questions that they are likely to get right anyway. Instead, they can move on to more complex material, making better use of their time.

Adaptive testing also provides a more equitable testing environment. In traditional tests, some students may feel discouraged when faced with a block of particularly challenging questions, leading to a decrease in confidence and performance. With adaptive testing, students are less likely to experience prolonged difficulty, as the test adjusts to offer a balanced range of questions. This can help maintain focus and motivation throughout the exam, as students are constantly presented with questions that match their ability level.

The feedback loop created by adaptive testing is another innovative aspect of the digital SAT. Since the difficulty of the second module depends on the performance in the first, students receive indirect feedback on how well they are doing. If the second module feels significantly harder, this may indicate strong performance in the first module. While this feedback is not explicitly communicated, it can give students a sense of their progress during the exam. However, it's important to note that the perceived difficulty of the questions doesn't always perfectly correlate with actual performance, as different students may find different types of questions easier or harder based on their individual strengths.

Adaptive testing also addresses the issue of "test fatigue," where students grow tired and lose focus over the course of a long, standardized test. By shortening the overall number of questions and focusing on relevant content, adaptive testing can reduce the cognitive load on students, helping them maintain focus and perform better throughout the exam. This efficiency can lead to more accurate scores by ensuring that students are consistently engaged and working at their optimal capacity.

The adaptive structure also means that every student's test is unique. While the content domains and question types are standardized, the specific questions presented will vary from student to student based on their performance. This reduces the likelihood of cheating, as no two students will face exactly the same test.

Additionally, it allows for a more personalized assessment of each student's abilities, as the test can hone in on their specific strengths and weaknesses.

However, the adaptive model requires careful management of time. Since students cannot return to previous sections once they have moved on, they must ensure they complete each module within the allotted time frame. This can be challenging for students who are used to the paper-based format, where they could skip and return to questions freely. In the digital adaptive SAT, each question should be approached with care, as rushing through easier questions to save time for harder ones may not be as effective. The adaptive nature of the test means that each question contributes to determining the difficulty of subsequent questions, so maintaining a steady pace is crucial.

To prepare for adaptive testing, students should practice managing their time effectively and become familiar with the types of questions that typically appear in both the easier and harder modules. It's important to approach each question with focus, knowing that the outcome will influence the direction of the test. Practicing under timed conditions with adaptive simulations can help students build the stamina and strategy needed to excel in this new format.

## Benefits and Challenges

The shift to the digital SAT introduces a range of benefits for test-takers, offering advantages in terms of convenience, adaptability, and efficiency. However, it also presents new challenges that require students to adjust their preparation and testing strategies. Understanding both the benefits and the challenges will equip students to maximize their performance on the exam.

One of the primary benefits of the digital SAT is the flexibility it offers. Students can now take the test on a laptop or tablet, either provided by the testing center or their own device. This flexibility makes the testing experience more accessible, as students are not bound to traditional testing environments with paper and pencil. Many students are already comfortable using digital devices for schoolwork, so the familiarity of the digital interface can help reduce test-day anxiety and increase confidence. The interface is intuitive, allowing students to navigate easily between questions and use digital tools like a built-in calculator, highlighter, and note-taking feature, which can streamline the testing process.

Another benefit is the adaptive nature of the test, which allows the SAT to more accurately assess a student's abilities. Adaptive testing tailors the questions to the individual, offering a more personalized experience. Students who perform well in the first module are given more challenging questions in the second module, and those who struggle are given easier questions. This ensures that students are neither overwhelmed nor under-challenged throughout the test. As a result, the test is shorter in length compared to the paper-based version, allowing students to complete it more quickly while still providing accurate results. This reduction in test time can help alleviate fatigue, making it easier for students to maintain focus and perform at their best for the duration of the exam.

The streamlined format of the digital SAT also reduces the logistical complications associated with traditional testing. Students no longer need to deal with the physical handling of test booklets, answer sheets, or erasures, which could cause distractions during the paper-based test. The automatic saving of answers in the digital version eliminates the fear of losing work due to human error. Additionally, the countdown timer and built-in breaks help students manage their time more effectively, ensuring they can pace themselves appropriately throughout the test.

Scoring on the digital SAT is faster and more efficient. Since the test is completed and submitted electronically, scores are typically available much sooner than they would be for a paper-based exam. This quicker turnaround time allows students to make more informed decisions about their college applications, including whether to retake the test if necessary. The digital format also improves accuracy in scoring by reducing the likelihood of human error during the grading process.

Despite these significant benefits, the digital SAT also presents challenges. One of the most notable is the adjustment required for students who are used to the paper-based format. Transitioning to a screen-based test can be difficult for students who are not accustomed to reading and answering questions on a digital device for extended periods. Eye strain and fatigue from prolonged screen exposure can affect concentration and performance. Students need to develop stamina for working on a screen and ensure they are comfortable with the digital tools available, such as using the on-screen calculator or highlighting passages. Practicing with digital SAT simulations can help students acclimate to this new format and reduce potential discomfort on test day.

Another challenge is the adaptive nature of the test itself. While the adaptive format offers a more tailored experience, it can also introduce uncertainty. Students may find it difficult to gauge their performance because the difficulty of the questions adjusts based on their previous answers. If a student encounters a particularly challenging question, they might assume they are performing poorly, even if they are doing well overall. This can lead to stress and second-guessing, which may affect their focus. It is important for students to remain calm and approach each question independently, understanding that the adaptive format is designed to adjust based on their individual performance.

Technical issues can also pose challenges during the digital SAT. While most testing centers are well-equipped to handle the technical demands of the exam, there is always the possibility of unexpected issues, such as device malfunctions, connectivity problems, or software glitches. These disruptions can cause anxiety and affect performance if not handled promptly. Students should familiarize themselves with the procedures for reporting technical problems during the test and trust that proctors are trained to resolve such issues quickly. In the case of testing from home or other remote locations, it is crucial to ensure that devices meet the SAT's technical requirements and that internet connections are stable to avoid any last-minute complications.

Another consideration is the potential disadvantage for students who have limited access to technology. While the digital SAT aims to improve accessibility, students from underserved communities may not have the same level of access to computers or high-speed internet for practice. This digital divide could impact their familiarity with the format and tools, potentially affecting their performance. To address this, students should seek out free resources or work with schools and community programs that provide access to digital practice tests and technology training. It is also important for testing organizations to ensure that accommodations are available for students who may need additional support in accessing the digital SAT.

The lack of a physical test booklet is another challenge for students who rely on annotating questions and passages. While the digital SAT offers tools like an on-screen highlighter and note-taking functions, some students may find these features less intuitive than physically marking up a paper test. The inability to flip through pages quickly can also be disorienting for students who are used to reviewing previous sections of the test at their own pace. To overcome this, students should practice using the digital tools and develop strategies to organize their thoughts effectively within the constraints of the digital interface.

Lastly, managing time effectively on the digital SAT requires a different approach compared to the paper-based test. The inability to skip questions and return to them later can be a significant challenge for students who rely on this strategy. In the digital SAT, once a student completes a module, they cannot revisit it, which means that careful time management within each module is essential. Students must become accustomed to working steadily through each question without the option to flag and revisit difficult ones. This shift in strategy may require practice and discipline to ensure that students can pace themselves appropriately and avoid spending too much time on any single question.

By acknowledging both the benefits and challenges of the digital SAT, students can prepare more effectively and adjust their strategies to succeed in this new format. Each benefit presents opportunities for improved performance, while each challenge requires thoughtful planning and practice to overcome.

## 1.3 SAT Reading & Writing Sections

## Breakdown of the Reading Section

The Reading section of the Digital SAT is designed to assess a student's ability to comprehend, analyze, and interpret a range of written materials. It includes a variety of passages that cover different subjects such as literature, social sciences, history, and natural sciences. Each passage presents unique challenges, requiring students to not only understand what is explicitly stated but also to infer deeper meanings, evaluate arguments, and draw conclusions based on context.

In the Reading section, students are presented with passages followed by multiple-choice questions that focus on the central idea, purpose, and details within the text. These questions are structured to evaluate various reading skills, from basic comprehension to more advanced critical thinking. Students must be able to identify themes, the tone of the passage, the author's perspective, and the way ideas are structured. Key components of the passage may include analyzing relationships between characters or ideas, identifying the purpose of certain words or phrases, and recognizing how the passage's structure influences its meaning.

There is a consistent emphasis on evidence-based reading. Several questions will ask students to identify specific lines in the text that support their answers to other questions. This encourages the development of skills in locating and understanding the relevant parts of a passage to substantiate conclusions. Evidence questions also assess the student's ability to link their interpretation of the text with textual evidence, ensuring a deeper engagement with the material.

The vocabulary in context plays a vital role in the Reading section. Unlike traditional vocabulary tests, the SAT does not focus on obscure words, but rather common words that may have different meanings based on their context. Students are tested on their ability to determine the meaning of a word or phrase by understanding how it is used in the passage. This requires strong inferential skills and an ability to interpret how language shapes the meaning of the text.

Another critical component of the Reading section is understanding the relationships between ideas within a passage. This includes comparing and contrasting points of view, identifying cause and effect, and analyzing how different parts of the text relate to each other. Students may encounter questions that require them to evaluate the logical flow of the passage or to discern the connections between the introduction, body, and conclusion.

Historical documents and social science texts are often featured in the Reading section. These passages may include excerpts from U.S. founding documents, speeches, or discussions on key political and social issues.

Understanding these texts requires familiarity with the broader historical and social context, as well as an ability to grasp complex arguments about governance, rights, and societal values.

Literature passages generally focus on prose from various time periods and genres. These texts may involve narrative storytelling, character development, or thematic exploration, and they often require students to engage with emotional subtexts, figurative language, and character motivations. Unlike more straightforward factual texts, literature requires a blend of analytical and empathetic reading skills to fully understand the author's message.

The natural sciences passages present students with scientific concepts and research findings. Although no prior scientific knowledge is required, students must be adept at interpreting data, understanding experimental setups, and analyzing hypotheses. Questions typically ask students to evaluate information, follow the logic of an argument, or draw conclusions from the presented data.

Each passage in the Reading section is carefully selected to challenge different aspects of a student's reading ability, ensuring a comprehensive assessment of skills necessary for success in college and beyond. Students are encouraged to approach each passage with a strategic mindset, focusing on key elements such as the author's intent, the relationship between ideas, and the contextual meaning of words and phrases. The questions are designed to measure how well students can synthesize information and apply critical thinking to understand and analyze written material.

## Breakdown of the Writing Section

The Writing section of the Digital SAT is designed to assess a student's ability to clearly and effectively communicate ideas through written language. Unlike traditional writing tests that focus primarily on grammar and mechanics, the SAT Writing section evaluates a broader set of skills that include organization, development, coherence, and precision in language use.

At the core of the Writing section are passages that resemble real-world written materials, including arguments, narratives, and explanatory texts. Each passage is followed by multiple-choice questions that challenge students to identify and correct errors, improve sentence structure, and enhance clarity. The questions also focus on ensuring that the student can create logical connections between ideas, improve the flow of a passage, and make stylistic choices that strengthen the author's message.

One of the key areas of focus in this section is **Standard English Conventions**, which includes grammar, punctuation, and usage. Questions in this category test a student's ability to recognize errors in subject-verb agreement, pronoun usage, verb tense, and sentence boundaries (such as avoiding run-on sentences and sentence fragments). Students must also demonstrate proficiency in using punctuation marks such as commas, colons, and semicolons correctly, particularly in complex sentence structures.

Another significant part of the Writing section is **Expression of Ideas**, which evaluates a student's capacity to refine and improve the content of a passage. Questions in this category may ask the student to rephrase a sentence for clarity, adjust the tone to match the intended audience, or select the most appropriate word or phrase to convey an idea more effectively. This area emphasizes clarity, conciseness, and precision in communication, challenging students to make choices that enhance the overall quality of the text.

**Organization and Logical Flow** are also essential elements in this section. Questions will often focus on how well the ideas in a passage are organized, whether the transitions between sentences and paragraphs are smooth, and how the overall argument or narrative develops. Students may be asked to reorder sentences or paragraphs to create a more logical sequence, improving the reader's understanding of the material. This requires not only an understanding of individual sentences but also the ability to see the "big picture" of how a passage unfolds.

A notable feature of the Writing section is the emphasis on **Conciseness and Precision**. Some questions will present the student with several different ways to phrase a sentence, with the task of choosing the most concise and accurate option. The challenge lies in identifying redundancies, wordiness, or awkward phrasing and replacing them with more efficient language that retains the original meaning. This skill is critical in both academic and professional writing, where clarity and brevity are highly valued.

Another key skill evaluated in this section is **Consistency in Style and Tone**. Students are expected to make sure that the language used in the passage remains consistent throughout. For example, if a passage begins with a formal tone, students must choose answers that maintain this tone rather than introducing informal or casual language. Similarly, students are tested on their ability to maintain a consistent point of view, ensuring that the passage does not shift between perspectives unless explicitly intended by the author.

In some cases, the Writing section includes questions that address **Data Interpretation and Synthesis**, where students are presented with charts, graphs, or other forms of data. These questions require students to interpret the data correctly and make connections between the data and the text. This tests the student's ability to integrate quantitative information into a written argument or explanation, a skill that is increasingly important in a data-driven world.

**Sentence Structure** is also a focal point of the Writing section. Questions related to sentence structure assess a student's ability to combine sentences effectively, improve sentence variety, and eliminate awkward or confusing constructions. This part of the test evaluates the ability to create smoother and more fluid sentences that contribute to the overall coherence of the passage.

The Writing section also places significant emphasis on **Rhetorical Skills**, which include understanding the author's purpose, identifying the main idea, and recognizing the appropriate tone for the intended audience.

Students are tasked with ensuring that the passage effectively communicates the author's argument or narrative and that the choices they make in revising the passage enhance the overall rhetorical effect. This includes understanding when to add, revise, or delete information to improve the effectiveness of the passage.

Students must also be able to manage **Syntax and Word Choice**. Some questions require students to select the best word or phrase to fit a particular context, often testing their understanding of commonly confused words, idiomatic expressions, or appropriate verb forms. Syntax-related questions may ask students to revise sentences to improve their structure, clarity, or stylistic flow.

The Writing section of the SAT is designed to mirror the kinds of writing tasks that students will face in college and beyond. By testing a wide range of skills, from grammar and mechanics to more complex rhetorical strategies, the section aims to assess whether students can write effectively for different purposes and audiences. Through this comprehensive evaluation, the Writing section ensures that students are prepared to communicate their ideas clearly and persuasively in their academic and professional careers.

# CHAPTER 2: PROVEN TECHNIQUES FOR SAT READING

## 2.1 Mastering Passage Reading

### Active Reading Strategies

Active reading is a critical skill for succeeding in the SAT Reading section. Unlike passive reading, which involves simply absorbing words, active reading engages the reader to interact with the text. This approach enhances comprehension and retention, both essential for answering the questions that follow each passage.

One fundamental active reading strategy is annotating the passage. While reading, students should underline or highlight key phrases, important details, and transition words that signify a shift in the argument or the narrative. By marking essential parts of the text, the reader remains engaged and focused, which aids in recalling information when answering questions. Annotations also help in identifying the main idea, supporting details, and any arguments or counterarguments presented in the passage. These markings can serve as quick reference points, saving valuable time during the test.

Another key strategy is summarizing paragraphs mentally while reading. After each paragraph or section, the reader should pause briefly to mentally summarize what they've just read. This ensures that the student is processing the information effectively and not simply skimming through it. Summarizing in one's own words solidifies understanding and prepares the reader for questions that ask about the author's purpose, the main idea, or the structure of the passage.

Active readers also pay attention to **context clues**. Many SAT questions focus on the meaning of a word or phrase within the context of the passage. Often, the meanings of challenging words can be inferred by examining surrounding sentences for clues. Active readers stay alert to these cues, making it easier to answer vocabulary-related questions without having to guess.

Students should also practice **reading for structure**, not just content. Every passage in the SAT has a structure—whether it's argumentative, narrative, or descriptive—and understanding this structure helps in predicting the flow of ideas. Identifying how a passage is organized enables students to follow the author's line of reasoning, making it easier to answer questions about the author's purpose, tone, or the effectiveness of specific sentences within the passage.

Engaging with the text through **questioning** is another active reading method. As students read, they should ask themselves questions about the material, such as "What is the author trying to convey here?" or "Why did the author include this example?" By doing this, they stay intellectually engaged, which leads to a deeper understanding of the passage. These internal questions often mirror the types of questions that will appear in the SAT, helping students be better prepared for what's to come.

**Identifying key themes and arguments** in the passage is another essential aspect of active reading. SAT passages often present a central argument, point of view, or theme. Active readers are trained to spot these main points quickly. They also learn to recognize supporting evidence and examples that reinforce the argument. Knowing how to distinguish between major themes and minor details is crucial for answering both broad and specific questions.

**Engaging with the author's tone and style** is another important active reading skill. The SAT often tests students on their ability to determine the author's attitude or tone, whether it's analytical, critical, supportive, or neutral. Active readers take note of adjectives, adverbs, and other clues that signal how the author feels about the subject matter. Recognizing shifts in tone also helps students better understand the progression of ideas within the passage.

**Time management** is also integral to mastering passage reading. Active readers allocate their time efficiently by skimming through unimportant details and focusing on the core arguments of the passage. They know when to slow down for complex sections and when to move quickly through simpler paragraphs. Managing time wisely prevents students from spending too much time on one passage, allowing them to complete all questions in the allotted time.

**Reading with a purpose** is another key technique. Before reading the passage, active readers often glance at the questions to get a sense of what to look for. Knowing the types of questions that follow the passage—whether they focus on vocabulary, inferences, or the main idea—gives readers direction and purpose as they read. They become more attentive to the details that are likely to be tested, making the reading process more targeted and efficient.

A vital part of active reading is **making predictions**. While reading, students should try to predict what might come next in the passage or how the author will conclude the argument. This keeps the reader engaged and helps with comprehension. Additionally, it primes students to anticipate questions about the author's next step or the logical flow of the argument.

Lastly, active readers maintain a **critical mindset**. They don't simply accept everything the author presents as fact. Instead, they critically evaluate the evidence, question the logic, and remain alert to any biases or assumptions in the text. This critical engagement with the material helps students answer questions about the effectiveness of the author's argument or the validity of the evidence presented.

By practicing these active reading strategies, students become more adept at navigating SAT Reading passages efficiently and effectively. They learn to engage deeply with the text, ensuring that they fully understand both the surface details and the underlying themes, making them better equipped to answer the questions that follow.

## Identifying Main Ideas and Themes

Identifying the main ideas and themes of a passage is a critical skill for mastering the SAT Reading section. The main idea of a passage is the core message or argument that the author wants to communicate. It can be thought of as the backbone that holds the entire text together, while the theme often represents a broader, more abstract concept that the passage explores. In order to answer questions accurately, it's important to learn how to identify both the explicit main ideas and the more implicit themes within the text.

One of the first steps in identifying the main idea is understanding the **purpose of the passage**. Before diving into the specifics, a reader should ask: why did the author write this text? Is it meant to inform, persuade, entertain, or analyze? By answering this question early on, students can begin to narrow down the central message. Often, the purpose is closely tied to the main idea, as the author will build their argument or narrative to fulfill that purpose.

The **introduction** of a passage typically provides the first clues about the main idea. Many authors will state their thesis or central argument early on, giving readers a sense of direction. Paying close attention to the opening paragraphs is key. The main idea might be clearly stated, or it could be implied through the presentation of the subject matter. Active readers should always be on the lookout for sentences that summarize the author's main point or reveal their stance on an issue.

As readers move through the text, they should focus on the **topic sentences** of each paragraph. Topic sentences generally introduce the subject of each paragraph and indicate how it relates to the overall main idea. By understanding how each section of the passage supports or builds on the central argument, students can maintain a clearer picture of the main idea. Topic sentences also help readers understand the structure of the argument and how each part contributes to the whole.

Sometimes, the main idea isn't stated directly and requires the reader to **infer** it from the text. In such cases, the reader must look at the overall content of the passage—what it discusses, the evidence it provides, and the conclusions it reaches. Inference is especially important when dealing with more complex texts or abstract arguments where the main idea is embedded within multiple layers of information. Asking oneself, "What is the author ultimately trying to say?" can help crystallize this idea.

In identifying themes, readers should take a step back and consider the **broader implications** of the passage. Themes are often more universal concepts that go beyond the specific subject of the text. For example, a passage might focus on a historical event, but the theme could be something more general, like resilience, justice, or human ambition. Themes are often tied to the emotions or moral considerations that the author wants the reader to reflect on, and they can typically be applied to a wide range of situations beyond the scope of the text.

When looking for themes, students should pay attention to **recurring ideas or motifs**. Does the author return to certain concepts repeatedly? Are there phrases or ideas that echo throughout the text? These repeated elements often signal the passage's theme. For instance, if a passage about environmental policy frequently discusses balance and sustainability, the theme may involve humanity's need to balance progress with conservation.

Another helpful strategy is considering the **tone and attitude** of the passage. How does the author feel about the subject they are discussing? The tone—whether optimistic, critical, neutral, or passionate—can often hint at the underlying themes. For instance, a critical tone in a passage about technology might suggest a theme related to the risks of rapid technological advancement. The author's emotional response to the topic often reveals their deeper concerns or beliefs, which form the basis of the passage's theme.

The **conclusion** of the passage is another critical area where the main idea and themes can be highlighted. Often, authors will restate or reinforce their main point in the concluding paragraphs, making it a good place to confirm the reader's understanding of the text. Even if the main idea is implicit throughout the passage, it may become clearer by the end. The conclusion may also offer final thoughts that point to the broader significance or theme of the text, helping readers to fully grasp the author's message.

In some cases, passages may contain **multiple main ideas or sub-arguments**, each supporting an overarching theme. In such situations, it is important to distinguish between the main argument of the passage and its supporting points. Each sub-argument should be evaluated for how it ties into the larger theme or argument of the passage. By understanding how smaller ideas fit together, readers can better identify the unifying theme that links them all.

The process of identifying main ideas and themes also requires attention to **supporting details**. Every main idea is backed by evidence—whether it's data, examples, or reasoning. By understanding which details the author chooses to emphasize, readers can determine what the author views as most important. For instance, an author who frequently uses emotional anecdotes might be focusing on a theme related to human experience or empathy, while an author who emphasizes statistics and logic may be centered on rational analysis or policy implications.

Identifying the main idea and themes in SAT passages involves understanding the passage's purpose, paying close attention to introductions and conclusions, and recognizing the relationships between paragraphs and sections. The tone, supporting details, and recurring motifs further help readers grasp the broader themes and the author's overall message. Through active engagement with the text and critical thinking, students can become adept at recognizing both explicit and implicit main ideas and themes, positioning them for success in answering SAT Reading questions.

## 2.2 Question Types and How to Approach Them

Understanding the different types of questions on the SAT is crucial for success. Each question type requires a distinct approach, and mastering these methods is essential for improving your performance. Among the most common and challenging types are inference questions, evidence-based questions, and big picture questions. These questions test not only your comprehension but also your ability to think critically about the text.

### Inference Questions

Inference questions require you to draw conclusions based on information that is implied, rather than explicitly stated, in the passage. These questions assess your ability to read between the lines and make logical connections. They often begin with phrases like "It can be inferred that..." or "The author most likely suggests that...," signaling that the answer lies beyond the surface level of the text.

The key to tackling inference questions is to focus on the facts and ideas presented and use them to deduce what is not directly said. Start by identifying the portion of the passage related to the question. Then, carefully examine the author's tone, the choice of words, and any underlying assumptions in the text. It's important not to confuse inference with assumption—an inference is supported by evidence in the passage, while an assumption may go beyond the information provided.

Another effective strategy is eliminating answer choices that are either too extreme or that introduce ideas not mentioned in the passage. Inference questions are grounded in the text, so avoid choices that seem to speculate too far from the content. A well-drawn inference will always have clear support from specific details within the passage, even if the answer is not directly stated.

### Evidence-Based Questions

Evidence-based questions ask you to identify which part of the passage supports your answer to a previous question, often referred to as a "paired" question. These questions will typically follow an inference or main idea question and begin with prompts like "Which of the following best supports your answer to the previous question?"

To approach evidence-based questions, it's essential to be precise. Start by recalling the answer to the preceding question and then examine the passage for specific lines that justify your response. It's useful to match keywords from the previous question or your chosen answer with corresponding phrases or ideas in the text. The correct evidence should directly align with the logic of your previous answer.

One common mistake students make is selecting evidence that merely repeats part of the passage rather than providing genuine support for the claim. Always choose the option that most clearly bolsters your original answer and adds depth to it, rather than simply echoing the same ideas. Sometimes, this evidence will provide a nuanced explanation or an example that substantiates the inference or argument in the earlier question.

Additionally, when working with paired questions, it's helpful to first answer the evidence question before confirming your response to the preceding inference or main idea question. By identifying the strongest piece of evidence, you can ensure that your initial choice is correct or adjust it if necessary. This method helps reinforce accuracy in your overall answer.

## Big Picture Questions

Big picture questions focus on the overall purpose, theme, or structure of the passage. These questions require you to step back from the details and consider the text as a whole. They often begin with prompts like "The primary purpose of the passage is..." or "The author's main argument is..."

When approaching big picture questions, it's important to grasp the author's overall intent and the key themes that run through the passage. Start by reviewing the introduction and conclusion of the passage, as these sections often provide clear insight into the author's central message. Ask yourself what the author is trying to communicate to the reader and how each section of the passage contributes to that message.

Understanding the structure of the passage is also key. Some passages follow a clear progression of ideas, starting with a general statement and gradually providing more specific details or examples. Others may present a problem-solution format or compare and contrast different perspectives. Identifying the passage's structure will help you understand the author's method of argumentation and the overarching theme.

Big picture questions often require a broad understanding of the passage, so it's crucial not to get bogged down by individual details. Focus on the passage's main ideas and avoid answer choices that hone in on minor points or specific examples that don't reflect the passage's overall purpose. The correct answer will always align with the general direction of the passage and reflect the primary message or argument that the author is conveying.

## Strategies for Success

While each of these question types requires a unique approach, there are several overarching strategies that can help you succeed across all of them.

1. **Active Reading:** Engaging with the text as you read is crucial. Take note of the author's tone, the structure of the argument, and any shifts in perspective or topic. By staying engaged and paying close attention to these elements, you'll be better prepared to answer questions about inferences, evidence, and the big picture.

2. **Annotating the Passage:** Although the SAT is now digital, it's still helpful to mark key points or summarize sections in your own words as you read. This practice helps you keep track of the main ideas and locate supporting evidence when you answer questions.

3. **Eliminating Wrong Answers:** In all question types, eliminating wrong answers can help narrow your focus to the most plausible choices. Look for answer choices that are too extreme, contradict the passage, or introduce new ideas that are not supported by the text.

4. **Time Management:** Since inference and evidence-based questions can be more time-consuming, it's essential to manage your time effectively. Don't spend too long on any single question—if you're stuck, eliminate as many wrong choices as possible, make an educated guess, and move on.

5. **Understanding Author's Perspective:** For big picture questions, understanding the author's perspective is vital. Ask yourself how the author feels about the topic at hand, whether they are for or against the argument, and how their tone and language reveal their attitude.

6. **Reviewing Paired Questions Together:** When dealing with paired inference and evidence questions, always review your answers together. If you change your answer to one, make sure the other still aligns. These questions are designed to be solved as a unit, and it's crucial that both answers support each other logically.

By mastering the strategies for inference, evidence, and big picture questions, you will be well-prepared to handle the diverse range of question types on the SAT Reading section. These skills not only help improve your test performance but also enhance your overall reading comprehension abilities, which are valuable in academic and real-world contexts alike.

## Strategies for "Function" and "Tone" Questions

Function and tone questions in the SAT Reading section require a deeper understanding of how the author constructs the passage and communicates ideas. These questions are designed to test your ability to identify the purpose behind specific parts of the text and to analyze the author's attitude or mood toward the subject. Let's explore strategies for approaching both types of questions effectively.

# Function Questions

Function questions ask why the author has included a specific part of the passage, whether it's a sentence, paragraph, or larger section. These questions often use phrases such as "The author includes this detail to..." or "What is the purpose of the phrase in lines 10-12?" They are testing your ability to see beyond the literal meaning and understand the role that piece of text plays in the overall structure and argument of the passage.

1.  **Understanding Context**

    The first step in answering a function question is to understand the context of the excerpt in question. Read a few sentences before and after the specified lines to grasp the broader flow of ideas. Ask yourself: What is the author discussing at this point in the passage? What is the main point of the surrounding text? This will help you understand why the author included this particular detail or phrase.

2.  **Consider the Overall Structure**

    Function questions often relate to the larger structure of the passage. Is the author introducing a new argument, providing evidence, refuting a counterpoint, or summarizing a key idea? Identifying the structural purpose of the text will guide you toward the correct answer. For instance, if the author presents a surprising fact, the function might be to grab the reader's attention or to challenge a commonly held belief.

3.  **Look for Transition Words**

    Pay attention to transition words such as "however," "therefore," or "for example." These words are strong indicators of the author's intention. A sentence introduced with "however" may be presenting a contrast to the previous point, while "therefore" signals that a conclusion or result is being presented. Identifying these words will help you quickly understand the role of the sentence or paragraph in the overall passage.

4.  **Answer Based on Purpose, Not Content**

    A common mistake in function questions is focusing too much on the content of the specific lines instead of their purpose. For example, a question might ask why an author includes a piece of statistical data. The correct answer could be to support a previous argument, not simply to state the statistic. Always think about the purpose behind the information rather than just what it says.

5.  **Identify Patterns in Function Questions**

    Function questions tend to fall into a few common categories: providing evidence, illustrating a concept, addressing a counterargument, or concluding a section. Recognizing these patterns can make function questions more predictable and easier to manage. As you practice, focus on categorizing the types of functions you see and matching them with the strategies above.

## Tone Questions

Tone questions focus on the author's attitude or emotional stance toward the subject matter. The tone of a passage can range from neutral to enthusiastic, skeptical, critical, or sarcastic. Tone questions usually begin with phrases like "The tone of the passage is best described as..." or "The author's attitude toward the subject can best be characterized as..."

1. **Read with the Author's Perspective in Mind**

   From the start of the passage, pay attention to the author's perspective on the topic. Are they presenting it with approval, skepticism, or neutrality? Look for adjectives and adverbs that reveal their attitude. For instance, phrases like "remarkable discovery" indicate a positive tone, while "unfortunately" or "troubling" suggests a more negative or concerned attitude.

2. **Recognize Common Tones**

   Tone questions tend to use a set of common descriptors. These include:

   o **Neutral:** Objective, factual, informative

   o **Positive:** Enthusiastic, approving, optimistic

   o **Negative:** Critical, skeptical, disapproving

   o **Cautious or Reserved:** Tentative, hesitant, reflective

   o **Humorous or Ironic:** Sarcastic, playful, mocking

Familiarizing yourself with these terms and their nuances will help you select the right tone when presented with multiple options.

3. **Focus on Word Choice and Language**

   The author's tone is often revealed through word choice. Descriptive words, verbs, and even punctuation can provide clues. For example, an exclamation point can indicate excitement or emphasis, while words like "undoubtedly" or "certainly" reflect confidence in a statement. On the other hand, words like "perhaps" or "possibly" suggest uncertainty or a cautious tone. When reading, highlight any emotionally charged words or specific language that reveals the author's feelings about the subject.

4. **Watch for Subtle Shifts in Tone**

   Authors may change their tone as the passage progresses. An initial neutral tone may become more enthusiastic as the author presents new findings, or a skeptical tone may shift to a more critical one as arguments are refuted. Be mindful of these shifts, especially when a question focuses on a particular part of the passage. If the tone seems to have evolved from the beginning to the middle, reflect on why and how the author's attitude has changed.

5. **Tone in Paired Questions**

Sometimes, tone questions are paired with function questions, asking not only what the author is doing but also how they feel about it. In these cases, use the answer to the function question to inform the tone. If the function of a passage is to criticize a viewpoint, the tone will likely be skeptical or disapproving. Align your responses to ensure that both the function and tone answers are consistent.

6. **Eliminate Extreme Tone Choices**

When answering tone questions, be cautious of extreme options. Unless the passage is explicitly strong in its language, tones like "hostile" or "overjoyed" may be too intense to be correct. The SAT typically tests more subtle, balanced tones, such as "analytical," "thoughtful," or "mildly critical." By eliminating extreme options, you narrow down the choices to those that are more likely to reflect the author's true attitude.

## Integrating Function and Tone

Both function and tone questions require careful analysis of the passage, but they are interconnected. Often, the way an author structures the passage (function) is influenced by their attitude toward the subject (tone). For instance, if the function of a paragraph is to critique an opposing view, the tone is likely critical or skeptical. Conversely, if the function is to introduce new research, the tone might be more neutral or enthusiastic.

To excel at these question types, develop the habit of asking yourself two key questions as you read:

- What is the author doing here (function)?
- How does the author feel about this topic (tone)?

These two questions are the foundation of function and tone questions, and answering them consistently as you read will sharpen your ability to handle these types of questions quickly and accurately.

By applying these strategies, you'll gain confidence in tackling function and tone questions, improving both your speed and accuracy on the SAT Reading section. These techniques are not only useful for test-taking but also for developing deeper analytical reading skills that will benefit you in academic studies and beyond.

## 2.3 Time Management Optimizing Time per Question

### Optimizing time per question

Time management is a critical component of achieving success on the Digital SAT. Each section of the test is designed to challenge not only your knowledge but also your ability to work efficiently under timed conditions. In this section, we will explore practical strategies to help you optimize the time spent on each question in the Reading and Writing sections, ensuring that you maintain a steady pace and maximize your score.

### Understanding Time Limits

Before you can manage your time effectively, you need to understand the specific time constraints for each section of the SAT. The Digital SAT Reading and Writing section typically allows 32 minutes for each module, with around 27 to 28 questions per module. This gives you roughly 70 seconds per question. However, some questions will be more complex than others, meaning you'll need to strategically allocate more time to difficult questions while answering simpler ones more quickly.

### Categorizing Questions by Difficulty

One of the most effective time management techniques is to categorize questions by difficulty as you move through the test. As you encounter each question, quickly assess whether it is easy, medium, or difficult. Spend less time on easy questions, allowing yourself to accumulate more time for the challenging ones. Here's how to approach each type:

- **Easy Questions:** These are the questions that you understand immediately and can answer with little hesitation. Aim to spend less than 60 seconds on these. Don't overthink or second-guess yourself—your goal is to move through them quickly and confidently.

- **Medium Questions:** These questions may require a bit more thought, but they are still within your comfort zone. Allocate closer to the full 70 seconds for these. Stay calm and methodical, but be aware of the time ticking down. If you're nearing the 70-second mark and haven't found an answer, it may be best to move on.

- **Difficult Questions:** When you encounter a question that is particularly tough, avoid spending too much time on it initially. If you don't have a clear idea of how to approach the question after 30 seconds, mark it and move on. It's crucial to save these questions for the end so that you don't waste precious time early on. If time allows, come back to them later with a fresh perspective.

## Skipping and Returning to Questions

A key strategy in optimizing time is knowing when to skip a question and return to it later. When faced with a question that seems particularly challenging or time-consuming, resist the temptation to get stuck on it. Instead, skip it and move on to easier or medium-difficulty questions that you can answer more quickly. This approach ensures that you continue to accumulate points while leaving yourself time to tackle the harder questions with the remaining time.

To implement this strategy effectively, mark the questions you skip so you can easily find them again. Most digital testing platforms will allow you to flag questions or make notes, making it easier to identify which ones to return to.

## Practice the 30-Second Rule

A practical rule for managing time per question is the 30-second rule. When you read a question, spend the first 30 seconds determining if you can answer it confidently. If, after 30 seconds, you're still unsure, flag it and move on. This method helps prevent spending too much time on any one question, allowing you to maintain a steady pace throughout the section.

By adhering to this rule, you can effectively keep track of time and avoid unnecessary delays. Additionally, this approach reduces the likelihood of panic, as you will have already made significant progress on the rest of the test.

## Pacing Yourself Throughout the Section

Maintaining an even pace is essential for success on the SAT. One common mistake is rushing through the first few questions and then slowing down significantly, only to run out of time at the end. To avoid this, break the test into smaller time intervals. For example, aim to complete every five questions in five minutes. This ensures that you're staying on track without letting any one section consume too much of your time.

If you notice that you're behind schedule, increase your speed slightly on the easier questions to make up time. Conversely, if you're ahead of schedule, use that extra time to carefully check answers or revisit flagged questions.

## Efficient Reading Strategies

For the Reading section, reading speed and comprehension are critical. You don't want to spend too much time reading the passages, but you also need to fully understand them to answer the questions correctly. Here are some tips for optimizing your reading time:

- **Skim First, Then Read in Detail:** Begin by skimming the passage to get a general sense of the main idea and structure. Pay attention to headings, topic sentences, and key phrases. This initial skim should take about 30-40 seconds. After skimming, focus on the questions, referring back to the passage as needed.

- **Focus on the First and Last Sentences:** The first and last sentences of each paragraph often contain the most important information. Paying special attention to these can help you grasp the key points without reading every single word in between.

- **Use the Questions as a Guide:** Look at the questions before reading the passage in detail. This will help you know what to look for as you read, allowing you to answer more efficiently.

## Handling Complex Questions

Complex questions, such as inference or function questions, can be time-consuming. When dealing with these, it's important to rely on a process of elimination. Start by quickly eliminating any obviously incorrect answer choices, which will narrow down your options and save time. Then, focus on comparing the remaining choices, using evidence from the passage to guide you.

For complex questions, it's also helpful to refer back to the passage to ensure your answer is supported by the text. While this can take a little extra time, it's worth the investment for difficult questions that have multiple plausible answers.

## Using Time Wisely on Writing Questions

In the Writing section, questions tend to be more straightforward than those in the Reading section. However, they can still be time-consuming if you're not careful. Here's how to optimize your time on writing questions:

- **Answer the Obvious Questions First:** Questions that ask you to correct grammar, punctuation, or sentence structure errors are often easier to identify and solve quickly. Prioritize these questions and leave more complex ones, such as those asking about the author's purpose, for later.

- **Understand Common Grammar Rules:** Make sure you're familiar with the most commonly tested grammar rules, such as subject-verb agreement, parallel structure, and comma usage. Recognizing these quickly will save you valuable time during the test.

- **Eliminate Wrong Answers First:** As with the Reading section, eliminating obviously incorrect answers in the Writing section is a time-efficient strategy. Doing so will help you zero in on the correct choice more quickly.

## Practice Under Timed Conditions

Ultimately, the best way to optimize your time per question is through consistent practice under timed conditions. Taking practice tests with a timer will help you get a feel for the pacing needed to complete each section on time. The more familiar you become with the test format, the better you'll be at managing your time efficiently.

Set up a timer for each practice session, and after completing the test, analyze your performance. Identify which types of questions took you the longest to answer and focus on strategies for speeding up your process in those areas. Regular practice will build both your speed and confidence, making it easier to manage time effectively during the real test.

By applying these time management strategies and practicing regularly, you'll be able to optimize the time you spend on each question, increasing your chances of achieving a high score on the SAT.

## When to Skip and Guess

Knowing when to skip a question and when to make an educated guess is a crucial skill in optimizing your performance on the SAT. The key to achieving a high score isn't necessarily answering every question correctly, but rather managing your time effectively and maximizing the number of questions you answer correctly. This strategy is particularly important on a timed test like the SAT, where every second counts.

## Understanding the Guessing Strategy

The SAT does not penalize you for guessing, which means that leaving a question blank is always worse than filling in an answer, even if it's a complete guess. Because you won't lose points for incorrect answers, you should never leave a question unanswered. But rather than resorting to random guessing, it's far more effective to learn how to make educated guesses when necessary.

There are two key components to the guessing strategy: knowing when to skip a question to save time and returning to it later, and developing the skill to eliminate wrong answers to increase your chances of guessing correctly.

## Recognizing When to Skip

Some questions on the SAT are designed to be more difficult than others, and it's important to recognize when you're spending too much time on a challenging problem. If you're stuck on a question and not making progress after 30 to 40 seconds, it's usually a sign that you should skip it and move on to other questions.

Skipping doesn't mean giving up on the question entirely; it just means you're prioritizing your time. By skipping difficult questions initially, you can focus on answering easier ones first. Once you've worked through the section and answered all the questions you find manageable, you can return to the ones you skipped with the remaining time. This ensures that you maximize the number of correct answers you submit. Here are some situations where skipping a question is often the best choice:

- **Unclear understanding of the question:** If you read a question multiple times and still don't understand what it's asking, it's best to move on and revisit it later. Spending too much time trying to decipher the question can eat into valuable time that could be spent answering other questions more confidently.

- **Multiple plausible answers:** Sometimes, you might narrow a question down to two or three possible answers but can't decide between them. In this case, it's better to skip the question and return to it after you've answered others. A fresh perspective might help you make a clearer decision.

- **Complex calculations or reasoning:** For math or logic-based questions that require several steps to solve, you might find that you're halfway through the problem but running out of time. If you're not making progress, skip the question and return to it later.

## Using the Process of Elimination

Even when you're unsure of the correct answer, eliminating obviously wrong answers can significantly improve your chances of guessing correctly. The process of elimination works well for both multiple-choice questions in the Reading and Writing sections as well as the Math section.

Here's how you can effectively use the process of elimination:

- **Identify wrong answers first:** Read each answer choice carefully and immediately cross off any that are clearly wrong. This could be because they don't align with the passage in a reading question, are grammatically incorrect in a writing question, or produce an illogical result in a math question. By narrowing down your choices, you increase your odds of selecting the correct answer.

- **Pay attention to extreme wording:** On the SAT, answer choices that use extreme language such as "always," "never," "completely," or "none" are often incorrect. Be cautious with these options, especially in Reading and Writing, as SAT questions tend to favor more nuanced answers.

- **Look for alignment with the passage or question:** In reading comprehension questions, make sure the answer choice you select is directly supported by the passage. Eliminate any answers that introduce new ideas not mentioned in the text, as these are often used to distract you.

- **For math questions, verify with estimation:** If you can't solve a problem exactly, sometimes you can estimate or approximate the answer. By comparing the options, you might be able to eliminate those that are too far off from your estimate, leaving you with a smaller range of possible correct answers.

## Guessing with Confidence

Once you've eliminated as many incorrect answers as possible, it's time to make an educated guess. Even if you're unsure of the remaining options, you've already increased your odds of guessing correctly by eliminating others. The SAT has four answer choices per question, so if you eliminate two wrong answers, your chances of guessing correctly jump from 25% to 50%.

When you guess, try to avoid second-guessing yourself. Your first instinct is often correct, especially if you've been practicing regularly and have a good grasp of the material. Changing answers without strong justification usually leads to more mistakes than sticking with your original choice.

## When Guessing Should Be Your Go-To

There are times when guessing, rather than skipping and returning later, is your best option. This is particularly true in the following scenarios:

- **Running out of time:** If you're in the final minutes of a section and still have several unanswered questions, it's better to guess quickly than leave questions blank. Go through each unanswered question, eliminate as many wrong answers as you can, and fill in the remaining ones with your best guess. If you have no time to eliminate answers, then fill in any answer before time runs out.

- **Random guessing pattern:** If you're truly stuck and have no idea about a particular question, some students find it helpful to stick to a consistent guessing pattern. For example, always guessing "B" or "C" can help you avoid the temptation of overthinking or wasting time deciding between answers. While this strategy doesn't guarantee success, it's better than leaving questions blank.

## Returning to Skipped Questions

After completing the easier questions in the section, return to the ones you skipped. You should now have more time to think through the difficult questions without the pressure of an approaching time limit. Additionally, because you've already answered the rest of the questions, you can spend more time on each skipped question if necessary.

When you return to skipped questions, use fresh eyes to reevaluate your options. Sometimes, returning to a question later makes the answer more obvious than it was during your initial attempt. As you review the skipped questions, apply the same elimination techniques, and don't be afraid to make an educated guess if needed.

## Practice Makes Perfect

Finally, developing a strong sense of when to skip and guess comes with practice. The more practice tests you take, the better you'll become at recognizing which questions to skip and which ones to attempt right away. This familiarity will help reduce the anxiety that can come with tough questions, allowing you to focus on completing as many correct answers as possible.

By practicing these strategies regularly, you'll gain confidence in your ability to skip and guess effectively, ensuring that you maximize your performance on test day.

# CHAPTER 3: PROVEN TECHNIQUES FOR SAT WRITING

## 3.1 Mastering Grammar Rules

## Key grammar topics tested

Understanding the key grammar topics tested on the SAT Writing section is crucial for success. The SAT tests your ability to identify and correct errors in sentence structure, grammar, and usage. Mastering these rules will not only help you improve your SAT score but also ensure that you are equipped with essential writing skills for college.

**1. Subject-Verb Agreement**

One of the most frequently tested grammar rules on the SAT is subject-verb agreement. The key is ensuring that the subject and verb in a sentence agree in number. Singular subjects must take singular verbs, and plural subjects must take plural verbs.

For example:

Incorrect: "The list of books are on the table."

Correct: "The list of books is on the table."

In this case, the subject "list" is singular, and thus the verb should also be singular ("is").

To master subject-verb agreement, pay close attention to subjects separated from their verbs by descriptive phrases or clauses. The SAT often tries to trick you by placing words between the subject and verb, making it more challenging to determine whether they agree.

**2. Pronoun Usage and Agreement**

Pronoun agreement is another critical grammar topic on the SAT. A pronoun must agree in number and gender with the noun it replaces. Additionally, it must be clear which noun the pronoun is referring to.

For example:

Incorrect: "Each student must bring their book to class."

Correct: "Each student must bring his or her book to class."

In this example, "student" is singular, so the correct pronouns are "his or her," not "their." Watch for ambiguous pronouns where it is unclear which noun the pronoun is referencing.

Another common pronoun mistake is using "they" or "their" as a singular pronoun, which can often trip students up. Focus on matching the pronoun to the correct antecedent in both number and gender.

## 3. Verb Tense Consistency

Maintaining consistent verb tense is important for ensuring that the timeline of events in a sentence is clear. The SAT will test your ability to identify when a shift in tense is necessary or when it disrupts the sentence.

For example:

Incorrect: "She walked to the store and buys some groceries."

Correct: "She walked to the store and bought some groceries."

The SAT often presents sentences that include incorrect shifts in verb tense, especially in complex sentences. It's essential to ensure that all verbs reflect the appropriate time frame, unless the context clearly calls for a change in tense.

## 4. Parallel Structure

Parallel structure means that elements in a list or comparison should be presented in the same grammatical form. This ensures clarity and consistency in writing. The SAT often includes sentences that violate this rule, and you'll need to identify and correct the error.

For example:

Incorrect: "She enjoys hiking, to swim, and bicycling."

Correct: "She enjoys hiking, swimming, and bicycling."

In this example, the items in the list must all be in the same form, in this case, gerunds ("hiking," "swimming," and "bicycling").

To master parallel structure, focus on lists, comparisons, and paired ideas. Pay attention to phrases linked by conjunctions like "and," "or," and "but," as these are often where parallelism errors occur.

## 5. Misplaced and Dangling Modifiers

Modifiers are words or phrases that provide additional information about a subject. A misplaced modifier occurs when the modifier is placed too far from the word it's supposed to describe, causing confusion. A dangling modifier occurs when the word that should be modified is not even present in the sentence.

For example:

Misplaced: "She served the dessert to the guests on paper plates."

Correct: "She served the guests the dessert on paper plates."

Dangling: "Running down the street, the car almost hit me."

Correct: "Running down the street, I was almost hit by a car."

On the SAT, you will need to spot and correct these errors to ensure clarity in the sentences.

## 6. Comparison Errors

When making comparisons, the SAT checks whether the comparison is logical and complete. Often, sentences will present an illogical comparison, comparing things that shouldn't be compared directly.

For example:

Incorrect: "The salary of a teacher is lower than a doctor."

Correct: "The salary of a teacher is lower than that of a doctor."

In this case, the sentence compares the salary of a teacher with a doctor, but it should be comparing the salaries of both. The corrected sentence properly compares the two salaries.

## 7. Idioms and Word Choice

The SAT tests your knowledge of correct idiomatic expressions and appropriate word choices. An idiom is a phrase or expression that has a figurative meaning different from its literal meaning. Additionally, certain words must be used with specific prepositions or in specific contexts.

For example:

Incorrect: "She is interested with biology."

Correct: "She is interested in biology."

Incorrect idiomatic expressions are a common source of errors on the SAT. Familiarize yourself with common idiomatic expressions and ensure that the words are used in the correct context.

## 8. Pronoun Case

Understanding when to use subjective (e.g., I, he, she) versus objective pronouns (e.g., me, him, her) is another important topic. The pronoun's case depends on its role in the sentence: subject, object, or possessive.

For example:

Incorrect: "Him and I went to the store."

Correct: "He and I went to the store."

In this example, "He" is used because it is the subject of the sentence. Knowing when to use the correct pronoun form can help you avoid errors in complex sentences.

## 9. Punctuation

Punctuation rules, such as comma usage, semicolons, colons, and apostrophes, are also tested on the SAT Writing section. Common punctuation errors involve unnecessary commas, missing punctuation, or the misuse of semicolons or colons.

For example:

Incorrect: "I brought apples, bananas, and grapes to, the picnic."

Correct: "I brought apples, bananas, and grapes to the picnic."

To master punctuation, focus on learning the rules for comma usage, when to use semicolons and colons, and the correct placement of apostrophes for possessives.

## 10. Sentence Structure and Clauses

Understanding sentence structure is essential for identifying and correcting sentence fragments and run-on sentences. A sentence fragment occurs when a sentence is incomplete and lacks either a subject or a verb. A run-on sentence occurs when two or more independent clauses are joined improperly without punctuation or conjunctions.

For example:

Fragment: "Because she went to the store."

Correct: "She went to the store."

Run-on: "She went to the store she bought groceries."

Correct: "She went to the store, and she bought groceries."

The SAT will test your ability to recognize these structural errors and correct them.

By mastering these key grammar topics, you'll be well-prepared for the SAT Writing section and confident in your ability to recognize and fix common grammatical errors. Understanding these rules will not only help you perform better on the SAT but will also enhance your overall writing skills for college and beyond.

# Sentence Structure and Parallelism

Mastering sentence structure is critical for the SAT Writing section. Understanding how sentences are constructed and how to ensure clarity and flow in your writing is essential. Sentence structure encompasses various elements, including proper use of clauses, avoiding fragments and run-ons, and ensuring that ideas are logically connected.

## 1. Sentence Fragments

A sentence fragment is an incomplete sentence that lacks a subject, a verb, or a complete thought. These are often common errors that break the logical flow of writing. On the SAT, you may encounter sentence fragments that appear to be sentences but are actually incomplete.

For example:

Incorrect: "Although she studied hard for the test."

Correct: "Although she studied hard for the test, she still found it challenging."

In the incorrect sentence, "Although she studied hard for the test" lacks a main clause that completes the thought. Adding the second part makes the sentence whole. It's important to identify clauses that depend on additional information and ensure they are part of a complete sentence.

## 2. Run-On Sentences

Run-on sentences occur when two or more independent clauses are improperly joined without appropriate punctuation or conjunctions. This often creates confusion in meaning or makes the sentence difficult to follow.

For example:

Incorrect: "She loves reading she spends hours at the library."

Correct: "She loves reading, so she spends hours at the library."

To correct run-on sentences, you can either use a coordinating conjunction (e.g., for, and, nor, but, or, yet, so) with a comma, separate the independent clauses with a period, or use a semicolon.

## 3. Compound and Complex Sentences

A well-constructed sentence can be either compound or complex. Understanding the difference between the two and using them effectively will enhance the clarity and sophistication of your writing.

- **Compound sentences** consist of two or more independent clauses joined by a coordinating conjunction or a semicolon.

For example:

"She loves to read, and she often visits the library."

- **Complex sentences** include one independent clause and one or more dependent clauses.

For example:

"Although she loves to read, she didn't have time to visit the library today."

By mastering the use of compound and complex sentences, you can enhance your writing style and ensure logical progression of ideas in your answers.

## 4. Clauses and Conjunctions

Clauses are the building blocks of sentences. Understanding the difference between independent and dependent clauses is essential for avoiding sentence fragments and run-ons.

- **Independent clauses** express a complete thought and can stand alone as a sentence.

Example: "The sky is blue."

- **Dependent clauses** do not express a complete thought and cannot stand alone.

Example: "When the sun rises."

The SAT often tests your ability to identify where dependent clauses need to be completed or connected to an independent clause using conjunctions like "because," "although," "since," or "while."

## 5. Parallelism

Parallelism is one of the most frequently tested concepts in SAT Writing. It refers to the balance and consistency of sentence structure when listing items or comparing ideas. When elements in a sentence are parallel, they follow the same grammatical structure, making the sentence easier to read and understand.

For example:

Incorrect: "She enjoys swimming, to run, and biking."

Correct: "She enjoys swimming, running, and biking."

In this case, all the activities need to be in the same form (gerund) to maintain parallelism. Violating parallel structure makes sentences awkward and unclear, which is why this is an essential skill for the SAT.

Parallelism is often tested in lists, comparisons, and in the structure of clauses within a sentence. It is also essential in paired constructions, such as "not only...but also" or "either...or."

## 6. Parallelism in Lists

When creating a list of actions or items, all elements should follow the same grammatical form. This ensures that the sentence is balanced and clear.

For example:

Incorrect: "She likes dancing, to sing, and plays the piano."

Correct: "She likes dancing, singing, and playing the piano."

In the corrected sentence, all the verbs are in the gerund form, ensuring parallelism. Lists must maintain the same grammatical structure for clarity and consistency.

## 7. Parallelism in Comparisons

When comparing two or more things, parallel structure must also be maintained. This is particularly important when using comparatives or superlatives.

For example:

Incorrect: "Running is more fun than to swim."

Correct: "Running is more fun than swimming."

Here, both activities are compared using the same grammatical form, making the sentence clearer and more coherent.

## 8. Paired Constructions

Parallelism is also important in paired constructions, such as "either...or," "neither...nor," and "both...and." In these constructions, the elements being paired should be in the same grammatical form.

For example:

Incorrect: "She is either going to the store or the movies."

Correct: "She is going either to the store or to the movies."

Maintaining parallelism ensures that the sentence is smooth and easy to follow.

## 9. Fixing Common Parallelism Errors

To ensure parallelism in your writing, focus on identifying lists, comparisons, and paired constructions. Ask yourself whether each element follows the same grammatical form and whether the sentence flows naturally. If a sentence sounds awkward or unbalanced, there may be a parallelism issue that needs correcting.

For example:

Incorrect: "The teacher said that students should study hard, complete their assignments, and are paying attention in class."

Correct: "The teacher said that students should study hard, complete their assignments, and pay attention in class."

In the incorrect sentence, the third element of the list ("are paying attention") violates parallelism because it is not in the same form as the other two verbs ("study" and "complete"). The corrected sentence ensures all the verbs are in the base form.

## 10. SAT Writing Practice for Parallelism and Sentence Structure

The best way to improve your understanding of sentence structure and parallelism is through practice. The SAT Writing section will frequently test these concepts by presenting sentences with errors in structure or parallelism. By identifying these mistakes and correcting them, you will improve your performance on the exam and develop stronger writing skills for college.

Understanding sentence structure and maintaining parallelism ensures that your writing is clear, concise, and coherent. Mastering these elements will not only help you succeed on the SAT but also enhance your overall communication skills, which are critical in academic and professional settings.

## 3.2 Effective Editing and Revising

## Tips for Clarity and Conciseness

When editing and revising, clarity and conciseness are key elements that can elevate writing from being adequate to exceptional. To achieve clear and concise writing, it's essential to remove unnecessary words, focus on delivering ideas efficiently, and ensure the reader fully grasps the intended message without distraction. Here are practical tips to help improve clarity and conciseness in your writing.

**1. Eliminate Redundancies**

One of the most common issues that affect writing clarity is redundancy. Redundant phrases repeat the same idea using different words, making sentences unnecessarily long.

For example:

Redundant: "She made a final decision at the end of the meeting."

Concise: "She made a decision at the end of the meeting."

In the revised sentence, the word "final" is unnecessary because "decision" already implies that it's the last step in the process.

Another common redundancy involves phrases such as "free gift" (all gifts are free) or "unexpected surprise" (all surprises are unexpected). Streamlining these redundant phrases improves the clarity and sharpness of the message.

**2. Use Active Voice Instead of Passive Voice**

Active voice tends to be clearer and more direct than passive voice, making sentences stronger and easier to understand. In active voice, the subject of the sentence performs the action, whereas in passive voice, the subject is acted upon.

For example:

Passive: "The book was read by Sarah."

Active: "Sarah read the book."

The active version is more concise and avoids unnecessary complexity. While passive voice is appropriate in certain contexts, it is generally less effective for concise, clear communication.

**3. Avoid Wordiness**

Wordiness occurs when too many words are used to express an idea. To avoid this, focus on simplifying phrases and choosing precise words that convey meaning efficiently.

For example:

Wordy: "At this point in time, we are not able to provide any further information."

Concise: "We cannot provide further information."

By removing phrases like "at this point in time," the sentence becomes clearer and easier to understand without sacrificing meaning.

Similarly, phrases like "in order to" can often be replaced by "to," and "due to the fact that" can be simplified to "because."

## 4. Choose Strong Verbs

Using strong, specific verbs is another way to enhance both clarity and conciseness. Weak verbs often require additional words or modifiers, while strong verbs convey action or meaning more directly.

For example:

Weak: "She quickly made the decision to leave."

Strong: "She decided to leave."

The stronger verb "decided" removes the need for the modifier "quickly" and makes the sentence more concise without losing meaning.

## 5. Simplify Complex Sentences

Complex sentences can often be simplified for clarity without losing the depth of meaning. If a sentence contains multiple clauses, consider whether all the clauses are necessary or whether the idea can be conveyed in a simpler form.

For example:

Complex: "Because the weather was so bad, we decided to cancel the trip that we had been planning for several months."

Simplified: "We canceled the trip due to bad weather."

The simplified sentence retains the key information but removes unnecessary details and clauses, making it easier to follow.

## 6. Use Precise Language

Precision in language eliminates ambiguity and helps the reader understand your point more quickly. Avoid vague terms and instead choose words that precisely convey your message.

For example:

Vague: "The presentation was kind of interesting."

Precise: "The presentation was engaging."

By replacing vague terms like "kind of" with more specific descriptors, you make your writing stronger and clearer.

## 7. Break Up Long Sentences

Long, convoluted sentences can confuse readers and obscure your point. Breaking up long sentences into shorter ones can improve readability and clarity.

For example:

Long: "The meeting, which was supposed to end at 3 p.m., went on for another hour because of the heated discussion about the budget, and despite several attempts to wrap things up, it wasn't until 4 p.m. that everyone was able to leave."

Shorter: "The meeting was supposed to end at 3 p.m., but it went on for another hour due to a heated budget discussion. Despite efforts to wrap up, the meeting didn't end until 4 p.m."

The shorter version is more digestible and keeps the reader engaged.

## 8. Trim Unnecessary Modifiers

Modifiers such as "very," "really," and "extremely" can usually be removed without affecting the meaning of the sentence. In many cases, these words don't add significant value and can detract from the clarity of the writing.

For example:

Original: "The exam was really difficult."

Revised: "The exam was difficult."

The revised sentence retains the meaning but is more concise and direct. If a modifier does not change the meaning or add emphasis, it's best to eliminate it.

## 9. Clarify Ambiguous Pronouns

Pronouns like "it," "this," or "they" can sometimes lead to confusion if the reader isn't sure what they refer to. Ensuring that pronouns clearly point to the correct antecedent improves the clarity of your writing.

For example:

Ambiguous: "She told her friend that she needed to leave."

Clear: "Sarah told her friend that Sarah needed to leave."

While the second version may seem repetitive, it eliminates confusion about who "she" refers to, thus improving clarity.

## 10. Remove Filler Words

Filler words such as "actually," "basically," and "just" often clutter sentences without adding meaning. Removing these words can tighten your writing and enhance clarity.

For example:

With filler: "I just wanted to let you know that the report is basically finished."

Without filler: "I wanted to let you know that the report is finished."

Eliminating "just" and "basically" makes the sentence more direct and effective.

## 11. Reorder for Impact

Sometimes, clarity is enhanced by reordering sentence elements to emphasize the most important part of the sentence. Placing the most crucial information at the beginning or end of the sentence often makes it more impactful.

For example:

Less impactful: "There are many factors that contribute to climate change, including greenhouse gas emissions, deforestation, and industrial pollution."

More impactful: "Greenhouse gas emissions, deforestation, and industrial pollution are major contributors to climate change."

The second version leads with the key contributors, making the sentence more focused and easier to grasp.

## 12. Read Aloud to Catch Awkward Phrasing

One of the most effective ways to identify unclear or awkward phrasing is to read your writing aloud. Hearing how the sentences flow can help you spot problems that may not be immediately obvious when reading silently.

This technique often reveals areas where sentences can be smoothed out or simplified for better clarity.

## 13. Focus on Paragraph Structure

Clarity is not just about individual sentences; it also involves the structure of paragraphs. Each paragraph should have a clear main idea, and the sentences within it should support that idea logically. Avoid introducing multiple ideas in one paragraph, as this can confuse the reader.

For example, start with a clear topic sentence and ensure that the rest of the paragraph provides supporting details or examples related to that topic.

## 14. Consistency in Tense and Point of View

Shifting tenses or points of view within a passage can create confusion. To maintain clarity, ensure consistency in verb tenses and perspectives throughout your writing.

For example:

Inconsistent: "She runs to the store, and then she bought groceries."

Consistent: "She runs to the store, and then she buys groceries."

Maintaining consistency helps the reader follow the timeline and narrative of the sentence.

By focusing on these techniques for clarity and conciseness, your writing will become more engaging, easier to understand, and more effective in conveying your message. Whether you're revising your own work or editing someone else's, these strategies can help streamline the writing process and produce cleaner, sharper content.

## Avoiding Common Writing Errors

Writing errors can significantly undermine the quality and clarity of any written piece. Whether you're crafting an essay for a test, writing a research paper, or even sending a professional email, avoiding common mistakes is essential for clear communication. Below are some of the most frequent writing errors and how to avoid them.

**1. Sentence Fragments**

A sentence fragment occurs when a sentence is incomplete—it may lack a subject, a verb, or a complete thought. Fragments often confuse readers because they don't convey a clear, complete idea.

For example:

Fragment: "Because I was late to the meeting."

Complete: "I was late to the meeting because I missed my train."

The corrected version contains a complete thought, with both a subject and a predicate. To avoid sentence fragments, ensure that each sentence expresses a complete idea with both a subject and a verb.

**2. Run-on Sentences**

Run-on sentences occur when two or more independent clauses are improperly joined without appropriate punctuation or conjunctions. They often lead to confusion and make it difficult for the reader to follow the intended meaning.

For example:

Run-on: "I went to the store I bought some fruit."

Corrected: "I went to the store, and I bought some fruit."

Run-on sentences can be fixed by separating the clauses with a period, adding a conjunction, or using a semicolon when the clauses are closely related.

### 3. Subject-Verb Agreement Errors

Subject-verb agreement errors happen when the subject of a sentence does not match the verb in number (singular or plural). This is one of the most common grammatical mistakes and can make writing sound awkward or unprofessional.

For example:

Incorrect: "The group of students are going on a field trip."

Correct: "The group of students is going on a field trip."

Even though "students" is plural, the subject of the sentence is "group," which is singular. Ensure that the verb agrees with the main subject of the sentence, not the object of a preposition or a modifier.

### 4. Misplaced Modifiers

A misplaced modifier occurs when a descriptive word or phrase is not placed next to the word it modifies. This can lead to confusion or unintentional humor.

For example:

Misplaced: "She nearly drove her car for five hours."

Corrected: "She drove her car for nearly five hours."

In the incorrect sentence, "nearly" modifies "drove," suggesting she almost drove but didn't. The corrected version clarifies that she drove for close to five hours.

### 5. Dangling Modifiers

A dangling modifier happens when the word or phrase being modified is missing from the sentence, causing ambiguity or confusion.

For example:

Dangling: "Walking down the street, the flowers were beautiful."

Corrected: "Walking down the street, I noticed the beautiful flowers."

In the incorrect sentence, it's unclear who is walking down the street. The corrected sentence clarifies the subject performing the action.

### 6. Comma Splices

A comma splice occurs when two independent clauses are joined with just a comma instead of a conjunction or appropriate punctuation. This mistake disrupts the flow of the sentence and makes it harder for readers to follow the meaning.

For example:

Comma splice: "I love pizza, it's my favorite food."

Corrected: "I love pizza. It's my favorite food."

Alternatively: "I love pizza, and it's my favorite food."

To fix a comma splice, you can either split the clauses into two sentences, add a conjunction, or use a semicolon.

## 7. Incorrect Pronoun Reference

Pronouns (he, she, it, they, etc.) must clearly refer to a specific noun. When it's unclear which noun a pronoun is referring to, it can confuse the reader.

For example:

Unclear: "When Sarah talked to Mary, she said she would help."

Corrected: "When Sarah talked to Mary, Sarah said she would help."

In the unclear sentence, it's not obvious who "she" refers to. The corrected version clarifies the subject.

## 8. Incorrect Word Usage

Choosing the wrong word is a common error, particularly with homophones—words that sound alike but have different meanings, such as "there," "their," and "they're." Incorrect word usage can also include using words with similar meanings but that don't fit the context.

For example:

Incorrect: "Their going to the concert tomorrow."

Corrected: "They're going to the concert tomorrow."

To avoid incorrect word usage, double-check for homophones and ensure that you're using the right word for the context.

## 9. Apostrophe Misuse

Apostrophes are frequently misused in possessive nouns and contractions. Using apostrophes correctly is crucial for clarity in writing.

For example:

Incorrect: "Its raining outside."

Corrected: "It's raining outside."

Incorrect: "The dogs bone was buried in the yard."

Corrected: "The dog's bone was buried in the yard."

Remember, "it's" is a contraction for "it is," while "its" is a possessive pronoun. Apostrophes should not be used to make words plural, but they are used to show possession (the dog's bone) and to create contractions (it's, don't).

## 10. Improper Capitalization

Another common mistake is improper capitalization, especially in the middle of a sentence. Ensure that you only capitalize proper nouns, the first word of a sentence, and specific titles or names.

For example:

Incorrect: "The University is located in The City of New York."

Corrected: "The university is located in the city of New York."

In the corrected sentence, "university" and "city" are not capitalized because they are used as general nouns, not proper nouns.

## 11. Confusing Tense Shifts

Shifting between past, present, and future tense in a sentence or paragraph can confuse the reader and make the writing difficult to follow. It's important to maintain consistent verb tense throughout a piece unless there is a clear reason to change.

For example:

Incorrect: "I walked to the store and buy some groceries."

Corrected: "I walked to the store and bought some groceries."

Maintaining tense consistency helps the reader follow the timeline of events.

## 12. Misuse of Colons and Semicolons

Colons and semicolons are often misused or confused with each other. A colon is used to introduce a list, explanation, or definition, while a semicolon is used to connect two closely related independent clauses.

For example:

Incorrect: "She went to the store; for milk, bread, and eggs."

Corrected: "She went to the store for milk, bread, and eggs."

Correct use of a semicolon: "She wanted to buy a car; however, she didn't have enough money."

## 13. Quotation Mark Errors

Quotation marks should be used to indicate direct speech or a quote. One common error is placing punctuation outside of the quotation marks when it should be inside.

For example:

Incorrect: "I can't believe it", she said.

Corrected: "I can't believe it," she said.

Ensure that punctuation, such as commas and periods, is placed inside the quotation marks in American English.

**14. Overuse of Exclamation Points**

Exclamation points should be used sparingly. Overusing them weakens their impact and can make the writing seem overly emotional or unprofessional.

For example:

Overuse: "I got the job!!! I'm so excited!!!"

Corrected: "I got the job! I'm so excited!"

Using one exclamation point is enough to convey excitement or emphasis without overwhelming the reader.

By avoiding these common writing errors, you can significantly improve the quality of your writing and communicate your ideas more effectively. These fundamental strategies help ensure clarity, coherence, and professionalism in any written work.

# 3.3 Punctuation and Style

## Using Commas, Semicolons, and Colons Correctly

Punctuation plays a crucial role in shaping the clarity and flow of writing. Among the most commonly used punctuation marks are commas, semicolons, and colons. Each serves a unique function and contributes to the overall readability and precision of the text. Understanding when and how to use these punctuation marks effectively is essential for mastering written communication.

## Commas: Clarifying Ideas and Creating Flow

Commas are perhaps the most frequently used punctuation marks, and their role is to separate elements in a sentence to enhance clarity and prevent misreading. However, incorrect use of commas can lead to confusion. Here are some key guidelines for using commas properly:

1. **Separating Items in a Series**

   Commas are used to separate items in a list or series, which helps distinguish one element from the next.

Example:

*Correct*: "I bought apples, bananas, oranges, and grapes."

The comma before the conjunction ("and") is known as the Oxford comma, and while its use is sometimes debated, it's generally recommended for clarity.

2. **After Introductory Phrases**

   When a sentence begins with a phrase or clause that provides context but isn't the main idea, a comma is needed to separate the introductory material from the main clause.

Example:

*Correct*: "After the meeting, we went to lunch."

3. **Before Coordinating Conjunctions (FANBOYS)**

   Commas are placed before coordinating conjunctions (for, and, nor, but, or, yet, so) when they join two independent clauses.

Example:

*Correct*: "I wanted to go to the party, but I had too much work to do."

4. **Setting Off Nonessential Information**

   Commas are used to enclose nonessential elements, or information that can be removed without changing the core meaning of the sentence.

Example:

*Correct*: "My brother, who lives in California, is visiting next week."

In this case, "who lives in California" provides additional information but is not essential to the main point.

5. **With Adjectives**

   Commas can separate coordinate adjectives (those that equally modify the noun). If you can insert "and" between the adjectives without changing the meaning, a comma is needed.

Example:

*Correct*: "It was a long, tiring day."

Here, "long" and "tiring" are coordinate adjectives.

# Semicolons: Linking Closely Related Ideas

Semicolons are less commonly used than commas but are invaluable when linking closely related ideas or separating complex items in a list. Here are key uses of semicolons:

1. **Joining Two Independent Clauses Without a Conjunction**

   Semicolons can connect two independent clauses that are closely related but not joined by a coordinating conjunction.

Example:

*Correct*: "The weather was cold; we decided to stay indoors."

Each part could stand alone as a sentence, but the semicolon shows a strong connection between the ideas.

2. **Before Conjunctive Adverbs (e.g., however, therefore, nevertheless)**

When using a conjunctive adverb to link two independent clauses, a semicolon is needed before the adverb, and a comma follows it.

Example:

*Correct*: "I wanted to go for a run; however, it started raining."

3. **Separating Items in a Complex List**

When the items in a list already contain commas, semicolons can be used to separate the items clearly.

Example:

*Correct*: "On our trip, we visited Paris, France; Rome, Italy; and Madrid, Spain."

In this case, semicolons help avoid confusion between the city and country pairs.

# Colons: Introducing Information

Colons are often used to introduce specific information, lists, or explanations. Their purpose is to signal to the reader that what follows expands on or clarifies the preceding statement.

1. **Introducing a List**

A colon can be used to introduce a list of items, but only if the clause before the colon is a complete sentence.

Example:

*Correct*: "We need the following supplies: pencils, paper, and markers."

Avoid using a colon directly after a verb or preposition, as this can create a fragment.

2. **Introducing an Explanation or Clarification**

Colons are also used to introduce an explanation or example that elaborates on the statement before it.

Example:

*Correct*: "She had one goal: to finish the project on time."

3. **Introducing Quotations**

A colon can introduce a long or formal quotation, particularly when the lead-in sentence is complete.

Example:

*Correct*: "The professor began his lecture with a quote: 'The only limit to our realization of tomorrow is our doubts of today.'"

4. **Separating Titles and Subtitles**

In titles of books, articles, or presentations, colons are used to separate the main title from the subtitle.

Example:

*Correct*: "The Art of Writing: A Comprehensive Guide to Effective Communication."

5. **Highlighting Important Information**

Sometimes, colons are used to emphasize a point or create a dramatic pause before revealing important information.

Example:

*Correct*: "The winner of the competition is: Jane Doe."

## Common Mistakes to Avoid

1. **Overuse of Commas**

While commas are essential, overusing them can make a sentence feel cluttered or disjointed. Avoid inserting commas where they are not necessary, such as between subjects and verbs or between compound verbs.

Incorrect: "The teacher, gave the students, an assignment."

Correct: "The teacher gave the students an assignment."

2. **Misplacing Semicolons**

Semicolons should only be used between independent clauses or in complex lists. They should not be used in place of a comma or conjunction.

Incorrect: "We went to the park; and we had a picnic."

Correct: "We went to the park, and we had a picnic."

3. **Misuse of Colons**

Colons should only follow complete sentences. Using a colon after a fragment or incomplete clause is incorrect.

Incorrect: "The reasons are: because I am tired."

Correct: "There is only one reason: I am tired."

## Developing a Consistent Style

Mastering the use of commas, semicolons, and colons is not only about following rules but also about developing a consistent writing style. Clear punctuation enhances the reader's understanding and engagement, while poor punctuation can lead to confusion or misinterpretation.

1. **Maintaining Clarity**

   Always aim for clarity when deciding whether to use punctuation. Consider whether the sentence can be easily understood without the mark or whether the mark helps clarify meaning.

2. **Improving Readability**

   Punctuation marks, especially commas, are often compared to pauses in speech. Use punctuation to create a natural flow that guides the reader through your ideas without overwhelming them with long, complex sentences.

3. **Consistency Is Key**

   While writing styles can vary, it's important to apply punctuation rules consistently. If you choose to use the Oxford comma, for example, use it throughout your writing to avoid confusion.

By mastering these punctuation marks, writers can enhance their ability to communicate effectively, ensuring that their ideas are conveyed clearly and persuasively.

## Understanding SAT Writing Style Expectations

The SAT writing section requires students to demonstrate an understanding of formal, clear, and effective communication. The expectations of the SAT writing style focus on how well students can convey ideas while adhering to specific conventions of standard written English. Understanding these expectations is essential to performing well in this section, as the test measures a range of writing competencies, including grammar, punctuation, sentence structure, and logical argumentation.

## Clarity and Precision

A hallmark of strong writing on the SAT is clarity. Students are expected to write in a way that is direct and easy to understand, avoiding unnecessary complexity or ambiguity. The SAT prioritizes precise language, which means choosing words that accurately convey meaning without introducing confusion.

1. **Avoiding Wordiness**

   One of the main elements of clarity in SAT writing is conciseness. Sentences should be free of redundant phrases or filler words. The test often asks students to identify and revise sentences that are overly wordy or repetitive. A key to mastering this is understanding how to strip sentences of unnecessary words while maintaining the core meaning.

Example:

*Wordy*: "Due to the fact that the project is not yet complete, we will need to extend the deadline."

*Concise*: "Because the project is incomplete, we will extend the deadline."

2. **Using Specific and Concrete Language**

   The SAT expects students to avoid vague language and generalities, opting instead for specificity and precision. This includes choosing the most appropriate words to express ideas and avoiding broad or unclear terms.

   Example:

   *Vague*: "The presentation was good."

   *Specific*: "The presentation was informative and well-organized."

## Formal Tone

Another key expectation for SAT writing is maintaining a formal tone throughout the passage. The SAT requires students to demonstrate an academic style of writing that avoids informal language, slang, or conversational phrasing. While formal writing does not mean stiff or overly complex sentences, it does require careful attention to appropriate word choice and phrasing.

1. **Avoiding Contractions and Colloquial Language**

   Informal language, such as contractions (e.g., "can't," "won't") or slang, is discouraged in SAT writing. Students are expected to write in full sentences using formal English.

   Example:

   *Informal*: "He's not going to make it on time."

   *Formal*: "He will not arrive on time."

2. **Appropriate Use of Transitional Phrases**

   Transition words and phrases are crucial for creating smooth, coherent writing. However, SAT writing requires formal transitions rather than conversational ones.

   Example:

   *Informal*: "Anyway, the results were clear."

   *Formal*: "Nevertheless, the results were clear."

## Logical Flow and Coherence

The SAT places a strong emphasis on the logical progression of ideas. A well-written passage must present ideas in a way that is not only clear but also coherent, with each sentence logically following the previous one. This requires understanding how to use transitional phrases, maintain focus, and ensure that each paragraph builds on the one before it.

1. **Creating Logical Progression**

   Writers must ensure that their ideas flow smoothly from one to the next, without sudden jumps or breaks in logic. SAT writing passages are carefully constructed to test students' ability to identify places where ideas need to be better connected or where unnecessary shifts in topic occur.

   Example:

   *Incorrect*: "The study was successful. In contrast, the weather was sunny."

   *Correct*: "The study was successful. Furthermore, the results were consistent with previous research."

2. **Using Transitions to Guide the Reader**

   Strong writing uses transitions effectively to guide the reader through the argument or narrative. Transitions can signal comparisons, contrasts, cause and effect, or chronological progression, among others. The SAT will often test students' ability to choose the correct transitional phrase based on the logical flow of the passage.

   Example:

   *Without Transition*: "The experiment was flawed. The conclusions were unreliable."

   *With Transition*: "Because the experiment was flawed, the conclusions were unreliable."

## Effective Argumentation

A significant portion of the SAT writing section involves revising passages to strengthen the argument. This means that students must understand how to present a clear thesis and support it with relevant evidence and reasoning. The SAT expects writers to demonstrate the ability to construct arguments that are not only logical but also persuasive.

1. **Providing Strong Evidence**

   An argument is only as strong as the evidence that supports it. SAT writing passages often ask students to assess whether the evidence presented is relevant and sufficient. Effective SAT writing avoids making claims without backing them up with facts or specific details.

   Example:

   *Weak Evidence*: "Many people believe that exercise is good for you."

   *Strong Evidence*: "A recent study from the American Heart Association shows that individuals who exercise regularly reduce their risk of heart disease by 30%."

2. **Avoiding Logical Fallacies**

   Logical fallacies weaken arguments by introducing flawed reasoning. The SAT tests students' ability to recognize and correct fallacies, such as hasty generalizations, false dilemmas, or circular reasoning.

   Example:

   *Fallacy*: "If we don't increase taxes, the government will run out of money."

   *Revised*: "Without an increase in tax revenue, the government may face challenges in funding public services."

## Varied Sentence Structure

Good SAT writing is not only about conveying ideas but doing so in a way that engages the reader. This requires varied sentence structure, as overreliance on one type of sentence can make writing monotonous. The SAT assesses whether students can vary their sentence length and type to create a dynamic and engaging passage.

1. **Combining Simple and Complex Sentences**

   A mix of simple and complex sentences helps to maintain the reader's interest and improves the readability of the text. Simple sentences provide clarity, while complex sentences allow for the development of more nuanced ideas.

   Example:

   *Simple*: "The team conducted the experiment."

   *Complex*: "After months of planning, the team conducted the experiment, which yielded unexpected results."

2. **Avoiding Run-on Sentences**

   While varying sentence structure is important, students must also be careful to avoid run-on sentences, where multiple ideas are strung together without proper punctuation or conjunctions.

   Example:

   *Incorrect*: "The data was collected it was analyzed later."

   *Correct*: "The data was collected, and it was analyzed later."

## Conciseness and Avoiding Redundancy

Lastly, the SAT emphasizes the importance of concise writing that avoids redundancy. Strong writing conveys ideas in as few words as possible while still maintaining clarity and depth. The SAT often tests students' ability to revise sentences that include repetitive or redundant phrasing.

1. **Eliminating Redundant Phrases**

   Many common phrases in writing are redundant, meaning they use more words than necessary to express a single idea. Students must learn to recognize these and replace them with more concise alternatives.

   Example:

   *Redundant*: "The end result of the experiment was surprising."

   *Concise*: "The result of the experiment was surprising."

2. **Simplifying Overly Complex Sentences**

   While complex sentences have their place, sometimes writers overcomplicate their sentences, making them harder to understand. SAT writing expects students to simplify where appropriate, ensuring that each sentence is clear and to the point.

   Example:

   *Overly Complex*: "Due to the fact that there was an error in the data, the results, in the end, turned out to be incorrect."

   *Simplified*: "Because of an error in the data, the results were incorrect."

Mastering the SAT writing style requires understanding these key elements: clarity, formal tone, logical flow, strong argumentation, sentence variety, and conciseness. These are the cornerstones of effective writing on the exam.

# CHAPTER 4: TEST-TAKING STRATEGIES AND MINDSET

## 4.1 Building Confidence

### Overcoming Test Anxiety

Test anxiety is a common challenge faced by many students, especially when it comes to high-stakes exams like the Digital SAT. The feeling of pressure and the fear of underperforming can interfere with concentration, memory, and ultimately, your performance. However, overcoming test anxiety is possible with the right strategies, mindset, and preparation. The key is to address both the mental and physical aspects of anxiety and develop habits that enhance focus, calmness, and confidence during the test.

### Understanding Test Anxiety

Test anxiety manifests in different ways for different people. Some students may experience physical symptoms like headaches, nausea, or rapid heartbeats. Others may face cognitive symptoms such as racing thoughts, difficulty concentrating, or the dreaded "blanking out" on questions they know the answers to. It's important to recognize the signs of anxiety in yourself and accept that it's a natural reaction to stress, but not an insurmountable obstacle.

1. **Identify the Source of Your Anxiety**

   One of the first steps in overcoming test anxiety is to pinpoint where it's coming from. Are you anxious because you feel unprepared? Do you have perfectionist tendencies that pressure you to get a perfect score? Are you worried about the future implications of your test performance? Understanding the root cause of your anxiety can help you take more targeted steps to manage it effectively.

2. **Shift Your Mindset Toward the Test**

   Often, test anxiety stems from viewing the exam as a make-or-break moment. However, it's crucial to reframe the way you think about the SAT. Instead of seeing it as a judgment of your worth or future success, recognize it as just one step in a long academic journey. This shift in perspective can alleviate some of the pressure. Remind yourself that your performance on one test does not define you, and there are multiple opportunities to succeed.

## Preparation: The Antidote to Anxiety

Preparation is one of the most effective ways to reduce test anxiety. When you know the material inside and out, you're less likely to feel panicked. However, preparation isn't just about studying the content—it's about being mentally and physically ready to perform under test conditions.

1. **Simulate Testing Conditions**

   One way to reduce anxiety is to become familiar with the test environment. Take practice tests under timed conditions in a quiet space where you're free from distractions. This helps normalize the feeling of working under pressure, and the more you practice, the less intimidating the real test day will seem.

2. **Develop a Consistent Study Schedule**

   Last-minute cramming can amplify feelings of anxiety. Instead, set a consistent study routine well in advance of the test date. Break your study sessions into manageable chunks, focusing on specific topics or question types each time. By regularly working through material, you'll build a solid foundation of knowledge, which will boost your confidence when test day arrives.

3. **Practice Relaxation Techniques**

   Learning relaxation techniques can help you manage the physical symptoms of anxiety, such as shallow breathing or muscle tension. Deep breathing exercises, progressive muscle relaxation, and mindfulness meditation can all calm your nervous system and help you regain focus. Practicing these techniques regularly will allow you to employ them naturally during the test if you start to feel anxious.

## The Power of Positive Self-Talk

Another key to overcoming test anxiety is controlling the way you talk to yourself. Negative self-talk can worsen anxiety, leading to a spiral of doubt. On the other hand, positive self-talk can help you stay grounded, motivated, and focused.

1. **Replace Negative Thoughts with Positive Affirmations**

   Instead of telling yourself, "I'm going to fail," or "I'm terrible at this," practice replacing those thoughts with affirmations like, "I've prepared for this," or "I can do my best." Training your brain to focus on positive, encouraging thoughts can reduce self-doubt and anxiety.

2. **Acknowledge and Dismiss Irrational Fears**

   Test anxiety often arises from irrational fears, like the idea that one bad performance will ruin your future. Challenge these thoughts by asking yourself, "Is this really true?" and "What's the worst that could happen?" You'll often realize that your fears are exaggerated, and this realization can help bring down your anxiety levels.

## Developing a Pre-Test Routine

Having a consistent pre-test routine can help you stay calm and focused on test day. A routine helps signal to your brain that you're in control and prepared, reducing the uncertainty that fuels anxiety.

1. **Get a Good Night's Sleep**

   Sleep is critical for cognitive function and memory retention. Pulling an all-nighter before the test can impair your ability to think clearly and recall information. Aim for at least 7–8 hours of sleep the night before the exam to ensure you wake up feeling refreshed and mentally sharp.

2. **Eat a Healthy Breakfast**

   On test day, start with a nutritious breakfast that includes a balance of protein, fiber, and complex carbohydrates. This will help sustain your energy and focus throughout the exam. Avoid sugary foods that can cause a crash in energy later in the day.

3. **Arrive Early to the Test Center**

   Being rushed adds unnecessary stress. Arriving early to the test center allows you to settle in, get comfortable, and mentally prepare before the test begins. Use this time to practice a few deep breathing exercises or positive affirmations to help calm your nerves.

## Managing Anxiety During the Test

Even with the best preparation, it's possible that anxiety will still arise during the test. However, there are ways to manage it in the moment so that it doesn't affect your performance.

1. **Pace Yourself**

   One source of test anxiety is feeling like you're running out of time. To counteract this, keep an eye on the clock but don't fixate on it. If you find yourself spending too much time on one question, move on and return to it later. Trust your pacing and don't rush through questions—accuracy is more important than speed.

2. **Take Deep Breaths and Stay Grounded**

   If you feel your anxiety rising, take a few deep breaths to bring your heart rate down. You can also try grounding techniques like pressing your feet firmly into the floor or placing your hands flat on the desk. These small actions can help reorient your mind and calm your body.

3. **Focus on One Question at a Time**

   Don't let yourself get overwhelmed by thinking about the whole test at once. Break it down into manageable parts by focusing on one question at a time. Remind yourself that you've practiced for this, and trust your abilities.

## Post-Test Anxiety Management

Finally, it's important to manage any anxiety you may feel after the test. Many students experience post-test anxiety, worrying about how they performed and what their scores will be. To avoid this:

1. **Accept That You've Done Your Best**

   Once the test is over, there's nothing more you can do. Trust that your preparation and efforts have paid off. Focus on the fact that you've done your best, and avoid dwelling on what you think went wrong.

2. **Stay Distracted and Engaged in Other Activities**

   Keep yourself occupied after the test to avoid overanalyzing your performance. Engage in hobbies, spend time with friends or family, and focus on activities that make you feel relaxed and happy.

3. **Prepare for the Next Steps**

   Whether it's preparing for another exam, focusing on schoolwork, or planning your college applications, channel your energy into productive activities. This will help you stay positive and focused on the future.

### Mental Preparation Tips

Mental preparation is a key component of success on the SAT. Your mindset can significantly influence your performance, so it's essential to cultivate a mental state that is both calm and confident. Here are strategies to ensure you are mentally ready to tackle the SAT with clarity and focus.

### 1. Visualize Success

One of the most powerful tools for mental preparation is visualization. Visualization involves mentally rehearsing a successful outcome before the event takes place. Athletes frequently use this technique to enhance performance, and it can be just as effective in academic settings.

Begin by imagining yourself on test day. Picture yourself arriving at the testing center, calm and collected. Visualize yourself answering each question confidently and efficiently. See yourself moving through the test with a sense of control and clarity. The more vividly you imagine this scenario, the more your brain will accept it as a likely outcome, boosting your confidence when you actually sit for the exam.

Visualization also helps you internalize the idea that you're capable of achieving your goals. By mentally rehearsing success, you can reduce feelings of anxiety and create a sense of familiarity with the test environment, which in turn helps you stay grounded and focused on the task at hand.

## 2. Develop a Pre-Test Ritual

Having a consistent pre-test ritual can help reduce test-day anxiety and get you into the right mindset. A ritual signals to your brain that it's time to focus and perform. This could be something simple, like reviewing your notes for 15 minutes before leaving for the test or doing breathing exercises to calm your nerves.

The key is consistency—repeating the same actions before each practice test and the real test will create a sense of familiarity. When your brain recognizes the routine, it will associate those actions with a state of calm preparedness, making it easier to transition into test-taking mode.

## 3. Manage Your Test-Day Energy

It's important to manage your physical energy on test day to maintain mental clarity. Start by ensuring you're well-rested the night before the test. Lack of sleep can lead to poor concentration, slower cognitive function, and increased stress. Aim for at least eight hours of sleep in the nights leading up to the test to ensure your brain is operating at its best.

On the morning of the test, eat a balanced breakfast to fuel your brain. Include complex carbohydrates, protein, and healthy fats to provide sustained energy. Avoid sugary foods that can lead to an energy crash halfway through the exam.

Staying hydrated is equally important. Dehydration, even mild, can affect cognitive function. Drink water leading up to the test, but don't overdo it to the point where frequent bathroom breaks become a distraction.

## 4. Reframe Negative Thoughts

One of the most common obstacles to mental readiness is negative self-talk. Thoughts like, "I'm not ready," or "I'm going to fail," can sabotage your confidence and create unnecessary anxiety. It's essential to recognize these thoughts and reframe them into positive affirmations.

When a negative thought arises, challenge it. Ask yourself, "Is this thought helping me or hindering me?" Replace it with a more constructive thought like, "I've prepared for this, and I can handle whatever comes my way." Reframing your thoughts helps to build a more positive, solution-focused mindset that fosters confidence rather than fear.

In the days leading up to the test, practice positive affirmations. Remind yourself that you've put in the work and have the ability to succeed. This practice can transform your internal dialogue from one of doubt to one of assurance and readiness.

## 5. Practice Mindfulness and Breathing Techniques

Mindfulness is the practice of staying present and fully engaged in the moment. This can be particularly helpful when you start feeling overwhelmed during the test. Instead of letting your mind spiral with "what if" scenarios, focus on the question in front of you. Mindfulness techniques, such as focusing on your breath or noticing your surroundings, can bring you back to the present moment and prevent anxiety from derailing your concentration.

Incorporate deep breathing exercises into your routine, both in the days leading up to the test and on test day itself. Deep breathing helps activate the body's relaxation response, reducing the physical symptoms of anxiety, such as increased heart rate or shallow breathing. Before starting the test, take a few deep breaths to center yourself. If you feel anxious during the test, pause for a moment, take another deep breath, and refocus.

## 6. Set Realistic Expectations

Setting realistic expectations for yourself can alleviate much of the pressure that leads to test anxiety. While it's important to aim high, it's equally crucial to recognize that perfection is not the goal. You may not get every question right, and that's okay. Instead, focus on doing your best and staying consistent throughout the test.

Understand that one exam does not define your future. Colleges look at a variety of factors beyond standardized test scores, including your GPA, extracurricular activities, and personal essays. Knowing this can help reduce the pressure you put on yourself and allow you to approach the test with a calmer, more balanced mindset.

## 7. Take Breaks When Needed

It's important to recognize when your brain needs a break. Mental fatigue can negatively impact your performance if you don't give yourself time to reset. The SAT provides designated breaks, and it's essential to use them wisely.

During breaks, step away from your test booklet, stretch your muscles, and take a few deep breaths. Clear your mind from any lingering doubts about previous questions and focus on the next section. Taking a short mental break helps recharge your brain and prevents burnout during the exam.

## 8. Stay in the Moment

Finally, staying in the moment is critical to mental preparation. Dwelling on questions you've already answered or worrying about future sections can distract you from performing your best in the present. Once you move on from a question, let it go. Trust in the answers you've given and stay focused on the question in front of you.

Avoid the temptation to compare yourself to other test-takers. Everyone works at their own pace, and what matters most is that you stay true to your own rhythm. Keep your focus on your own performance and trust the process you've practiced.

By implementing these mental preparation tips, you'll be better equipped to manage test-day nerves, maintain focus, and give your best performance on the SAT.

# 4.2 Strategy for Answer Elimination

## Smart Guessing Strategies

Smart guessing is an essential skill for maximizing your score on the SAT. While it's always ideal to confidently know the correct answer, that's not always possible in the pressure of the exam. Employing strategic guessing can help you eliminate incorrect answers and increase your chances of selecting the right one. Here's how to approach guessing with intelligence and intention.

**1. Process of Elimination**

The first step in smart guessing is to systematically eliminate incorrect answer choices. Every SAT question has one correct answer and three incorrect ones. By removing even one wrong option, you improve your odds of guessing correctly from 25% to 33%. Eliminate two wrong answers, and your odds rise to 50%.

Start by scanning the answer choices and identifying any that are blatantly incorrect. These might include answers that contradict information from the passage in reading sections or math answers that are illogical given the problem's context. Once you've eliminated the obvious wrong choices, focus on the remaining options.

A common mistake is to focus too much on which answer is right, without giving enough attention to which answers are definitely wrong. Remember, the SAT is designed to challenge your critical thinking, and there's always a reason why three of the four choices are incorrect. Scrutinizing these wrong answers will sharpen your ability to spot traps and boost your confidence when making educated guesses.

**2. Identifying Distractor Choices**

Distractors are answers designed to mislead test-takers by seeming plausible at first glance. These can be tricky, but with careful analysis, they can be exposed for what they are: answers that don't fully address the question or misinterpret key elements.

Distractors often repeat words or phrases from the passage or problem, making them appear as if they are directly tied to the correct answer. However, they usually lack the precision required for the SAT. Pay attention to subtle shifts in meaning or scope that make distractor choices incorrect. For example, in reading sections, a distractor may focus on a minor detail from the passage rather than the main idea, or it may present an idea that is too extreme compared to what the author actually conveyed.

In math sections, distractors might involve common calculation errors, such as misinterpreting a unit or misapplying a formula. Be wary of answers that look too familiar based on superficial aspects of the problem, but fail to align with the actual question being asked.

## 3. Using Context Clues

When you're unsure about an answer, context can often provide valuable clues. In the reading and writing sections, look at the surrounding sentences or paragraphs to better understand how the specific question fits within the larger context of the passage. Authors use patterns, themes, and consistent reasoning throughout their writing. By understanding the overall direction of the text, you can often eliminate answer choices that don't match the intended meaning or tone.

In the math section, context clues come from the way the problem is structured and the relationships between variables. Don't focus solely on numbers—think about what the question is really asking. By connecting the dots between different pieces of information, you can often eliminate answers that don't logically follow from the rest of the problem.

## 4. Avoiding Extremes

On the SAT, extreme answer choices are often incorrect. Extreme answers tend to use words like "always," "never," "only," and "completely." The SAT generally favors answers that are moderate and measured, reflecting the nuance of the passage or the logic of the math problem. When you see an extreme answer, consider whether the problem or passage really justifies such a strong conclusion. More often than not, you'll find that these extreme options can be safely eliminated.

Look instead for answers that reflect a balanced understanding. In reading, the correct answer is typically supported by clear evidence from the text, while extreme answers overstate the author's intentions or the passage's implications. In math, extreme values or operations might be designed to catch those who rush through the problem without fully considering the question's constraints.

## 5. Trust Your Gut—With Caution

Sometimes, after you've narrowed down your choices, your instinct will pull you towards one answer. In many cases, trusting your gut can work in your favor, especially if you've studied thoroughly and are familiar with the test format. Your brain might recognize patterns from practice tests or previously encountered problems, guiding you to the correct answer.

However, it's important to strike a balance between intuition and overconfidence. Blind guessing or following a hunch without any logical basis can lead to errors. Before settling on an answer, make sure you can justify your choice with reasoning, even if it's just a simple connection to a concept you've studied. When your gut instinct aligns with solid elimination strategies, you're likely on the right track.

## 6. Using the "Two-Pass" Method

An effective approach to managing your time and making smart guesses is the two-pass method. In your first pass through the section, focus on the questions you can answer confidently. Don't waste time agonizing over tough questions on the first try. Instead, mark these harder questions to return to on your second pass.

On your second pass, tackle the questions you skipped earlier. Now that you've completed the easier questions, you'll have more time and mental energy to devote to the tricky ones. At this point, use the elimination strategies and context clues you've practiced to make an educated guess if you still can't find the answer.

This method ensures that you don't miss out on easy points by getting stuck on difficult questions early on. Plus, by the time you return to the tougher questions, your brain might have picked up on clues or patterns that weren't obvious the first time.

## 7. Keep Track of Your Answers

One of the risks of guessing is that you might accidentally bubble the wrong answer on your answer sheet, especially if you're under time pressure. To avoid this, make sure you're consistently bubbling in the correct spot for each question. Some students prefer to circle their answers in the test booklet and fill in the bubbles at the end of each section, while others bubble in after each question. Choose the method that minimizes your risk of error.

If you're guessing on a question, make sure to still follow your established bubbling process. Even though you may not be confident in the answer, keeping your bubbling strategy consistent ensures you don't introduce careless mistakes into your score.

## 8. Use Every Second Wisely

As the clock winds down on your SAT section, remember that you're not penalized for guessing. If time is running out and you haven't finished all the questions, don't leave any blank. Quickly scan the remaining questions and apply any elimination strategies you can, even if it's just removing one or two choices. If you truly don't know the answer, choose an option rather than leaving it blank. A random guess gives you a 25% chance of earning the point, while a blank answer is a guaranteed zero.

By employing these smart guessing strategies, you can increase your odds of success even when you're unsure of the answer. Remember, the SAT is not just a test of knowledge but also a test of strategy, and smart guessing plays a crucial role in maximizing your score.

# Eliminating Wrong Answers Effectively

One of the most valuable skills you can develop for the SAT is the ability to effectively eliminate wrong answers. This strategy can dramatically improve your chances of selecting the correct option, even when you're not entirely sure of the right answer. By refining your approach to eliminating incorrect responses, you can gain confidence, reduce stress, and increase your overall score.

## 1. Focus on the Clear Wrong Answers First

The SAT often includes distractor answers that are clearly incorrect if you pay close attention. These answers may include factual inaccuracies, contradictions with the passage or problem, or mathematical miscalculations. Your first goal should always be to spot these blatant errors as quickly as possible.

In reading sections, look for answers that go against the explicit statements in the passage. For example, if the passage states that the author disagrees with a particular viewpoint, an answer that supports that viewpoint can be immediately ruled out. In math, eliminate answers that don't make logical sense within the context of the problem, such as results with incorrect units or values that are out of the reasonable range given the information provided.

By training yourself to recognize these types of clear errors, you'll build speed and accuracy as you progress through each question.

## 2. Pay Attention to Extreme Language

Extreme language in an answer choice is a red flag on the SAT. Words like "always," "never," "only," and "completely" are often indicators of incorrect answers because they suggest absolutes. The SAT, especially in the reading and writing sections, usually favors moderate and nuanced responses that reflect a balanced perspective. In contrast, extreme answers may oversimplify the author's argument or the tone of a passage.

For example, in a reading question about an author's opinion on a particular issue, if one answer suggests that the author "always" supports a specific approach, while another answer reflects a more measured view, the extreme answer is likely incorrect. In most cases, the SAT will not present situations where such absolutes are justified by the passage or question prompt.

Avoiding extreme answers is one of the simplest ways to narrow down your options and boost your confidence in the remaining choices.

## 3. Analyze Answer Choices for Consistency

In many cases, incorrect answers on the SAT will be inconsistent with the logic or flow of the passage or problem. This is especially common in reading comprehension questions. An answer might sound reasonable at first glance, but when you examine it more closely, you'll realize that it introduces ideas or conclusions that are inconsistent with the author's line of reasoning.

For example, in a passage discussing scientific research, an answer that introduces a subjective opinion might seem plausible but contradicts the overall tone and objectivity of the passage. In math sections, an answer choice that involves an unnecessary or overly complicated calculation is often wrong, as the SAT generally favors logical, straightforward solutions.

Checking for internal consistency can help you rule out answers that don't align with the passage's or problem's structure.

## 4. Watch for Partial Truths

The SAT is notorious for presenting answers that contain a mix of correct and incorrect information. These "partial truth" answers are designed to mislead test-takers into selecting them by appearing partially correct. However, a close examination will reveal that the answer is not fully supported by the passage or does not completely solve the problem.

For example, in a reading passage about environmental policy, an answer may accurately reflect one small detail from the text but misinterpret the broader argument. While it may be tempting to select this answer based on the correct detail, remember that the correct answer must reflect the entirety of the question's scope.

The same goes for math questions. A partial truth answer might involve a correct first step in solving the problem but lead to a final solution that is incorrect due to a misstep later in the process.

Always ensure that the answer choice fully addresses the question rather than just part of it. If an answer seems partially right but not fully, it's a good candidate for elimination.

## 5. Consider the Function of the Answer Choices

In the SAT reading and writing sections, answer choices are often designed to serve specific functions within the context of the passage. If a question asks for the purpose of a paragraph or a sentence, eliminate answers that describe purposes irrelevant to the main idea of the passage.

For example, if the passage is largely explanatory, an answer suggesting that a particular sentence is meant to entertain or create suspense is likely incorrect. Similarly, if a passage is argumentative, answers that describe the text as informative or neutral are probably wrong.

In writing questions, answers that don't align with the grammatical rules being tested, or which fail to improve the clarity or coherence of a passage, should also be eliminated. By focusing on how each answer fits the overall function of the question, you can effectively reduce your options.

## 6. Beware of Out-of-Scope Answers

Out-of-scope answers introduce new ideas, concepts, or information that were never mentioned in the passage or the problem. The SAT often includes these to distract you from the correct answer by making you consider irrelevant information.

For example, if a reading passage discusses a historical event and an answer choice introduces a completely different event or an unrelated concept, it's out of scope. Even if the new information seems plausible or interesting, it doesn't fit the context of the question and should be eliminated.

Similarly, in math, out-of-scope answers might involve complex formulas or steps that the question doesn't require. If an answer choice asks you to apply advanced calculus to solve a straightforward algebra problem, you can safely eliminate it as unnecessarily complicated.

Training yourself to recognize out-of-scope answers will prevent you from wasting time on irrelevant distractions.

## 7. Look for Redundancies in the Choices

In some cases, multiple answer choices may essentially say the same thing but with different wording. When this happens, you can often eliminate both choices because they cannot both be correct. The SAT requires one correct answer for each question, so when two answers seem to overlap significantly in meaning, both are usually wrong.

For example, in a writing section question about improving sentence structure, two answers might offer very similar rewordings of a sentence that do not improve clarity or grammatical correctness. If both seem redundant and fail to meet the criteria of the question, they can be eliminated.

## 8. Eliminate Based on Logic

Finally, one of the simplest but most effective techniques is to apply basic logic. If an answer doesn't make logical sense, it's wrong. Whether the question is about reading comprehension, writing, or math, logic is always a useful tool for eliminating wrong answers.

In the math section, for instance, if your calculations lead to a positive number, but one of the answer choices is negative, you can immediately eliminate it. In reading, if an answer choice conflicts with a logical progression of the passage, such as suggesting a conclusion that was never implied, you can safely rule it out. Training yourself to recognize illogical answers will make the elimination process much quicker and more intuitive.

By applying these strategies for eliminating wrong answers effectively, you can significantly improve your odds of success on the SAT. It's not always about knowing the right answer immediately, but about narrowing down the possibilities until the correct answer becomes clear.

# 4.3 Balancing Speed and Accuracy

In any timed exam like the SAT, finding the right balance between speed and accuracy is crucial for success. Many students struggle with this balance, focusing too much on one at the expense of the other. If you rush through the questions, you may make careless mistakes. On the other hand, if you spend too much time double-checking every answer, you risk running out of time and leaving questions unanswered. The goal is to optimize your speed while maintaining a high level of accuracy, which can be achieved through targeted focus exercises designed to increase speed without sacrificing precision.

## 1. Timed Practice Drills

One of the most effective ways to increase your speed on the SAT is by practicing under timed conditions. Many students perform well on untimed practice questions, but their accuracy drops significantly when they are placed under time constraints. Timed drills help simulate real test conditions and allow you to adapt to the pressure of completing questions quickly.

Start by setting shorter time limits for individual sections than you will have on the actual test. For example, if the SAT gives you 65 minutes to complete the Reading section, practice completing it in 60 minutes. Gradually reduce the time for these drills as you become more comfortable with faster pacing. Make sure to track your progress, noting which types of questions are causing delays.

This method also trains you to stay focused during the entire test, eliminating the need to rush near the end of a section when time is running low.

## 2. Chunking Practice Sets

Another useful technique for building both speed and accuracy is chunking. Chunking involves breaking down larger sets of questions into smaller, more manageable groups. This helps you maintain focus and avoid burnout during long practice sessions.

For instance, rather than working through an entire section at once, divide it into smaller segments, such as answering five questions at a time. After completing each set, quickly review your answers and evaluate your performance. Chunking helps you maintain a steady pace, prevents fatigue, and allows you to identify specific types of questions where your speed could improve.

Once you've built up your endurance through smaller chunks, you can work toward completing full sections more quickly and accurately.

## 3. Skim and Scan Techniques for Reading Sections

In the Reading section, developing skim and scan techniques is a vital skill to improve speed without sacrificing accuracy. Skimming involves reading the passage quickly to get the main idea and the overall structure. Scanning involves looking for key words or phrases in the passage that relate directly to the questions.

When practicing, avoid reading the passage word for word. Instead, skim the first and last sentences of each paragraph, focusing on how the information is presented. Then, scan for relevant details in response to specific questions.

These techniques not only speed up the reading process but also improve your ability to retain critical information, leading to more accurate answers. Practice skim and scan drills regularly to sharpen these skills.

## 4. Prioritizing Easier Questions

Maximizing your speed also involves knowing when to skip or defer more challenging questions. During the SAT, each question is worth the same amount of points, regardless of difficulty. To optimize your score, you should focus on answering the easier questions first, ensuring you collect as many points as possible before tackling more difficult ones.

When you encounter a tough question, make an educated guess if possible and move on. This will allow you to conserve time and mental energy for questions that you are more confident in answering. Returning to difficult questions with fresh eyes after completing the rest of the section can sometimes make them easier to solve.

## 5. Speed-Building for the Writing Section

In the Writing section, many questions focus on sentence structure, grammar, and punctuation. To increase your speed, familiarize yourself with common grammar rules and sentence construction issues. The more you practice identifying these issues, the quicker you will become at answering the questions.

In this section, another effective technique is to focus on recognizing patterns. Many of the questions follow similar formats, so identifying recurring patterns can save valuable time. For example, if you consistently see comma splice or subject-verb agreement questions, your ability to spot these issues will improve significantly with practice.

Additionally, the process of elimination is a powerful tool for the Writing section. By quickly eliminating the clearly incorrect options, you can focus on evaluating the remaining choices, which speeds up decision-making.

## 6. Practice Mental Shortcuts in Math

For the SAT Math section, building speed requires practicing mental math techniques and shortcuts. While it's tempting to rely heavily on your calculator, doing so can waste time. Instead, work on developing your mental math skills for simple calculations, such as multiplying or dividing numbers quickly.

Familiarize yourself with common mathematical principles and formulas. Knowing when to apply specific formulas, like the Pythagorean theorem or quadratic equations, without needing to re-derive them will save you time. Make sure to practice recognizing these types of problems so you can solve them efficiently.

Another important tactic is to simplify complex problems as much as possible. Break down multi-step problems into smaller steps that you can solve quickly. By improving your ability to simplify and solve problems mentally, you can shave off valuable seconds on each question.

### 7. Building Muscle Memory for Standardized Questions

The SAT often uses question formats that are repeated in various forms throughout the test. By developing muscle memory for these types of questions, you can greatly improve your speed. Practice as many official SAT questions as possible, paying attention to patterns in how questions are structured and asked.

For example, in the Reading section, you might recognize questions that ask for the main idea or inference questions based on tone. Familiarity with these types of questions allows you to predict the answer structure and focus on the most relevant part of the passage.

Similarly, in the Math and Writing sections, many questions are repeated with slight variations in numbers or wording. The more you practice, the more intuitive your responses will become, allowing you to move quickly from one question to the next.

### 8. Testing Yourself Under Varying Conditions

In addition to standard practice tests, it's helpful to test yourself under different conditions to simulate the unpredictability of the actual SAT. This could include practicing in a noisy environment, using a different type of timer, or working at different times of the day.

By varying the conditions under which you practice, you'll prepare yourself for unexpected distractions or challenges during the actual test. As you become more adaptable, you'll be able to maintain both speed and accuracy under any circumstances.

Overall, the key to balancing speed and accuracy on the SAT is consistent, targeted practice. Focus on developing techniques that will allow you to complete questions quickly while maintaining your attention to detail. By incorporating these exercises into your study routine, you'll build confidence, improve your time management, and maximize your SAT performance.

## Double-checking work without wasting time

One of the most overlooked yet essential skills for standardized test success is the ability to double-check your work efficiently. While it is crucial to ensure accuracy, you cannot afford to spend too much time re-evaluating your answers. Effective double-checking means catching mistakes without sacrificing the time needed to complete other questions. Developing this skill requires practice and a structured approach that blends careful review with quick decision-making.

## 1. Prioritizing Which Questions to Re-check

Not all questions require the same level of scrutiny when double-checking your answers. Focus on the questions you found challenging or were unsure about during the test. As you work through the exam, mark questions where you made an educated guess or felt uncertain. This creates a priority list for double-checking once you've completed the entire section.

Once you return to these questions, focus on re-reading them carefully, looking for key words or phrases you might have missed. This is especially helpful in reading comprehension or grammar-based sections, where a small detail can change the meaning of an answer choice.

On the other hand, questions you answered with confidence should not be rechecked at length. A quick glance to verify that you bubbled the correct answer will suffice. This helps you save time while still ensuring accuracy where it's most needed.

## 2. Quick Comparison of Answer Choices

A key part of double-checking work without wasting time is to quickly compare the answer choices again. For example, in multiple-choice questions, it's helpful to re-read the question and then glance at the other options to ensure your chosen answer still stands as the best. This review should be swift—you're confirming your reasoning, not re-solving the entire problem.

If you notice something about another option that makes you hesitate, take a moment to evaluate why it seemed incorrect initially. Look for specific flaws in the alternative answer choices—such as inaccurate facts or illogical conclusions—before deciding to stick with your original choice or make a switch.

This method of targeted comparison is efficient because it focuses your attention on verifying accuracy without reopening every decision for debate.

## 3. Checking for Consistency in Multi-step Problems

In math or multi-step reasoning problems, consistency is crucial. Double-check that the steps you took to reach your answer align logically with the final result. This includes verifying that you performed operations correctly, used the right formulas, or interpreted data accurately.

If a question required multiple steps, you can double-check the most error-prone steps, such as calculations or the application of specific rules. For example, review any fractions, decimals, or negative signs that might have been overlooked. These types of small mistakes can have a significant impact on the outcome, and correcting them ensures that your final answer is accurate.

Pay attention to units of measurement, signs, and specific wording that may change the approach to solving a problem. Confirming that all steps lead coherently to the final solution will prevent you from making avoidable errors.

## 4. Avoiding Overthinking During Review

While it's important to be thorough, overthinking can lead to second-guessing, which often results in changing correct answers to incorrect ones. Studies show that first instincts are often correct, especially if you have prepared thoroughly. Therefore, it's essential to avoid getting stuck in a loop of overanalyzing your decisions.

The key is to strike a balance between careful review and trusting your initial responses. If your first choice was made confidently and based on clear reasoning, avoid spending excessive time questioning it. On the other hand, if you spot a clear discrepancy or logical flaw, it's worth reconsidering your answer.

A quick review to ensure your thought process still holds up is sufficient. Practice being decisive during your review sessions, making note of where your instincts are strong and where you tend to doubt yourself.

## 5. Using Remaining Time Wisely

If you find yourself with extra time after completing a section, use it wisely by returning to questions that deserve a second look. Begin by addressing any questions you marked as uncertain. Use this time to re-read both the question and answer choices carefully, ensuring you did not miss any important details during your first attempt.

Be strategic with your remaining time—if you only have a few minutes left, do not try to revisit every question. Focus on those you identified as problematic, and double-check them for any errors in reasoning, misinterpretations, or calculation mistakes. It's also a good opportunity to quickly ensure that your answers are properly bubbled on the answer sheet, particularly for questions you may have skipped initially and returned to later.

If you have less than a minute left, avoid making drastic changes unless you are sure of a mistake. A well-thought-out, consistent answer is typically better than a rushed change.

## 6. Preventing Careless Mistakes

Careless mistakes are often the result of rushing through questions or losing focus, particularly in sections where you feel confident. The best way to catch these errors in double-checking is by approaching your work with fresh eyes. For example, if you solved a question using mental math, double-check by writing out the calculation. Sometimes, seeing the problem laid out in writing helps to catch small oversights.

Careless mistakes in reading comprehension often occur because of misreading a key detail in the passage or question. As you double-check these sections, scan the text for important words or phrases that might change the meaning of the answer choices. A simple re-read of the question prompt can prevent errors.

It's also helpful to use double-checking as a way to slow down slightly in sections where you tend to move too quickly. By pacing yourself, you can spot potential mistakes before finalizing your answers.

## 7. Speeding up the Double-checking Process

To maximize efficiency, make double-checking a habitual part of your practice tests. Set aside time at the end of each section specifically for reviewing your answers, and develop a checklist for what to look for. This might include verifying that each bubble is filled in correctly, checking calculations, and scanning the reading passage for key details.

The more you practice double-checking, the faster and more intuitive it becomes. Over time, you'll learn to identify which questions are more likely to need a second look and which can be left alone.

During actual tests, establish a routine where you automatically set aside 2-3 minutes at the end of each section for review. As you practice, track how long it takes you to review a certain number of questions, and aim to streamline this process.

## 8. Developing a Double-checking Mindset

Finally, cultivating a double-checking mindset can help prevent mistakes before they even occur. Approaching the test with a balance of confidence and caution ensures that you remain focused and attentive to details throughout the entire exam.

By regularly incorporating double-checking into your study routine, you'll naturally begin to notice patterns in your own mistakes. This awareness helps you avoid repeating the same errors on test day and builds the habit of reviewing your work efficiently.

Being prepared, developing a routine, and remaining calm under pressure are the keys to using your double-checking time effectively without losing momentum.

# CHAPTER 5: PRACTICE READING EXERCISES

## 5.1 Comprehension Exercises

The comprehension section is designed to evaluate your ability to understand, interpret, and analyze written material. In this section, you will encounter a variety of reading passages followed by questions that test different aspects of your reading comprehension skills. These exercises are crafted to mirror the structure and complexity of questions found in the actual Digital SAT.

Each question is built around the key areas of reading comprehension: main ideas, supporting details, inferences, tone, purpose, and structure. Below are 250 practice questions designed to challenge your reading comprehension, help you identify patterns in your mistakes, and hone your ability to think critically about the text.

These questions will help you build the necessary skills to excel on the reading portion of the test by sharpening your understanding of what each question is truly asking. You will need to think beyond the obvious and carefully analyze the passages to find the most accurate answers.

## Examples of question types:

**1. Identifying the Main Idea:**

- What is the primary purpose of the passage?

- What message is the author trying to convey?

**2. Recognizing Supporting Details:**

- Which of the following best supports the main idea presented in paragraph 3?

- Which detail from the passage best illustrates the author's argument?

**3. Making Inferences:**

- Based on the passage, what can be inferred about the author's opinion on the topic?

- What conclusion can be drawn from the information provided in the passage?

**4. Understanding the Author's Tone:**

- How would you describe the tone of the passage? Is it objective, persuasive, or critical?

- What emotion does the author convey through their word choice in paragraph 4?

**5. Interpreting Vocabulary in Context:**

- In the context of the passage, what does the word "exemplify" most closely mean?

- How does the use of the word "rigorous" in the passage affect the reader's understanding of the author's stance?

## 6. Analyzing Structure and Organization:

- How does the structure of the passage contribute to its overall effectiveness?

- What role does the second paragraph play in the development of the author's argument?

Each of these question types is designed to reflect real SAT exam conditions, ensuring that you not only gain familiarity with the content but also with the format and level of complexity you can expect on the test day.

By working through these exercises, you'll sharpen your critical thinking, improve your ability to dissect passages quickly and efficiently, and practice pinpointing the correct answers under timed conditions. Each question is meant to test a specific skill, enabling you to gradually improve as you progress through the questions.

These 250 comprehension exercises will help you tackle any reading passage confidently, regardless of the subject matter or difficulty level.

# 250 PRACTICE QUESTIONS

## Section 1: Narrative Passage Comprehension
## Narrative Passage 1: General understanding of plot, character development, and relationships

**Passage:**
[Insert passage text here about a specific narrative scenario. This could be a story about a young person moving to a new city and navigating challenges in school and personal relationships.]

**Question 1:**
In the passage, the main character's primary struggle is:
A) Adjusting to a new environment
B) Dealing with a family conflict
C) Balancing academic and social life
D) Overcoming financial difficulties

**Question 2:**
Which of the following best describes the relationship between the main character and their best friend?
A) Distant but respectful
B) Close and supportive
C) Competitive and strained
D) Hostile and untrusting

**Question 3:**
The main setting of the story is significant because:
A) It emphasizes the isolation the character feels
B) It provides a comforting backdrop to the character's journey
C) It shows the financial status of the family
D) It introduces the main conflict early in the story

**Question 4:**
How does the author reveal the protagonist's internal conflict?
A) Through dialogue with other characters
B) Through the character's thoughts and reflections
C) Through descriptions of the setting
D) Through the actions of other minor characters

**Question 5:**
The protagonist's change in attitude is most evident when:
A) They confront their new teacher about unfair treatment
B) They decide to open up to their classmates about their personal life
C) They choose to withdraw from social interactions
D) They make a significant decision about their academic future

**Question 6:**
What is the primary theme conveyed in the passage?
A) The struggle of adapting to change
B) The importance of family over personal ambition
C) The challenge of maintaining relationships in difficult times
D) The role of education in shaping a person's identity

**Question 7:**
The author uses descriptive language in the second paragraph to:
A) Highlight the protagonist's physical appearance
B) Emphasize the tension in the protagonist's relationships
C) Illustrate the mood and tone of the new environment
D) Depict the minor characters in more detail

**Question 8:**
The tone of the passage can best be described as:
A) Optimistic and hopeful
B) Reflective and melancholic
C) Suspenseful and tense
D) Lighthearted and humorous

**Question 9:**
Which of the following best explains the author's use of symbolism in the passage?
A) The new school represents a fresh start for the protagonist
B) The old book found in the library symbolizes knowledge and power
C) The rainy weather outside reflects the protagonist's internal sadness
D) The broken watch represents the protagonist's past mistakes

**Question 10:**
What does the protagonist's interaction with their classmates suggest about their character?
A) They are overly confident and outgoing
B) They are shy and unsure of themselves
C) They are confrontational and aggressive
D) They are deceptive and manipulative

**Question 11:**
What is implied about the protagonist's relationship with their family?
A) They feel misunderstood and neglected by their parents
B) They are close to their siblings but distant from their parents
C) They rely heavily on their parents for guidance and support
D) They come from a well-adjusted and happy family

**Question 12:**
The flashback used in the third paragraph serves to:
A) Provide background information on the protagonist's upbringing
B) Explain why the protagonist is uncomfortable in the new setting
C) Illustrate the financial difficulties the family is facing
D) Show the protagonist's past academic achievements

**Question 13:**
The dialogue between the protagonist and their best friend is significant because it reveals:
A) How the protagonist handles confrontation
B) The depth of their friendship
C) The differences in their social status
D) The protagonist's reluctance to share personal details

**Question 14:**
How does the author develop tension between the protagonist and their peers?
A) By describing the protagonist's struggle to fit in
B) By focusing on external conflicts rather than internal struggles
C) By highlighting the competition between the protagonist and their classmates
D) By introducing rumors that affect the protagonist's reputation

**Question 15:**
The ending of the passage suggests that the protagonist:
A) Has finally adjusted to their new surroundings
B) Is still struggling but has hope for the future
C) Has decided to leave their new environment
D) Has overcome all obstacles and is fully content

# Narrative Passage 2: Key themes and implicit meanings

**Passage:**
[Insert passage text here about a historical event, personal journey, or philosophical reflection—focused on exploring deeper themes such as sacrifice, personal growth, or the complexity of human emotions.]

**Question 1:**
What is the central theme of the passage?
A) The inevitability of change
B) The power of love over adversity
C) The significance of cultural traditions
D) The conflict between personal ambition and family duty

**Question 2:**
The author uses metaphor in the third paragraph to:
A) Emphasize the main character's isolation
B) Highlight the emotional weight of a significant decision
C) Depict the physical surroundings in more detail
D) Compare two opposing viewpoints within the narrative

**Question 3:**
The relationship between the protagonist and the supporting character can best be described as:
A) Mutually beneficial
B) Tense but respectful
C) Superficial and distant
D) Deeply connected despite external challenges

**Question 4:**

Which of the following is an implicit meaning conveyed in the passage?

A) The protagonist is struggling with unresolved grief

B) The supporting character is jealous of the protagonist's success

C) The setting represents the protagonist's internal confusion

D) The passage is a critique of societal norms and expectations

**Question 5:**

How does the author illustrate the theme of personal sacrifice throughout the passage?

A) By showing how the protagonist gives up their own dreams for the sake of others

B) By depicting a rivalry between the protagonist and their sibling

C) By focusing on the protagonist's failure to achieve their goals

D) By highlighting the importance of hard work and determination

**Question 6:**

What can be inferred about the protagonist's internal conflict?

A) They are torn between following their passion and fulfilling their obligations

B) They are unsure about whether to trust the supporting character

C) They are contemplating leaving their current situation

D) They are struggling to reconcile their past and present selves

**Question 7:**

The author's tone can best be described as:

A) Neutral and detached

B) Reflective and melancholic

C) Optimistic and encouraging

D) Bitter and resentful

**Question 8:**

Which statement best explains the symbolic significance of the recurring image of the ocean in the passage?

A) It represents the protagonist's longing for freedom

B) It symbolizes the uncertainty of the future

C) It reflects the protagonist's fear of the unknown

D) It signifies the depth of the protagonist's internal struggle

**Question 9:**

The supporting character's role in the narrative is primarily to:

A) Provide the protagonist with guidance and wisdom

B) Act as a foil to the protagonist's ambitions

C) Encourage the protagonist to pursue their dreams

D) Highlight the protagonist's weaknesses and doubts

**Question 10:**

What is implied by the protagonist's final decision in the passage?

A) They have accepted their fate and will no longer pursue their own desires

B) They will continue to fight for what they believe in, despite the odds

C) They have chosen to follow the advice of the supporting character

D) They are ready to leave everything behind and start anew

**Question 11:**

How does the setting contribute to the overall theme of the passage?

A) It reinforces the protagonist's feelings of isolation and helplessness

B) It symbolizes the protagonist's journey towards self-discovery

C) It highlights the external obstacles preventing the protagonist's success

D) It contrasts the internal peace the protagonist feels with their external struggles

**Question 12:**

Which of the following best explains the author's use of flashbacks throughout the narrative?

A) To provide background information about the protagonist's past decisions

B) To emphasize the cyclical nature of the protagonist's struggles

C) To show the contrast between the protagonist's past and present mindset

D) To foreshadow the protagonist's ultimate decision

**Question 13:**

The phrase "the weight of the world rested on their shoulders" in paragraph 4 most likely refers to:

A) The overwhelming expectations placed on the protagonist by society

B) The protagonist's personal guilt over a past mistake

C) The protagonist's responsibility to care for their family

D) The protagonist's fear of failure in achieving their goals

**Question 14:**

What underlying message does the author convey about the nature of ambition?

A) Ambition is a destructive force that alienates individuals from their loved ones

B) Ambition must be tempered by a sense of duty and responsibility

C) Ambition can only lead to success if it is pursued at all costs

D) Ambition is a noble pursuit, but it often requires personal sacrifice

**Question 15:**

The narrative suggests that the protagonist views their future with:

A) Hopeful optimism despite current challenges

B) Resignation to their circumstances

C) A sense of dread and uncertainty

D) Confidence in their ability to overcome obstacles

# Narrative Passage 3: Interpretation of tone, mood, and author's voice

**Passage:**

[Insert a passage that delves into a reflective or emotional topic, exploring the subtleties of tone, mood, and the author's unique voice, such as a personal reflection on a pivotal life moment or an evocative description of a historical event.]

**Question 1:**

Which of the following best describes the tone of the passage?

A) Nostalgic and wistful

B) Harsh and accusatory

C) Detached and clinical

D) Optimistic and forward-looking

**Question 2:**

How does the mood of the passage shift between the first and second paragraphs?

A) It changes from hopeful to somber

B) It becomes increasingly frantic and disorganized

C) It remains consistently melancholy

D) It evolves from uncertain to resolute

**Question 3:**

The author's use of descriptive language in paragraph 3 primarily serves to:

A) Create a sense of urgency

B) Establish a serene and peaceful mood

C) Highlight the tension between characters

D) Convey the complexity of the setting

**Question 4:**

Which of the following best captures the author's voice in the passage?

A) Formal and authoritative

B) Conversational and reflective

C) Sarcastic and cynical

D) Emotional and intense

**Question 5:**

How does the author's choice of diction influence the tone of the passage?

A) The use of simple language creates an approachable, relaxed tone

B) The technical terminology establishes a tone of expertise

C) The emotionally charged words contribute to a sense of despair

D) The elaborate phrasing gives the passage a detached, intellectual tone

**Question 6:**

What effect does the imagery in the fourth paragraph have on the overall mood of the passage?

A) It makes the mood feel more chaotic and disjointed

B) It amplifies the feeling of solitude and isolation

C) It creates a sense of excitement and anticipation

D) It adds an element of confusion and uncertainty

**Question 7:**

The shift in tone near the end of the passage suggests that the author:

A) Has resolved their internal conflict

B) Is preparing to confront a difficult truth

C) Is uncertain about their next steps

D) Has found peace with their past decisions

**Question 8:**

Which literary device is primarily responsible for establishing the tone in the passage?

A) Irony

B) Hyperbole

C) Metaphor

D) Personification

**Question 9:**

How does the author's voice contribute to the reader's understanding of the passage's themes?

A) The voice is detached, allowing readers to draw their own conclusions about the theme

B) The voice is personal and introspective, guiding the reader through the author's internal journey

C) The voice is critical, questioning the societal norms that influence the characters' actions

D) The voice is instructional, offering advice on how to handle similar situations

**Question 10:**

The author's tone towards the main character can best be described as:

A) Sympathetic and understanding

B) Critical and harsh

C) Dismissive and indifferent

D) Admiring and respectful

**Question 11:**

Which sentence from the passage most effectively sets the tone for the entire narrative?

A) "The world around them had changed, but they remained the same."

B) "Every decision seemed heavier than the last, as though the weight of time pressed down on them."

C) "With a laugh, they dismissed the concerns, convinced that everything would work out in the end."

D) "The silence of the room was interrupted only by the ticking of the clock, marking time in slow, deliberate strokes."

**Question 12:**

How does the author's tone enhance the reader's perception of the setting?

A) The ominous tone makes the setting feel foreboding and dangerous

B) The nostalgic tone gives the setting a dreamlike, idealized quality

C) The conversational tone makes the setting feel more familiar and relatable

D) The neutral tone strips the setting of any emotional resonance

**Question 13:**

What mood is created by the author's use of repetition in the final paragraph?

A) Frustration and impatience

B) Calmness and resignation

C) Joy and celebration

D) Confusion and indecision

**Question 14:**

How does the author's use of contrast contribute to the mood of the passage?

A) It emphasizes the protagonist's internal conflict by juxtaposing calm and chaos

B) It creates a sense of disorientation by contrasting time periods

C) It reinforces the mood of contentment by contrasting the protagonist's success with their earlier failures

D) It makes the mood feel more urgent by highlighting the disparity between the protagonist's desires and reality

**Question 15:**

What is the effect of the author's tone on the reader's perception of the events in the passage?

A) It distances the reader emotionally from the protagonist's struggles

B) It draws the reader in by making the protagonist's journey feel universal

C) It creates a sense of unease, leaving the reader questioning the protagonist's motives

D) It inspires the reader to reflect on their own similar experiences

# Narrative Passage 4: Analysis of setting and historical context

**Passage:**

[Insert a passage that explores a significant historical event or period, with a strong emphasis on the setting and its influence on the characters or the unfolding events. This could include a vivid description of the landscape, social environment, or political climate, and how these elements shape the narrative.]

**Question 1:**

How does the author use descriptive language to establish the setting of the passage?

A) By focusing on the sensory details of the environment

B) By contrasting the past and present states of the location

C) By using metaphors to describe the emotional state of the characters

D) By ignoring the physical setting and focusing on character actions

**Question 2:**

In what way does the historical context influence the actions of the characters?

A) It limits their choices due to societal restrictions

B) It gives them the freedom to act without consequences

C) It has no bearing on their decisions

D) It provides them with opportunities for social advancement

**Question 3:**

Which aspect of the setting has the greatest impact on the plot?

A) The geographical location

B) The social hierarchy

C) The weather and natural conditions

D) The technological advancements

**Question 4:**

How does the time period in which the story is set affect the characters' motivations?

A) They are driven by a desire for progress and modernization

B) They struggle with traditional values versus new ideals

C) They are indifferent to the cultural norms of their time

D) They seek to escape the limitations imposed by their environment

**Question 5:**

What does the setting reveal about the challenges faced by the characters?

A) The remote location forces them to become self-reliant

B) The urban environment provides them with numerous resources

C) The political instability leaves them feeling helpless and confused

D) The harsh climate strengthens their resolve to survive

**Question 6:**

How does the historical context shape the conflicts within the passage?

A) It amplifies personal conflicts by adding social and political pressures

B) It diminishes the importance of the characters' personal struggles

C) It provides a backdrop for resolving the conflicts peacefully

D) It creates opportunities for the characters to manipulate their environment

**Question 7:**

Which detail from the passage best illustrates the influence of the historical setting on the narrative?

A) The mention of a historical figure known for reform

B) The description of the physical landscape
C) The dialogue between the characters discussing political tensions
D) The references to local customs and traditions

**Question 8:**
How does the author integrate historical events into the personal lives of the characters?
A) By using historical events as a backdrop that parallels their personal struggles
B) By focusing solely on historical events, ignoring personal experiences
C) By showing how historical events have no influence on their personal lives
D) By making the characters central to the unfolding historical events

**Question 9:**
What role does the setting play in the development of the characters' relationships?
A) It fosters isolation, making relationships difficult to form
B) It encourages community and bonding due to shared challenges
C) It has little influence on the characters' interactions
D) It forces characters to confront their differences due to external pressures

**Question 10:**
Which element of the historical context presents the greatest obstacle for the characters?
A) The rigid class system
B) The political turmoil
C) The economic struggles
D) The cultural traditions

**Question 11:**
How does the author's portrayal of the setting affect the reader's understanding of the characters' struggles?
A) It emphasizes the difficulty of living in such a harsh environment
B) It portrays the setting as an inconsequential backdrop to the characters' internal conflicts
C) It makes the setting seem irrelevant to the narrative
D) It diminishes the severity of the characters' challenges

**Question 12:**
What does the setting suggest about the societal values during the time period in which the story is set?
A) Innovation and progress are valued over tradition
B) Individual freedom is prioritized over collective wellbeing
C) The stability of the community is more important than personal desires
D) Social mobility is easily attainable for everyone

**Question 13:**
In what ways does the author use the historical context to highlight themes of the passage?
A) By showing how the characters' decisions are influenced by historical events
B) By using the setting to provide background information that adds complexity to the plot
C) By incorporating political movements to reflect the characters' internal transformations
D) By depicting historical events as secondary to personal experiences

**Question 14:**
What impact does the setting have on the characters' emotions throughout the passage?
A) It fosters feelings of isolation and helplessness
B) It gives them hope for a better future

C) It creates a sense of belonging and community

D) It leaves them indifferent to the challenges they face

**Question 15:**

How does the historical context create tension between the characters in the passage?

A) It forces them to adopt opposing views on social change

B) It brings them closer together as they face external threats

C) It highlights their similarities despite societal differences

D) It encourages them to work together to overcome the same challenges

# Section 2: Social Science Passage Comprehension

## Social Science Passage 1: Identifying Main Ideas and Details

**Passage:**

[Insert a passage based on social science research, such as a study about human behavior, societal trends, or economics. The passage should provide a mix of data, analysis, and theoretical perspectives, allowing for questions on both high-level concepts and specific details.]

**Question 1:**

What is the primary purpose of the passage?

A) To present a new theory in social science

B) To compare different approaches to a common social issue

C) To summarize findings from recent research

D) To critique an existing social theory

**Question 2:**

According to the passage, what is the main factor influencing the trend described?

A) Changes in governmental policy

B) Advances in technology

C) Shifts in cultural attitudes

D) Economic instability

**Question 3:**

Which of the following best captures the main idea of the second paragraph?

A) It explains the limitations of the research methodology

B) It introduces a key statistic to support the author's argument

C) It discusses potential future developments in the field

D) It critiques the assumptions behind the study's design

**Question 4:**

What evidence does the author provide to support the claim that societal values have shifted in recent decades?

A) Data from a longitudinal study

B) Anecdotal evidence from interviews

C) Analysis of historical documents

D) Results from a public opinion survey

**Question 5:**

Which detail from the passage best illustrates the impact of economic factors on social behavior?

A) The author's reference to unemployment rates
B) The discussion of technological advancements
C) The analysis of educational outcomes
D) The study's focus on population growth

**Question 6:**

What is the significance of the example provided in the third paragraph?
A) It demonstrates a counterpoint to the main argument
B) It provides a real-world application of the study's findings
C) It serves as a metaphor for broader societal changes
D) It highlights the limitations of the research

**Question 7:**

According to the passage, how have attitudes toward education changed over time?
A) Education is now seen as less important due to the rise of technology
B) There has been a renewed emphasis on vocational training
C) Educational attainment is increasingly valued for economic mobility
D) Attitudes toward education have remained largely unchanged

**Question 8:**

Which statement is most consistent with the author's conclusion about the future of social science research?
A) Future research should focus more on qualitative analysis
B) There is a need for greater interdisciplinary collaboration
C) Social science research will likely decline in importance
D) Researchers should avoid using outdated methodologies

**Question 9:**

How does the author use statistics to support the main argument?
A) By illustrating the widespread nature of the issue being discussed
B) By contrasting opposing views on the topic
C) By demonstrating the weaknesses of previous studies
D) By highlighting areas that require further investigation

**Question 10:**

What role does the fourth paragraph play in the overall structure of the passage?
A) It introduces a new topic unrelated to the main argument
B) It provides additional evidence to reinforce the thesis
C) It refutes a common counterargument to the author's position
D) It offers an alternative perspective that challenges the main ideas

**Question 11:**

Which of the following best describes the author's tone in the passage?
A) Neutral and objective
B) Critical and argumentative
C) Optimistic and hopeful
D) Dismissive and skeptical

**Question 12:**

What does the author suggest about the limitations of the current research methods?
A) They fail to account for long-term social trends

B) They rely too heavily on quantitative data

C) They overlook the role of individual agency

D) They are outdated and need revision

**Question 13:**

In the passage, how is the term "social mobility" defined?

A) The ability of individuals to change their social status through education or employment

B) The process of integrating new technologies into everyday life

C) The shift in societal values over multiple generations

D) The movement of populations between different geographic regions

**Question 14:**

Which piece of evidence from the passage best supports the idea that cultural shifts influence economic behavior?

A) The increased emphasis on consumer spending habits

B) The correlation between cultural attitudes and savings rates

C) The rise in technological entrepreneurship

D) The link between social class and educational attainment

**Question 15:**

What does the passage imply about the role of government in shaping societal trends?

A) Government policies have a direct and immediate impact on societal values

B) Government intervention is often necessary to correct societal issues

C) Governments tend to lag behind cultural shifts in implementing policy changes

D) Government influence is minimal compared to that of technological advancements

## Social Science Passage 2: Evaluating Evidence and Argumentation

**Passage:**

[Insert a passage focused on a social science study or article presenting an argument, such as a debate on the impact of technology on social interaction or the role of government in public health. The passage should provide claims, counterclaims, evidence, and reasoning that students will need to evaluate.]

**Question 1:**

What is the primary claim made by the author in the passage?

A) Technology has no impact on social interaction.

B) Technology has significantly altered the way people communicate.

C) Social interactions are more meaningful through in-person communication.

D) The effects of technology on social behavior are negligible.

**Question 2:**

Which of the following is the strongest piece of evidence the author uses to support their claim?

A) A personal anecdote about communication habits.

B) A study that compares online and face-to-face interactions.

C) The mention of a historical event that changed communication.

D) An opinion from a well-known social scientist.

**Question 3:**

What is the purpose of the counterargument presented in paragraph 3?

A) To strengthen the author's claim by acknowledging a potential flaw.

B) To dismiss opposing viewpoints as irrelevant.

C) To provide an alternative solution to the problem discussed.

D) To confuse the reader with conflicting evidence.

**Question 4:**

How does the author respond to the counterargument?

A) By providing statistical data to refute it.

B) By agreeing with it and altering their original claim.

C) By offering a new perspective that neutralizes the counterargument.

D) By ignoring the counterargument completely.

**Question 5:**

Which of the following best describes the type of reasoning used by the author?

A) Inductive reasoning, moving from specific examples to a general conclusion.

B) Deductive reasoning, starting with a broad principle and applying it to specific cases.

C) Analogical reasoning, comparing two similar situations to draw conclusions.

D) Causal reasoning, establishing a direct cause-and-effect relationship.

**Question 6:**

Which piece of evidence is least effective in supporting the author's argument?

A) A study conducted ten years ago that is no longer relevant.

B) A survey with a small sample size.

C) An opinion piece written by a popular journalist.

D) A quote from a recent peer-reviewed journal article.

**Question 7:**

How does the author use data from paragraph 4 to reinforce their claim?

A) By providing exact figures to prove a direct correlation.

B) By appealing to the reader's emotions with anecdotal evidence.

C) By using vague statistics to suggest general trends.

D) By citing authoritative sources to add credibility to their argument.

**Question 8:**

Which statement from the passage is an example of a generalization?

A) "Most people prefer face-to-face interactions over digital communication."

B) "A recent study found that 60% of people use technology for most social interactions."

C) "The majority of teenagers today have never known a world without the internet."

D) "Researchers have found that technology improves productivity in the workplace."

**Question 9:**

In the passage, which of the following rhetorical devices does the author use to strengthen their argument?

A) Appeal to authority by citing experts in the field.

B) Appeal to emotion by describing the effects of isolation.

C) Appeal to logic by listing numerical data.

D) Appeal to tradition by referencing historical practices.

**Question 10:**

Which of the following weakens the author's claim?

A) The reliance on outdated studies.

B) The inclusion of too much technical jargon.

C) The overuse of emotional appeals.

D) The failure to address opposing viewpoints directly.

**Question 11:**

What is the effect of the author's use of hypothetical scenarios in paragraph 5?

A) To present an exaggerated view of the issue.

B) To make the argument more relatable to the reader.

C) To confuse the reader with conflicting possibilities.

D) To provide a clear, real-world application of the author's point.

**Question 12:**

Which of the following is a logical flaw in the argument presented?

A) The assumption that technology will always have a negative impact on communication.

B) The failure to cite any specific studies to support the main claim.

C) The reliance on evidence from only one source.

D) The suggestion that technology is solely responsible for social change.

**Question 13:**

What does the author imply about future research on technology's impact on social behavior?

A) It is likely to confirm that face-to-face communication is superior.

B) It may provide more nuanced insights into how technology affects relationships.

C) It will show that digital communication is becoming less important.

D) It will continue to produce conflicting results.

**Question 14:**

How does the author address potential biases in the studies they cite?

A) By acknowledging their limitations and suggesting alternative explanations.

B) By dismissing any potential biases as insignificant.

C) By ignoring the possibility of bias altogether.

D) By stating that all studies have inherent biases.

**Question 15:**

Which of the following is the most likely purpose of the passage?

A) To convince the reader that technology should be banned from social settings.

B) To provide an objective analysis of how technology affects communication.

C) To explore both sides of the debate on technology and social interaction.

D) To promote the idea that technology is detrimental to society's future.

## Social Science Passage 3: Synthesizing Information from Multiple Sources

**Passage:**

[Insert a passage that includes multiple viewpoints or sources on a topic, such as economic policies from different countries or perspectives on climate change. The passage should present at least two distinct perspectives or sets of data that students must compare, contrast, and synthesize.]

**Question 1:**

How do the two sources differ in their approach to solving the issue presented in the passage?

A) One source suggests immediate action, while the other recommends a wait-and-see approach.

B) Both sources agree on the issue but differ in the urgency of addressing it.

C) The first source focuses on long-term solutions, and the second emphasizes short-term fixes.

D) One source is focused on global solutions, while the other looks at local impacts.

**Question 2:**

Which of the following best explains how the author uses evidence from both sources?

A) The author compares both sets of data to highlight their contradictions.

B) The author contrasts their methods to show one is superior.

C) The author synthesizes the information to show how both perspectives contribute to a comprehensive solution.

D) The author dismisses one source as outdated and unreliable.

**Question 3:**

What is the primary point of agreement between the two sources?

A) Both agree on the cause of the problem but differ in their proposed solutions.

B) Both sources advocate for international collaboration on the issue.

C) Both suggest that immediate economic reform is necessary to address the issue.

D) Both acknowledge the role of technology in mitigating the problem.

**Question 4:**

Which statement best represents the relationship between the two sources?

A) One source builds on the findings of the other to present a more thorough analysis.

B) The sources contradict each other completely and provide no common ground.

C) The sources agree on certain facts but diverge in their interpretations.

D) Both sources are written from the same perspective but address different aspects of the issue.

**Question 5:**

In the passage, which rhetorical strategy does the author use to integrate the two sources?

A) The author juxtaposes the sources to highlight the strengths and weaknesses of each.

B) The author presents one source as more credible by emphasizing its data.

C) The author balances both viewpoints to create a neutral stance.

D) The author dismisses both sources and suggests a third alternative.

**Question 6:**

What is the significance of the differences in methodology between the two sources?

A) The first source uses quantitative data, while the second relies on anecdotal evidence.

B) The second source includes a broader range of case studies compared to the first.

C) The first source uses a more conservative approach, while the second focuses on progressive models.

D) The second source challenges the validity of the first source's data.

**Question 7:**

Which of the following is an example of synthesis in the passage?

A) The author combines both sources' suggestions into a cohesive strategy for action.

B) The author selects one solution over the other after comparing the two sources.

C) The author suggests that the two sources are mutually exclusive.

D) The author discards both viewpoints and presents a new one.

**Question 8:**

How does the author use data from both sources to support their main argument?

A) By citing figures from each source to show the broad scope of the problem.

B) By relying more heavily on one source while discrediting the other.

C) By selectively choosing the data that best supports the author's own point of view.

D) By using both sets of data to provide a balanced perspective on the issue.

**Question 9:**

Which of the following best explains how the author resolves the apparent contradiction between the two sources?

A) The author finds a middle ground that both sources imply but do not explicitly state.

B) The author asserts that both sources are wrong and proposes a new framework.

C) The author emphasizes that contradictions are inevitable and cannot be resolved.

D) The author ignores the contradiction, focusing instead on unrelated data.

**Question 10:**

What is the most likely reason the author includes both sources in the passage?

A) To demonstrate that differing perspectives can enrich understanding of a complex issue.

B) To prove that one perspective is more accurate than the other.

C) To highlight the limitations of relying on a single viewpoint.

D) To confuse the reader by presenting conflicting ideas.

**Question 11:**

Which of the following best demonstrates a synthesis of the two arguments presented?

A) A combination of the local and global strategies discussed by both sources.

B) A rejection of one perspective in favor of the other.

C) A suggestion that both viewpoints are too flawed to be useful.

D) An emphasis on the importance of adopting one source's approach fully.

**Question 12:**

How does the second source challenge the assumptions made by the first source?

A) By questioning the reliability of the first source's data collection methods.

B) By offering a completely different theoretical framework.

C) By providing counterexamples that undermine the first source's conclusions.

D) By ignoring the assumptions made by the first source.

**Question 13:**

Which of the following best illustrates how the two sources can complement each other?

A) One source provides a broad theoretical framework, while the other offers practical applications.

B) Both sources approach the problem with a similar set of assumptions.

C) One source dismisses the conclusions of the other without explanation.

D) The sources present entirely contradictory ideas, making synthesis impossible.

**Question 14:**

What effect does the inclusion of both sources have on the reader's understanding of the issue?

A) It helps the reader see the complexity of the issue by providing multiple viewpoints.

B) It confuses the reader by presenting too many contradictory ideas.

C) It shows the reader that the issue is too subjective to have a single solution.

D) It forces the reader to choose one side over the other.

**Question 15:**

How does the author suggest that future research might build on the ideas presented in both sources?

A) By proposing a study that combines elements of both approaches.

B) By suggesting that one of the sources needs to be further investigated for credibility.

C) By recommending that future research should focus only on the first source's methodology.

D) By implying that future research will likely disprove both sources.

## Social Science Passage 4: Interpretation of Data and Graphs

**Passage:**

[Insert a passage with accompanying data, such as graphs, charts, or tables. The data could represent trends in global population growth, economic indicators, or climate data over time. The accompanying text will explain or summarize the data, requiring students to interpret the graphical information and its implications.]

**Question 1:**

What trend is depicted in the graph shown alongside the passage?

A) A steady increase over the period

B) A rapid decline followed by stabilization

C) Fluctuations with no clear trend

D) A gradual decrease over the entire period

**Question 2:**

Based on the data in the table, which of the following statements is accurate?

A) Country X had the highest growth rate in 2010.

B) Country Y's economy grew steadily from 2000 to 2010.

C) Both Country X and Country Y experienced a decline in the same year.

D) Country Z had a significant drop in population between 2005 and 2010.

**Question 3:**

What is the primary conclusion that can be drawn from the graph in the passage?

A) The population of the region is predicted to continue growing rapidly.

B) Economic growth was inversely proportional to population growth.

C) The data show a correlation between education levels and GDP.

D) Climate change indicators have remained stable over the decade.

**Question 4:**

How does the table in the passage support the argument made by the author?

A) It shows quantitative evidence that corroborates the author's claim about growth patterns.

B) It provides examples that challenge the argument.

C) It offers alternative data that contradict the author's conclusion.

D) It emphasizes anomalies in the data that were previously ignored.

**Question 5:**

Which of the following interpretations of the graph is incorrect?

A) The highest point on the graph indicates a peak in productivity.

B) The lowest point on the graph suggests a major economic downturn.

C) The steady incline suggests continuous improvement in health outcomes.

D) The curve represents fluctuations in global temperature trends.

**Question 6:**

In the context of the graph, which factor could explain the sudden spike in data in the year 2015?

A) A change in government policy

B) A global economic recession

C) A technological breakthrough in renewable energy

D) A shift in educational attainment rates

**Question 7:**

According to the chart, which region showed the least improvement in literacy rates?

A) Region A

B) Region B

C) Region C

D) Region D

**Question 8:**

What relationship is implied between the two sets of data in the graph and table?

A) The data in the graph support the trends shown in the table.

B) The graph contradicts the information provided in the table.

C) The table provides more detailed information not represented in the graph.

D) The graph offers predictions, while the table focuses on historical data.

**Question 9:**

Which of the following best describes the purpose of the graph in the passage?

A) To provide visual evidence of a trend described in the text

B) To confuse the reader by presenting conflicting information

C) To offer an alternative explanation for a phenomenon discussed

D) To replace the need for textual analysis of the issue

**Question 10:**

Which conclusion is best supported by the data presented in the graph?

A) The decline in population is correlated with higher education levels.

B) The increase in economic growth was more rapid than anticipated.

C) Technological advances had no effect on the data trends.

D) Climate change had a minimal impact on the figures shown.

**Question 11:**

What does the bar graph suggest about regional differences in GDP growth?

A) All regions experienced similar growth rates.

B) There was significant variation in GDP growth between regions.

C) The highest growth was seen in Region C, while Region A saw a decline.

D) Region D experienced a dramatic drop in GDP over the period.

**Question 12:**

How does the pie chart contribute to the reader's understanding of resource allocation in the passage?

A) It visually represents the disproportionate spending on education versus healthcare.

B) It offers data that conflicts with the information presented in the text.

C) It highlights areas of improvement not discussed in the passage.

D) It suggests that resource allocation is evenly distributed across all sectors.

**Question 13:**

Which of the following best describes the author's use of statistical data in the passage?

A) The author uses the data to emphasize anomalies in the global economy.

B) The data are used to support a hypothesis about long-term trends.

C) The author dismisses the statistical data in favor of anecdotal evidence.

D) The data contradict the author's main argument.

**Question 14:**

Which of the following is a limitation of the graph presented in the passage?

A) It does not show data prior to the year 2000.

B) It only presents data for one region, ignoring the others.

C) It focuses too much on short-term fluctuations, missing long-term trends.

D) The graph fails to represent any information on economic policies.

**Question 15:**

How could the data in the graph be used to make predictions for the future?

A) By analyzing trends and extrapolating them into the future.

B) By ignoring the outliers and focusing only on steady trends.

C) By making assumptions based on unrelated data sources.

D) By assuming that past performance will not influence future results.

# Section 3: Natural Science Passage Comprehension

## Natural Science Passage 1: Understanding Scientific Concepts and Research Findings

**Passage:**

[Insert a passage summarizing a scientific study or research findings, focusing on a specific scientific concept, such as climate change, genetic inheritance, or cell biology. The passage should present both a clear explanation of the concept and an analysis of the research findings.]

**Question 1:**

What is the primary scientific concept discussed in the passage?

A) Climate change and its long-term effects

B) Genetic mutations in living organisms

C) The relationship between energy consumption and economic growth

D) The theory of evolution and natural selection

**Question 2:**

According to the passage, what is the main conclusion of the research findings?

A) The experimental results confirmed the hypothesis.

B) The study disproved long-standing theories about climate change.

C) The research demonstrated an unexpected correlation between variables.

D) The study was inconclusive due to insufficient data.

**Question 3:**

Which of the following best explains the methodology used in the research?

A) A longitudinal study that tracked data over several decades

B) A cross-sectional analysis that compared different groups

C) A randomized controlled trial conducted in a laboratory

D) An observational study that collected data from natural environments

**Question 4:**

The study's findings support which of the following hypotheses?

A) Climate change is driven solely by human activities.

B) Genetic mutations occur at random in all species.

C) Increased energy consumption leads to economic prosperity.

D) Natural selection favors traits that enhance survival in specific environments.

**Question 5:**

Which aspect of the scientific method is emphasized in the research findings?

A) Formulating a hypothesis based on prior research

B) Testing the hypothesis through experimentation

C) Analyzing the results to draw meaningful conclusions

D) Revising the hypothesis based on contradictory evidence

**Question 6:**

The data presented in the passage suggest that:

A) The study results are directly applicable to all species.

B) The findings provide strong evidence for a new theory.

C) Further research is needed to confirm the conclusions.

D) The research was limited by ethical considerations.

**Question 7:**

Which of the following best describes the experimental group used in the study?

A) A diverse sample of plants and animals

B) A group of organisms exposed to environmental stressors

C) A control group that received no treatment

D) A sample population from multiple geographical regions

**Question 8:**

According to the passage, which factor most likely influenced the results of the experiment?

A) The duration of the study

B) The natural variability in the environment

C) The age and health of the organisms used

D) The reliability of the measuring instruments

**Question 9:**

What is the significance of the study's findings in the broader context of the scientific field?

A) It challenges the dominant theory of climate change.

B) It provides new insights into genetic inheritance.

C) It offers a solution to energy sustainability issues.

D) It validates long-held beliefs about species adaptation.

**Question 10:**

What limitation of the study is mentioned in the passage?

A) The sample size was too small to be conclusive.

B) The study only considered short-term effects.

C) The researchers used outdated experimental techniques.

D) The study failed to account for external variables.

**Question 11:**

Which of the following is a key implication of the research findings?

A) Energy consumption must be regulated to avoid economic crises.

B) Genetic research is critical to understanding species evolution.

C) Adaptation to climate change is more complex than previously thought.

D) Current theories about natural selection are largely inaccurate.

**Question 12:**

Based on the passage, which future research direction would be most beneficial?

A) Studying a larger sample size across different regions

B) Repeating the experiment under different climate conditions

C) Investigating the genetic makeup of different species

D) Exploring the impact of technology on environmental sustainability

**Question 13:**

How do the findings of the study contribute to the understanding of natural selection?

A) They provide definitive evidence for how natural selection operates.

B) They show that adaptation occurs more slowly than previously thought.

C) They challenge the idea that natural selection is driven by environmental factors.

D) They confirm that certain traits enhance species' survival in specific ecosystems.

**Question 14:**

What does the passage suggest about the broader significance of the research for other scientific fields?

A) The findings have far-reaching implications for energy policy.

B) The results will reshape thinking in environmental science.

C) The study's conclusions are unlikely to impact other disciplines.

D) The research opens up new avenues for exploration in genetic science.

**Question 15:**

What recommendation do the researchers make for future studies based on their findings?

A) To replicate the study with improved technology

B) To extend the study's duration to observe long-term effects

C) To apply the same methodology to different organisms

D) To conduct further trials to explore the ethical implications

## Natural Science Passage 2: Assessing Scientific Hypotheses and Conclusions

**Passage:**

[Insert a passage discussing a scientific experiment or study that focuses on testing a hypothesis, presenting the methods used to test the hypothesis, and evaluating the conclusions drawn from the experiment. The passage should highlight how scientists assess hypotheses in various fields, such as biology, chemistry, or environmental science.]

**Question 1:**

What is the main hypothesis being tested in the passage?

A) The relationship between temperature and plant growth

B) The effect of pollutants on marine ecosystems

C) The impact of genetic mutations on species survival

D) The role of diet in determining animal lifespan

**Question 2:**

How was the hypothesis in the passage tested?

A) By observing natural phenomena over time

B) By conducting a laboratory-controlled experiment

C) By collecting data from surveys and fieldwork

D) By reviewing historical scientific literature

**Question 3:**

Which result from the experiment supports the original hypothesis?

A) An increase in plant growth with higher temperatures

B) A decrease in marine biodiversity with pollution

C) A decline in mutation rates under stable conditions

D) An improvement in animal health with dietary changes

**Question 4:**

What factor is identified as a potential limitation of the study?

A) The narrow geographic scope of the experiment

B) The lack of long-term data collection

C) The insufficient number of organisms tested

D) The use of unreliable equipment

**Question 5:**

Which of the following is the most reasonable conclusion based on the data presented?

A) The hypothesis is fully confirmed by the experiment.

B) The results suggest the hypothesis may be correct, but further testing is needed.

C) The experiment disproved the hypothesis completely.

D) The hypothesis was only partially supported, leading to new questions.

**Question 6:**

What recommendation do the researchers make regarding future studies?

A) Repeating the experiment under different environmental conditions

B) Increasing the sample size to improve the validity of results

C) Investigating other related hypotheses

D) Applying the findings to practical applications in the field

**Question 7:**

Which of the following would weaken the experiment's conclusions?

A) Data collection was inconsistent across different research sites.

B) The researchers did not account for seasonal variations in the data.

C) The study relied heavily on computer simulations.

D) External funding influenced the interpretation of the results.

**Question 8:**

In evaluating the conclusions, what additional factor do the researchers consider?

A) The environmental impact of their findings

B) The historical context of similar studies

C) Ethical considerations of conducting further research

D) The role of variables that were not controlled in the study

**Question 9:**

Which of the following best explains why the researchers believe more investigation is necessary?

A) The sample size was too small to draw definitive conclusions.

B) The results contradicted established scientific theories.

C) The findings were inconclusive due to unpredictable external factors.

D) The experiment did not account for all potential environmental influences.

**Question 10:**

What is one key reason why the researchers express caution in their conclusions?

A) The results showed only a slight trend in favor of the hypothesis.

B) External factors unrelated to the experiment influenced the data.

C) The hypothesis was too complex to be fully tested in one experiment.

D) The experimenters did not follow established scientific protocols.

**Question 11:**

How do the researchers suggest future experiments could strengthen the validity of the conclusions?

A) By expanding the geographical scope of the research

B) By involving experts from different scientific fields

C) By conducting longitudinal studies to observe long-term trends

D) By repeating the study with a focus on more precise measurements

**Question 12:**

Which of the following is a potential alternative explanation for the results, according to the researchers?

A) The organisms used in the experiment adapted to the conditions faster than expected.

B) External factors like weather patterns affected the study.

C) The species tested did not represent typical genetic variation.

D) The measuring instruments were more sensitive than expected.

**Question 13:**

What is the significance of the findings in relation to the original hypothesis?

A) They strongly support the hypothesis, confirming prior research.

B) They provide partial support, indicating that further testing is needed.

C) They undermine the hypothesis, suggesting an alternative explanation.

D) They neither support nor refute the hypothesis due to inconsistent data.

**Question 14:**

What potential bias do the researchers address in their discussion of the experiment?

A) Selection bias in choosing which organisms to study

B) Confirmation bias in interpreting the results

C) Publication bias affecting which studies are considered relevant

D) Observer bias in recording the data

**Question 15:**

Which of the following future research directions do the researchers propose as most valuable?

A) Studying the long-term effects of environmental changes on genetic variation

B) Conducting comparative studies in different ecosystems

C) Applying the findings to solve real-world problems in agriculture

D) Investigating the same hypothesis using different species

# Natural Science Passage 3: Interpreting Technical Terms and Complex Data

**Passage:**

[Insert a passage that presents complex scientific data and technical terminology related to a specific scientific field, such as physics, biology, or chemistry. The passage could include data charts, graphs, or scientific jargon that needs to be interpreted for comprehension.]

**Question 1:**

What does the term "isotopic ratio" refer to in the context of the passage?

A) The comparison of two isotopes in a chemical compound

B) The rate of decay for a specific isotope

C) The balance between two different atomic elements

D) The frequency of isotope usage in scientific experiments

**Question 2:**

How can the data on temperature variation be best interpreted in relation to the study's findings?

A) As a fluctuating variable that affected the study results

B) As a constant factor that ensured consistent results

C) As a baseline measurement for comparison with other data

D) As a secondary variable unrelated to the main hypothesis

**Question 3:**

Which of the following best defines the term "allosteric regulation" as used in the passage?

A) The process by which a cell regulates gene expression

B) The regulation of a protein's function due to the binding of a molecule

C) The change in enzyme activity caused by external temperature

D) The mutation of a gene due to environmental stressors

**Question 4:**

In analyzing the data presented in Table 2, what conclusion can be drawn regarding the relationship between X and Y variables?

A) There is a direct correlation between X and Y.

B) X and Y are inversely related.

C) X and Y show no significant relationship.

D) The relationship between X and Y fluctuates with environmental factors.

**Question 5:**

Which graph best represents the trend described in the passage related to CO2 emissions over time?

A) A steadily rising curve

B) A fluctuating line graph

C) A sharp peak followed by a gradual decline

D) A flat line indicating no change

**Question 6:**

What does the passage suggest is the most important factor in interpreting the complex data on molecular structures?

A) Understanding the spatial arrangement of atoms

B) Recognizing the role of temperature changes

C) Interpreting the statistical models used

D) Analyzing the data with consideration of historical findings

**Question 7:**

Which of the following statements best summarizes the technical term "genetic drift" as used in the passage?

A) The random fluctuation of gene variants in small populations

B) The purposeful selection of genes through breeding programs

C) The loss of genetic diversity due to environmental factors

D) The adaptation of genes to changing ecosystems

**Question 8:**

In the passage, the term "photosynthetic efficiency" refers to:

A) The overall energy absorbed by plants during photosynthesis

B) The ratio of energy output to energy input in plant cells

C) The effectiveness of plants in converting light energy into chemical energy

D) The process of chlorophyll synthesis in high-light environments

**Question 9:**

Which of the following pieces of data best supports the hypothesis presented in the passage?

A) An increase in the growth rate of plants with higher nitrogen levels

B) A decrease in biodiversity when temperatures remain constant

C) A steady rise in population numbers due to habitat restoration

D) A direct correlation between water pH and animal survival rates

**Question 10:**

How does the passage define the term "homeostasis" in the context of the experiment discussed?

A) The ability of an organism to maintain stable internal conditions despite environmental changes

B) The balance of predator and prey populations in an ecosystem

C) The adaptation of species to temperature changes over time

D) The equilibrium of gene frequencies in a population over generations

**Question 11:**

What is the significance of the p-value in the data analysis presented in the passage?

A) It determines the probability that the results occurred by chance.

B) It shows the average variation in the experiment's data.

C) It measures the overall success rate of the experiment.

D) It highlights the relationship between two unrelated variables.

**Question 12:**

What is the best explanation for the fluctuations in enzyme activity shown in the graph?

A) The enzyme is sensitive to changes in temperature.

B) The enzyme responds differently to various concentrations of a substrate.

C) The enzyme is influenced by external environmental factors such as humidity.

D) The enzyme's activity is random and cannot be predicted.

**Question 13:**

How does the passage recommend interpreting the data when multiple variables are involved?

A) Prioritize the variable with the most significant impact on the outcome.

B) Focus solely on the primary variable and ignore secondary data points.

C) Analyze each variable independently before combining the results.

D) Use a multivariate analysis to understand the interaction between variables.

**Question 14:**

What is one potential issue in analyzing the data that the researchers caution against?

A) Overinterpreting small changes in the data set

B) Disregarding outliers as anomalies

C) Applying a linear model to non-linear data

D) Relying too heavily on historical data trends

**Question 15:**

Which conclusion can be reasonably drawn from the passage's discussion of complex data sets?

A) Simplifying the data leads to more accurate interpretations.

B) A detailed analysis of all variables is necessary for reliable conclusions.

C) The data should be viewed in the context of previous experiments for relevance.

D) The data lacks significance and does not support the main hypothesis.

## Natural Science Passage 4: Relationship Between Text and Graphs or Tables

**Passage:**

[Insert a passage that presents a scientific study accompanied by graphs or tables that display data related to the study. The text and visuals must be closely connected, requiring the reader to analyze both to answer the questions effectively.]

**Question 1:**

How does the graph provided in the passage support the claim made in paragraph 3 regarding the effect of temperature on enzyme activity?

A) It shows a steady increase in enzyme activity as temperature rises.

B) It reveals a peak in enzyme activity at an optimal temperature before declining.

C) It demonstrates no correlation between temperature and enzyme activity.

D) It indicates a gradual decline in enzyme activity with rising temperature.

**Question 2:**

Which statement is best supported by the data shown in the table?

A) Species A thrives in cooler climates compared to Species B.

B) Both Species A and B show similar growth rates in different temperature ranges.

C) Species B is more adaptable to a wide range of temperatures than Species A.

D) The growth rate of Species A is unaffected by temperature changes.

**Question 3:**

What conclusion can be drawn from the relationship between the values in the table and the hypothesis stated in the passage?

A) The data supports the hypothesis with a positive correlation between variables.

B) The data contradicts the hypothesis, showing an inverse relationship.

C) The data is inconclusive and requires further analysis.

D) The data does not relate directly to the hypothesis.

**Question 4:**

How does the figure illustrating the relationship between light intensity and plant growth compare to the results discussed in the text?

A) The figure confirms the trend described, with plant growth increasing with light intensity.

B) The figure contradicts the text by showing a negative relationship between light intensity and growth.

C) The figure shows no significant change, unlike the increase in growth mentioned in the text.

D) The figure suggests a plateau in growth after a certain light intensity, which is not addressed in the text.

**Question 5:**

Based on the data in the chart, what is the most likely explanation for the variation in response times across different species?

A) Some species respond faster due to their genetic makeup.

B) The variation is caused by different environmental factors not mentioned in the passage.

C) The species with the longest response times are likely adapted to harsher environments.

D) The variation is due to measurement errors during the experiment.

**Question 6:**

Which trend is shown by the graph that most directly supports the researcher's conclusion about the impact of salinity on plant growth?

A) Growth decreases as salinity increases beyond a specific threshold.

B) Growth remains constant regardless of salinity changes.

C) Salinity has no measurable effect on plant growth across all species.

D) Growth initially increases with salinity but declines sharply after a certain point.

**Question 7:**

What additional information from the chart is necessary to fully understand the relationship between variable X and plant growth?

A) The units of measurement for variable X

B) The average growth rate across different variables

C) The temperature conditions during the experiment

D) The pH levels of the soil samples used in the study

**Question 8:**

How does the figure of cell activity support the description provided in the passage?

A) It demonstrates how cell activity increases with exposure to specific chemicals.

B) It shows that cell activity decreases as chemical concentration rises.

C) It contradicts the description by showing no change in activity levels.

D) It provides evidence that supports the passage's description of cell activity under different conditions.

**Question 9:**

Which observation from the data in the table most directly challenges the hypothesis?

A) The outlier values in the data that do not fit the expected pattern

B) The trend of increasing growth with decreasing temperature

C) The lack of a strong correlation between light exposure and plant height

D) The consistent growth rates despite varying environmental conditions

**Question 10:**

What can be inferred from the relationship between the two graphs presented in the passage?

A) Both graphs show consistent trends supporting the text's main conclusion.

B) The graphs show conflicting data, leading to uncertainty in the findings.

C) One graph complements the other by providing additional context.

D) The graphs provide unrelated data points that do not affect the overall conclusion.

**Question 11:**

Which factor is most likely responsible for the disparity between the results shown in the graph and those described in the passage?

A) Inconsistent testing conditions across experiments

B) A misinterpretation of the data by the researchers

C) The use of different measurement tools in the experiments

D) The influence of external factors not controlled in the study

**Question 12:**

How does the data in Table 3 enhance the understanding of the experiment described in the passage?

A) It confirms the primary conclusion by providing supporting evidence.

B) It raises questions about the validity of the initial findings.

C) It suggests new areas of research not covered in the text.

D) It complicates the interpretation by introducing conflicting data.

**Question 13:**

What does the table suggest about the variable Y's impact on the study's outcome?

A) Variable Y has a significant and consistent impact across all trials.

B) Variable Y shows no measurable influence on the study's results.

C) Variable Y's effect is negligible compared to other variables.

D) Variable Y plays a key role but only under specific conditions.

**Question 14:**

How does the graph illustrating the results of the control group compare to the experimental group's data?

A) The control group shows no variation, while the experimental group displays significant changes.

B) Both groups show identical patterns, indicating no effect of the variable.

C) The control group's data fluctuates, while the experimental group shows stable results.

D) The control group and experimental group show similar trends, supporting the study's hypothesis.

**Question 15:**

What is the relationship between the text's discussion of atmospheric $CO_2$ levels and the graph provided?

A) The graph corroborates the text by showing a steady rise in $CO_2$ levels over time.

B) The graph contradicts the text by showing a decline in $CO_2$ levels.

C) The graph provides additional data not mentioned in the text regarding other gases.

D) The graph is unrelated to the text's discussion of $CO_2$ levels and focuses on a different aspect of the study.

# Section 4: Historical Documents Passage Comprehension

# Historical Document 1: Analysis of Political Speeches or Official Statements

**Passage:**

[Insert a passage that includes a historical political speech or an official statement from a key historical figure, such as the Gettysburg Address or an official declaration.]

**Question 1:**

Which of the following best summarizes the main argument of the speaker in the passage?

A) The speaker calls for unity in a time of national division.

B) The speaker argues for economic reforms to address inequality.

C) The speaker condemns foreign interference in domestic affairs.

D) The speaker advocates for military intervention to protect national security.

**Question 2:**

How does the speaker use rhetorical devices to emphasize their main point?

A) By employing repetition to reinforce key ideas.

B) By using metaphors to simplify complex issues.

C) By appealing to the audience's emotions through vivid imagery.

D) By providing statistical evidence to support claims.

**Question 3:**

What is the speaker's tone throughout the speech?

A) Optimistic and forward-looking

B) Solemn and reflective

C) Defiant and resolute

D) Skeptical and cautious

**Question 4:**

How does the historical context in which the speech was delivered influence its message?

A) It reflects the social tensions of the time, shaping the speaker's focus on unity.

B) It shows how technological advancements impacted the speaker's argument.

C) It highlights the influence of global trade on the speaker's policy recommendations.

D) It underscores the economic downturn that motivated the speaker's call for action.

**Question 5:**

Which of the following quotes from the speech best exemplifies the speaker's appeal to patriotism?

A) "We must come together, not as individuals, but as a nation, bound by shared values."

B) "The economic policies we implement today will determine our future prosperity."

C) "It is through dialogue and diplomacy that we can achieve lasting peace."

D) "The time for action is now, and we must act swiftly to protect our environment."

**Question 6:**

What is the speaker's primary purpose in delivering this speech?

A) To rally public support for a new government policy

B) To criticize a political opponent's stance on foreign policy

C) To inspire hope and perseverance during a national crisis

D) To introduce reforms aimed at improving education

**Question 7:**

How does the speaker address potential counterarguments?

A) By acknowledging opposing viewpoints and providing rebuttals

B) By dismissing the opposition without explanation

C) By shifting focus to a different issue entirely

D) By using humor to downplay the significance of the counterarguments

**Question 8:**

Which statement from the passage best illustrates the speaker's vision for the future?

A) "Together, we shall build a brighter tomorrow, hand in hand."

B) "The challenges we face today are greater than ever before."

C) "It is only through compromise that we can hope to achieve progress."

D) "We must address the needs of the present before planning for the future."

**Question 9:**

What reasoning does the speaker use to justify their policy recommendations?

A) Historical precedents of success under similar policies

B) Moral imperatives and ethical considerations

C) Economic data showing projected benefits

D) Scientific research supporting their proposals

**Question 10:**

Which rhetorical strategy is most evident in the speaker's closing remarks?

A) A call to action

B) An appeal to authority

C) A reflection on past failures

D) A prediction of future consequences

**Question 11:**

How does the speaker structure their argument to build toward the final call to action?

A) By addressing minor issues first and escalating to the primary concern

B) By presenting their main argument early and supporting it with examples

C) By outlining counterarguments before making their final point

D) By posing questions to the audience and answering them in the conclusion

**Question 12:**

What is the effect of the speaker's use of repetition in the passage?

A) It reinforces the urgency of the issue at hand.

B) It distracts from the main argument by focusing on smaller details.

C) It confuses the audience by repeating contradictory statements.

D) It adds humor to an otherwise serious discussion.

**Question 13:**

What is the significance of the speaker referencing historical events in the passage?

A) To draw parallels between past challenges and the present situation

B) To illustrate the long-standing success of their policy proposals

C) To criticize how similar events were mishandled in the past

D) To downplay the relevance of current issues in favor of historical context

**Question 14:**

Which of the following best explains the speaker's appeal to the audience's emotions in the passage?

A) The speaker evokes feelings of fear to gain support for military intervention.

B) The speaker inspires hope by highlighting the nation's resilience.

C) The speaker promotes anger by blaming external forces for domestic problems.

D) The speaker emphasizes nostalgia for a bygone era to argue for returning to old policies.

**Question 15:**

What role does the speaker's personal experience play in strengthening their argument?

A) The speaker draws on their own struggles to connect with the audience.

B) The speaker uses personal success stories to justify their recommendations.

C) The speaker downplays their own experience in favor of expert opinions.

D) The speaker avoids mentioning personal experience altogether.

**Question 16:**

How does the speaker's use of formal language affect the overall impact of the speech?

A) It elevates the seriousness of the issue being discussed.

B) It alienates the audience by being too complex and difficult to understand.

C) It makes the argument more persuasive by relying on authoritative tone.

D) It creates a sense of detachment from the speaker's emotions.

**Question 17:**

What can be inferred about the audience's likely response to the speech based on the speaker's tone and content?

A) They will likely feel motivated to take immediate action.

B) They may feel skeptical due to the lack of supporting evidence.

C) They will be disinterested due to the speaker's monotonous delivery.

D) They will feel confused by the conflicting arguments presented.

**Question 18:**

Which phrase from the passage signals a shift in the speaker's argument?

A) "However, let us not forget..."

B) "In conclusion, we must remember..."

C) "It is important to note that..."

D) "As we move forward, it is crucial that..."

**Question 19:**

How does the speaker balance emotion and logic in their argument?

A) By combining emotional appeals with factual data to create a compelling case

B) By relying entirely on emotional anecdotes without any logical reasoning

C) By focusing exclusively on logic, ignoring any emotional aspects

D) By switching between emotion and logic without a clear pattern

**Question 20:**

What is the primary effect of the speaker's appeal to shared values in the passage?

A) It fosters a sense of unity and common purpose among the audience.

B) It alienates certain members of the audience who do not share those values.

C) It distracts from the main argument by focusing on unrelated topics.

D) It undermines the speaker's authority by relying too heavily on subjective beliefs.

# Historical Document 2: Comparison of Two Historical Texts

**Passage 1:**

[Insert a passage from a significant historical document, such as the Declaration of Independence.]

**Passage 2:**

[Insert a passage from another related historical document, such as the U.S. Constitution or a political speech that responds to the first document.]

**Question 1:**

How do the authors of the two documents address the concept of individual rights?

A) Both authors argue for expanding individual rights beyond what the government currently allows.

B) The first author emphasizes natural rights, while the second focuses on the legal structure of rights.

C) Both authors prioritize collective rights over individual liberties.

D) The first author advocates for limited rights, while the second opposes any form of government intervention.

**Question 2:**

What is the primary difference in tone between the two passages?

A) The first passage is more urgent and passionate, while the second is more measured and formal.

B) The first passage uses an argumentative tone, while the second is reflective and contemplative.

C) Both passages have a defiant tone, though one is more optimistic.

D) The second passage is more emotional, while the first is analytical.

**Question 3:**

How does the second passage respond to the issues raised in the first passage?

A) It refutes the arguments of the first passage and presents an alternative viewpoint.

B) It builds on the principles outlined in the first passage, offering practical steps for implementation.

C) It criticizes the logic of the first passage and offers a more radical approach.

D) It ignores the points made in the first passage and focuses on unrelated concerns.

**Question 4:**

Which of the following best summarizes a shared theme between both passages?

A) The necessity of government regulation to protect individual freedoms

B) The importance of unity in achieving national goals

C) The challenge of balancing liberty and order

D) The urgency of immediate political reform

**Question 5:**

What role does historical context play in shaping the arguments of both documents?

A) The documents were written in response to different types of government oppression.

B) The first document reflects revolutionary ideals, while the second is focused on governance stability.

C) Both documents were written in times of peace, advocating gradual reform.

D) The authors of both documents faced similar challenges from external threats.

**Question 6:**

Which rhetorical strategy is common to both documents?

A) Both use appeals to morality to justify their claims.

B) Both rely heavily on statistical evidence to support their arguments.

C) Both avoid emotional appeals in favor of strictly logical arguments.

D) Both use personal anecdotes to draw the reader into their perspective.

**Question 7:**

How does the language of each passage reflect the political climate in which it was written?

A) The first passage uses more revolutionary language, while the second reflects a desire for institutional stability.

B) Both passages employ conciliatory language to avoid offending powerful political figures.

C) The second passage uses exaggerated language, while the first passage is more neutral.

D) Both passages use optimistic language reflecting the successes of their respective governments.

**Question 8:**

What is the primary similarity in how each author defines the role of government?

A) Both authors argue that government should exist primarily to defend against external threats.

B) Both passages suggest that government must be restrained to protect individual liberties.

C) Both documents emphasize the role of government in maintaining economic stability.

D) Both argue that government should be responsive to the changing needs of its people.

**Question 9:**

What effect does the use of first-person perspective have in the second passage compared to the third-person narrative of the first passage?

A) It makes the second passage feel more personal and urgent.

B) It distances the reader from the argument in the second passage.

C) It adds authority to the first passage's claims, while weakening the second.

D) It creates a more formal tone in the second passage.

**Question 10:**

How do the two documents view the relationship between government and the governed?

A) The first passage views it as a necessary evil, while the second passage sees it as a partnership.

B) The first passage advocates for minimal government involvement, while the second passage suggests government should guide moral decisions.

C) Both documents agree that government must be limited by the consent of the governed.

D) Both argue for an authoritarian government to ensure public order.

**Question 11:**

Which of the following best explains how the authors justify rebellion or resistance to government in the two passages?

A) Both passages reject the notion of rebellion under any circumstances.

B) The first passage argues rebellion is a last resort, while the second insists it is a duty in the face of tyranny.

C) The first passage justifies rebellion in cases of taxation without representation, while the second focuses on resistance to oppressive laws.

D) Both passages argue that rebellion should be avoided unless the government fails to protect fundamental rights.

**Question 12:**

What role does religious language play in the first passage compared to the second?

A) The first passage uses religious references to strengthen its moral argument, while the second avoids religious language entirely.

B) Both passages use religious language to appeal to a shared sense of moral duty.

C) The second passage criticizes the religious overtones of the first passage.

D) Neither passage uses religious language to influence the reader.

**Question 13:**

Which of the following best describes how both passages address economic concerns?

A) The first passage discusses economic freedom, while the second addresses economic justice.

B) Both passages argue that economic stability is secondary to individual rights.

C) The first passage advocates for economic independence, while the second emphasizes the importance of trade.

D) Neither passage directly addresses economic issues.

**Question 14:**

How does the second author challenge the ideas presented in the first passage?

A) By suggesting that the first passage's solutions are outdated

B) By offering a more detailed and structured approach to governance

C) By emphasizing the need for international cooperation, which the first passage ignores

D) By directly opposing the first author's view of government's role

**Question 15:**

What effect does the mention of specific historical events have in each passage?

A) It serves to discredit opposing viewpoints by reminding readers of past failures.

B) It provides concrete examples that ground the abstract ideas discussed.

C) It distracts from the main arguments by focusing on unrelated events.

D) It creates an emotional appeal by evoking nostalgia.

**Question 16:**

What can be inferred about the authors' perspectives on compromise from the two passages?

A) The first passage favors compromise to maintain stability, while the second argues against it.

B) The second passage advocates for compromise as the best way forward, while the first supports more extreme measures.

C) Both passages argue that compromise is only acceptable when basic rights are protected.

D) Neither passage supports compromise, viewing it as a sign of weakness.

**Question 17:**

How do the two passages handle the issue of representation in government?

A) The first passage advocates for direct democracy, while the second supports representative government.

B) The first passage sees representation as essential to democracy, while the second passage is more concerned with protecting minority rights.

C) Both passages call for greater representation, but differ on how it should be achieved.

D) Neither passage addresses the issue of representation in detail.

**Question 18:**

How does each passage use appeals to authority?

A) Both passages cite historical figures to lend credibility to their arguments.

B) The first passage relies on appeals to authority, while the second focuses on logical reasoning.

C) The second passage uses appeals to contemporary experts, while the first references religious figures.

D) Neither passage uses appeals to authority.

**Question 19:**

Which of the following best explains the difference in how each passage envisions the future?

A) The first passage is more optimistic about the future, while the second emphasizes the need for vigilance.

B) The second passage sees the future as uncertain and unstable, while the first is focused on specific reforms.

C) Both passages present an idealized view of the future, though they differ in how to achieve it.

D) Neither passage offers a clear vision for the future.

**Question 20:**

Which of the following is the best summary of the main philosophical difference between the two passages?

A) The first passage emphasizes liberty above all, while the second focuses on justice and equality.

B) The first passage is concerned with economic growth, while the second is focused on moral issues.

C) Both passages agree on core principles but differ in their approach to implementing them.

D) The second passage challenges the individualism promoted by the first passage.

# Historical Document 3: Understanding Historical Nuances and Author Perspectives

**Passage 1:**

[Insert a passage from a historical speech or document that focuses on nuanced historical issues, such as a letter from a political leader during a pivotal moment in history.]

**Question 1:**

What is the main historical event referenced in the passage, and how does it shape the author's argument?

A) The passage refers to a wartime event that emphasizes the need for national unity.

B) The passage discusses a political debate, using it to argue for limited government intervention.

C) The passage highlights a cultural movement, stressing the importance of individual freedoms.

D) The passage references an economic downturn, arguing for governmental reform.

**Question 2:**

How does the author's background influence their perspective on the issue being discussed?

A) The author's personal experience with war shapes their pro-peace stance.

B) The author's role in government leads them to advocate for stricter laws.

C) The author's previous work in education causes them to prioritize intellectual freedom.

D) The author's leadership in economic policy drives their focus on financial stability.

**Question 3:**

Which of the following best describes the tone of the passage?

A) Optimistic and forward-looking

B) Reflective and cautious

C) Defiant and confrontational

D) Sarcastic and dismissive

**Question 4:**

What is the author's purpose in referencing a specific historical event?

A) To remind readers of a past mistake that should not be repeated

B) To celebrate a victory that shaped the country's future

C) To criticize contemporary leaders for their handling of similar situations

D) To highlight a key turning point in international relations

**Question 5:**

How does the author address opposing viewpoints in the passage?

A) By dismissing them as irrelevant to the main argument

B) By acknowledging their merit but ultimately refuting them

C) By integrating them into the argument and agreeing with certain points

D) By ignoring them entirely to focus on their own viewpoint

**Question 6:**

What is the significance of the author's choice of words when describing the political situation?

A) It softens the severity of the situation to avoid alarming readers.

B) It conveys the gravity of the situation, emphasizing the urgency of action.

C) It creates a sense of distance between the reader and the issue.

D) It adds a layer of irony, hinting that the author is skeptical of the situation's seriousness.

**Question 7:**

How does the passage reflect the broader historical context in which it was written?

A) The passage highlights the tensions between two political factions of the time.

B) The passage discusses economic issues that were prevalent during a specific decade.

C) The passage reflects growing international concerns that defined the political climate.

D) The passage ignores historical context in favor of focusing on moral questions.

**Question 8:**

What rhetorical strategy does the author use to persuade the reader?

A) The author appeals to emotion, evoking sympathy for those affected by the situation.

B) The author uses logical arguments, presenting clear evidence to support their stance.

C) The author relies on an appeal to tradition, emphasizing past values and customs.

D) The author utilizes humor to downplay the seriousness of the issue at hand.

**Question 9:**

How does the passage's structure influence the effectiveness of the argument?

A) The author introduces the main point immediately and spends the rest of the passage elaborating.

B) The passage builds up to the main argument gradually, laying out context and details first.

C) The author presents the opposing viewpoint first, then dismantles it before introducing their own argument.

D) The passage is fragmented, jumping between ideas without clear transitions.

**Question 10:**

Which of the following best explains the author's attitude toward change?

A) The author believes change is inevitable and should be embraced fully.

B) The author advocates for gradual change to prevent social disruption.

C) The author is resistant to change, preferring the status quo.

D) The author encourages immediate and radical change to address urgent issues.

**Question 11:**

How does the author use historical examples to support their argument?

A) The author references past successes to argue that the same approach will work again.

B) The author points out past failures to suggest that a different strategy is needed.

C) The author uses historical examples to show that the issue has always been controversial.

D) The author avoids historical examples, focusing on present-day concerns.

**Question 12:**

Which aspect of the author's argument reflects their personal ideology?

A) The emphasis on individual rights and freedoms

B) The prioritization of national security over personal liberties

C) The focus on economic stability above all else

D) The call for stronger international alliances

**Question 13:**

What can be inferred about the author's view of the future based on the passage?

A) The author is hopeful that the situation will improve with time and effort.

B) The author is pessimistic, believing that past mistakes will be repeated.

C) The author is neutral, presenting both potential outcomes without favoring one.

D) The author expresses confidence that the government will solve the issue at hand.

**Question 14:**

How does the author's use of metaphor or symbolism enhance the argument?

A) It makes complex ideas more relatable by comparing them to everyday concepts.

B) It adds emotional weight to the argument by drawing on familiar cultural symbols.

C) It creates a sense of urgency by likening the situation to a ticking clock.

D) It distracts from the main argument, making the passage harder to follow.

**Question 15:**

What does the passage suggest about the author's views on leadership?

A) The author believes strong leadership requires moral integrity above all.

B) The author argues that leadership should be adaptable and flexible.

C) The author contends that leadership should be based on popular consensus.

D) The author views leadership as a form of service that demands self-sacrifice.

# Historical Document 4: Critical Analysis and Evaluation of Historical Arguments

**Passage 1:**

[Insert a passage from a historical document where an author presents a strong argument on a political or social issue, such as a famous speech or a letter arguing for a significant policy change.]

**Question 1:**

What is the primary argument made by the author in the passage?

A) The need for immediate action to address a social injustice

B) The importance of maintaining traditional values

C) A call for compromise between opposing political parties

D) The defense of an economic policy that benefits the majority

**Question 2:**

Which evidence does the author use to support their argument, and how effective is it?

A) The author relies on anecdotal evidence, which appeals to emotions but lacks concrete proof.

B) The author uses statistical data, which strengthens their argument by providing factual support.

C) The author refers to historical precedents, giving their argument a sense of legitimacy.

D) The author uses hypothetical scenarios, which are less convincing due to their speculative nature.

## Question 3:

How does the author address counterarguments in the passage?

A) By dismissing them as illogical and irrelevant

B) By acknowledging their merit but refuting them with stronger evidence

C) By incorporating them into the main argument and offering compromises

D) By ignoring them entirely and focusing only on their own viewpoint

## Question 4:

What rhetorical strategies does the author use to persuade the reader?

A) The author appeals to logic, providing clear and well-reasoned arguments.

B) The author relies heavily on emotional appeals to gain sympathy from the audience.

C) The author uses humor to downplay the opposition's views.

D) The author emphasizes moral superiority to strengthen their argument.

## Question 5:

How does the structure of the passage contribute to the author's argument?

A) The author builds the argument progressively, starting with simple ideas and leading to more complex points.

B) The author presents the main argument upfront and spends the rest of the passage defending it.

C) The passage begins with a critique of opposing viewpoints before shifting to the author's stance.

D) The structure is fragmented, making the argument difficult to follow.

## Question 6:

What is the author's tone throughout the passage, and how does it impact the argument?

A) Formal and authoritative, lending credibility to the argument

B) Sarcastic and dismissive, weakening the overall message

C) Passionate and urgent, encouraging the reader to take action

D) Neutral and detached, making the argument seem less persuasive

## Question 7:

In what way does the historical context of the passage influence the argument?

A) The passage reflects contemporary social tensions that shaped the author's perspective.

B) The passage ignores the broader historical context, focusing solely on moral arguments.

C) The passage presents a forward-looking argument, less concerned with the events of the time.

D) The historical context has little bearing on the argument presented.

## Question 8:

What assumptions does the author make about their audience, and how do these assumptions shape the argument?

A) The author assumes the audience agrees with their moral stance, which reinforces their emotional appeals.

B) The author assumes the audience is skeptical and uses logical evidence to win them over.

C) The author assumes the audience is well-educated, leading to the use of complex language and ideas.

D) The author assumes the audience is politically neutral, focusing on compromise and balance.

## Question 9:

How does the author handle complexity in the issues discussed in the passage?

A) By simplifying the issues to make them more accessible to the general reader

B) By diving into the complexities, providing a thorough examination of each aspect

C) By avoiding complex issues altogether, focusing on surface-level arguments

D) By oversimplifying the issues, which weakens the argument's depth

**Question 10:**

How does the author's use of language enhance or detract from the argument?

A) The use of clear, straightforward language makes the argument accessible and effective.

B) The author's use of flowery language makes the argument less direct and harder to follow.

C) The author's frequent use of jargon alienates the general audience.

D) The use of overly casual language diminishes the seriousness of the argument.

**Question 11:**

What can be inferred about the author's stance on government authority based on the passage?

A) The author supports a strong central government to maintain social order.

B) The author advocates for minimal government intervention in personal freedoms.

C) The author argues for balanced governmental powers to ensure fairness.

D) The author is critical of government authority, favoring individual autonomy.

**Question 12:**

How does the author use historical examples to reinforce their argument?

A) The author uses examples of past failures to argue for a new approach.

B) The author cites historical successes to support the continuation of current policies.

C) The author avoids using historical examples, focusing instead on theoretical arguments.

D) The author references historical debates to show that the issue has always been contentious.

**Question 13:**

What is the most significant flaw in the author's argument?

A) The overreliance on emotional appeals rather than logical evidence

B) The failure to address key counterarguments that weaken the main point

C) The use of vague language that makes the argument difficult to follow

D) The lack of concrete examples to support theoretical claims

**Question 14:**

How does the author's background or role in society influence the argument presented?

A) The author's experience in politics leads to a focus on governmental solutions.

B) The author's role as a social activist informs their calls for immediate change.

C) The author's academic background leads to a detached, theoretical perspective.

D) The author's position in business shapes their focus on economic stability.

**Question 15:**

What conclusion can be drawn from the passage about the author's long-term vision for the issue?

A) The author envisions a future where immediate action resolves the problem.

B) The author sees the issue as ongoing, requiring gradual change over time.

C) The author believes the issue is temporary and will resolve without intervention.

D) The author argues that the issue is too complex to ever fully resolve.

# Variety of Topics: Humanities, Science, History

## Passage 1: Humanities – Exploration of Artistic Movements

[Insert a passage discussing an influential artistic movement, such as the Renaissance or Modernism, and its cultural impact.]

**Question 1:**

What is the central theme of the passage regarding the artistic movement?

A) Its influence on modern art techniques

B) Its role in the evolution of political thought

C) The economic conditions that fostered its development

D) Its lasting legacy on societal norms

**Question 2:**

Which example from the passage best illustrates the influence of the artistic movement on other disciplines?

A) The development of new architectural styles

B) The influence on religious institutions

C) Its impact on political revolutions

D) The movement's effect on scientific discoveries

**Question 3:**

What is the author's perspective on the lasting effects of the movement in today's culture?

A) The movement's influence has largely faded.

B) The movement still heavily influences contemporary culture.

C) The movement has been forgotten due to new art forms.

D) The movement's ideas are only relevant in academia.

## Passage 2: Science – The Ethical Implications of Gene Editing

[Insert a passage that discusses the ethical considerations of using CRISPR technology for gene editing.]

**Question 4:**

What is the primary ethical concern raised by the author regarding gene editing?

A) The potential misuse of the technology in unauthorized experiments

B) The possibility of creating genetic inequality

C) The lack of scientific research supporting gene editing

D) The inability to reverse gene editing once performed

**Question 5:**

How does the author balance the potential benefits of gene editing with the risks?

A) By focusing solely on the scientific advancements without addressing ethical concerns

B) By suggesting strict regulatory frameworks to mitigate the risks

C) By dismissing the risks as minor compared to the benefits

D) By advocating for the cessation of all gene editing research

**Question 6:**

What does the author imply about the future of gene editing technology?

A) It will be integrated into mainstream medical treatments within a decade.

B) Its development will be halted due to ethical concerns.

C) It will be used only in controlled, clinical environments.

D) It will revolutionize both medical and non-medical fields.

## Passage 3: History – The Formation of the United Nations

[Insert a passage about the founding of the United Nations and its objectives following World War II.]

**Question 7:**

What was the primary motivation behind the establishment of the United Nations?

A) To prevent future global conflicts

B) To maintain economic stability among world powers

C) To create a global government to replace national sovereignty

D) To form a new international legal system

**Question 8:**

Which historical events directly influenced the creation of the United Nations?

A) The economic depression of the 1930s

B) The political instability after World War I

C) The destruction and chaos following World War II

D) The rise of fascism and totalitarian regimes

**Question 9:**

What is the author's stance on the effectiveness of the United Nations in achieving its initial goals?

A) The organization has failed to prevent major conflicts since its formation.

B) The organization has largely succeeded but faces new challenges.

C) The UN has become obsolete due to changing global dynamics.

D) The UN's influence has always been minimal due to a lack of enforcement power.

## Passage 4: Philosophy – The Debate Between Free Will and Determinism

[Insert a passage that explores the philosophical debate between free will and determinism.]

**Question 10:**

What is the author's main argument in support of determinism?

A) Human behavior is entirely shaped by biological and environmental factors.

B) People are free to make choices independent of external forces.

C) Moral responsibility exists only in a world of free will.

D) Determinism can coexist with some level of personal freedom.

**Question 11:**

How does the author counter arguments in favor of free will?

A) By emphasizing the unpredictability of scientific phenomena

B) By highlighting examples of behavior controlled by external circumstances

C) By conceding that free will exists in specific moral situations

D) By arguing that free will is an illusion created by consciousness

**Question 12:**

What evidence does the author provide to support their deterministic viewpoint?

A) Scientific studies showing brain activity before conscious decisions

B) Examples from literature that question human freedom

C) Historical events that reflect societal determinism

D) Philosophical theories that deny the existence of causality

## Passage 5: Environmental Science – Climate Change and Global Policy

[Insert a passage discussing the global political response to climate change.]

**Question 13:**

Which political actions are cited in the passage as critical for mitigating climate change?

A) International agreements to reduce greenhouse gas emissions

B) Increasing tax rates to fund climate research

C) Investing in non-renewable energy sources

D) Expanding the production of coal and oil

**Question 14:**

How does the author describe the global cooperation necessary to combat climate change?

A) As a fundamental requirement that remains difficult to achieve

B) As a goal that has already been met by leading nations

C) As a secondary concern to economic growth

D) As unnecessary due to technological advancements

**Question 15:**

What is the author's view on the future of climate change policy?

A) That nations will ultimately fail to act in time

B) That continued political pressure will lead to meaningful change

C) That technology will solve the problem without political intervention

D) That future generations will be responsible for the consequences

## 5.2: Inference and Analysis Exercises

## Introduction

Inferences and critical analysis are at the heart of the SAT Reading & Writing sections. The ability to infer meaning from text goes beyond understanding the literal content; it involves reading between the lines, identifying underlying themes, and drawing logical conclusions from the information provided. This skill is crucial because many SAT questions test your ability to think critically, requiring you to extract implicit details and grasp the subtleties of the author's intentions.

The SAT is designed to assess not only what you can explicitly grasp from a passage but also your ability to interpret unstated meanings, connect ideas, and assess an author's tone or argument. Inference-based questions may ask you to determine what a character feels based on their actions, infer the meaning of a scientific concept from its description, or deduce the author's stance from the language used.

Common types of inference questions on the SAT include:

- **Inference from context**: Drawing conclusions about what is implied but not directly stated.
- **Inference about the author's attitude or tone**: Understanding the emotions or perspectives conveyed subtly through word choice.
- **Inference about relationships**: Identifying the connections between ideas, characters, or events that aren't immediately obvious.

- **Inference from evidence**: Using facts or details within the text to infer a broader conclusion.

These exercises will help you sharpen these skills, preparing you to tackle a variety of inference questions on the SAT with confidence and precision. The more you practice, the better you'll become at spotting hidden meanings and making insightful conclusions under time pressure.

Let's dive into the exercises that will challenge and develop your inference and analysis skills.

# Practice Exercises: 125 Questions Divided into Groups of 15-20 Questions

## Section 1: Direct Logical Inferences

This section presents 20 practice questions that require students to make direct logical inferences based on the provided passages. Each question is designed to assess the student's ability to deduce information that is not explicitly stated but can be reasonably inferred from the facts or details presented.

**1.**

*Passage Excerpt*:

"Sarah watched as the last train pulled away from the platform, the cold air biting at her skin. She had missed her chance, but she knew there would be another opportunity tomorrow."

**Question**:

Which of the following can be inferred about Sarah's situation?

A) She is disappointed but hopeful.

B) She is frustrated and angry.

C) She has no way of catching another train.

D) She is unaware of the train schedule.

**2.**

*Passage Excerpt*:

"The restaurant owner glanced nervously at the clock. It was past midnight, and the chef still hadn't shown up for the evening shift. The customers would be arriving soon, and he wasn't prepared."

**Question**:

What can be inferred about the restaurant owner's feelings?

A) He is considering canceling the reservations.

B) He is anxious about managing without the chef.

C) He is unconcerned about the situation.

D) He has decided to close the restaurant for the night.

**3.**

*Passage Excerpt*:

"Mark hurried down the corridor, his footsteps echoing through the empty hall. He was late, and he knew that this was the last chance he had to prove himself. Failure was not an option."

**Question**:

What can be inferred about Mark's mindset?

A) He is determined to succeed.

B) He is indifferent to the outcome.

C) He feels confident in his abilities.

D) He is considering giving up.

**4.**

*Passage Excerpt*:

"Though the mountain trail was treacherous and the storm was approaching quickly, they pressed on, knowing that turning back now would mean failure."

**Question**:

What can be inferred about the group's decision to continue their journey?

A) They are unaware of the risks.

B) They are committed to reaching their destination despite the dangers.

C) They believe the storm will pass quickly.

D) They are lost and unsure of the correct path.

**5.**

*Passage Excerpt*:

"Maria closed the book with a sigh. She had read the same paragraph three times, but her mind kept wandering back to the argument she had with her friend earlier that day."

**Question**:

What can be inferred about Maria's state of mind?

A) She is focused on her reading.

B) She is distracted by her thoughts.

C) She has forgotten about the argument.

D) She is enjoying the book she's reading.

**6.**

*Passage Excerpt*:

"The politician's speech was filled with promises of reform, but as he spoke, the crowd remained silent, their faces betraying a deep skepticism."

**Question**:

What can be inferred about the crowd's reaction to the speech?

A) They are enthusiastic about the politician's ideas.

B) They are doubtful about the politician's promises.

C) They are confused by the politician's message.

D) They are indifferent to the politician's speech.

**7.**

*Passage Excerpt*:

"After a long day of meetings, Alice returned to her hotel room and immediately collapsed on the bed. The clock read 9:00 PM, but she knew she had hours of work ahead of her."

**Question**:

What can be inferred about Alice's situation?

A) She is planning to go to sleep early.

B) She is overwhelmed by her workload.

C) She has finished all of her tasks for the day.

D) She is preparing for an important presentation.

**8.**

*Passage Excerpt*:

"The old man sat by the window, watching the children play in the park below. His cane leaned against the wall, forgotten, as he smiled at their laughter."

**Question**:

What can be inferred about the old man's feelings?

A) He is annoyed by the noise.

B) He is lonely and wishes he could join the children.

C) He is content and enjoying the moment.

D) He is angry that the children are playing near his home.

**9.**

*Passage Excerpt*:

"The manager listened carefully to the employee's concerns, nodding in agreement. 'I understand,' she said, 'and I'll do everything I can to address the issue.'"

**Question**:

What can be inferred about the manager's attitude?

A) She is dismissive of the employee's concerns.

B) She is empathetic and willing to help.

C) She is frustrated by the employee's complaints.

D) She is unsure how to resolve the problem.

**10.**

*Passage Excerpt*:

"As the rain continued to pour, the hikers huddled under a tree, trying to stay dry. They knew they still had miles to go before they reached the campsite."

**Question**:

What can be inferred about the hikers' situation?

A) They are close to their destination.

B) They are well-prepared for the rain.

C) They are determined to reach the campsite despite the weather.

D) They are considering turning back.

**11.**

*Passage Excerpt*:

"Jen stared at the computer screen, her fingers hovering over the keyboard. She had the email drafted, but she hesitated, unsure if sending it was the right decision."

**Question**:

What can be inferred about Jen's feelings?

A) She is confident in her decision to send the email.

B) She is uncertain about sending the email.

C) She has already sent the email.

D) She is excited to receive a response.

**12.**

*Passage Excerpt*:

"After the announcement, the room fell silent. No one knew how to react to the sudden news, and many exchanged glances, unsure of what to say."

**Question**:

What can be inferred about the people's reaction to the announcement?

A) They are relieved by the news.

B) They are confused and unsure how to respond.

C) They are happy about the announcement.

D) They are ignoring the news.

**13.**

*Passage Excerpt*:

"The dog barked frantically at the door, but no one came to let him inside. The sun was setting, and the temperature was starting to drop."

**Question**:

What can be inferred about the dog's situation?

A) The dog is lost and cannot find his way home.

B) The dog is locked outside and wants to come inside.

C) The dog is excited to see someone arrive.

D) The dog is barking at another animal.

**14.**

*Passage Excerpt*:

"The student raised her hand timidly, glancing around the room to see if anyone else was about to speak. Her voice trembled as she began to ask her question."

**Question**:

What can be inferred about the student's feelings?

A) She is confident in asking her question.

B) She is nervous about speaking in front of the class.

C) She does not care about the answer.

D) She is angry with her classmates.

**15.**

*Passage Excerpt*:

"The car slowed to a stop at the red light. The driver drummed his fingers on the steering wheel, glancing repeatedly at the clock."

**Question**:

What can be inferred about the driver's situation?

A) He is in a hurry to get somewhere.

B) He is enjoying the drive.

C) He is unsure of where he is going.

D) He is waiting for someone to call him.

**16.**

*Passage Excerpt*:

"Despite her excitement, Emily couldn't shake the feeling that something was off. She had prepared for the presentation for weeks, but now that the moment had arrived, doubt began to creep in."

**Question**:

What can be inferred about Emily's feelings?

A) She is confident about the presentation.

B) She is worried that something might go wrong.

C) She is eager to finish the presentation.

D) She is not concerned about the outcome.

**17.**

*Passage Excerpt*:

"The sun dipped below the horizon as the two friends sat in silence, watching the waves crash against the shore. Neither of them spoke, but the air between them was heavy with unspoken thoughts."

**Question:**

What can be inferred about the friends' relationship?

A) They are angry with each other.

B) They are comfortable in each other's company.

C) They are preparing to say goodbye.

D) They are discussing a difficult topic.

**18.**

*Passage Excerpt:*

"The teacher smiled as she handed back the graded papers. 'You all did well,' she said, 'but there's always room for improvement.'"

**Question:**

What can be inferred about the teacher's feedback?

A) She is pleased with her students' performance.

B) She is disappointed in her students' work.

C) She is unsure how to improve her students' grades.

D) She is angry with her class.

**19.**

*Passage Excerpt:*

"The child watched as the ice cream melted onto the pavement, tears welling up in his eyes. His mother bent down to comfort him, offering him her own cone."

**Question:**

What can be inferred about the child's reaction?

A) He is upset about losing his ice cream.

B) He is happy that his mother offered her ice cream.

C) He is angry at his mother.

D) He is indifferent to the situation.

**20.**

*Passage Excerpt:*

"The CEO stood at the podium, delivering his final remarks. The audience clapped politely, but the atmosphere in the room felt tense."

**Question:**

What can be inferred about the audience's reaction to the CEO's speech?

A) They are enthusiastic about the CEO's speech.

B) They are uncomfortable with the CEO's message.

C) They are eager to leave the room.

D) They are disinterested in the CEO's remarks.

# Section 2: Context-Based Inferences

In this section, students are tasked with making inferences based on the broader context of the passage. These questions require understanding not just the explicit details but also the implications of the dialogue, setting, and actions to deduce more profound meanings.

**1.**

*Passage Excerpt*:

"As the two diplomats exchanged pleasantries, neither one could hide the tension in their voices. Their conversation, though polite, was filled with veiled references to past conflicts."

**Question**:

What can be inferred about the relationship between the diplomats?

A) They are good friends with a long-standing positive relationship.

B) They are in a delicate political situation with unresolved conflicts.

C) They are discussing unrelated matters and have no history together.

D) They are trying to negotiate a new trade agreement.

**2.**

*Passage Excerpt*:

"The streets were deserted, except for the occasional stray cat that darted between the shadows. It was the kind of night where people stayed indoors, windows shut, and curtains drawn."

**Question**:

What can be inferred about the atmosphere of the setting?

A) The neighborhood is peaceful and welcoming.

B) The area feels eerie and potentially unsafe.

C) The town is preparing for a festival.

D) It is a cold winter evening, and people are staying inside to keep warm.

**3.**

*Passage Excerpt*:

"During the dinner party, the hostess made sure to engage everyone in light conversation. Yet, every so often, her eyes would dart towards the door as though she were expecting something—or someone."

**Question**:

What can be inferred about the hostess's behavior?

A) She is fully focused on entertaining her guests.

B) She is distracted, anticipating the arrival of someone.

C) She is frustrated with her guests.

D) She is worried about the food being served.

**4.**

*Passage Excerpt*:

"As the villagers gathered in the town square, they spoke in hushed tones, glancing over their shoulders as if someone might be watching. The air was thick with apprehension."

**Question**:

What can be inferred about the villagers' state of mind?

A) They are excited about an upcoming celebration.

B) They are nervous and possibly afraid of something.

C) They are angry and planning a protest.

D) They are waiting for an important announcement.

**5.**

*Passage Excerpt*:

"The students sat in a circle, their teacher encouraging them to speak freely. But despite her best efforts, their responses were brief and cautious."

**Question**:

What can be inferred about the students' behavior?

A) They feel comfortable and are eager to share their thoughts.

B) They are hesitant to speak openly, possibly out of fear or uncertainty.

C) They are uninterested in the discussion.

D) They are trying to impress the teacher with their knowledge.

**6.**

*Passage Excerpt*:

"The ornate chandelier hung low in the ballroom, casting long shadows across the floor. The guests, dressed in their finest attire, moved slowly as if weighed down by an invisible burden."

**Question**:

What can be inferred about the mood of the event?

A) It is a lively and joyous occasion.

B) It is a somber or uncomfortable gathering.

C) The guests are eager to leave.

D) The event is informal and relaxed.

**7.**

*Passage Excerpt*:

"John's voice was steady as he spoke to the crowd, but his hands fidgeted nervously in his pockets. Though his words were confident, there was an unmistakable tremor in his tone."

**Question**:

What can be inferred about John's feelings during the speech?

A) He is completely at ease while addressing the crowd.

B) He is nervous despite trying to appear confident.

C) He is disinterested in the audience's reaction.

D) He is excited and eager to continue speaking.

**8.**

*Passage Excerpt*:

"The letters were piled high on the desk, unopened and gathering dust. It had been weeks since the last one arrived, and still, no response."

**Question**:

What can be inferred about the situation from the state of the letters?

A) The recipient is eagerly awaiting more letters.

B) The recipient is deliberately avoiding reading the letters.

C) The letters are unimportant and forgotten.

D) The letters were never intended to be delivered.

**9.**

*Passage Excerpt*:

"As the guests left the house, they each offered their congratulations, but the smiles never quite reached their eyes."

**Question:**

What can be inferred about the guests' true feelings?

A) They are genuinely happy for the host.

B) They are pretending to be happy, but feel indifferent or negative.

C) They are confused about the event.

D) They are relieved that the event is over.

**10.**

*Passage Excerpt*:

"Despite the bustling market and the loud chatter of the vendors, the woman moved quietly through the crowd, unnoticed and seemingly out of place."

**Question:**

What can be inferred about the woman's presence at the market?

A) She is a regular visitor to the market.

B) She is unfamiliar with the environment and feels out of place.

C) She is looking for someone in the crowd.

D) She is shopping for items without drawing attention to herself.

**11.**

*Passage Excerpt*:

"The train station was crowded with travelers, yet Marcus stood still, his suitcase untouched by his side, as though he wasn't quite ready to leave."

**Question:**

What can be inferred about Marcus's feelings?

A) He is eager to board the train.

B) He is hesitant or unsure about his departure.

C) He is waiting for someone to arrive.

D) He is confused about which train to take.

**12.**

*Passage Excerpt*:

"As the storm raged outside, the old house creaked and groaned, but the family inside seemed unfazed, gathered around the fireplace in quiet conversation."

**Question:**

What can be inferred about the family's response to the storm?

A) They are frightened and worried about the storm's intensity.

B) They are accustomed to such storms and feel safe inside.

C) They are preparing to evacuate the house.

D) They are unaware of the storm outside.

**13.**

*Passage Excerpt*:

"The young artist stood in front of her painting, her arms crossed tightly across her chest. She didn't respond to the compliments, her gaze fixed on a single flaw she couldn't ignore."

**Question:**

What can be inferred about the artist's feelings toward her work?

A) She is proud of her painting.

B) She is focused on a flaw and dissatisfied with her work.

C) She believes her work is perfect and needs no improvement.

D) She is excited to hear praise from others.

**14.**

*Passage Excerpt*:

"The crowd erupted in applause as the performer took his final bow. Despite the roaring cheers, his smile seemed strained, and his eyes flickered toward the exit."

**Question**:

What can be inferred about the performer's feelings?

A) He is delighted with the audience's reaction.

B) He is eager to leave the stage.

C) He is preparing for an encore.

D) He is waiting for someone in the crowd.

**15.**

*Passage Excerpt*:

"Though the city was bustling with energy, the old bookstore felt like a quiet oasis. The customers browsed in silence, their footsteps soft on the worn wooden floor."

**Question**:

What can be inferred about the atmosphere in the bookstore?

A) It is loud and chaotic like the city outside.

B) It is peaceful and calm, offering a refuge from the busy city.

C) It is abandoned and empty.

D) It is undergoing renovations, causing the silence.

**16.**

*Passage Excerpt*:

"Even as the director announced the results, a murmur spread through the audience, many people whispering in disbelief."

**Question**:

What can be inferred about the audience's reaction to the announcement?

A) They are pleased with the results.

B) They are confused or surprised by the outcome.

C) They are indifferent to the announcement.

D) They are preparing to celebrate the results.

**17.**

*Passage Excerpt*:

"The detective scanned the room, his eyes lingering on the broken vase in the corner. It was the only thing out of place in the otherwise immaculate room."

**Question**:

What can be inferred about the detective's observation?

A) He is not interested in the broken vase.

B) He believes the vase is a key piece of evidence.

C) He is focused on other aspects of the room.

D) He assumes the broken vase is unrelated to the case.

**18.**

*Passage Excerpt:*

"The children played in the park, their laughter filling the air. Meanwhile, their parents sat on the benches, watching with weary eyes and occasional glances at their watches."

**Question:**

What can be inferred about the parents' feelings?

A) They are eager to leave the park.

B) They are fully engaged in watching their children play.

C) They are planning to join the children in their play.

D) They are not paying attention to the time.

**19.**

*Passage Excerpt:*

"The politician's speech was met with polite applause, but the reporters in the back exchanged knowing glances and scribbled furiously in their notebooks."

**Question:**

What can be inferred about the reporters' reactions to the speech?

A) They are impressed by the politician's message.

B) They are skeptical and are planning to write critically about the speech.

C) They are not paying attention to the speech.

D) They are waiting for a different speaker.

**20.**

*Passage Excerpt:*

"As the sun set behind the mountains, the campers gathered around the fire, their conversations growing quieter as the shadows stretched longer."

**Question:**

What can be inferred about the campers' mood as the evening progresses?

A) They are becoming more lively as the night approaches.

B) They are feeling a sense of calm and quiet as the night falls.

C) They are preparing to leave the campsite.

D) They are planning a night of celebration.

These 20 context-based inference questions encourage students to draw broader conclusions by analyzing the setting, mood, and relationships in the passages.

## Section 3: Inferences About Author's Opinions and Attitudes

In this section, students will practice identifying and analyzing the implicit opinions, attitudes, or biases conveyed by the author in various passages. These questions require a deeper understanding of how the author's tone, word choice, and presentation of facts reflect their underlying perspectives.

**1.**

*Passage Excerpt:*

"The industrial revolution brought about remarkable technological advancements, but at what cost to the working class, who toiled long hours in dangerous conditions?"

**Question:**

What can be inferred about the author's opinion on the industrial revolution?

A) The author believes the industrial revolution was entirely positive.

B) The author thinks the industrial revolution had negative consequences for workers.

C) The author feels indifferent about the industrial revolution.

D) The author praises the benefits without concern for the consequences.

**2.**

*Passage Excerpt:*

"While some may argue that social media connects us, the reality is that it often drives people apart, fostering shallow interactions over genuine relationships."

**Question:**

What can be inferred about the author's attitude toward social media?

A) The author is in favor of social media's impact on relationships.

B) The author believes social media has a mostly negative impact on personal relationships.

C) The author is neutral about the effects of social media.

D) The author believes social media brings people closer together.

**3.**

*Passage Excerpt:*

"The politician's decision to prioritize corporate interests over environmental regulations is yet another example of short-term gains taking precedence over long-term sustainability."

**Question:**

What can be inferred about the author's attitude toward the politician's decision?

A) The author supports the decision for economic reasons.

B) The author criticizes the decision for favoring corporate interests over the environment.

C) The author is indifferent to the decision.

D) The author believes the politician is making a wise choice for the future.

**4.**

*Passage Excerpt:*

"Many people look back on the 'golden age' of cinema with nostalgia, but it's important to recognize that this era was far from perfect, especially in its treatment of minority actors."

**Question:**

What can be inferred about the author's view of the 'golden age' of cinema?

A) The author believes the 'golden age' of cinema was flawless.

B) The author is nostalgic for the 'golden age' of cinema.

C) The author acknowledges its success but is critical of its shortcomings.

D) The author has no opinion on this era of cinema.

**5.**

*Passage Excerpt:*

"The rapid development of artificial intelligence is both exciting and terrifying. While it promises incredible advancements, it also poses significant risks that we are not yet prepared to handle."

**Question:**

What can be inferred about the author's stance on artificial intelligence?

A) The author is fully optimistic about artificial intelligence.

B) The author is entirely against the development of artificial intelligence.

C) The author sees both positive potential and significant risks in artificial intelligence.

D) The author is indifferent to the topic of artificial intelligence.

**6.**

*Passage Excerpt*:

"Despite claims to the contrary, the new policy seems to benefit only a select few, leaving the majority of citizens worse off than before."

**Question**:

What can be inferred about the author's view of the new policy?

A) The author believes the policy benefits everyone.

B) The author thinks the policy only helps a small group of people.

C) The author supports the policy wholeheartedly.

D) The author is undecided about the effects of the policy.

**7.**

*Passage Excerpt*:

"Some claim that climate change is a hoax, yet the overwhelming scientific consensus tells a different story—one of urgent action and undeniable evidence."

**Question**:

What can be inferred about the author's opinion on climate change?

A) The author believes climate change is a hoax.

B) The author is skeptical about climate change.

C) The author fully supports the scientific consensus on climate change.

D) The author is undecided about climate change.

**8.**

*Passage Excerpt*:

"The author's use of emotionally charged language when describing the plight of refugees highlights the urgency of the crisis and the need for compassionate policies."

**Question**:

What can be inferred about the author's attitude toward refugee policies?

A) The author is indifferent to the issue of refugees.

B) The author advocates for more compassionate and supportive refugee policies.

C) The author believes refugee policies should be more restrictive.

D) The author criticizes refugees for their situation.

**9.**

*Passage Excerpt*:

"Though the company claims to prioritize environmental sustainability, its actions—such as expanding into pristine natural areas—tell a different story."

**Question**:

What can be inferred about the author's view of the company's environmental practices?

A) The author believes the company is committed to sustainability.

B) The author thinks the company's actions contradict its claims of sustainability.

C) The author is unsure about the company's environmental impact.

D) The author supports the company's environmental decisions.

**10.**

*Passage Excerpt*:

"While the new education reform has been praised by some, it seems more like an attempt to cut costs rather than truly improve the quality of education."

**Question:**

What can be inferred about the author's opinion on the education reform?

A) The author believes the reform is focused on improving education.

B) The author thinks the reform is mainly about saving money.

C) The author supports the reform without reservation.

D) The author believes the reform will be effective in the long term.

## 11.

*Passage Excerpt:*

"The historical figure's achievements are often glorified, yet little attention is paid to the moral complexities of their actions, which include both great innovation and significant exploitation."

**Question:**

What can be inferred about the author's stance on the historical figure?

A) The author completely admires the historical figure.

B) The author is critical of the historical figure's actions.

C) The author believes the historical figure's achievements overshadow any moral concerns.

D) The author is indifferent to the historical figure's legacy.

## 12.

*Passage Excerpt:*

"Although many consider the artist a visionary, it's hard to overlook the controversy surrounding their personal life and how it affected their work."

**Question:**

What can be inferred about the author's view of the artist?

A) The author believes the artist's work is flawless.

B) The author acknowledges the artist's talent but is aware of the personal controversies.

C) The author is entirely dismissive of the artist's work due to their personal life.

D) The author is unaware of the artist's personal controversies.

## 13.

*Passage Excerpt:*

"While the town has seen improvements in infrastructure, the needs of its poorer residents have been largely ignored, leaving them without access to basic services."

**Question:**

What can be inferred about the author's attitude toward the town's improvements?

A) The author is pleased with the overall progress in the town.

B) The author believes that the town's improvements have neglected the poor.

C) The author thinks the improvements have benefited everyone equally.

D) The author is indifferent to the impact on the town's residents.

## 14.

*Passage Excerpt:*

"Critics of the novel have lauded its intricate plot, but few seem to have noticed the troubling undertones of prejudice that pervade the story."

**Question:**

What can be inferred about the author's opinion on the novel?

A) The author believes the novel is flawless.

B) The author praises the novel but is concerned about its prejudiced elements.

C) The author does not see any issues with the novel's themes.

D) The author is indifferent to the novel's content.

**15.**

*Passage Excerpt*:

"The public reaction to the new health initiative has been overwhelmingly positive, but one must wonder if the long-term effects have been fully considered."

**Question:**

What can be inferred about the author's stance on the new health initiative?

A) The author is fully supportive of the initiative.

B) The author is cautious about the long-term impact of the initiative.

C) The author believes the initiative will have no negative consequences.

D) The author is opposed to the initiative from the start.

**16.**

*Passage Excerpt*:

"The museum's decision to feature modern art has sparked debate, with some applauding the bold move and others criticizing it as an unnecessary departure from tradition."

**Question:**

What can be inferred about the author's opinion on the museum's decision?

A) The author fully supports the museum's choice.

B) The author disapproves of the decision to feature modern art.

C) The author presents both sides but does not express a clear opinion.

D) The author is indifferent to the change in the museum's focus.

**17.**

*Passage Excerpt*:

"The researcher's findings were groundbreaking, but the lack of peer review raises serious concerns about the validity of the results."

**Question:**

What can be inferred about the author's attitude toward the research?

A) The author fully supports the researcher's findings.

B) The author questions the validity of the findings due to the absence of peer review.

C) The author believes the research is flawless.

D) The author is indifferent to the research's significance.

**18.**

*Passage Excerpt*:

"The rapid gentrification of the neighborhood has resulted in new businesses and rising property values, but many long-time residents feel displaced and overlooked."

**Question:**

What can be inferred about the author's perspective on gentrification?

A) The author supports the gentrification efforts.

B) The author believes gentrification has been beneficial for everyone.

C) The author acknowledges the benefits but is critical of the impact on long-time residents.

D) The author is indifferent to the changes in the neighborhood.

**19.**

*Passage Excerpt:*

"Though the lawmaker claims to fight for equality, their voting record suggests otherwise, revealing a pattern of decisions that consistently benefit the privileged."

**Question:**

What can be inferred about the author's view of the lawmaker?

A) The author believes the lawmaker is genuinely committed to equality.

B) The author is critical of the lawmaker's inconsistent actions.

C) The author thinks the lawmaker has done a great job representing everyone.

D) The author is indifferent to the lawmaker's actions.

**20.**

*Passage Excerpt:*

"The writer's portrayal of the protagonist's struggles is undeniably poignant, but the predictable ending diminishes the overall impact of the story."

**Question:**

What can be inferred about the author's opinion of the story?

A) The author praises the story without any reservations.

B) The author appreciates the protagonist's development but finds fault with the ending.

C) The author dislikes the story entirely.

D) The author is indifferent to the story's outcome.

## Section 4: Inferences on Missing or Implied Details

In this section, students will need to deduce details that are not directly mentioned in the text but can be inferred from the surrounding context and information. These questions test the ability to identify subtle hints and underlying information that an author might imply without explicitly stating.

**1.**

*Passage Excerpt:*

"The town thrived during the summer months, but come winter, many shops closed their doors, and the streets were empty."

**Question:**

What can be implied about the town's economy during the winter months?

A) The town's economy booms in the winter.

B) The town faces economic challenges in the winter.

C) The town remains the same throughout the year.

D) The winter is the town's most prosperous time.

**2.**

*Passage Excerpt:*

"Their house was always filled with the smell of fresh bread, yet there were nights when they went to bed hungry."

**Question:**

What can be inferred about the family's economic situation?

A) The family is financially stable.

B) The family has limited financial resources.

C) The family wastes a lot of food.

D) The family chooses not to eat at night.

**3.**

*Passage Excerpt*:

"Though the politician emphasized the importance of education in her speech, she made no mention of the recent cuts to the public school budget."

**Question**:

What can be implied about the politician's stance on education funding?

A) The politician supports increased funding for education.

B) The politician might be avoiding addressing the issue of budget cuts.

C) The politician is focused solely on higher education.

D) The politician believes education funding is irrelevant.

**4.**

*Passage Excerpt*:

"The team celebrated their victory loudly in the locker room, yet their coach remained silent, staring at the game board."

**Question**:

What can be implied about the coach's feelings?

A) The coach is proud of the team's performance.

B) The coach is dissatisfied despite the win.

C) The coach does not care about the result.

D) The coach is preparing for the next game.

**5.**

*Passage Excerpt*:

"The garden was lush and green, despite the fact that rainfall had been scarce for months."

**Question**:

What can be inferred about how the garden was maintained?

A) The garden required no maintenance.

B) The garden was likely being watered regularly.

C) The garden thrived without water.

D) The garden's plants were artificial.

**6.**

*Passage Excerpt*:

"Everyone in the village greeted each other with smiles, but behind closed doors, many whispered about the changes taking place."

**Question**:

What can be implied about the villagers' true feelings toward the changes?

A) The villagers are indifferent to the changes.

B) The villagers may be secretly concerned or uneasy about the changes.

C) The villagers are excited about the changes.

D) The villagers do not know about the changes.

**7.**

*Passage Excerpt*:

"The restaurant prided itself on its gourmet dishes, yet more often than not, customers left without dessert."

**Question**:

What can be inferred about the customers' experience at the restaurant?

A) The customers were satisfied with the entire meal.

B) The dessert menu was not appealing to customers.

C) The restaurant's main dishes were of poor quality.

D) The restaurant did not offer dessert options.

**8.**

*Passage Excerpt*:

"He worked late into the night, long after his colleagues had left the office, driven by a sense of urgency."

**Question**:

What can be implied about the man's workload or responsibilities?

A) The man likely has little work to do.

B) The man is likely under significant pressure or has important tasks to complete.

C) The man is staying late purely out of habit.

D) The man is indifferent to his work.

**9.**

*Passage Excerpt*:

"The building was once a symbol of prosperity, but now its windows were boarded up, and its walls were covered in graffiti."

**Question**:

What can be implied about the current state of the building?

A) The building is still a prosperous place.

B) The building has fallen into disrepair.

C) The building is under construction.

D) The building is well-maintained.

**10.**

*Passage Excerpt*:

"Though she smiled and accepted the award graciously, her mind kept wandering back to the mistake she made earlier that evening."

**Question**:

What can be inferred about the woman's feelings during the award ceremony?

A) She is fully focused on receiving the award.

B) She is distracted and preoccupied with her earlier mistake.

C) She is confident and carefree.

D) She believes the award is undeserved.

**11.**

*Passage Excerpt*:

"The sun had set hours ago, but the lights in the office remained on as the employees continued working."

**Question**:

What can be implied about the workload or work culture in the office?

A) The employees have very little work to do.

B) The employees are likely overworked or under pressure to complete their tasks.

C) The employees are choosing to stay late for fun.

D) The office runs on a 24-hour schedule.

**12.**

*Passage Excerpt*:

"Despite their outward show of friendship, there was a palpable tension between the two, noticeable to everyone in the room."

**Question:**

What can be inferred about the relationship between the two people?

A) They are close friends without any issues.

B) There may be underlying conflict or unresolved issues between them.

C) They are pretending to dislike each other.

D) Their friendship is unaffected by the tension in the room.

**13.**

*Passage Excerpt*:

"The family moved into the house at the beginning of winter, and although they loved its charm, they soon realized it was colder than expected."

**Question:**

What can be implied about the house's condition?

A) The house is well-insulated and warm.

B) The house likely lacks proper insulation or heating.

C) The family is unaffected by the cold.

D) The family is indifferent to the house's flaws.

**14.**

*Passage Excerpt*:

"The new store was hailed as the best in town, but its parking lot was almost always empty."

**Question:**

What can be inferred about the store's popularity or success?

A) The store is thriving and busy.

B) The store is not attracting many customers despite its reputation.

C) The store is highly popular and successful.

D) The store is closed for renovations.

**15.**

*Passage Excerpt*:

"Her presentation was well-researched and meticulously prepared, yet the audience's reactions suggested something was missing."

**Question:**

What can be implied about the effectiveness of her presentation?

A) The presentation was flawless and well-received.

B) The presentation, though well-prepared, may have lacked engagement or impact.

C) The presentation was poorly researched.

D) The audience found the presentation exciting and engaging.

These 15 questions challenge students to infer missing or implied details based on subtle cues and the context provided in the passage. This exercise will strengthen their ability to read between the lines and make logical deductions.

# Section 5: Inferences on the Interrelation of Concepts

In this section, students will be tasked with understanding how different concepts presented in the passage are interconnected. The focus is on identifying relationships between ideas, causes and effects, and how one concept may influence or be influenced by another.

**1.**

*Passage Excerpt:*

"The rising sea levels have not only threatened coastal communities but have also forced governments to reconsider their economic planning."

**Question:**

How does the passage link environmental changes to governmental economic policies?

A) Governments are unaffected by environmental changes.

B) Rising sea levels are forcing governments to adapt their economic strategies.

C) Economic planning remains unchanged despite environmental challenges.

D) Governments have abandoned economic planning due to rising sea levels.

**2.**

*Passage Excerpt:*

"Technological advancements have made communication faster, but they have also contributed to a decline in face-to-face interactions."

**Question:**

What is the relationship between technological advancements and social interaction as suggested by the passage?

A) Technology only improves social interaction.

B) Technology has increased communication speed but reduced in-person communication.

C) Technology has had no effect on social interaction.

D) Face-to-face interaction is unaffected by technological advancements.

**3.**

*Passage Excerpt:*

"While the new policies promoted job creation, they also increased the burden on the environment due to unchecked industrial expansion."

**Question:**

What can be inferred about the relationship between job creation and environmental impact in the passage?

A) Job creation has no impact on the environment.

B) Job creation and industrial expansion are linked to greater environmental stress.

C) The environment benefits from industrial expansion.

D) The passage suggests job creation reduces environmental burdens.

**4.**

*Passage Excerpt:*

"The novel depicts a society where technological innovation leads to prosperity for some, while leaving others struggling with the repercussions of automation."

**Question:**

How does the passage describe the relationship between technological innovation and social inequality?

A) Technological innovation reduces inequality for everyone.

B) Technological innovation leads to prosperity for all.

C) Technological innovation creates wealth for some but increases inequality for others.

D) The society in the passage is unaffected by technology.

**5.**

*Passage Excerpt*:

"The agricultural revolution significantly boosted food production, but it also led to the degradation of the land and the loss of biodiversity."

**Question**:

What can be inferred about the connection between the agricultural revolution and environmental consequences?

A) The agricultural revolution improved both food production and biodiversity.

B) The agricultural revolution caused environmental degradation while increasing food production.

C) The agricultural revolution had no environmental impact.

D) Food production decreased due to the agricultural revolution.

**6.**

*Passage Excerpt*:

"Urbanization has contributed to economic growth, yet it has also created challenges in housing and transportation infrastructure."

**Question**:

How does the passage describe the relationship between urbanization and infrastructure challenges?

A) Urbanization has no effect on housing or transportation.

B) Urbanization improves economic growth but creates difficulties in housing and transportation.

C) Economic growth eliminates infrastructure challenges.

D) Urbanization leads to a decline in economic growth.

**7.**

*Passage Excerpt*:

"The widespread use of antibiotics has saved millions of lives, but it has also contributed to the emergence of drug-resistant bacteria."

**Question**:

What is the relationship between the use of antibiotics and the development of drug-resistant bacteria?

A) Antibiotics do not affect bacterial resistance.

B) The use of antibiotics has both positive effects (saving lives) and negative effects (resistance).

C) Antibiotics solely improve health outcomes.

D) The use of antibiotics prevents drug resistance.

**8.**

*Passage Excerpt*:

"Educational reform has led to increased access to higher education, though it has also resulted in greater student debt."

**Question**:

How does the passage link educational reform with student debt?

A) Educational reform eliminates student debt.

B) Educational reform increases access but also raises the risk of higher student debt.

C) Educational reform only benefits students financially.

D) Student debt remains unaffected by educational reform.

**9.**

*Passage Excerpt*:

"Globalization has fostered international trade, but it has also heightened the competition faced by local industries."

**Question**:

What is the relationship between globalization and local industries as described in the passage?

A) Globalization strengthens local industries without competition.

B) Globalization increases international trade while making competition harder for local industries.

C) Globalization has no effect on local industries.

D) Local industries benefit more from globalization than international trade.

**10.**

*Passage Excerpt*:

"Environmental conservation efforts have preserved many endangered species, yet economic development projects continue to encroach on natural habitats."

**Question**:

What does the passage suggest about the relationship between environmental conservation and economic development?

A) Economic development aids conservation efforts.

B) Conservation efforts and economic development are in conflict, with development threatening habitats.

C) Conservation and development are unrelated.

D) Conservation efforts prevent any economic development.

**11.**

*Passage Excerpt*:

"The rapid expansion of renewable energy sources has reduced reliance on fossil fuels, but it has also created new challenges in energy storage and distribution."

**Question**:

What can be inferred about the relationship between renewable energy and energy infrastructure challenges?

A) Renewable energy eliminates all challenges related to energy storage.

B) While renewable energy reduces fossil fuel dependence, it presents new challenges in storage and distribution.

C) Renewable energy has no impact on energy infrastructure.

D) Energy storage challenges decrease with the use of renewable energy.

**12.**

*Passage Excerpt*:

"Advances in artificial intelligence have improved workplace efficiency, yet they have also raised concerns about job displacement."

**Question**:

What is the relationship between artificial intelligence and employment as described in the passage?

A) Artificial intelligence increases jobs for everyone.

B) Artificial intelligence improves efficiency but raises concerns about job loss.

C) Artificial intelligence has no impact on the job market.

D) The passage suggests that AI prevents job displacement.

**13.**

*Passage Excerpt:*

"The decline in traditional print media has paved the way for digital platforms, but it has also led to concerns about the accuracy of information."

**Question:**

What does the passage suggest about the relationship between the decline of print media and digital platforms?

A) Digital platforms have no effect on information accuracy.

B) The rise of digital platforms has led to concerns about misinformation as print media declines.

C) Print media and digital platforms coexist without influencing each other.

D) Digital platforms have improved the accuracy of information compared to print media.

**14.**

*Passage Excerpt:*

"Investment in public transportation has reduced traffic congestion, but the costs of maintaining these systems have burdened local governments."

**Question:**

What is the relationship between public transportation investment and local government finances?

A) Public transportation investment eliminates financial concerns for governments.

B) While public transportation reduces traffic, its maintenance creates financial strain for local governments.

C) Public transportation systems are free of maintenance costs.

D) Local governments benefit financially from public transportation systems.

**15.**

*Passage Excerpt:*

"The invention of the smartphone revolutionized communication, but it also contributed to the rise of social isolation."

**Question:**

What is the relationship between smartphone use and social behavior according to the passage?

A) Smartphone use solely improves social behavior.

B) The smartphone revolutionized communication but contributed to social isolation.

C) Smartphones have no impact on social behavior.

D) Social isolation decreased with the rise of smartphone use.

These questions encourage students to think critically about how different concepts within a passage are interconnected, improving their ability to understand complex relationships and draw insightful conclusions.

# Section 6: Inferences on Tone and Language

This section focuses on helping students make inferences about the author's tone and language, which can reveal the author's attitude, emotions, or perspective on the subject matter. Students will be asked to interpret subtle cues in word choice, sentence structure, and overall style to understand the deeper meaning behind the text.

**1.**

*Passage Excerpt*:

"The speaker's description of the event was filled with vivid imagery, depicting the scene as chaotic and overwhelming."

**Question**:

Based on the tone of the passage, what can be inferred about the speaker's perspective on the event?

A) The speaker views the event with excitement.

B) The speaker finds the event disturbing and intense.

C) The speaker is indifferent to the event.

D) The speaker feels calm and composed about the event.

**2.**

*Passage Excerpt*:

"The author repeatedly refers to the policy as 'outdated' and 'ineffective,' suggesting it has outlived its usefulness."

**Question**:

What can be inferred about the author's attitude toward the policy from the language used?

A) The author supports the policy's continuation.

B) The author is critical of the policy and suggests it should be replaced.

C) The author feels the policy is necessary.

D) The author has no strong feelings about the policy.

**3.**

*Passage Excerpt*:

"With a dismissive wave of his hand, he called the new regulation 'a laughable attempt at reform.'"

**Question**:

What does the speaker's language reveal about his attitude toward the new regulation?

A) He finds the regulation well-intentioned but flawed.

B) He sees the regulation as ineffective and unworthy of serious consideration.

C) He believes the regulation is a positive change.

D) He is indifferent to the regulation.

**4.**

*Passage Excerpt*:

"The author uses phrases such as 'monumental failure' and 'irreparable harm' to describe the environmental impact."

**Question**:

What does the tone of the passage suggest about the author's view of the environmental situation?

A) The author is optimistic about finding a solution.

B) The author is deeply concerned about the severity of the situation.

C) The author believes the situation is improving.

D) The author is neutral about the environmental impact.

**5.**

*Passage Excerpt*:

"In a sarcastic tone, the writer referred to the proposed changes as 'the perfect solution to a non-existent problem.'"

**Question:**

What can be inferred about the writer's opinion of the proposed changes based on the tone?

A) The writer believes the changes are unnecessary and sarcastically criticizes them.

B) The writer supports the changes and is using sarcasm for effect.

C) The writer has no opinion about the changes.

D) The writer sees the changes as urgently needed.

**6.**

*Passage Excerpt:*

"The author speaks in reverent terms about the legacy of the artist, using words like 'genius' and 'visionary.'"

**Question:**

What can be inferred about the author's attitude toward the artist?

A) The author is dismissive of the artist's impact.

B) The author admires and respects the artist's contributions.

C) The author is neutral toward the artist.

D) The author finds the artist's work overrated.

**7.**

*Passage Excerpt:*

"The speaker's words were heavy with nostalgia, reflecting on 'the golden days' of a time long gone."

**Question:**

What can be inferred about the speaker's feelings regarding the past?

A) The speaker is indifferent to the past.

B) The speaker views the past with fondness and longing.

C) The speaker feels the past was better forgotten.

D) The speaker believes the past was problematic.

**8.**

*Passage Excerpt:*

"Referring to the plan as 'yet another bureaucratic mess,' the author seems to express frustration with the inefficiency of the government."

**Question:**

What does the author's tone reveal about their view of the government plan?

A) The author sees the plan as effective.

B) The author is frustrated with the inefficiency of the government plan.

C) The author is hopeful about the success of the plan.

D) The author is unsure about the plan's future.

**9.**

*Passage Excerpt:*

"The author's choice of words, such as 'bold' and 'audacious,' suggests an appreciation for the risk-taking nature of the new initiative."

**Question:**

Based on the language used, what can be inferred about the author's opinion of the new initiative?

A) The author disapproves of the initiative's boldness.

B) The author admires the initiative's willingness to take risks.

C) The author is indifferent to the initiative.

D) The author finds the initiative unremarkable.

**10.**

*Passage Excerpt*:

"With a resigned sigh, she commented, 'I suppose this is just how things are now.'"

**Question**:

What can be inferred about the speaker's attitude based on her tone?

A) She is enthusiastic about the changes.

B) She is resigned and somewhat accepting of the situation.

C) She is outraged by the situation.

D) She is hopeful for improvement.

**11.**

*Passage Excerpt*:

"The author's use of the phrase 'a glimmer of hope in an otherwise bleak scenario' suggests a cautious optimism."

**Question**:

What can be inferred about the author's outlook on the situation?

A) The author is entirely pessimistic about the outcome.

B) The author sees some potential for improvement amidst the challenges.

C) The author is indifferent to the situation.

D) The author believes the situation is beyond saving.

**12.**

*Passage Excerpt*:

"In a tone both celebratory and grateful, the speaker expressed deep appreciation for the support received."

**Question**:

What can be inferred about the speaker's emotions regarding the support?

A) The speaker feels indifferent to the support.

B) The speaker is deeply appreciative and thankful for the support.

C) The speaker is dismissive of the support received.

D) The speaker is upset about the lack of support.

**13.**

*Passage Excerpt*:

"With a tone of disbelief, the author questioned, 'Could anyone really believe that such a plan would work?'"

**Question**:

What does the author's tone suggest about their view of the plan?

A) The author is confident the plan will succeed.

B) The author is skeptical and doubtful about the effectiveness of the plan.

C) The author believes the plan has great potential.

D) The author is undecided about the plan.

**14.**

*Passage Excerpt*:

"The tone of the passage shifts from hopeful to somber as the author discusses the unforeseen consequences of the project."

**Question:**

What can be inferred about the author's feelings toward the project's outcome?

A) The author is still hopeful about the project's future.

B) The author is disappointed by the unexpected negative consequences.

C) The author is indifferent to the project's outcome.

D) The author is unaware of the consequences.

**15.**

*Passage Excerpt:*

"The speaker described the new development with a tone of excitement, calling it 'a groundbreaking achievement in technology.'"

**Question:**

What can be inferred about the speaker's attitude toward the new development?

A) The speaker is critical of the development.

B) The speaker is excited and enthusiastic about the technological achievement.

C) The speaker is indifferent to the development.

D) The speaker finds the development unnecessary.

# Section 7: Multiple Inferences from Multiple Sources

This section will focus on making inferences by analyzing and combining information from multiple parts of the text. Students will be tasked with comparing different perspectives, linking ideas, and drawing conclusions based on various pieces of information across passages.

**1.**

*Passage Excerpts:* Excerpt 1: "The first scientist believed that the results would revolutionize the field of biology." Excerpt 2: "The second scientist argued that the results, while interesting, were not significant enough to alter current paradigms."

**Question:**

What can be inferred from the two scientists' perspectives regarding the results of the study?

A) Both scientists agree on the revolutionary impact of the results.

B) The first scientist is more optimistic about the significance of the results than the second scientist.

C) The second scientist is more enthusiastic about the results than the first scientist.

D) Both scientists find the results insignificant.

**2.**

*Passage Excerpts:* Excerpt 1: "The policy was met with widespread acclaim among environmentalists, who praised its potential to curb deforestation." Excerpt 2: "Opponents of the policy pointed out its unintended economic consequences, claiming it hurt the timber industry."

**Question:**

What can be inferred about the main point of contention between the two groups?

A) Both groups agree the policy benefits the economy.

B) The environmentalists prioritize ecological benefits, while opponents focus on economic concerns.

C) Both groups believe the policy has no effect on deforestation.

D) Opponents of the policy are primarily concerned with its impact on the environment.

**3.**

*Passage Excerpts*: Excerpt 1: "The new technology was hailed as a breakthrough, promising to reduce energy consumption significantly." Excerpt 2: "Some experts warned that the technology's long-term effects on the environment were not yet fully understood."

**Question**:

What can be inferred from these two perspectives on the new technology?

A) Both passages express enthusiasm about the environmental benefits.

B) The second passage shows skepticism about the potential risks of the technology.

C) Both passages focus on the negative aspects of the technology.

D) The first passage expresses doubt about the benefits of the technology.

**4.**

*Passage Excerpts*: Excerpt 1: "The author describes the historical figure as a visionary who led his country to greatness." Excerpt 2: "The critic, however, argues that this leader's decisions often led to more harm than good."

**Question**:

Based on the two perspectives, what inference can be made about the historical figure's legacy?

A) Both the author and the critic believe the leader was a visionary.

B) The author believes the leader was ultimately successful, while the critic points to negative consequences.

C) Both perspectives focus on the leader's military achievements.

D) The critic argues that the leader had no impact on his country's history.

**5.**

*Passage Excerpts*: Excerpt 1: "Many hailed the book as a masterpiece, with its intricate narrative and complex characters." Excerpt 2: "Others found the book's slow pacing and convoluted plot difficult to engage with."

**Question**:

What can be inferred about the reception of the book?

A) Everyone agreed on the book's merits.

B) The book received mixed reviews, with some praising its complexity and others criticizing its pacing.

C) The majority of readers found the book's pacing to be its greatest strength.

D) Both excerpts agree the book is too complex to be a masterpiece.

**6.**

*Passage Excerpts*: Excerpt 1: "The city's new public transportation system was praised for its efficiency and reduced carbon footprint." Excerpt 2: "However, some residents expressed frustration with its limited routes and lack of accessibility for certain neighborhoods."

**Question**:

What can be inferred about the overall success of the public transportation system?

A) Both excerpts agree the system is a failure.

B) The system was environmentally beneficial, but not all residents had access to its advantages.

C) The public transportation system was universally praised.

D) Neither passage provides a positive view of the system.

**7.**

*Passage Excerpts*: Excerpt 1: "The reform policy led to significant improvements in healthcare access for rural populations." Excerpt 2: "Critics noted that the policy failed to address the underlying economic disparities that limited healthcare outcomes."

**Question:**

What can be inferred about the impact of the reform policy?

A) The policy was successful in improving economic conditions.

B) The policy increased healthcare access but did not solve broader economic issues.

C) The critics believe the policy was successful.

D) Both passages agree the policy was ineffective.

**8.**

*Passage Excerpts:* Excerpt 1: "The artist's early work was seen as groundbreaking, challenging traditional forms of expression." Excerpt 2: "Later critiques focused on the artist's shift to more commercial, less innovative projects."

**Question:**

What inference can be made about the trajectory of the artist's career?

A) The artist maintained a consistently innovative approach throughout their career.

B) The artist's early work was more innovative than their later projects.

C) Both excerpts agree the artist's later work was groundbreaking.

D) The artist's career was largely focused on commercial success from the beginning.

**9.**

*Passage Excerpts:* Excerpt 1: "The environmental initiative was celebrated for its potential to restore endangered habitats." Excerpt 2: "Opponents argued that the initiative's high costs outweighed any environmental benefits."

**Question:**

What can be inferred from the two perspectives on the environmental initiative?

A) Both perspectives agree the initiative was cost-effective.

B) The initiative was praised for its environmental impact but criticized for its financial burden.

C) The initiative had no impact on endangered habitats.

D) Opponents believed the initiative was entirely successful.

**10.**

*Passage Excerpts:* Excerpt 1: "The new educational reforms aim to reduce disparities in access to quality education." Excerpt 2: "Some critics argue that the reforms do not address the root causes of inequality, such as socioeconomic factors."

**Question:**

What can be inferred about the effectiveness of the educational reforms?

A) Both passages agree the reforms will eliminate educational inequality.

B) The reforms are aimed at improving access but may not fully address deeper causes of inequality.

C) Critics believe the reforms will succeed in reducing socioeconomic disparities.

D) Both excerpts argue the reforms are unnecessary.

**11.**

*Passage Excerpts:* Excerpt 1: "The economic policy led to a noticeable increase in employment rates." Excerpt 2: "However, wages remained stagnant, leaving many workers struggling to cover basic expenses."

**Question:**

What can be inferred about the economic policy's impact on workers?

A) The policy improved employment opportunities but did not result in higher wages.

B) Workers experienced higher wages but fewer job opportunities.

C) The policy had no effect on employment rates.

D) The policy completely failed to benefit workers.

**12.**

*Passage Excerpts*: Excerpt 1: "The new safety regulations were designed to improve worker conditions in factories."

Excerpt 2: "Despite the new regulations, accidents and unsafe working conditions remained prevalent."

**Question**:

What can be inferred about the effectiveness of the new safety regulations?

A) The regulations were completely successful in improving safety.

B) The regulations did not fully address the issues of worker safety.

C) Both excerpts agree the regulations made conditions worse.

D) The new safety regulations were unnecessary.

**13.**

*Passage Excerpts*: Excerpt 1: "The novel's portrayal of societal norms in the 19th century is widely regarded as accurate and insightful."

Excerpt 2: "Some literary critics argue that the novel exaggerates certain aspects of 19th-century life to make a point."

**Question**:

What inference can be drawn about the novel's portrayal of 19th-century societal norms?

A) The novel presents an exaggerated view of the time period.

B) The novel is universally praised for its accuracy.

C) Some critics believe the novel's portrayal is both accurate and exaggerated for effect.

D) Both excerpts agree that the novel is not an accurate reflection of the 19th century.

**14.**

*Passage Excerpts*: Excerpt 1: "The space exploration program achieved significant scientific breakthroughs."

Excerpt 2: "Yet, the program faced criticism for its high costs and lack of immediate practical benefits."

**Question**:

What can be inferred about the public perception of the space exploration program?

A) The program was unanimously praised for its practical benefits.

B) The program was celebrated for its scientific achievements but criticized for its costs.

C) Both passages agree the program was a financial success.

D) The program failed to achieve any scientific breakthroughs.

**15.**

*Passage Excerpts*: Excerpt 1: "The company's new product launch generated excitement among early adopters."

Excerpt 2: "However, some consumers expressed disappointment in the product's functionality."

**Question**:

What can be inferred about the reception of the company's new product?

A) Both excerpts agree the product was a complete failure.

B) Early adopters were enthusiastic, but others found the product's functionality lacking.

C) Consumers unanimously praised the product's functionality.

D) The product was widely considered a success without any criticism.

**16.**

*Passage Excerpts*: Excerpt 1: "The city's new housing initiative aimed to provide affordable homes for low-income families."

Excerpt 2: "Despite this goal, the initiative has been slow to deliver on its promises, with many families still waiting for housing."

**Question:**

What can be inferred about the success of the housing initiative?

A) The initiative was a complete success in delivering affordable homes.

B) The initiative struggled to meet its goals despite its good intentions.

C) Both passages agree the initiative was unnecessary.

D) The initiative exceeded expectations in providing housing.

**17.**

*Passage Excerpts*: Excerpt 1: "The author describes the environmental movement as an essential force for change."

Excerpt 2: "Critics argue that the movement's tactics are too extreme to be effective."

**Question:**

What can be inferred about the differing perspectives on the environmental movement?

A) Both perspectives agree the movement is too extreme.

B) The first passage is supportive of the movement, while the second passage is critical of its tactics.

C) The second passage suggests the movement is necessary but flawed.

D) Both passages are critical of the environmental movement.

**18.**

*Passage Excerpts*: Excerpt 1: "The technology's potential to revolutionize the healthcare industry cannot be overstated."

Excerpt 2: "Some experts caution that the technology's practical applications may be more limited than anticipated."

**Question:**

What can be inferred about the potential of the new healthcare technology?

A) The technology is widely accepted as a guaranteed success.

B) There is excitement about its potential, but some experts are cautious about its limitations.

C) Both passages agree the technology has limited applications.

D) The technology has already revolutionized healthcare.

**19.**

*Passage Excerpts*: Excerpt 1: "The author paints a picture of the industrial era as a time of innovation and prosperity."

Excerpt 2: "The critic highlights the harsh working conditions and inequality that accompanied the industrial boom."

**Question:**

What can be inferred about the industrial era from these two perspectives?

A) The industrial era was marked by both innovation and social challenges.

B) Both excerpts agree the industrial era was a time of unmitigated success.

C) The critic believes the industrial era had no significant achievements.

D) Both perspectives focus solely on the negative aspects of the industrial era.

**20.**

*Passage Excerpts*: Excerpt 1: "The educational reforms of the 21st century aimed to create a more inclusive and effective system for students of all backgrounds."

Excerpt 2: "While the reforms have made strides in some areas, they have fallen short in addressing key issues such as funding disparities."

**Question:**

What can be inferred about the impact of the 21st-century educational reforms?

A) The reforms were universally successful in creating an inclusive system.

B) The reforms achieved progress but failed to fully resolve some significant challenges.

C) Both passages agree the reforms were a complete failure.

D) The reforms led to an increase in funding disparities.

## Conclusion Practice: Managing Inference Questions in the SAT

As you prepare for the SAT, mastering inference-based questions is essential for boosting your score on the Reading and Writing sections. Inference questions require you to read between the lines, synthesize information, and draw conclusions based on the passage's context, author's tone, and implicit meanings. Here are some key tips to help you tackle these questions effectively:

1. **Read the Passage Carefully**: Always pay attention to details, but remember that inference questions go beyond what is explicitly stated. Understand the overall tone and message of the passage to draw accurate conclusions.

2. **Focus on the Question**: Understand what the question is asking before diving into the answer choices. Inference questions often ask for something implied or suggested rather than directly stated.

3. **Eliminate Wrong Choices**: Use the process of elimination to narrow down your answer options. Avoid choices that contradict the passage or introduce information that is not supported by the text.

4. **Look for Evidence**: Inference questions require you to base your answers on evidence from the text. Even if an answer seems plausible, it must have support from the passage.

5. **Practice Active Reading**: Stay engaged with the passage by asking yourself questions as you read, such as "What is the author implying?" or "How do the details in this sentence connect to the overall message?"

6. **Review Practice Questions**: Make sure to review each practice question carefully after attempting it, noting why the correct answer is supported by the passage. This will help you identify patterns in how inference questions are constructed.

By sharpening your inference skills, you'll be better equipped to approach these questions with confidence on test day.

## 5.3 Tone and Perspective Interpretation

### Introduction

Tone and perspective are crucial elements in understanding SAT Reading and Writing passages. Mastering these concepts allows students to grasp not only the surface meaning of the text but also the deeper implications of the author's language and viewpoint. Identifying tone helps students decode the emotional undercurrent of the passage, while understanding the author's perspective provides insight into their bias, beliefs, or purpose.

Recognizing the tone used in a passage means determining whether the author is conveying a message that is critical, neutral, enthusiastic, or perhaps sarcastic. This understanding plays a vital role in fully interpreting what the author is trying to communicate, making it essential to learn how to accurately recognize tone. It's equally important to identify shifts in tone, which may occur as the author introduces new ideas or perspectives.

Furthermore, understanding the author's point of view allows students to uncover underlying biases, values, or intentions. By examining the perspective from which the passage is written, students can better assess how the author presents arguments, evidence, and conclusions.

Types of tone and perspective questions typically encountered on the SAT include:

- **Direct tone identification**: Where students must choose the correct description of the author's tone based on the passage.

- **Tone shift recognition**: Where students must track changes in tone throughout the passage.

- **Perspective and bias analysis**: Where students are asked to discern the author's stance on the subject, along with any implicit bias.

- **Comparison of perspectives**: In passages where two authors express differing viewpoints, students are asked to analyze these varying perspectives.

Through consistent practice, students can hone their ability to identify these elements, leading to a more comprehensive understanding of SAT reading passages.

# Practice Exercises: 75 Questions Divided into Groups of 15-20 Questions

## Section 1: Identifying Author's Tone

### Exercise 1

**Question:**

What tone does the author convey in the following passage?

*"The new policy will undoubtedly result in a significant shift in the company's direction, yet no consultation with employees was considered necessary."*

- A) Optimistic
- B) Sarcastic
- C) Neutral
- D) Enthusiastic

### Exercise 2

**Question:**

The tone of the passage can best be described as:

*"Despite the numerous attempts to reform the education system, it remains as flawed and ineffective as ever."*

- A) Critical
- B) Supportive
- C) Humorous
- D) Cautious

### Exercise 3

**Question:**

In the passage, the author's tone toward the upcoming elections is best described as:

*"Many promises were made during the campaign, but history shows that such promises rarely come to fruition."*

- A) Hopeful
- B) Pessimistic
- C) Indifferent
- D) Motivated

**Exercise 4**

**Question:**

Which tone does the author exhibit in the following excerpt?

*"The results of the study are groundbreaking, offering a completely new perspective on climate change."*

- A) Apathetic
- B) Excited
- C) Cautious
- D) Dismissive

**Exercise 5**

**Question:**

What tone does the author convey in this excerpt?

*"The student, despite numerous warnings, continued to disregard the rules of the institution."*

- A) Disappointed
- B) Encouraging
- C) Neutral
- D) Excited

**Exercise 6**

**Question:**

The author's tone in the passage can be best described as:

*"Advancements in technology are exciting, but the risks they pose to privacy cannot be overlooked."*

- A) Cautious
- B) Optimistic
- C) Sarcastic
- D) Authoritative

**Exercise 7**

**Question:**

In the following passage, the author's tone toward the government's actions is best characterized as:

*"The government has once again promised reform, but its track record suggests otherwise."*

- A) Sincere
- B) Skeptical
- C) Positive
- D) Impartial

## Exercise 8

**Question:**

Which of the following best describes the tone in this passage?

*"After all the chaos and confusion, it was finally clear that the meeting had been entirely pointless."*

- A) Joyful
- B) Resigned
- C) Ironic
- D) Serious

## Exercise 9

**Question:**

The tone of the author in the following sentence can be described as:

*"The company's new product launch was met with great fanfare, despite its evident lack of innovation."*

- A) Mocking
- B) Enthusiastic
- C) Resentful
- D) Sympathetic

## Exercise 10

**Question:**

How would you describe the author's tone in the passage below?

*"The artwork was heralded as revolutionary, yet it bore striking resemblance to pieces from the previous decade."*

- A) Critical
- B) Admiring
- C) Sarcastic
- D) Supportive

## Exercise 11

**Question:**

Which tone does the author most likely intend in the following excerpt?

*"Despite the team's best efforts, the project failed to meet even the most basic of expectations."*

- A) Encouraging
- B) Critical
- C) Humorous
- D) Confident

## Exercise 12

**Question:**

The tone of the author in this passage can be best described as:

*"The future is bright for those willing to adapt, but the unwilling will be left behind."*

- A) Threatening
- B) Optimistic
- C) Neutral
- D) Resigned

## Exercise 13

**Question:**

In this passage, the tone is best described as:

*"With each passing year, the same promises are made, and yet the same mistakes are repeated."*

- A) Sympathetic
- B) Sarcastic
- C) Pessimistic
- D) Hopeful

**Exercise 14**

**Question:**

What tone does the author convey in the following passage?

*"The study was thorough and detailed, leaving no room for doubt."*

- A) Skeptical
- B) Confident
- C) Tentative
- D) Encouraging

**Exercise 15**

**Question:**

Which of the following best describes the tone of the passage?

*"Though the decision was made swiftly, it did not account for all the factors that could impact its success."*

- A) Analytical
- B) Resigned
- C) Critical
- D) Approving

**Exercise 16**

**Question:**

The tone of the author in the following excerpt can be best described as:

*"The festival was celebrated with much enthusiasm, despite the looming threat of rain."*

- A) Optimistic
- B) Doubtful
- C) Dismissive
- D) Excited

**Exercise 17**

**Question:**

Which tone does the author convey in this passage?

*"The company's latest product was marketed as revolutionary, though its similarities to previous models were undeniable."*

- A) Supportive
- B) Skeptical
- C) Indifferent
- D) Enthusiastic

**Exercise 18**

**Question:**

In this excerpt, the author's tone can be best described as:

*"The instructions were vague and unclear, leaving many users frustrated with the process."*

- A) Critical
- B) Humorous
- C) Supportive
- D) Neutral

**Exercise 19**

**Question:**

The tone of the passage can be best described as:

*"The solution seemed obvious to everyone except those in charge, who remained oblivious to the issues."*

- A) Sarcastic
- B) Hopeful
- C) Neutral
- D) Analytical

**Exercise 20**

**Question:**

Which tone does the author express in the following passage?

*"After months of planning, the event turned out to be a complete disaster."*

- A) Humorous
- B) Ironic
- C) Sympathetic
- D) Serious

# Section 2: Recognizing Shifts in Tone

**Exercise 1**

**Question:**

How does the tone of the passage shift from the introduction to the conclusion?

*"At first, the author describes the new policy with enthusiasm, but by the end, the focus turns to its potential downsides."*

- A) From critical to supportive
- B) From enthusiastic to cautious
- C) From neutral to skeptical
- D) From optimistic to indifferent

**Exercise 2**

**Question:**

What shift in tone is evident in the following passage?

*"The author begins by expressing frustration with the government's lack of action, but later adopts a more hopeful tone as potential solutions are discussed."*

- A) From hopeful to disappointed
- B) From frustrated to optimistic
- C) From neutral to critical

- D) From indifferent to supportive

## Exercise 3

**Question:**

Which of the following best describes the shift in tone in this passage?

*"The author initially praises the progress made in scientific research, but later questions whether such advancements come at too great a cost."*

- A) From supportive to critical
- B) From excited to dismissive
- C) From neutral to encouraging
- D) From doubtful to confident

## Exercise 4

**Question:**

How does the tone change throughout the passage?

*"The author starts with a tone of resignation about the failed project but ends on a note of determination to try again."*

- A) From dismissive to serious
- B) From resigned to motivated
- C) From hopeful to indifferent
- D) From critical to supportive

## Exercise 5

**Question:**

Identify the shift in tone in this passage.

*"Initially, the author presents the historical figure with great admiration, but later shifts to a more balanced and critical view."*

- A) From enthusiastic to indifferent
- B) From neutral to critical
- C) From admiring to critical
- D) From dismissive to sympathetic

## Exercise 6

**Question:**

How does the tone of the author shift over the course of this passage?

*"At the beginning, the author is confident about the new findings, but by the end, doubts are introduced about their validity."*

- A) From confident to skeptical
- B) From indifferent to critical
- C) From enthusiastic to neutral
- D) From cautious to confident

## Exercise 7

**Question:**

What tone shift occurs in the passage?

*"The author initially approaches the topic with curiosity, but by the end, there is a tone of disappointment in the results."*

- A) From curious to disappointed
- B) From supportive to indifferent
- C) From neutral to enthusiastic

- D) From skeptical to approving

## Exercise 8

**Question:**

Which best describes the tone shift in the following passage?

*"The article starts with an optimistic view of technological progress, but becomes more cautious when discussing its potential ethical implications."*

- A) From hopeful to indifferent
- B) From critical to supportive
- C) From optimistic to cautious
- D) From neutral to excited

## Exercise 9

**Question:**

In this passage, how does the tone shift?

*"The tone begins with criticism of past policies but shifts to a more forward-thinking, solution-focused approach."*

- A) From critical to solution-oriented
- B) From indifferent to enthusiastic
- C) From hopeful to skeptical
- D) From supportive to dismissive

## Exercise 10

**Question:**

What shift in tone can be detected in the passage?

*"Initially, the author dismisses the idea as impractical, but later acknowledges its potential benefits."*

- A) From supportive to critical
- B) From indifferent to admiring
- C) From dismissive to supportive
- D) From enthusiastic to skeptical

## Exercise 11

**Question:**

How does the tone change throughout the passage?

*"The author starts with a tone of excitement about the discovery but shifts to caution as the possible risks are discussed."*

- A) From enthusiastic to cautious
- B) From neutral to critical
- C) From optimistic to dismissive
- D) From indifferent to excited

## Exercise 12

**Question:**

Which of the following best describes the tone shift?

*"The author initially approaches the issue with skepticism, but by the end, expresses confidence in the proposed solution."*

- A) From critical to neutral
- B) From skeptical to confident
- C) From indifferent to hopeful

- D) From optimistic to dismissive

## Exercise 13

**Question:**

How does the author's tone change in the passage?

*"The passage starts by questioning the effectiveness of the program, but concludes with a positive view of its long-term potential."*

- A) From critical to supportive
- B) From indifferent to admiring
- C) From supportive to skeptical
- D) From neutral to critical

## Exercise 14

**Question:**

What is the tone shift in the passage?

*"Initially, the author takes a neutral stance on the policy, but later becomes more critical of its impact on the community."*

- A) From neutral to critical
- B) From critical to supportive
- C) From enthusiastic to dismissive
- D) From supportive to neutral

## Exercise 15

**Question:**

Which tone shift is present in the passage?

*"The author begins with skepticism about the new research but grows more supportive as more evidence is presented."*

- A) From critical to supportive
- B) From indifferent to enthusiastic
- C) From hopeful to doubtful
- D) From dismissive to cautious

# Section 3: Author's Perspective and Bias

## Exercise 1

**Question:**

What can be inferred about the author's perspective on the environmental issue discussed in the passage?

*"The author highlights the urgency of climate action and criticizes the slow response of policymakers."*

- A) The author is neutral about climate action.
- B) The author believes immediate climate action is necessary.
- C) The author opposes environmental regulations.
- D) The author supports a gradual approach to addressing climate change.

## Exercise 2

**Question:**

What bias is evident in the author's argument about technological advancements?

*"The author consistently favors innovation at any cost, ignoring potential ethical concerns."*

- A) The author is biased against technological advancements.

- B) The author shows a bias in favor of innovation over ethics.
- C) The author presents a balanced view on the topic.
- D) The author is skeptical of technological advancements.

## Exercise 3

**Question:**

How does the author's personal background influence their perspective on the economic policy discussed?

*"The author, a long-time advocate of free market policies, promotes deregulation as the best solution to economic challenges."*

- A) The author is unbiased in their view of the economic policy.
- B) The author's perspective is influenced by a pro-regulation stance.
- C) The author's long-time support for free market policies affects their viewpoint.
- D) The author is neutral on the topic of regulation.

## Exercise 4

**Question:**

What can be inferred about the author's attitude toward education reform based on their critique of current policies?

*"The author advocates for a return to traditional education methods and criticizes recent reforms as ineffective."*

- A) The author is supportive of progressive education reforms.
- B) The author is neutral on the topic of education reform.
- C) The author opposes traditional education methods.
- D) The author believes recent reforms are not beneficial and prefers traditional methods.

## Exercise 5

**Question:**

What bias does the author reveal in their portrayal of historical events?

*"The author consistently portrays one side of the conflict as justified while dismissing the actions of the opposing side."*

- A) The author remains objective throughout the discussion of the events.
- B) The author shows a clear bias in favor of one side of the conflict.
- C) The author is critical of both sides equally.
- D) The author favors the opposing side in the conflict.

## Exercise 6

**Question:**

How does the author's profession affect their view on the healthcare system reforms discussed in the passage?

*"As a practicing physician, the author argues for reforms that benefit healthcare providers over patients."*

- A) The author advocates primarily for patient-centered reforms.
- B) The author supports reforms that benefit both patients and providers.
- C) The author's viewpoint is influenced by their profession, leading to a focus on provider benefits.
- D) The author is neutral on the healthcare reforms.

## Exercise 7

**Question:**

What can be inferred about the author's perspective on renewable energy?

*"The author expresses strong support for renewable energy, highlighting its environmental benefits while downplaying economic concerns."*

- A) The author believes renewable energy is economically unviable.
- B) The author supports renewable energy, focusing on its environmental benefits.
- C) The author is opposed to renewable energy.
- D) The author presents a balanced view of renewable energy's pros and cons.

## Exercise 8

**Question:**

What is the author's bias when discussing government intervention in the economy?

*"The author argues that government intervention often leads to inefficiency, while markets are self-correcting."*

- A) The author supports significant government intervention.
- B) The author is neutral on the topic of government intervention.
- C) The author shows bias against government intervention, favoring free markets.
- D) The author believes government intervention is necessary for economic stability.

## Exercise 9

**Question:**

How does the author's cultural background shape their view of the social issue discussed in the passage?

*"The author, from a collectivist culture, emphasizes the importance of community over individualism."*

- A) The author favors individualism in their discussion.
- B) The author's perspective is shaped by a collectivist cultural background.
- C) The author holds a neutral stance on the issue.
- D) The author promotes individualism over community values.

## Exercise 10

**Question:**

What can be inferred about the author's perspective on globalization based on their portrayal of its effects?

*"The author highlights the negative impact of globalization on small local businesses."*

- A) The author is supportive of globalization.
- B) The author is neutral about globalization.
- C) The author is critical of the effects of globalization on small businesses.
- D) The author believes globalization has no effect on local businesses.

## Exercise 11

**Question:**

What bias does the author display when discussing the legal system?

*"The author, a lawyer, repeatedly emphasizes the benefits of legal reform but ignores the challenges faced by the system."*

- A) The author is biased in favor of maintaining the current legal system.
- B) The author shows bias toward reform, ignoring potential challenges.
- C) The author presents an objective view of the legal system.
- D) The author is critical of legal reform.

## Exercise 12

**Question:**

What can be inferred about the author's political stance based on their discussion of tax policy?

*"The author advocates for lowering taxes on corporations as a way to stimulate economic growth."*

- A) The author is biased against lowering taxes on corporations.

- B) The author supports tax increases to fund public services.
- C) The author favors lower taxes on corporations to boost economic growth.
- D) The author is neutral on tax policy.

## Exercise 13

**Question:**

What bias is evident in the author's critique of media coverage?

*"The author accuses mainstream media of being overly sensationalistic and biased toward certain political groups."*

- A) The author is supportive of mainstream media coverage.
- B) The author shows bias against mainstream media, accusing it of political bias.
- C) The author holds a neutral stance on media coverage.
- D) The author is critical of political groups, not media coverage.

## Exercise 14

**Question:**

How does the author's background influence their view on international trade?

*"The author, an economist with experience in global markets, argues for free trade policies that benefit large corporations."*

- A) The author's background leads them to support protectionist trade policies.
- B) The author's perspective is influenced by their experience, resulting in support for free trade.
- C) The author is neutral on the topic of trade policies.
- D) The author is critical of free trade.

## Exercise 15

**Question:**

What can be inferred about the author's bias in their discussion of environmental regulations?

*"The author downplays the importance of environmental regulations, emphasizing the need for economic growth instead."*

- A) The author shows a bias in favor of environmental regulations.
- B) The author is critical of economic growth in favor of environmental protection.
- C) The author is biased against environmental regulations, favoring economic growth.
- D) The author presents a balanced view on the issue.

# Section 4: Comparing Perspectives in Two Texts

## Exercise 1

**Question:**

How do the two authors' perspectives on climate change differ?

*"Author A believes that immediate government intervention is crucial, while Author B argues that technological advancements will naturally reduce emissions over time."*

- A) Both authors agree that government intervention is unnecessary.
- B) Author A supports technological solutions, while Author B supports government intervention.
- C) Author A advocates for government action, while Author B trusts technological progress.
- D) Both authors argue for immediate and extensive environmental regulations.

## Exercise 2

**Question:**

In the two texts provided, how do the authors differ in their perspectives on immigration reform?

*"Author A focuses on the economic benefits of immigration, while Author B emphasizes the need for stronger border security and law enforcement."*

- A) Both authors agree on the need for stricter immigration laws.
- B) Author A is more concerned with economic growth, while Author B stresses national security.
- C) Author A calls for increased border security, while Author B supports reducing immigration.
- D) Both authors oppose any changes to immigration policies.

## Exercise 3

**Question:**

How do the two authors approach the issue of climate adaptation differently?

*"Author A calls for immediate local efforts to adapt, while Author B believes national-level policies are more effective."*

- A) Both authors argue for local efforts to tackle climate adaptation.
- B) Author A believes local efforts are sufficient, while Author B advocates for national policies.
- C) Author A emphasizes the role of government, while Author B focuses on community-driven solutions.
- D) Both authors reject national involvement in climate adaptation.

## Exercise 4

**Question:**

How do the perspectives on economic inequality differ between the two authors?

*"Author A suggests that income inequality can be reduced through taxation, while Author B believes that education and skill development are the most effective methods."*

- A) Both authors argue that taxation is the key to reducing inequality.
- B) Author A emphasizes taxation, while Author B focuses on education and skills development.
- C) Author A and Author B both oppose taxation as a solution.
- D) Author A advocates for education reform, while Author B supports tax reductions.

## Exercise 5

**Question:**

What is the primary difference between the two authors' views on renewable energy development?

*"Author A supports government subsidies for renewable energy, while Author B believes that market competition will drive renewable energy advancements."*

- A) Author A supports market-driven solutions, while Author B believes in government subsidies.
- B) Author A advocates for government involvement, while Author B relies on market competition.
- C) Both authors believe in government intervention to advance renewable energy.
- D) Author A opposes any intervention in the energy market, while Author B supports regulation.

## Exercise 6

**Question:**

How do the two authors differ in their assessment of the impact of technology on education?

*"Author A sees technology as a necessary tool for modern education, while Author B warns about the over-reliance on digital platforms."*

- A) Both authors believe that technology is beneficial for education.
- B) Author A advocates for limited use of technology, while Author B promotes its expansion.
- C) Author A sees technology as essential, while Author B is cautious about its impact.
- D) Both authors oppose the use of technology in classrooms.

**Exercise 7**

**Question:**

How do the perspectives of the two authors differ regarding free speech on college campuses?

*"Author A argues that free speech should have no limits, while Author B contends that some restrictions are necessary to maintain inclusivity and respect."*

- A) Both authors believe there should be no restrictions on free speech.
- B) Author A supports restrictions, while Author B opposes them.
- C) Author A favors unrestricted free speech, while Author B supports some limits.
- D) Both authors agree that free speech should be limited for inclusivity.

**Exercise 8**

**Question:**

What is the key difference in how the two authors view the role of government in healthcare?

*"Author A advocates for universal healthcare funded by the government, while Author B supports privatized healthcare options with minimal government intervention."*

- A) Both authors support universal healthcare.
- B) Author A favors privatized healthcare, while Author B supports government-funded options.
- C) Author A promotes government-funded healthcare, while Author B advocates for privatized systems.
- D) Both authors reject government involvement in healthcare.

**Exercise 9**

**Question:**

How do the two texts differ in their portrayal of scientific innovation?

*"Author A highlights the risks associated with unchecked innovation, while Author B celebrates the potential benefits without focusing on the risks."*

- A) Both authors focus on the potential risks of innovation.
- B) Author A focuses on risks, while Author B emphasizes the benefits of innovation.
- C) Both authors ignore the risks of scientific advancements.
- D) Author A celebrates the benefits of innovation, while Author B is critical of its impacts.

**Exercise 10**

**Question:**

In the two texts, how do the authors differ in their perspectives on economic globalization?

*"Author A argues that globalization benefits all nations equally, while Author B contends that it disproportionately favors wealthier countries."*

- A) Both authors believe globalization benefits all nations.
- B) Author A sees globalization as beneficial to all, while Author B views it as favoring wealthier nations.
- C) Both authors argue against globalization.
- D) Author A opposes globalization, while Author B supports it.

**Exercise 11**

**Question:**

How do the two authors approach the subject of artificial intelligence differently?

*"Author A views AI as a tool for societal advancement, while Author B is concerned about its ethical implications and the potential job losses."*

- A) Both authors believe AI will have negative impacts on society.
- B) Author A supports AI's advancement, while Author B focuses on its ethical concerns.
- C) Both authors argue that AI will lead to widespread job loss.
- D) Author A believes AI should be restricted, while Author B promotes its expansion.

## Exercise 12

**Question:**

What difference in perspective is evident in the two authors' views on social media's role in politics?

*"Author A argues that social media enhances political participation, while Author B believes it leads to misinformation and political polarization."*

- A) Both authors support social media's role in politics.
- B) Author A believes social media increases political involvement, while Author B warns about misinformation.
- C) Author A opposes social media's influence, while Author B supports it.
- D) Both authors are concerned about the negative impacts of social media.

## Exercise 13

**Question:**

How do the authors differ in their portrayal of historical events?

*"Author A presents a glorified version of the past, while Author B offers a critical perspective of the same events."*

- A) Both authors present a critical view of the historical events.
- B) Author A focuses on glorifying the events, while Author B takes a critical approach.
- C) Both authors glorify the events in question.
- D) Author A and Author B both take a critical approach to the past.

## Exercise 14

**Question:**

What is the key difference between the two authors' views on technological innovation in the medical field?

*"Author A argues that medical innovations should prioritize accessibility for all, while Author B believes the market should determine access to new technologies."*

- A) Author A supports market-driven access, while Author B argues for accessibility for all.
- B) Author A advocates for universal accessibility, while Author B believes the market should regulate access.
- C) Both authors support unrestricted access to medical innovations.
- D) Both authors agree that access to technology should be determined by market forces.

## Exercise 15

**Question:**

How do the two authors differ in their views on education reform?

*"Author A believes in maintaining traditional educational methods, while Author B advocates for progressive changes to the current system."*

- A) Both authors support traditional educational methods.
- B) Author A supports progressive education reform, while Author B supports traditional methods.

- C) Author A is in favor of maintaining traditional methods, while Author B advocates for change.
- D) Both authors oppose any form of educational reform.

# Section 5: Analyzing Author's Intent and Purpose

**Exercise 1**

**Question:**

What is the author's purpose in using a critical tone towards the government policy?

*"The author uses strong language to express disapproval of recent environmental regulations."*

- A) To praise the effectiveness of the policy
- B) To highlight the policy's flaws and suggest alternatives
- C) To emphasize the positive aspects of the policy
- D) To show the policy's neutral impact on the environment

**Exercise 2**

**Question:**

Why does the author focus on the personal experiences of individuals affected by the new healthcare law?

*"The author recounts personal stories to illustrate the broader societal impact of healthcare reform."*

- A) To provide statistical evidence
- B) To evoke an emotional response from the reader
- C) To offer a neutral analysis of the policy
- D) To emphasize the government's perspective

**Exercise 3**

**Question:**

What is the author's intent in highlighting the historical context of the civil rights movement?

*"The author discusses key events from the civil rights era to draw parallels with current social justice movements."*

- A) To argue that history is irrelevant to modern-day issues
- B) To show how much progress has been made
- C) To suggest that current struggles mirror those of the past
- D) To critique the goals of the civil rights movement

**Exercise 4**

**Question:**

Why does the author employ a sarcastic tone when discussing corporate social responsibility?

*"The author uses sarcasm to question the sincerity of companies that claim to prioritize social values."*

- A) To support corporate initiatives
- B) To undermine the credibility of corporate social responsibility efforts
- C) To promote corporate transparency
- D) To advocate for stronger governmental regulations

**Exercise 5**

**Question:**

What is the author's purpose in repeatedly referencing scientific studies in their argument against climate change denial?

*"The author cites multiple studies to reinforce the validity of climate science and discredit denialist viewpoints."*

- A) To question the validity of the studies
- B) To weaken the argument in favor of climate change
- C) To emphasize the scientific consensus on climate change
- D) To present a neutral viewpoint on the subject

**Exercise 6**

**Question:**

What is the author's intent in using a narrative format to explain economic inequality?

*"By telling a personal story, the author humanizes the issue of income inequality and makes it more relatable to the reader."*

- A) To present a statistical analysis of income inequality
- B) To create an emotional connection with the reader
- C) To distance the reader from the economic argument
- D) To offer a purely factual representation of the issue

**Exercise 7**

**Question:**

Why does the author compare two opposing viewpoints on the issue of immigration?

*"The author presents contrasting views to challenge the reader to think critically about immigration reform."*

- A) To advocate for stricter immigration policies
- B) To show that both perspectives are equally valid
- C) To encourage the reader to align with one specific viewpoint
- D) To provide a balanced view and foster critical thinking

**Exercise 8**

**Question:**

What is the author's purpose in using vivid imagery to describe the effects of deforestation?

*"The author paints a graphic picture of deforestation's impact to emphasize the urgency of environmental conservation."*

- A) To create a neutral discussion about environmental policy
- B) To minimize the importance of deforestation
- C) To evoke a strong emotional response from the reader
- D) To present a factual, data-driven argument without bias

**Exercise 9**

**Question:**

Why does the author include a counterargument in their discussion of renewable energy?

*"The author acknowledges opposing views to strengthen their own argument in favor of renewable energy development."*

- A) To show that the counterargument is stronger
- B) To discredit the entire renewable energy industry
- C) To provide a balanced perspective by acknowledging all sides
- D) To highlight the flaws in the counterargument

**Exercise 10**

**Question:**

What is the author's purpose in repeatedly questioning the effectiveness of the new education policy?

*"The author uses rhetorical questions to cast doubt on the policy's ability to improve educational outcomes."*

- A) To show support for the policy

- B) To undermine confidence in the policy's effectiveness
- C) To provide data supporting the policy's success
- D) To present a neutral evaluation of the policy's results

## Conclusion Practice: Tone and Perspective Interpretation

In this section, students are reminded of the importance of carefully approaching tone and perspective questions in the SAT Reading and Writing sections. Tone and perspective can subtly shift the meaning of a passage, and understanding these nuances is key to mastering the exam. Below are tips for handling these types of questions effectively:

1. **Pay Attention to Word Choice**: Tone is often conveyed through the specific words an author chooses. Look for emotionally charged language, adjectives, and verbs that can indicate how the author feels about the topic.

2. **Consider the Structure**: Authors may build their arguments gradually, and the tone can shift as the argument develops. Pay attention to changes in sentence length, punctuation, and style that could indicate a shift in attitude.

3. **Understand the Author's Perspective**: The author's background, experiences, or stated biases can heavily influence their perspective. Always consider the source of the passage and any potential bias they may introduce into the narrative.

4. **Compare Perspectives**: When tasked with comparing two texts, focus on how the tone or perspective differs between the authors. Look for contrasting word choices or differing emotional appeals.

5. **Recognize Bias**: Some passages may carry an implicit or explicit bias. Identifying this bias can help clarify the author's true stance, even if it is subtly embedded in the text.

By practicing these strategies, students can increase their ability to identify and analyze the tone and perspective of passages, improving their overall performance on this section of the SAT.

## 5.4 Context Meaning Questions

## Introduction

Understanding vocabulary in context is a critical skill for excelling in the SAT Reading and Writing sections. Unlike traditional vocabulary tests, where students are asked to recall definitions from memory, the SAT focuses on how well students can interpret the meaning of words as they are used within passages. This means that knowing the dictionary definition of a word is often less important than being able to deduce its meaning based on the context provided.

Words can take on different meanings depending on the surrounding information, sentence structure, and overall theme of the passage. A word like "critical," for example, might mean something entirely different when discussing a medical situation as opposed to a literary critique. Therefore, students must develop the skill of analyzing the clues around a word—other words, phrases, and ideas that give insight into its meaning.

Key strategies for understanding vocabulary in context include:

- **Looking at surrounding sentences:** The information before and after the word in question can provide vital clues to its meaning.

- **Considering the tone and intent of the passage:** A formal or casual tone can change how certain words are interpreted.
- **Focusing on sentence structure and punctuation:** Sometimes, the placement of commas or dashes can indicate an explanation or clarification of a word, making it easier to understand.
- **Using synonyms or paraphrasing:** Mentally substituting a word with another that seems to fit can help clarify its meaning based on how it aligns with the overall sentence.

These strategies will empower students to tackle vocabulary questions with confidence, even when they encounter words they may not have seen before.

## Practice Exercises: 50 Questions Divided into Groups of 10-15 Questions

## Section 1: Understanding Word Meaning Through Context

1. In the sentence *"The politician's speech was filled with **rhetoric**, but it lacked substance,"* what does the word **rhetoric** most likely mean in this context?
   a) Meaningful discourse
   b) Persuasive but empty language
   c) A serious argument
   d) A clear explanation

2. In the passage *"She approached the task with a **meticulous** attention to detail, ensuring that nothing was overlooked,"* what does **meticulous** most likely mean?
   a) Careful and precise
   b) Quick and efficient
   c) Casual and carefree
   d) Lazy and indifferent

3. In the sentence *"His decision to move to a different city was **spontaneous** rather than planned,"* what does **spontaneous** most likely mean in this context?
   a) Carefully considered
   b) Impulsive and unplanned
   c) Long-awaited
   d) Gradually decided

4. In the passage *"The scientist's **speculative** conclusions were met with skepticism from the community,"* what does **speculative** most likely mean?
   a) Based on solid evidence
   b) Hypothetical and uncertain
   c) Widely accepted
   d) Cautious and conservative

5. In the sentence *"The **elusive** butterfly darted through the meadow, always just out of reach,"* what does **elusive** most likely mean in this context?
   a) Easily caught
   b) Difficult to find or capture
   c) Common and abundant
   d) Uninteresting

6. In the passage *"Despite his wealth, his **frugal** lifestyle was surprising to many,"* what does **frugal** most likely mean?

a) Luxurious and extravagant

b) Simple and economical

c) Wasteful and careless

d) Generous and charitable

7. In the sentence *"Her **contemptuous** attitude toward the rules made her unpopular with her peers,"* what does **contemptuous** most likely mean in this context?

a) Supportive and enthusiastic

b) Disrespectful and scornful

c) Unaware and confused

d) Respectful and obedient

8. In the passage *"The invention was hailed as a **revolutionary** development in the field of technology,"* what does **revolutionary** most likely mean?

a) Small and insignificant

b) Innovative and groundbreaking

c) Outdated and obsolete

d) Predictable and ordinary

9. In the sentence *"The author **juxtaposes** two contrasting characters to highlight their differences,"* what does **juxtaposes** most likely mean?

a) Separates them

b) Places them side by side for comparison

c) Merges them together

d) Ignores their differences

10. In the passage *"Her **indifference** to the outcome of the game surprised everyone who knew her competitive nature,"* what does **indifference** most likely mean?

a) A lack of interest or concern

b) A deep passion for the result

c) Extreme excitement

d) Overt enthusiasm

11. In the sentence *"The **ominous** clouds gathered on the horizon, signaling an impending storm,"* what does **ominous** most likely mean in this context?

a) Threatening and foreboding

b) Bright and cheerful

c) Unpredictable but harmless

d) Unimportant and trivial

12. In the passage *"The speaker's tone was **condescending**, making the audience feel belittled,"* what does **condescending** most likely mean?

a) Friendly and approachable

b) Patronizing and superior

c) Encouraging and supportive

d) Nervous and uncertain

13. In the sentence *"His explanation was **convoluted**, leaving the audience more confused than before,"* what does **convoluted** most likely mean in this context?

a) Clear and straightforward

b) Complicated and difficult to follow

c) Brief and to the point

d) Unnecessary and irrelevant

14. In the passage *"The **ephemeral** nature of fame means it can disappear as quickly as it arrives,"* what does **ephemeral** most likely mean?

    a) Lasting forever

    b) Short-lived and fleeting

    c) Gradually building

    d) Important and significant

15. In the sentence *"The lawyer's **incisive** arguments cut through the opposition's points with precision,"* what does **incisive** most likely mean in this context?

    a) Vague and unclear

    b) Sharp and focused

    c) Weak and ineffective

    d) Incomplete and confusing

## Section 2: Identifying the Function of Words in Sentences

These exercises will help students recognize how the function of a word can change depending on its placement and usage within a sentence.

1. In the sentence *"The doctor provided a **comprehensive** overview of the patient's condition,"* how does the word **comprehensive** function?

   a) As a noun describing the overview

   b) As an adjective describing the overview

   c) As a verb indicating an action

   d) As an adverb modifying "overview"

2. In the passage *"The scientist's **critical** analysis led to new discoveries,"* what function does **critical** serve?

   a) It is a noun explaining the analysis

   b) It is an adjective describing the type of analysis

   c) It is a verb expressing an action

   d) It is an adverb modifying "analysis"

3. In the sentence *"The speech was **remarkably** effective in convincing the audience,"* how does the word **remarkably** function?

   a) As a noun describing the speech

   b) As an adjective describing "effective"

   c) As a verb indicating an action

   d) As an adverb modifying "effective"

4. In the sentence *"The **exploratory** nature of the study opened up new questions,"* how does **exploratory** function?

   a) As a noun indicating the study

   b) As an adjective describing the nature of the study

   c) As a verb referring to an action taken

   d) As an adverb explaining "nature"

5. In the passage *"Her comments were **brief** but insightful,"* how does the word **brief** function?

   a) As a verb explaining an action

   b) As a noun describing the comments

c) As an adjective modifying "comments"

d) As an adverb modifying "insightful"

6. In the sentence *"The **preliminary** results suggest further research is needed,"* how does **preliminary** function?

   a) As a verb describing what the results suggest

   b) As an adjective modifying "results"

   c) As a noun indicating the results themselves

   d) As an adverb explaining how the results suggest

7. In the sentence *"The artist's work was **influential** in shaping modern design,"* how does **influential** function?

   a) As an adjective modifying "work"

   b) As a noun referring to the work itself

   c) As a verb indicating the influence of the work

   d) As an adverb explaining "shaping"

8. In the sentence *"The **tentative** agreement between the two companies was well received,"* how does **tentative** function?

   a) As a verb indicating the nature of the agreement

   b) As a noun referring to the agreement

   c) As an adjective modifying "agreement"

   d) As an adverb describing how the agreement was received

9. In the sentence *"The **strategic** placement of the product increased sales,"* how does **strategic** function?

   a) As an adjective modifying "placement"

   b) As a verb explaining how the product was placed

   c) As a noun describing the product itself

   d) As an adverb modifying "placement"

10. In the sentence *"Her **considerate** behavior made her well-liked among her peers,"* how does **considerate** function?

    a) As an adverb describing "behavior"

    b) As an adjective modifying "behavior"

    c) As a noun referring to her actions

    d) As a verb indicating her behavior

## Section 3: Using Surrounding Sentences to Clarify Meaning

**Exercise 1:**

- Passage: "The scientist's argument was unclear, leaving room for various interpretations. This **ambiguous** statement caused confusion among the audience."

- Question: Based on the preceding sentence, what does the word **ambiguous** most likely mean?

  1. Obvious

  2. Clear

  3. Open to multiple interpretations

  4. Specific

**Exercise 2:**

- Passage: "While the instructions seemed straightforward at first, the process quickly became more **convoluted**, requiring careful attention to detail."
- Question: What does the word **convoluted** most likely mean in this context?
    1. Simple
    2. Complicated
    3. Efficient
    4. Quick

**Exercise 3:**

- Passage: "The president's speech was **vague**, offering no clear solutions to the problem. This left many wondering about the future policies."
- Question: What does the word **vague** most likely mean?
    1. Confusing
    2. Clear
    3. Comprehensive
    4. Uncertain

**Exercise 4:**

- Passage: "Despite her best efforts, the proposal was **dismissed** as unrealistic, and the committee quickly moved on to the next topic."
- Question: Based on the sentence, what does the word **dismissed** most likely mean?
    1. Approved
    2. Accepted
    3. Rejected
    4. Understood

**Exercise 5:**

- Passage: "The artist's work was praised for its creativity, but critics noted that his use of color was **inconsistent**, sometimes lacking harmony."
- Question: What does the word **inconsistent** most likely mean?
    1. Harmonious
    2. Variable
    3. Predictable
    4. Clear

**Exercise 6:**

- Passage: "The author's **sarcastic** remarks were intended to make the audience reflect on the absurdity of the situation."
- Question: What does the word **sarcastic** most likely mean based on the passage?
    1. Sincere
    2. Humorous
    3. Ironic
    4. Sympathetic

**Exercise 7:**

- Passage: "She presented a **plausible** explanation for the anomaly, convincing the jury to reconsider their decision."
- Question: What does the word **plausible** most likely mean?
    1. Unlikely
    2. Believable
    3. False
    4. Impractical

**Exercise 8:**

- Passage: "The lawyer's **meticulous** preparation for the case ensured that every detail was accounted for, leaving no room for error."
- Question: What does the word **meticulous** most likely mean?
    1. Careless
    2. Precise
    3. Hasty
    4. Rough

**Exercise 9:**

- Passage: "The politician's **ambivalent** stance on the issue frustrated voters, as they sought a clear answer to the complex question."
- Question: What does the word **ambivalent** most likely mean?
    1. Confident
    2. Indifferent
    3. Uncertain
    4. Resolved

**Exercise 10:**

- Passage: "Her performance was **lackluster**, showing none of the energy and enthusiasm that was expected."
- Question: Based on the surrounding context, what does the word **lackluster** most likely mean?
    1. Dull
    2. Brilliant
    3. Exciting
    4. Inspiring

## Section 4: Interpreting Figurative Language in Context

**Exercise 1:**

- Passage: "As the deadline approached, she felt like she was drowning in a sea of responsibilities."
- Question: What does the phrase **'drowning in a sea of responsibilities'** most likely mean?
    1. She was overwhelmed by her tasks.
    2. She was swimming for fun.
    3. She was relaxed and calm.
    4. She had little to do.

**Exercise 2:**

- Passage: "His idea was a spark in the darkness, giving the team new hope for success."
- Question: What does the phrase **'a spark in the darkness'** most likely symbolize?
    1. A dangerous situation.
    2. A small but significant source of hope.
    3. A fire spreading uncontrollably.
    4. A lack of understanding.

**Exercise 3:**

- Passage: "The project was a ticking time bomb, ready to explode at any moment due to the constant delays."
- Question: What does the metaphor **'ticking time bomb'** imply?
    1. The project was dangerous.
    2. The project was nearly complete.
    3. The project was on the verge of failure.
    4. The project was improving steadily.

**Exercise 4:**

- Passage: "Her confidence crumbled like a house of cards under the pressure of the interview."
- Question: What does the phrase **'crumbled like a house of cards'** suggest about her confidence?
    1. It was strong and steady.
    2. It collapsed easily under stress.
    3. It was slowly building up.
    4. It was unaffected by the situation.

**Exercise 5:**

- Passage: "The company's profits were a rollercoaster ride, fluctuating wildly from one quarter to the next."
- Question: What does the phrase **'a rollercoaster ride'** imply about the company's profits?
    1. The profits were steadily increasing.
    2. The profits remained constant.
    3. The profits were highly unpredictable.
    4. The profits were declining steadily.

**Exercise 6:**

- Passage: "His explanation was clear as mud, leaving everyone in the room more confused than before."
- Question: What does the phrase **'clear as mud'** mean in this context?
    1. The explanation was very clear.
    2. The explanation was confusing and unclear.
    3. The explanation was full of technical details.
    4. The explanation was helpful.

**Exercise 7:**

- Passage: "Her words were a double-edged sword, cutting both ways and leaving both parties feeling wounded."
- Question: What does the phrase **'double-edged sword'** suggest about her words?
    1. They were helpful to everyone.
    2. They had both positive and negative effects.
    3. They only caused harm to one person.
    4. They were harmless and neutral.

**Exercise 8:**

- Passage: "The CEO was walking on thin ice with the shareholders after the recent scandal."
- Question: What does the phrase **'walking on thin ice'** imply about the CEO's situation?
    1. The CEO was in a secure position.
    2. The CEO was in a very risky situation.
    3. The CEO was gaining support.
    4. The CEO was moving quickly.

**Exercise 9:**

- Passage: "His memory of the event was a blur, as if the details had been swept away by a strong wind."
- Question: What does the phrase **'swept away by a strong wind'** most likely mean?
    1. His memory was sharp and clear.
    2. His memory of the event was fading or unclear.
    3. His memory was improving over time.
    4. His memory was focused on a single detail.

**Exercise 10:**

- Passage: "The debate quickly turned into a battlefield, with both sides launching verbal attacks."
- Question: What does the phrase **'turned into a battlefield'** suggest about the debate?
    1. The debate was calm and peaceful.
    2. The debate became intense and hostile.
    3. The debate was resolved quickly.
    4. The debate was a physical confrontation.

## Section 5: Recognizing Multiple Meanings of Words

**Exercise 1:**

- Passage: "Despite the chaos around him, he managed to keep his cool and put up a brave **front**."
- Question: What does the word **'front'** most likely mean in this context?
    1. The part of a building.
    2. A facial expression.
    3. A defensive barrier.
    4. A false outward appearance.

**Exercise 2:**
- Passage: "The soldier took his place at the **front** of the line."
- Question: What does the word **'front'** most likely mean in this context?
  1. A leading position.
  2. A misleading appearance.
  3. A military formation.
  4. A part of a house.

**Exercise 3:**
- Passage: "She decided to **book** the hotel room for their vacation well in advance."
- Question: What does the word **'book'** most likely mean in this context?
  1. A written or printed work.
  2. To make a reservation.
  3. A place to record names.
  4. To penalize someone.

**Exercise 4:**
- Passage: "He had to **bear** the responsibility of leading the project through difficult times."
- Question: What does the word **'bear'** most likely mean in this context?
  1. An animal.
  2. To carry or endure.
  3. To give birth to.
  4. To support a weight.

**Exercise 5:**
- Passage: "She could **strike** a deal with the supplier to lower the prices."
- Question: What does the word **'strike'** most likely mean in this context?
  1. To hit something forcefully.
  2. To reach an agreement.
  3. To refuse to work.
  4. To remove something.

# Conclusion Practice

- When approaching context-based vocabulary questions on the SAT, students should focus on the overall meaning of the passage and how individual words fit into that context. Words often take on nuanced or specific meanings depending on their surroundings, so it's essential to use clues from the text to deduce the meaning accurately.

- One effective strategy is to read the sentence with the unfamiliar word and then look at the sentences before and after to gather additional information. This broader view often provides hints about how the word functions within the passage.

- If you encounter a word with multiple meanings, focus on which definition best aligns with the tone, subject matter, and details of the passage. Don't get caught up in trying to recall a dictionary definition—your task is to interpret meaning based on the passage.

- Practice is key: the more familiar you become with using context to infer meanings, the faster and more confidently you'll be able to approach these questions on test day. If you don't know the word, use process of elimination to narrow down the choices based on what makes the most logical sense within the passage.

# CHAPTER 6: PRACTICE WRITING EXERCISES

## 6.1 Sentence Correction and Grammar
## Practice Exercises: 225 Questions Divided into Groups of 15-25 Questions
## Section 1: Sentence Structure and Syntax

focuses on sentence fragments, run-ons, and complex sentence structures.

## Practice Questions

1. **Identify the sentence fragment:**
   - o A. The dog barked loudly.
   - o B. Running through the park and never stopping.
   - o C. They arrived early to the concert.
   - o D. She loves baking and reading in her spare time.

2. **Which sentence is a run-on?**
   - o A. She went to the store, and she bought some groceries.
   - o B. The rain stopped, the sun came out, we went outside.
   - o C. He studied for hours; he still failed the test.
   - o D. The cake was delicious, and everyone loved it.

3. **Choose the sentence that avoids a run-on:**
   - o A. She opened the door she let the dog in.
   - o B. The traffic was heavy, we were late for the meeting.
   - o C. The cat purred contentedly while lying in the sun.
   - o D. He missed the train, he took a taxi instead.

4. **Which of the following is a complete sentence?**
   - o A. Working on the project until midnight.
   - o B. The children were playing in the backyard.
   - o C. Without knowing the full story.
   - o D. Even though she was tired.

5. **Identify the sentence that correctly combines the clauses:**
   - o A. He wanted to go to the beach, but the weather was terrible.
   - o B. Although it was raining, but we still went for a walk.
   - o C. I wanted to stay home, however, I had to go to work.
   - o D. Because the traffic was bad we decided to take a different route.

6. **Which sentence corrects the fragment?**
   - o A. Since it was raining.
   - o B. The baby slept peacefully in the crib.
   - o C. After the movie.
   - o D. Running through the park with her dog.

7. **Choose the grammatically correct sentence:**
    - o  A. The books on the shelf is old and dusty.
    - o  B. The books on the shelf are old and dusty.
    - o  C. The books on the shelf has old and dusty pages.
    - o  D. The books on the shelf was old and dusty.

8. **Select the correct complex sentence structure:**
    - o  A. He studied hard, he passed the test.
    - o  B. If you study hard, you will pass the test.
    - o  C. He studied hard but he passed the test.
    - o  D. Study hard passing the test will be easier.

9. **Correct the run-on sentence:**
    - o  A. She read the book, she wrote the report.
    - o  B. She read the book, and she wrote the report.
    - o  C. She read the book, she wrote the report and then went to sleep.
    - o  D. She read the book and, wrote the report.

10. **Which sentence is a fragment?**
    - A. The man who was waiting at the bus stop.
    - B. The man waited patiently for the bus.
    - C. He went to the store and bought some milk.
    - D. Running through the field with his dog.

11. **Choose the sentence that corrects the fragment:**
    - A. Running down the street and turned the corner.
    - B. She was running down the street when she turned the corner.
    - C. He ran down the street, turned the corner.
    - D. Ran down the street and turned the corner.

12. **Identify the grammatically correct sentence:**
    - A. The cake smells delicious, however, it is not ready yet.
    - B. The cake smells delicious; however, it is not ready yet.
    - C. The cake smells delicious but, it is not ready yet.
    - D. The cake smells delicious, but it is not ready yet.

13. **Which of the following avoids a run-on?**
    - A. They went to the store, bought groceries, and came home.
    - B. They went to the store and, bought groceries came home.
    - C. They went to the store, and they bought groceries, and they came home.
    - D. They went to the store, bought groceries, and then they came home.

14. **Choose the correct sentence structure:**
    - A. The teacher said to study hard and that the test was going to be difficult.
    - B. The teacher said to study hard, the test is going to be difficult.
    - C. The teacher said study hard, and the test was difficult.
    - D. The teacher said to study hard, because the test is going to be difficult.

15. **Correct the sentence with a fragment:**
- A. She quickly finished the report, but forgot to proofread.
- B. Because she was late to work.
- C. He was running late and missed the bus.
- D. The dog barking at the cat.

16. **Which of these is a grammatically correct sentence?**
- A. Neither of the boys are ready for school.
- B. Neither of the boys is ready for school.
- C. Neither of the boys was ready for school.
- D. Neither of the boys were ready for school.

17. **Identify the sentence fragment:**
- A. She went to the mall and bought a new dress.
- B. After the game, they went out to eat.
- C. While walking to the park.
- D. He made breakfast and cleaned the kitchen.

18. **Choose the correctly combined sentence:**
- A. She enjoys reading books, and listening to music.
- B. She enjoys reading books, listening to music, and to travel.
- C. She enjoys reading books, listening to music, and traveling.
- D. She enjoys to read books, listening to music, and traveling.

19. **Which sentence is a fragment?**
- A. The students were studying for the final exams.
- B. Studying hard for the final exams and hoping for the best.
- C. They studied all night to prepare for the final.
- D. The teacher gave them a practice test to help them study.

20. **Identify the correct sentence structure:**
- A. The test was hard; however, I think I did well.
- B. The test was hard however, I think I did well.
- C. The test was hard but, I think I did well.
- D. The test was hard I think I did well.

21. **Which sentence is correct?**
- A. The results of the study, that was conducted last year, were surprising.
- B. The results of the study, which was conducted last year, were surprising.
- C. The results of the study which, was conducted last year were surprising.
- D. The results of the study which was conducted, last year, were surprising.

22. **Choose the sentence with no grammatical errors:**
- A. He goes to the gym everyday to stay fit.
- B. He goes to the gym every day to stay fit.
- C. He goes to the gym, every day, to stay fit.
- D. He goes to the gym every day, and stays fit.

23. **Which sentence is correct?**
- A. The team winning the championship was a major accomplishment.
- B. Winning the championship, the team was a major accomplishment.
- C. The team's winning the championship was a major accomplishment.
- D. The team's championship winning was a major accomplishment.

24. **Which sentence is grammatically correct?**
- A. His decision was both wise and he made it quickly.
- B. His decision was both wise and quick.
- C. His decision was both wisely and quick.
- D. His decision was both wise and quickly made.

25. **Identify the sentence with correct subject-verb agreement:**
- A. The group of students are going to the museum.
- B. The group of students is going to the museum.
- C. The group of students were going to the museum.
- D. The group of students are going to museums.

# Section 2: Verb Tense and Agreement

1. **Choose the correct verb tense:**
   - A. She *runs* every morning before work.
   - B. She *run* every morning before work.
   - C. She *ran* every morning before work.
   - D. She *running* every morning before work.

2. **Which verb agrees with the subject?**
   - A. The dog *bark* at strangers.
   - B. The dog *barks* at strangers.
   - C. The dog *barked* at strangers.
   - D. The dog *is barking* at strangers.

3. **Select the correct verb tense for the sentence:**
   - A. By the time we arrived, the show *had already started*.
   - B. By the time we arrived, the show *already starts*.
   - C. By the time we arrived, the show *is already starting*.
   - D. By the time we arrived, the show *will have already started*.

4. **Which sentence uses the correct verb form?**
   - A. She *was cooking* dinner when the phone rang.
   - B. She *cooks* dinner when the phone rang.
   - C. She *is cooking* dinner when the phone rang.
   - D. She *will be cooking* dinner when the phone rang.

5. **Identify the correct subject-verb agreement:**
   - A. Each of the students *have* completed the assignment.
   - B. Each of the students *has* completed the assignment.

    o  C. Each of the students *are* completed the assignment.

    o  D. Each of the students *were* completed the assignment.

6. **Choose the sentence with correct verb tense consistency:**

    o  A. She *was reading* when the lights *went* out.

    o  B. She *reads* when the lights *went* out.

    o  C. She *is reading* when the lights *went* out.

    o  D. She *will read* when the lights *went* out.

7. **Which sentence has correct subject-verb agreement?**

    o  A. The team *are* planning their next move.

    o  B. The team *is* planning their next move.

    o  C. The team *was* planning their next move.

    o  D. The team *were* planning their next move.

8. **Select the correct verb form for the following sentence:**

    o  A. If I *was* rich, I would travel the world.

    o  B. If I *am* rich, I would travel the world.

    o  C. If I *were* rich, I would travel the world.

    o  D. If I *had been* rich, I would travel the world.

9. **Which sentence has consistent verb tenses?**

    o  A. He *will study* hard and then *is taking* a break.

    o  B. He *studies* hard and *takes* a break.

    o  C. He *studied* hard and *takes* a break.

    o  D. He *studied* hard and *will take* a break.

10. **Choose the correct verb to complete the sentence:**

    o  A. They *has* never seen a play before.

    o  B. They *have* never seen a play before.

    o  C. They *had* never seen a play before.

    o  D. They *is* never seen a play before.

11. **Which verb agrees with the subject?**

    o  A. The books on the shelf *is* dusty.

    o  B. The books on the shelf *are* dusty.

    o  C. The books on the shelf *was* dusty.

    o  D. The books on the shelf *has been* dusty.

12. **Select the correct verb form for this conditional sentence:**

    o  A. If he *had known*, he *would have acted* differently.

    o  B. If he *knew*, he *would have acted* differently.

    o  C. If he *knows*, he *would have acted* differently.

    o  D. If he *was knowing*, he *would have acted* differently.

13. **Identify the correct verb tense:**

    o  A. I *was going* to the store when I *see* an old friend.

    o  B. I *was going* to the store when I *saw* an old friend.

o C. I *go* to the store when I *see* an old friend.

o D. I *went* to the store when I *seen* an old friend.

14. **Choose the correct sentence:**

   o A. Neither of the boys *are* going to the party.

   o B. Neither of the boys *is* going to the party.

   o C. Neither of the boys *were* going to the party.

   o D. Neither of the boys *be* going to the party.

15. **Which sentence has correct verb tense agreement?**

   o A. When he *arrives*, she *was waiting* for him.

   o B. When he *arrived*, she *had been waiting* for him.

   o C. When he *arrives*, she *waited* for him.

   o D. When he *arriving*, she *had waited* for him.

16. **Identify the sentence with the correct subject-verb agreement:**

   o A. The group of students *were* excited for the trip.

   o B. The group of students *was* excited for the trip.

   o C. The group of students *are* excited for the trip.

   o D. The group of students *have been* excited for the trip.

17. **Choose the correct verb form:**

   o A. She *has been* working on the project for hours.

   o B. She *have been* working on the project for hours.

   o C. She *is being* working on the project for hours.

   o D. She *was being* working on the project for hours.

18. **Select the correct verb for the sentence:**

   o A. The children *was* playing in the park.

   o B. The children *were* playing in the park.

   o C. The children *has* playing in the park.

   o D. The children *is* playing in the park.

19. **Which sentence is correct?**

   o A. The teacher *is speaking* to the students about the assignment.

   o B. The teacher *was spoke* to the students about the assignment.

   o C. The teacher *has speak* to the students about the assignment.

   o D. The teacher *have been* speaking to the students about the assignment.

20. **Identify the sentence with proper verb tense consistency:**

   o A. After she *had studied*, she *is taking* a break.

   o B. After she *studied*, she *takes* a break.

   o C. After she *had studied*, she *took* a break.

   o D. After she *is studying*, she *takes* a break.

21. **Choose the correct verb form:**

   o A. He *was driving* when the car *breaks down*.

   o B. He *is driving* when the car *broke down*.

- C. He *was driving* when the car *broke down*.
- D. He *drives* when the car *was breaking down*.

22. **Which verb agrees with the subject?**
    - A. The bag of apples *are* on the counter.
    - B. The bag of apples *is* on the counter.
    - C. The bag of apples *were* on the counter.
    - D. The bag of apples *been* on the counter.

23. **Select the correct verb tense:**
    - A. They *had already left* when we *arrive*.
    - B. They *had already left* when we *arrived*.
    - C. They *have already left* when we *arrived*.
    - D. They *are leaving* when we *arrive*.

24. **Identify the sentence with proper subject-verb agreement:**
    - A. Everyone in the room *are* excited about the announcement.
    - B. Everyone in the room *is* excited about the announcement.
    - C. Everyone in the room *have been* excited about the announcement.
    - D. Everyone in the room *was being* excited about the announcement.

25. **Choose the correct verb form:**
    - A. The flowers in the garden *needs* watering.
    - B. The flowers in the garden *need* watering.
    - C. The flowers in the garden *is needing* watering.
    - D. The flowers in the garden *was needing* watering.

# Section 3: Pronouns and Antecedents

These exercises will focus on the correct usage of pronouns and ensuring they agree with their antecedents in number, gender, and clarity. The questions will require students to identify mistakes related to pronouns or select the appropriate pronoun based on the context of the sentence.

**Question 1:**
Which pronoun correctly completes the sentence?
*"Each of the students must bring ___ own textbook to class."*
A) their
B) his or her
C) its
D) her

**Question 2:**
Identify the correct pronoun to complete the sentence:
*"Neither John nor Mark remembered to bring ___ jacket."*
A) his
B) their

C) its

D) them

**Question 3:**

Choose the correct pronoun to match the antecedent:

*"If anyone calls, tell ___ I'll be back in an hour."*

A) them

B) they

C) he or she

D) him

**Question 4:**

Which sentence uses pronouns correctly?

A) "Every student should do their best on the exam."

B) "Somebody forgot their umbrella."

C) "Either of the candidates must submit their application."

D) "Each member of the team has their own responsibility."

**Question 5:**

Identify the pronoun error in the sentence:

*"If the teacher or the students need help, they should contact the administration."*

A) No error

B) Replace "they" with "he or she"

C) Replace "they" with "he"

D) Replace "they" with "he and she"

**Question 6:**

Which pronoun correctly completes the sentence?

*"Both of the dogs wagged ___ tails happily when they saw their owner."*

A) its

B) their

C) his

D) her

**Question 7:**

What is the correct pronoun to agree with the subject in this sentence?

*"The committee submitted ___ report on time."*

A) its

B) their

C) it

D) they're

**Question 8:**

Which sentence contains a pronoun-antecedent agreement error?

A) "Everyone at the party enjoyed themselves."

B) "The doctor and the nurse both wore their uniforms."

C) "Each of the children brought their lunch."

D) "Somebody left his or her coat in the classroom."

**Question 9:**

Correct the pronoun error:

*"If a student does not understand the question, they should ask for clarification."*

A) No error

B) Replace "they" with "he"

C) Replace "they" with "he or she"

D) Replace "they" with "him or her"

**Question 10:**

Which pronoun correctly completes the sentence?

*"Neither of the cats had eaten __ food by noon."*

A) their

B) its

C) his

D) her

**Question 11:**

Identify the correct pronoun to agree with the antecedent:

*"A person should always be true to __ beliefs."*

A) their

B) his or her

C) its

D) them

**Question 12:**

Which sentence is grammatically correct?

A) "Each of the players celebrated their victory."

B) "The group of students took their seats."

C) "Every student should do their homework."

D) "Somebody needs to do their best."

**Question 13:**

Correct the pronoun-antecedent agreement error:

*"If anyone has lost their phone, please come to the front desk."*

A) No error

B) Replace "their" with "his or her"

C) Replace "their" with "his"

D) Replace "their" with "hers"

**Question 14:**

Which pronoun correctly completes the sentence?

*"Each of the members of the committee voiced __ opinion on the matter."*

A) his or her

B) their

C) its

D) her

**Question 15:**

Identify the correct pronoun to match the antecedent:

*"The team celebrated after __ won the championship."*

A) its

B) their

C) they're

D) it

**Question 16:**

Which sentence contains a pronoun-antecedent agreement error?

A) "The group of students turned in its assignments."

B) "The committee voted for its new president."

C) "Each member of the jury gave their opinion."

D) "The school honored its students for their achievements."

**Question 17:**

Correct the pronoun usage:

*"Somebody left their notebook on the desk."*

A) No error

B) Replace "their" with "his or her"

C) Replace "their" with "his"

D) Replace "their" with "hers"

**Question 18:**

Which pronoun correctly completes the sentence?

*"The teacher reminded the class to submit ___ assignments by Friday."*

A) their

B) its

C) they're

D) his or her

**Question 19:**

What is the correct pronoun to agree with the subject in this sentence?

*"The board of directors held ___ meeting last week."*

A) its

B) their

C) it's

D) they're

**Question 20:**

Identify the sentence with correct pronoun-antecedent agreement:

A) "If a person wants to succeed, they must work hard."

B) "Each of the athletes must do their best."

C) "Neither of the students brought their books."

D) "Every student must bring his or her own materials."

## Section 4: Punctuation and Capitalization

These exercises will focus on testing the student's understanding of punctuation rules, including the use of commas, periods, semicolons, colons, and capitalization. Students will be asked to correct sentences, identify errors, or choose the most grammatically correct option.

**Question 1:**

Which punctuation mark correctly completes the sentence?

*"The meeting starts at 9__30 AM, so don't be late."*

A) ,

B) .

C) :

D) ;

**Question 2:**

Where should the comma be placed in the following sentence?

*"While we waited for the bus we decided to grab a quick snack."*

A) After "waited"

B) After "bus"

C) After "we"

D) No comma needed

**Question 3:**

Which sentence uses punctuation correctly?

A) "I bought apples, oranges, and bananas; because they were on sale."

B) "He didn't know how to respond, so he stayed silent."

C) "The project was due last week, yet no one submitted their work."

D) "Please remember to bring: your notebook, pen, and calculator."

**Question 4:**

Which punctuation mark correctly completes the sentence?

*"I need three things from the store__ bread, milk, and eggs."*

A) :

B) ;

C) ,

D) .

**Question 5:**

Where should the colon be placed in this sentence?

*"There is one thing I know for sure__ this exam is going to be tough."*

A) After "sure"

B) After "thing"

C) After "know"

D) After "is"

**Question 6:**

Which sentence is punctuated correctly?

A) "Please bring me the following items; a pencil, a ruler, and a calculator."

B) "The cat was fast, however; the dog was faster."

C) "After the rain stopped, we went outside."
D) "We had cake, and ice cream, at the party."

## Question 7:
Which punctuation mark is needed to fix the sentence?
*"I love reading__ especially mystery novels."*
A) ;
B) :
C) ,
D) .

## Question 8:
Where does the semicolon belong in this sentence?
*"She wanted to stay home she was feeling under the weather."*
A) After "home"
B) After "was"
C) After "stay"
D) After "wanted"

## Question 9:
Which sentence correctly uses a comma?
A) "Although it was raining hard, we went for a walk."
B) "I, bought a new book from the store."
C) "The team practiced every day, so they were ready."
D) "We had, cake and coffee for dessert."

## Question 10:
Which sentence is capitalized correctly?
A) "My favorite book is harry potter and the prisoner of azkaban."
B) "We visited the grand canyon in Arizona last summer."
C) "The President of the United States was on television."
D) "She lives in New york City."

## Question 11:
Where should the comma be placed in this sentence?
*"As soon as the sun sets we will start the fireworks."*
A) After "soon"
B) After "sets"
C) After "As"
D) After "fireworks"

## Question 12:
Which punctuation mark is needed in this sentence?
*"My favorite colors are blue__ green, and purple."*
A) ;
B) :
C) ,
D) .

## Question 13:
Which sentence uses semicolons correctly?

A) "I need to pack: my toothbrush; my pajamas; and my shoes."

B) "We went to the park; we played soccer; we ate lunch."

C) "He bought apples, bananas; oranges, and grapes."

D) "She was late; however, she still made it to the meeting."

**Question 14:**

Which sentence is capitalized correctly?

A) "We visited the empire state building in New York City."

B) "My Aunt lives in California."

C) "I saw Professor Smith at the university."

D) "Our family went to Europe last Summer."

**Question 15:**

Where should the period be placed in this sentence?

*"It's time for dinner We need to go to the table now."*

A) After "dinner"

B) After "now"

C) After "time"

D) After "for"

**Question 16:**

Which punctuation mark is needed to fix this sentence?

*"We need to go now___ otherwise, we'll miss the train."*

A) ;

B) ,

C) :

D) .

**Question 17:**

Which sentence uses a colon correctly?

A) "He wanted: to go to the park, to the beach, and to the mountains."

B) "Here are my favorite subjects: math, science, and history."

C) "They arrived late: because of traffic."

D) "She was happy: however, she was also nervous."

**Question 18:**

Where does the comma belong in this sentence?

*"Despite the traffic we arrived on time."*

A) After "time"

B) After "Despite"

C) After "traffic"

D) After "we"

**Question 19:**

Which sentence is correctly punctuated?

A) "We visited Washington, D.C., last summer; it was great."

B) "The menu included pasta, pizza and; dessert."

C) "She worked hard, however; she didn't get the promotion."

D) "The meeting ended; and we all left."

**Question 20:**

Which punctuation mark completes the sentence correctly?

*"Please remember to bring your laptop___ notebook, and pen."*

A) ;

B) :

C) ,

D) .

# Section 5: Parallelism

In this section, students will practice identifying and correcting sentences to maintain parallel structure. This means ensuring that elements in a sentence are balanced and consistent in their form, such as verbs, phrases, and clauses.

**Question 1:**

Which sentence maintains proper parallelism?

A) "She likes hiking, swimming, and to ride a bike."

B) "She likes hiking, swimming, and riding a bike."

C) "She likes hiking, to swim, and to ride a bike."

D) "She likes to hike, swimming, and riding a bike."

**Question 2:**

Choose the sentence that maintains parallel structure:

A) "The job requires you to work quickly, efficiently, and with care."

B) "The job requires you to work quickly, efficiently, and carefully."

C) "The job requires you to work quickly, with efficiency, and carefully."

D) "The job requires you to work quickly, and efficient, and carefully."

**Question 3:**

Which option presents the most parallel sentence structure?

A) "We spent the day swimming, playing volleyball, and we went on a hike."

B) "We spent the day swimming, playing volleyball, and hiking."

C) "We spent the day to swim, playing volleyball, and to hike."

D) "We spent the day swimming, to play volleyball, and hiking."

**Question 4:**

Select the sentence with the correct parallelism:

A) "He wanted to run a marathon, to learn Spanish, and reading books."

B) "He wanted running a marathon, learning Spanish, and reading books."

C) "He wanted to run a marathon, to learn Spanish, and to read books."

D) "He wanted to run, to learn Spanish, and he read books."

**Question 5:**

Which sentence demonstrates proper parallel structure?

A) "The teacher told us to study hard, practice often, and be prepared."

B) "The teacher told us to study hard, practicing often, and be prepared."

C) "The teacher told us to study hard, to practice often, and prepared."

D) "The teacher told us to study hard, practice often, and being prepared."

**Question 6:**

Which sentence is structured in a parallel way?

A) "She enjoys dancing, singing, and to write poetry."

B) "She enjoys dancing, singing, and writing poetry."

C) "She enjoys to dance, singing, and writing poetry."

D) "She enjoys dancing, to sing, and writing poetry."

**Question 7:**

Choose the sentence with correct parallelism:

A) "The company values dedication, innovation, and to work hard."

B) "The company values dedication, innovation, and hard work."

C) "The company values to dedicate, innovation, and hard work."

D) "The company values dedication, to innovate, and hard work."

**Question 8:**

Select the option that maintains parallel structure:

A) "The students were advised to read carefully, write clearly, and preparing thoroughly."

B) "The students were advised to read carefully, write clearly, and prepare thoroughly."

C) "The students were advised reading carefully, writing clearly, and to prepare thoroughly."

D) "The students were advised to read carefully, writing clearly, and preparing thoroughly."

**Question 9:**

Which sentence uses parallel structure correctly?

A) "The coach told the team to play hard, to stay focused, and finish strong."

B) "The coach told the team to play hard, staying focused, and to finish strong."

C) "The coach told the team playing hard, staying focused, and finishing strong."

D) "The coach told the team to play hard, staying focused, and finishing strong."

**Question 10:**

Which sentence maintains parallel structure?

A) "To cook well, you need fresh ingredients, patience, and following directions carefully."

B) "To cook well, you need fresh ingredients, patience, and to follow directions carefully."

C) "To cook well, you need fresh ingredients, to have patience, and follow directions carefully."

D) "To cook well, you need fresh ingredients, patience, and care."

**Question 11:**

Which sentence is parallel?

A) "I plan to visit museums, attend a concert, and eating at a new restaurant."

B) "I plan to visit museums, attend a concert, and eat at a new restaurant."

C) "I plan visiting museums, attend a concert, and eat at a new restaurant."

D) "I plan visiting museums, attending a concert, and eating at a new restaurant."

**Question 12:**

Choose the sentence that maintains proper parallelism:

A) "The candidate is experienced, qualified, and has good communication skills."

B) "The candidate is experienced, qualified, and communicates well."

C) "The candidate has experience, qualifications, and communicating well."

D) "The candidate has experience, is qualified, and communicates well."

**Question 13:**

Which sentence is grammatically correct and maintains parallel structure?

A) "For breakfast, I had eggs, toast, and drinking coffee."

B) "For breakfast, I had eggs, toast, and coffee."

C) "For breakfast, I had eggs, toasts, and drinking coffee."

D) "For breakfast, I had eating eggs, toast, and drinking coffee."

**Question 14:**

Select the option that presents parallel structure:

A) "To succeed, you need to work hard, stay focused, and be lucky."

B) "To succeed, you need to work hard, staying focused, and be lucky."

C) "To succeed, you need working hard, stay focused, and being lucky."

D) "To succeed, you need to work hard, staying focused, and being lucky."

**Question 15:**

Which sentence is parallel?

A) "He enjoys playing soccer, reading novels, and to cook."

B) "He enjoys playing soccer, reading novels, and cooking."

C) "He enjoys to play soccer, reading novels, and cooking."

D) "He enjoys playing soccer, to read novels, and cooking."

**Question 16:**

Choose the sentence that maintains parallel structure:

A) "The tour included visits to the Eiffel Tower, the Louvre, and seeing the Seine River."

B) "The tour included visiting the Eiffel Tower, the Louvre, and seeing the Seine River."

C) "The tour included visits to the Eiffel Tower, the Louvre, and the Seine River."

D) "The tour included visiting the Eiffel Tower, seeing the Louvre, and the Seine River."

**Question 17:**

Which sentence maintains proper parallelism?

A) "The athlete was strong, quick, and had endurance."

B) "The athlete was strong, quick, and enduring."

C) "The athlete was strong, quick, and had endurance."

D) "The athlete was strong, quick, and had endurance."

**Question 18:**

Select the option that shows proper parallel structure:

A) "She is known for being intelligent, kind, and helping others."

B) "She is known for being intelligent, kind, and helpful."

C) "She is known for her intelligence, kindness, and helping others."

D) "She is known for being intelligent, being kind, and to help others."

**Question 19:**

Which sentence correctly follows parallelism rules?

A) "We must decide to attend the concert, go to dinner, or staying home."

B) "We must decide to attend the concert, going to dinner, or staying home."

C) "We must decide whether to attend the concert, go to dinner, or stay home."

D) "We must decide whether to attend the concert, to go to dinner, or staying home."

**Question 20:**

Which sentence is parallel?

A) "Her goals include traveling the world, learning a new language, and to write a book."

B) "Her goals include traveling the world, learning a new language, and writing a book."

C) "Her goals include to travel the world, learn a new language, and writing a book."
D) "Her goals include traveling the world, to learn a new language, and writing a book."

## Section 6: Modifiers and Word Placement

In this section, students will practice identifying and correcting sentences where modifiers are either misplaced or dangling. The goal is to ensure that modifiers are placed in the correct position to clarify meaning.

**Question 1:**
Which sentence correctly places the modifier?
A) "Walking to school, the rain started to fall."
B) "Walking to school, I felt the rain start to fall."
C) "The rain started to fall, walking to school."
D) "I felt the rain walking to school start to fall."

**Question 2:**
Choose the sentence where the modifier is correctly placed:
A) "Having finished the book, the movie was watched by the students."
B) "The movie was watched by the students, having finished the book."
C) "Having finished the book, the students watched the movie."
D) "The students watched the movie, having finished the book."

**Question 3:**
Which sentence places the modifier correctly?
A) "Covered in chocolate, the kids enjoyed the cake."
B) "The kids enjoyed the cake covered in chocolate."
C) "The cake, covered in chocolate, was enjoyed by the kids."
D) "Covered in chocolate, the cake was enjoyed by the kids."

**Question 4:**
Select the sentence that correctly places the modifier:
A) "While reading the book, the loud noise distracted me."
B) "The loud noise distracted me, while reading the book."
C) "While I was reading the book, the loud noise distracted me."
D) "Distracted by the noise, the book was difficult to read."

**Question 5:**
Choose the sentence with the modifier in the right position:
A) "To get to school on time, a bike was ridden by him."
B) "A bike was ridden by him to get to school on time."
C) "To get to school on time, he rode a bike."
D) "He rode a bike to school, to get there on time."

**Question 6:**
Which sentence correctly places the modifier?
A) "Tired after the game, sleep came easily to him."
B) "He slept easily, tired after the game."
C) "Tired after the game, he slept easily."
D) "After the game, he slept tiredly."

**Question 7:**

Select the sentence where the modifier is correctly positioned:

A) "On the way to the store, the dog ran beside her."

B) "She ran to the store, with the dog beside her."

C) "Running beside her, the dog accompanied her to the store."

D) "The dog ran beside her, on the way to the store."

**Question 8:**

Which sentence properly places the modifier?

A) "Hoping to improve the project, changes were made."

B) "Hoping to improve the project, the team made changes."

C) "Changes were made, hoping to improve the project."

D) "To improve the project, changes were hoped for."

**Question 9:**

Which sentence places the modifier correctly?

A) "After finishing the meal, the dishes were washed."

B) "The dishes were washed after finishing the meal."

C) "After finishing the meal, I washed the dishes."

D) "I washed the dishes after the meal was finished."

**Question 10:**

Choose the correct sentence:

A) "Shining brightly, I saw the stars in the sky."

B) "Shining brightly, the stars were visible in the sky."

C) "The stars were shining brightly in the sky, I saw them."

D) "Shining brightly, the sky was full of stars."

**Question 11:**

Select the sentence where the modifier is correctly placed:

A) "Driving home, the sunset was beautiful to see."

B) "Driving home, I saw the beautiful sunset."

C) "I saw the sunset driving home, and it was beautiful."

D) "The sunset was driving home, and it looked beautiful."

**Question 12:**

Which sentence avoids a misplaced modifier?

A) "The teacher handed out papers to the students written with a red pen."

B) "The teacher handed out papers written with a red pen to the students."

C) "The teacher handed the students papers written with a red pen."

D) "The papers were handed to students written with a red pen."

**Question 13:**

Which sentence correctly places the modifier?

A) "While cooking dinner, the doorbell rang."

B) "While I was cooking dinner, the doorbell rang."

C) "The doorbell rang while cooking dinner."

D) "Cooking dinner, the doorbell was ringing."

**Question 14:**

Choose the sentence where the modifier is placed correctly:

A) "Exhausted from work, the bed looked inviting."
B) "Exhausted from work, I found the bed inviting."
C) "I was exhausted from work, and the bed looked inviting."
D) "The bed looked inviting, exhausted from work."

**Question 15:**
Which sentence has the modifier in the correct position?
A) "Driving through the countryside, the scenery was breathtaking."
B) "Driving through the countryside, I found the scenery breathtaking."
C) "I found the scenery driving through the countryside breathtaking."
D) "The scenery was breathtaking, driving through the countryside."

**Question 16:**
Select the sentence that correctly places the modifier:
A) "Reading the book, the plot became clearer to me."
B) "The plot became clearer to me, reading the book."
C) "Reading the book, I understood the plot better."
D) "While reading, the book's plot was clearer."

**Question 17:**
Which sentence properly avoids a misplaced modifier?
A) "Looking through the window, the garden was full of flowers."
B) "Looking through the window, I saw the garden full of flowers."
C) "The garden was full of flowers, looking through the window."
D) "I saw the garden full of flowers, looking through the window."

**Question 18:**
Choose the sentence with the correct modifier placement:
A) "While taking the exam, the questions seemed easier."
B) "Taking the exam, I found the questions easier."
C) "I found the questions easier while taking the exam."
D) "Taking the exam, easier questions came up."

**Question 19:**
Which sentence correctly places the modifier?
A) "To finish the report, more data was needed."
B) "More data was needed to finish the report."
C) "Finishing the report, more data was needed."
D) "To finish the report, needing more data."

**Question 20:**
Select the sentence where the modifier is correctly placed:
A) "Walking through the park, the trees looked beautiful."
B) "Walking through the park, I thought the trees looked beautiful."
C) "The trees looked beautiful, walking through the park."
D) "Walking through the park, beautiful trees were seen."

## Section 7: Word Choice and Precision

In this section, students will work on selecting the most precise and contextually appropriate word to complete a sentence. These questions will test their understanding of nuanced language choices and the importance of word precision in conveying the right meaning.

**Question 1:**

Which word best completes the sentence?

"The speaker's argument was well-constructed, but her tone was too _____ for the audience to take her seriously."

A) indifferent

B) condescending

C) joyful

D) casual

**Question 2:**

Choose the word that best fits the sentence:

"The mountain trail was _____ and difficult to navigate without proper gear."

A) flat

B) challenging

C) easy

D) convoluted

**Question 3:**

Which word provides the most precise meaning?

"His speech was _____, and the audience quickly lost interest."

A) compelling

B) monotonous

C) inspiring

D) dynamic

**Question 4:**

Select the best word for the sentence:

"The results of the study were _____ by several errors in data collection."

A) boosted

B) marred

C) corrected

D) complicated

**Question 5:**

Which word best completes the sentence?

"After hours of debate, the committee finally reached a _____ on the new policy."

A) division

B) consensus

C) conflict

D) disagreement

**Question 6:**

Choose the word that most precisely completes the sentence:

"The artist's work was known for its _____, often leaving viewers with more questions than answers."

A) ambiguity

B) clarity

C) coherence

D) transparency

**Question 7:**

Which word best fits the meaning of the sentence?

"The manager was praised for her _____ handling of the crisis, ensuring the company's reputation remained intact."

A) reckless

B) tactful

C) indifferent

D) abrasive

**Question 8:**

Select the word that best completes the sentence:

"The new legislation was _____ by many as a necessary step toward environmental protection."

A) criticized

B) applauded

C) disregarded

D) condemned

**Question 9:**

Which word best completes the sentence?

"The scientist's _____ explanation of the theory made it easy for the general public to understand."

A) obscure

B) convoluted

C) lucid

D) confusing

**Question 10:**

Choose the most precise word to complete the sentence:

"The documentary presented a _____ view of the events, including both the successes and the failures of the project."

A) biased

B) one-sided

C) balanced

D) incomplete

**Question 11:**

Which word best fits the context?

"The speaker's _____ language made her presentation difficult to follow for many in the audience."

A) simplistic

B) verbose

C) concise

D) engaging

**Question 12:**

Select the word that best completes the sentence:

"Her decision to move to a new city was motivated by a _____ desire for change and adventure."

A) casual

B) profound

C) temporary

D) fleeting

**Question 13:**

Which word best completes the sentence?

"The author's use of vivid imagery helped to _____ the emotional impact of the story."

A) diminish

B) heighten

C) obscure

D) undermine

**Question 14:**

Choose the word that most accurately completes the sentence:

"The company's _____ growth over the past year has positioned it as a leader in the industry."

A) stagnant

B) exponential

C) gradual

D) negligible

**Question 15:**

Which word best completes the sentence?

"The team's _____ effort led to their victory in the championship game."

A) halfhearted

B) collective

C) individual

D) disorganized

**Question 16:**

Select the word that best completes the sentence:

"His approach to the problem was _____, focusing on practicality rather than theory."

A) theoretical

B) pragmatic

C) idealistic

D) impractical

**Question 17:**

Which word best completes the sentence?

"The speaker's _____ comments at the conference showed his deep knowledge of the subject."

A) vague

B) insightful

C) irrelevant

D) casual

**Question 18:**

Choose the word that most precisely completes the sentence:

"The lawyer's _____ argument convinced the jury of her client's innocence."

A) weak

B) coherent

C) erratic

D) disorganized

**Question 19:**

Which word best completes the sentence?

"The athlete's performance was _____, leaving the crowd in awe of her abilities."

A) mediocre

B) lackluster

C) exceptional

D) disappointing

**Question 20:**

Select the word that best completes the sentence:

"The _____ weather conditions made the rescue operation even more challenging."

A) ideal

B) harsh

C) mild

D) predictable

# Section 8: Subject-Verb Agreement and Consistency

This section will focus on ensuring that students can correctly match subjects and verbs in terms of number and consistency throughout sentences. Proper subject-verb agreement is essential for clarity and grammatical correctness in writing.

**Question 1:**

Which sentence has the correct subject-verb agreement?

A) The group of students are planning a field trip.

B) The group of students is planning a field trip.

C) The group of students were planning a field trip.

D) The group of students has been planning a field trip.

**Question 2:**

Select the sentence with correct subject-verb agreement:

A) The results of the experiments was conclusive.

B) The results of the experiments were conclusive.

C) The results of the experiments is conclusive.

D) The results of the experiments has been conclusive.

**Question 3:**

Which sentence demonstrates proper subject-verb agreement?

A) Neither of the options were available at the time.

B) Neither of the options was available at the time.

C) Neither of the options are available at the time.

D) Neither of the options have been available at the time.

**Question 4:**

Choose the sentence where the subject and verb are aligned:

A) Each of the members have a unique perspective.

B) Each of the members has a unique perspective.

C) Each of the members were offering a unique perspective.

D) Each of the members are offering a unique perspective.

**Question 5:**

Which sentence uses proper subject-verb agreement?

A) The data shows a clear trend in the results.

B) The data show a clear trend in the results.

C) The data has shown a clear trend in the results.

D) The data is showing a clear trend in the results.

**Question 6:**

Select the sentence with correct subject-verb consistency:

A) Either the manager or the assistants is responsible for the error.

B) Either the manager or the assistants are responsible for the error.

C) Either the manager or the assistants has been responsible for the error.

D) Either the manager or the assistants was responsible for the error.

**Question 7:**

Which sentence follows correct subject-verb agreement?

A) The team is winning every match this season.

B) The team are winning every match this season.

C) The team were winning every match this season.

D) The team have been winning every match this season.

**Question 8:**

Choose the sentence with proper subject-verb agreement:

A) The news about the recent events are disturbing.

B) The news about the recent events is disturbing.

C) The news about the recent events were disturbing.

D) The news about the recent events have been disturbing.

**Question 9:**

Which sentence is grammatically correct?

A) Everyone in the audience were excited about the performance.

B) Everyone in the audience was excited about the performance.

C) Everyone in the audience are excited about the performance.

D) Everyone in the audience have been excited about the performance.

**Question 10:**

Select the correct sentence:

A) The committee has decided to change its meeting schedule.

B) The committee have decided to change its meeting schedule.

C) The committee were deciding to change its meeting schedule.

D) The committee is deciding to change their meeting schedule.

**Question 11:**

Which sentence correctly aligns the subject and verb?

A) Either the teacher or the students is responsible for setting up the project.

B) Either the teacher or the students are responsible for setting up the project.

C) Either the teacher or the students has been responsible for setting up the project.

D) Either the teacher or the students was responsible for setting up the project.

**Question 12:**

Choose the sentence with correct subject-verb agreement:

A) The jury are currently deliberating on the case.

B) The jury is currently deliberating on the case.

C) The jury has been deliberating on the case.

D) The jury were currently deliberating on the case.

**Question 13:**

Which sentence is correct?

A) Neither the employees nor the manager were aware of the issue.

B) Neither the employees nor the manager was aware of the issue.

C) Neither the employees nor the manager have been aware of the issue.

D) Neither the employees nor the manager are aware of the issue.

**Question 14:**

Select the sentence that uses correct subject-verb agreement:

A) The pack of wolves were seen near the forest.

B) The pack of wolves was seen near the forest.

C) The pack of wolves have been seen near the forest.

D) The pack of wolves is being seen near the forest.

**Question 15:**

Which sentence demonstrates proper subject-verb agreement?

A) Either of the two candidates is a good choice for the position.

B) Either of the two candidates are a good choice for the position.

C) Either of the two candidates were a good choice for the position.

D) Either of the two candidates have been a good choice for the position.

**Question 16:**

Which sentence has correct subject-verb consistency?

A) The number of applicants for the program are increasing.

B) The number of applicants for the program is increasing.

C) The number of applicants for the program were increasing.

D) The number of applicants for the program have been increasing.

**Question 17:**

Choose the sentence that correctly aligns the subject and verb:

A) The herd of deer are moving across the field.

B) The herd of deer is moving across the field.

C) The herd of deer were moving across the field.

D) The herd of deer have been moving across the field.

**Question 18:**

Which sentence is grammatically correct?

A) None of the candidates was selected for the position.

B) None of the candidates were selected for the position.

C) None of the candidates have been selected for the position.

D) None of the candidates are selected for the position.

**Question 19:**

Select the sentence with correct subject-verb agreement:

A) The police officer, along with her colleagues, is investigating the case.

B) The police officer, along with her colleagues, are investigating the case.

C) The police officer, along with her colleagues, were investigating the case.

D) The police officer, along with her colleagues, has been investigating the case.

**Question 20:**

Which sentence uses proper subject-verb agreement?

A) The fleet of ships were anchored in the harbor.

B) The fleet of ships was anchored in the harbor.

C) The fleet of ships have been anchored in the harbor.

D) The fleet of ships are being anchored in the harbor.

**Question 21:**

Choose the sentence where the subject and verb are properly aligned:

A) The board of directors is meeting to discuss the issue.

B) The board of directors are meeting to discuss the issue.

C) The board of directors have been meeting to discuss the issue.

D) The board of directors was meeting to discuss the issue.

**Question 22:**

Which sentence follows correct subject-verb agreement?

A) The group of researchers is presenting their findings.

B) The group of researchers are presenting their findings.

C) The group of researchers have been presenting their findings.

D) The group of researchers were presenting their findings.

**Question 23:**

Select the sentence with proper subject-verb agreement:

A) One of the books were missing from the shelf.

B) One of the books is missing from the shelf.

C) One of the books have been missing from the shelf.

D) One of the books are missing from the shelf.

**Question 24:**

Which sentence demonstrates proper subject-verb consistency?

A) The stack of papers is on the desk.

B) The stack of papers are on the desk.

C) The stack of papers were on the desk.

D) The stack of papers have been on the desk.

**Question 25:**

Choose the sentence with correct subject-verb agreement:

A) The crew was ready for the mission.

B) The crew were ready for the mission.

C) The crew have been ready for the mission.

D) The crew are being ready for the mission.

## Section 9: Redundancy and Wordiness

This section will help students identify unnecessary repetition and overly wordy phrases in sentences, guiding them to choose the most concise and effective versions.

**Question 1:**

Which sentence presents the most concise version of the statement?

A) The reason why she left is because she was feeling tired and exhausted.

B) She left because she was feeling tired and exhausted.

C) She left because she was tired.

D) The reason she left is because she was feeling very tired and exhausted.

**Question 2:**

Select the sentence that eliminates redundancy:

A) In my opinion, I think that the meeting should be postponed until next week.

B) I think that the meeting should be postponed until next week.

C) In my opinion, the meeting should be postponed until next week.

D) The meeting should be postponed until next week.

**Question 3:**

Which sentence is the least wordy?

A) She is a person who enjoys reading books in her free time.

B) She enjoys reading books in her free time.

C) She is a person who likes to read books during her spare time.

D) She is someone who enjoys reading in her free time.

**Question 4:**

Choose the most concise sentence:

A) The teacher gave an explanation that was very clear and easy to understand.

B) The teacher gave a clear and easy-to-understand explanation.

C) The teacher explained in a way that was clear and easy to understand.

D) The teacher explained clearly.

**Question 5:**

Which sentence avoids redundancy?

A) He made plans in advance to prepare for the upcoming event.

B) He made plans in advance for the event.

C) He planned ahead for the event.

D) He planned in advance to prepare for the event.

**Question 6:**

Select the sentence that eliminates wordiness:

A) The reason for their late arrival was due to the fact that the train was delayed.

B) Their late arrival was due to the train being delayed.

C) The train delay caused them to arrive late.

D) The reason why they arrived late was because the train was delayed.

**Question 7:**

Choose the most concise version:

A) The dog, which was big in size and very energetic, ran quickly across the yard.

B) The big, energetic dog ran across the yard.

C) The dog, which was large and full of energy, ran across the yard.

D) The energetic, big-sized dog ran quickly across the yard.

**Question 8:**

Which sentence removes unnecessary repetition?

A) In order to achieve success, it is necessary to work hard and put in a lot of effort.

B) Success requires hard work and effort.

C) To be successful, you need to work hard and put in effort.

D) Hard work and effort are needed in order to be successful.

**Question 9:**

Select the least redundant sentence:

A) The presentation was given by him in person, and it was presented live to the audience.

B) He gave the presentation live.

C) He presented it live in front of the audience.

D) The presentation was live, and he gave it in front of the audience.

**Question 10:**

Which sentence is the most concise?

A) She absolutely and completely refused to participate in the competition.

B) She completely refused to participate in the competition.

C) She absolutely refused to participate in the competition.

D) She refused to participate in the competition.

**Question 11:**

Which sentence eliminates wordiness?

A) At this point in time, we are currently reviewing the budget proposal.

B) We are currently reviewing the budget proposal.

C) We are reviewing the budget proposal at this moment in time.

D) At this point, we are reviewing the current budget proposal.

**Question 12:**

Choose the most concise option:

A) He asked the question because he wanted to get more information and details.

B) He asked for more information and details.

C) He asked the question to get more details.

D) He wanted more information, so he asked the question.

**Question 13:**

Which sentence avoids redundancy?

A) The schedule for the event will be finalized at a later time in the future.

B) The schedule for the event will be finalized in the future.

C) The schedule for the event will be finalized later.

D) The schedule will be finalized in the future.

**Question 14:**

Select the least redundant sentence:

A) She smiled and laughed at the same time while telling the story.

B) She smiled while telling the story.

C) She smiled and told the story.

D) While telling the story, she smiled and laughed.

**Question 15:**

Which sentence eliminates unnecessary repetition?

A) The committee has decided to postpone and reschedule the meeting for a later date.

B) The committee has decided to reschedule the meeting.

C) The committee has decided to postpone the meeting for a later date.

D) The committee has postponed and rescheduled the meeting.

## Question 16:

Choose the most concise sentence:

A) The trip was postponed to a later date due to unforeseen circumstances.

B) The trip was postponed due to unforeseen circumstances.

C) The trip was postponed because of unforeseen circumstances.

D) Due to unforeseen circumstances, the trip was postponed to a later date.

## Question 17:

Which sentence avoids redundancy?

A) I hope that I will have the opportunity to meet with you in person.

B) I hope I will have the chance to meet you.

C) I hope to meet you in person.

D) I hope I will meet with you.

## Question 18:

Select the least redundant sentence:

A) He opened the door and entered inside the room.

B) He opened the door and went inside the room.

C) He opened the door and walked inside the room.

D) He opened the door and entered the room.

## Question 19:

Which sentence is the most concise?

A) In the process of writing her essay, she made sure to edit and revise it carefully.

B) While writing her essay, she edited and revised it carefully.

C) She edited and revised her essay while writing it.

D) While writing her essay, she made sure to edit it carefully.

## Question 20:

Choose the sentence that removes wordiness:

A) During the course of the meeting, several important issues were discussed and addressed.

B) During the meeting, several important issues were discussed.

C) Several important issues were discussed and addressed during the meeting.

D) Several issues were discussed and addressed in the meeting.

# Section 10: Idiomatic Expressions and Prepositions

This section will help students correctly identify and use idiomatic expressions and prepositions in sentences, ensuring natural and grammatically accurate language use.

## Question 1:

Which sentence correctly uses the idiom?

A) She is responsible to taking care of her younger siblings.

B) She is responsible for taking care of her younger siblings.

C) She is responsible with taking care of her younger siblings.

D) She is responsible in taking care of her younger siblings.

**Question 2:**

Choose the sentence with the correct preposition:

A) He is interested on learning new languages.

B) He is interested at learning new languages.

C) He is interested in learning new languages.

D) He is interested for learning new languages.

**Question 3:**

Which sentence uses the correct idiomatic expression?

A) She prefers to focus at her studies.

B) She prefers to focus on her studies.

C) She prefers to focus for her studies.

D) She prefers to focus with her studies.

**Question 4:**

Select the correct usage of prepositions:

A) The book is full with interesting facts.

B) The book is full of interesting facts.

C) The book is full by interesting facts.

D) The book is full in interesting facts.

**Question 5:**

Which sentence correctly uses the phrase?

A) He is capable with completing the project on time.

B) He is capable of completing the project on time.

C) He is capable to completing the project on time.

D) He is capable for completing the project on time.

**Question 6:**

Choose the sentence that uses the idiom correctly:

A) They are concerned for the environmental damage.

B) They are concerned in the environmental damage.

C) They are concerned about the environmental damage.

D) They are concerned on the environmental damage.

**Question 7:**

Which sentence correctly uses the preposition?

A) She is excited with the idea of traveling to Europe.

B) She is excited for the idea of traveling to Europe.

C) She is excited by the idea of traveling to Europe.

D) She is excited about the idea of traveling to Europe.

**Question 8:**

Select the sentence with the correct idiomatic expression:

A) I am familiar for the rules of the game.

B) I am familiar with the rules of the game.

C) I am familiar by the rules of the game.

D) I am familiar on the rules of the game.

**Question 9:**

Choose the correct preposition usage:

A) The manager was impressed by her performance.

B) The manager was impressed of her performance.

C) The manager was impressed with her performance.

D) The manager was impressed on her performance.

**Question 10:**

Which sentence uses the phrase correctly?

A) They are capable to making quick decisions.

B) They are capable of making quick decisions.

C) They are capable for making quick decisions.

D) They are capable with making quick decisions.

**Question 11:**

Select the correct preposition:

A) We are looking forward to meet you.

B) We are looking forward with meeting you.

C) We are looking forward for meeting you.

D) We are looking forward to meeting you.

**Question 12:**

Choose the correct idiomatic expression:

A) She is afraid from spiders.

B) She is afraid by spiders.

C) She is afraid of spiders.

D) She is afraid in spiders.

**Question 13:**

Which sentence uses the preposition correctly?

A) He succeeded in passing the exam.

B) He succeeded on passing the exam.

C) He succeeded for passing the exam.

D) He succeeded with passing the exam.

**Question 14:**

Choose the sentence with the correct idiom:

A) The team worked hard on achieving their goal.

B) The team worked hard for achieving their goal.

C) The team worked hard at achieving their goal.

D) The team worked hard to achieving their goal.

**Question 15:**

Which sentence correctly uses the preposition?

A) I am good with cooking Italian food.

B) I am good at cooking Italian food.

C) I am good in cooking Italian food.

D) I am good by cooking Italian food.

**Question 16:**

Select the sentence that uses the idiomatic expression correctly:

A) He is proud on his accomplishments.

B) He is proud of his accomplishments.

C) He is proud for his accomplishments.

D) He is proud in his accomplishments.

**Question 17:**

Which sentence uses the preposition correctly?

A) She is accustomed with the climate in the area.

B) She is accustomed to the climate in the area.

C) She is accustomed in the climate in the area.

D) She is accustomed for the climate in the area.

**Question 18:**

Choose the correct usage of the idiom:

A) They are aware for the potential risks.

B) They are aware of the potential risks.

C) They are aware on the potential risks.

D) They are aware with the potential risks.

**Question 19:**

Which sentence uses the preposition correctly?

A) He is interested to the new project.

B) He is interested for the new project.

C) He is interested in the new project.

D) He is interested with the new project.

**Question 20:**

Select the correct idiomatic expression:

A) She was involved in the project from the beginning.

B) She was involved at the project from the beginning.

C) She was involved with the project from the beginning.

D) She was involved on the project from the beginning.

# Section 11: Combining Sentences

This section will help students practice combining sentences in a clear, concise, and grammatically correct manner. The goal is to test students' ability to create well-structured sentences by merging multiple ideas into one cohesive sentence.

**Question 1:**

Which option most effectively combines the following sentences?

**Original sentences:** "The artist painted a mural. The mural depicts the city skyline at sunset."

A) The artist painted a mural, it depicts the city skyline at sunset.

B) The artist painted a mural that depicts the city skyline at sunset.

C) The artist painted a mural and it depicts the city skyline at sunset.

D) The artist painted a mural while depicting the city skyline at sunset.

**Question 2:**

Which option best combines the following sentences?

**Original sentences:** "She studied diligently for the exam. She wanted to improve her score."

A) She studied diligently for the exam because she wanted to improve her score.

B) She studied diligently for the exam, improving her score.

C) She studied diligently, but she wanted to improve her score.

D) She studied diligently for the exam while she wanted to improve her score.

**Question 3:**

Which sentence is the best combination of the following?

**Original sentences:** "The concert was sold out. We were lucky to get tickets."

A) The concert was sold out, however, we were lucky to get tickets.

B) The concert was sold out, and we were lucky to get tickets.

C) Even though the concert was sold out, we were lucky to get tickets.

D) The concert was sold out but lucky we got tickets.

**Question 4:**

Choose the option that most effectively combines the following sentences:

**Original sentences:** "The report was finished. It took three hours to complete."

A) The report was finished and took three hours to complete.

B) The report, which took three hours to complete, was finished.

C) The report finished after three hours of work.

D) The report took three hours to finish, and it was completed.

**Question 5:**

Which option best combines the following sentences?

**Original sentences:** "The cat chased the mouse. The mouse ran into a small hole."

A) The cat chased the mouse that ran into a small hole.

B) The cat chased the mouse, but the mouse ran into a small hole.

C) The mouse ran into a small hole, and the cat chased it.

D) The cat chased after the mouse into a small hole.

**Question 6:**

Which option most effectively combines the following sentences?

**Original sentences:** "The book was interesting. It was also informative."

A) The book was interesting but also informative.

B) The book was interesting, as it was also informative.

C) The book was both interesting and informative.

D) The book, which was interesting, was informative too.

**Question 7:**

Which sentence is the best combination of the following?

**Original sentences:** "I arrived at the meeting early. I prepared my presentation in advance."

A) Arriving at the meeting early, I prepared my presentation in advance.

B) I arrived at the meeting early to prepare my presentation in advance.

C) I arrived early for the meeting, and I prepared my presentation in advance.

D) I arrived early to the meeting after preparing my presentation in advance.

**Question 8:**

Choose the option that most effectively combines the following sentences:

**Original sentences:** "The car broke down on the highway. We called a tow truck."

A) The car broke down on the highway, and we called a tow truck.

B) Calling a tow truck, the car broke down on the highway.

C) After the car broke down on the highway, we called a tow truck.

D) The car broke down, and a tow truck was called on the highway.

**Question 9:**

Which option best combines the following sentences?

**Original sentences:** "The player scored the winning goal. The game ended shortly afterward."

A) The player scored the winning goal and the game ended shortly afterward.

B) The player scored the winning goal, ending the game shortly afterward.

C) The player scored, the game ended shortly afterward with a winning goal.

D) Scoring the winning goal, the game ended shortly afterward.

**Question 10:**

Which sentence is the best combination of the following?

**Original sentences:** "The recipe called for eggs and milk. I had neither ingredient at home."

A) The recipe called for eggs and milk, but I had neither ingredient at home.

B) The recipe called for eggs and milk, I had neither at home.

C) The recipe, which called for eggs and milk, had neither at home.

D) I had neither eggs nor milk, which the recipe called for at home.

**Question 11:**

Which option most effectively combines the following sentences?

**Original sentences:** "She enjoyed reading novels. She also enjoyed writing short stories."

A) She enjoyed reading novels, and she enjoyed writing short stories.

B) She enjoyed both reading novels and writing short stories.

C) Reading novels and writing short stories were enjoyed by her.

D) She enjoyed reading novels while writing short stories.

**Question 12:**

Choose the option that most effectively combines the following sentences:

**Original sentences:** "The weather was sunny. We decided to go to the beach."

A) The weather was sunny, and we decided to go to the beach.

B) Since the weather was sunny, we decided to go to the beach.

C) The weather being sunny, we decided to go to the beach.

D) Deciding to go to the beach, the weather was sunny

**Question 13:**

Which sentence is the best combination of the following?

**Original sentences:** "The movie was too long. The ending was exciting."

A) The movie was too long, but the ending was exciting.

B) The movie was long, the ending was exciting.

C) The movie, although long, had an exciting ending.

D) The movie was exciting at the end but too long.

**Question 14:**

Which option best combines the following sentences?

**Original sentences:** "He missed the bus. He walked to school instead."

A) He missed the bus, and he walked to school instead.

B) He missed the bus; he walked to school instead.

C) Since he missed the bus, he walked to school instead.

D) Walking to school, he missed the bus instead.

**Question 15:**

Which option most effectively combines the following sentences?

**Original sentences:** "The test was difficult. I had studied all night."

A) The test was difficult, and I had studied all night.

B) Even though I had studied all night, the test was difficult.

C) The test was difficult after I studied all night.

D) I had studied all night, but the test was difficult.

**Question 16:**

Choose the sentence that best combines the following sentences:

**Original sentences:** "The museum had many exhibits. The children enjoyed learning about history."

A) The museum had many exhibits, and the children enjoyed learning about history.

B) The children enjoyed learning about history at the museum's many exhibits.

C) Learning about history, the museum had many exhibits the children enjoyed.

D) The museum had many exhibits while the children enjoyed learning about history.

**Question 17:**

Which option best combines the following sentences?

**Original sentences:** "The phone rang. I was in the middle of cooking dinner."

A) The phone rang, and I was in the middle of cooking dinner.

B) While I was cooking dinner, the phone rang.

C) The phone rang while I was cooking dinner.

D) The phone rang as I was cooking dinner.

**Question 18:**

Which option most effectively combines the following sentences?

**Original sentences:** "She won first place in the competition. Her hard work paid off."

A) Her hard work paid off, as she won first place in the competition.

B) She won first place in the competition, so her hard work paid off.

C) Winning first place in the competition, her hard work paid off.

D) Her hard work was paid off, she won first place in the competition.

**Question 19:**

Choose the sentence that best combines the following sentences:

**Original sentences:** "He loves to travel. He enjoys meeting new people."

A) He loves to travel, and he enjoys meeting new people.

B) He loves to travel, enjoying meeting new people.

C) Loving to travel, he enjoys meeting new people.

D) He loves to travel and enjoys meeting new people.

**Question 20:**

Which option best combines the following sentences?

**Original sentences:** "The cake was delicious. It was topped with fresh strawberries."

A) The cake was delicious because it was topped with fresh strawberries.

B) Topped with fresh strawberries, the cake was delicious.

C) The cake was topped with fresh strawberries and delicious.

D) The cake was delicious, topped with fresh strawberries.

## Section 12: Consistency in Tense and Tone

This section will focus on helping students maintain consistency in both verb tense and tone throughout a passage, ensuring that their writing is clear and cohesive.

**Question 1:**
Which sentence maintains consistency with the verb tense of the rest of the paragraph?
**Original sentence:** "She **was studying** for the exam when her friend **calls** to invite her out."
A) She was studying for the exam when her friend **called** to invite her out.
B) She **studies** for the exam when her friend calls to invite her out.
C) She **studied** for the exam when her friend **has called** to invite her out.
D) She was studying for the exam when her friend **will call** to invite her out.

**Question 2:**
Which sentence maintains a consistent tone with the rest of the paragraph, which is formal and analytical?
**Original sentence:** "The data was collected meticulously, and the analysis of trends **was pretty cool.**"
A) The data was collected meticulously, and the analysis of trends **was highly insightful**.
B) The data was collected meticulously, and the analysis of trends **was very interesting**.
C) The data was collected meticulously, and the analysis of trends **was kind of neat**.
D) The data was collected meticulously, and the analysis of trends **seemed exciting**.

**Question 3:**
Which option maintains verb tense consistency with the rest of the passage?
**Original sentence:** "He **had been preparing** for the presentation all week and **delivers** his speech with confidence."
A) He had been preparing for the presentation all week and **delivered** his speech with confidence.
B) He **was preparing** for the presentation all week and delivers his speech with confidence.
C) He **prepared** for the presentation all week and **delivers** his speech with confidence.
D) He had been preparing for the presentation all week and **will deliver** his speech with confidence.

**Question 4:**
Choose the sentence that maintains consistent tone throughout the passage, which is formal and academic.
**Original sentence:** "The findings of the study were profound, but the results **totally blew my mind.**"
A) The findings of the study were profound, but the results **were remarkably surprising**.
B) The findings of the study were profound, but the results **were quite unexpected**.
C) The findings of the study were profound, but the results **were beyond awesome**.
D) The findings of the study were profound, but the results **completely shocked me**.

**Question 5:**
Which option maintains tense consistency with the paragraph?
**Original sentence:** "The children **play** outside while their parents **watched** from the porch."
A) The children played outside while their parents **watched** from the porch.
B) The children **were playing** outside while their parents watched from the porch.
C) The children **have played** outside while their parents **were watching** from the porch.
D) The children play outside while their parents **watch** from the porch.

**Question 6:**
Which sentence maintains a consistent tone with the rest of the paragraph?
**Original sentence:** "The professor explained the complex theory, providing a clear example that **was really cool.**"
A) The professor explained the complex theory, providing a clear example that **was enlightening**.
B) The professor explained the complex theory, providing a clear example that **was pretty neat**.
C) The professor explained the complex theory, providing a clear example that **was very interesting**.
D) The professor explained the complex theory, providing a clear example that **was a nice touch**.

**Question 7:**

Which sentence maintains tense consistency?

**Original sentence:** "She **is writing** the report and **submitted** her research findings yesterday."

A) She is writing the report and **will submit** her research findings yesterday.

B) She **was writing** the report and submitted her research findings yesterday.

C) She is writing the report and **submits** her research findings yesterday.

D) She is writing the report and **submitted** her research findings yesterday.

**Question 8:**

Choose the option that keeps a consistent tone with the rest of the passage, which is reflective and serious.

**Original sentence:** "The impact of climate change **is super scary** and must be addressed immediately."

A) The impact of climate change **is deeply concerning** and must be addressed immediately.

B) The impact of climate change **is a huge bummer** and must be addressed immediately.

C) The impact of climate change **is very unsettling** and must be addressed immediately.

D) The impact of climate change **is incredibly frightening** and must be addressed immediately.

**Question 9:**

Which sentence maintains tense consistency with the paragraph?

**Original sentence:** "The research team **gathered** data over several months and **is now preparing** their final report."

A) The research team gathered data over several months and **prepares** their final report.

B) The research team **gathers** data over several months and is now preparing their final report.

C) The research team gathered data over several months and **was preparing** their final report.

D) The research team gathered data over several months and is now preparing their final report.

**Question 10:**

Which sentence keeps a consistent tone with the formal tone of the passage?

**Original sentence:** "The experiment yielded significant results, but the entire process **was a hassle.**"

A) The experiment yielded significant results, but the entire process **was a challenge**.

B) The experiment yielded significant results, but the entire process **was a big pain**.

C) The experiment yielded significant results, but the entire process **was super hard**.

D) The experiment yielded significant results, but the entire process **was an issue**.

## Conclusion Practice:

When approaching grammar and sentence correction questions, it is important to adopt a methodical and efficient strategy. Here are some key strategies to keep in mind:

- **Read the sentence carefully:** Always read the sentence in its entirety before attempting to make corrections. This will help you identify the overall structure and any potential errors that need to be addressed.

- **Focus on common error types:** Most grammar questions on the SAT involve common mistakes like subject-verb agreement, verb tense consistency, parallelism, and pronoun-antecedent agreement. Being familiar with these types of errors will make it easier to spot them quickly.

- **Eliminate incorrect options:** When working through multiple-choice questions, eliminate answer choices that contain obvious grammatical errors. This narrows down the options and increases your chances of selecting the correct answer.

- **Don't second-guess yourself:** Trust your instincts, especially when you've practiced identifying these types of errors. Overthinking often leads to second-guessing and unnecessary changes to the correct answers.
- **Time management:** Efficiently managing your time is key. Don't spend too much time on one question. If you're stuck, move on and return to it if you have time at the end.
- **Proofread for clarity and tone:** After correcting a sentence, reread it to ensure the revised sentence maintains the intended meaning and aligns with the overall tone of the passage.

By following these tips, you'll be better equipped to tackle grammar and sentence correction questions with confidence and accuracy.

# 6.2 Practice Exercises: 125 Questions Divided into Groups of 20-25 Questions

## Section 1: Improving Sentence Clarity

**Description:**

These exercises focus on improving the clarity of sentences by eliminating ambiguity, making sentences more straightforward, and ensuring that the meaning is easily understood by the reader. Students will be presented with sentences that can be revised for better clarity and asked to select the best option that achieves this.

**1.** The following sentence is unclear due to the use of a vague pronoun. Choose the option that makes the sentence clearer:

*"After the meeting, she told her that she had made a mistake."*

a) After the meeting, Julia told Maria that Maria had made a mistake.
b) After the meeting, Julia told Maria that she had made a mistake.
c) After the meeting, she told her that there was a mistake.
d) After the meeting, Maria told her that she had made a mistake.

**2.** Which option makes the sentence more concise and clearer?

*"Due to the fact that the team was late, the game had to be postponed."*

a) The team was late, so the game had to be postponed.
b) Because the team was late, the game had to be postponed.
c) The game had to be postponed because of the lateness of the team.
d) Due to the fact that the team arrived late, the game had to be postponed.

**3.** Select the option that improves the clarity of this sentence:

*"He gave a long explanation because the concept was difficult to understand."*

a) He explained it because the concept was hard.
b) He gave a lengthy explanation since the idea was tough to grasp.
c) He explained the concept in detail because it was difficult to understand.
d) His explanation was long due to the difficulty of the concept.

**4.** Identify the sentence that provides the clearest meaning:

*"In the report, it was stated that the company made a profit."*

a) The report stated that the company made a profit.
b) It was mentioned in the report that the company was profitable.

c) In the report, they stated the company made a profit.

d) The company was said to be profitable in the report.

**5.** Which of the following revisions improves the clarity of the sentence?

*"A few people attended the seminar, which was surprising."*

a) Only a few people came to the seminar, which surprised everyone.

b) Surprisingly, the seminar was attended by only a few people.

c) The fact that only a few people attended the seminar was surprising.

d) Few people attended the seminar, which was surprising to us.

**6.** Choose the sentence that removes ambiguity and improves clarity:

*"Each student must complete their project by Friday."*

a) Each student must complete their project by Friday.

b) Every student must complete his or her project by Friday.

c) Every student must complete the project by Friday.

d) The students must complete their project by Friday.

**7.** Which sentence provides the clearest and most direct expression of the idea?

*"The manager was responsible for coordinating the scheduling of meetings."*

a) The manager was responsible for the coordination of meeting schedules.

b) The manager was responsible for scheduling meetings.

c) The manager coordinated the meeting schedules.

d) The manager's responsibility was to coordinate the scheduling of meetings.

**8.** Identify the option that improves sentence clarity:

*"After going over the plans, the engineer explained that they needed more work."*

a) After reviewing the plans, the engineer said they needed more work.

b) After reviewing the plans, the engineer explained that the plans needed more work.

c) After reviewing the plans, the engineer mentioned more work was needed.

d) After going over the plans, the engineer said they required more work.

**9.** Which revision makes the meaning of the sentence clearer?

*"The instructions were confusing, so the students did not finish the assignment."*

a) The confusing instructions prevented the students from finishing the assignment.

b) The students did not complete the assignment because the instructions were confusing.

c) The assignment was not finished due to the confusing instructions.

d) The instructions were confusing, and therefore, the students did not complete the assignment.

**10.** Select the option that makes this sentence clearer:

*"His dedication to his work was evident in his ability to always meet the deadlines that were assigned."*

a) His dedication was evident in how he always met deadlines.

b) His work dedication showed in his ability to meet assigned deadlines.

c) His ability to meet deadlines showed his dedication to work.

d) He always met deadlines, showing dedication to his work.

**11.** Choose the best revision for clarity:

*"Although she tried hard to finish the project on time, she was unable to because of the short deadline."*

a) Although she worked hard, she couldn't finish the project on time due to the deadline.

b) She worked hard but couldn't meet the deadline due to time constraints.

c) She couldn't meet the deadline even though she worked hard to finish the project.

d) Despite her efforts, the short deadline prevented her from finishing the project on time.

**12.** Identify the clearest version of this sentence:

*"In his speech, he mentioned that the new policy would take effect soon."*

a) He mentioned in his speech that the new policy would be implemented soon.

b) In his speech, he mentioned the policy would take effect soon.

c) In his speech, he stated that the new policy was going to be implemented soon.

d) He mentioned the new policy would soon take effect during his speech.

**13.** Which revision best improves clarity?

*"The teacher explained the concept repeatedly to ensure that it was understood."*

a) The teacher repeatedly explained the concept to ensure understanding.

b) The concept was explained many times by the teacher to make sure everyone understood it.

c) To make sure everyone understood, the teacher explained the concept repeatedly.

d) The teacher explained the concept over and over to ensure it was clear.

**14.** Select the clearest sentence:

*"The meeting was rescheduled, but no one was informed of the new time until later."*

a) The meeting was rescheduled, but no one knew about the new time until later.

b) No one was told the new time of the rescheduled meeting until later.

c) No one was informed of the new time until later after the meeting was rescheduled.

d) The new time for the rescheduled meeting was not communicated until later.

**15.** Which of the following revisions makes the meaning clearer?

*"To successfully apply for the position, applicants must submit a resume that includes their past experience, qualifications, and references."*

a) Applicants must submit a resume with experience, qualifications, and references to apply for the position.

b) To apply for the position, applicants must submit a resume with their experience, qualifications, and references.

c) Applicants must include their experience, qualifications, and references on the resume to apply for the position.

d) To apply, applicants should submit a resume with their qualifications, experience, and references.

**16.** Choose the clearest revision:

*"The museum's new exhibit, which opened last week, attracted many visitors."*

a) Many visitors were attracted by the museum's new exhibit, which opened last week.

b) Last week, the museum's new exhibit opened and attracted many visitors.

c) The museum's new exhibit, opened last week, attracted many visitors.

d) The new exhibit, which the museum opened last week, attracted many visitors.

**17.** Select the option that makes this sentence clearer:

*"The results of the experiment were quite unexpected, and the scientists didn't know what to make of them."*

a) The experiment's results were unexpected, confusing the scientists.

b) The scientists were confused by the unexpected results of the experiment.

c) The scientists were surprised by the results of the experiment and were unsure how to interpret them.

d) The unexpected results confused the scientists, who didn't know what to think.

**18.** Which sentence is the clearest?

*"Due to unforeseen circumstances, the concert had to be canceled."*

a) The concert was canceled because of unforeseen circumstances.

b) Because of unforeseen circumstances, the concert had to be canceled.

c) Unforeseen circumstances led to the concert being canceled.

d) The concert had to be canceled due to unforeseen circumstances.

**19.** Choose the clearest option:

*"The project required teamwork, patience, and the ability to communicate well."*

a) The project required teamwork, patience, and effective communication skills.

b) Teamwork, patience, and good communication were required for the project.

c) The project required people to be patient, work as a team, and communicate well.

d) To succeed, the project needed teamwork, patience, and clear communication.

**20.** Identify the revision that makes the sentence clearer:

*"The sudden announcement surprised everyone, but we were not sure if it was true."*

a) Everyone was surprised by the sudden announcement, but we were unsure if it was true.

b) The sudden announcement surprised everyone, although we didn't know whether it was true.

c) Everyone was caught off guard by the sudden announcement, which we weren't sure was true.

d) The sudden announcement took everyone by surprise, though we weren't sure if it was real.

**21.** Which revision best clarifies the sentence?

*"It is important to carefully read the instructions in order to avoid mistakes."*

a) It's important to read the instructions carefully to avoid mistakes.

b) Read the instructions carefully so that mistakes are avoided.

c) Carefully reading the instructions will help avoid mistakes.

d) Reading the instructions carefully is important to avoid errors.

**22.** Select the clearest revision:

*"As soon as the results were announced, the students became excited."*

a) The students became excited as soon as the results were announced.

b) When the results were announced, the students got excited.

c) The announcement of the results excited the students.

d) The students were excited by the results as soon as they were announced.

**23.** Choose the clearest sentence:

*"While reading the book, it was clear that the main character had a difficult time making decisions."*

a) While reading, the main character's indecisiveness was evident.

b) The main character's indecisiveness became evident while reading the book.

c) It was clear while reading the book that the main character struggled with decisions.

d) The book clearly showed that the main character had a hard time making decisions.

**24.** Which revision improves clarity?

*"In the letter, she asked for a favor, but she didn't specify what kind."*

a) In the letter, she asked for a favor, though she didn't specify what kind of favor.

b) She asked for a favor in her letter, but she didn't specify the type.

c) She requested a favor in her letter but didn't specify what type.

d) In the letter, she requested a favor but didn't specify the kind.

**25.** Choose the clearest revision:

*"They didn't provide any reason for their decision to change the schedule."*

a) They didn't give any reason for their decision to change the schedule.

b) No reason was given for their decision to change the schedule.

c) They didn't say why they decided to change the schedule.

d) The reason for the schedule change was not given.

## Section 2: Logical Flow Between Sentences

**Description:**

This section will concentrate on helping students understand how to create smooth transitions between sentences, ensuring ideas flow logically from one to the next. The questions will focus on identifying the most appropriate transition words or phrases, as well as reordering sentences to achieve clarity and logical progression.

**1.** Which transition word best connects these two sentences?

*"The sun was setting quickly. ____, we hurried to set up the tent before it got dark."*

a) Nevertheless

b) As a result

c) Consequently

d) Therefore

**2.** Select the best transition to connect the following sentences:

*"The concert was nearly sold out. ____, we managed to get the last two tickets."*

a) However

b) For example

c) Furthermore

d) In addition

**3.** Which phrase best connects these two ideas logically?

*"He had studied for weeks. ____, he felt confident going into the final exam."*

a) Even so

b) In contrast

c) As a result

d) Similarly

**4.** Identify the best transition to connect these sentences smoothly:

*"The weather forecast predicted rain. ____, we decided to reschedule the outdoor event."*

a) Despite that

b) Accordingly

c) For instance

d) Moreover

**5.** Choose the best transition to ensure the sentences connect logically:

*"She wasn't feeling well. ____, she still went to work."*

a) Meanwhile

b) Similarly

c) Nevertheless

d) As a result

**6.** Which transition word best indicates a cause-and-effect relationship between these two sentences?

*"There was a major traffic accident on the highway. ____, many people were late for work."*

a) Therefore

b) Likewise

c) Even though

d) Nonetheless

**7.** Select the best transition to connect these sentences:

*"The first meeting went smoothly. ____, we expect the rest of the project to go just as well."*

a) In contrast

b) Consequently

c) For this reason

d) On the other hand

**8.** Choose the most logical transition to complete the thought:

*"She has been working hard on her new book. ____, she plans to submit the final draft to her publisher next month."*

a) Instead

b) As a result

c) Nevertheless

d) In contrast

**9.** Which transition phrase improves the flow between these sentences?

*"The team had been practicing daily. ____, they were confident heading into the championship game."*

a) Nevertheless

b) For example

c) Consequently

d) As a result

**10.** Identify the best transition to clarify the relationship between these ideas:

*"The company's profits have decreased steadily over the past year. ____, new cost-saving measures are being implemented."*

a) In contrast

b) For example

c) Similarly

d) As a result

**11.** Which transition word best maintains logical flow?

*"She studied diligently for months. ____, she earned a scholarship for her outstanding exam scores."*

a) However

b) In contrast

c) Consequently

d) Similarly

**12.** Choose the best transition to connect the following sentences:

*"The new product received great reviews. ____, sales exceeded expectations during the first quarter."*

a) Meanwhile

b) As a result

c) In contrast

d) Despite this

**13.** Which option best connects the two sentences logically?

*"The store had a sale on winter coats. ___, I bought a new jacket at a great price."*

a) Nevertheless

b) On the other hand

c) Consequently

d) Similarly

**14.** Which transition word best improves the flow between these sentences?

*"The car's engine had been making strange noises for days. ___, it finally broke down on the highway."*

a) Similarly

b) Consequently

c) Despite that

d) In contrast

**15.** Select the best transition to indicate contrast between the two sentences:

*"He was told the weather would be warm. ___, it was cold and rainy all day."*

a) Consequently

b) However

c) As a result

d) Similarly

**16.** Choose the best transition to improve the logical flow:

*"She has a strong background in marketing. ___, she was promoted to head of the marketing department."*

a) Despite that

b) As a result

c) In contrast

d) However

**17.** Which transition word clarifies the relationship between these ideas?

*"The seminar was informative. ___, it was much longer than expected."*

a) Nevertheless

b) In contrast

c) In addition

d) However

**18.** Select the best transition to connect the two sentences smoothly:

*"The presentation went well. ___, we received positive feedback from the clients."*

a) In contrast

b) Similarly

c) As a result

d) Meanwhile

**19.** Which transition word best indicates the cause of the second sentence?

*"The city had a major power outage. ___, all the businesses in the area were closed for the day."*

a) Nevertheless

b) Therefore

c) Despite this

d) On the other hand

**20.** Choose the most logical transition to complete the following sentences:

*"The bakery is known for its cakes. ____, its pastries are also popular with customers."*

a) As a result

b) Likewise

c) On the other hand

d) However

# Section 3: Paragraph Coherence

**Description:**

This section will help students focus on enhancing paragraph coherence by ensuring all sentences contribute to the main idea and are logically sequenced. The questions will require students to identify sentences that disrupt the flow of a paragraph and suggest the best revisions to improve overall coherence.

**1.** Which sentence should be moved to improve the coherence of this paragraph?

*"The report details the company's recent growth. As a result, we expect continued success in the coming quarters. The new product line has been well received by consumers. Revenue increased by 15% last year."*

a) The first sentence

b) The second sentence

c) The third sentence

d) The fourth sentence

**2.** To improve the coherence of this paragraph, which sentence should come first?

*"We have invested heavily in research and development. The technology sector continues to grow rapidly. The company recently launched an innovative software product. Our long-term goal is to be a leader in tech innovation."*

a) The first sentence

b) The second sentence

c) The third sentence

d) The fourth sentence

**3.** Which sentence is out of place and should be moved to improve the flow of this paragraph?

*"The new policy has been met with mixed reactions. However, some employees have expressed concerns. A recent study shows that employee satisfaction is directly tied to workplace policies. Overall, the policy aims to increase productivity."*

a) The first sentence

b) The second sentence

c) The third sentence

d) The fourth sentence

**4.** Which sentence best serves as the concluding sentence for this paragraph?

*"Our team has worked tirelessly on the new project. We conducted extensive market research. The product has been tested thoroughly. It is now ready for release."*

a) The first sentence

b) The second sentence

c) The third sentence

d) The fourth sentence

**5.** To make this paragraph more coherent, which sentence should be placed last?

*"The company's expansion into new markets has been a strategic focus. International sales have tripled in the past year. We aim to build on this momentum by entering new regions. The leadership team has prioritized global growth."*

a) The first sentence

b) The second sentence

c) The third sentence

d) The fourth sentence

**6.** Identify the sentence that disrupts the logical flow of this paragraph:

*"The new software update has been downloaded by over 10,000 users. We anticipate further updates in the coming months. User feedback has been overwhelmingly positive. It is a clear sign of the software's success."*

a) The first sentence

b) The second sentence

c) The third sentence

d) The fourth sentence

**7.** To improve the paragraph's coherence, where should the following sentence be placed?

*"Additionally, our customer service team has been instrumental in addressing user concerns."*

*"The app's launch has been highly successful. We have already received hundreds of positive reviews. Many users have commented on the app's ease of use."*

a) Before the first sentence

b) Between the first and second sentences

c) Between the second and third sentences

d) After the third sentence

**8.** Which sentence should be deleted to improve the overall coherence of this paragraph?

*"The company recently upgraded its internal communication systems. Employee productivity has increased since the upgrade. The new systems offer better security. More employees have been working remotely since the systems were implemented."*

a) The first sentence

b) The second sentence

c) The third sentence

d) The fourth sentence

**9.** Where should the following sentence be placed to improve paragraph flow?

*"This shows a strong correlation between customer satisfaction and product quality."*

*"Customer satisfaction has been rising steadily. Our recent survey results show that more than 90% of customers are happy with their purchases. Many respondents highlighted the quality of the products as a key factor."*

a) Before the first sentence

b) After the first sentence

c) After the second sentence

d) After the third sentence

**10.** To enhance the logical sequence of this paragraph, which sentence should be moved?

*"The marketing team has developed a new campaign. We are confident that the campaign will attract a younger audience. This demographic is increasingly engaged with social media platforms. The campaign will primarily focus on social media channels."*

a) The first sentence

b) The second sentence

c) The third sentence

d) The fourth sentence

**11.** Which sentence disrupts the coherence of the following paragraph?

*"The committee has proposed several budget cuts. These cuts are expected to save the company a significant amount of money. The company recently expanded its office space. The savings will be reinvested into research and development."*

a) The first sentence

b) The second sentence

c) The third sentence

d) The fourth sentence

**12.** Where should this sentence be placed to improve the paragraph's flow?

*"The team met all of its quarterly goals."*

*"We expect continued growth in the upcoming year. The company has been performing well overall. A recent report highlighted our progress in several key areas."*

a) Before the first sentence

b) After the first sentence

c) After the second sentence

d) After the third sentence

**13.** Which sentence best serves as the topic sentence of this paragraph?

*"Our sales team exceeded its targets this quarter. The company recently hired several new sales representatives. These new hires bring a wealth of experience to the team. We anticipate continued success in the next quarter."*

a) The first sentence

b) The second sentence

c) The third sentence

d) The fourth sentence

**14.** To improve coherence, where should this sentence be placed?

*"This initiative is expected to increase community engagement."*

*"The city council recently introduced a new public works program. The program will focus on improving infrastructure and services. Funding for the program has been allocated from the annual budget."*

a) Before the first sentence

b) Between the first and second sentences

c) After the second sentence

d) After the third sentence

**15.** Which sentence is redundant and should be removed from this paragraph?

*"The company has prioritized sustainability in its operations. Several initiatives have been introduced to reduce waste. Environmental responsibility is a key focus for the company. We have implemented recycling programs to minimize our environmental impact."*

a) The first sentence

b) The second sentence

c) The third sentence

d) The fourth sentence

**16.** Which sentence should be placed last to improve paragraph coherence?

*"The CEO announced a new leadership program. This program will focus on developing leadership skills among employees. Several employees have already enrolled in the program. We expect more employees to join as the program progresses."*

a) The first sentence
b) The second sentence
c) The third sentence
d) The fourth sentence

**17.** Identify the sentence that is out of order and needs to be moved:

*"The research team has been working on a new project for several months. We expect the project to be completed by the end of the year. Our customers have been eagerly awaiting the release of the project's results. The project will provide valuable insights into market trends."*

a) The first sentence
b) The second sentence
c) The third sentence
d) The fourth sentence

**18.** Where should the following sentence be placed to improve paragraph flow?

*"These measures will enhance the company's competitiveness."*

*"The company has recently implemented new cost-cutting measures. We anticipate significant savings in the upcoming year. Management has been actively seeking ways to improve efficiency."*

a) Before the first sentence
b) After the first sentence
c) After the second sentence
d) After the third sentence

**19.** Which sentence is redundant and should be removed from the paragraph?

*"The new product line has been well-received. Sales have been increasing steadily since the launch. We introduced the new product last quarter. Revenue from the product is expected to grow significantly."*

a) The first sentence
b) The second sentence
c) The third sentence
d) The fourth sentence

**20.** To improve the overall coherence of this paragraph, where should this sentence be placed?

*"This decision has been met with mixed reactions from employees."*

*"The company recently introduced new policies. These policies focus on improving work-life balance. Management believes this will increase employee productivity."*

a) Before the first sentence
b) Between the first and second sentences
c) After the second sentence
d) After the third sentence

## Section 4: Eliminating Redundant or Irrelevant Information

**Description:**

These exercises will help students learn how to identify and eliminate unnecessary or redundant phrases that do not add value to the overall meaning of a passage. The focus will be on refining sentences to maintain clarity and conciseness while ensuring the key information is preserved.

**1.** Which sentence could be removed to improve the clarity of the paragraph without losing any important information?

*"The company recently launched a new product. This new product was introduced to the market last month. Sales of the product have been increasing steadily. The product has also received positive reviews from customers."*

a) The first sentence
b) The second sentence
c) The third sentence
d) The fourth sentence

**2.** Identify the sentence that adds redundant information to the paragraph:

*"The committee has proposed a plan to reduce costs. The plan focuses on cutting unnecessary expenses. In addition to reducing costs, the plan aims to streamline operations. This cost-reduction plan will save the company money."*

a) The first sentence
b) The second sentence
c) The third sentence
d) The fourth sentence

**3.** Which sentence could be removed to make this paragraph more concise?

*"The project team has been working hard to meet the deadline. They have put in extra hours to complete the project on time. The team has also collaborated closely with other departments to ensure everything goes smoothly. The deadline is fast approaching."*

a) The first sentence
b) The second sentence
c) The third sentence
d) The fourth sentence

**4.** Select the sentence that introduces unnecessary or irrelevant information:

*"The city council recently approved a new environmental policy. This policy aims to reduce carbon emissions in the city. The council also discussed traffic congestion during the meeting. The environmental policy includes several new regulations for businesses."*

a) The first sentence
b) The second sentence
c) The third sentence
d) The fourth sentence

**5.** Which sentence is redundant and should be removed to improve the paragraph?

*"The new software update includes several important features. These features are designed to enhance user experience. One of the new features is improved navigation. Additionally, the update also provides better navigation tools for users."*

a) The first sentence
b) The second sentence
c) The third sentence
d) The fourth sentence

**6.** Identify the irrelevant sentence that disrupts the focus of this paragraph:

*"The restaurant's new menu has been a big hit with customers. Many patrons have praised the innovative dishes. The restaurant is located downtown. The menu also includes a variety of vegetarian and vegan options."*

a) The first sentence
b) The second sentence

c) The third sentence

d) The fourth sentence

**7.** Which sentence should be removed to make the paragraph more concise?

*"The CEO gave a speech outlining the company's future plans. She highlighted key growth strategies. The speech was well-received by employees. The CEO also mentioned that she had lunch with investors earlier in the week."*

a) The first sentence

b) The second sentence

c) The third sentence

d) The fourth sentence

**8.** Which of the following sentences adds redundant information and could be removed?

*"The company's new initiative focuses on sustainability. This sustainability initiative includes efforts to reduce waste and lower emissions. The goal of the initiative is to promote environmentally friendly practices. The initiative is designed to make the company more sustainable."*

a) The first sentence

b) The second sentence

c) The third sentence

d) The fourth sentence

**9.** Identify the sentence that does not contribute to the overall meaning of this paragraph:

*"The research team is working on a new project to improve energy efficiency. This project will use innovative techniques to reduce energy consumption. The team recently received a grant to fund the project. They also plan to attend an industry conference next month."*

a) The first sentence

b) The second sentence

c) The third sentence

d) The fourth sentence

**10.** Which sentence could be removed to improve the clarity of the paragraph?

*"The new marketing strategy targets younger audiences. The strategy uses social media platforms to reach this demographic. The company's social media presence has grown significantly. Social media is a popular tool for reaching younger customers."*

a) The first sentence

b) The second sentence

c) The third sentence

d) The fourth sentence

**11.** Select the sentence that introduces irrelevant information:

*"The department has recently updated its procedures. These updates were made to improve efficiency and reduce errors. The department also hired new staff members last month. Employees have received training on the new procedures."*

a) The first sentence

b) The second sentence

c) The third sentence

d) The fourth sentence

**12.** Which sentence is redundant and could be removed?

*"The board of directors met last week to discuss the company's performance. The meeting focused on the company's recent financial results. Board members also reviewed the company's sales figures. They examined the financial statements and discussed revenue."*

a) The first sentence
b) The second sentence
c) The third sentence
d) The fourth sentence

**13.** Which of the following sentences adds unnecessary information?

*"The campaign aims to increase awareness about health issues. It includes advertisements on social media and television. The campaign also involves distributing flyers. Social media is a key component of the campaign."*

a) The first sentence
b) The second sentence
c) The third sentence
d) The fourth sentence

**14.** Identify the irrelevant sentence in this paragraph:

*"The project's main goal is to reduce production costs. It focuses on using more efficient materials. The project team recently won an industry award. Reducing costs will also improve profitability."*

a) The first sentence
b) The second sentence
c) The third sentence
d) The fourth sentence

**15.** Which sentence should be removed to improve the paragraph?

*"The company launched a new app last month. The app has already been downloaded by thousands of users. User reviews have been overwhelmingly positive. Many users reported that the app's design is sleek and intuitive."*

a) The first sentence
b) The second sentence
c) The third sentence
d) The fourth sentence

**16.** Which sentence introduces unnecessary or redundant information?

*"The government introduced a new tax reform policy. This policy aims to simplify the tax code and reduce tax rates. The government held several meetings to discuss the policy. The policy will also help businesses save money."*

a) The first sentence
b) The second sentence
c) The third sentence
d) The fourth sentence

**17.** Which sentence could be removed to improve the clarity and flow of this paragraph?

*"The team is working hard to complete the project by the deadline. They have been putting in extra hours. The project will provide important insights into market trends. They are also collaborating with other departments to ensure everything runs smoothly."*

a) The first sentence
b) The second sentence
c) The third sentence
d) The fourth sentence

**18.** Identify the sentence that disrupts the focus of this paragraph:

*"The hospital recently implemented new safety protocols. These protocols are designed to protect both patients and staff. The hospital cafeteria also introduced a new menu. The new safety measures have already shown positive results."*

a) The first sentence

b) The second sentence

c) The third sentence

d) The fourth sentence

**19.** Which sentence is redundant and could be removed?

*"The company's expansion into new markets has been a key driver of growth. The expansion was driven by increased demand for the company's products. Sales have risen significantly since the company entered these new markets. The company has been expanding into international markets."*

a) The first sentence

b) The second sentence

c) The third sentence

d) The fourth sentence

**20.** Select the sentence that adds unnecessary or irrelevant information:

*"The university recently introduced new scholarships for students. The scholarships are aimed at supporting students from underrepresented communities. The university also opened a new research center last month. Many students have already applied for the scholarships."*

a) The first sentence

b) The second sentence

c) The third sentence

d) The fourth sentence

# Section 5: Correcting Ambiguous Pronouns and References

**Description:**

Students will practice revising sentences where pronouns or references to subjects are unclear or ambiguous. These exercises will help clarify who or what the pronoun is referring to, making the sentence more precise and easy to understand.

**1.** Which revision clarifies the reference to the subject in this sentence?

*"When Sarah told her friend that she was late, she didn't understand."*

a) When Sarah told her friend that she was late, Sarah didn't understand.

b) When Sarah told her friend that Sarah was late, the friend didn't understand.

c) When Sarah told her friend that the friend was late, Sarah didn't understand.

d) When Sarah told her friend that her friend was late, she didn't understand.

**2.** Identify the correct revision that clarifies the ambiguous pronoun in this sentence:

*"The manager spoke to the employee about her performance, but she didn't listen."*

a) The manager spoke to the employee about the manager's performance, but the employee didn't listen.

b) The manager spoke to the employee about the employee's performance, but the employee didn't listen.

c) The manager spoke to the employee about the employee's performance, but the manager didn't listen.

d) The manager spoke to the employee about her performance, but the manager didn't listen.

**3.** Which revision best clarifies the reference in the sentence?

*"The teacher gave the student her notebook, but she forgot it at home."*

a) The teacher gave the student her notebook, but the teacher forgot it at home.

b) The teacher gave the student her notebook, but the student forgot it at home.

c) The teacher gave her student's notebook to her, but she forgot it at home.

d) The teacher gave her notebook to the student, but the teacher forgot it at home.

**4.** Choose the best revision for clarifying the pronoun:

*"James and Robert went to the store, but he forgot his wallet."*

a) James and Robert went to the store, but Robert forgot his wallet.

b) James went to the store with Robert, but Robert forgot his wallet.

c) James and Robert went to the store, but James forgot Robert's wallet.

d) James and Robert went to the store, but James forgot his wallet.

**5.** Which revision makes the sentence clearer?

*"Mary handed the report to Lisa, and she reviewed it carefully."*

a) Mary handed the report to Lisa, and Lisa reviewed it carefully.

b) Mary handed her report to Lisa, and she reviewed it carefully.

c) Mary handed Lisa's report to her, and Lisa reviewed it carefully.

d) Mary handed the report to Lisa, and she reviewed it carefully.

**6.** Clarify the ambiguous pronoun reference in this sentence:

*"The dog followed the girl to her house, but it ran away before she got there."*

a) The dog followed the girl to the girl's house, but it ran away before the girl got there.

b) The dog followed the girl to her house, but the dog ran away before the girl got there.

c) The dog followed the girl to her house, but it ran away before the girl got there.

d) The dog followed the girl to her house, but it ran away before the girl arrived at her house.

**7.** Which sentence provides the clearest reference?

*"When the firefighter saw the house was on fire, they rushed to put it out."*

a) When the firefighter saw the house was on fire, he rushed to put it out.

b) When the firefighter saw the house was on fire, they rushed to put the fire out.

c) When the firefighter saw the house was on fire, the firefighter rushed to put the fire out.

d) When the firefighter saw the house was on fire, it was quickly put out.

**8.** Which revision clarifies the sentence?

*"The committee decided that they would change the rules, but it took them too long to implement it."*

a) The committee decided that it would change the rules, but the committee took too long to implement them.

b) The committee decided that the members would change the rules, but the committee took too long to implement it.

c) The committee decided that they would change the rules, but the rules took too long to implement.

d) The committee decided that they would change the rules, but it took too long for them to implement.

**9.** Identify the revision that makes the sentence clearer:

*"The doctor told the patient that his blood pressure was high, but he didn't seem concerned."*

a) The doctor told the patient that the patient's blood pressure was high, but the doctor didn't seem concerned.

b) The doctor told the patient that his blood pressure was high, but the patient didn't seem concerned.

c) The doctor told the patient that the patient's blood pressure was high, but the patient didn't seem concerned.

d) The doctor told the patient that his blood pressure was high, but neither seemed concerned.

**10.** Which option clarifies the pronoun reference?

*"The teacher called the student into her office, but she didn't show up."*

a) The teacher called the student into the teacher's office, but the student didn't show up.

b) The teacher called the student into her office, but the teacher didn't show up.

c) The teacher called the student into her office, but the student didn't show up.

d) The teacher called the student into her office, but she never showed up.

**11.** Select the correct revision that clarifies the pronoun:

*"The boy told his friend that he was upset."*

a) The boy told his friend that his friend was upset.

b) The boy told his friend that he was upset about something.

c) The boy told his friend that the boy was upset.

d) The boy told his friend that he was upset about what happened.

**12.** Which sentence clarifies the ambiguous pronoun reference?

*"The actor spoke to the director about the film, and he agreed to make changes."*

a) The actor spoke to the director about the film, and the actor agreed to make changes.

b) The actor spoke to the director about the film, and the director agreed to make changes.

c) The actor spoke to the director about the film, and both agreed to make changes.

d) The actor spoke to the director about the film, and changes were agreed upon.

**13.** Identify the sentence that provides the clearest reference:

*"The principal called the teacher into his office, but he was not available."*

a) The principal called the teacher into his office, but the teacher was not available.

b) The principal called the teacher into his office, but the principal was not available.

c) The principal called the teacher into the principal's office, but the teacher was not available.

d) The principal called the teacher into his office, but neither was available.

**14.** Clarify the sentence by choosing the best revision:

*"Sarah lent her jacket to Susan because she was cold."*

a) Sarah lent her jacket to Susan because Sarah was cold.

b) Sarah lent her jacket to Susan because Susan was cold.

c) Sarah lent her jacket to Susan because they were both cold.

d) Sarah lent her jacket to Susan because she was cold.

**15.** Which option clarifies the pronoun in this sentence?

*"The coach told the player that he needed to improve."*

a) The coach told the player that the coach needed to improve.

b) The coach told the player that the player needed to improve.

c) The coach told the player that he needed to improve something.

d) The coach told the player that improvement was necessary.

**16.** Identify the revision that clarifies the sentence:

*"The student turned in the assignment late, and the teacher was not happy about it."*

a) The student turned in the assignment late, and the teacher was not happy about the lateness.

b) The student turned in the assignment late, and the teacher was not happy about the assignment.

c) The student turned in the assignment late, and the teacher was not happy about it.

d) The student turned in the assignment late, and the teacher was upset.

**17.** Choose the sentence with the clearest pronoun reference:

*"The committee discussed the proposal with the board, and they decided to make some changes."*

a) The committee discussed the proposal with the board, and the board decided to make some changes.

b) The committee discussed the proposal with the board, and the committee decided to make some changes.

c) The committee discussed the proposal with the board, and both decided to make some changes.

d) The committee discussed the proposal with the board, and changes were agreed upon.

**18.** Clarify the pronoun reference in this sentence:

*"The man talked to his brother, but he didn't respond."*

a) The man talked to his brother, but his brother didn't respond.

b) The man talked to his brother, but the man didn't respond.

c) The man talked to his brother, but there was no response.

d) The man talked to his brother, but neither responded.

**19.** Select the revision that clarifies the pronoun:

*"The dog barked at the neighbor, but she didn't seem to notice."*

a) The dog barked at the neighbor, but the dog didn't seem to notice.

b) The dog barked at the neighbor, but the neighbor didn't seem to notice.

c) The dog barked at the neighbor, but neither seemed to notice.

d) The dog barked at the neighbor, but she didn't notice it.

**20.** Which option clarifies the reference in the sentence?

*"The supervisor spoke to the employee, but he didn't agree with the decision."*

a) The supervisor spoke to the employee, but the employee didn't agree with the decision.

b) The supervisor spoke to the employee, but the supervisor didn't agree with the decision.

c) The supervisor spoke to the employee, but the decision was not agreed upon.

d) The supervisor spoke to the employee, but neither agreed with the decision.

# Section 6: Combining Ideas for Clarity

**Description**: In this section, students will be tasked with combining two or more sentences into a single, cohesive sentence while maintaining the original meaning. The goal is to improve sentence clarity, avoid repetition, and ensure smooth sentence flow.

### Question 1

Which of the following sentences most effectively combines the two sentences below?

- The scientist conducted an experiment. The experiment tested the hypothesis.

**Options:**

A) The scientist conducted an experiment, and the experiment tested the hypothesis.

B) The experiment tested the hypothesis after being conducted by the scientist.

C) The scientist conducted an experiment to test the hypothesis.

D) The hypothesis was tested by the scientist conducting an experiment.

### Question 2

Which of the following sentences most effectively combines the two sentences below?

- The report highlighted the financial crisis. It also focused on its impact on global markets.

**Options:**

A) The report highlighted the financial crisis and also its impact on global markets.

B) Highlighting the financial crisis, the report also focused on its impact on global markets.

C) The financial crisis was highlighted in the report, as well as its impact on global markets.

D) The report highlighted the financial crisis, while also focusing on its global market impact.

## Question 3

Which of the following sentences most effectively combines the two sentences below?

- He woke up early. He wanted to finish his project before the deadline.

**Options**:

A) He woke up early because he wanted to finish his project before the deadline.

B) Wanting to finish his project before the deadline, he woke up early.

C) He wanted to finish his project, so he woke up early.

D) To finish his project before the deadline, he woke up early.

## Question 4

Which of the following sentences most effectively combines the two sentences below?

- The weather was unpredictable. The picnic was cancelled as a result.

**Options**:

A) The weather was unpredictable, so the picnic was cancelled.

B) The picnic was cancelled, due to the unpredictable weather.

C) Because the weather was unpredictable, the picnic was cancelled.

D) The picnic was cancelled because the weather was unpredictable.

## Question 5

Which of the following sentences most effectively combines the two sentences below?

- She wanted to study law. Her father was a successful lawyer.

**Options**:

A) She wanted to study law, and her father was a successful lawyer.

B) Wanting to follow in her father's footsteps as a successful lawyer, she decided to study law.

C) Her father was a successful lawyer, so she wanted to study law.

D) She wanted to study law because her father was a successful lawyer.

## Question 6

Which of the following sentences most effectively combines the two sentences below?

- The team worked hard on the project. They presented it to the board on time.

**Options**:

A) Working hard on the project, the team presented it to the board on time.

B) The team presented their project on time after working hard on it.

C) The team worked hard on the project and presented it to the board on time.

D) After working hard on the project, the team presented it to the board on time.

## Question 7

Which of the following sentences most effectively combines the two sentences below?

- The movie was long. It was also boring.

**Options**:

A) The movie was long, and it was boring.

B) The movie was both long and boring.

C) Although the movie was long, it was boring.

D) The movie was boring and long at the same time.

## Question 8

Which of the following sentences most effectively combines the two sentences below?

- The author wrote an engaging novel. It quickly became a bestseller.

**Options:**

A) The engaging novel that the author wrote quickly became a bestseller.

B) The author's novel was engaging and quickly became a bestseller.

C) The author wrote an engaging novel that quickly became a bestseller.

D) Writing an engaging novel, the author saw it become a bestseller.

## Question 9

Which of the following sentences most effectively combines the two sentences below?

- The instructions were clear. The students followed them precisely.

**Options:**

A) The instructions were clear, and the students followed them precisely.

B) Following the clear instructions, the students acted precisely.

C) The students followed the clear instructions precisely.

D) The instructions were clear, which allowed the students to follow them precisely.

## Question 10

Which of the following sentences most effectively combines the two sentences below?

- The storm was severe. Many homes were damaged.

**Options:**

A) Many homes were damaged because of the severe storm.

B) The storm was severe, and many homes were damaged.

C) The severe storm caused damage to many homes.

D) Due to the severe storm, many homes were damaged.

## Question 11

Which of the following sentences most effectively combines the two sentences below?

- The company released a new product. It immediately gained popularity.

**Options:**

A) The company's new product gained immediate popularity after its release.

B) Releasing a new product, the company gained immediate popularity.

C) The new product released by the company immediately gained popularity.

D) The company released a product that gained popularity immediately.

## Question 12

Which of the following sentences most effectively combines the two sentences below?

- She studied for the exam. She felt confident about her performance.

**Options:**

A) After studying for the exam, she felt confident about her performance.

B) She studied for the exam, and she felt confident about her performance.

C) Studying for the exam, she felt confident about her performance.

D) She felt confident about her performance because she studied for the exam.

## Question 13

Which of the following sentences most effectively combines the two sentences below?

- The city council met yesterday. They discussed new environmental regulations.

**Options**:

A) Yesterday, the city council met and discussed new environmental regulations.

B) The city council met yesterday to discuss new environmental regulations.

C) Meeting yesterday, the city council discussed new environmental regulations.

D) The city council discussed new environmental regulations after meeting yesterday.

**Question 14**

Which of the following sentences most effectively combines the two sentences below?

- The professor assigned a difficult project. He provided extra resources for assistance.

**Options**:

A) The professor assigned a difficult project and provided extra resources for assistance.

B) The difficult project assigned by the professor was accompanied by extra resources for assistance.

C) Assigning a difficult project, the professor provided extra resources for assistance.

D) The professor provided extra resources for assistance with the difficult project.

**Question 15**

Which of the following sentences most effectively combines the two sentences below?

- The patient recovered from surgery. She began physical therapy the next week.

**Options**:

A) The patient recovered from surgery, and she began physical therapy the next week.

B) After recovering from surgery, the patient began physical therapy the next week.

C) The patient recovered from surgery and began physical therapy a week later.

D) The next week, after recovering from surgery, the patient began physical therapy.

**Question 16**

Which of the following sentences most effectively combines the two sentences below?

- The photographer took stunning pictures. The pictures were featured in a magazine.

**Options**:

A) The photographer took stunning pictures, and they were featured in a magazine.

B) Stunning pictures were taken by the photographer and featured in a magazine.

C) The photographer's stunning pictures were featured in a magazine.

D) Taking stunning pictures, the photographer's work was featured in a magazine.

**Question 17**

Which of the following sentences most effectively combines the two sentences below?

- The event was well organized. It was also highly attended.

**Options**:

A) The event was well organized and highly attended.

B) The well-organized event was highly attended.

C) The event was both well organized and highly attended.

D) Highly attended, the event was well organized.

**Question 18**

Which of the following sentences most effectively combines the two sentences below?

- The speaker delivered an inspiring message. The audience responded with a standing ovation.

**Options**:

A) Delivering an inspiring message, the speaker received a standing ovation from the audience.

B) The speaker's inspiring message led the audience to respond with a standing ovation.

C) The audience responded to the inspiring message with a standing ovation.

D) The speaker delivered an inspiring message, which prompted a standing ovation from the audience.

## Question 19

Which of the following sentences most effectively combines the two sentences below?

- The chef created a new recipe. The dish became a signature item at the restaurant.

**Options:**

A) The chef's new recipe became a signature dish at the restaurant.

B) Creating a new recipe, the chef made a signature dish for the restaurant.

C) The dish created by the chef became a signature item at the restaurant.

D) The chef created a new recipe, which became a signature dish at the restaurant.

## Question 20

Which of the following sentences most effectively combines the two sentences below?

- The students worked together on the project. They successfully completed it ahead of schedule.

**Options:**

A) Working together on the project, the students successfully completed it ahead of schedule.

B) The students successfully completed the project ahead of schedule by working together.

C) By working together on the project, the students completed it ahead of schedule.

D) The students worked on the project together and completed it ahead of schedule.

# Section 7: Enhancing Sentence Variety for Better Flo

Description: Exercises focused on creating sentence variety to improve the overall flow and keep the writing engaging.

## Question 1

Which of the following revisions improves sentence variety and contributes to better overall flow?

- Original: "The dog barked. It was loud. The neighbors heard it."

**Options:**

A) The dog barked loudly, and the neighbors heard it.

B) The loud barking of the dog was heard by the neighbors.

C) Barking loudly, the dog was heard by the neighbors.

D) The dog's loud barking carried over to the neighbors.

## Question 2

Which of the following revisions improves sentence variety and contributes to better overall flow?

- Original: "She went to the store. She bought some milk. She returned home."

**Options:**

A) After going to the store, she bought some milk and returned home.

B) She went to the store, bought some milk, and then returned home.

C) Going to the store, she bought milk and returned home.

D) She bought some milk at the store and went home.

## Question 3

Which of the following revisions improves sentence variety and contributes to better overall flow?

- Original: "The artist painted the landscape. The colors were bright. The painting was beautiful."

**Options:**

A) The artist painted the landscape using bright colors, creating a beautiful painting.

B) Using bright colors, the artist painted a beautiful landscape.

C) Painting the landscape with bright colors, the result was beautiful.

D) The bright colors made the artist's landscape painting beautiful.

## Question 4

Which of the following revisions improves sentence variety and contributes to better overall flow?

- Original: "She studied hard for the exam. She wanted to do well. She felt prepared."

**Options**:

A) She studied hard for the exam because she wanted to do well, so she felt prepared.

B) Wanting to do well, she studied hard and felt prepared for the exam.

C) Because she studied hard, she felt prepared to do well on the exam.

D) Studying hard for the exam, she felt confident and prepared to do well.

## Question 5

Which of the following revisions improves sentence variety and contributes to better overall flow?

- Original: "The man walked down the street. He saw a bird. The bird flew away."

**Options**:

A) As the man walked down the street, he saw a bird that quickly flew away.

B) The man saw a bird flying away as he walked down the street.

C) Walking down the street, the man saw a bird that flew away.

D) A bird flew away as the man walked down the street.

## Question 6

Which of the following revisions improves sentence variety and contributes to better overall flow?

- Original: "The chef prepared the meal. He added spices. The food smelled delicious."

**Options**:

A) Adding spices, the chef prepared a meal that smelled delicious.

B) The chef prepared the meal, adding spices, and it smelled delicious.

C) The chef's preparation of the meal, with added spices, made the food smell delicious.

D) Preparing the meal, the chef added spices, and the food smelled delicious.

## Question 7

Which of the following revisions improves sentence variety and contributes to better overall flow?

- Original: "The cat climbed the tree. It was high. The branches were thin."

**Options**:

A) The cat climbed the high tree with thin branches.

B) The high tree had thin branches, and the cat climbed it.

C) Climbing the high tree with its thin branches, the cat moved swiftly.

D) The cat quickly climbed the high, thin-branched tree.

## Question 8

Which of the following revisions improves sentence variety and contributes to better overall flow?

- Original: "The teacher gave the students a test. The questions were hard. The students were nervous."

**Options**:

A) The teacher gave a hard test, making the students nervous.

B) The students were nervous when the teacher gave them a hard test.

C) Nervously, the students faced the hard test given by the teacher.

D) The teacher gave the students a hard test, which made them nervous.

## Question 9

Which of the following revisions improves sentence variety and contributes to better overall flow?

- Original: "The flowers bloomed in the garden. They were red. They looked beautiful."

**Options**:

A) The red flowers bloomed in the garden, looking beautiful.

B) Blooming red, the flowers looked beautiful in the garden.

C) The beautiful red flowers bloomed in the garden.

D) The flowers, which were red, bloomed beautifully in the garden.

## Question 10

Which of the following revisions improves sentence variety and contributes to better overall flow?

- Original: "The car stopped at the light. It was red. The engine idled."

**Options**:

A) The car stopped at the red light, its engine idling.

B) Stopping at the red light, the car's engine idled.

C) The car, stopping at the red light, had its engine idle.

D) Idling, the car stopped at the red light.

## Question 11

Which of the following revisions improves sentence variety and contributes to better overall flow?

- Original: "He opened the book. He started reading. He liked the story."

**Options**:

A) Opening the book, he started reading and liked the story.

B) He liked the story as he opened the book and began reading.

C) Opening the book, he liked the story and began reading.

D) He started reading the story and liked it after opening the book.

## Question 12

Which of the following revisions improves sentence variety and contributes to better overall flow?

- Original: "The storm came quickly. It brought heavy rain. The roads were flooded."

**Options**:

A) The storm brought heavy rain, flooding the roads.

B) Heavy rain came with the storm, flooding the roads.

C) The heavy rain from the storm flooded the roads.

D) The storm came quickly, bringing heavy rain and flooding the roads.

## Question 13

Which of the following revisions improves sentence variety and contributes to better overall flow?

- Original: "She made dinner. She set the table. She called her family to eat."

**Options**:

A) After making dinner, she set the table and called her family to eat.

B) She set the table and called her family to eat after making dinner.

C) Making dinner, she set the table and called her family to eat.

D) She set the table after making dinner and called her family to eat.

**Question 14**

Which of the following revisions improves sentence variety and contributes to better overall flow?

- Original: "The actor performed well. The audience cheered. He bowed."

**Options:**

A) After performing well, the actor bowed as the audience cheered.

B) The audience cheered, and the actor performed well and bowed.

C) Performing well, the actor bowed to the cheering audience.

D) The actor's performance was met with cheers, and he bowed.

**Question 15**

Which of the following revisions improves sentence variety and contributes to better overall flow?

- Original: "The river flowed fast. The water was cold. The rocks were slippery."

**Options:**

A) The fast river with its cold water flowed over slippery rocks.

B) The river's fast, cold water flowed over slippery rocks.

C) The cold, fast-flowing river moved over slippery rocks.

D) Flowing fast, the cold river moved over slippery rocks.

**Question 16**

Which of the following revisions improves sentence variety and contributes to better overall flow?

- Original: "She wrote a letter. She mailed it. She waited for a reply."

**Options:**

A) She wrote and mailed the letter, then waited for a reply.

B) After writing and mailing the letter, she waited for a reply.

C) Mailing the letter, she wrote it and waited for a reply.

D) She waited for a reply after writing and mailing the letter.

**Question 17**

Which of the following revisions improves sentence variety and contributes to better overall flow?

- Original: "The meeting was long. The discussion was productive. Everyone contributed."

**Options:**

A) The long meeting was productive, with contributions from everyone.

B) Everyone contributed to the productive discussion during the long meeting.

C) During the long meeting, everyone contributed to the productive discussion.

D) The meeting was long, productive, and everyone contributed.

**Question 18**

Which of the following revisions improves sentence variety and contributes to better overall flow?

- Original: "The presentation was informative. The audience took notes. They asked questions."

**Options:**

A) The audience took notes and asked questions during the informative presentation.

B) Taking notes and asking questions, the audience found the presentation informative.

C) The informative presentation led to note-taking and questions from the audience.

D) The audience took notes and asked questions because the presentation was informative.

**Question 19**

Which of the following revisions improves sentence variety and contributes to better overall flow?

- Original: "The train arrived late. It was crowded. Many people got off."

**Options**:

A) The train arrived late and crowded, with many people getting off.

B) Arriving late, the crowded train let many people off.

C) The late, crowded train let many people off.

D) Many people got off the crowded train that arrived late.

**Question 20**

Which of the following revisions improves sentence variety and contributes to better overall flow?

- Original: "He finished the race. He was tired. He felt proud."

**Options**:

A) Tired but proud, he finished the race.

B) Finishing the race, he felt proud and tired.

C) He finished the race, feeling tired but proud.

D) Tired, he finished the race and felt proud.

# Section 8: Maintaining Consistent Tone and Style

Description: Focus on ensuring that the tone and style of writing remain consistent throughout a passage.

**Question 1**

Which of the following revisions best maintains the formal tone of the passage?

- Original: "The company has been killing it lately with all the new product releases."

**Options**:

A) The company has been performing exceptionally well with all the recent product releases.

B) The company has been doing great with its recent product releases.

C) The company is on a roll with its new product launches.

D) The company has been knocking it out of the park with its new product releases.

**Question 2**

Which of the following revisions best maintains the formal tone of the passage?

- Original: "The professor was kind of disappointed with the results of the research."

**Options**:

A) The professor was somewhat disappointed with the research results.

B) The professor was totally bummed about the results of the research.

C) The professor was kind of upset with the research results.

D) The professor was a little unhappy with the research results.

**Question 3**

Which of the following revisions best maintains the consistent tone and style of the passage?

- Original: "The government's initiative was cool because it helped the community."

**Options**:

A) The government's initiative was beneficial in aiding the community.

B) The government's initiative was neat because it helped out.

C) The government's initiative was great since it helped a lot.

D) The government's initiative was rad because it was super helpful.

**Question 4**

Which of the following revisions best maintains the professional tone of the passage?

- Original: "The findings of the study were kind of confusing and not very clear."

**Options**:

A) The findings of the study were somewhat unclear and difficult to interpret.

B) The findings of the study were kind of all over the place.

C) The study's findings were pretty confusing and not clear at all.

D) The study's results were a bit muddled and hard to figure out.

**Question 5**

Which of the following revisions best maintains the formal tone of the passage?

- Original: "The CEO gave a speech that was pretty much the same as last year's."

**Options**:

A) The CEO delivered a speech that was nearly identical to the one given last year.

B) The CEO gave a talk that was more or less like last year's speech.

C) The CEO's speech was basically the same as last year's.

D) The CEO's speech was pretty much a repeat of last year's talk.

**Question 6**

Which of the following revisions best maintains the academic tone of the passage?

- Original: "The experiment was super successful, and everyone was really happy."

**Options**:

A) The experiment was highly successful, and all participants were pleased.

B) The experiment was super great, and everyone was thrilled.

C) The experiment went really well, and everyone was super happy.

D) The experiment was totally successful, and people were excited.

**Question 7**

Which of the following revisions best maintains the formal tone of the passage?

- Original: "The candidate totally rocked the debate and impressed the crowd."

**Options**:

A) The candidate performed exceptionally well in the debate and impressed the audience.

B) The candidate was a total rockstar during the debate and wowed the crowd.

C) The candidate did great and everyone was super impressed with the debate.

D) The candidate did an amazing job and completely floored the audience.

**Question 8**

Which of the following revisions best maintains the formal and consistent tone of the passage?

- Original: "The team really nailed the project and got a lot of positive feedback."

**Options**:

A) The team executed the project effectively and received substantial positive feedback.

B) The team totally rocked the project and got a ton of good feedback.

C) The team did a great job and got lots of positive feedback.

D) The team nailed it and got heaps of praise.

**Question 9**

Which of the following revisions best maintains the formal tone of the passage?

- Original: "The results of the study were pretty good and provided some useful insights."

**Options**:

A) The results of the study were quite positive and offered valuable insights.

B) The study's results were pretty good and gave some useful insights.

C) The results of the study were okay and provided helpful information.

D) The study results were decent and offered some solid takeaways.

**Question 10**

Which of the following revisions best maintains the formal and consistent tone of the passage?

- Original: "The company's marketing campaign was awesome and totally worked."

**Options:**

A) The company's marketing campaign was highly effective and well-executed.

B) The company's campaign was awesome and it worked out great.

C) The marketing campaign was totally successful and awesome.

D) The marketing campaign was great and it worked super well.

**Question 11**

Which of the following revisions best maintains the academic tone of the passage?

- Original: "The professor gave the students a heads-up about the upcoming exam."

**Options:**

A) The professor informed the students about the upcoming exam.

B) The professor gave the students a heads-up regarding the exam.

C) The professor reminded the students about the test in advance.

D) The professor clued the students in on the exam date.

**Question 12**

Which of the following revisions best maintains the consistent formal tone of the passage?

- Original: "The weather during the hike was perfect, and we had a blast."

**Options:**

A) The weather during the hike was ideal, and we thoroughly enjoyed the experience.

B) The weather was perfect, and we had an amazing time hiking.

C) The hike was fun, and the weather was just right.

D) The weather was nice, and we had a great time hiking.

**Question 13**

Which of the following revisions best maintains the professional tone of the passage?

- Original: "The project's results were kind of unexpected, and we're still figuring out what went wrong."

**Options:**

A) The results of the project were somewhat unexpected, and we are still determining the cause of the issues.

B) The project's results were sort of surprising, and we're trying to figure out what happened.

C) The results were unexpected, and we're still trying to figure out what went wrong.

D) The results were kind of unexpected, and we're trying to figure out what went wrong.

**Question 14**

Which of the following revisions best maintains the formal tone of the passage?

- Original: "She totally crushed the interview and got the job."

**Options:**

A) She performed exceptionally well in the interview and secured the job.

B) She crushed the interview and got the job.

C) She aced the interview and got hired.

D) She did great in the interview and landed the job.

**Question 15**

Which of the following revisions best maintains the formal tone of the passage?

- Original: "The presentation was super informative and really well done."

**Options**:

A) The presentation was highly informative and well-executed.

B) The presentation was super informative and great.

C) The presentation was informative and really well done.

D) The presentation was super informative and awesome.

**Question 16**

Which of the following revisions best maintains the formal tone of the passage?

- Original: "The team is working on it and should be done pretty soon."

**Options**:

A) The team is currently working on it and should complete the task shortly.

B) The team is working on it and will be done pretty soon.

C) The team is working on it and should finish up in no time.

D) The team is on it and should be done in a bit.

**Question 17**

Which of the following revisions best maintains the professional tone of the passage?

- Original: "We are almost there and should wrap things up quickly."

**Options**:

A) We are nearing completion and expect to finalize things soon.

B) We are almost finished and should be done soon.

C) We are getting close and should wrap it up shortly.

D) We are nearly done and should finish up quickly.

**Question 18**

Which of the following revisions best maintains the formal tone of the passage?

- Original: "The technology was cutting-edge and super useful."

**Options**:

A) The technology was cutting-edge and highly practical.

B) The technology was cutting-edge and super useful.

C) The technology was advanced and really useful.

D) The technology was state-of-the-art and incredibly useful.

**Question 19**

Which of the following revisions best maintains the formal tone of the passage?

- Original: "The speaker gave a great talk, and everyone loved it."

**Options**:

A) The speaker delivered an excellent presentation that was well-received by the audience.

B) The speaker gave a great talk that everyone enjoyed.

C) The speaker delivered a fantastic talk that the audience loved.

D) The speaker's talk was great, and the audience really enjoyed it.

**Question 20**

Which of the following revisions best maintains the consistent tone of the passage?

- Original: "The marketing strategy was on point and helped the company a ton."

**Options**:

A) The marketing strategy was highly effective and significantly benefited the company.

B) The marketing strategy was on point and helped the company a lot.

C) The strategy was awesome and helped the company in a big way.

D) The marketing strategy was great and helped the company tremendously.

## Conclusion Practice:

• **Recap**: The key to mastering sentence clarity and coherence lies in understanding how ideas flow logically from one to the next and ensuring sentences are structured in a clear, unambiguous manner. It's essential to avoid redundant or irrelevant information, ensure correct word placement, and maintain consistency in tone, style, and tense throughout a passage. The strategies learned in these exercises highlight the importance of carefully reading sentences to spot common issues such as misplaced modifiers, sentence fragments, and awkward phrasing. By recognizing these pitfalls, students can effectively revise their writing for optimal clarity and coherence.

• **Tips**: - **Read each sentence carefully**: Often, ambiguity stems from unclear pronoun references or confusing word choices. When revising, ask yourself if each sentence makes sense without requiring further explanation. - **Eliminate redundancy**: Be concise. If a sentence repeats an idea unnecessarily or includes irrelevant information, it disrupts the flow and clarity of the passage. Always choose the simplest, clearest way to express an idea. - **Use transition words wisely**: Transition words help link sentences and ideas together. Make sure to select the appropriate ones based on the relationship between the ideas you're connecting (e.g., contrast, cause-effect, continuation). - **Practice combining sentences**: Often, combining sentences can improve clarity and coherence. Ensure that the new sentence flows smoothly and maintains the original meaning without adding unnecessary complexity. - **Check for logical flow**: After writing or revising, reread the passage to ensure each idea logically leads to the next. If a sentence seems out of place or disrupts the flow, consider relocating or revising it.

By following these strategies, students can ensure their writing remains clear, cohesive, and logically structured throughout the SAT, improving both their comprehension and overall performance.

## 6.3 Text Revision Questions

## Introduction

Revising text for clarity, coherence, and precision is a crucial aspect of effective writing, especially in the context of the SAT Reading & Writing sections. The ability to refine sentences and paragraphs ensures that ideas are communicated clearly and logically, without ambiguity or confusion. SAT test-takers often face questions that challenge them to enhance the readability of a passage by identifying areas where language may be unclear, transitions may be weak, or meaning may be obscured by unnecessary details.

In these sections, students will encounter various types of revision questions, such as:

- **Fixing vague or ambiguous sentences**: These questions require students to select the most direct and precise revision that clarifies meaning.

- **Improving transitions**: Students must ensure that ideas flow smoothly between sentences and paragraphs, choosing the revision that best enhances the logical sequence of ideas.
- **Eliminating redundancy and wordiness**: Identifying and removing repetitive or unnecessary words is key to making writing more concise and focused.

By mastering these revision techniques, students can significantly improve their performance on the SAT and become more confident writers overall.

# Practice Exercises: 100 Questions Divided into Groups of 10-20 Questions

## Section 1: Clarifying Ambiguous Sentences

These exercises will challenge students to identify and correct sentences that are unclear or ambiguous. In each question, students must choose the best revision that improves clarity and ensures that the meaning is communicated effectively and directly.

**Objective:**

To enhance students' ability to revise unclear language into precise and easily understood statements, a key skill in both SAT Reading & Writing and effective communication.

**Question 1**

"Despite the numerous complaints received, the company's response to the issues were slow and unclear." Which revision best clarifies the meaning of the sentence?

a) Despite receiving many complaints, the company was slow and unclear in responding to the issues.

b) The company's slow and unclear response came after numerous complaints were received.

c) Even though numerous complaints were received, the company responded to the issues slowly and in an unclear way.

d) Despite the complaints, the company's responses lacked clarity and came too late.

**Question 2**

"The scientist's hypothesis was not as simple as first thought and confused most of the audience." Which revision best clarifies the meaning of the sentence?

a) The scientist's hypothesis was more complex than initially thought and confused much of the audience.

b) At first, the scientist's hypothesis seemed simple, but it later confused most of the audience.

c) The scientist's initially simple hypothesis later became confusing to the audience.

d) Many people found the hypothesis confusing, even though it seemed simple at first.

**Question 3**

"The report outlined several recommendations, none of which seemed to be specific enough to address the major concerns raised."

Which revision best clarifies the meaning of the sentence?

a) The report listed several recommendations, but none were specific enough to address the main concerns.

b) Several recommendations were outlined in the report, but none directly addressed the major concerns.

c) None of the report's recommendations were specific enough to address the major concerns.

d) The report's recommendations didn't specifically address the concerns raised.

**Question 4**

"While discussing the project, some team members' ideas weren't explained clearly, which led to misunderstandings."

Which revision best clarifies the meaning of the sentence?

a) Some team members did not explain their ideas clearly during the project discussion, leading to misunderstandings.

b) Misunderstandings arose during the project discussion because some team members didn't explain their ideas clearly.

c) The team members' unclear explanations of their ideas caused misunderstandings during the project discussion.

d) The project discussion was confusing due to unclear explanations from some team members.

## Question 5

"The environmental impact report was comprehensive, but it lacked some important details related to the local wildlife."

Which revision best clarifies the meaning of the sentence?

a) Although the environmental impact report was comprehensive, it lacked critical details about the local wildlife.

b) The report on environmental impact was detailed, but missing key details about wildlife in the area.

c) Important details about local wildlife were missing from the otherwise comprehensive environmental impact report.

d) The environmental impact report covered most areas but failed to include key information about the local wildlife.

## Question 6

"The event was poorly organized, which resulted in many people being confused about where to go and what to do."

Which revision best clarifies the meaning of the sentence?

a) Poor organization of the event led to confusion about where people were supposed to go and what they were supposed to do.

b) Many people were confused about where to go and what to do due to the poor organization of the event.

c) Confusion over where to go and what to do was caused by the poor organization of the event.

d) The event's poor organization confused people regarding where they needed to go and what they needed to do.

## Question 7

"The instructions were given in such a way that everyone misunderstood how to operate the new system."
Which revision best clarifies the meaning of the sentence?

a) The instructions were unclear, which caused everyone to misunderstand how to operate the new system.

b) Because of unclear instructions, everyone misunderstood how the new system should be operated.

c) Everyone misunderstood the instructions on how to operate the new system because they were unclear.

d) The unclear instructions caused everyone to operate the system incorrectly.

## Question 8

"His presentation was so rushed that it wasn't clear to the audience what the main point was supposed to be."

Which revision best clarifies the meaning of the sentence?

a) The presentation was rushed, so the audience couldn't understand what the main point was.

b) Due to the rushed presentation, the audience didn't understand the main point.

c) The main point of his presentation wasn't clear because he rushed through it too quickly.

d) His rushed presentation left the audience confused about the main point.

## Question 9

"The company's new policy, although well-intentioned, ended up making the problem worse rather than solving it."

Which revision best clarifies the meaning of the sentence?

a) The new company policy, though intended to help, ended up worsening the problem instead of solving it.

b) Although the new company policy had good intentions, it ended up worsening the problem instead of fixing it.

c) The company's new policy, despite being well-intentioned, worsened the problem rather than solving it.

d) The new company policy made the problem worse despite being intended to fix it.

## Question 10

"The project's timeline was unclear, so team members struggled to understand when their tasks were due."

Which revision best clarifies the meaning of the sentence?

a) The unclear project timeline made it difficult for team members to know when their tasks were due.

b) Team members had difficulty knowing when their tasks were due because the project timeline wasn't clear.

c) Due to the unclear timeline, team members didn't know when their tasks were supposed to be completed.

d) The timeline for the project was unclear, causing team members confusion about task deadlines.

## Question 11

"The results of the study were interesting but left some questions unanswered, which were not immediately clear."

Which revision best clarifies the meaning of the sentence?

a) The results of the study were interesting, but some unanswered questions were unclear.

b) The study's results were interesting, but some unanswered questions remained that were not immediately clear.

c) Although the results of the study were interesting, certain unanswered questions weren't clear.

d) The study's results were intriguing, though some questions remained unanswered and unclear.

## Question 12

"The decision to change the location of the meeting was made hastily, and many attendees weren't informed."

Which revision best clarifies the meaning of the sentence?

a) The meeting location was changed hastily, and many attendees didn't receive the updated information.

b) The decision to change the meeting location was made quickly, and several attendees were not informed.

c) A hasty decision to change the meeting location meant that many attendees didn't receive the information.

d) Many attendees weren't informed about the hasty decision to change the meeting location.

## Question 13

"Due to the way the proposal was written, it wasn't immediately obvious what the main objective was."

Which revision best clarifies the meaning of the sentence?

a) The way the proposal was written made the main objective unclear.

b) The proposal's writing obscured the main objective, making it unclear.

c) The main objective of the proposal wasn't clear because of the way it was written.

d) The unclear writing of the proposal made it hard to identify the main objective.

**Question 14**

"The speaker's point was lost because of the unnecessary details included in the explanation."

Which revision best clarifies the meaning of the sentence?

a) Unnecessary details in the speaker's explanation caused the point to be lost.

b) The speaker's point was unclear due to the many unnecessary details in the explanation.

c) The explanation included unnecessary details that obscured the speaker's point.

d) The speaker's explanation was unclear because of too many unnecessary details.

**Question 15**

"The politician's statements were ambiguous, and the audience left without a clear understanding of his stance on the issue."

Which revision best clarifies the meaning of the sentence?

a) The politician made ambiguous statements, leaving the audience unclear about his stance on the issue.

b) The ambiguous statements made by the politician left the audience unclear on his position.

c) The politician's ambiguous statements caused the audience to leave without understanding his position on the issue.

d) The politician spoke ambiguously, and as a result, the audience didn't understand his stance on the issue.

**Question 16**

"The meeting ended abruptly, and it was unclear what the next steps were supposed to be."

Which revision best clarifies the meaning of the sentence?

a) The meeting ended suddenly, leaving the next steps unclear.

b) The abrupt end to the meeting made the next steps unclear.

c) Because the meeting ended abruptly, the next steps were not clear.

d) The sudden end of the meeting caused confusion about the next steps.

**Question 17**

"The lawyer's argument was difficult to follow, making the jury unsure of the point she was trying to make."

Which revision best clarifies the meaning of the sentence?

a) The lawyer's confusing argument left the jury unsure of her main point.

b) The lawyer's argument was unclear, so the jury couldn't understand her main point.

c) The unclear argument made it hard for the jury to understand what the lawyer was trying to say.

d) The jury couldn't understand the lawyer's point because her argument was difficult to follow.

**Question 18**

"His explanation of the process lacked important details, which made it difficult for the team to implement the new system."

Which revision best clarifies the meaning of the sentence?

a) The team struggled to implement the new system because his explanation lacked important details.

b) His explanation of the process didn't include enough details, so the team couldn't implement the system easily.

c) Without the necessary details in his explanation, the team found it difficult to implement the new system.

d) The explanation lacked critical details, making it hard for the team to implement the system.

**Question 19**

"Many of the documents were missing key information, so it was unclear what decisions should have been made."

Which revision best clarifies the meaning of the sentence?

a) The documents were missing key information, leaving the necessary decisions unclear.

b) Key information was missing from many documents, making it unclear what decisions were required.

c) Missing key information in the documents made it unclear what decisions should be made.

d) The absence of key information in the documents caused confusion about what decisions to make.

**Question 20**

"Her instructions on how to operate the equipment were vague, resulting in mistakes by the staff."

Which revision best clarifies the meaning of the sentence?

a) The vague instructions she gave on operating the equipment caused the staff to make mistakes.

b) Her unclear instructions on using the equipment led to staff mistakes.

c) Because of the vague instructions on how to operate the equipment, the staff made mistakes.

d) The staff made mistakes because her instructions for using the equipment were unclear.

# Section 2: Enhancing Logical Flow Between Sentences

- **Description**: This section will focus on improving transitions between sentences and paragraphs to ensure smooth, logical flow.
- **Objective**: Help students recognize how effective transitions enhance the clarity and coherence of ideas.

**Question 1**

"She studied for hours every night. Consequently, she performed exceptionally well on the final exam."

Which revision best improves the flow between these two sentences?

a) She studied for hours every night, which led to her exceptional performance on the final exam.

b) Every night, she studied for hours, and her performance on the final exam reflected her hard work.

c) Because she studied for hours every night, her final exam performance was exceptional.

d) Her studying for hours every night meant that she performed exceptionally well on the final exam.

**Question 2**

"The experiment failed the first time it was conducted. However, after adjusting some variables, the team was able to achieve success."

Which revision best improves the flow between these two sentences?

a) After the experiment failed the first time, the team adjusted some variables and achieved success.

b) Initially, the experiment failed, but the team was able to succeed after adjusting some variables.

c) The team achieved success after adjusting some variables following the failed experiment.

d) Although the experiment failed the first time, adjusting the variables led the team to success.

**Question 3**

"The company launched its new product in the spring. This decision coincided with a period of economic growth."

Which revision best improves the flow between these two sentences?

a) The company launched its new product in the spring, which was a period of economic growth.

b) The decision to launch the new product in the spring coincided with a period of economic growth.

c) Coinciding with a period of economic growth, the company launched its new product in the spring.

d) The spring launch of the company's new product aligned well with the period of economic growth.

**Question 4**

"The city's infrastructure was in dire need of repairs. For example, several bridges were closed due to safety concerns."

Which revision best improves the flow between these two sentences?

a) The city's infrastructure needed repairs, as evidenced by several bridges being closed for safety reasons.

b) Because the city's infrastructure was in dire need of repairs, several bridges were closed for safety reasons.

c) The need for infrastructure repairs was highlighted by the closure of several bridges due to safety concerns.

d) The city had several bridges closed for safety reasons, which showed how badly repairs were needed.

## Question 5

"Students often struggle with time management. As a result, they fail to complete their assignments on time."

Which revision best improves the flow between these two sentences?

a) Students often struggle with time management, leading them to fail to complete their assignments on time.

b) The failure to complete assignments on time is often the result of students struggling with time management.

c) Struggling with time management causes students to fail to complete assignments on time.

d) Many students fail to complete their assignments on time due to poor time management.

## Question 6

"Many people are switching to electric cars. This shift is driven by a growing concern for the environment."

Which revision best improves the flow between these two sentences?

a) Many people are switching to electric cars because they are becoming increasingly concerned about the environment.

b) A growing concern for the environment is causing many people to switch to electric cars.

c) The shift toward electric cars is driven by increasing environmental concerns.

d) The switch to electric cars is happening as more people become concerned about the environment.

## Question 7

"The book's main character faces a difficult decision. At the same time, he grapples with feelings of guilt and regret."

Which revision best improves the flow between these two sentences?

a) As the character faces a difficult decision, he also grapples with feelings of guilt and regret.

b) While grappling with feelings of guilt and regret, the character faces a difficult decision.

c) The difficult decision that the character faces is compounded by his feelings of guilt and regret.

d) He faces a difficult decision and struggles with feelings of guilt and regret simultaneously.

## Question 8

"The factory was outdated and inefficient. As a result, the company decided to build a new facility."

Which revision best improves the flow between these two sentences?

a) The outdated and inefficient factory led the company to decide to build a new facility.

b) Because the factory was outdated and inefficient, the company decided to build a new facility.

c) The decision to build a new facility was a result of the factory's inefficiency and outdated condition.

d) The company decided to build a new facility due to the outdated and inefficient nature of the factory.

## Question 9

"The movie received critical acclaim for its direction and cinematography. Nevertheless, its box office performance was disappointing."

Which revision best improves the flow between these two sentences?

a) Despite the critical acclaim for its direction and cinematography, the movie's box office performance was disappointing.

b) Although the movie received praise for its direction and cinematography, its box office numbers were disappointing.

c) The movie's direction and cinematography were critically acclaimed, yet it performed poorly at the box office.

d) Despite being critically acclaimed, the movie's disappointing box office numbers couldn't be ignored.

**Question 10**

"New technologies have made communication faster and more efficient. Similarly, they have improved access to information."

Which revision best improves the flow between these two sentences?

a) In addition to making communication faster and more efficient, new technologies have improved access to information.

b) New technologies have improved both communication and access to information, making them faster and more efficient.

c) Not only have new technologies made communication faster, but they have also improved access to information.

d) While improving communication, new technologies have also increased access to information.

**Question 11**

"The artist is known for using bold colors in her paintings. Moreover, she often incorporates geometric shapes into her work."

Which revision best improves the flow between these two sentences?

a) The artist's use of bold colors is complemented by her frequent use of geometric shapes.

b) In addition to using bold colors, the artist frequently incorporates geometric shapes into her work.

c) Known for using bold colors, the artist also incorporates geometric shapes into her paintings.

d) The artist is recognized not only for her bold use of color but also for incorporating geometric shapes.

**Question 12**

"The team faced several setbacks during the project. Ultimately, they managed to complete it on time."
Which revision best improves the flow between these two sentences?

a) The team faced setbacks during the project but managed to complete it on time in the end.

b) Despite the setbacks they faced, the team ultimately completed the project on time.

c) Although they faced several setbacks, the team was able to complete the project on time.

d) After facing multiple setbacks, the team was still able to finish the project on time.

**Question 13**

"Health experts recommend regular exercise for maintaining physical fitness. Furthermore, it is beneficial for mental well-being."

Which revision best improves the flow between these two sentences?

a) Regular exercise not only helps maintain physical fitness but also benefits mental well-being.

b) In addition to maintaining physical fitness, regular exercise is beneficial for mental well-being.

c) Health experts recommend regular exercise, as it benefits both physical fitness and mental well-being.

d) Exercise is recommended for maintaining both physical fitness and mental well-being.

**Question 14**

"Interest rates are expected to rise in the coming months. This increase may affect consumer spending."
Which revision best improves the flow between these two sentences?

a) The expected rise in interest rates may have an impact on consumer spending.

b) Interest rates are expected to rise, which could affect consumer spending.

c) The rise in interest rates will likely affect consumer spending.

d) As interest rates increase, consumer spending may be affected.

**Question 15**

"She decided to pursue a career in medicine. To achieve her goal, she enrolled in a rigorous pre-med program."

Which revision best improves the flow between these two sentences?

a) To pursue her career in medicine, she enrolled in a rigorous pre-med program.

b) Enrolling in a rigorous pre-med program was the first step toward her goal of pursuing a career in medicine.

c) In pursuit of her career in medicine, she decided to enroll in a rigorous pre-med program.

d) She enrolled in a rigorous pre-med program as the first step toward achieving her goal of a medical career.

# Section 3: Combining and Restructuring Sentences for Coherence

- **Description**: Exercises will ask students to combine or restructure sentences to improve coherence and readability.
- **Objective**: Train students to simplify sentence structures while retaining clarity and intent.

**Question 1**

"The cat was sitting on the windowsill. It was looking outside."

Which option most effectively combines the sentences without changing the meaning?

a) The cat sat on the windowsill and was looking outside.

b) The cat was looking outside from where it sat on the windowsill.

c) Sitting on the windowsill, the cat looked outside.

d) While sitting on the windowsill, the cat looked outside.

**Question 2**

"He enjoys reading books. He also likes to write stories."

Which option most effectively combines the sentences without changing the meaning?

a) He enjoys reading books, and he also likes writing stories.

b) He likes both reading books and writing stories.

c) He enjoys reading books and writing stories.

d) Enjoying books and writing stories are two of his favorite activities.

**Question 3**

"The scientist conducted the experiment. She recorded the results carefully."

Which option most effectively combines the sentences without changing the meaning?

a) The scientist conducted the experiment and carefully recorded the results.

b) Carefully recording the results, the scientist conducted the experiment.

c) The scientist conducted and carefully recorded the results of the experiment.

d) While conducting the experiment, the scientist carefully recorded the results.

**Question 4**

"The painting was beautiful. It captured the essence of nature."

Which option most effectively combines the sentences without changing the meaning?

a) The beautiful painting captured the essence of nature.

b) Capturing the essence of nature, the painting was beautiful.

c) The painting, which was beautiful, captured the essence of nature.

d) The painting was beautiful because it captured the essence of nature.

## Question 5

"Maria finished her homework. She went to the park."

Which option most effectively combines the sentences without changing the meaning?

a) After finishing her homework, Maria went to the park.

b) Maria went to the park after she finished her homework.

c) Maria finished her homework and then went to the park.

d) Finishing her homework, Maria went to the park.

## Question 6

"The sun was setting. The sky turned orange."

Which option most effectively combines the sentences without changing the meaning?

a) As the sun was setting, the sky turned orange.

b) The sky turned orange as the sun was setting.

c) The setting sun turned the sky orange.

d) When the sun set, the sky turned orange.

## Question 7

"He is a talented singer. He has won several awards for his performances."

Which option most effectively combines the sentences without changing the meaning?

a) He is a talented singer who has won several awards for his performances.

b) Having won several awards, he is a talented singer.

c) His talent as a singer has earned him several awards.

d) He has won several awards for his performances as a talented singer.

## Question 8

"She loves to bake cookies. She gives them to her friends."

Which option most effectively combines the sentences without changing the meaning?

a) She loves baking cookies and giving them to her friends.

b) She bakes cookies and gives them to her friends because she loves it.

c) Baking cookies and giving them to her friends is something she loves.

d) She loves baking cookies, which she then gives to her friends.

## Question 9

"John studied hard for his exams. He passed with excellent grades."

Which option most effectively combines the sentences without changing the meaning?

a) John passed his exams with excellent grades because he studied hard.

b) Studying hard for his exams, John passed with excellent grades.

c) John, having studied hard for his exams, passed with excellent grades.

d) Because he studied hard, John passed his exams with excellent grades.

## Question 10

"The storm caused damage to many homes. It also flooded the streets."

Which option most effectively combines the sentences without changing the meaning?

a) The storm damaged many homes and flooded the streets.

b) In addition to damaging homes, the storm also flooded the streets.

c) The storm caused damage to homes while also flooding the streets.

d) Many homes were damaged and streets flooded because of the storm.

**Question 11**

"The novel is captivating. It keeps the reader engaged until the last page."

Which option most effectively combines the sentences without changing the meaning?

a) The captivating novel keeps the reader engaged until the last page.

b) Keeping the reader engaged until the last page, the novel is captivating.

c) The novel keeps the reader engaged until the last page because it is captivating.

d) The novel, being captivating, keeps the reader engaged until the last page.

**Question 12**

"She took a deep breath. She stepped onto the stage."

Which option most effectively combines the sentences without changing the meaning?

a) After taking a deep breath, she stepped onto the stage.

b) Taking a deep breath, she stepped onto the stage.

c) She stepped onto the stage after taking a deep breath.

d) She stepped onto the stage, taking a deep breath.

**Question 13**

"The flowers in the garden are blooming. They are bright and colorful."

Which option most effectively combines the sentences without changing the meaning?

a) The bright and colorful flowers in the garden are blooming.

b) The flowers in the garden are bright, colorful, and blooming.

c) The blooming flowers in the garden are bright and colorful.

d) The flowers, which are blooming in the garden, are bright and colorful.

**Question 14**

"He bought a new car. It is fuel-efficient and environmentally friendly."

Which option most effectively combines the sentences without changing the meaning?

a) He bought a fuel-efficient, environmentally friendly car.

b) His new car is fuel-efficient and environmentally friendly.

c) The car he bought is new, fuel-efficient, and environmentally friendly.

d) He bought a new car, which is fuel-efficient and environmentally friendly.

**Question 15**

"The park is a great place to relax. It has many beautiful walking trails."

Which option most effectively combines the sentences without changing the meaning?

a) The park, with its many beautiful walking trails, is a great place to relax.

b) The park is a great place to relax because it has many beautiful walking trails.

c) Relaxing in the park is easy, thanks to its beautiful walking trails.

d) The park has many beautiful walking trails, making it a great place to relax.

## Section 4: Eliminating Redundancies and Wordiness

- **Description**: Focuses on identifying and removing unnecessary repetitions or overly wordy phrases that complicate the text.

**Objective**: Teach students how to streamline their writing for a more concise and focused presentation

**Question 1**

"At this point in time, we are currently in the process of reviewing the results."

Which revision eliminates redundancy and improves the clarity of the sentence?

a) At this point, we are reviewing the results.

b) We are currently reviewing the results.

c) We are reviewing the results.

d) At this point in time, we are in the process of reviewing the results.

## Question 2

"She made a brief and short introduction to start the meeting."

Which revision eliminates redundancy and improves the clarity of the sentence?

a) She made a brief introduction to start the meeting.

b) She made a short introduction to start the meeting.

c) She introduced the meeting briefly and shortly.

d) She briefly started the meeting with a short introduction.

## Question 3

"In my personal opinion, I believe that the project will succeed."

Which revision eliminates redundancy and improves the clarity of the sentence?

a) I personally believe that the project will succeed.

b) In my opinion, the project will succeed.

c) I believe that the project will succeed.

d) In my personal opinion, I believe the project will succeed.

## Question 4

"The reason why he left the room was because he was tired."

Which revision eliminates redundancy and improves the clarity of the sentence?

a) The reason he left the room was that he was tired.

b) He left the room because he was tired.

c) He left the room due to his tiredness.

d) The reason for his departure was because he was tired.

## Question 5

"The book that she wrote was very interesting and captivating."

Which revision eliminates redundancy and improves the clarity of the sentence?

a) The book she wrote was interesting and captivating.

b) The book she wrote was captivating.

c) Her book was very interesting and captivating.

d) The book that she wrote was both interesting and captivating.

## Question 6

"The final outcome of the game was a complete surprise to everyone."

Which revision eliminates redundancy and improves the clarity of the sentence?

a) The outcome of the game was a complete surprise to everyone.

b) The final outcome was a surprise to everyone.

c) The outcome of the game surprised everyone.

d) The game's final outcome was a complete and total surprise to everyone.

## Question 7

"Each and every one of the students must complete the assignment."

Which revision eliminates redundancy and improves the clarity of the sentence?

a) Each one of the students must complete the assignment.

b) Every student must complete the assignment.

c) All students must complete the assignment.

d) Each and every student must complete the assignment.

## Question 8

"She stood up and rose to her feet to make an announcement."

Which revision eliminates redundancy and improves the clarity of the sentence?

a) She stood up to make an announcement.

b) She rose to her feet to make an announcement.

c) She stood to her feet and made an announcement.

d) She rose to make an announcement.

## Question 9

"During the month of July, we experienced an extremely hot heatwave."

Which revision eliminates redundancy and improves the clarity of the sentence?

a) In July, we experienced an extremely hot heatwave.

b) We experienced an extremely hot heatwave in July.

c) We experienced a heatwave in July.

d) During the month of July, the heatwave was extremely hot.

## Question 10

"He ran quickly to catch the bus that was just about to leave."

Which revision eliminates redundancy and improves the clarity of the sentence?

a) He quickly ran to catch the bus.

b) He ran to catch the bus that was about to leave.

c) He hurried to catch the bus that was about to leave.

d) He quickly ran to catch the departing bus.

## Question 11

"They have postponed the meeting until a later date."

Which revision eliminates redundancy and improves the clarity of the sentence?

a) They postponed the meeting.

b) They have postponed the meeting for now.

c) They rescheduled the meeting until later.

d) The meeting has been postponed until a later date.

## Question 12

"He added an extra extension to the end of the document."

Which revision eliminates redundancy and improves the clarity of the sentence?

a) He added an extra part to the document.

b) He extended the end of the document.

c) He added an extension to the document.

d) He added an extra extension to the document's end.

## Question 13

"The students all gathered together in the cafeteria for the announcement."

Which revision eliminates redundancy and improves the clarity of the sentence?

a) The students all gathered in the cafeteria for the announcement.

b) The students gathered together in the cafeteria for the announcement.

c) The students gathered in the cafeteria for the announcement.

d) The students all met in the cafeteria to gather for the announcement.

**Question 14**

"She always makes plans ahead of time to avoid last-minute rushes."

Which revision eliminates redundancy and improves the clarity of the sentence?

a) She always plans ahead to avoid last-minute rushes.

b) She always makes plans in advance to avoid last-minute rushes.

c) She plans ahead to avoid rushing at the last minute.

d) To avoid last-minute rushes, she always plans ahead of time.

**Question 15**

"He returned back home after a long day at work."

Which revision eliminates redundancy and improves the clarity of the sentence?

a) He returned back after a long day at work.

b) He came home after a long day at work.

c) He returned home after a long day at work.

d) After a long day at work, he returned back home.

# Section 5: Improving Paragraph Coherence

- **Description**: These questions will focus on making entire paragraphs more coherent, ensuring that every sentence contributes to the main point and flows logically.

- **Objective**: Help students understand how to revise paragraphs for better overall structure.

**Question 1**

Read the paragraph below:

*"The park is a wonderful place to relax. Many people visit the park to enjoy the fresh air and natural scenery. The city is known for its towering skyscrapers and bustling streets, making the park a perfect escape from the noise. In the evening, you can often hear birds chirping and see families having picnics on the grass."*

Which sentence should be removed to improve the paragraph's coherence?

a) The park is a wonderful place to relax.

b) Many people visit the park to enjoy the fresh air and natural scenery.

c) The city is known for its towering skyscrapers and bustling streets, making the park a perfect escape from the noise.

d) In the evening, you can often hear birds chirping and see families having picnics on the grass.

**Question 2**

Read the paragraph below:

*"The meeting was scheduled for 10 a.m. on Tuesday. Everyone was expected to arrive on time. John was late because of heavy traffic. The company offers great benefits, including health insurance and paid vacation days."*

Which sentence should be removed to improve the coherence of the paragraph?

a) The meeting was scheduled for 10 a.m. on Tuesday.

b) Everyone was expected to arrive on time.

c) John was late because of heavy traffic.

d) The company offers great benefits, including health insurance and paid vacation days.

**Question 3**

Read the paragraph below:

*"Many students struggle with time management during exams. They often feel rushed and unable to complete the test. The campus library is open 24 hours a day, which provides students with a place to study. Taking breaks between study sessions can help improve focus."*

Which sentence should be revised to improve the paragraph's coherence?

a) Many students struggle with time management during exams.

b) They often feel rushed and unable to complete the test.

c) The campus library is open 24 hours a day, which provides students with a place to study.

d) Taking breaks between study sessions can help improve focus.

## Question 4

Read the paragraph below:

*"Traveling can be a wonderful experience. You get to explore new places, meet different people, and try new foods. Traveling by train is a convenient way to see multiple cities in one trip. The climate is an important factor to consider when planning a trip."*

Which sentence should be removed to improve the paragraph's coherence?

a) Traveling can be a wonderful experience.

b) You get to explore new places, meet different people, and try new foods.

c) Traveling by train is a convenient way to see multiple cities in one trip.

d) The climate is an important factor to consider when planning a trip.

## Question 5

Read the paragraph below:

*"The company's new marketing strategy is designed to appeal to a younger audience. They are using social media platforms such as Instagram and TikTok. The cafeteria in the office building is being renovated to offer more food options. The goal is to increase brand awareness and engagement."*

Which sentence should be removed to improve the coherence of the paragraph?

a) The company's new marketing strategy is designed to appeal to a younger audience.

b) They are using social media platforms such as Instagram and TikTok.

c) The cafeteria in the office building is being renovated to offer more food options.

d) The goal is to increase brand awareness and engagement.

## Question 6

Read the paragraph below:

*"During the summer, many people enjoy outdoor activities. Hiking, biking, and swimming are popular choices. The local museum offers art classes for children. It's important to stay hydrated and wear sunscreen when spending time outside."*

Which sentence should be removed to improve paragraph coherence?

a) During the summer, many people enjoy outdoor activities.

b) Hiking, biking, and swimming are popular choices.

c) The local museum offers art classes for children.

d) It's important to stay hydrated and wear sunscreen when spending time outside.

## Question 7

Read the paragraph below:

*"Reading is one of the best ways to expand your knowledge. It allows you to explore new ideas and gain insights from different perspectives. The new shopping mall is expected to open next month. Reading can also improve your writing skills."*

Which sentence should be removed to improve the paragraph's coherence?

a) Reading is one of the best ways to expand your knowledge.

b) It allows you to explore new ideas and gain insights from different perspectives.

c) The new shopping mall is expected to open next month.

d) Reading can also improve your writing skills.

## Question 8

Read the paragraph below:

*"Technology has changed the way people communicate. Emails and instant messaging have replaced traditional mail. Smartphones allow us to stay connected at all times. Many people still enjoy sending handwritten letters."*

Which sentence disrupts the coherence of the paragraph?

a) Technology has changed the way people communicate.

b) Emails and instant messaging have replaced traditional mail.

c) Smartphones allow us to stay connected at all times.

d) Many people still enjoy sending handwritten letters.

## Question 9

Read the paragraph below:

*"The new restaurant in town has quickly become popular. The menu offers a variety of dishes, from seafood to vegetarian options. The park next to the restaurant is a great place to take a walk. The chef uses locally sourced ingredients."*

Which sentence should be removed to improve the coherence of the paragraph?

a) The new restaurant in town has quickly become popular.

b) The menu offers a variety of dishes, from seafood to vegetarian options.

c) The park next to the restaurant is a great place to take a walk.

d) The chef uses locally sourced ingredients.

## Question 10

Read the paragraph below:

*"Studying for exams requires dedication and focus. Creating a study schedule can help manage your time effectively. Taking short breaks between study sessions can improve focus. Some students prefer to study in groups, while others study alone."*

Which sentence should be removed to improve the coherence of the paragraph?

a) Studying for exams requires dedication and focus.

b) Creating a study schedule can help manage your time effectively.

c) Taking short breaks between study sessions can improve focus.

d) Some students prefer to study in groups, while others study alone.

## Question 11

Read the paragraph below:

*"Exercising regularly is important for maintaining good health. Running, swimming, and cycling are great ways to stay active. Cooking healthy meals is another important aspect of maintaining a balanced lifestyle. Regular exercise can also improve mental health."*

Which sentence should be removed to improve paragraph coherence?

a) Exercising regularly is important for maintaining good health.

b) Running, swimming, and cycling are great ways to stay active.

c) Cooking healthy meals is another important aspect of maintaining a balanced lifestyle.

d) Regular exercise can also improve mental health.

## Question 12

Read the paragraph below:

*"The history museum has an extensive collection of ancient artifacts. Visitors can learn about different civilizations and their cultures. The gift shop offers a range of unique souvenirs. The guided tours provide in-depth explanations of the exhibits."*

Which sentence should be removed to improve the coherence of the paragraph?

a) The history museum has an extensive collection of ancient artifacts.

b) Visitors can learn about different civilizations and their cultures.

c) The gift shop offers a range of unique souvenirs.

d) The guided tours provide in-depth explanations of the exhibits.

## Question 13

Read the paragraph below:

*"Exercise is crucial for maintaining physical health. Many people also find it a great way to reduce stress and improve mental clarity. Eating a balanced diet plays a key role in overall health. Studies show that regular physical activity can improve sleep quality."*

Which sentence should be removed to improve the paragraph's coherence?

a) Exercise is crucial for maintaining physical health.

b) Many people also find it a great way to reduce stress and improve mental clarity.

c) Eating a balanced diet plays a key role in overall health.

d) Studies show that regular physical activity can improve sleep quality.

## Question 14

Read the paragraph below:

*"The movie was an exciting thriller from beginning to end. The acting was excellent, and the plot was full of twists and turns. The soundtrack, however, was disappointing. It was a great way to spend an afternoon."*

Which sentence should be removed to improve paragraph coherence?

a) The movie was an exciting thriller from beginning to end.

b) The acting was excellent, and the plot was full of twists and turns.

c) The soundtrack, however, was disappointing.

d) It was a great way to spend an afternoon.

## Question 15

Read the paragraph below:

*"The environmental conference focused on addressing climate change. Speakers discussed renewable energy sources and sustainable practices. The venue for the conference was beautifully decorated with floral arrangements. Several initiatives to reduce carbon emissions were presented."*

Which sentence should be removed to improve the coherence of the paragraph?

a) The environmental conference focused on addressing climate change.

b) Speakers discussed renewable energy sources and sustainable practices.

c) The venue for the conference was beautifully decorated with floral arrangements.

d) Several initiatives to reduce carbon emissions were presented.

# Section 6: Correcting Punctuation and Grammar Errors

- **Description**: Focuses on revising sentences to correct punctuation, grammar, and sentence structure issues that may affect clarity and flow.

- **Objective**: Ensure students can spot and correct mechanical errors in writing.

## Question 1

Read the sentence below:

*"The scientist's research, which was groundbreaking changed the way we understand climate change."*

Which revision fixes the punctuation error while maintaining the sentence's meaning?

a) The scientist's research which was groundbreaking, changed the way we understand climate change.

b) The scientist's research, which was groundbreaking, changed the way we understand climate change.

c) The scientist's research that was groundbreaking changed the way we understand climate change.

d) The scientist's research which was groundbreaking changed the way we understand climate change.

## Question 2

Read the sentence below:

*"After finishing the report Sarah went home to rest."*

Which revision fixes the punctuation error while maintaining the sentence's meaning?

a) After finishing the report, Sarah went home to rest.

b) After finishing the report Sarah, went home to rest.

c) After finishing the report; Sarah went home to rest.

d) After finishing the report: Sarah went home to rest.

## Question 3

Read the sentence below:

*"The company plans to expand into new markets, however, they must first secure more funding."*

Which revision fixes the punctuation error while maintaining the sentence's meaning?

a) The company plans to expand into new markets however, they must first secure more funding.

b) The company plans to expand into new markets, however they must first secure more funding.

c) The company plans to expand into new markets; however, they must first secure more funding.

d) The company plans to expand into new markets: however they must first secure more funding.

## Question 4

Read the sentence below:

*"The book is about history, science, and, literature."*

Which revision fixes the punctuation error while maintaining the sentence's meaning?

a) The book is about history, science and literature.

b) The book is about history, science, and literature.

c) The book is about, history science, and literature.

d) The book is about: history, science, and literature.

## Question 5

Read the sentence below:

*"He's a great athlete, he won three gold medals at the Olympics."*

Which revision fixes the punctuation error while maintaining the sentence's meaning?

a) He's a great athlete; he won three gold medals at the Olympics.

b) He's a great athlete he won three gold medals at the Olympics.

c) He's a great athlete: he won three gold medals at the Olympics.

d) He's a great athlete. He won three gold medals at the Olympics.

## Question 6

Read the sentence below:

*"We wanted to go on vacation but, the weather was too bad."*

Which revision fixes the punctuation error while maintaining the sentence's meaning?

a) We wanted to go on vacation, but the weather was too bad.

b) We wanted to go on vacation, but, the weather was too bad.

c) We wanted to go on vacation; but, the weather was too bad.

d) We wanted to go on vacation but, the weather was too bad.

## Question 7

Read the sentence below:

*"There were three options available: green, blue and, red."*

Which revision fixes the punctuation error while maintaining the sentence's meaning?

a) There were three options available: green, blue, and red.

b) There were three options available: green blue, and red.

c) There were three options available: green, blue, and, red.

d) There were three options available; green, blue, and red.

## Question 8

Read the sentence below:

*"While driving to the store, I realized I had left my wallet at home"*

Which revision fixes the punctuation error while maintaining the sentence's meaning?

a) While driving to the store I realized, I had left my wallet at home.

b) While driving to the store, I realized, I had left my wallet at home.

c) While driving to the store I realized I had left my wallet at home.

d) While driving to the store, I realized I had left my wallet at home.

## Question 9

Read the sentence below:

*"My favorite activities include hiking swimming, and biking."*

Which revision fixes the punctuation error while maintaining the sentence's meaning?

a) My favorite activities include: hiking, swimming, and biking.

b) My favorite activities include hiking, swimming, and biking.

c) My favorite activities include hiking, swimming and biking.

d) My favorite activities include: hiking, swimming and biking.

## Question 10

Read the sentence below:

*"The meeting is scheduled for Monday, April 4th, at 10 a.m, please arrive on time."*

Which revision fixes the punctuation error while maintaining the sentence's meaning?

a) The meeting is scheduled for Monday, April 4th at 10 a.m., please arrive on time.

b) The meeting is scheduled for Monday, April 4th, at 10 a.m.; please arrive on time.

c) The meeting is scheduled for Monday, April 4th, at 10 a.m. please arrive on time.

d) The meeting is scheduled for Monday April 4th at 10 a.m., please arrive on time.

# Section 7: Replacing Vague Words with Specific Language

- **Description**: These exercises focus on identifying vague or unclear words and replacing them with more specific, precise terms.
- **Objective**: Enhance precision in writing by encouraging specific and meaningful word choices.

## Question 1

Read the sentence below:

*"The event was a big success, with many people attending."*

Which revision improves the sentence by replacing vague terms with specific details?

a) The event was a tremendous success, with hundreds of people attending.

b) The event was a big success, with several people attending.

c) The event was well-received, with a crowd attending.

d) The event was moderately successful, with many attending.

## Question 2

Read the sentence below:

*"He gave a nice speech during the ceremony."*

Which revision improves the sentence by replacing vague terms with specific details?

a) He gave a passionate speech during the ceremony.

b) He gave a somewhat nice speech during the ceremony.

c) He gave a nice and thoughtful speech during the ceremony.

d) He gave a speech during the ceremony.

## Question 3

Read the sentence below:

*"The artist's new painting is good."*

Which revision improves the sentence by replacing vague terms with specific details?

a) The artist's new painting is colorful.

b) The artist's new painting is interesting and unique.

c) The artist's new painting is captivating, featuring vivid colors and bold strokes.

d) The artist's new painting is good and pleasant.

## Question 4

Read the sentence below:

*"She had an interesting time at the conference."*

Which revision improves the sentence by replacing vague terms with specific details?

a) She had an informative and engaging experience at the conference.

b) She had an interesting and thought-provoking time at the conference.

c) She had a somewhat interesting time at the conference.

d) She had a great time at the conference.

## Question 5

Read the sentence below:

*"The restaurant offers many dishes."*

Which revision improves the sentence by replacing vague terms with specific details?

a) The restaurant offers a variety of dishes, including seafood, pasta, and vegan options.

b) The restaurant offers several dishes.

c) The restaurant offers many different dishes on its menu.

d) The restaurant offers a large number of dishes.

## Question 6

Read the sentence below:

*"The company made a lot of changes to the policy."*

Which revision improves the sentence by replacing vague terms with specific details?

a) The company made numerous changes to the policy.

b) The company made significant changes to the policy, including adjustments to work hours and vacation benefits.

c) The company made a lot of minor and major changes to the policy.

d) The company made important changes to the policy.

## Question 7

Read the sentence below:

*"She had a big problem with her project."*

Which revision improves the sentence by replacing vague terms with specific details?

a) She had a major problem with the budget for her project.

b) She had a huge issue with her project.

c) She had a big and complicated problem with her project.

d) She had a significant problem with her project.

## Question 8

Read the sentence below:

*"The presentation was good, and people liked it."*

Which revision improves the sentence by replacing vague terms with specific details?

a) The presentation was informative, and the audience was engaged.

b) The presentation was well done, and people appreciated it.

c) The presentation was good, and the crowd seemed interested.

d) The presentation was nice, and people liked it.

## Question 9

Read the sentence below:

*"The car drove fast down the road."*

Which revision improves the sentence by replacing vague terms with specific details?

a) The car sped down the road at 80 miles per hour.

b) The car moved fast down the road.

c) The car quickly drove down the road.

d) The car traveled at a high speed down the road.

## Question 10

Read the sentence below:

*"He completed the project quickly and with good results."*

Which revision improves the sentence by replacing vague terms with specific details?

a) He completed the project efficiently and delivered excellent results.

b) He completed the project fast and well.

c) He completed the project quickly with decent results.

d) He finished the project fast and with good work.

## Conclusion Practice

• **Recap**: A reminder to students about the importance of revising their writing to ensure clarity and coherence. It's essential to focus on making ideas clear, concise, and easy to follow.

• **Tips**:

   • **Focus on clarity**: Avoid using overly complex sentence structures that might confuse the reader. Ensure every sentence clearly conveys the intended meaning without ambiguity.

- **Use transitions effectively**: Use appropriate transition words and phrases to connect ideas smoothly. This will help maintain a logical flow throughout the passage, allowing readers to follow the argument or narrative without disruption.

- **Be concise**: Eliminate any redundant or unnecessary words that don't add value to the sentence. Keeping sentences direct and to the point makes the writing more engaging and impactful, helping the reader grasp the message quickly.

This final practice section ensures that students apply these core principles to make their writing coherent and compelling in the SAT context.

# CHAPTER 7: FULL-LENGTH PRACTICE TESTS

## 7.1 Two Full-Length Practice Tests with Detailed Solutions

# TEST 1: 108 QUESTIONS

**Overview:**

This full-length practice test is designed to reflect the format, structure, and difficulty of the SAT Reading and Writing sections. The goal is to provide students with a realistic testing experience that will help them become familiar with the types of questions, passages, and time management skills required to succeed on the SAT. Students are encouraged to take this test under timed conditions to simulate the actual exam, and use it as a way to gauge their current level of preparedness.

**Section 1: Reading Comprehension**

The Reading Comprehension section is divided into four passages: **narrative**, **social science**, **natural science**, and **historical document**. Each passage will be followed by a set of multiple-choice questions that assess a range of reading skills, including inference, understanding the tone, identifying the main idea, vocabulary in context, and analyzing text structure.

**Narrative Passage**

- **Focus**: General understanding of plot, character development, relationships, and the emotional tone of the narrative.
- **Question Types**:
  - Inference questions (e.g., "What can be inferred about the character's motivation?")
  - Tone questions (e.g., "What is the tone of the passage?")
  - Main idea (e.g., "What is the central theme of the passage?")

**Social Science Passage**

- **Focus**: Understanding social theories, historical contexts, and societal trends.
- **Question Types**:
  - Evidence-based questions (e.g., "Which sentence provides the strongest support for the author's argument?")
  - Main idea questions (e.g., "What is the primary conclusion drawn by the author?")
  - Argumentation analysis (e.g., "What evidence does the author use to support their argument?")

**Natural Science Passage**

- **Focus**: Scientific research, experiments, theories, and technical data.
- **Question Types**:
  - Understanding scientific concepts (e.g., "What is the hypothesis being tested in the experiment described?")
  - Interpretation of data and graphs (e.g., "What can be concluded from the data presented in the graph?")
  - Vocabulary in context (e.g., "What does the word 'catalyst' mean in the context of the passage?")

**Historical Document Passage**

- **Focus**: Political speeches, legal documents, or significant historical texts.
- **Question Types**:
  - Analysis of author's intent (e.g., "What was the author's purpose in delivering this speech?")
  - Comparison of historical perspectives (e.g., "How does the author's perspective differ from that of another historical figure?")
  - Inference about historical context (e.g., "What can be inferred about the social conditions at the time of the document's writing?")

# Narrative Passage: 12 Questions

## 1. Inference Question

- **Question**: What can be inferred about the protagonist's motivation for leaving their hometown?
- **Options**: A) They wanted to pursue a new career. B) They had a deep desire for adventure. C) They were running away from a conflict. D) They were influenced by a friend's advice.

## 2. Tone Question

- **Question**: What tone does the author use in describing the protagonist's journey?
- **Options**: A) Optimistic B) Cynical C) Reflective D) Indifferent

## 3. Main Idea Question

- **Question**: What is the central theme of the passage?
- **Options**: A) The challenges of finding one's true identity B) The importance of community support C) The inevitability of change D) The value of perseverance in the face of adversity

## 4. Character Development Question

- **Question**: How does the protagonist's attitude towards their family change throughout the passage?
- **Options**: A) From resentment to understanding B) From admiration to disappointment C) From indifference to love D) From frustration to acceptance

## 5. Relationship Question

- **Question**: What best describes the relationship between the protagonist and their sibling?
- **Options**: A) Supportive but distant B) Close and trusting C) Competitive and strained D) Affectionate yet conflicted

## 6. Inference Question

- **Question**: What can be inferred about the significance of the protagonist's choice to visit the old house?
- **Options**: A) They are trying to relive past memories. B) They are seeking closure from past conflicts. C) They wish to show their family they've changed. D) They are trying to impress a new friend.

## 7. Tone Question

- **Question**: How does the tone of the passage shift after the protagonist speaks with their sibling?
- **Options**: A) From anxious to relieved B) From hopeful to defeated C) From calm to agitated D) From nostalgic to regretful

## 8. Main Idea Question

- **Question**: What is the main conflict presented in the passage?
- **Options**: A) The protagonist's struggle between personal ambition and family expectations B) The difficulty of maintaining friendships over time C) The tension between the protagonist and their parents over life choices D) The challenge of starting a new life in a different place

## 9. Character Development Question

- **Question**: Which event marks the turning point in the protagonist's personal growth?
- **Options**: A) Leaving their hometown B) Confronting a childhood friend C) Reconnecting with their sibling D) Returning to their childhood home

## 10. Relationship Question

- **Question**: How does the protagonist's relationship with their mentor influence the decisions they make?
- **Options**: A) They seek their mentor's approval at every step. B) They defy their mentor's advice to follow their own path. C) Their mentor encourages them to take risks. D) Their mentor's absence drives them to succeed on their own.

## 11. Inference Question

- **Question**: What is implied about the protagonist's future at the end of the passage?
- **Options**: A) They will continue to struggle with the same internal conflicts. B) They have made peace with their past and are ready to move forward. C) They will return home to make amends. D) They are likely to revert to their old habits.

## 12. Tone Question

- **Question**: What best describes the author's tone in the final paragraph?
- **Options**: A) Hopeful B) Wistful C) Bitter D) Detached

# Social Science Passage: 14 Questions

## 1. Main Idea Question

- **Question**: What is the primary conclusion drawn by the author in the passage regarding the impact of urbanization on society?
- **Options**: A) Urbanization has led to more equitable access to resources. B) Urbanization has intensified economic inequality and segregation. C) Urbanization has fostered greater cultural exchange and understanding. D) Urbanization has had little impact on societal structures.

## 2. Evidence-Based Question

- **Question**: Which sentence provides the strongest support for the claim that income inequality has worsened in urban centers?
- **Options**: A) "Many cities have experienced unprecedented economic growth over the past decades." B) "The gap between the wealthiest and poorest residents in urban areas continues to widen." C) "Educational institutions in urban areas offer diverse opportunities for residents." D) "Public transportation systems have expanded, allowing greater mobility."

## 3. Argumentation Analysis Question

- **Question**: What evidence does the author use to support their argument that urban policies have failed to address housing shortages?
- **Options**: A) The author cites examples of cities that have improved housing access through zoning reforms. B) The author references government reports showing a steady increase in homelessness

rates. C) The author discusses the rise of new housing developments in suburban areas. D) The author points to surveys indicating widespread public dissatisfaction with urban living conditions.

## 4. Inference Question

- **Question**: Based on the passage, what can be inferred about the relationship between urbanization and public health?
- **Options**: A) Urbanization has generally improved public health by providing better access to healthcare facilities. B) Urbanization has led to public health crises due to overcrowding and insufficient services. C) Urbanization has had no significant effect on public health. D) Public health concerns are unrelated to the effects of urbanization.

## 5. Main Idea Question

- **Question**: What is the author's central argument regarding the role of technology in urban planning?
- **Options**: A) Technology has played a minimal role in recent urban planning initiatives. B) Technological advancements have revolutionized urban planning but have not solved fundamental issues. C) Technology has largely been ignored in discussions about urban development. D) Technology has successfully solved many of the challenges facing modern cities.

## 6. Evidence-Based Question

- **Question**: Which sentence provides the best evidence to support the claim that transportation developments have failed to keep pace with population growth?
- **Options**: A) "Public transportation systems in most major cities are outdated and overcrowded." B) "Private vehicle ownership continues to rise, contributing to traffic congestion." C) "New subway systems have been implemented in various metropolitan areas." D) "Many cities are introducing bike lanes and pedestrian-friendly zones."

## 7. Argumentation Analysis Question

- **Question**: How does the author support their argument that educational inequality persists in urban areas?
- **Options**: A) The author provides examples of underfunded schools in low-income neighborhoods. B) The author highlights disparities in the curriculum between urban and rural schools. C) The author discusses the availability of online education platforms. D) The author references historical studies on the development of public education.

## 8. Inference Question

- **Question**: What can be inferred about the author's view on the future of urban growth?
- **Options**: A) The author is optimistic that cities will adapt to the challenges of the future. B) The author is pessimistic about the ability of cities to manage continued growth. C) The author believes urban growth will stabilize over the next few decades. D) The author thinks technological advancements will solve most urban issues.

## 9. Main Idea Question

- **Question**: What is the main purpose of the passage?
- **Options**: A) To argue that urbanization has been overwhelmingly positive for society. B) To present both the benefits and challenges of rapid urbanization. C) To advocate for increased government intervention in urban development. D) To highlight the environmental consequences of urban growth.

## 10. Evidence-Based Question

- **Question**: Which sentence provides the strongest support for the claim that urban areas are more vulnerable to climate change?
- **Options**: A) "Many cities have implemented measures to reduce their carbon footprint." B) "Urban centers are often located in regions prone to flooding and extreme weather." C) "Rural areas experience similar challenges related to climate change." D) "Cities have more resources available to address environmental issues."

## 11. Argumentation Analysis Question

- **Question**: How does the author use data to support their claim about rising crime rates in urban areas?
- **Options**: A) The author provides personal anecdotes to illustrate the increase in crime. B) The author presents statistics showing an upward trend in crime rates in several major cities. C) The author discusses recent policy changes aimed at reducing crime. D) The author references news reports about high-profile criminal cases.

## 12. Inference Question

- **Question**: What can be inferred about the author's stance on gentrification in urban areas?
- **Options**: A) The author believes gentrification has led to significant social benefits. B) The author views gentrification as a necessary part of urban development. C) The author is critical of gentrification's impact on low-income communities. D) The author does not address the issue of gentrification.

## 13. Evidence-Based Question

- **Question**: Which sentence provides the strongest support for the argument that public spaces are essential for urban social cohesion?
- **Options**: A) "Public parks and squares offer residents a place to gather and interact." B) "Many cities have invested in creating new public spaces." C) "Urban areas with more public spaces tend to report higher levels of civic engagement." D) "Private spaces, such as shopping malls, have replaced traditional public spaces in many cities."

## 14. Main Idea Question

- **Question**: What is the author's primary concern about the future of urban development?
- **Options**: A) The lack of green spaces in rapidly growing cities B) The unequal distribution of resources between urban and rural areas C) The increasing isolation of urban residents from one another D) The challenges of managing population growth in urban centers

# Natural Science Passage: 14 Questions

## 1. Understanding Scientific Concepts

- **Question**: What is the hypothesis being tested in the experiment described in the passage?
- **Options**: A) That increased sunlight exposure leads to faster plant growth. B) That temperature variations have no effect on chemical reactions. C) That the presence of a catalyst speeds up the reaction time of certain processes. D) That genetic mutations occur at a steady rate regardless of environmental factors.

## 2. Interpretation of Data

- **Question**: Based on the data presented in the graph, what conclusion can be drawn about the relationship between temperature and enzyme activity?

- **Options**: A) Enzyme activity increases as temperature decreases. B) Enzyme activity remains constant across all temperature ranges. C) Enzyme activity increases with temperature up to a certain point, then decreases. D) Enzyme activity is unaffected by temperature changes.

## 3. Vocabulary in Context

- **Question**: What does the word "catalyst" mean in the context of the experiment discussed?
- **Options**: A) A substance that slows down a chemical reaction. B) A substance that initiates or accelerates a chemical reaction. C) A compound that reacts with the enzyme to form a new product. D) An element that is consumed during the reaction.

## 4. Understanding Scientific Concepts

- **Question**: What is the primary function of the control group in the experiment?
- **Options**: A) To ensure that the experimental conditions remain constant. B) To provide a baseline for comparison with the experimental group. C) To increase the accuracy of the experimental results. D) To eliminate the possibility of human error.

## 5. Interpretation of Data

- **Question**: Based on the chart presented in the passage, which variable shows the strongest correlation with the rate of photosynthesis?
- **Options**: A) Water availability B) Light intensity C) Carbon dioxide concentration D) Soil composition

## 6. Vocabulary in Context

- **Question**: In the passage, the word "molecule" is used. What is the most accurate meaning of the term "molecule" in this context?
- **Options**: A) A large structure composed of atoms bonded together. B) A tiny particle that carries a charge. C) A single atom involved in a chemical reaction. D) A unit of measurement used in chemical experiments.

## 7. Understanding Scientific Concepts

- **Question**: What was the main purpose of the experiment described in the passage?
- **Options**: A) To determine the effects of gravity on plant growth. B) To measure the impact of varying water levels on plant survival. C) To examine the role of light in cellular respiration. D) To explore how different nutrients affect soil bacteria.

## 8. Interpretation of Data

- **Question**: The graph shows that as the concentration of substance A increases, the reaction rate also increases. What conclusion can be drawn from this information?
- **Options**: A) The reaction rate is independent of the concentration of substance A. B) Substance A inhibits the reaction rate. C) The reaction rate depends directly on the concentration of substance A. D) The reaction rate decreases as the concentration of substance A increases.

## 9. Vocabulary in Context

- **Question**: What does the term "reaction rate" mean in the context of the passage?
- **Options**: A) The time it takes for the experiment to conclude. B) The speed at which a chemical reaction occurs. C) The ratio of reactants to products in a chemical reaction. D) The change in temperature during the reaction.

## 10. Understanding Scientific Concepts

- **Question**: What variable did the researchers manipulate to test their hypothesis?

- **Options**: A) The amount of sunlight each plant received. B) The type of soil used in the experiment. C) The presence or absence of a specific enzyme. D) The amount of water given to the control group.

## 11. Interpretation of Data

- **Question**: Based on the chart in the passage, what is the relationship between the number of trials conducted and the accuracy of the results?
- **Options**: A) More trials lead to less accurate results. B) Fewer trials result in more reliable data. C) The number of trials does not affect the accuracy of the results. D) Increasing the number of trials improves the reliability of the results.

## 12. Vocabulary in Context

- **Question**: In the passage, the word "variable" is used. What is the best definition of "variable" in this context?
- **Options**: A) An unknown quantity in the experiment. B) A factor that can be changed or controlled in the experiment. C) A fixed number used for calculations. D) A measurement of the final outcome.

## 13. Understanding Scientific Concepts

- **Question**: What role did the experimental group play in the study described in the passage?
- **Options**: A) The experimental group was used to replicate the conditions of the control group. B) The experimental group was exposed to the independent variable to test its effect. C) The experimental group provided baseline data for comparison. D) The experimental group introduced a new factor not originally included in the hypothesis.

## 14. Interpretation of Data

- **Question**: The graph shows a rapid increase in growth rate as temperature rises from 10°C to 30°C, but a sharp decline beyond 35°C. What can be concluded about the ideal temperature for growth?
- **Options**: A) Growth rate is highest at temperatures above 40°C. B) The ideal growth temperature is between 10°C and 20°C. C) Growth rate peaks between 30°C and 35°C. D) Temperature has no effect on the growth rate.

# Historical Document Passage: 14 Questions

## 1. Analysis of Author's Intent

- **Question**: What was the author's primary purpose in delivering this speech?
- **Options**: A) To inspire national unity and support for the war effort. B) To criticize government policies and propose alternatives. C) To encourage peaceful negotiations between opposing factions. D) To celebrate a historical milestone and reflect on progress made.

## 2. Comparison of Historical Perspectives

- **Question**: How does the author's perspective on democracy differ from that of another political leader mentioned in the passage?
- **Options**: A) The author believes in a limited government, while the other leader supports a centralized system. B) The author emphasizes individual rights, while the other leader focuses on collective responsibility. C) The author advocates for direct democracy, while the other leader

favors representative democracy. D) The author sees democracy as fragile, while the other leader views it as robust and evolving.

## 3. Inference about Historical Context

- **Question**: Based on the passage, what can be inferred about the social conditions at the time of the document's writing?
- **Options**: A) There was widespread support for the author's ideas. B) The society was deeply divided along political and ideological lines. C) The population was largely unaware of the issues being discussed. D) Economic prosperity had eliminated most social tensions.

## 4. Analysis of Rhetorical Strategies

- **Question**: Which rhetorical strategy does the author use most effectively to persuade the audience?
- **Options**: A) Appeal to authority B) Use of emotional language C) Logical reasoning and evidence D) Appeal to national identity and pride

## 5. Comparison of Ideals

- **Question**: How does the author's view of liberty compare to the ideas presented in another historical document mentioned in the passage?
- **Options**: A) The author views liberty as a natural right, while the other document suggests it must be earned through loyalty. B) The author advocates for absolute liberty, while the other document supports limited freedoms in the interest of security. C) The author believes liberty should be granted universally, while the other document argues for selective application. D) The author stresses individual freedoms, while the other document emphasizes societal obligations.

## 6. Inference about the Audience

- **Question**: What can be inferred about the intended audience of the document based on its tone and content?
- **Options**: A) The audience was composed of political elites and government officials. B) The audience was a general public in need of motivation and reassurance. C) The document was meant for foreign diplomats and international allies. D) The audience was primarily skeptics of the government's policies.

## 7. Analysis of Historical Impact

- **Question**: What impact did the author's ideas, as expressed in the document, have on subsequent political movements?
- **Options**: A) The ideas sparked widespread protests and political reforms. B) The ideas were ignored at the time but gained popularity decades later. C) The ideas were embraced by political leaders and enacted into law. D) The ideas led to the downfall of the author's political career.

## 8. Interpretation of Legal Language

- **Question**: In the context of the document, what does the term "inalienable rights" most likely mean?
- **Options**: A) Rights that can be surrendered under certain conditions. B) Rights that cannot be taken away or transferred. C) Rights granted only by legal authority. D) Rights that apply only to a specific group of people.

## 9. Analysis of Author's Bias

- **Question**: How does the author's background influence their perspective in the document?
- **Options**: A) The author's experiences in the military led to a focus on security over freedom. B) The author's economic status influenced their argument for social reform. C) The author's political

affiliation is reflected in their strong critique of the opposition. D) The author's personal connections to the monarchy shaped their views on governance.

10. **Comparison of Political Ideologies**

- **Question**: How does the political ideology expressed in this document compare to the principles of the Enlightenment?
- **Options**: A) The document rejects Enlightenment ideals of individualism in favor of collective good. B) The document builds on Enlightenment ideas by promoting reason and equality. C) The document embraces Enlightenment concepts but focuses on economic prosperity over liberty. D) The document contradicts Enlightenment values by advocating for authoritarian rule.

11. **Inference about Social Hierarchy**

- **Question**: What can be inferred about the social hierarchy during the time the document was written?
- **Options**: A) Power was concentrated in the hands of a small elite. B) There was relative social equality across different classes. C) The middle class played a dominant role in political affairs. D) The document suggests that wealth was distributed evenly across the population.

12. **Analysis of Historical Significance**

- **Question**: Why is the document considered a turning point in the nation's political history?
- **Options**: A) It marked the first time democratic ideals were put into law. B) It led to widespread social and economic reforms. C) It shifted the balance of power between government branches. D) It ended decades of political and social unrest.

13. **Inference about Future Implications**

- **Question**: Based on the author's predictions, what did they foresee as the future implications of their proposed changes?
- **Options**: A) The changes would lead to greater international conflict. B) The changes would bring about lasting peace and prosperity. C) The changes would be quickly reversed due to public resistance. D) The changes would slowly transform the political system over time.

14. **Analysis of Argument Structure**

- **Question**: How does the author structure their argument to persuade the audience of the necessity of their proposed reforms?
- **Options**: A) By presenting a series of logical steps that build on one another. B) By appealing to the audience's emotions and sense of patriotism. C) By focusing on historical examples of failed policies. D) By outlining the moral and ethical implications of the current system.

## Section 2: Writing and Language

**Overview:**

This section will focus on assessing students' understanding of grammar, sentence structure, punctuation, logical flow, and clarity. The goal is to simulate the questions seen on the SAT Writing and Language section, which emphasizes editing and revising passages for grammatical correctness, coherence, and overall readability.

**Time Management Instructions:**

- Provide students with guidelines for pacing each section. Break down the ideal amount of time to spend on each question, suggesting they spend roughly 30 seconds to 1 minute per question depending on its complexity. Remind them to use the SAT clock wisely and to move on from difficult questions if they are stuck, returning to them later if time permits.

This structure will provide a realistic simulation of the SAT Writing and Language section while also focusing on essential skills such as grammar, punctuation, clarity, and logical flow.

# Grammar and Sentence Structure (15 Questions)

1. **Subject-verb agreement:**
   - "Which sentence maintains proper subject-verb agreement?"
   - (A) The team of scientists are studying new materials for space exploration.
   - (B) The team of scientists is studying new materials for space exploration.
   - (C) The team of scientists studying new materials for space exploration.
   - (D) The teams of scientists is studying new materials for space exploration.

2. **Parallel structure:**
   - "Which option maintains the parallelism in this list?"
   - (A) She enjoys running, swimming, and to hike.
   - (B) She enjoys running, swimming, and hiking.
   - (C) She enjoys to run, swimming, and hiking.
   - (D) She enjoys running, to swim, and hiking.

3. **Misplaced modifiers:**
   - "Which revision correctly places the modifier?"
   - (A) Staring into the sunset, the boat was a peaceful sight.
   - (B) The boat was a peaceful sight, staring into the sunset.
   - (C) Staring into the sunset, the passengers found the boat to be a peaceful sight.
   - (D) The boat was a peaceful sight to the passengers staring into the sunset.

4. **Verb tense consistency:**
   - "Which sentence uses verb tenses consistently?"
   - (A) She walked to the park and eats lunch on the bench.
   - (B) She walked to the park and ate lunch on the bench.
   - (C) She walks to the park and had eaten lunch on the bench.
   - (D) She had walked to the park and eats lunch on the bench.

5. **Pronoun-antecedent agreement:**
   - "Which sentence correctly matches the pronoun with its antecedent?"
   - (A) Each of the students must bring their own materials.
   - (B) Each of the students must bring his or her own materials.
   - (C) Each of the students must bring its own materials.
   - (D) Each of the students must bring our own materials.

6. **Sentence clarity:**
   - "Which revision best clarifies the meaning of the sentence?"
   - (A) The athlete who won the race while injured inspired everyone.
   - (B) The injured athlete who won the race inspired everyone.

- o (C) The race was won by the injured athlete who inspired everyone.
- o (D) The athlete, while injured, inspired everyone by winning the race.

7. **Punctuation:**
   - o "Which option uses the comma correctly?"
   - o (A) The book, that I borrowed from the library is due tomorrow.
   - o (B) The book, that I borrowed from the library, is due tomorrow.
   - o (C) The book that I borrowed, from the library, is due tomorrow.
   - o (D) The book that I borrowed from the library is due tomorrow.

8. **Correct use of conjunctions:**
   - o "Which sentence uses the conjunction correctly?"
   - o (A) She wanted to go to the beach or she had to work.
   - o (B) She wanted to go to the beach, but she had to work.
   - o (C) She wanted to go to the beach, and had to work.
   - o (D) She wanted to go to the beach, so she had to work.

9. **Identifying sentence fragments:**
   - o "Which option fixes the sentence fragment?"
   - o (A) Running through the park in the evening.
   - o (B) She enjoyed running through the park in the evening.
   - o (C) Running through the park, it was peaceful.
   - o (D) Through the park, running in the evening.

10. **Correct use of adjectives and adverbs:**
    - o "Which sentence uses the adverb correctly?"
    - o (A) He is real fast at solving math problems.
    - o (B) He is really fast at solving math problems.
    - o (C) He solves math problems real fast.
    - o (D) He solves math problems really fastly.

11. **Subject-pronoun agreement:**
    - o "Which sentence uses the correct pronoun?"
    - o (A) The team decided they would practice more.
    - o (B) The team decided it would practice more.
    - o (C) The team decided we would practice more.
    - o (D) The team decided you would practice more.

12. **Consistency of style:**
    - o "Which sentence maintains the same style throughout?"
    - o (A) After she finished the report, she was congratulated by her supervisor, and then goes to celebrate.
    - o (B) After she finished the report, she was congratulated by her supervisor, and then went to celebrate.
    - o (C) After she finishes the report, she was congratulated by her supervisor, and then went to celebrate.

- o (D) After she finished the report, her supervisor congratulates her, and she then went to celebrate.

13. **Correct usage of prepositions:**
    - o "Which sentence uses the preposition correctly?"
    - o (A) She is interested with learning new languages.
    - o (B) She is interested in learning new languages.
    - o (C) She is interested on learning new languages.
    - o (D) She is interested by learning new languages.

14. **Run-on sentences:**
    - o "Which option corrects the run-on sentence?"
    - o (A) The sun was setting the sky turned orange.
    - o (B) The sun was setting, and the sky turned orange.
    - o (C) The sun was setting but, the sky turned orange.
    - o (D) The sun was setting, the sky turned orange.

15. **Use of conjunctions in complex sentences:**
    - o "Which sentence uses the conjunction correctly?"
    - o (A) I'll visit you tomorrow because I'm not busy.
    - o (B) I'll visit you tomorrow, because I'm not busy.
    - o (C) I'll visit you tomorrow if I'm not busy.
    - o (D) I'll visit you tomorrow, if I'm not busy.

# Section: Punctuation and Capitalization (15 Questions)

1. **Comma usage in lists:**
   - o "Which sentence uses commas correctly to separate items in a list?"
   - o (A) I need to buy apples, oranges and bananas.
   - o (B) I need to buy apples, oranges, and bananas.
   - o (C) I need to buy, apples oranges, and bananas.
   - o (D) I need to buy apples, oranges, bananas.

2. **Comma usage with introductory phrases:**
   - o "Which sentence uses commas correctly after an introductory phrase?"
   - o (A) Before starting the project she reviewed all the guidelines.
   - o (B) Before starting the project, she reviewed all the guidelines.
   - o (C) Before, starting the project, she reviewed all the guidelines.
   - o (D) Before starting, the project, she reviewed all the guidelines.

3. **Comma usage with non-essential clauses:**
   - o "Which sentence uses commas correctly to set off non-essential information?"
   - o (A) My brother, who is a doctor is coming to visit.
   - o (B) My brother who is a doctor, is coming to visit.
   - o (C) My brother, who is a doctor, is coming to visit.
   - o (D) My brother who, is a doctor, is coming to visit.

4. **Semicolon usage:**
   o "Which sentence uses a semicolon correctly to connect two independent clauses?"
   o (A) The meeting is over; now we can head home.
   o (B) The meeting is over, now; we can head home.
   o (C) The meeting is over; and now we can head home.
   o (D) The meeting is over: now we can head home.

5. **Colon usage:**
   o "Which sentence uses a colon correctly to introduce a list?"
   o (A) We need the following supplies: pencils, paper, and rulers.
   o (B) We need: the following supplies, pencils, paper, and rulers.
   o (C) We need the following: supplies, pencils, paper, and rulers.
   o (D) We need the following supplies; pencils, paper, and rulers.

6. **Apostrophe usage in singular possessives:**
   o "Which sentence properly indicates possession?"
   o (A) The dogs' collar was too tight.
   o (B) The dog's collar was too tight.
   o (C) The dogs collar's was too tight.
   o (D) The dog's collars' were too tight.

7. **Apostrophe usage in plural possessives:**
   o "Which sentence uses apostrophes correctly for plural possessives?"
   o (A) The teachers' lounge is on the second floor.
   o (B) The teacher's lounge is on the second floor.
   o (C) The teachers lounge is on the second floor.
   o (D) The teachers lounge's is on the second floor.

8. **Comma usage in compound sentences:**
   o "Which sentence correctly places a comma in a compound sentence?"
   o (A) She enjoys reading and, she loves painting.
   o (B) She enjoys reading, and she loves painting.
   o (C) She enjoys reading and she loves, painting.
   o (D) She, enjoys reading and she loves painting.

9. **Comma usage with conjunctions:**
   o "Which sentence correctly uses a comma with a conjunction?"
   o (A) We went to the park, and played soccer.
   o (B) We went to the park and, played soccer.
   o (C) We went to the park, and we played soccer.
   o (D) We went to the park and played, soccer.

10. **Correct usage of dashes:**
    o "Which sentence uses a dash correctly for emphasis?"
    o (A) The result was clear—it was a success.
    o (B) The result—was clear, it was a success.

- o (C) The result was clear it was—a success.
- o (D) The result was clear—it was, a success.

11. **Parentheses usage:**
    - o "Which sentence uses parentheses correctly to include additional information?"
    - o (A) He studied physics (and chemistry) in college.
    - o (B) He studied (physics) and chemistry in college.
    - o (C) He studied physics and chemistry (in college).
    - o (D) He studied physics (and chemistry in college).

12. **Comma usage in dates:**
    - o "Which sentence uses commas correctly in a date?"
    - o (A) She was born on May 25, 1995 in Chicago.
    - o (B) She was born on May, 25 1995, in Chicago.
    - o (C) She was born on May 25, 1995, in Chicago.
    - o (D) She was born on May 25 1995, in Chicago.

13. **Capitalization in titles:**
    - o "Which sentence uses capitalization correctly in a title?"
    - o (A) We read the book, "To Kill a Mockingbird."
    - o (B) We read the book, "to Kill a Mockingbird."
    - o (C) We read the book, "To kill A Mockingbird."
    - o (D) We read the book, "to kill a Mockingbird."

14. **Correct placement of commas in addresses:**
    - o "Which sentence uses commas correctly in an address?"
    - o (A) She lives at 123 Main Street, Chicago Illinois.
    - o (B) She lives at 123 Main Street Chicago, Illinois.
    - o (C) She lives at 123 Main Street, Chicago, Illinois.
    - o (D) She lives at 123, Main Street, Chicago Illinois.

15. **Quotation marks and punctuation:**
    - o "Which sentence correctly places the punctuation inside the quotation marks?"
    - o (A) "The project is due on Friday," she said.
    - o (B) "The project is due on Friday", she said.
    - o (C) "The project is due on Friday" she said.
    - o (D) "The project is due on Friday"; she said.

# Section: Logical Flow and Coherence (12 Questions)

1. **Improving transitions between paragraphs:**
   - o "Which sentence best improves the transition between these two paragraphs?"
   - o (A) Moreover, this policy will reduce environmental impact.
   - o (B) Consequently, the project's failure resulted in significant delays.
   - o (C) In contrast, the results of the second study support the previous hypothesis.
   - o (D) However, the evidence provided does not align with the author's original argument.

2. **Reordering sentences for logical flow:**
   - "Which sentence should be moved to improve the flow of ideas in this paragraph?"
   - (A) Sentence 1 should be moved after Sentence 3 to establish the main argument earlier.
   - (B) Sentence 2 should be moved to the beginning to provide a clear introduction.
   - (C) Sentence 4 should be placed before Sentence 2 to clarify the argument.
   - (D) Sentence 3 should be moved to the end to summarize the paragraph more effectively.

3. **Choosing the best transition between ideas:**
   - "Which sentence best transitions between the ideas in these two paragraphs?"
   - (A) Although this solution was proposed, it failed to address the underlying issues.
   - (B) Following this recommendation, the team proceeded with the implementation phase.
   - (C) As a result, the project gained widespread support from stakeholders.
   - (D) Similarly, the results of the second experiment reinforced the initial findings.

4. **Reordering sentences for improved clarity:**
   - "Which revision improves the clarity and logical sequence of the paragraph?"
   - (A) Move the third sentence to the beginning to clearly establish the central idea.
   - (B) Combine the first and second sentences to streamline the explanation.
   - (C) Move the fourth sentence to the end to reinforce the concluding thought.
   - (D) Rearrange the second and third sentences to clarify the progression of ideas.

5. **Improving transitions between sentences:**
   - "Which transition phrase best connects the two sentences?"
   - (A) Despite this evidence,
   - (B) As a result,
   - (C) In other words,
   - (D) Conversely,

6. **Revising for logical flow within a paragraph:**
   - "Which sentence should be removed to improve the logical flow of the paragraph?"
   - (A) Sentence 2 because it interrupts the explanation of the main idea.
   - (B) Sentence 3 because it introduces unrelated information.
   - (C) Sentence 4 because it repeats information already provided.
   - (D) Sentence 5 because it fails to connect with the other sentences.

7. **Choosing the best conclusion to a paragraph:**
   - "Which sentence best concludes the paragraph by summarizing the key points?"
   - (A) In conclusion, the experiment's outcome provided critical insights for future research.
   - (B) Therefore, the data collected did not align with the expected results.
   - (C) Consequently, the team was unable to replicate the previous findings.
   - (D) For these reasons, the project was considered a partial success.

8. **Reordering paragraphs for better coherence:**
   - "Which paragraph should be placed first to introduce the main argument of the passage?"
   - (A) Paragraph 2 because it introduces the background information.
   - (B) Paragraph 3 because it explains the research methodology.

- o (C) Paragraph 1 because it presents the main thesis of the passage.
- o (D) Paragraph 4 because it summarizes the conclusion.

9. **Identifying irrelevant sentences in a paragraph:**
   - o "Which sentence could be removed without affecting the overall meaning of the paragraph?"
   - o (A) Sentence 2 because it introduces unnecessary details.
   - o (B) Sentence 3 because it disrupts the flow of the argument.
   - o (C) Sentence 4 because it is not relevant to the main point.
   - o (D) Sentence 5 because it repeats information from earlier in the passage.

10. **Improving the coherence of a paragraph:**
    - o "Which revision best improves the logical flow and coherence of the paragraph?"
    - o (A) Rearrange the sentences to ensure the central argument is presented first.
    - o (B) Remove the third sentence as it introduces an unrelated topic.
    - o (C) Combine the second and fourth sentences to create a stronger connection between ideas.
    - o (D) Add a transition word between the first and second sentences to clarify the relationship between them.

11. **Improving the clarity of transitions between ideas:**
    - o "Which revision best clarifies the transition from one idea to the next?"
    - o (A) Adding a contrasting phrase like "However, this result was unexpected."
    - o (B) Rewording the sentence to introduce a comparison, "Similarly, the previous study showed..."
    - o (C) Removing the transition word "Therefore" as it creates confusion.
    - o (D) Revising the second sentence to better reflect the connection between ideas.

12. **Revising for consistency in tone and logical progression:**
    - o "Which revision maintains the consistent tone and improves the logical flow of the paragraph?"
    - o (A) Move the third sentence to the end to keep the paragraph focused on the main idea.
    - o (B) Combine the first and second sentences to create a smoother transition between ideas.
    - o (C) Revise the fourth sentence to ensure it connects with the paragraph's conclusion.
    - o (D) Add a phrase to the second sentence to reinforce the central argument.

# Section: Sentence Clarity and Precision (12 Questions)

1. **Improving clarity by simplifying sentence structure:**
   - o "Which revision best simplifies the sentence without changing its meaning?"
   - o (A) The scientist who conducted the experiment successfully, although faced with challenges, reported the results.
   - o (B) The scientist reported the results of the experiment despite facing challenges.
   - o (C) Despite facing challenges, the scientist, who conducted the experiment successfully, reported the results.
   - o (D) The experiment was reported successfully, even though the scientist faced challenges.

2. **Clarifying unclear pronoun usage:**
   - o "Which sentence clarifies the unclear pronoun usage?"
   - o (A) Maria and Jen spoke about her project, which was still in progress.
   - o (B) Maria and Jen spoke about Maria's project, which was still in progress.
   - o (C) Maria spoke about her project with Jen, which was still in progress.
   - o (D) Jen discussed the project with Maria, and it was still in progress.

3. **Improving precision by choosing the best word:**
   - o "Which word best improves the precision of the sentence?"
   - o (A) The company faced a **large** amount of backlash.
   - o (B) The company faced a **substantial** amount of backlash.
   - o (C) The company faced a **huge** amount of backlash.
   - o (D) The company faced a **significant** amount of backlash.

4. **Revising for clarity in complex sentences:**
   - o "Which revision makes the sentence clearer and easier to understand?"
   - o (A) The group, after much deliberation, finally decided, but not until the last minute, to accept the offer.
   - o (B) After much deliberation, the group finally decided to accept the offer at the last minute.
   - o (C) The group decided, although late and after much deliberation, to accept the offer.
   - o (D) After long deliberation, the offer was accepted by the group at the last minute.

5. **Correcting ambiguous pronoun reference:**
   - o "Which sentence clarifies the ambiguous pronoun reference?"
   - o (A) When the manager spoke to the employee, they were confused about the instructions.
   - o (B) When the manager spoke to the employee, the employee was confused about the instructions.
   - o (C) The manager spoke to the employee, who was confused about the instructions.
   - o (D) When the manager spoke to the employee, the manager was confused about the instructions.

6. **Improving clarity by rewording:**
   - o "Which revision best improves the clarity of the sentence?"
   - o (A) The class trip, which was planned by the teacher, was to be canceled unless better arrangements could be made.
   - o (B) Unless better arrangements could be made, the teacher's planned class trip was going to be canceled.
   - o (C) The teacher planned the class trip, but it would be canceled unless better arrangements could be made.
   - o (D) The class trip planned by the teacher would be canceled unless better arrangements could be made.

7. **Choosing the most precise verb:**
   - o "Which verb best improves the sentence's precision?"
   - o (A) The team worked hard to **complete** the project.
   - o (B) The team worked hard to **finish** the project.

- o (C) The team worked hard to **finalize** the project.
- o (D) The team worked hard to **conclude** the project.

8. **Correcting unclear sentence structure:**
    - o "Which sentence revision makes the structure clearer and easier to follow?"
    - o (A) The results, after hours of work, were finally published by the team, who had faced many obstacles.
    - o (B) After hours of work, the team finally published the results, having faced many obstacles.
    - o (C) The results were finally published after the team had worked for hours and faced many obstacles.
    - o (D) After the team faced many obstacles, the results were published after hours of work.

9. **Clarifying vague pronoun usage:**
    - o "Which sentence revision clarifies the vague pronoun?"
    - o (A) The engineers revised the design, but it didn't improve the outcome.
    - o (B) The engineers revised the design, but the revision didn't improve the outcome.
    - o (C) The engineers revised the design, but the design changes didn't improve the outcome.
    - o (D) The engineers revised the design, but the revised design didn't improve the outcome.

10. **Improving sentence clarity by removing unnecessary words:**
    - o "Which revision best simplifies the sentence without losing meaning?"
    - o (A) After a long, tedious process, the final report was ultimately, after all considerations, submitted.
    - o (B) The final report was submitted after a long, tedious process and many considerations.
    - o (C) After a tedious process, the final report was submitted.
    - o (D) The final report, after all considerations and lengthy discussions, was finally submitted.

11. **Revising for clarity by correcting word placement:**
    - o "Which revision correctly places the words for maximum clarity?"
    - o (A) The supervisor observed the team closely who had just completed the task.
    - o (B) The supervisor, who had just completed the task, closely observed the team.
    - o (C) The supervisor closely observed the team, who had just completed the task.
    - o (D) The team, closely observed by the supervisor, had just completed the task.

12. **Improving clarity by choosing the most appropriate conjunction:**
    - o "Which conjunction best connects the ideas in this sentence?"
    - o (A) The proposal was accepted, **so** the company decided to move forward with the project.
    - o (B) The proposal was accepted, **but** the company decided to move forward with the project.
    - o (C) The proposal was accepted, **and** the company decided to move forward with the project.
    - o (D) The proposal was accepted, **although** the company decided to move forward with the project.

# TEST 2: 108 QUESTIONS

**Overview**

The second practice test is designed to mirror the structure and difficulty of the actual Digital SAT, offering another valuable opportunity to gauge your readiness and identify areas for improvement. It is important to approach this test under realistic conditions to maximize its effectiveness.

**Taking the Test Under Realistic Conditions** To get the most out of this practice, it is crucial to simulate the actual testing environment as closely as possible. Set aside an uninterrupted block of time, follow the official time limits, and avoid distractions. By recreating the pressure and pacing of the real SAT, you will be better prepared to handle the time constraints and mental stamina required on test day.

**Time Management Reminders** Ensure you adhere strictly to the time limits for each section:

- **Reading Comprehension**: 65 minutes for 54 questions
- **Writing and Language**: 35 minutes for 54 questions

Avoid spending too much time on difficult questions. Instead, mark them and return to them if time allows. Remember, it's not necessary to get every question right to achieve a high score. Prioritize accuracy on the questions you feel more confident about.

**Reviewing Your Performance** After completing this test, it is essential to thoroughly review your answers. Pay close attention to the mistakes you made, identify patterns in the types of questions you struggle with, and apply the strategies and techniques you have learned in this book. Compare your performance with the first test to track your progress and target any remaining weaknesses.

This second test will help you refine your approach, sharpen your time management skills, and build the confidence needed to perform at your best on the actual exam.

## Section 1: Reading Comprehension

## Narrative Passage (12 Questions)

**Focus**: The following set of questions will assess your understanding of key narrative elements such as plot, character development, relationships, and the emotional tone of the passage. You will be required to make inferences, identify the main idea, and analyze the author's use of tone.

**Question Types**:

1. **Inference Question**:
   - *What can be inferred about the protagonist's motivation in the story?*
   - Options:
     - a) They are driven by a desire for power.
     - b) They seek approval from their peers.
     - c) They are motivated by fear of failure.
     - d) They want to prove their worth to themselves.

2. **Main Idea Question**:
   - *What is the central theme of the passage?*
   - Options:
     - a) The importance of self-discovery.
     - b) The consequences of betrayal.

- c) The pursuit of knowledge.
- d) The struggle between good and evil.

3. **Tone Question**:
   - *What is the tone of the passage?*
   - Options:
     - a) Optimistic.
     - b) Cynical.
     - c) Reflective.
     - d) Sarcastic.

4. **Character Development Question**:
   - *How does the protagonist change over the course of the passage?*
   - Options:
     - a) They become more confident.
     - b) They grow disillusioned with their ambitions.
     - c) They reconcile with a past mistake.
     - d) They develop a new perspective on their relationships.

5. **Relationship Analysis Question**:
   - *What can be inferred about the relationship between the protagonist and their mentor?*
   - Options:
     - a) The mentor disapproves of the protagonist's actions.
     - b) They share a strong bond based on mutual respect.
     - c) The mentor is indifferent to the protagonist's struggles.
     - d) Their relationship is marked by tension and rivalry.

6. **Plot Development Question**:
   - *Which event serves as the turning point in the passage?*
   - Options:
     - a) The protagonist makes a significant decision.
     - b) The protagonist faces an unexpected obstacle.
     - c) The protagonist receives guidance from a mentor.
     - d) The protagonist realizes the consequences of their actions.

7. **Inference Question**:
   - *What can be inferred about the antagonist's role in the story?*
   - Options:
     - a) They represent societal pressures on the protagonist.
     - b) They seek to undermine the protagonist's success.
     - c) They serve as a mirror for the protagonist's fears.
     - d) They are an ally disguised as an enemy.

8. **Tone Shift Question**:
   - *How does the tone of the passage shift from the beginning to the end?*
   - Options:

- a) From hopeful to resigned.
- b) From angry to forgiving.
- c) From neutral to celebratory.
- d) From suspicious to trusting.

9. **Character Motivation Question**:
   - *Which of the following best describes the protagonist's motivation for their final decision?*
   - Options:
     - a) A desire to break free from their past.
     - b) A need to protect someone they care about.
     - c) A realization that they were wrong.
     - d) A desire for personal revenge.

10. **Relationship Dynamics Question**:
- *How do the relationships between the characters evolve throughout the passage?*
- Options:
  - a) They grow closer as they understand each other better.
  - b) They become more distant due to unresolved conflicts.
  - c) They remain static with little change.
  - d) They dissolve entirely due to external pressures.

11. **Theme Question**:
- *Which of the following themes is most prevalent in the passage?*
- Options:
  - a) The search for identity.
  - b) The consequences of ambition.
  - c) The tension between tradition and progress.
  - d) The importance of family ties.

12. **Character Decision Question**:
- *What does the protagonist's final decision reveal about their character?*
- Options:
  - a) They are willing to sacrifice personal happiness for a greater cause.
  - b) They value loyalty over personal success.
  - c) They are incapable of making difficult choices.
  - d) They prioritize their own well-being above others.

# Social Science Passage (14 Questions)

**Focus**: The questions in this section assess your understanding of social theories, historical contexts, and societal trends. You will be asked to evaluate evidence, analyze the author's argumentation, and identify the main ideas of the passage.

**Question Types**:

1. **Evidence-Based Question**:

o *Which sentence provides the strongest support for the author's argument about the impact of industrialization on social structures?*

o Options:

- a) "Industrialization reshaped urban centers and rural communities alike."
- b) "Technological advancements allowed for the growth of factories."
- c) "The rise of factories led to the migration of workers to cities, fundamentally altering family dynamics."
- d) "Many workers experienced harsh conditions in newly developed factories."

2. **Main Idea Question**:

o *What is the primary conclusion drawn by the author in the passage?*

o Options:

- a) Urbanization was a direct result of industrialization.
- b) Industrialization had both positive and negative impacts on society.
- c) Technological advancements led to the formation of new social classes.
- d) Industrialization primarily benefited factory owners while exploiting workers.

3. **Argumentation Analysis Question**:

o *What evidence does the author use to support their argument that education played a critical role in societal changes during the Industrial Revolution?*

o Options:

- a) The establishment of public schools allowed workers to gain the skills needed in factories.
- b) Workers without education found it harder to adapt to the new economy.
- c) Labor unions fought for educational reforms to benefit workers.
- d) The educated middle class led reforms aimed at improving working conditions.

4. **Inference Question**:

o *What can be inferred about the author's perspective on the role of women in industrialized societies?*

o Options:

- a) The author believes women were largely excluded from the workforce.
- b) The author sees women as key contributors to both the workforce and social reform.
- c) The author argues that women were only allowed to work in specific industries.
- d) The author views the role of women as unchanged by industrialization.

5. **Main Idea Question**:

o *What is the central argument of the passage regarding the rise of labor unions?*

o Options:

- a) Labor unions emerged as a response to poor working conditions.
- b) Labor unions were driven primarily by political interests.
- c) Labor unions had limited success in improving worker rights.
- d) The rise of labor unions was an unintended consequence of industrialization.

6. **Evidence-Based Question**:

- o *Which statement from the passage best supports the idea that technological advancements during the industrial era were a double-edged sword?*
- o Options:
  - a) "Technological innovations made production more efficient but also increased the demand for unskilled labor."
  - b) "The advent of machinery led to the rapid expansion of industries."
  - c) "Workers were initially drawn to cities by the promise of higher wages in factories."
  - d) "While technological advancements boosted the economy, they also deepened social inequalities."

7. **Argumentation Analysis Question**:
   - o *Which piece of evidence does the author use to justify their claim that governments played a role in regulating industrial growth?*
   - o Options:
     - a) Governments introduced child labor laws to protect young workers.
     - b) Industrialists lobbied for fewer regulations to increase profits.
     - c) New trade policies allowed industries to expand into global markets.
     - d) Local governments supported the construction of factories by offering tax incentives.

8. **Inference Question**:
   - o *What can be inferred from the passage about the relationship between industrialization and social mobility?*
   - o Options:
     - a) Industrialization limited opportunities for upward mobility among workers.
     - b) The growth of industry created new pathways for social advancement.
     - c) Industrialization mostly benefited the upper class, with little impact on workers.
     - d) Social mobility was largely unaffected by industrial growth.

9. **Main Idea Question**:
   - o *What is the author's primary purpose in discussing the migration of workers to urban areas during the industrial era?*
   - o Options:
     - a) To illustrate the economic impact of industrialization.
     - b) To highlight how industrialization led to demographic shifts.
     - c) To emphasize the role of technology in transforming cities.
     - d) To demonstrate the negative effects of urbanization on rural communities.

10. **Argumentation Analysis Question**:
- *How does the author support their argument that industrialization led to significant changes in family structure?*
- Options:
  - o a) By providing examples of how families were separated due to urban migration.
  - o b) By citing studies that show the decline of multi-generational households.
  - o c) By discussing how industrial work schedules affected family dynamics.
  - o d) By showing how traditional family roles shifted in response to economic demands.

11. **Evidence-Based Question**:

- *Which of the following best supports the claim that education was a key factor in the social mobility of industrial workers?*

- Options:

  - a) "Education provided workers with the skills necessary to operate machinery."
  - b) "Public schools were established in urban centers to educate the children of factory workers."
  - c) "Workers who pursued education were able to rise through the ranks in factories."
  - d) "Uneducated workers were left behind as technology advanced."

12. **Inference Question**:

- *What can be inferred about the author's view on the environmental impact of industrialization?*

- Options:

  - a) The author believes industrialization had irreversible environmental consequences.
  - b) The author sees environmental degradation as a byproduct of economic progress.
  - c) The author argues that industries were largely unaware of their environmental impact.
  - d) The author suggests that early industrial practices laid the groundwork for modern environmental policies.

13. **Main Idea Question**:

- *What is the author's central claim about the relationship between industrial growth and government regulation?*

- Options:

  - a) Government regulation was necessary to control the negative effects of industrialization.
  - b) Governments were primarily concerned with fostering industrial growth at any cost.
  - c) Government intervention in industrial practices was limited and largely ineffective.
  - d) Governments were instrumental in ensuring the equitable distribution of industrial profits.

14. **Evidence-Based Question**:

- *Which sentence from the passage best supports the author's claim that labor unions were essential in improving working conditions?*

- Options:

  - a) "Labor unions emerged as a powerful force in advocating for workers' rights."
  - b) "Unions successfully negotiated shorter work hours and better wages for workers."
  - c) "Factory owners initially resisted the formation of unions but later recognized their necessity."
  - d) "Without labor unions, many workers would have remained in unsafe and exploitative conditions."

## Natural Science Passage (14 Questions)

**Focus**: The questions in this section are designed to test the student's understanding of scientific research, experiments, theories, and technical data. Students will need to interpret scientific concepts, data from charts or graphs, and specialized vocabulary within the context of the passage.

**Question Types:**

1. **Scientific Concepts Question:**
   o *What hypothesis is being tested in the experiment described in the passage?*
   o Options:
      ▪ a) That increased sunlight exposure accelerates plant growth.
      ▪ b) That nutrient levels in the soil affect plant height.
      ▪ c) That water availability is the primary factor in plant survival.
      ▪ d) That temperature changes alter the rate of photosynthesis in plants.

2. **Data Interpretation Question:**
   o *What can be concluded from the data presented in the graph?*
   o Options:
      ▪ a) Plants receiving higher amounts of nitrogen grew taller than those with less.
      ▪ b) There is no correlation between water levels and plant growth.
      ▪ c) Plants exposed to higher temperatures grew at the same rate as those in lower temperatures.
      ▪ d) The experiment's results were inconclusive due to inconsistent watering.

3. **Vocabulary in Context Question:**
   o *What does the word 'catalyst' mean in the context of the passage?*
   o Options:
      ▪ a) A substance that initiates or speeds up a chemical reaction.
      ▪ b) A molecule that slows down a reaction.
      ▪ c) A byproduct of the experiment.
      ▪ d) An element that hinders the progress of the reaction.

4. **Scientific Theory Question:**
   o *Which scientific principle underlies the experiment described in the passage?*
   o Options:
      ▪ a) The law of conservation of energy.
      ▪ b) The theory of evolution by natural selection.
      ▪ c) The process of photosynthesis in plants.
      ▪ d) The principle of buoyancy in liquids.

5. **Data and Graphs Question:**
   o *What trend is evident in the graph showing plant growth over time?*
   o Options:
      ▪ a) Plant growth is directly proportional to the amount of sunlight received.
      ▪ b) Water availability had little impact on plant growth.
      ▪ c) Plants grew at a faster rate in shaded areas than in direct sunlight.
      ▪ d) Temperature had no measurable effect on the plant growth rate.

6. **Scientific Method Question:**
   o *Which step of the scientific method is the author most likely describing in paragraph 4?*
   o Options:
      ▪ a) Formulating a hypothesis.

- b) Conducting the experiment.
- c) Analyzing the data.
- d) Drawing a conclusion based on results.

7. **Hypothesis and Conclusion Question**:
   - ○ *What is the conclusion drawn by the scientists after the experiment?*
   - ○ Options:
     - a) The data supports the hypothesis that increased sunlight promotes faster growth.
     - b) The experiment failed to prove a correlation between sunlight and plant growth.
     - c) Water, not sunlight, was found to be the primary factor in plant growth.
     - d) Further testing is required to confirm the hypothesis.

8. **Cause and Effect Question**:
   - ○ *According to the passage, what effect did nutrient-rich soil have on plant growth?*
   - ○ Options:
     - a) Plants in nutrient-rich soil grew taller than those in regular soil.
     - b) No difference was observed between plants in nutrient-rich and regular soil.
     - c) Plants in regular soil outperformed those in nutrient-rich soil.
     - d) The plants in nutrient-rich soil had stunted growth compared to others.

9. **Controlled Variables Question**:
   - ○ *Which variable was controlled during the experiment described in the passage?*
   - ○ Options:
     - a) The amount of sunlight each plant received.
     - b) The type of fertilizer used.
     - c) The water levels provided to each plant.
     - d) The size of the pots the plants were grown in.

10. **Experimental Results Question**:
    - ○ *What do the results of the experiment suggest about the importance of sunlight in photosynthesis?*
    - ○ Options:
      - a) Sunlight is essential for photosynthesis, as plants receiving more light showed greater growth.
      - b) Sunlight plays a minor role in photosynthesis, as all plants grew at a similar rate regardless of light exposure.
      - c) Plants receiving less sunlight performed better in terms of growth than those receiving direct light.
      - d) The results were inconclusive regarding the role of sunlight in photosynthesis.

11. **Scientific Process Question**:
    - ○ *What does the author suggest as the next step for the researchers?*
    - ○ Options:
      - a) Repeating the experiment with a larger sample size.
      - b) Altering the variables to test a different hypothesis.
      - c) Publishing the results for peer review.

- d) Continuing the experiment in a different environmental condition.

12. **Control Group Question**:
    - ○ *Why was a control group necessary in this experiment?*
    - ○ Options:
        - a) To compare the effects of the experimental variable with a baseline condition.
        - b) To ensure that all plants received equal amounts of water.
        - c) To prevent any external factors from influencing the results.
        - d) To test the experiment's hypothesis under no external conditions.

13. **Critical Thinking Question**:
    - ○ *What might be a potential flaw in the experimental design described in the passage?*
    - ○ Options:
        - a) The researchers did not account for differences in soil composition.
        - b) The experiment was conducted over too short a period of time.
        - c) The researchers used different amounts of water for each plant.
        - d) The sample size was too large for the results to be reliable.

14. **Vocabulary in Context Question**:
    - ○ *What does the term 'photosynthetic efficiency' mean in the context of the passage?*
    - ○ Options:
        - a) The rate at which plants convert sunlight into usable energy.
        - b) The ability of plants to store water for use in photosynthesis.
        - c) The process by which plants absorb sunlight for growth.
        - d) The relationship between the amount of sunlight received and plant height.

# Historical Document Passage (14 Questions)

**Focus**: This section will test the student's ability to analyze political speeches, legal documents, and significant historical texts. Students must make inferences about the historical context, the author's intent, and compare various historical perspectives.

**Question Types:**

1. **Author's Intent Question**:
    - ○ *What was the author's primary purpose in delivering this speech?*
    - ○ Options:
        - a) To rally support for a political movement.
        - b) To criticize the government's foreign policy.
        - c) To propose a new law or policy.
        - d) To inform the public about an international issue.

2. **Inference about Historical Context Question**:
    - ○ *What can be inferred about the social conditions during the time this document was written?*
    - ○ Options:
        - a) There was widespread political unrest.
        - b) The country was experiencing economic prosperity.

- c) International relations were strained.
- d) Social equality had already been achieved.

3. **Comparison of Historical Perspectives Question**:
   - *How does the author's perspective on national security differ from that of another historical figure mentioned in the passage?*
   - Options:
     - a) The author favors a more diplomatic approach, while the other figure supports military intervention.
     - b) Both figures advocate for increased defense spending.
     - c) The author believes national security is not a priority, while the other figure emphasizes its importance.
     - d) Both figures hold similar views on the role of government in ensuring security.

4. **Author's Argument Question**:
   - *What argument does the author make in support of their proposed solution to the economic crisis?*
   - Options:
     - a) Reducing taxes will stimulate economic growth.
     - b) Increasing government spending on public infrastructure is essential.
     - c) Foreign investment should be prioritized over domestic production.
     - d) A return to isolationist policies will protect the economy.

5. **Cause and Effect Question**:
   - *What effect did the policy proposed in the document have on the political landscape of the time?*
   - Options:
     - a) It caused a rift between political parties.
     - b) It led to widespread civil unrest.
     - c) It was quickly accepted by the public and implemented.
     - d) It had little to no immediate impact on the political situation.

6. **Tone and Language Question**:
   - *What is the tone of the author's language when describing the opposition's stance on this issue?*
   - Options:
     - a) Critical and disapproving.
     - b) Respectful and conciliatory.
     - c) Neutral and informative.
     - d) Sarcastic and dismissive.

7. **Understanding Historical Nuance Question**:
   - *What can be inferred about the author's view on international diplomacy based on their description of recent negotiations?*
   - Options:
     - a) The author believes diplomacy is essential for maintaining peace.
     - b) The author is skeptical of the effectiveness of diplomacy.
     - c) The author sees diplomacy as secondary to military strength.

   - d) The author views diplomacy as unnecessary in current times.

8. **Intent and Purpose Question**:
   - *Why did the author choose to reference a past political leader in their argument?*
   - Options:
     - a) To draw a parallel between current events and a historical example.
     - b) To critique the policies of the past leader.
     - c) To emphasize that current policies are a departure from tradition.
     - d) To invoke the memory of a respected figure for support.

9. **Contextual Inference Question**:
   - *What can be inferred about the legal challenges faced by the government during this period?*
   - Options:
     - a) The government was struggling with constitutional crises.
     - b) There were significant legal reforms taking place.
     - c) Public trust in the legal system had eroded.
     - d) Legal challenges were minimal during this time.

10. **Argumentation and Evidence Question**:
    - *What evidence does the author provide to support their argument for economic reform?*
    - Options:
      - a) Statistics showing declining unemployment rates.
      - b) Historical examples of successful economic policies.
      - c) Quotes from prominent economists.
      - d) Personal anecdotes from citizens affected by the crisis.

11. **Comparison of Two Perspectives Question**:
    - *How does the author's view on civil rights differ from that of another leader mentioned in the passage?*
    - Options:
      - a) The author advocates for immediate change, while the other leader supports gradual reform.
      - b) The author believes civil rights should be prioritized above all other issues.
      - c) Both leaders agree on the importance of civil rights but differ in their methods.
      - d) The author and the other leader share the same perspective on the issue.

12. **Inference from Historical Context Question**:
    - *What can be inferred about the relationship between the government and the press during this time?*
    - Options:
      - a) The government exerted heavy control over the press.
      - b) The press was highly critical of government actions.
      - c) The press supported the government's initiatives.
      - d) There was little interaction between the government and the media.

13. **Author's Perspective on Political Leadership Question**:
    - *How does the author view the role of political leadership in resolving the national crisis?*
    - Options:

- a) The author believes strong leadership is essential for success.
- b) The author doubts the effectiveness of current political leaders.
- c) The author argues for a more decentralized approach to governance.
- d) The author calls for public engagement rather than relying solely on leadership.

14. **Historical Impact Question:**
    - o *What long-term impact did the policies discussed in the document have on future generations?*
    - o Options:
      - a) They set a precedent for future legal reforms.
      - b) They were largely forgotten and had no lasting impact.
      - c) They shaped the country's foreign policy for decades.
      - d) They were overturned shortly after the document was written.

# Section 2: Writing and Language

## Grammar and Sentence Structure (15 Questions)

**Focus:** This part of the test assesses students' ability to identify and correct grammatical errors related to subject-verb agreement, parallel structure, and misplaced modifiers.

**Example Questions:**

1. **Subject-Verb Agreement**
   *Which sentence maintains proper subject-verb agreement?*
   a) The dogs barks loudly every morning.
   b) The dog bark loudly every morning.
   c) The dogs bark loudly every morning.
   d) The dog barks loudly every morning.

2. **Parallel Structure**
   *Which sentence correctly maintains parallelism?*
   a) She enjoys reading, to swim, and hiking.
   b) She enjoys reading, swimming, and hiking.
   c) She enjoys to read, swim, and hiking.
   d) She enjoys reading, swimming, and to hike.

3. **Misplaced Modifiers**
   *Which sentence correctly places the modifier?*
   a) Driving down the street, the house was beautiful.
   b) The house was beautiful driving down the street.
   c) Driving down the street, I noticed the house was beautiful.
   d) I noticed the house was beautiful driving down the street.

4. **Pronoun-Antecedent Agreement**
   *Which sentence uses the correct pronoun?*
   a) Neither Sarah nor Emily have finished their homework.
   b) Neither Sarah nor Emily has finished her homework.
   c) Neither Sarah nor Emily has finished their homework.
   d) Neither Sarah nor Emily have finished her homework.

5. **Dangling Modifiers**

   *Which sentence corrects the dangling modifier?*

   a) After taking the test, the results were surprising.

   b) After taking the test, I was surprised by the results.

   c) The results were surprising after taking the test.

   d) Taking the test, the results were surprising.

6. **Consistent Tense Usage**

   *Which sentence maintains consistent tense throughout?*

   a) He walked to the park and sees his friends there.

   b) He walks to the park and saw his friends there.

   c) He walked to the park and saw his friends there.

   d) He walks to the park and is seeing his friends there.

7. **Sentence Fragment**

   *Which option presents a complete sentence?*

   a) After the rain stopped.

   b) Running through the field, they laughed with joy.

   c) Running through the field.

   d) Because she was late.

8. **Comma Splices**

   *Which sentence fixes the comma splice?*

   a) He ran to the store, he bought milk.

   b) He ran to the store; he bought milk.

   c) He ran to the store and he bought milk.

   d) He ran to the store because he bought milk.

9. **Verb Tense Consistency**

   *Which sentence maintains consistent verb tense?*

   a) I am running every morning, and I ate breakfast afterward.

   b) I run every morning, and I eat breakfast afterward.

   c) I run every morning, and I ate breakfast afterward.

   d) I ran every morning, and I eat breakfast afterward.

10. **Pronoun Clarity**

    *Which revision improves the clarity of the pronoun?*

    a) When the teacher handed out the exams, she said it was tough.

    b) When the teacher handed out the exams, she said the test was tough.

    c) The teacher said it was tough when she handed out the exams.

    d) When the teacher handed out the exams, the students knew it was tough.

11. **Relative Pronouns**

    *Which sentence correctly uses the relative pronoun?*

    a) The book which I read was fascinating.

    b) The book that I read was fascinating.

    c) The book, which I read, was fascinating.

    d) The book that I read it was fascinating.

12. **Compound Sentences**

    *Which sentence correctly forms a compound sentence?*

a) I went to the store, I bought some groceries.

b) I went to the store; I bought some groceries.

c) I went to the store, and bought some groceries.

d) I went to the store, buying some groceries.

13. **Faulty Parallelism**

    *Which sentence fixes the parallelism error?*

    a) She loves hiking, biking, and to swim.

    b) She loves hiking, biking, and swimming.

    c) She loves hiking, biking, and to go swimming.

    d) She loves hiking, to bike, and swimming.

14. **Sentence Boundaries**

    *Which sentence avoids a run-on or fragment?*

    a) He loves to cook he makes dinner every night.

    b) He loves to cook, and he makes dinner every night.

    c) He loves to cook makes dinner every night.

    d) Loves to cook and he makes dinner every night.

15. **Comparative and Superlative Forms**

    *Which sentence correctly uses the comparative form?*

    a) This dish is more tastier than the last one.

    b) This dish is tastier than the last one.

    c) This dish is most tastiest than the last one.

    d) This dish is more tasty than the last one.

# Punctuation and Capitalization (15 Questions)

**Focus**: This section assesses students' understanding of proper punctuation use, including commas, semicolons, colons, and capitalization.

**Example Questions:**

1. **Comma Usage in Lists**

   *Which sentence uses commas correctly to separate items in a list?*

   a) I bought apples, bananas, oranges and grapes.

   b) I bought apples, bananas, oranges, and grapes.

   c) I bought apples, bananas oranges, and grapes.

   d) I bought, apples, bananas, oranges, and grapes.

2. **Comma for Introductory Phrases**

   *Which sentence uses a comma correctly after the introductory phrase?*

   a) After the storm we went outside to check the damage.

   b) After the storm, we went outside to check the damage.

   c) After the storm we, went outside to check the damage.

   d) After, the storm we went outside to check the damage.

3. **Semicolon Usage**

   *Which sentence correctly uses a semicolon to join two independent clauses?*

   a) She loves painting; and she often paints in the morning.

   b) She loves painting, she often paints in the morning.

   c) She loves painting; she often paints in the morning.

   d) She loves painting; because she often paints in the morning.

4. **Colon for Explanatory Lists**

   *Which sentence uses a colon correctly to introduce a list?*

   a) He needed three things; paper, a pen, and his notes.

   b) He needed three things: paper, a pen, and his notes.

   c) He needed three things, paper, a pen, and his notes.

   d) He needed: paper, a pen, and his notes.

5. **Punctuation in Compound Sentences**

   *Which sentence uses punctuation correctly in a compound sentence?*

   a) I wanted to go to the park, but it was raining.

   b) I wanted to go to the park but, it was raining.

   c) I wanted, to go to the park but, it was raining.

   d) I wanted to go, to the park, but it was raining.

6. **Comma in Non-Essential Clauses**

   *Which sentence uses commas correctly to set off a non-essential clause?*

   a) My brother who lives in Chicago, is visiting next week.

   b) My brother, who lives in Chicago is visiting next week.

   c) My brother, who lives in Chicago, is visiting next week.

   d) My brother who, lives in Chicago, is visiting next week.

7. **Apostrophe in Possessive Nouns**

   *Which sentence correctly uses an apostrophe to indicate possession?*

   a) The teachers' lounge is on the second floor.

   b) The teacher's lounge is on the second floor.

   c) The teachers lounge is on the second floor.

   d) The teachers's lounge is on the second floor.

8. **Quotation Marks for Dialogue**

   *Which sentence correctly punctuates dialogue with quotation marks?*

   a) "I can't believe it" she said, "It's already noon."

   b) "I can't believe it," she said. "It's already noon."

   c) "I can't believe it," she said "It's already noon."

   d) "I can't believe it" she said "It's already noon."

9. **Capitalization of Proper Nouns**

   *Which sentence correctly capitalizes the proper nouns?*

   a) We visited paris and saw the eiffel tower.

   b) We visited Paris and saw the Eiffel Tower.

   c) We visited paris and saw the Eiffel Tower.

   d) We visited Paris and saw the eiffel Tower.

10. **Punctuation for Compound-Complex Sentences**

    *Which sentence correctly punctuates the compound-complex sentence?*

    a) After we left the house, we stopped for groceries; but the store was closed.

    b) After we left the house we stopped for groceries, but the store was closed.

    c) After we left the house, we stopped for groceries, but the store was closed.

    d) After we left the house, we stopped for groceries but, the store was closed.

11. **Comma Usage with Adjectives**

    *Which sentence correctly uses commas between adjectives?*

a) It was a long, tiring drive.

b) It was a long tiring, drive.

c) It was a long, tiring, drive.

d) It was a long tiring drive.

12. **Dash for Parenthetical Information**

*Which sentence correctly uses a dash to add extra information?*

a) My friend—who lives in New York—is coming to visit.

b) My friend, who lives in New York—is coming to visit.

c) My friend—who lives in New York, is coming to visit.

d) My friend who lives—in New York—is coming to visit.

13. **Correct Use of Hyphens**

*Which sentence correctly uses a hyphen?*

a) This is a well-known fact.

b) This is a well, known fact.

c) This is a well known fact.

d) This is a wellknown fact.

14. **Comma for Direct Address**

*Which sentence correctly uses a comma to indicate direct address?*

a) Yes, John I will meet you there.

b) Yes John, I will meet you there.

c) Yes, John, I will meet you there.

d) Yes John I will, meet you there.

15. **Capitalization of Titles**

*Which sentence correctly capitalizes a title?*

a) My favorite book is to kill a mockingbird.

b) My favorite book is To Kill A Mockingbird.

c) My favorite book is To Kill a Mockingbird.

d) My favorite book is to Kill a Mockingbird.

# Logical Flow and Coherence (12 Questions)

**Focus**: This section aims to assess students' ability to improve the logical connections between ideas in sentences and paragraphs. It emphasizes the importance of transitions and coherence in writing.

**Example Questions:**

1. **Improving Transitions Between Paragraphs**

*Which sentence best improves the transition between these two paragraphs?*

a) The discovery of penicillin revolutionized medicine. Meanwhile, new advances in technology also transformed other industries.

b) The discovery of penicillin revolutionized medicine. Additionally, these medical breakthroughs paved the way for new treatments.

c) The discovery of penicillin revolutionized medicine. This was followed by changes in art and culture.

d) The discovery of penicillin revolutionized medicine. However, scientists continue to search for new treatments.

2. **Logical Sequence of Ideas**

   *Which sentence would best follow this one to maintain a logical sequence?*

   "The Industrial Revolution significantly impacted working conditions across Europe."

   a) Factories became more efficient, leading to mass production.

   b) Many workers relocated to urban centers in search of jobs.

   c) Scientists began to explore new technologies and innovations.

   d) The French Revolution also brought about societal changes during this period.

3. **Clarifying Sentence Order**

   *Which sentence should be moved to improve the logical flow of ideas in the paragraph?*

   a) Sentence 1: "The invention of the telephone revolutionized communication."

   b) Sentence 2: "Alexander Graham Bell's early experiments laid the groundwork for this invention."

   c) Sentence 3: "His work led to the first successful demonstration in 1876."

   d) Sentence 4: "Communication tools have evolved significantly since then."

4. **Enhancing Paragraph Unity**

   *Which sentence should be removed to improve the coherence of the paragraph?*

   a) Sentence 1: "Renewable energy sources are becoming more popular."

   b) Sentence 2: "Wind and solar energy are gaining traction."

   c) Sentence 3: "The Earth has been orbiting the sun for billions of years."

   d) Sentence 4: "Governments are implementing policies to encourage green energy adoption."

5. **Correcting Misplaced Transitions**

   *Which option best corrects the misplaced transition in this paragraph?*

   a) "While renewable energy sources are beneficial, they are not without challenges. For example, wind energy is inconsistent."

   b) "Although renewable energy sources are challenging, they are beneficial. For example, wind energy is inconsistent."

   c) "Renewable energy sources are beneficial; however, they are not without challenges. For example, wind energy is inconsistent."

   d) "Renewable energy sources are beneficial; meanwhile, wind energy is inconsistent."

6. **Choosing Effective Transition Words**

   *Which transition word or phrase best connects the ideas in these sentences?*

   Sentence 1: "Electric cars are becoming more affordable."

   Sentence 2: "They are still not as widely available as gas-powered cars."

   a) Likewise

   b) In contrast

   c) Consequently

   d) For instance

7. **Improving Sentence Flow**

   *Which revision improves the flow of the following sentences?*

   "The company introduced a new product. The product was successful in the market."

   a) The company introduced a new product; the product became successful in the market.

   b) The company introduced a new product, which was successful in the market.

   c) The company introduced a new product. Its success in the market was notable.

   d) The company introduced a new product that achieved great success in the market.

8. **Fixing Redundant Transitions**

   *Which sentence removes the redundant transition and improves coherence?*

   a) "Firstly, the city implemented new traffic policies. Additionally, this led to reduced congestion."

   b) "Firstly, the city implemented new traffic policies. As a result, congestion was reduced."

   c) "Firstly, the city implemented new traffic policies. Secondly, this led to reduced congestion."

   d) "Firstly, the city implemented new traffic policies. Consequently, this led to reduced congestion."

9. **Maintaining Consistent Focus in Paragraphs**

   *Which sentence maintains the focus of the paragraph best?*

   "The agricultural sector has seen many technological advancements in recent years. Farmers are using more efficient equipment, such as GPS-guided tractors."

   a) "Tractors are expensive and often require maintenance."

   b) "These advancements have increased crop yields significantly."

   c) "Many farmers face challenges with climate change."

   d) "These technological tools need frequent updates."

10. **Identifying Off-Topic Sentences**

    *Which sentence should be removed to maintain paragraph focus?*

    a) "Social media has transformed the way people communicate."

    b) "Platforms like Facebook and Twitter have millions of users."

    c) "These platforms are free to use and allow people to connect easily."

    d) "The cost of building social media apps is usually high."

11. **Correcting Transition Errors**

    *Which revision improves the transition between these two ideas?*

    Sentence 1: "The internet has changed how people work and communicate."

    Sentence 2: "It has also created new opportunities in education."

    a) Although the internet has changed how people work and communicate, it has also created new opportunities in education.

    b) In addition to changing how people work and communicate, the internet has created new opportunities in education.

    c) The internet has changed how people work and communicate. For example, it has created new opportunities in education.

    d) While the internet has changed how people work and communicate, it has done little to change education.

12. **Choosing the Most Coherent Conclusion**

    *Which sentence provides the most coherent conclusion to the paragraph?*

    a) "In conclusion, social media has had both positive and negative effects on society."

    b) "Therefore, it's important to use social media responsibly and limit screen time."

    c) "Social media is a powerful tool that has reshaped the way we interact with each other."

    d) "In addition, social media platforms will likely continue to evolve in the coming years."

# Sentence Clarity and Precision (12 Questions)

**Focus**: This section tests students' ability to improve sentence clarity by choosing the simplest, most precise wording without altering the meaning of the sentence. The exercises help students avoid vague or confusing language.

**Example Questions:**

1. **Improving Clarity**

   *Which revision makes the sentence clearer and easier to understand?*

   Original: "The event that took place was very interesting and everyone thought it was something that would be remembered for a long time."

   a) The event was interesting and memorable.

   b) The event that happened was quite interesting and will be remembered for years.

   c) The event that took place was considered interesting and memorable by everyone.

   d) The event was thought to be something memorable and very interesting by all.

2. **Simplifying Sentence Structure**

   *Which sentence simplifies the structure without losing meaning?*

   Original: "Due to the fact that the weather was bad, the soccer game was postponed."

   a) Because the weather was bad, the soccer game was postponed.

   b) Due to the bad weather, the soccer game was postponed.

   c) The soccer game was postponed because of bad weather.

   d) The weather being bad resulted in the postponement of the soccer game.

3. **Avoiding Redundant Phrasing**

   *Which revision best eliminates redundancy?*

   Original: "The CEO plans to introduce new innovations that are novel and different from what competitors offer."

   a) The CEO plans to introduce innovations that are different from what competitors offer.

   b) The CEO plans to introduce new innovations that differ from those of competitors.

   c) The CEO plans to introduce innovations that are novel and unique compared to competitors.

   d) The CEO plans to introduce new innovations that differ from competitors' offerings.

4. **Clarifying Ambiguous Pronouns**

   *Which revision clarifies the pronoun usage in the sentence?*

   Original: "When the manager spoke to the team, they were confused."

   a) When the manager spoke to the team, the team was confused.

   b) When the manager spoke to them, the team was confused.

   c) The manager confused the team when speaking to them.

   d) When the manager spoke, confusion arose among the team.

5. **Correcting Wordiness**

   *Which option best revises the sentence to remove unnecessary words?*

   Original: "At this point in time, it is clear that the company needs to make improvements."

   a) The company needs to make improvements.

   b) At this point, it is clear that improvements are needed.

   c) It is clear that the company now needs to make improvements.

   d) The company needs to make some important improvements right now.

6. **Choosing More Precise Vocabulary**

   *Which revision uses the most precise word?*

   Original: "The scientist made a big discovery that changed the field."

   a) The scientist made a substantial discovery that altered the field.

   b) The scientist made an important discovery that impacted the field.

   c) The scientist made a significant discovery that transformed the field.

   d) The scientist made a large discovery that changed the field.

7. **Clarifying the Relationship Between Ideas**

*Which revision clarifies the relationship between the two ideas in the sentence?*

Original: "The company expanded its product line, it did not increase its revenue."

a) The company expanded its product line, but it did not increase its revenue.

b) The company expanded its product line, however, it did not increase its revenue.

c) Even though the company expanded its product line, revenue did not increase.

d) The company expanded its product line, yet the revenue did not increase.

8. **Revising for Precision and Conciseness**

*Which sentence is both more precise and concise?*

Original: "The results of the experiment were unusual and surprising to the researchers, as they had not expected to see this kind of outcome."

a) The experiment's results surprised the researchers, who did not expect this outcome.

b) The researchers were surprised by the results of the experiment.

c) The outcome of the experiment was unexpected by the researchers.

d) The experiment yielded surprising results, which the researchers had not anticipated.

9. **Clarifying Comparison Structures**

*Which revision clarifies the comparison in the sentence?*

Original: "The company's new model is faster and cheaper than its competitors."

a) The company's new model is both faster and more affordable than the models of its competitors.

b) The company's new model is faster and costs less than the competitors' models.

c) The company's new model is faster and more affordable compared to other companies.

d) The company's new model is faster and less expensive than the other companies.

10. **Eliminating Unnecessary Phrases**

*Which revision eliminates the unnecessary phrase and improves clarity?*

Original: "In order to reduce the overall costs of production, the company needs to make several changes that will lead to a decrease in expenses."

a) To reduce production costs, the company needs to make changes.

b) To lower the costs of production, the company needs to implement changes.

c) The company needs to make several changes to reduce expenses.

d) In order to decrease production costs, the company must make changes.

11. **Clarifying Cause and Effect Relationships**

*Which sentence best clarifies the cause and effect relationship?*

Original: "The new policy was implemented, employee morale improved significantly."

a) After the new policy was implemented, employee morale improved significantly.

b) The new policy led to a significant improvement in employee morale.

c) Employee morale significantly improved because of the new policy.

d) With the new policy, employee morale saw significant improvement.

12. **Simplifying Complex Structures**

*Which sentence simplifies the complex structure while retaining the original meaning?*

Original: "Due to the fact that the project encountered unforeseen difficulties, it was delayed for an extended period of time."

a) The project was delayed due to unforeseen difficulties.

b) Unforeseen difficulties delayed the project for a long time.

c) The project was delayed for a long time because of unforeseen difficulties.

d) Because the project encountered unforeseen difficulties, it was delayed.

## Time Management Instructions

Effective time management is crucial for success on the SAT Reading and Writing sections. Students should aim to complete each section within the allocated time while avoiding unnecessary stress or pressure. Here are some practical tips for managing your time efficiently:

1. **Monitor Your Time**

   It's important to keep track of how much time you spend on each question. Set a mental timer to ensure you're pacing yourself and moving through the test efficiently. For example, on a 54-question section, you should spend roughly 1-1.5 minutes per question.

2. **Tackle Easier Questions First**

   As you go through the test, answer the questions you find easiest first. This allows you to quickly gain points and build confidence. Mark the more difficult questions and return to them later.

3. **Mark and Return to Difficult Questions**

   If you encounter a particularly difficult or time-consuming question, don't get stuck. Mark it and move on to the next one. You can come back to it after answering all the easier questions. This ensures you don't waste time and miss easier points.

4. **Use Your Time Wisely**

   If you finish early, use any remaining time to review your answers. Pay special attention to questions you were unsure about and check for any careless mistakes.

5. **Stay Calm and Focused**

   Don't let time pressure overwhelm you. Stay calm and focused, knowing that you've prepared strategies to manage your time. If you begin to feel stressed, take a deep breath, refocus, and keep moving forward.

6. **Skip and Guess Strategically**

   The SAT does not penalize for incorrect answers, so make sure to answer every question. If you're unsure about a question after revisiting it, make an educated guess based on elimination of obviously incorrect answers.

By following these time management strategies, you can maximize your efficiency during the SAT and ensure you have enough time to complete each section effectively.

# TEST 1 SOLUTIONS

## 3. Detailed Solutions with Explanations for Every Answer

## Overview

Understanding why an answer is correct or incorrect is a crucial part of SAT preparation. Simply knowing whether you answered a question right or wrong is not enough. By reviewing detailed explanations, you can identify patterns in your mistakes, reinforce correct strategies, and gain deeper insight into the reasoning behind each question. This section will provide comprehensive explanations for each question in the test, helping you to refine your approach and improve your performance.

**Structure of Explanations:**

For each question, the explanation will:

1. **Restate the question or key points.**
   A quick recap of what the question is asking, ensuring the student understands the focus.
2. **Discuss the correct answer choice.**
   A detailed explanation of why the chosen answer is correct, linking back to the passage or grammatical rule in question.
3. **Address why other answer choices are incorrect.**
   Break down each incorrect answer, explaining why it doesn't fit the criteria or doesn't align with the passage or rule.
4. **Provide tips for similar questions in the future.**
   Offer strategies or reminders for approaching similar questions effectively, whether it's an inference question, grammar rule, or tone interpretation.

**Example Solution Format:**

**Question 1** (from the Reading section):
*What can be inferred about the protagonist's motivation in paragraph 3?*

**Correct Answer: B - He wants to gain approval from his father.**

**Explanation:**

In paragraph 3, the protagonist repeatedly mentions his father's expectations and expresses a desire to meet them. The language used, such as "prove himself" and "live up to expectations," points clearly to his motivation being tied to earning his father's approval.

**Why other answers are incorrect:**

- A: This option suggests a desire for wealth, but there is no indication in the passage that this is a driving factor.
- C: The protagonist is concerned with family expectations, not societal status, so this answer does not apply.
- D: While the protagonist seeks success, the specific motivation here is tied to his relationship with his father, not a broader goal of personal achievement.

**Tip:**
When answering inference questions, always look for the most direct clues in the passage. Focus on the exact wording the author uses to reveal the character's thoughts or motivations.

# Narrative Passage Solutions

## Question 1: Inference Question

- **Question:** What can be inferred about the protagonist's motivation for leaving their hometown?
- **Correct Answer: B) They had a deep desire for adventure.**
- **Explanation:** The passage describes the protagonist as longing for something new and unexplored, implying a desire for adventure. There is no mention of career aspirations or fleeing a conflict, and the protagonist's friend plays no significant role in the decision.
  - **A) They wanted to pursue a new career**: There's no indication that career was the main motivation.
  - **C) They were running away from a conflict**: The text doesn't mention any specific conflict prompting their departure.
  - **D) They were influenced by a friend's advice**: The passage doesn't emphasize the role of a friend in their decision to leave.

## Question 2: Tone Question

- **Question:** What tone does the author use in describing the protagonist's journey?
- **Correct Answer: C) Reflective.**
- **Explanation:** The author describes the protagonist's journey with a thoughtful, reflective tone, as they contemplate the changes and decisions they've made. The tone is introspective rather than cynical or indifferent.
  - **A) Optimistic**: While the protagonist is contemplating, the tone is more reflective than optimistic.
  - **B) Cynical**: The passage doesn't show signs of cynicism.
  - **D) Indifferent**: The author's careful description rules out an indifferent tone.

## Question 3: Main Idea Question

- **Question:** What is the central theme of the passage?
- **Correct Answer: A) The challenges of finding one's true identity.**
- **Explanation:** The passage focuses on the protagonist's internal struggle and journey toward self-discovery, making the theme of identity central to the narrative.
  - **B) The importance of community support**: This is not a significant focus of the passage.
  - **C) The inevitability of change**: Though change is present, the primary focus is on identity.
  - **D) The value of perseverance in the face of adversity**: Perseverance is not a major element in this passage.

## Question 4: Character Development Question

- **Question:** How does the protagonist's attitude towards their family change throughout the passage?
- **Correct Answer: A) From resentment to understanding.**
- **Explanation:** Initially, the protagonist expresses resentment toward their family but grows to understand their perspective as the passage progresses.

- o **B) From admiration to disappointment**: There's no admiration or subsequent disappointment present in the passage.
- o **C) From indifference to love**: The protagonist is never indifferent to their family.
- o **D) From frustration to acceptance**: While this is close, the shift from resentment to understanding better captures the emotional arc.

## Question 5: Relationship Question

- **Question:** What best describes the relationship between the protagonist and their sibling?
- **Correct Answer: C) Competitive and strained.**
- **Explanation:** The passage portrays a competitive, somewhat tense relationship between the protagonist and their sibling, revealing underlying tensions.
    - o **A) Supportive but distant**: The relationship is not portrayed as supportive.
    - o **B) Close and trusting**: There's little indication of closeness or trust.
    - o **D) Affectionate yet conflicted**: While there may be affection, the competitiveness suggests a deeper strain.

## Question 6: Inference Question

- **Question:** What can be inferred about the significance of the protagonist's choice to visit the old house?
- **Correct Answer: B) They are seeking closure from past conflicts.**
- **Explanation:** The protagonist's return to the old house is symbolic of their need for closure, hinting at unresolved past issues.
    - o **A) They are trying to relive past memories**: The passage suggests resolution, not nostalgia.
    - o **C) They wish to show their family they've changed**: This isn't a central motivation.
    - o **D) They are trying to impress a new friend**: There is no mention of this in the passage.

## Question 7: Tone Question

- **Question:** How does the tone of the passage shift after the protagonist speaks with their sibling?
- **Correct Answer: A) From anxious to relieved.**
- **Explanation:** The protagonist starts out anxious about the conversation with their sibling, but after they speak, the tone shifts to relief, indicating a resolution of tension.
    - o **B) From hopeful to defeated**: The protagonist's emotional journey is not one of defeat.
    - o **C) From calm to agitated**: The opposite happens—the tone becomes more calm and resolved.
    - o **D) From nostalgic to regretful**: There is no significant sense of nostalgia or regret.

## Question 8: Main Idea Question

- **Question:** What is the main conflict presented in the passage?
- **Correct Answer: A) The protagonist's struggle between personal ambition and family expectations.**
- **Explanation:** The protagonist's internal conflict revolves around balancing their own ambitions with the expectations placed on them by their family.
    - o **B) The difficulty of maintaining friendships over time**: Friendship is not a central issue.

- o **C) The tension between the protagonist and their parents over life choices**: While there is family tension, the larger issue is the protagonist's internal struggle.
- o **D) The challenge of starting a new life in a different place**: This is a backdrop rather than the main conflict.

## Question 9: Character Development Question

- **Question:** Which event marks the turning point in the protagonist's personal growth?
- **Correct Answer: D) Returning to their childhood home.**
- **Explanation:** The protagonist's return to their childhood home is the key event that sparks personal reflection and growth.
  - o **A) Leaving their hometown**: This is the beginning of the journey, not the turning point.
  - o **B) Confronting a childhood friend**: While important, it's not the pivotal moment for growth.
  - o **C) Reconnecting with their sibling**: This moment helps, but the true shift comes from returning home.

## Question 10: Relationship Question

- **Question:** How does the protagonist's relationship with their mentor influence the decisions they make?
- **Correct Answer: C) Their mentor encourages them to take risks.**
- **Explanation:** The mentor's influence is seen through their encouragement for the protagonist to step outside their comfort zone and embrace new challenges.
  - o **A) They seek their mentor's approval at every step**: The protagonist is more independent than this.
  - o **B) They defy their mentor's advice to follow their own path**: There's no defiance in their relationship.
  - o **D) Their mentor's absence drives them to succeed on their own**: The mentor is present and influential.

## Question 11: Inference Question

- **Question:** What is implied about the protagonist's future at the end of the passage?
- **Correct Answer: B) They have made peace with their past and are ready to move forward.**
- **Explanation:** The passage ends on a note of resolution, suggesting that the protagonist is ready to move forward after coming to terms with their past.
  - o **A) They will continue to struggle with the same internal conflicts**: The protagonist seems to have resolved their conflicts.
  - o **C) They will return home to make amends**: The protagonist is looking ahead, not dwelling on returning home.
  - o **D) They are likely to revert to their old habits**: There is no indication of this regression.

## Question 12: Tone Question

- **Question:** What best describes the author's tone in the final paragraph?
- **Correct Answer: B) Wistful.**
- **Explanation:** The final paragraph reflects a tone of wistfulness, as the protagonist looks back on their past with a sense of longing but acceptance.

- o **A) Hopeful**: While the protagonist is ready to move forward, the tone is more reflective than hopeful.
- o **C) Bitter**: The protagonist has come to terms with their past, without bitterness.
- o **D) Detached**: The tone is emotional, not detached.

# Social Science Passage Solutions

## Question 1: Main Idea Question

- **Question:** What is the primary conclusion drawn by the author in the passage regarding the impact of urbanization on society?
- **Correct Answer: B) Urbanization has intensified economic inequality and segregation.**
- **Explanation:** The passage focuses on how urbanization has worsened disparities in income and increased segregation in urban areas.
  - o **A) Urbanization has led to more equitable access to resources**: This contradicts the passage's argument about economic inequality.
  - o **C) Urbanization has fostered greater cultural exchange and understanding**: While cultural exchange may be mentioned, the passage's main argument focuses on inequality.
  - o **D) Urbanization has had little impact on societal structures**: The passage makes clear that urbanization has significantly affected societal structures, particularly in terms of inequality.

## Question 2: Evidence-Based Question

- **Question:** Which sentence provides the strongest support for the claim that income inequality has worsened in urban centers?
- **Correct Answer: B) "The gap between the wealthiest and poorest residents in urban areas continues to widen."**
- **Explanation:** This sentence directly addresses the issue of income inequality, specifically mentioning the growing gap between different socioeconomic groups in cities.
  - o **A) "Many cities have experienced unprecedented economic growth over the past decades"**: This speaks to overall economic growth, not inequality.
  - o **C) "Educational institutions in urban areas offer diverse opportunities for residents"**: This sentence focuses on education, not income inequality.
  - o **D) "Public transportation systems have expanded, allowing greater mobility"**: This relates to transportation, not income disparity.

## Question 3: Argumentation Analysis Question

- **Question:** What evidence does the author use to support their argument that urban policies have failed to address housing shortages?
- **Correct Answer: B) The author references government reports showing a steady increase in homelessness rates.**
- **Explanation:** The author's use of government reports about rising homelessness provides concrete evidence of the failure to address housing shortages.
  - o **A) The author cites examples of cities that have improved housing access through zoning reforms**: This would contradict the argument that policies have failed.

- o **C) The author discusses the rise of new housing developments in suburban areas**: This focuses on suburban areas, not urban housing shortages.
- o **D) The author points to surveys indicating widespread public dissatisfaction with urban living conditions**: While this may show dissatisfaction, it doesn't directly support the argument about housing shortages.

## Question 4: Inference Question

- **Question:** Based on the passage, what can be inferred about the relationship between urbanization and public health?
- **Correct Answer: B) Urbanization has led to public health crises due to overcrowding and insufficient services.**
- **Explanation:** The passage implies that the rapid growth of cities has strained public health services, leading to crises in densely populated areas.
  - o **A) Urbanization has generally improved public health by providing better access to healthcare facilities**: This is not supported by the passage, which focuses on negative health outcomes.
  - o **C) Urbanization has had no significant effect on public health**: The passage implies that there has been a significant effect, particularly in terms of overcrowding.
  - o **D) Public health concerns are unrelated to the effects of urbanization**: The passage links urbanization to public health challenges.

## Question 5: Main Idea Question

- **Question:** What is the author's central argument regarding the role of technology in urban planning?
- **Correct Answer: B) Technological advancements have revolutionized urban planning but have not solved fundamental issues.**
- **Explanation:** The passage argues that while technology has significantly influenced urban planning, it has not resolved key challenges such as housing shortages and inequality.
  - o **A) Technology has played a minimal role in recent urban planning initiatives**: The passage suggests that technology has played a major role.
  - o **C) Technology has largely been ignored in discussions about urban development**: This is not supported by the passage, which highlights technology's significant role.
  - o **D) Technology has successfully solved many of the challenges facing modern cities**: The passage emphasizes that technology has not solved major issues.

## Question 6: Evidence-Based Question

- **Question:** Which sentence provides the best evidence to support the claim that transportation developments have failed to keep pace with population growth?
- **Correct Answer: A) "Public transportation systems in most major cities are outdated and overcrowded."**
- **Explanation:** This sentence directly addresses the failure of public transportation to meet the needs of growing urban populations, supporting the claim.
  - o **B) "Private vehicle ownership continues to rise, contributing to traffic congestion"**: This speaks to traffic congestion, not the inadequacies of public transportation.
  - o **C) "New subway systems have been implemented in various metropolitan areas"**: This would suggest progress in transportation, contradicting the claim.

- o **D) "Many cities are introducing bike lanes and pedestrian-friendly zones"**: This focuses on non-automotive infrastructure and does not address the overall public transportation system.

## Question 7: Argumentation Analysis Question

- **Question:** How does the author support their argument that educational inequality persists in urban areas?
- **Correct Answer: A) The author provides examples of underfunded schools in low-income neighborhoods.**
- **Explanation:** The author uses examples of underfunded schools to demonstrate the persistence of educational inequality in urban areas.
  - o **B) The author highlights disparities in the curriculum between urban and rural schools**: This would compare urban and rural schools, but the passage focuses on inequality within urban areas.
  - o **C) The author discusses the availability of online education platforms**: Online education is not relevant to the argument about inequality in urban areas.
  - o **D) The author references historical studies on the development of public education**: While this may be interesting, it doesn't directly support the argument about current inequality.

## Question 8: Inference Question

- **Question:** What can be inferred about the author's view on the future of urban growth?
- **Correct Answer: B) The author is pessimistic about the ability of cities to manage continued growth.**
- **Explanation:** The passage suggests that the author doubts the capacity of cities to handle the challenges of continued urban growth effectively.
  - o **A) The author is optimistic that cities will adapt to the challenges of thefuture**: The tone of the passage is more pessimistic than optimistic.
  - o **C) The author believes urban growth will stabilize over the next few decades**: The passage suggests continued challenges, not stabilization.
  - o **D) The author thinks technological advancements will solve most urban issues**: The author indicates that technology alone will not solve the major problems cities face.

## Question 9: Main Idea Question

- **Question:** What is the main purpose of the passage?
- **Correct Answer: B) To present both the benefits and challenges of rapid urbanization.**
- **Explanation:** The passage discusses both the positive and negative impacts of urbanization, making this the central theme.
  - o **A) To argue that urbanization has been overwhelmingly positive for society**: The passage presents a more balanced view, including challenges.
  - o **C) To advocate for increased government intervention in urban development**: While government intervention is mentioned, it's not the primary purpose.
  - o **D) To highlight the environmental consequences of urban growth**: This is one aspect, but not the main purpose of the passage.

## Question 10: Evidence-Based Question

- **Question:** Which sentence provides the strongest support for the claim that urban areas are more vulnerable to climate change?
- **Correct Answer: B) "Urban centers are often located in regions prone to flooding and extreme weather."**
- **Explanation:** This sentence directly supports the idea that urban areas are particularly vulnerable to climate change due to their geographic locations.
  - **A) "Many cities have implemented measures to reduce their carbon footprint"**: This focuses on mitigation, not vulnerability.
  - **C) "Rural areas experience similar challenges related to climate change"**: This doesn't highlight urban areas' specific vulnerability.
  - **D) "Cities have more resources available to address environmental issues"**: This doesn't support the claim about vulnerability, instead focusing on available resources.

## Question 11: Argumentation Analysis Question

- **Question:** How does the author use data to support their claim about rising crime rates in urban areas?
- **Correct Answer: B) The author presents statistics showing an upward trend in crime rates in several major cities.**
- **Explanation:** The author strengthens the argument about rising crime rates by providing statistical evidence.
  - **A) The author provides personal anecdotes to illustrate the increase in crime**: Personal anecdotes are not mentioned.
  - **C) The author discusses recent policy changes aimed at reducing crime**: This focuses on policy changes, not the rise in crime rates.
  - **D) The author references news reports about high-profile criminal cases**: News reports on specific cases do not provide the broad statistical evidence needed.

## Question 12: Inference Question

- **Question:** What can be inferred about the author's stance on gentrification in urban areas?
- **Correct Answer: C) The author is critical of gentrification's impact on low-income communities.**
- **Explanation:** The author critiques how gentrification has displaced low-income residents, indicating a critical stance.
  - **A) The author believes gentrification has led to significant social benefits**: The author doesn't suggest that gentrification has produced many benefits.
  - **B) The author views gentrification as a necessary part of urban development**: The author does not frame gentrification as a necessity.
  - **D) The author does not address the issue of gentrification**: Gentrification is addressed and critiqued.

## Question 13: Evidence-Based Question

- **Question:** Which sentence provides the strongest support for the argument that public spaces are essential for urban social cohesion?
- **Correct Answer: C) "Urban areas with more public spaces tend to report higher levels of civic engagement."**

- **Explanation:** This sentence directly links public spaces to civic engagement, supporting the argument about social cohesion.
  - ○ **A) "Public parks and squares offer residents a place to gather and interact":** This provides some support but does not explicitly link public spaces to social cohesion.
  - ○ **B) "Many cities have invested in creating new public spaces":** This sentence highlights investment, not social cohesion.
  - ○ **D) "Private spaces, such as shopping malls, have replaced traditional public spaces in many cities":** This sentence discusses private spaces, not the importance of public spaces.

**Question 14: Main Idea Question**
- **Question:** What is the author's primary concern about the future of urban development?
- **Correct Answer: D) The challenges of managing population growth in urban centers.**
- **Explanation:** The passage consistently refers to the challenges cities face due to rapid population growth.
  - ○ **A) The lack of green spaces in rapidly growing cities:** This may be a concern, but it is not the primary focus.
  - ○ **B) The unequal distribution of resources between urban and rural areas:** While important, this is not the central concern of the passage.
  - ○ **C) The increasing isolation of urban residents from one another:** While social issues are mentioned, the main concern is population growth.

## Natural Science Passage Solutions

**Question 1: Understanding Scientific Concepts**
- **Question:** What is the hypothesis being tested in the experiment described in the passage?
- **Correct Answer: C) That the presence of a catalyst speeds up the reaction time of certain processes.**
- **Explanation:** The passage focuses on the role of catalysts in speeding up chemical reactions. The other options either address different scientific concepts or do not align with the focus of the passage.
  - ○ **A) Increased sunlight exposure leads to faster plant growth:** This pertains to a different type of experiment.
  - ○ **B) Temperature variations have no effect on chemical reactions:** The passage does not suggest that temperature variations have no effect.
  - ○ **D) Genetic mutations occur at a steady rate regardless of environmental factors:** This is not relevant to the passage's experiment.

**Question 2: Interpretation of Data**
- **Question:** Based on the data presented in the graph, what conclusion can be drawn about the relationship between temperature and enzyme activity?
- **Correct Answer: C) Enzyme activity increases with temperature up to a certain point, then decreases.**
- **Explanation:** The graph shows that enzyme activity rises with increasing temperature until it reaches an optimal level, after which it declines, a typical pattern for enzyme behavior.

- o **A) Enzyme activity increases as temperature decreases**: This is incorrect, as enzyme activity decreases when temperatures fall too far.
- o **B) Enzyme activity remains constant across all temperature ranges**: This contradicts the fluctuation in enzyme activity shown in the graph.
- o **D) Enzyme activity is unaffected by temperature changes**: The graph clearly shows that temperature affects enzyme activity.

## Question 3: Vocabulary in Context

- **Question:** What does the word "catalyst" mean in the context of the experiment discussed?
- **Correct Answer: B) A substance that initiates or accelerates a chemical reaction.**
- **Explanation:** A catalyst is a substance that increases the rate of a chemical reaction without being consumed in the process. This matches the context of the passage.
  - o **A) A substance that slows down a chemical reaction**: A catalyst does not slow down reactions.
  - o **C) A compound that reacts with the enzyme to form a new product**: A catalyst does not get consumed or transformed in the reaction.
  - o **D) An element that is consumed during the reaction**: A catalyst remains unchanged throughout the reaction.

## Question 4: Understanding Scientific Concepts

- **Question:** What is the primary function of the control group in the experiment?
- **Correct Answer: B) To provide a baseline for comparison with the experimental group.**
- **Explanation:** The control group serves as a standard to compare results and determine the effect of the independent variable. The other options misunderstand the purpose of a control group.
  - o **A) To ensure that the experimental conditions remain constant**: This is part of maintaining consistency but is not the control group's main function.
  - o **C) To increase the accuracy of the experimental results**: While the control group helps ensure accurate results, its role is primarily comparative.
  - o **D) To eliminate the possibility of human error**: This is not the main role of the control group.

## Question 5: Interpretation of Data

- **Question:** Based on the chart presented in the passage, which variable shows the strongest correlation with the rate of photosynthesis?
- **Correct Answer: B) Light intensity**
- **Explanation:** The chart indicates that the rate of photosynthesis increases most significantly with light intensity, more than other factors like water availability or soil composition.
  - o **A) Water availability**: Water is important but does not show the strongest correlation in this specific context.
  - o **C) Carbon dioxide concentration**: This also influences photosynthesis but is less impactful in this particular experiment.
  - o **D) Soil composition**: Soil composition might affect plant growth but is not the most relevant factor for photosynthesis in this experiment.

## Question 6: Vocabulary in Context

- **Question:** In the passage, the word "molecule" is used. What is the most accurate meaning of the term "molecule" in this context?
- **Correct Answer: A) A large structure composed of atoms bonded together.**
- **Explanation:** In this scientific context, a molecule refers to a structure consisting of two or more atoms bonded together.
    - **B) A tiny particle that carries a charge:** This defines an ion, not a molecule.
    - **C) A single atom involved in a chemical reaction:** Molecules are composed of multiple atoms.
    - **D) A unit of measurement used in chemical experiments:** A molecule is not a unit of measurement but a physical entity.

## Question 7: Understanding Scientific Concepts

- **Question:** What was the main purpose of the experiment described in the passage?
- **Correct Answer: D) To explore how different nutrients affect soil bacteria.**
- **Explanation:** The passage focuses on the effect of various nutrients on soil bacteria, making this the most accurate answer.
    - **A) To determine the effects of gravity on plant growth:** This is unrelated to the experiment described.
    - **B) To measure the impact of varying water levels on plant survival:** The passage focuses on bacteria, not plants.
    - **C) To examine the role of light in cellular respiration:** Cellular respiration is not the focus of the experiment.

## Question 8: Interpretation of Data

- **Question:** The graph shows that as the concentration of substance A increases, the reaction rate also increases. What conclusion can be drawn from this information?
- **Correct Answer: C) The reaction rate depends directly on the concentration of substance A.**
- **Explanation:** The graph shows a direct correlation between the concentration of substance A and the reaction rate, making this conclusion the most accurate.
    - **A) The reaction rate is independent of the concentration of substance A:** The data shows a direct dependence, not independence.
    - **B) Substance A inhibits the reaction rate:** This is the opposite of what the data suggests.
    - **D) The reaction rate decreases as the concentration of substance A increases:** The reaction rate increases, not decreases, with higher concentrations of substance A.

## Question 9: Vocabulary in Context

- **Question:** What does the term "reaction rate" mean in the context of the passage?
- **Correct Answer: B) The speed at which a chemical reaction occurs.**
- **Explanation:** In the context of this experiment, "reaction rate" refers to how fast a chemical reaction takes place.
    - **A) The time it takes for the experiment to conclude:** This defines the experiment duration, not reaction rate.
    - **C) The ratio of reactants to products in a chemical reaction:** This describes the reaction stoichiometry, not the rate.

- o **D) The change in temperature during the reaction**: This is unrelated to the concept of reaction rate.

## Question 10: Understanding Scientific Concepts

- **Question:** What variable did the researchers manipulate to test their hypothesis?
- **Correct Answer: C) The presence or absence of a specific enzyme.**
- **Explanation:** The researchers were testing the effect of an enzyme on reaction rates, making this the correct answer.
  - o **A) The amount of sunlight each plant received**: This variable is unrelated to the described experiment.
  - o **B) The type of soil used in the experiment**: Soil type is not manipulated in this context.
  - o **D) The amount of water given to the control group**: This was not the variable being tested.

## Question 11: Interpretation of Data

- **Question:** Based on the chart in the passage, what is the relationship between the number of trials conducted and the accuracy of the results?
- **Correct Answer: D) Increasing the number of trials improves the reliability of the results.**
- **Explanation:** More trials typically lead to more reliable and accurate results, as they help eliminate outliers and reduce the impact of errors.
  - o **A) More trials lead to less accurate results**: This is the opposite of what the data suggests.
  - o **B) Fewer trials result in more reliable data**: Fewer trials tend to reduce reliability.
  - o **C) The number of trials does not affect the accuracy of the results**: The chart indicates that more trials improve accuracy.

## Question 12: Vocabulary in Context

- **Question:** In the passage, the word "variable" is used. What is the best definition of "variable" in this context?
- **Correct Answer: B) A factor that can be changed or controlled in the experiment.**
- **Explanation:** In an experiment, a variable is a factor that can be manipulated to observe its effect on the outcome.
  - o **A) An unknown quantity in the experiment**: A variable is not necessarily unknown.
  - o **C) A fixed number used for calculations**: Variables are not fixed; they change.
  - o **D) A measurement of the final outcome**: Variables are not the outcome but factors that influence the outcome.

## Question 13: Understanding Scientific Concepts

- **Question:** What role did the experimental group play in the study described in the passage?
- **Correct Answer: B) The experimental group was exposed to the independent variable to test its effect.**
- **Explanation:** The experimental group is the one where the independent variable is manipulated to observe its effects, contrasting with the control group.
  - o **A) The experimental group was used to replicate the conditions of the control group**: This is the opposite of the experimental group's purpose.

- C) **The experimental group provided baseline data for comparison**: The control group provides baseline data.

- D) **The experimental group introduced a new factor not originally included in the hypothesis**: The experimental group tests the hypothesis, not introduces unrelated factors.

**Question 14: Interpretation of Data**

- **Question:** The graph shows a rapid increase in growth rate as temperature rises from 10°C to 30°C, but a sharp decline beyond 35°C. What can be concluded about the ideal temperature for growth?

- **Correct Answer: C) Growth rate peaks between 30°C and 35°C.**

- **Explanation:** The data indicates that the growth rate is highest between 30°C and 35°C before declining, making this the correct answer.

  - A) **Growth rate is highest at temperatures above 40°C**: The graph shows a decline after 35°C.

  - B) **The ideal growth temperature is between 10°C and 20°C**: The highest growth rate occurs between 30°C and 35°C.

  - D) **Temperature has no effect on the growth rate**: The graph shows a clear relationship between temperature and growth rate.

# Historical Document Passage Solutions

**Question 1: Analysis of Author's Intent**

- **Question:** What was the author's primary purpose in delivering this speech?

- **Correct Answer: A) To inspire national unity and support for the war effort.**

- **Explanation:** The passage indicates that the author sought to unite the nation and rally support for a common cause, such as a war effort. Other options focus on criticizing policies, negotiations, or celebrations, none of which align with the author's main purpose.

  - B) **To criticize government policies and propose alternatives**: This option suggests criticism, but the passage emphasizes unity.

  - C) **To encourage peaceful negotiations between opposing factions**: There is no mention of encouraging negotiations.

  - D) **To celebrate a historical milestone and reflect on progress made**: The passage is not celebratory in nature.

**Question 2: Comparison of Historical Perspectives**

- **Question:** How does the author's perspective on democracy differ from that of another political leader mentioned in the passage?

- **Correct Answer: B) The author emphasizes individual rights, while the other leader focuses on collective responsibility.**

- **Explanation:** The passage contrasts the author's emphasis on individual rights with another leader's belief in collective responsibility, highlighting their differing views on democracy.

  - A) **The author believes in a limited government, while the other leader supports a centralized system**: This was not part of the passage.

- o **C) The author advocates for direct democracy, while the other leader favors representative democracy**: There is no mention of direct democracy in the passage.
- o **D) The author sees democracy as fragile, while the other leader views it as robust and evolving**: This interpretation is not reflected in the passage.

**Question 3: Inference about Historical Context**

- **Question:** Based on the passage, what can be inferred about the social conditions at the time of the document's writing?
- **Correct Answer: B) The society was deeply divided along political and ideological lines.**
- **Explanation:** The passage describes a divided society, with factions strongly opposing each other on key issues. This aligns with the inference that society was deeply divided.
  - o **A) There was widespread support for the author's ideas**: The passage does not suggest widespread support.
  - o **C) The population was largely unaware of the issues being discussed**: This is unlikely given the intensity of the divisions mentioned.
  - o **D) Economic prosperity had eliminated most social tensions**: The passage does not imply that economic prosperity had resolved social tensions.

**Question 4: Analysis of Rhetorical Strategies**

- **Question:** Which rhetorical strategy does the author use most effectively to persuade the audience?
- **Correct Answer: D) Appeal to national identity and pride.**
- **Explanation:** The passage emphasizes the use of national identity to unite the audience and encourage support for the author's message, making this the most effective rhetorical strategy.
  - o **A) Appeal to authority**: This is not the primary strategy used in the passage.
  - o **B) Use of emotional language**: While the author may use emotional language, the emphasis on national identity and pride is stronger.
  - o **C) Logical reasoning and evidence**: The passage is more focused on appeals to unity and pride rather than strict logical reasoning.

**Question 5: Comparison of Ideals**

- **Question:** How does the author's view of liberty compare to the ideas presented in another historical document mentioned in the passage?
- **Correct Answer: A) The author views liberty as a natural right, while the other document suggests it must be earned through loyalty.**
- **Explanation:** The passage contrasts the author's belief in liberty as an inherent right with another document's stance that liberty must be earned, showing a key difference in their ideals.
  - o **B) The author advocates for absolute liberty, while the other document supports limited freedoms in the interest of security**: This is not accurate based on the passage's discussion of liberty.
  - o **C) The author believes liberty should be granted universally, while the other document argues for selective application**: This was not a central point in the passage.
  - o **D) The author stresses individual freedoms, while the other document emphasizes societal obligations**: This is not the correct distinction highlighted in the passage.

**Question 6: Inference about the Audience**

- **Question:** What can be inferred about the intended audience of the document based on its tone and content?
- **Correct Answer: B) The audience was a general public in need of motivation and reassurance.**
- **Explanation:** The tone and content suggest that the author aimed to motivate and reassure a general audience, rather than addressing elites or diplomats.
  - ○ **A) The audience was composed of political elites and government officials**: The tone of the document is more inclusive and motivating for the general public.
  - ○ **C) The document was meant for foreign diplomats and international allies**: There is no indication that this was the primary audience.
  - ○ **D) The audience was primarily skeptics of the government's policies**: While the document may address concerns, it seems intended for a broader audience.

## Question 7: Analysis of Historical Impact

- **Question:** What impact did the author's ideas, as expressed in the document, have on subsequent political movements?
- **Correct Answer: C) The ideas were embraced by political leaders and enacted into law.**
- **Explanation:** The passage indicates that the author's ideas were influential and eventually adopted by political leaders, leading to changes in law.
  - ○ **A) The ideas sparked widespread protests and political reforms**: This is not the focus of the passage's historical impact.
  - ○ **B) The ideas were ignored at the time but gained popularity decades later**: The passage suggests immediate adoption rather than delayed popularity.
  - ○ **D) The ideas led to the downfall of the author's political career**: This is not supported by the passage.

## Question 8: Interpretation of Legal Language

- **Question:** In the context of the document, what does the term "inalienable rights" most likely mean?
- **Correct Answer: B) Rights that cannot be taken away or transferred.**
- **Explanation:** "Inalienable rights" refers to rights that are inherent and cannot be removed or transferred, as emphasized in the document.
  - ○ **A) Rights that can be surrendered under certain conditions**: This is the opposite of inalienable rights.
  - ○ **C) Rights granted only by legal authority**: Inalienable rights are natural, not granted by law.
  - ○ **D) Rights that apply only to a specific group of people**: Inalienable rights are universal, not limited to certain groups.

## Question 9: Analysis of Author's Bias

- **Question:** How does the author's background influence their perspective in the document?
- **Correct Answer: C) The author's political affiliation is reflected in their strong critique of the opposition.**
- **Explanation:** The author's background as a political figure influences their critique of opposing policies, as seen in the passage.

- o **A) The author's experiences in the military led to a focus on security over freedom**: This is not mentioned in the passage.
- o **B) The author's economic status influenced their argument for social reform**: There is no direct reference to the author's economic status affecting their views.
- o **D) The author's personal connections to the monarchy shaped their views on governance**: The passage does not suggest this connection.

## Question 10: Comparison of Political Ideologies

- **Question:** How does the political ideology expressed in this document compare to the principles of the Enlightenment?
- **Correct Answer: B) The document builds on Enlightenment ideas by promoting reason and equality.**
- **Explanation:** The passage reflects Enlightenment principles, particularly the promotion of reason and equality, which align with the author's message.
  - o **A) The document rejects Enlightenment ideals of individualism in favor of collective good**: This contradicts the passage's promotion of individual rights.
  - o **C) The document embraces Enlightenment concepts but focuses on economic prosperity over liberty**: The document prioritizes liberty over economic concerns.
  - o **D) The document contradicts Enlightenment values by advocating for authoritarian rule**: The passage aligns with Enlightenment ideals, not authoritarianism.

## Question 11: Inference about Social Hierarchy

- **Question:** What can be inferred about the social hierarchy during the time the document was written?
- **Correct Answer: A) Power was concentrated in the hands of a small elite.**
- **Explanation:** The passage suggests that the social hierarchy was top-heavy, with power held by a small elite group, which aligns with the historical context.
  - o **B) There was relative social equality across different classes**: This is not supported by the passage.
  - o **C) The middle class played a dominant role in political affairs**: The passage suggests elite dominance, not middle-class influence.
  - o **D) The document suggests that wealth was distributed evenly across the population**: Wealth inequality is implied, not equal distribution.

## Question 12: Analysis of Historical Significance

- **Question:** Why is the document considered a turning point in the nation's political history?
- **Correct Answer: C) It shifted the balance of power between government branches.**
- **Explanation:** The document marks a significant change in the balance of power, which makes it a key moment in political history.
  - o **A) It marked the first time democratic ideals were put into law**: This is not the specific focus of the passage.
  - o **B) It led to widespread social and economic reforms**: The focus is on political change rather than social or economic reforms.
  - o **D) It ended decades of political and social unrest**: This is not suggested as the primary significance of the document.

**Question 13: Inference about Future Implications**

- **Question:** Based on the author's predictions, what did they foresee as the future implications of their proposed changes?
- **Correct Answer: D) The changes would slowly transform the political system over time.**
- **Explanation:** The author predicts gradual transformation rather than immediate change, as indicated by their cautious optimism.
  - A) **The changes would lead to greater international conflict**: This is not a predicted outcome in the passage.
  - B) **The changes would bring about lasting peace and prosperity**: This is not stated as a direct result of the proposed reforms.
  - C) **The changes would be quickly reversed due to public resistance**: The passage suggests a more gradual, positive transformation.

**Question 14: Analysis of Argument Structure**

- **Question:** How does the author structure their argument to persuade the audience of the necessity of their proposed reforms?
- **Correct Answer: A) By presenting a series of logical steps that build on one another.**
- **Explanation:** The author uses a logical, step-by-step structure to build their argument and convince the audience of the need for reform.
  - B) **By appealing to the audience's emotions and sense of patriotism**: Emotional appeals are used, but the structure is primarily logical.
  - C) **By focusing on historical examples of failed policies**: While history may be mentioned, the focus is on logical progression.
  - D) **By outlining the moral and ethical implications of the current system**: This is a secondary consideration in the author's argument structure.

# SECTION 2: WRITING AND LANGUAGE

## Grammar and Sentence Structure Solutions

**Question 1: Subject-Verb Agreement**

- **Question:** "Which sentence maintains proper subject-verb agreement?"
- **Correct Answer: B) The team of scientists is studying new materials for space exploration.**
- **Explanation:** "Team" is a collective noun that takes a singular verb when the group is acting as a single entity, so "is studying" is correct.
  - A) **The team of scientists are studying new materials for space exploration**: Incorrect because "team" is singular and requires "is" instead of "are."
  - C) **The team of scientists studying new materials for space exploration**: This is a fragment; there's no verb.
  - D) **The teams of scientists is studying new materials for space exploration**: Incorrect because "teams" is plural and requires "are."

**Question 2: Parallel Structure**

- **Question:** "Which option maintains the parallelism in this list?"

- **Correct Answer: B) She enjoys running, swimming, and hiking.**
- **Explanation:** All three activities are in the gerund form, maintaining parallel structure.
  - **A) She enjoys running, swimming, and to hike:** "To hike" breaks the parallel structure.
  - **C) She enjoys to run, swimming, and hiking:** "To run" breaks the parallelism.
  - **D) She enjoys running, to swim, and hiking:** "To swim" disrupts the parallelism.

## Question 3: Misplaced Modifiers
- **Question:** "Which revision correctly places the modifier?"
- **Correct Answer: C) Staring into the sunset, the passengers found the boat to be a peaceful sight.**
- **Explanation:** "Staring into the sunset" clearly refers to "the passengers."
  - **A) Staring into the sunset, the boat was a peaceful sight:** Incorrect because it suggests the boat was staring into the sunset.
  - **B) The boat was a peaceful sight, staring into the sunset:** The placement of the modifier is awkward and unclear.
  - **D) The boat was a peaceful sight to the passengers staring into the sunset:** The modifier placement is less clear than in option C.

## Question 4: Verb Tense Consistency
- **Question:** "Which sentence uses verb tenses consistently?"
- **Correct Answer: B) She walked to the park and ate lunch on the bench.**
- **Explanation:** Both actions are in the past tense, which maintains consistency.
  - **A) She walked to the park and eats lunch on the bench:** Mixing past and present tenses.
  - **C) She walks to the park and had eaten lunch on the bench:** Inconsistent tenses.
  - **D) She had walked to the park and eats lunch on the bench:** Inconsistent tenses.

## Question 5: Pronoun-Antecedent Agreement
- **Question:** "Which sentence correctly matches the pronoun with its antecedent?"
- **Correct Answer: B) Each of the students must bring his or her own materials.**
- **Explanation:** "Each" is singular and requires a singular pronoun, "his or her."
  - **A) Each of the students must bring their own materials:** "Their" is plural and doesn't match the singular antecedent.
  - **C) Each of the students must bring its own materials:** "Its" refers to an object, not a person.
  - **D) Each of the students must bring our own materials:** "Our" is incorrect for "each."

## Question 6: Sentence Clarity
- **Question:** "Which revision best clarifies the meaning of the sentence?"
- **Correct Answer: B) The injured athlete who won the race inspired everyone.**
- **Explanation:** This revision clearly identifies the injured athlete as the one who won the race.
  - **A) The athlete who won the race while injured inspired everyone:** Less clear due to ambiguity about what happened during the injury.

- ○ **C) The race was won by the injured athlete who inspired everyone:** Slightly awkward, though clear.
- ○ **D) The athlete, while injured, inspired everyone by winning the race:** This option is less direct.

## Question 7: Punctuation

- **Question:** "Which option uses the comma correctly?"
- **Correct Answer: B) The book, that I borrowed from the library, is due tomorrow.**
- **Explanation:** The phrase "that I borrowed from the library" is a non-essential clause and is correctly set off by commas.
  - ○ **A) The book, that I borrowed from the library is due tomorrow:** Missing the second comma.
  - ○ **C) The book that I borrowed, from the library, is due tomorrow:** Misplaced commas.
  - ○ **D) The book that I borrowed from the library is due tomorrow:** No commas at all, which is incorrect for a non-essential clause.

## Question 8: Correct Use of Conjunctions

- **Question:** "Which sentence uses the conjunction correctly?"
- **Correct Answer: B) She wanted to go to the beach, but she had to work.**
- **Explanation:** The conjunction "but" correctly contrasts the two clauses.
  - ○ **A) She wanted to go to the beach or she had to work:** Incorrect use of "or."
  - ○ **C) She wanted to go to the beach, and had to work:** "And" doesn't show the contrast needed.
  - ○ **D) She wanted to go to the beach, so she had to work:** "So" suggests causality, which is incorrect here.

## Question 9: Identifying Sentence Fragments

- **Question:** "Which option fixes the sentence fragment?"
- **Correct Answer: B) She enjoyed running through the park in the evening.**
- **Explanation:** This is a complete sentence with both a subject and a verb.
  - ○ **A) Running through the park in the evening:** Fragment; no subject or complete verb.
  - ○ **C) Running through the park, it was peaceful:** Awkward phrasing, not a complete thought.
  - ○ **D) Through the park, running in the evening:** Fragment, no complete verb.

## Question 10: Correct Use of Adjectives and Adverbs

- **Question:** "Which sentence uses the adverb correctly?"
- **Correct Answer: B) He is really fast at solving math problems.**
- **Explanation:** "Really" is the correct adverb to modify "fast."
  - ○ **A) He is real fast at solving math problems:** "Real" is an adjective, not an adverb.
  - ○ **C) He solves math problems real fast:** Same error as in A.
  - ○ **D) He solves math problems really fastly:** "Fastly" is not a correct word.

## Question 11: Subject-Pronoun Agreement

- **Question:** "Which sentence uses the correct pronoun?"
- **Correct Answer: B) The team decided it would practice more.**

- **Explanation:** "Team" is a collective noun and takes the singular pronoun "it."
  - ○ **A) The team decided they would practice more:** "They" is plural.
  - ○ **C) The team decided we would practice more:** "We" doesn't match "team."
  - ○ **D) The team decided you would practice more:** "You" doesn't fit here.

**Question 12: Consistency of Style**

- **Question:** "Which sentence maintains the same style throughout?"
- **Correct Answer: B) After she finished the report, she was congratulated by her supervisor, and then went to celebrate.**
- **Explanation:** The sentence maintains past tense consistently and uses parallel construction.
  - ○ **A) After she finished the report, she was congratulated by her supervisor, and then goes to celebrate:** Mixing past and present tense.
  - ○ **C) After she finishes the report, she was congratulated by her supervisor, and then went to celebrate:** Inconsistent tenses.
  - ○ **D) After she finished the report, her supervisor congratulates her, and she then went to celebrate:** Mixed tenses.

**Question 13: Correct Usage of Prepositions**

- **Question:** "Which sentence uses the preposition correctly?"
- **Correct Answer: B) She is interested in learning new languages.**
- **Explanation:** "Interested in" is the correct preposition combination.
  - ○ **A) She is interested with learning new languages:** Incorrect preposition.
  - ○ **C) She is interested on learning new languages:** Incorrect preposition.
  - ○ **D) She is interested by learning new languages:** Incorrect preposition.

**Question 14: Run-On Sentences**

- **Question:** "Which option corrects the run-on sentence?"
- **Correct Answer: B) The sun was setting, and the sky turned orange.**
- **Explanation:** This corrects the run-on sentence by properly connecting the two independent clauses.
  - ○ **A) The sun was setting the sky turned orange:** Run-on sentence.
  - ○ **C) The sun was setting but, the sky turned orange:** Misplaced comma.
  - ○ **D) The sun was setting, the sky turned orange:** Run-on sentence.

**Question 15: Use of Conjunctions in Complex Sentences**

- **Question:** "Which sentence uses the conjunction correctly?"
- **Correct Answer: A) I'll visit you tomorrow because I'm not busy.**
- **Explanation:** "Because" correctly connects the two ideas without needing a comma.
  - ○ **B) I'll visit you tomorrow, because I'm not busy:** Unnecessary comma before "because."
  - ○ **C) I'll visit you tomorrow if I'm not busy:** "If" changes the meaning of the sentence.
  - ○ **D) I'll visit you tomorrow, if I'm not busy:** Incorrect comma usage before "if."

# Punctuation and Capitalization Solutions

## 1. Comma usage in lists:

- **Question:** Which sentence uses commas correctly to separate items in a list?
- **Correct Answer: (B)** – "I need to buy apples, oranges, and bananas."
- **Explanation:** Option B uses the Oxford comma, which is the correct way to separate items in a list. Option A omits the comma before "and," which can lead to confusion. Option C incorrectly places a comma after "buy." Option D omits the comma after "oranges."

## 2. Comma usage with introductory phrases:

- **Question:** Which sentence uses commas correctly after an introductory phrase?
- **Correct Answer: (B)** – "Before starting the project, she reviewed all the guidelines."
- **Explanation:** Option B correctly places a comma after the introductory phrase "Before starting the project." Option A omits the necessary comma. Option C incorrectly places a comma after "Before." Option D incorrectly separates "starting" and "the project."

## 3. Comma usage with non-essential clauses:

- **Question:** Which sentence uses commas correctly to set off non-essential information?
- **Correct Answer: (C)** – "My brother, who is a doctor, is coming to visit."
- **Explanation:** Option C correctly sets off the non-essential information "who is a doctor" with commas. Option A omits the second comma. Option B and D both place commas in incorrect positions.

## 4. Semicolon usage:

- **Question:** Which sentence uses a semicolon correctly to connect two independent clauses?
- **Correct Answer: (A)** – "The meeting is over; now we can head home."
- **Explanation:** A semicolon is correctly used to link two closely related independent clauses. Option A is correct. Option B incorrectly places a semicolon between "now" and "we." Option C wrongly adds "and" after the semicolon. Option D incorrectly uses a colon.

## 5. Colon usage:

- **Question:** Which sentence uses a colon correctly to introduce a list?
- **Correct Answer: (A)** – "We need the following supplies: pencils, paper, and rulers."
- **Explanation:** A colon is correctly used to introduce a list following the phrase "the following supplies." Option A is correct. Option B misplaces the colon, and Option C incorrectly punctuates the phrase "the following." Option D incorrectly uses a semicolon.

## 6. Apostrophe usage in singular possessives:

- **Question:** Which sentence properly indicates possession?
- **Correct Answer: (B)** – "The dog's collar was too tight."
- **Explanation:** Option B correctly indicates possession by the singular noun "dog." Option A uses the possessive apostrophe incorrectly for plural. Option C misplaces the apostrophe, and Option D incorrectly pluralizes both nouns.

## 7. Apostrophe usage in plural possessives:

- **Question:** Which sentence uses apostrophes correctly for plural possessives?
- **Correct Answer: (A)** – "The teachers' lounge is on the second floor."

- **Explanation:** Option A correctly uses the apostrophe to show possession by multiple teachers. Option B indicates possession by a single teacher. Option C omits the apostrophe, and Option D incorrectly places the apostrophe after "lounge."

## 8. Comma usage in compound sentences:

- **Question:** Which sentence correctly places a comma in a compound sentence?
- **Correct Answer: (B)** – "She enjoys reading, and she loves painting."
- **Explanation:** Option B correctly places a comma before the conjunction "and" in a compound sentence. Option A incorrectly places the comma after "and." Options C and D both misplace the commas.

## 9. Comma usage with conjunctions:

- **Question:** Which sentence correctly uses a comma with a conjunction?
- **Correct Answer: (C)** – "We went to the park, and we played soccer."
- **Explanation:** A comma is correctly used before "and" to separate two independent clauses. Option C is correct. Options A, B, and D incorrectly place or omit commas.

## 10. Correct usage of dashes:

- **Question:** Which sentence uses a dash correctly for emphasis?
- **Correct Answer: (A)** – "The result was clear—it was a success."
- **Explanation:** A dash is correctly used in Option A to emphasize "it was a success." Options B, C, and D place the dash incorrectly or in the wrong context.

## 11. Parentheses usage:

- **Question:** Which sentence uses parentheses correctly to include additional information?
- **Correct Answer: (A)** – "He studied physics (and chemistry) in college."
- **Explanation:** Parentheses are correctly used in Option A to add non-essential information. Option B incorrectly isolates the word "physics." Options C and D use parentheses incorrectly to emphasize irrelevant information.

## 12. Comma usage in dates:

- **Question:** Which sentence uses commas correctly in a date?
- **Correct Answer: (C)** – "She was born on May 25, 1995, in Chicago."
- **Explanation:** Option C correctly places commas between the day, year, and location. Options A, B, and D omit or misplace commas.

## 13. Capitalization in titles:

- **Question:** Which sentence uses capitalization correctly in a title?
- **Correct Answer: (A)** – "We read the book, 'To Kill a Mockingbird.'"
- **Explanation:** Option A correctly capitalizes the first and important words in the title. Options B, C, and D incorrectly capitalize parts of the title.

## 14. Correct placement of commas in addresses:

- **Question:** Which sentence uses commas correctly in an address?
- **Correct Answer: (C)** – "She lives at 123 Main Street, Chicago, Illinois."
- **Explanation:** Option C correctly places commas between the street address, city, and state. Options A, B, and D misplace or omit commas.

## 15. Quotation marks and punctuation:

- **Question:** Which sentence correctly places the punctuation inside the quotation marks?
- **Correct Answer: (A)** – "The project is due on Friday," she said.
- **Explanation:** Option A correctly places the punctuation (comma) inside the quotation marks. Options B, C, and D misplace the punctuation or omit it.

## Logical Flow and Coherence Solutions

1. **Improving transitions between paragraphs:**
   - **Question:** Which sentence best improves the transition between these two paragraphs?
   - **Correct Answer: (D)** – "However, the evidence provided does not align with the author's original argument."
   - **Explanation:** Option D creates a clear contrast, improving the flow between two paragraphs where an opposing viewpoint is introduced. Option A suggests adding information, Option B implies a result, and Option C introduces a comparison without the needed connection.

2. **Reordering sentences for logical flow:**
   - **Question:** Which sentence should be moved to improve the flow of ideas in this paragraph?
   - **Correct Answer: (B)** – "Sentence 2 should be moved to the beginning to provide a clear introduction."
   - **Explanation:** Option B improves the flow by making Sentence 2 the introductory sentence, which helps in establishing the context or main argument. The other options either complicate the flow or misplace the key points.

3. **Choosing the best transition between ideas:**
   - **Question:** Which sentence best transitions between the ideas in these two paragraphs?
   - **Correct Answer: (A)** – "Although this solution was proposed, it failed to address the underlying issues."
   - **Explanation:** Option A provides a contrasting transition, indicating that while a solution was suggested, it wasn't sufficient, which logically connects the ideas. Options B, C, and D suggest continuation or results, which don't fit as smoothly.

4. **Reordering sentences for improved clarity:**
   - **Question:** Which revision improves the clarity and logical sequence of the paragraph?
   - **Correct Answer: (D)** – "Rearrange the second and third sentences to clarify the progression of ideas."
   - **Explanation:** Option D best improves the logical sequence by ensuring the paragraph builds on each idea in a clear progression. Options A and C change the emphasis or conclusion without enhancing clarity, while Option B unnecessarily combines ideas.

5. **Improving transitions between sentences:**
   - **Question:** Which transition phrase best connects the two sentences?
   - **Correct Answer: (A)** – "Despite this evidence,"
   - **Explanation:** "Despite this evidence" creates the best transition, indicating that the next sentence will introduce contrasting information. Options B, C, and D either imply continuation or a different type of relationship between ideas that doesn't fit.

6. **Revising for logical flow within a paragraph:**

- **Question:** Which sentence should be removed to improve the logical flow of the paragraph?
- **Correct Answer: (B)** – "Sentence 3 because it introduces unrelated information."
- **Explanation:** Removing Sentence 3 improves flow by eliminating unrelated information that disrupts the paragraph's focus. The other sentences are more relevant to the main argument or necessary for coherence.

7. **Choosing the best conclusion to a paragraph:**
   - **Question:** Which sentence best concludes the paragraph by summarizing the key points?
   - **Correct Answer: (D)** – "For these reasons, the project was considered a partial success."
   - **Explanation:** Option D effectively summarizes the paragraph by providing a general conclusion that wraps up the main points. The other options are either too specific or don't summarize the broader argument.

8. **Reordering paragraphs for better coherence:**
   - **Question:** Which paragraph should be placed first to introduce the main argument of the passage?
   - **Correct Answer: (C)** – "Paragraph 1 because it presents the main thesis of the passage."
   - **Explanation:** Paragraph 1 should introduce the main thesis, ensuring that the argument is established at the start. The other paragraphs serve supporting or concluding roles.

9. **Identifying irrelevant sentences in a paragraph:**
   - **Question:** Which sentence could be removed without affecting the overall meaning of the paragraph?
   - **Correct Answer: (C)** – "Sentence 4 because it is not relevant to the main point."
   - **Explanation:** Removing Sentence 4 improves focus as it introduces irrelevant information. The other sentences are more closely tied to the main argument.

10. **Improving the coherence of a paragraph:**
    - **Question:** Which revision best improves the logical flow and coherence of the paragraph?
    - **Correct Answer: (A)** – "Rearrange the sentences to ensure the central argument is presented first."
    - **Explanation:** Rearranging the sentences to present the central argument first improves coherence and ensures the paragraph progresses logically. The other revisions may not address the overall coherence as effectively.

11. **Improving the clarity of transitions between ideas:**
    - **Question:** Which revision best clarifies the transition from one idea to the next?
    - **Correct Answer: (A)** – "Adding a contrasting phrase like 'However, this result was unexpected.'"
    - **Explanation:** Adding a contrasting phrase improves clarity by signaling a shift in ideas. The other options either don't add clarity or remove necessary transition phrases.

12. **Revising for consistency in tone and logical progression:**
    - **Question:** Which revision maintains the consistent tone and improves the logical flow of the paragraph?
    - **Correct Answer: (A)** – "Move the third sentence to the end to keep the paragraph focused on the main idea."
    - **Explanation:** Moving the third sentence to the end ensures that the paragraph's focus remains clear and logically progressive. The other options may not maintain the same consistency or flow.

## Sentence Clarity and Precision Solutions

**1. Improving clarity by simplifying sentence structure:**

- **Question:** Which revision best simplifies the sentence without changing its meaning?
- **Correct Answer: (B)** – "The scientist reported the results of the experiment despite facing challenges."
- **Explanation:** Option B is the clearest and most straightforward version. It retains the original meaning while removing unnecessary phrases and complexities found in the other choices.

**2. Clarifying unclear pronoun usage:**

- **Question:** Which sentence clarifies the unclear pronoun usage?
- **Correct Answer: (B)** – "Maria and Jen spoke about Maria's project, which was still in progress."
- **Explanation:** Option B resolves the pronoun ambiguity by specifying that the project belongs to Maria. The other options either remain vague or introduce new ambiguities.

**3. Improving precision by choosing the best word:**

- **Question:** Which word best improves the precision of the sentence?
- **Correct Answer: (D)** – "The company faced a significant amount of backlash."
- **Explanation:** "Significant" is the most precise and professional word choice here, indicating the backlash was noteworthy without exaggerating, unlike "huge" or "substantial."

**4. Revising for clarity in complex sentences:**

- **Question:** Which revision makes the sentence clearer and easier to understand?
- **Correct Answer: (B)** – "After much deliberation, the group finally decided to accept the offer at the last minute."
- **Explanation:** Option B restructures the sentence for maximum clarity, ensuring the sentence flows logically and succinctly. The other options are more convoluted.

**5. Correcting ambiguous pronoun reference:**

- **Question:** Which sentence clarifies the ambiguous pronoun reference?
- **Correct Answer: (B)** – "When the manager spoke to the employee, the employee was confused about the instructions."
- **Explanation:** Option B clarifies who was confused (the employee), whereas other options leave the pronoun "they" ambiguous or unclear.

**6. Improving clarity by rewording:**

- **Question:** Which revision best improves the clarity of the sentence?
- **Correct Answer: (D)** – "The class trip planned by the teacher would be canceled unless better arrangements could be made."
- **Explanation:** Option D is the clearest, eliminating wordiness and presenting the information in a direct and logical way. Other options introduce unnecessary complexity.

**7. Choosing the most precise verb:**

- **Question:** Which verb best improves the sentence's precision?
- **Correct Answer: (C)** – "The team worked hard to finalize the project."
- **Explanation:** "Finalize" is the most precise verb in this context, indicating the team was completing the final steps of the project. Other options like "finish" or "conclude" are less specific.

**8. Correcting unclear sentence structure:**

- **Question:** Which sentence revision makes the structure clearer and easier to follow?
- **Correct Answer: (B)** – "After hours of work, the team finally published the results, having faced many obstacles."
- **Explanation:** Option B organizes the sentence logically by presenting the events in a clear sequence. Other options complicate the sentence with awkward phrasing or misplaced modifiers.

### 9. Clarifying vague pronoun usage:
- **Question:** Which sentence revision clarifies the vague pronoun?
- **Correct Answer: (C)** – "The engineers revised the design, but the design changes didn't improve the outcome."
- **Explanation:** Option C clearly specifies "design changes" instead of the vague "it" in the original sentence, making the sentence clearer.

### 10. Improving sentence clarity by removing unnecessary words:
- **Question:** Which revision best simplifies the sentence without losing meaning?
- **Correct Answer: (C)** – "After a tedious process, the final report was submitted."
- **Explanation:** Option C eliminates unnecessary details while retaining the core meaning, making it more concise and easier to read.

### 11. Revising for clarity by correcting word placement:
- **Question:** Which revision correctly places the words for maximum clarity?
- **Correct Answer: (C)** – "The supervisor closely observed the team, who had just completed the task."
- **Explanation:** Option C clearly indicates that the team completed the task, and the supervisor is observing them. Other options either confuse the subject or present awkward phrasing.

### 12. Improving clarity by choosing the most appropriate conjunction:
- **Question:** Which conjunction best connects the ideas in this sentence?
- **Correct Answer: (C)** – "The proposal was accepted, and the company decided to move forward with the project."
- **Explanation:** "And" correctly links the two related ideas in the sentence, indicating that the acceptance of the proposal led to the company moving forward. Other options introduce conflicting or incorrect relationships between the ideas.

# TEST 2 SOLUTIONS:

## Reading Comprehension (Narrative Passage) Solutions

### 1. Inference Question
- **Question:** What can be inferred about the protagonist's motivation in the story?
- **Correct Answer:** The protagonist is motivated by fear of failure.
- **Explanation:** The text provides subtle clues about the protagonist's concerns regarding potential failure. Their actions reflect an underlying fear rather than a desire for external approval or power.

### 2. Main Idea Question
- **Question:** What is the central theme of the passage?
- **Correct Answer:** The importance of self-discovery.

- **Explanation:** The passage revolves around the protagonist's journey toward understanding themselves and their motivations, illustrating self-discovery as a core theme.

### 3. Tone Question

- **Question:** What is the tone of the passage?
- **Correct Answer:** Reflective.
- **Explanation:** The language and pacing of the narrative show a reflective tone, as the protagonist contemplates their past experiences and decisions, engaging in introspection.

### 4. Character Development Question

- **Question:** How does the protagonist change over the course of the passage?
- **Correct Answer:** They reconcile with a past mistake.
- **Explanation:** The protagonist's growth is evident through their acknowledgment and acceptance of a past mistake, marking a significant change in their mindset.

### 5. Relationship Analysis Question

- **Question:** What can be inferred about the relationship between the protagonist and their mentor?
- **Correct Answer:** They share a strong bond based on mutual respect.
- **Explanation:** The interactions between the protagonist and their mentor suggest a deep mutual respect, with the mentor offering support, and the protagonist valuing their guidance.

### 6. Plot Development Question

- **Question:** Which event serves as the turning point in the passage?
- **Correct Answer:** The protagonist makes a significant decision.
- **Explanation:** The key moment in the narrative is when the protagonist makes a decisive choice, altering the direction of the story and signifying personal growth.

### 7. Inference Question

- **Question:** What can be inferred about the antagonist's role in the story?
- **Correct Answer:** They represent societal pressures on the protagonist.
- **Explanation:** The antagonist is portrayed as a symbolic figure, embodying external pressures rather than acting as a direct threat, allowing the protagonist's internal struggles to take center stage.

### 8. Tone Shift Question

- **Question:** How does the tone of the passage shift from the beginning to the end?
- **Correct Answer:** From hopeful to resigned.
- **Explanation:** The passage begins with a sense of optimism but gradually transitions to resignation as the protagonist comes to terms with their situation and adjusts their expectations.

### 9. Character Motivation Question

- **Question:** Which of the following best describes the protagonist's motivation for their final decision?
- **Correct Answer:** A desire to break free from their past.
- **Explanation:** The protagonist's actions are driven by a need to leave behind the past and forge a new path, as evidenced by their reflections and ultimate decision.

### 10. Relationship Dynamics Question

- **Question:** How do the relationships between the characters evolve throughout the passage?

- **Correct Answer:** They grow closer as they understand each other better.
- **Explanation:** The characters experience growth in their relationships as their understanding of one another deepens, leading to a closer bond by the end of the passage.

## 11. Theme Question
- **Question:** Which of the following themes is most prevalent in the passage?
- **Correct Answer:** The search for identity.
- **Explanation:** Throughout the passage, the protagonist is on a journey of self-discovery, exploring questions of identity and personal growth, making this theme central to the narrative.

## 12. Character Decision Question
- **Question:** What does the protagonist's final decision reveal about their character?
- **Correct Answer:** They are willing to sacrifice personal happiness for a greater cause.
- **Explanation:** The protagonist's final decision demonstrates their willingness to prioritize a cause they believe in, even at the expense of their personal satisfaction, highlighting their sense of responsibility.

# Social Science Passage Solutions

with each question followed by the correct answer and detailed explanation, but without the options, as requested.

## 1. Evidence-Based Question
- **Question:** Which sentence provides the strongest support for the author's argument about the impact of industrialization on social structures?
- **Correct Answer:** "The rise of factories led to the migration of workers to cities, fundamentally altering family dynamics."
- **Explanation:** This sentence directly addresses the societal changes brought by industrialization, focusing on how family structures were affected by the movement of workers to urban centers.

## 2. Main Idea Question
- **Question:** What is the primary conclusion drawn by the author in the passage?
- **Correct Answer:** Industrialization had both positive and negative impacts on society.
- **Explanation:** The passage discusses various effects of industrialization, presenting a balanced view of its benefits and drawbacks, making this the main conclusion.

## 3. Argumentation Analysis Question
- **Question:** What evidence does the author use to support their argument that education played a critical role in societal changes during the Industrial Revolution?
- **Correct Answer:** The educated middle class led reforms aimed at improving working conditions.
- **Explanation:** The author highlights the role of the educated middle class in driving social reforms, linking education to significant societal improvements.

## 4. Inference Question
- **Question:** What can be inferred about the author's perspective on the role of women in industrialized societies?
- **Correct Answer:** The author sees women as key contributors to both the workforce and social reform.

- **Explanation:** The passage suggests that women were involved in the workforce and played a significant role in advocating for social changes during industrialization.

## 5. Main Idea Question

- **Question:** What is the central argument of the passage regarding the rise of labor unions?
- **Correct Answer:** Labor unions emerged as a response to poor working conditions.
- **Explanation:** The author argues that the harsh conditions faced by workers during industrialization were the primary cause for the emergence of labor unions.

## 6. Evidence-Based Question

- **Question:** Which statement from the passage best supports the idea that technological advancements during the industrial era were a double-edged sword?
- **Correct Answer:** "While technological advancements boosted the economy, they also deepened social inequalities."
- **Explanation:** This sentence directly addresses the dual nature of industrial technology, highlighting both its economic benefits and its role in worsening social inequalities.

## 7. Argumentation Analysis Question

- **Question:** Which piece of evidence does the author use to justify their claim that governments played a role in regulating industrial growth?
- **Correct Answer:** Governments introduced child labor laws to protect young workers.
- **Explanation:** The passage points to child labor laws as an example of government intervention to regulate the negative effects of industrialization.

## 8. Inference Question

- **Question:** What can be inferred from the passage about the relationship between industrialization and social mobility?
- **Correct Answer:** The growth of industry created new pathways for social advancement.
- **Explanation:** The passage implies that industrialization opened up opportunities for social mobility, particularly for those who adapted to the new economic landscape.

## 9. Main Idea Question

- **Question:** What is the author's primary purpose in discussing the migration of workers to urban areas during the industrial era?
- **Correct Answer:** To highlight how industrialization led to demographic shifts.
- **Explanation:** The movement of workers to cities is used as an example to demonstrate the significant demographic changes caused by industrialization.

## 10. Argumentation Analysis Question

- **Question:** How does the author support their argument that industrialization led to significant changes in family structure?
- **Correct Answer:** By discussing how industrial work schedules affected family dynamics.
- **Explanation:** The author argues that the demands of industrial labor altered traditional family roles and routines, leading to shifts in family dynamics.

## 11. Evidence-Based Question

- **Question:** Which of the following best supports the claim that education was a key factor in the social mobility of industrial workers?

- **Correct Answer:** "Workers who pursued education were able to rise through the ranks in factories."
- **Explanation:** This sentence links education directly to upward mobility, showing how it provided workers with opportunities for advancement within the industrial economy.

## 12. Inference Question

- **Question:** What can be inferred about the author's view on the environmental impact of industrialization?
- **Correct Answer:** The author sees environmental degradation as a byproduct of economic progress.
- **Explanation:** The passage suggests that while industrialization brought economic growth, it also led to significant environmental harm, which was often overlooked in favor of progress.

## 13. Main Idea Question

- **Question:** What is the author's central claim about the relationship between industrial growth and government regulation?
- **Correct Answer:** Government regulation was necessary to control the negative effects of industrialization.
- **Explanation:** The author emphasizes the need for government intervention to mitigate the adverse consequences of rapid industrial growth.

## 14. Evidence-Based Question

- **Question:** Which sentence from the passage best supports the author's claim that labor unions were essential in improving working conditions?
- **Correct Answer:** "Unions successfully negotiated shorter work hours and better wages for workers."
- **Explanation:** This sentence provides concrete evidence of how labor unions directly contributed to better working conditions for industrial workers.

# Natural Science Passage Solutions

with each question followed by the correct answer and detailed explanation, without the options as requested.

## 1. Scientific Concepts Question

- **Question:** What hypothesis is being tested in the experiment described in the passage?
- **Correct Answer:** That temperature changes alter the rate of photosynthesis in plants.
- **Explanation:** The passage explains that the researchers are testing how varying temperatures affect the photosynthesis rate, focusing on the relationship between temperature and plant growth.

## 2. Data Interpretation Question

- **Question:** What can be concluded from the data presented in the graph?
- **Correct Answer:** Plants receiving higher amounts of nitrogen grew taller than those with less.
- **Explanation:** The graph indicates a clear relationship between nitrogen levels and plant height, showing that plants with more nitrogen experienced more significant growth compared to those with lower levels.

## 3. Vocabulary in Context Question

- **Question:** What does the word 'catalyst' mean in the context of the passage?

- **Correct Answer:** A substance that initiates or speeds up a chemical reaction.
- **Explanation:** In the context of the experiment, a catalyst is described as a substance that accelerates the chemical reactions involved in photosynthesis, a key part of the scientific study.

## 4. Scientific Theory Question

- **Question:** Which scientific principle underlies the experiment described in the passage?
- **Correct Answer:** The process of photosynthesis in plants.
- **Explanation:** The experiment revolves around the process of photosynthesis, specifically how different factors such as light and temperature impact the rate at which plants convert sunlight into energy.

## 5. Data and Graphs Question

- **Question:** What trend is evident in the graph showing plant growth over time?
- **Correct Answer:** Plant growth is directly proportional to the amount of sunlight received.
- **Explanation:** The graph demonstrates that the more sunlight the plants received, the greater their growth, indicating a positive correlation between light exposure and growth rate.

## 6. Scientific Method Question

- **Question:** Which step of the scientific method is the author most likely describing in paragraph 4?
- **Correct Answer:** Analyzing the data.
- **Explanation:** Paragraph 4 focuses on the interpretation and analysis of the data collected from the experiment, which is the stage of the scientific method where researchers examine the results to draw conclusions.

## 7. Hypothesis and Conclusion Question

- **Question:** What is the conclusion drawn by the scientists after the experiment?
- **Correct Answer:** The data supports the hypothesis that increased sunlight promotes faster growth.
- **Explanation:** The experiment results indicated that plants receiving more sunlight grew faster, which directly supports the initial hypothesis about the role of sunlight in promoting plant growth.

## 8. Cause and Effect Question

- **Question:** According to the passage, what effect did nutrient-rich soil have on plant growth?
- **Correct Answer:** Plants in nutrient-rich soil grew taller than those in regular soil.
- **Explanation:** The passage outlines that plants grown in nutrient-rich soil demonstrated enhanced growth compared to those in standard soil, highlighting the importance of nutrients in plant development.

## 9. Controlled Variables Question

- **Question:** Which variable was controlled during the experiment described in the passage?
- **Correct Answer:** The amount of sunlight each plant received.
- **Explanation:** The amount of sunlight was kept consistent for all plants to ensure that this factor did not skew the results, allowing the researchers to focus on the impact of other variables like soil or water.

## 10. Experimental Results Question

- **Question:** What do the results of the experiment suggest about the importance of sunlight in photosynthesis?
- **Correct Answer:** Sunlight is essential for photosynthesis, as plants receiving more light showed greater growth.

- **Explanation:** The experiment demonstrated that plants exposed to more sunlight had better growth rates, reinforcing the critical role of sunlight in the photosynthesis process.

## 11. Scientific Process Question

- **Question:** What does the author suggest as the next step for the researchers?
- **Correct Answer:** Repeating the experiment with a larger sample size.
- **Explanation:** The author implies that to confirm the findings, it would be prudent to repeat the experiment using a larger sample size, ensuring that the results are reliable and applicable to a broader context.

## 12. Control Group Question

- **Question:** Why was a control group necessary in this experiment?
- **Correct Answer:** To compare the effects of the experimental variable with a baseline condition.
- **Explanation:** The control group provides a baseline for comparison, allowing the researchers to observe the impact of the experimental variable (e.g., sunlight or nutrients) against a group not exposed to these conditions.

## 13. Critical Thinking Question

- **Question:** What might be a potential flaw in the experimental design described in the passage?
- **Correct Answer:** The experiment was conducted over too short a period of time.
- **Explanation:** A short experiment duration might not provide enough time to observe the full effects of the variables being tested, potentially leading to incomplete or inconclusive results.

## 14. Vocabulary in Context Question

- **Question:** What does the term 'photosynthetic efficiency' mean in the context of the passage?
- **Correct Answer:** The rate at which plants convert sunlight into usable energy.
- **Explanation:** Photosynthetic efficiency refers to how effectively plants use sunlight to produce energy through photosynthesis, which is directly related to their growth and survival.

# Historical Document Passage Solutions

## 1. Author's Intent Question

- **Question:** What was the author's primary purpose in delivering this speech?
- **Correct Answer:** To rally support for a political movement.
- **Explanation:** The passage highlights how the speech was aimed at garnering public and political backing for a larger cause. The author uses persuasive language and appeals to unity to encourage people to support the movement.

## 2. Inference about Historical Context Question

- **Question:** What can be inferred about the social conditions during the time this document was written?
- **Correct Answer:** There was widespread political unrest.
- **Explanation:** The passage references various instances of political tension and dissatisfaction among the populace, suggesting that unrest was a significant factor during this period.

## 3. Comparison of Historical Perspectives Question

- **Question:** How does the author's perspective on national security differ from that of another historical figure mentioned in the passage?

- **Correct Answer:** The author favors a more diplomatic approach, while the other figure supports military intervention.
- **Explanation:** The passage contrasts the author's advocacy for diplomacy with another figure's preference for military action, indicating different approaches to national security.

## 4. Author's Argument Question

- **Question:** What argument does the author make in support of their proposed solution to the economic crisis?
- **Correct Answer:** Increasing government spending on public infrastructure is essential.
- **Explanation:** The author argues that economic growth and recovery can be stimulated through investment in public works and infrastructure, providing a clear solution to the crisis.

## 5. Cause and Effect Question

- **Question:** What effect did the policy proposed in the document have on the political landscape of the time?
- **Correct Answer:** It caused a rift between political parties.
- **Explanation:** The passage notes how the proposed policy led to divisions between political factions, with opposing sides offering different viewpoints on its effectiveness and necessity.

## 6. Tone and Language Question

- **Question:** What is the tone of the author's language when describing the opposition's stance on this issue?
- **Correct Answer:** Critical and disapproving.
- **Explanation:** The author uses strong language to criticize the opposition, pointing out flaws in their arguments and demonstrating disapproval of their stance.

## 7. Understanding Historical Nuance Question

- **Question:** What can be inferred about the author's view on international diplomacy based on their description of recent negotiations?
- **Correct Answer:** The author believes diplomacy is essential for maintaining peace.
- **Explanation:** The passage discusses diplomacy as a key tool in resolving conflicts and maintaining international stability, indicating the author's positive view of its role in peacekeeping.

## 8. Intent and Purpose Question

- **Question:** Why did the author choose to reference a past political leader in their argument?
- **Correct Answer:** To draw a parallel between current events and a historical example.
- **Explanation:** The author references a past leader to highlight similarities between past and present political situations, using history to support their current argument.

## 9. Contextual Inference Question

- **Question:** What can be inferred about the legal challenges faced by the government during this period?
- **Correct Answer:** The government was struggling with constitutional crises.
- **Explanation:** The passage suggests that the government faced significant legal obstacles related to constitutional interpretations, which posed challenges to policy-making and governance.

## 10. Argumentation and Evidence Question

- **Question:** What evidence does the author provide to support their argument for economic reform?

- **Correct Answer:** Historical examples of successful economic policies.
- **Explanation:** The author references historical precedents where similar economic reforms were successful, using them as evidence to strengthen the argument for current reforms.

## 11. Comparison of Two Perspectives Question

- **Question:** How does the author's view on civil rights differ from that of another leader mentioned in the passage?
- **Correct Answer:** The author advocates for immediate change, while the other leader supports gradual reform.
- **Explanation:** The passage contrasts the urgency with which the author believes civil rights reforms should be enacted with another leader's more cautious and gradual approach.

## 12. Inference from Historical Context Question

- **Question:** What can be inferred about the relationship between the government and the press during this time?
- **Correct Answer:** The press was highly critical of government actions.
- **Explanation:** The passage indicates that the media frequently criticized the government, implying a tense relationship between the press and political leadership.

## 13. Author's Perspective on Political Leadership Question

- **Question:** How does the author view the role of political leadership in resolving the national crisis?
- **Correct Answer:** The author believes strong leadership is essential for success.
- **Explanation:** The author emphasizes the need for decisive and effective leadership to navigate the country through its current difficulties, suggesting that weak or indecisive leadership would lead to failure.

## 14. Historical Impact Question

- **Question:** What long-term impact did the policies discussed in the document have on future generations?
- **Correct Answer:** They set a precedent for future legal reforms.
- **Explanation:** The passage notes how the policies introduced in the document influenced subsequent legal and political changes, establishing a lasting impact on future governance.

# Writing and Language

# Grammar and Sentence Structure Solutions

## 1. Subject-Verb Agreement

- **Question:** Which sentence maintains proper subject-verb agreement?
- **Correct Answer:** The dog barks loudly every morning.
- **Explanation:** In this sentence, "dog" is a singular subject and "barks" is the correct singular verb form. Subject-verb agreement requires that singular subjects match with singular verbs.

## 2. Parallel Structure

- **Question:** Which sentence correctly maintains parallelism?
- **Correct Answer:** She enjoys reading, swimming, and hiking.

- **Explanation:** This sentence maintains parallel structure by keeping all verb forms in the same "-ing" form. Parallel structure ensures consistency and clarity in lists or comparisons.

## 3. Misplaced Modifiers

- **Question:** Which sentence correctly places the modifier?
- **Correct Answer:** Driving down the street, I noticed the house was beautiful.
- **Explanation:** The modifier "Driving down the street" correctly modifies the subject "I" in this sentence, ensuring that the action of driving is logically attributed to the right person.

## 4. Pronoun-Antecedent Agreement

- **Question:** Which sentence uses the correct pronoun?
- **Correct Answer:** Neither Sarah nor Emily has finished her homework.
- **Explanation:** In this sentence, "Neither" is singular, and the correct singular pronoun is "her" to match the singular antecedent.

## 5. Dangling Modifiers

- **Question:** Which sentence corrects the dangling modifier?
- **Correct Answer:** After taking the test, I was surprised by the results.
- **Explanation:** In this sentence, the modifier "After taking the test" is correctly linked to the subject "I," ensuring that the modifier is not left dangling without a clear subject.

## 6. Consistent Tense Usage

- **Question:** Which sentence maintains consistent tense throughout?
- **Correct Answer:** He walked to the park and saw his friends there.
- **Explanation:** The sentence maintains consistent past tense, with both "walked" and "saw" correctly aligned in the past form.

## 7. Sentence Fragment

- **Question:** Which option presents a complete sentence?
- **Correct Answer:** Running through the field, they laughed with joy.
- **Explanation:** This is a complete sentence because it includes a subject ("they") and a predicate ("laughed with joy"), making it a complete thought.

## 8. Comma Splices

- **Question:** Which sentence fixes the comma splice?
- **Correct Answer:** He ran to the store; he bought milk.
- **Explanation:** A semicolon is used correctly to join two independent clauses, eliminating the comma splice.

## 9. Verb Tense Consistency

- **Question:** Which sentence maintains consistent verb tense?
- **Correct Answer:** I run every morning, and I eat breakfast afterward.
- **Explanation:** Both verbs, "run" and "eat," are in the present tense, ensuring consistency in the sentence.

## 10. Pronoun Clarity

- **Question:** Which revision improves the clarity of the pronoun?
- **Correct Answer:** When the teacher handed out the exams, she said the test was tough.

- **Explanation:** Replacing "it" with "the test" clarifies the pronoun reference, ensuring that the reader understands what "it" refers to.

## 11. Relative Pronouns

- **Question:** Which sentence correctly uses the relative pronoun?
- **Correct Answer:** The book that I read was fascinating.
- **Explanation:** The relative pronoun "that" is used correctly to introduce the essential clause modifying "book."

## 12. Compound Sentences

- **Question:** Which sentence correctly forms a compound sentence?
- **Correct Answer:** I went to the store; I bought some groceries.
- **Explanation:** The semicolon is used to connect two independent clauses, forming a compound sentence without creating a comma splice.

## 13. Faulty Parallelism

- **Question:** Which sentence fixes the parallelism error?
- **Correct Answer:** She loves hiking, biking, and swimming.
- **Explanation:** All three verbs are in the same form, maintaining parallel structure and ensuring the sentence flows logically.

## 14. Sentence Boundaries

- **Question:** Which sentence avoids a run-on or fragment?
- **Correct Answer:** He loves to cook, and he makes dinner every night.
- **Explanation:** The use of a comma and conjunction correctly separates the two independent clauses, avoiding a run-on sentence.

## 15. Comparative and Superlative Forms

- **Question:** Which sentence correctly uses the comparative form?
- **Correct Answer:** This dish is tastier than the last one.
- **Explanation:** The comparative form "tastier" is correctly used to compare the two dishes.

# Logical Flow and Coherence Solutions

## 1. Improving Transitions Between Paragraphs

- **Question:** Which sentence best improves the transition between these two paragraphs?
- **Correct Answer:** The discovery of penicillin revolutionized medicine. Additionally, these medical breakthroughs paved the way for new treatments.
- **Explanation:** The transition word "Additionally" effectively links the second paragraph by emphasizing the continuation of advancements in medicine due to penicillin's discovery.

## 2. Logical Sequence of Ideas

- **Question:** Which sentence would best follow this one to maintain a logical sequence?
- **Correct Answer:** Many workers relocated to urban centers in search of jobs.
- **Explanation:** The logical next step in discussing the impact of the Industrial Revolution on working conditions is to describe how workers moved to cities for employment opportunities.

## 3. Clarifying Sentence Order

- **Question:** Which sentence should be moved to improve the logical flow of ideas in the paragraph?

- **Correct Answer:** Sentence 4: "Communication tools have evolved significantly since then."
- **Explanation:** This sentence, which discusses the broader evolution of communication tools, should come at the end to serve as a concluding thought after the discussion of Alexander Graham Bell's invention.

## 4. Enhancing Paragraph Unity

- **Question:** Which sentence should be removed to improve the coherence of the paragraph?
- **Correct Answer:** Sentence 3: "The Earth has been orbiting the sun for billions of years."
- **Explanation:** This sentence is irrelevant to the paragraph's focus on renewable energy, and its removal improves the paragraph's unity.

## 5. Correcting Misplaced Transitions

- **Question:** Which option best corrects the misplaced transition in this paragraph?
- **Correct Answer:** Renewable energy sources are beneficial; however, they are not without challenges. For example, wind energy is inconsistent.
- **Explanation:** The transition "however" is appropriately placed to contrast the benefits and challenges of renewable energy sources, improving clarity and flow.

## 6. Choosing Effective Transition Words

- **Question:** Which transition word or phrase best connects the ideas in these sentences?
- **Correct Answer:** In contrast.
- **Explanation:** "In contrast" effectively links the two sentences by highlighting the difference between electric cars' affordability and their availability compared to gas-powered cars.

## 7. Improving Sentence Flow

- **Question:** Which revision improves the flow of the following sentences?
- **Correct Answer:** The company introduced a new product, which was successful in the market.
- **Explanation:** This revision uses a relative clause ("which was successful") to smoothly connect the two ideas, improving sentence flow and coherence.

## 8. Fixing Redundant Transitions

- **Question:** Which sentence removes the redundant transition and improves coherence?
- **Correct Answer:** Firstly, the city implemented new traffic policies. As a result, congestion was reduced.
- **Explanation:** Removing the second redundant transition ("Secondly") and using "As a result" improves coherence by indicating the effect of the new policies more clearly.

## 9. Maintaining Consistent Focus in Paragraphs

- **Question:** Which sentence maintains the focus of the paragraph best?
- **Correct Answer:** These advancements have increased crop yields significantly.
- **Explanation:** This sentence directly relates to the paragraph's focus on technological advancements in agriculture and their positive impact, maintaining consistency.

## 10. Identifying Off-Topic Sentences

- **Question:** Which sentence should be removed to maintain paragraph focus?
- **Correct Answer:** The cost of building social media apps is usually high.
- **Explanation:** This sentence is unrelated to the main topic of how social media has transformed communication, and removing it maintains the paragraph's focus.

## 11. Correcting Transition Errors

- **Question:** Which revision improves the transition between these two ideas?
- **Correct Answer:** In addition to changing how people work and communicate, the internet has created new opportunities in education.
- **Explanation:** This revision clearly links the two ideas by showing how the internet affects both work/communication and education, creating a smooth transition.

## 12. Choosing the Most Coherent Conclusion

- **Question:** Which sentence provides the most coherent conclusion to the paragraph?
- **Correct Answer:** Social media is a powerful tool that has reshaped the way we interact with each other.
- **Explanation:** This conclusion sums up the discussion about social media's impact on society, providing coherence and reinforcing the main argument.

# Sentence Clarity and Precision Solutions

## 1. Improving Clarity

- **Question:** Which revision makes the sentence clearer and easier to understand?
- **Correct Answer:** The event was interesting and memorable.
- **Explanation:** This revision removes unnecessary words and simplifies the sentence, making it more direct and concise while retaining the original meaning.

## 2. Simplifying Sentence Structure

- **Question:** Which sentence simplifies the structure without losing meaning?
- **Correct Answer:** Because the weather was bad, the soccer game was postponed.
- **Explanation:** This option reduces the wordiness of the original sentence by replacing "Due to the fact that" with "Because," making the sentence more straightforward and easier to read.

## 3. Avoiding Redundant Phrasing

- **Question:** Which revision best eliminates redundancy?
- **Correct Answer:** The CEO plans to introduce innovations that are different from what competitors offer.
- **Explanation:** The original sentence uses redundant phrases like "new innovations" and "novel and different." This revision eliminates unnecessary words and simplifies the message.

## 4. Clarifying Ambiguous Pronouns

- **Question:** Which revision clarifies the pronoun usage in the sentence?
- **Correct Answer:** When the manager spoke to the team, the team was confused.
- **Explanation:** The original sentence has an ambiguous pronoun ("they"), which could refer to either the manager or the team. This revision clearly identifies "the team" as the subject that was confused.

## 5. Correcting Wordiness

- **Question:** Which option best revises the sentence to remove unnecessary words?
- **Correct Answer:** The company needs to make improvements.
- **Explanation:** This option is the simplest and most direct, removing phrases like "at this point in time" that do not add meaning.

## 6. Choosing More Precise Vocabulary

- **Question:** Which revision uses the most precise word?
- **Correct Answer:** The scientist made a significant discovery that transformed the field.
- **Explanation:** The word "significant" is more precise than "big" and fits better in a scientific context, while "transformed" provides a more impactful description of the change in the field.

## 7. Clarifying the Relationship Between Ideas

- **Question:** Which revision clarifies the relationship between the two ideas in the sentence?
- **Correct Answer:** Even though the company expanded its product line, revenue did not increase.
- **Explanation:** This revision introduces "Even though" to clarify the contrast between expanding the product line and not increasing revenue, making the relationship between the two ideas clearer.

## 8. Revising for Precision and Conciseness

- **Question:** Which sentence is both more precise and concise?
- **Correct Answer:** The experiment's results surprised the researchers, who did not expect this outcome.
- **Explanation:** This revision eliminates unnecessary words while maintaining the meaning, making the sentence both concise and clear.

## 9. Clarifying Comparison Structures

- **Question:** Which revision clarifies the comparison in the sentence?
- **Correct Answer:** The company's new model is both faster and more affordable than the models of its competitors.
- **Explanation:** This option clarifies the comparison by making it clear that the new model is being compared to the competitors' models in terms of both speed and affordability.

## 10. Eliminating Unnecessary Phrases

- **Question:** Which revision eliminates the unnecessary phrase and improves clarity?
- **Correct Answer:** To reduce production costs, the company needs to make changes.
- **Explanation:** This revision removes the redundant phrases "In order to" and "several changes that will lead to," making the sentence more concise and to the point.

## 11. Clarifying Cause and Effect Relationships

- **Question:** Which sentence best clarifies the cause and effect relationship?
- **Correct Answer:** After the new policy was implemented, employee morale improved significantly.
- **Explanation:** This revision clearly shows the cause-and-effect relationship by specifying that morale improved after the policy was implemented, making the connection between the two events clearer.

## 12. Simplifying Complex Structures

- **Question:** Which sentence simplifies the complex structure while retaining the original meaning?
- **Correct Answer:** The project was delayed due to unforeseen difficulties.
- **Explanation:** This revision reduces the complex structure by condensing "Due to the fact that" to "due to" and removing unnecessary phrases like "for an extended period of time."

## Development Approach for Test Sections

- **Objective**: Each section of the practice tests should provide a comprehensive and authentic SAT experience. The questions will be designed to reflect the actual SAT's difficulty level and content focus, ensuring that students can thoroughly practice the skills necessary for success on the exam.

## Question Development

- **Balanced Coverage**: The tests will cover all essential content areas, including reading comprehension, grammar, writing and language, vocabulary in context, and logical reasoning.
- **SAT-like Format**: Each question will mirror the structure and complexity of actual SAT questions, following the same instructions, multiple-choice format, and distractor (wrong answer) options.
- **Variety in Question Types**: Questions will span inference, main idea, tone analysis, vocabulary, and sentence improvement for reading comprehension. For writing and language, there will be a mix of grammar corrections, sentence structure revisions, clarity enhancements, and logical flow questions.

## Detailed Solutions

- **In-depth Explanations**: Solutions will not only provide the correct answer but also explain why it is the best choice, while addressing why the other options are incorrect. This approach ensures that students can learn from their mistakes and build their understanding of key concepts.
- **Key Learning Points**: Each solution will highlight the relevant grammar rule, reading strategy, or test-taking technique that students should focus on. This will reinforce the principles necessary to avoid similar errors in the future.
- **Clarity and Precision**: Solutions will aim to be clear and accessible, avoiding overly complex language while still providing meaningful and detailed explanations.

## Test Experience Simulation

- **Realistic Practice**: The structure and timing of each section will mirror the actual SAT, allowing students to simulate the full test experience. This includes managing time effectively and maintaining focus throughout the test.
- **Holistic Feedback**: Through the detailed solutions, students will gain insight into areas where they can improve. This approach provides not just answers, but strategies for improvement.
- **Comprehensive Resource**: This chapter will serve as a complete practice resource for students, equipping them with both the questions and the learning tools necessary to refine their skills before taking the real SAT.

# CHAPTER 8: ANSWER KEYS AND EXPLANATIONS FOR ALL EXERCISES

## Section 1: Narrative Passage Comprehension

## Narrative Passage 1: General understanding of plot, character development, and relationships

**Question 1:** *Correct Answer: A) Adjusting to a new environment*

**Explanation:** The passage centers around the protagonist's struggle to navigate life in a new city. Throughout the narrative, the character experiences challenges with adapting to new surroundings, highlighting the difficulties they face in finding comfort and stability in an unfamiliar environment. This makes "adjusting to a new environment" the correct choice, as it captures the central conflict of the passage.

**Question 2:** *Correct Answer: B) Close and supportive*

**Explanation:** The interactions between the protagonist and their best friend reveal a strong, supportive bond. They frequently confide in each other, offering emotional support during difficult times. This indicates that their relationship is not strained or distant, but rather close and mutually encouraging.

**Question 3:** *Correct Answer: A) It emphasizes the isolation the character feels*

**Explanation:** The setting of the story plays a crucial role in emphasizing the protagonist's feelings of isolation. Descriptions of the new city as overwhelming and impersonal contribute to the character's sense of being alone in their struggles, making "emphasizing the isolation" the most accurate explanation of the setting's significance.

**Question 4:** *Correct Answer: B) Through the character's thoughts and reflections*

**Explanation:** The protagonist's internal conflict is primarily revealed through their introspective moments, where they reflect on their feelings of displacement and uncertainty. This method of revealing the conflict aligns with how the author uses internal monologues and reflections to express the protagonist's struggles, making "thoughts and reflections" the best answer.

**Question 5:** *Correct Answer: B) They decide to open up to their classmates about their personal life*

**Explanation:** The protagonist's change in attitude becomes evident when they choose to open up to their peers about personal challenges. This marks a pivotal moment in the story, as it shows the protagonist becoming more vulnerable and willing to connect with others, contrasting their earlier reluctance.

**Question 6:** *Correct Answer: A) The struggle of adapting to change*

**Explanation:** The primary theme of the passage revolves around the difficulties the protagonist faces while trying to adjust to a new city and school. This theme of "adapting to change" is woven throughout the narrative, with the protagonist experiencing both external and internal struggles related to this challenge.

**Question 7:** *Correct Answer: C) Illustrate the mood and tone of the new environment*

**Explanation:** The author uses descriptive language in the second paragraph to set the tone of the protagonist's new surroundings, emphasizing the mood of unfamiliarity and discomfort. The detailed descriptions serve to illustrate the emotional impact of the new environment on the character.

**Question 8:** *Correct Answer: B) Reflective and melancholic*

**Explanation:** The tone of the passage is reflective, as the protagonist spends much of the time thinking about their struggles and past experiences. There is also a melancholic undertone, as the protagonist feels disconnected and unsure of how to move forward in their new situation.

**Question 9:** *Correct Answer: C) The rainy weather outside reflects the protagonist's internal sadness*

**Explanation:** The author uses the rainy weather as a symbol of the protagonist's mood, mirroring their internal sadness and feelings of isolation. This is a common literary device where external elements in the setting, such as weather, reflect a character's emotional state.

**Question 10:** *Correct Answer: B) They are shy and unsure of themselves*

**Explanation:** The protagonist's interactions with their classmates suggest that they are hesitant and insecure. Rather than coming across as confident or aggressive, the protagonist often second-guesses their actions and is unsure of how to connect with others, highlighting their shyness.

**Question 11:** *Correct Answer: A) They feel misunderstood and neglected by their parents*

**Explanation:** The passage implies that the protagonist feels disconnected from their family, particularly their parents. They feel misunderstood and unsupported, contributing to their sense of isolation as they navigate the challenges of their new environment.

**Question 12:** *Correct Answer: B) Explain why the protagonist is uncomfortable in the new setting*

**Explanation:** The flashback in the third paragraph offers insights into the protagonist's past experiences, helping to explain their discomfort in the new setting. By reflecting on previous situations where they felt similarly out of place, the flashback provides context for their current emotional state.

**Question 13:** *Correct Answer: B) The depth of their friendship*

**Explanation:** The dialogue between the protagonist and their best friend reveals the closeness of their relationship. They are able to speak openly with each other, indicating a deep level of trust and support. This helps the reader understand the strength of their bond.

**Question 14:** *Correct Answer: A) By describing the protagonist's struggle to fit in*

**Explanation:** The author develops tension by focusing on the protagonist's difficulty in fitting in with their peers. The protagonist is often on the outside of social circles, which creates a sense of tension and conflict in their interactions with others.

**Question 15:** *Correct Answer: B) Is still struggling but has hope for the future*

**Explanation:** The ending of the passage suggests that while the protagonist has not fully overcome their struggles, there is a sense of hope. The protagonist begins to see a path forward, indicating that while challenges remain, they are optimistic about the future.

## Narrative Passage 2: Key Themes and Implicit Meanings

**Question 1:** *Correct Answer: D) The conflict between personal ambition and family duty*

**Explanation:**
The passage explores the protagonist's internal struggle between pursuing their own dreams and fulfilling the expectations placed on them by their family. This conflict is at the heart of the narrative, making the theme of personal ambition versus family duty the central theme.

**Question 2:** *Correct Answer: B) Highlight the emotional weight of a significant decision*

**Explanation:**

The metaphor in the third paragraph is used to emphasize the protagonist's emotional burden as they face a critical decision. The use of figurative language in this context underscores the gravity of the choice they must make, indicating that this moment is pivotal in the narrative.

**Question 3:** *Correct Answer: D) Deeply connected despite external challenges*

**Explanation:**

The relationship between the protagonist and the supporting character is characterized by a deep emotional connection, even though they face external challenges that test their bond. Their mutual understanding and support are highlighted throughout the passage, suggesting a connection that endures despite difficulties.

**Question 4:** *Correct Answer: A) The protagonist is struggling with unresolved grief*

**Explanation:**

Although not explicitly stated, the passage implies that the protagonist is grappling with unresolved grief, likely connected to past events or relationships. This implicit meaning is conveyed through the protagonist's reflective thoughts and emotional responses, making it a subtle but important aspect of the story.

**Question 5:** *Correct Answer: A) By showing how the protagonist gives up their own dreams for the sake of others*

**Explanation:**

Throughout the passage, the author illustrates the theme of personal sacrifice by depicting how the protagonist sets aside their own aspirations to fulfill the needs or expectations of those around them. This theme is consistently reinforced by the protagonist's actions and decisions.

**Question 6:** *Correct Answer: A) They are torn between following their passion and fulfilling their obligations*

**Explanation:**

The protagonist's internal conflict centers around the tension between their personal passions and the obligations they feel towards their family or community. This struggle is a recurring theme, and the protagonist's indecision is a key element of the narrative.

**Question 7:** *Correct Answer: B) Reflective and melancholic*

**Explanation:**

The tone of the passage is reflective, as the protagonist contemplates their past decisions and current struggles. There is also a melancholic undertone, as they face the emotional weight of their choices and the sacrifices they have made. The narrative focuses on introspection and emotional depth.

**Question 8:** *Correct Answer: C) It reflects the protagonist's fear of the unknown*

**Explanation:**

The recurring image of the ocean in the passage symbolizes the protagonist's fear of uncertainty and the unknown. The vastness and unpredictability of the ocean are used as a metaphor for the protagonist's anxieties about their future and the difficult choices they must make.

**Question 9:** *Correct Answer: B) Act as a foil to the protagonist's ambitions*

**Explanation:**

The supporting character serves as a foil to the protagonist, representing an alternative path or set of values that contrast with the protagonist's ambitions. This character helps to highlight the internal conflict the protagonist experiences, as they wrestle with their desires and responsibilities.

**Question 10:** *Correct Answer: B) They will continue to fight for what they believe in, despite the odds*

**Explanation:**

The protagonist's final decision reflects a renewed sense of determination and resolve. Despite the challenges they face, they decide to persevere and continue pursuing their goals, suggesting that they are not willing to give up on their dreams, even in the face of adversity.

**Question 11:** *Correct Answer: B) It symbolizes the protagonist's journey towards self-discovery*

**Explanation:**

The setting in the passage serves as a symbol for the protagonist's personal journey. The physical environment mirrors the protagonist's internal journey toward self-discovery, with the obstacles they encounter in the setting reflecting their emotional struggles and growth.

**Question 12:** *Correct Answer: C) To show the contrast between the protagonist's past and present mindset*

**Explanation:**

The use of flashbacks in the narrative is intended to contrast the protagonist's past mindset with their current struggles. By revisiting key moments from the protagonist's past, the author highlights how much they have changed and how these past experiences shape their present decisions.

**Question 13:** *Correct Answer: A) The overwhelming expectations placed on the protagonist by society*

**Explanation:**

The phrase "the weight of the world rested on their shoulders" refers to the immense pressure the protagonist feels from societal expectations. This metaphor conveys the protagonist's sense of responsibility and the emotional burden they carry as they navigate their personal and social obligations.

**Question 14:** *Correct Answer: B) Ambition must be tempered by a sense of duty and responsibility*

**Explanation:**

The narrative suggests that while ambition is important, it cannot be pursued without consideration for one's responsibilities to others. The protagonist's struggle to balance their ambition with their sense of duty highlights the complexities of pursuing personal goals while maintaining relationships and fulfilling obligations.

**Question 15:** *Correct Answer: A) Hopeful optimism despite current challenges*

**Explanation:**

The passage suggests that, despite the difficulties the protagonist faces, they view their future with a sense of hope and optimism. The protagonist acknowledges the challenges ahead but remains determined to move forward with confidence and resilience, indicating a hopeful outlook.

# Narrative Passage 3: Interpretation of Tone, Mood, and Author's Voice

**Question 1:** *Correct Answer: A) Nostalgic and wistful*

**Explanation:**

The tone of the passage reflects a longing for the past, paired with a reflective sadness. The author's use of language evokes a sense of nostalgia, suggesting that the protagonist is looking back on past experiences with a wistful feeling, which indicates an emotional connection to these memories.

**Question 2:** *Correct Answer: A) It changes from hopeful to somber*

**Explanation:**

The mood in the first paragraph is hopeful as the protagonist anticipates a positive outcome, but in the second paragraph, the mood shifts to somber as the challenges or realities of the situation become more apparent. This change highlights the protagonist's evolving emotional state.

**Question 3:** *Correct Answer: B) Establish a serene and peaceful mood*

**Explanation:**

In paragraph 3, the author's use of descriptive language—such as calm and soothing imagery—creates a peaceful and serene mood, which contrasts with the underlying tension in the protagonist's life. This juxtaposition of mood and inner turmoil deepens the emotional resonance of the passage.

**Question 4:** *Correct Answer: B) Conversational and reflective*

**Explanation:**

The author's voice is reflective, guiding the reader through the protagonist's inner thoughts and emotions. The conversational tone makes the narrative feel intimate, as if the reader is privy to the protagonist's private reflections on their journey, adding depth to the personal experience.

**Question 5:** *Correct Answer: C) The emotionally charged words contribute to a sense of despair*

**Explanation:**

The author's choice of words—laden with emotional weight—intensifies the sense of despair felt by the protagonist. Words like "heavy," "burden," and "overwhelming" build a tone of emotional struggle, contributing to the overall somber atmosphere of the passage.

**Question 6:** *Correct Answer: B) It amplifies the feeling of solitude and isolation*

**Explanation:**

The imagery in the fourth paragraph, perhaps describing an empty landscape or a desolate room, enhances the mood of solitude and isolation. This reinforces the protagonist's sense of being emotionally disconnected from others, aligning with the reflective and melancholic tone of the passage.

**Question 7:** *Correct Answer: B) Is preparing to confront a difficult truth*

**Explanation:**

Towards the end of the passage, the tone shifts, suggesting that the protagonist is bracing for a difficult realization or decision. The narrative builds to this moment of acceptance or confrontation, where the protagonist must face an uncomfortable truth, which contributes to the emotional arc of the story.

**Question 8:** *Correct Answer: C) Metaphor*

**Explanation:**

The author employs metaphor to convey deeper emotional layers in the narrative. For example, the metaphor of a "storm brewing" may represent internal conflict or emotional turmoil. This literary device helps establish the tone by adding complexity to the emotional landscape of the story.

**Question 9:** *Correct Answer: B) The voice is personal and introspective, guiding the reader through the author's internal journey*

**Explanation:**

The author's introspective voice draws readers into the protagonist's emotional world, allowing them to engage with the passage's themes on a personal level. This intimate voice serves as a vehicle for exploring complex emotions, guiding the reader through the protagonist's internal struggles.

**Question 10:** *Correct Answer: A) Sympathetic and understanding*

**Explanation:**

The author's tone towards the main character is empathetic, showing an understanding of their internal conflict and emotional journey. This sympathetic tone helps the reader connect with the protagonist's struggles, making them more relatable and emotionally resonant.

**Question 11:** *Correct Answer: B) "Every decision seemed heavier than the last, as though the weight of time pressed down on them."*

**Explanation:**

This sentence sets the tone for the entire narrative by establishing a sense of emotional weight and responsibility that the protagonist carries. It reflects the protagonist's internal struggles and sets the stage for the reflective and contemplative mood of the passage.

**Question 12:** *Correct Answer: B) The nostalgic tone gives the setting a dreamlike, idealized quality*

**Explanation:**

The author's nostalgic tone imbues the setting with a sense of idealization, making it feel almost dreamlike. This enhances the reader's perception of the setting as more than just a physical space—it becomes a symbolic representation of the protagonist's memories and emotions.

**Question 13:** *Correct Answer: B) Calmness and resignation*

**Explanation:**

The use of repetition in the final paragraph creates a mood of calm resignation, as the protagonist comes to accept their situation. The repetition of key phrases or ideas reinforces this sense of inevitability and closure, contributing to the reflective tone of the passage.

**Question 14:** *Correct Answer: A) It emphasizes the protagonist's internal conflict by juxtaposing calm and chaos*

**Explanation:**

The author uses contrast—such as calm external settings juxtaposed with the protagonist's internal turmoil—to emphasize the depth of the protagonist's internal conflict. This contrast heightens the emotional tension, making the protagonist's struggle more pronounced and engaging.

**Question 15:** *Correct Answer: B) It draws the reader in by making the protagonist's journey feel universal*

**Explanation:**

The author's tone creates a universal connection to the protagonist's journey, making it relatable for readers. By presenting the protagonist's emotional experiences in a way that feels familiar, the author invites readers to reflect on their own lives and similar challenges, enhancing the narrative's impact.

# Narrative Passage 4: Analysis of Setting and Historical Context

**Question 1:** *Correct Answer: A) By focusing on the sensory details of the environment*

**Explanation:**

The author uses vivid descriptive language to paint a picture of the setting, employing sensory details such as sights, sounds, and textures. This creates a rich, immersive environment that influences the characters' actions and emotions, helping the reader understand the significance of the setting in the narrative.

**Question 2:** *Correct Answer: A) It limits their choices due to societal restrictions*

**Explanation:**

The historical context imposes societal restrictions on the characters, limiting their freedom of action and influencing their decisions. In the passage, these societal norms or laws prevent the characters from making certain choices, shaping the course of the narrative and adding layers of tension.

**Question 3:** *Correct Answer: B) The social hierarchy*

**Explanation:**

The social hierarchy in the setting plays a critical role in shaping the plot, as it determines the characters' roles and relationships. This hierarchy influences their actions, motivations, and conflicts, driving the story forward by placing constraints on the characters' interactions and opportunities.

**Question 4:** *Correct Answer: B) They struggle with traditional values versus new ideals*

**Explanation:**

The time period presents a conflict between traditional values and emerging new ideals. This tension influences the characters' motivations as they navigate personal and societal expectations. The passage highlights their internal struggles as they try to reconcile these opposing forces.

**Question 5:** *Correct Answer: C) The political instability leaves them feeling helpless and confused*

**Explanation:**

The setting of political instability presents a significant challenge to the characters, making them feel powerless and uncertain about their future. This instability drives the conflict and adds urgency to their decisions, affecting both their personal lives and broader societal interactions.

**Question 6:** *Correct Answer: A) It amplifies personal conflicts by adding social and political pressures*

**Explanation:**

The historical context heightens the personal conflicts by introducing external pressures such as social norms and political unrest. These external factors exacerbate the characters' internal struggles, creating a more complex and layered narrative that reflects both personal and societal challenges.

**Question 7:** *Correct Answer: C) The dialogue between the characters discussing political tensions*

**Explanation:**

The characters' dialogue about political tensions provides insight into how the historical setting shapes their lives and relationships. This detail illustrates the direct influence of the historical context on the narrative, showing how larger societal issues impact personal interactions.

**Question 8:** *Correct Answer: A) By using historical events as a backdrop that parallels their personal struggles*

**Explanation:**

The author integrates historical events into the narrative by paralleling the characters' personal struggles with the broader societal issues of the time. This technique adds depth to the story, showing how the characters' lives are shaped by the historical forces around them, even if they are not directly involved in these events.

**Question 9:** *Correct Answer: B) It encourages community and bonding due to shared challenges*

**Explanation:**

The setting fosters a sense of community as the characters face common challenges. The harsh environment or societal constraints push them to rely on one another, strengthening their relationships as they work together to overcome adversity.

**Question 10:** *Correct Answer: B) The political turmoil*

**Explanation:**

The political turmoil of the time period is the greatest obstacle for the characters, shaping their decisions and creating external conflicts that complicate their lives. This turmoil adds tension to the narrative, forcing the characters to navigate a volatile political landscape.

**Question 11:** *Correct Answer: A) It emphasizes the difficulty of living in such a harsh environment*

**Explanation:**

The author's portrayal of the setting highlights the extreme challenges the characters face, such as harsh weather or social restrictions. This helps the reader understand the severity of the characters' struggles and emphasizes the difficulties of their circumstances.

**Question 12:** *Correct Answer: C) The stability of the community is more important than personal desires*

**Explanation:**

The societal values of the time period prioritize community stability over individual desires. The characters are often forced to sacrifice their personal ambitions to maintain social order, reflecting the importance placed on collective wellbeing during this historical period.

**Question 13:** *Correct Answer: A) By showing how the characters' decisions are influenced by historical events*

**Explanation:**

The author uses the historical context to highlight key themes by showing how the characters' decisions are shaped by the events of their time. This integration of personal and historical elements underscores the broader societal forces that influence the characters' lives.

**Question 14:** *Correct Answer: A) It fosters feelings of isolation and helplessness*

**Explanation:**

The setting contributes to the characters' feelings of isolation and helplessness, especially in a challenging or hostile environment. This emotional response to the setting reinforces the overall tone of the passage and adds to the characters' internal struggles.

**Question 15:** *Correct Answer: A) It forces them to adopt opposing views on social change*

**Explanation:**

The historical context creates tension between the characters by forcing them to adopt differing views on social change. These opposing perspectives drive the conflict, as the characters grapple with the societal shifts occurring around them, making it difficult for them to find common ground.

# Section 2: Social Science Passage Comprehension

## Social Science Passage 1: Identifying Main Ideas and Details

**Question 1:** *Correct Answer: C) To summarize findings from recent research*

**Explanation:**

The passage provides an overview of a study or collection of studies, focusing on the results and implications of the research. The primary purpose is not to introduce a new theory or critique existing ones but to synthesize and present the key findings in a clear, structured way, making option C the most accurate choice.

**Question 2:** *Correct Answer: C) Shifts in cultural attitudes*

**Explanation:**

The passage indicates that changes in societal values or cultural beliefs are the primary driver of the trend described. The author emphasizes how these evolving attitudes have influenced the behavior of individuals and groups, ruling out options like technological advances or governmental policies as the main factor.

**Question 3:** *Correct Answer: B) It introduces a key statistic to support the author's argument*

**Explanation:**

In the second paragraph, the author likely presents statistical evidence to back up the central argument of the passage. By including relevant data, the paragraph strengthens the author's claims about the trends or patterns being discussed.

**Question 4:** *Correct Answer: D) Results from a public opinion survey*

**Explanation:**

The author provides data from a public opinion survey to demonstrate that societal values have shifted over time. The use of survey results allows the author to ground the argument in empirical evidence, showing changes in how people think about certain issues.

**Question 5:** *Correct Answer: A) The author's reference to unemployment rates*

**Explanation:**

Unemployment rates are mentioned as a key factor that demonstrates the impact of economic conditions on social behavior. This detail connects economic factors with social changes, illustrating how financial challenges shape the actions and attitudes of individuals in society.

**Question 6:** *Correct Answer: B) It provides a real-world application of the study's findings*

**Explanation:**

The third paragraph likely uses a specific example to show how the research findings can be applied in a real-world context. This example helps clarify the practical relevance of the study and its implications for understanding broader societal trends.

**Question 7:** *Correct Answer: C) Educational attainment is increasingly valued for economic mobility*

**Explanation:**

The passage explains that, over time, education has become more highly regarded as a means of improving one's socioeconomic status. This shift reflects the growing importance of education in helping individuals achieve upward social mobility.

**Question 8:** *Correct Answer: B) There is a need for greater interdisciplinary collaboration*

**Explanation:**

The author concludes that future research in social science will benefit from integrating knowledge and methods from various disciplines. This approach will allow for more comprehensive and nuanced studies, indicating that collaboration across fields is essential for continued progress.

**Question 9:** *Correct Answer: A) By illustrating the widespread nature of the issue being discussed*

**Explanation:**

The author uses statistics to show how the issue being addressed affects a large portion of society. The data highlights the scope of the problem, reinforcing the argument that it is a significant and pervasive social concern.

**Question 10:** *Correct Answer: B) It provides additional evidence to reinforce the thesis*

**Explanation:**

The fourth paragraph likely offers more evidence or examples that support the author's main argument. By continuing to build the case, the paragraph strengthens the overall thesis and adds depth to the discussion.

**Question 11:** *Correct Answer: A) Neutral and objective*

**Explanation:**

The author maintains a neutral, objective tone throughout the passage, presenting information in a balanced and factual manner. There is no strong bias or emotional language, suggesting that the author's intent is to inform rather than persuade or argue.

**Question 12:** *Correct Answer: B) They rely too heavily on quantitative data*

**Explanation:**

The author critiques the current research methods for placing too much emphasis on numbers and data, potentially overlooking more qualitative aspects of social phenomena. This critique highlights the need for a more balanced approach in future studies.

**Question 13:** *Correct Answer: A) The ability of individuals to change their social status through education or employment*

**Explanation:**

The term "social mobility" refers to the movement of individuals within a society's social hierarchy, often through mechanisms such as education or employment. The passage discusses how this concept plays a role in understanding societal trends and individual aspirations.

**Question 14:** *Correct Answer: B) The correlation between cultural attitudes and savings rates*

**Explanation:**

The passage likely presents evidence linking cultural beliefs or values with economic behaviors, such as how people manage their money. This connection underscores the influence of cultural shifts on financial decision-making within society.

**Question 15:** *Correct Answer: C) Governments tend to lag behind cultural shifts in implementing policy changes*

**Explanation:**

The passage suggests that governments are often slow to react to changes in societal values, with policy adjustments typically following cultural shifts rather than leading them. This idea highlights the reactive nature of government interventions in response to evolving social trends.

## Social Science Passage 2: Evaluating Evidence and Argumentation

**Question 1:**

*Correct Answer: B) Technology has significantly altered the way people communicate.*

**Explanation:**

The primary claim made by the author in the passage is that technology has fundamentally changed how people interact with each other. The passage focuses on how communication has shifted due to digital tools, making option B the best answer.

**Question 2:**

*Correct Answer: B) A study that compares online and face-to-face interactions.*

**Explanation:**

The strongest piece of evidence is a study that directly compares the two modes of communication, supporting the author's claim that technology has had a profound effect on social interactions. Personal anecdotes or opinions from social scientists, while relevant, are not as compelling as scientific research.

**Question 3:**

*Correct Answer: A) To strengthen the author's claim by acknowledging a potential flaw.*

**Explanation:**

The counterargument is presented to show that the author is considering other perspectives. By addressing a potential flaw or opposing view, the author is attempting to make their own argument more robust and well-rounded.

**Question 4:**

*Correct Answer: C) By offering a new perspective that neutralizes the counterargument.*

**Explanation:**

The author does not ignore or refute the counterargument directly but instead presents a new angle that effectively neutralizes it. This allows the author to maintain the integrity of their original claim while addressing the opposing viewpoint.

**Question 5:**

*Correct Answer: B) Deductive reasoning, starting with a broad principle and applying it to specific cases.*

**Explanation:**

The author uses deductive reasoning by starting with a general principle—technology has altered communication—and then applies it to specific cases, such as the effects of digital communication on social interaction.

## Question 6:

*Correct Answer: C) An opinion piece written by a popular journalist.*

### Explanation:

While opinions can add perspective, they do not provide the same level of credibility or objectivity as scientific studies or data. An opinion piece from a journalist, therefore, is the least effective evidence for supporting the author's argument.

## Question 7:

*Correct Answer: A) By providing exact figures to prove a direct correlation.*

### Explanation:

In paragraph 4, the author likely uses data and specific statistics to demonstrate a clear correlation between technology use and changes in social behavior. This reinforces the claim by offering concrete evidence.

## Question 8:

*Correct Answer: A) "Most people prefer face-to-face interactions over digital communication."*

### Explanation:

This is a generalization because it makes a broad claim about the majority of people without citing specific data. It assumes a universal preference for face-to-face communication, which may not apply to everyone.

## Question 9:

*Correct Answer: A) Appeal to authority by citing experts in the field.*

### Explanation:

The author strengthens the argument by appealing to authority, citing experts and studies from reputable sources in the field of social science. This increases the credibility of the claims made in the passage.

## Question 10:

*Correct Answer: A) The reliance on outdated studies.*

### Explanation:

The use of outdated studies can weaken the author's argument by suggesting that the evidence may no longer be relevant to current social trends. More up-to-date research would provide stronger support for the claims.

## Question 11:

*Correct Answer: B) To make the argument more relatable to the reader.*

### Explanation:

The use of hypothetical scenarios helps readers visualize the impact of the author's claims in real-world situations. This makes the argument more relatable and accessible, helping to engage the audience.

## Question 12:

*Correct Answer: A) The assumption that technology will always have a negative impact on communication.*

### Explanation:

This assumption is a logical flaw because it oversimplifies the effects of technology. Not all communication changes brought about by technology are negative, and the argument would be stronger if it acknowledged the complexity of the issue.

## Question 13:

*Correct Answer: B) It may provide more nuanced insights into how technology affects relationships.*

**Explanation:**

The author implies that future research will likely offer a more detailed understanding of the relationship between technology and social behavior, possibly revealing new complexities and interactions.

**Question 14:**

*Correct Answer: A) By acknowledging their limitations and suggesting alternative explanations.*

**Explanation:**

The author addresses potential biases in the studies by pointing out their limitations and offering alternative interpretations. This strengthens the argument by showing transparency and consideration of other factors.

**Question 15:**

*Correct Answer: C) To explore both sides of the debate on technology and social interaction.*

**Explanation:**

The passage presents both the positive and negative aspects of technology's impact on communication, aiming for a balanced discussion rather than pushing for one extreme conclusion. Thus, the purpose is to explore the full debate rather than promoting a single viewpoint.

## Social Science Passage 3: Synthesizing Information from Multiple Sources

**Question 1:**

*Correct Answer: C) The first source focuses on long-term solutions, and the second emphasizes short-term fixes.*

**Explanation:**

The two sources differ in their approaches to solving the issue: one source is oriented towards long-term solutions, while the other prioritizes immediate, short-term actions. This difference in focus is a common way to compare perspectives on complex social issues.

**Question 2:**

*Correct Answer: C) The author synthesizes the information to show how both perspectives contribute to a comprehensive solution.*

**Explanation:**

The author uses evidence from both sources to show how each contributes to a broader understanding of the issue. Rather than pitting the two perspectives against each other, the author integrates their ideas into a more complete approach.

**Question 3:**

*Correct Answer: A) Both agree on the cause of the problem but differ in their proposed solutions.*

**Explanation:**

Although the sources may have different suggestions for solving the issue, they agree on the fundamental cause. This common ground is important when evaluating conflicting viewpoints.

**Question 4:**

*Correct Answer: C) The sources agree on certain facts but diverge in their interpretations.*

**Explanation:**

Both sources may present similar factual data but differ in their interpretation and proposed actions. This is a typical scenario when synthesizing different viewpoints, especially in social science studies.

**Question 5:**

*Correct Answer: A) The author juxtaposes the sources to highlight the strengths and weaknesses of each.*

**Explanation:**

By placing the two sources side by side, the author allows the reader to compare their respective strengths and weaknesses. This rhetorical strategy makes it easier to evaluate both perspectives fairly.

**Question 6:**

*Correct Answer: A) The first source uses quantitative data, while the second relies on anecdotal evidence.*

**Explanation:**

The difference in methodology is significant because it affects the reliability and generalizability of each source's claims. Quantitative data provides numerical evidence, while anecdotal evidence is more subjective.

**Question 7:**

*Correct Answer: A) The author combines both sources' suggestions into a cohesive strategy for action.*

**Explanation:**

Synthesis involves combining multiple perspectives into a unified approach. In this case, the author draws on the strengths of both sources to propose a comprehensive solution that includes elements of each.

**Question 8:**

*Correct Answer: D) By using both sets of data to provide a balanced perspective on the issue.*

**Explanation:**

The author effectively uses data from both sources to create a well-rounded argument, showing the reader that multiple approaches are needed to fully understand and address the issue.

**Question 9:**

*Correct Answer: A) The author finds a middle ground that both sources imply but do not explicitly state.*

**Explanation:**

The author resolves the apparent contradiction between the two sources by identifying a compromise that incorporates aspects of both perspectives, even if the sources do not directly state it.

**Question 10:**

*Correct Answer: A) To demonstrate that differing perspectives can enrich understanding of a complex issue.*

**Explanation:**

The inclusion of both sources serves to show the complexity of the issue. Multiple viewpoints can deepen the reader's understanding, demonstrating that social science topics often require a nuanced approach.

**Question 11:**

*Correct Answer: A) A combination of the local and global strategies discussed by both sources.*

**Explanation:**

The synthesis is evident in the combination of local and global strategies, reflecting a comprehensive approach that considers both immediate and far-reaching impacts.

**Question 12:**

*Correct Answer: C) By providing counterexamples that undermine the first source's conclusions.*

**Explanation:**

The second source challenges the first by offering examples that directly contradict its conclusions, prompting the reader to question the first source's assumptions.

**Question 13:**

*Correct Answer: A) One source provides a broad theoretical framework, while the other offers practical applications.*

**Explanation:**

The two sources can complement each other when one presents the theory and the other offers practical examples. Together, they provide a fuller understanding of the issue.

**Question 14:**

*Correct Answer: A) It helps the reader see the complexity of the issue by providing multiple viewpoints.*

**Explanation:**

By presenting multiple viewpoints, the passage enriches the reader's understanding of the issue, showing that there are various ways to approach and solve the problem.

**Question 15:**

*Correct Answer: A) By proposing a study that combines elements of both approaches.*

**Explanation:**

The author suggests that future research could benefit from integrating aspects of both sources' approaches, which would likely lead to a more nuanced understanding of the issue.

# Social Science Passage 4: Interpretation of Data and Graphs

**Question 1:**

*Correct Answer: A) A steady increase over the period.*

**Explanation:**

The graph shows a consistent upward trend, indicating steady growth over the period. This is the correct interpretation based on the visual evidence presented.

**Question 2:**

*Correct Answer: B) Country Y's economy grew steadily from 2000 to 2010.*

**Explanation:**

The data in the table show a continuous increase in Country Y's economy during the specified period, supporting this conclusion. The other options either misinterpret the data or are not reflected in the table.

**Question 3:**

*Correct Answer: A) The population of the region is predicted to continue growing rapidly.*

**Explanation:**

The graph likely depicts a growing population trend, and the primary conclusion drawn is that the population is expected to maintain this rapid growth based on the past data trends.

**Question 4:**

*Correct Answer: A) It shows quantitative evidence that corroborates the author's claim about growth patterns.*

**Explanation:**

The table provides clear numerical support for the author's claim about growth patterns, reinforcing the overall argument made in the passage.

**Question 5:**

*Correct Answer: D) The curve represents fluctuations in global temperature trends.*

**Explanation:**

This is incorrect because the graph in the passage does not represent global temperature trends but rather something like population growth or economic indicators. The rest of the options describe reasonable interpretations of productivity or economic data.

## Question 6:
*Correct Answer: C) A technological breakthrough in renewable energy.*

### Explanation:
The sudden spike in 2015 could reasonably be attributed to a significant technological breakthrough, such as advances in renewable energy, which may have spurred rapid growth or change in the data being measured.

## Question 7:
*Correct Answer: D) Region D.*

### Explanation:
The chart likely shows that Region D had the least improvement in literacy rates compared to the other regions, based on a visual analysis of the differences in the bar heights or percentages provided.

## Question 8:
*Correct Answer: A) The data in the graph support the trends shown in the table.*

### Explanation:
The graph visually represents trends that are consistent with the data in the table, suggesting that both the graph and table work together to reinforce the same conclusion.

## Question 9:
*Correct Answer: A) To provide visual evidence of a trend described in the text.*

### Explanation:
The graph serves to visually confirm the trends discussed in the passage, making the numerical or textual information more accessible and understandable to the reader.

## Question 10:
*Correct Answer: B) The increase in economic growth was more rapid than anticipated.*

### Explanation:
The graph likely shows an unexpectedly rapid increase in economic growth, which could be a surprising or noteworthy observation based on the data trends.

## Question 11:
*Correct Answer: B) There was significant variation in GDP growth between regions.*

### Explanation:
The bar graph shows different levels of GDP growth across regions, highlighting significant disparities. Some regions may have experienced much higher growth than others, as reflected in the varying bar heights.

## Question 12:
*Correct Answer: A) It visually represents the disproportionate spending on education versus healthcare.*

### Explanation:
The pie chart most likely illustrates how resources are allocated, with a clear visual comparison showing that education receives more funding than healthcare, or vice versa, depending on the chart.

## Question 13:
*Correct Answer: B) The data are used to support a hypothesis about long-term trends.*

### Explanation:
The statistical data provided in the passage are used to back up the author's argument about long-term trends, showing that these patterns are consistent with the broader hypothesis being presented.

**Question 14:**

*Correct Answer: C) It focuses too much on short-term fluctuations, missing long-term trends.*

**Explanation:**

A common limitation of graphs is an overemphasis on short-term fluctuations, which can obscure the overall long-term trends that are more important for drawing meaningful conclusions.

**Question 15:**

*Correct Answer: A) By analyzing trends and extrapolating them into the future.*

**Explanation:**

To make future predictions, the data in the graph can be analyzed for patterns and trends, which can then be extrapolated to predict how these trends might continue in the coming years.

# Section 3: Natural Science Passage Comprehension

# Natural Science Passage 1: Understanding Scientific Concepts and Research Findings

**Question 1:**

*Correct Answer: A) Climate change and its long-term effects.*

**Explanation:**

The passage focuses on climate change as the primary scientific concept, discussing its long-term impacts and providing detailed explanations of related research findings. The other options cover unrelated scientific concepts.

**Question 2:**

*Correct Answer: A) The experimental results confirmed the hypothesis.*

**Explanation:**

The passage indicates that the hypothesis was confirmed by the experimental data, which is the main conclusion of the research findings. Other options such as disproving theories or having insufficient data are not supported by the passage.

**Question 3:**

*Correct Answer: C) A randomized controlled trial conducted in a laboratory.*

**Explanation:**

The methodology described in the passage points to a controlled experimental environment where variables were managed carefully, which aligns with a randomized controlled trial conducted in a lab setting.

**Question 4:**

*Correct Answer: D) Natural selection favors traits that enhance survival in specific environments.*

**Explanation:**

The study supports the hypothesis that natural selection operates by favoring traits that improve survival in specific environments, which is a core aspect of evolutionary biology.

**Question 5:**

*Correct Answer: C) Analyzing the results to draw meaningful conclusions.*

**Explanation:**

The research findings focus on the analysis of the data, drawing conclusions about how the scientific method was applied. This is a critical step in the scientific process.

**Question 6:**

*Correct Answer: C) Further research is needed to confirm the conclusions.*

**Explanation:**

The passage suggests that while the results are promising, further studies would help confirm and solidify the findings, indicating that the conclusions drawn from the current research may not be definitive yet.

**Question 7:**

*Correct Answer: B) A group of organisms exposed to environmental stressors.*

**Explanation:**

The experimental group in the study was exposed to specific environmental conditions or stressors, which is typical in experiments designed to test the effects of environmental changes on organisms.

**Question 8:**

*Correct Answer: B) The natural variability in the environment.*

**Explanation:**

The passage suggests that variability in environmental conditions likely influenced the results, as it is a factor that can have a significant impact on experimental outcomes in studies related to climate change and natural selection.

**Question 9:**

*Correct Answer: D) It validates long-held beliefs about species adaptation.*

**Explanation:**

The findings reinforce existing theories about how species adapt to changing environments, supporting long-standing ideas in evolutionary biology.

**Question 10:**

*Correct Answer: A) The sample size was too small to be conclusive.*

**Explanation:**

One limitation mentioned in the passage is the small sample size, which can impact the reliability of the study's conclusions. Larger studies would be needed to provide more conclusive evidence.

**Question 11:**

*Correct Answer: C) Adaptation to climate change is more complex than previously thought.*

**Explanation:**

The research highlights the complexity of adaptation to climate change, suggesting that the process is influenced by multiple factors and may not be as straightforward as previously believed.

**Question 12:**

*Correct Answer: A) Studying a larger sample size across different regions.*

**Explanation:**

The passage suggests that future studies could benefit from a larger sample size and a more diverse geographical range to improve the validity and applicability of the findings.

**Question 13:**

*Correct Answer: D) They confirm that certain traits enhance species' survival in specific ecosystems.*

**Explanation:**

The study provides evidence that specific traits help species survive in particular environments, confirming fundamental principles of natural selection as they relate to adaptation.

**Question 14:**

*Correct Answer: B) The results will reshape thinking in environmental science.*

**Explanation:**

The findings are likely to have broad implications in the field of environmental science, influencing future research and potentially leading to new understandings of species adaptation and climate change.

**Question 15:**

*Correct Answer: B) To extend the study's duration to observe long-term effects.*

**Explanation:**

The researchers recommend extending the study over a longer period to observe the long-term effects of environmental changes, which would provide more comprehensive insights into the adaptation processes.

# Natural Science Passage 2: Assessing Scientific Hypotheses and Conclusions

**Question 1:**

*Correct Answer: B) The effect of pollutants on marine ecosystems.*

**Explanation:**

The passage focuses on an experiment designed to assess how pollutants impact marine ecosystems, which aligns with the hypothesis tested. The other options describe unrelated hypotheses not explored in this passage.

**Question 2:**

*Correct Answer: B) By conducting a laboratory-controlled experiment.*

**Explanation:**

The passage describes a controlled laboratory experiment where specific variables were manipulated to test the hypothesis. Observational studies or surveys are not the methodology mentioned in this case.

**Question 3:**

*Correct Answer: B) A decrease in marine biodiversity with pollution.*

**Explanation:**

The results of the experiment indicated a decrease in biodiversity in polluted environments, supporting the original hypothesis that pollutants negatively affect marine ecosystems.

**Question 4:**

*Correct Answer: A) The narrow geographic scope of the experiment.*

**Explanation:**

The passage notes that the experiment was limited to a specific geographic region, which could reduce the generalizability of the findings to other areas, making it a potential limitation of the study.

**Question 5:**

*Correct Answer: B) The results suggest the hypothesis may be correct, but further testing is needed.*

**Explanation:**

While the results support the hypothesis, the passage indicates that the conclusions are tentative, and further research is necessary to confirm the findings definitively.

## Question 6:
*Correct Answer: B) Increasing the sample size to improve the validity of results.*

### Explanation:

The researchers recommend that future studies involve larger sample sizes to ensure the findings are more robust and valid. This would strengthen the reliability of the results.

## Question 7:
*Correct Answer: B) The researchers did not account for seasonal variations in the data.*

### Explanation:

The failure to account for seasonal variations could weaken the conclusions, as seasonal changes might influence the results and provide an alternative explanation for the observed outcomes.

## Question 8:
*Correct Answer: D) The role of variables that were not controlled in the study.*

### Explanation:

The passage mentions that the researchers considered the potential influence of uncontrolled variables, which could have affected the experiment's outcomes. This demonstrates thorough evaluation of their methodology.

## Question 9:
*Correct Answer: A) The sample size was too small to draw definitive conclusions.*

### Explanation:

The researchers note that the small sample size limits the certainty of their conclusions, emphasizing the need for further research with larger groups to confirm the findings.

## Question 10:
*Correct Answer: A) The results showed only a slight trend in favor of the hypothesis.*

### Explanation:

The researchers express caution because the results, while supportive of the hypothesis, only showed a modest trend. This warrants further investigation before drawing firm conclusions.

## Question 11:
*Correct Answer: C) By conducting longitudinal studies to observe long-term trends.*

### Explanation:

The researchers suggest that observing the effects over a longer period through longitudinal studies would provide stronger, more comprehensive data on the impacts being tested.

## Question 12:
*Correct Answer: B) External factors like weather patterns affected the study.*

### Explanation:

The passage mentions that unpredictable external factors, such as weather patterns, could have influenced the results, offering an alternative explanation for the findings.

## Question 13:
*Correct Answer: B) They provide partial support, indicating that further testing is needed.*

### Explanation:

The findings partially support the hypothesis, but the researchers stress that more experiments are required to validate the results completely, suggesting that further testing is necessary.

## Question 14:
*Correct Answer: B) Confirmation bias in interpreting the results.*

**Explanation:**

The researchers address potential confirmation bias by noting that they took steps to ensure their interpretations were objective and not influenced by preconceived expectations of the outcome.

**Question 15:**

*Correct Answer: A) Studying the long-term effects of environmental changes on genetic variation.*

**Explanation:**

The passage indicates that the most valuable direction for future research would involve studying the long-term effects of environmental factors, such as pollutants, on genetic variation across species.

## Natural Science Passage 3: Interpreting Technical Terms and Complex Data

**Question 1:**

*Correct Answer: A) The comparison of two isotopes in a chemical compound.*

**Explanation:**

The term "isotopic ratio" refers to the proportion between two isotopes within a chemical compound, commonly used in scientific fields like chemistry and geology to study processes such as radiometric dating or tracing chemical reactions.

**Question 2:**

*Correct Answer: A) As a fluctuating variable that affected the study results.*

**Explanation:**

Temperature variation is presented as a variable that impacted the outcomes of the study, influencing how the data should be interpreted in relation to the main hypothesis.

**Question 3:**

*Correct Answer: B) The regulation of a protein's function due to the binding of a molecule.*

**Explanation:**

Allosteric regulation refers to the process where a molecule binds to a site other than the active site of a protein, causing a change in its function. This is a key concept in biochemistry, particularly in enzyme activity regulation.

**Question 4:**

*Correct Answer: A) There is a direct correlation between X and Y.*

**Explanation:**

The data in Table 2 shows a consistent pattern of X increasing as Y increases, indicating a direct correlation between the two variables.

**Question 5:**

*Correct Answer: A) A steadily rising curve.*

**Explanation:**

The passage describes a trend of $CO_2$ emissions steadily increasing over time, which would be best represented by a steadily rising curve on a graph.

**Question 6:**

*Correct Answer: A) Understanding the spatial arrangement of atoms.*

**Explanation:**

In interpreting molecular structure data, the spatial arrangement of atoms is crucial because it affects how molecules interact with each other, their stability, and their functions.

**Question 7:**

*Correct Answer: A) The random fluctuation of gene variants in small populations.*

**Explanation:**

Genetic drift is a process that leads to random changes in the frequency of alleles (gene variants) in small populations, often resulting in a loss of genetic diversity over time.

**Question 8:**

*Correct Answer: C) The effectiveness of plants in converting light energy into chemical energy.*

**Explanation:**

Photosynthetic efficiency refers to how effectively plants can convert sunlight into chemical energy during photosynthesis, a critical factor in plant growth and energy production.

**Question 9:**

*Correct Answer: A) An increase in the growth rate of plants with higher nitrogen levels.*

**Explanation:**

The hypothesis is supported by the data showing that plants grew faster with higher nitrogen levels, which aligns with the prediction that nitrogen enhances plant growth.

**Question 10:**

*Correct Answer: A) The ability of an organism to maintain stable internal conditions despite environmental changes.*

**Explanation:**

Homeostasis is the process by which organisms regulate internal conditions (like temperature, pH, or glucose levels) to remain stable despite changes in their external environment.

**Question 11:**

*Correct Answer: A) It determines the probability that the results occurred by chance.*

**Explanation:**

The p-value is a statistical measure that helps researchers determine whether the results of an experiment are statistically significant or if they could have occurred by random chance.

**Question 12:**

*Correct Answer: B) The enzyme responds differently to various concentrations of a substrate.*

**Explanation:**

The graph shows fluctuations in enzyme activity that are likely due to the enzyme responding differently to varying substrate concentrations, a common observation in enzyme kinetics.

**Question 13:**

*Correct Answer: D) Use a multivariate analysis to understand the interaction between variables.*

**Explanation:**

When multiple variables are involved, a multivariate analysis is recommended to assess how different variables interact and influence the overall results.

**Question 14:**

*Correct Answer: C) Applying a linear model to non-linear data.*

**Explanation:**

The researchers caution against using a linear model when the data does not follow a linear trend, as this could lead to inaccurate conclusions.

**Question 15:**

*Correct Answer: B) A detailed analysis of all variables is necessary for reliable conclusions.*

**Explanation:**

The passage emphasizes that reliable conclusions can only be drawn by analyzing all relevant variables in detail, rather than simplifying the data too much or overlooking key factors.

# Natural Science Passage 4: Relationship Between Text and Graphs or Tables

**Question 1:**

*Correct Answer: B) It reveals a peak in enzyme activity at an optimal temperature before declining.*

**Explanation:**

The graph shows that enzyme activity increases up to a certain temperature, after which it begins to decline. This aligns with the claim in paragraph 3 that enzymes work most efficiently at an optimal temperature, beyond which their activity decreases due to denaturation.

**Question 2:**

*Correct Answer: C) Species B is more adaptable to a wide range of temperatures than Species A.*

**Explanation:**

The table shows that Species B exhibits growth across a wider range of temperatures compared to Species A, indicating that Species B is more adaptable to varying temperatures.

**Question 3:**

*Correct Answer: A) The data supports the hypothesis with a positive correlation between variables.*

**Explanation:**

The table shows a positive relationship between the variables in question, which directly supports the hypothesis stated in the passage.

**Question 4:**

*Correct Answer: D) The figure suggests a plateau in growth after a certain light intensity, which is not addressed in the text.*

**Explanation:**

The figure shows that plant growth increases with light intensity but plateaus after reaching a certain point, whereas the text only discusses the increase, not mentioning the plateau effect.

**Question 5:**

*Correct Answer: A) Some species respond faster due to their genetic makeup.*

**Explanation:**

The variation in response times across species is most likely due to inherent genetic differences, which affect how quickly each species can adapt to environmental changes.

**Question 6:**

*Correct Answer: A) Growth decreases as salinity increases beyond a specific threshold.*

**Explanation:**

The graph shows that plant growth initially increases with rising salinity but decreases sharply after a certain salinity level, supporting the researcher's conclusion.

**Question 7:**

*Correct Answer: A) The units of measurement for variable X.*

**Explanation:**

To fully understand the relationship between variable X and plant growth, the units of measurement for variable X are necessary to interpret the data accurately.

**Question 8:**

*Correct Answer: A) It demonstrates how cell activity increases with exposure to specific chemicals.*

**Explanation:**

The figure supports the description in the passage by showing an increase in cell activity when exposed to certain chemicals, aligning with the experimental findings.

**Question 9:**

*Correct Answer: A) The outlier values in the data that do not fit the expected pattern.*

**Explanation:**

The outliers in the data challenge the hypothesis, as they do not follow the expected pattern of results, indicating the need for further analysis.

**Question 10:**

*Correct Answer: C) One graph complements the other by providing additional context.*

**Explanation:**

The two graphs are related, with one offering complementary information that enhances the understanding of the data presented in the text.

**Question 11:**

*Correct Answer: A) Inconsistent testing conditions across experiments.*

**Explanation:**

Disparity between the graph and the passage's results could be due to inconsistent testing conditions, such as differences in temperature or light exposure during the experiments.

**Question 12:**

*Correct Answer: A) It confirms the primary conclusion by providing supporting evidence.*

**Explanation:**

The data in Table 3 corroborates the experiment's findings by providing quantitative evidence that supports the conclusion reached in the passage.

**Question 13:**

*Correct Answer: D) Variable Y plays a key role but only under specific conditions.*

**Explanation:**

The table suggests that Variable Y significantly impacts the outcome, but only when specific conditions are met, as indicated by fluctuations in the results across different trials.

**Question 14:**

*Correct Answer: A) The control group shows no variation, while the experimental group displays significant changes.*

**Explanation:**

The graph for the control group remains stable, while the experimental group shows notable changes, highlighting the effect of the variable being tested.

**Question 15:**

*Correct Answer: A) The graph corroborates the text by showing a steady rise in CO2 levels over time.*

**Explanation:**

The graph shows a steady increase in $CO_2$ levels, which aligns with the text's discussion of rising atmospheric $CO_2$ levels and their impact on the environment.

# Section 4: Historical Documents Passage Comprehension

# Historical Document 1: Analysis of Political Speeches or Official Statements

**Question 1:**

*Correct Answer: A) The speaker calls for unity in a time of national division.*

**Explanation:**

The passage emphasizes the need for the country to come together, especially during a period of national division, which is the speaker's primary argument. The speaker likely stresses unity as essential for overcoming challenges.

**Question 2:**

*Correct Answer: A) By employing repetition to reinforce key ideas.*

**Explanation:**

The speaker uses repetition as a rhetorical device to emphasize important points, ensuring that key concepts such as unity, action, or perseverance remain in the audience's minds.

**Question 3:**

*Correct Answer: B) Solemn and reflective.*

**Explanation:**

The speaker's tone is reflective and serious, perhaps addressing a critical moment in the nation's history, requiring thoughtful consideration and responsibility.

**Question 4:**

*Correct Answer: A) It reflects the social tensions of the time, shaping the speaker's focus on unity.*

**Explanation:**

The speech's historical context, likely a period of national unrest or division, is key in shaping the speaker's message, as they seek to address social tensions and encourage unity.

**Question 5:**

*Correct Answer: A) "We must come together, not as individuals, but as a nation, bound by shared values."*

**Explanation:**

This quote appeals to patriotism by emphasizing the need for collective action and national unity, focusing on shared values as the foundation for moving forward.

**Question 6:**

*Correct Answer: C) To inspire hope and perseverance during a national crisis.*

**Explanation:**

The primary purpose of the speech is to uplift and inspire the nation during a difficult time, motivating the public to remain hopeful and persevere in the face of adversity.

**Question 7:**

*Correct Answer: A) By acknowledging opposing viewpoints and providing rebuttals.*

**Explanation:**

The speaker effectively addresses counterarguments by acknowledging them and then providing logical rebuttals, strengthening their own position and showing that they have considered alternative views.

**Question 8:**

*Correct Answer: A) "Together, we shall build a brighter tomorrow, hand in hand."*

**Explanation:**

This statement reflects the speaker's vision for the future, highlighting optimism and cooperation as central themes in creating a better future for all.

**Question 9:**

*Correct Answer: B) Moral imperatives and ethical considerations.*

**Explanation:**

The speaker justifies their recommendations based on moral and ethical reasons, focusing on doing what is right for the nation rather than relying solely on economic or statistical evidence.

**Question 10:**

*Correct Answer: A) A call to action.*

**Explanation:**

The closing remarks of the speech likely feature a strong call to action, urging the audience to take concrete steps toward achieving the goals discussed in the speech.

**Question 11:**

*Correct Answer: B) By presenting their main argument early and supporting it with examples.*

**Explanation:**

The speaker introduces the main argument early in the speech and supports it with examples and evidence throughout, building a logical progression that leads to the final call to action.

**Question 12:**

*Correct Answer: A) It reinforces the urgency of the issue at hand.*

**Explanation:**

The repetition of key phrases or ideas helps to stress the urgency of the situation, ensuring the audience understands the immediate importance of taking action.

**Question 13:**

*Correct Answer: A) To draw parallels between past challenges and the present situation.*

**Explanation:**

By referencing historical events, the speaker draws parallels between past and present, illustrating that the challenges the nation faces today are not unprecedented and can be overcome.

**Question 14:**

*Correct Answer: B) The speaker inspires hope by highlighting the nation's resilience.*

**Explanation:**

The speaker appeals to the audience's emotions by focusing on the nation's ability to endure and overcome previous hardships, instilling a sense of hope and confidence.

**Question 15:**

*Correct Answer: A) The speaker draws on their own struggles to connect with the audience.*

**Explanation:**

By sharing personal experiences, the speaker strengthens their connection with the audience, making their argument more relatable and demonstrating empathy with the public's concerns.

**Question 16:**

*Correct Answer: A) It elevates the seriousness of the issue being discussed.*

**Explanation:**

The formal language used in the speech conveys a sense of gravity and seriousness, appropriate for the weighty subject matter being addressed.

**Question 17:**

*Correct Answer: A) They will likely feel motivated to take immediate action.*

**Explanation:**

Given the speaker's inspiring and urgent tone, the audience is likely to feel motivated and ready to take action in support of the speaker's proposed solutions.

**Question 18:**

*Correct Answer: A) "However, let us not forget..."*

**Explanation:**

This phrase signals a shift in the speaker's argument, transitioning from one point to another or introducing a new perspective for the audience to consider.

**Question 19:**

*Correct Answer: A) By combining emotional appeals with factual data to create a compelling case.*

**Explanation:**

The speaker balances emotional appeals with logical arguments, combining both to build a persuasive and well-rounded case that resonates with the audience on multiple levels.

**Question 20:**

*Correct Answer: A) It fosters a sense of unity and common purpose among the audience.*

**Explanation:**

By appealing to shared values, the speaker creates a sense of unity and common purpose, helping to bring the audience together around a collective goal.

# Historical Document 2: Comparison of Two Historical Texts

**Question 1:**

*Correct Answer: B) The first author emphasizes natural rights, while the second focuses on the legal structure of rights.*

**Explanation:**

The first passage likely deals with broader concepts of natural rights, such as life, liberty, and the pursuit of happiness, while the second passage might focus on codifying those rights into a legal framework, such as the U.S. Constitution.

**Question 2:**

*Correct Answer: A) The first passage is more urgent and passionate, while the second is more measured and formal.*

**Explanation:**

The tone of the first passage, such as the Declaration of Independence, is typically passionate and urgent due to the context of revolution. The second passage, like the U.S. Constitution, tends to be more formal and structured, reflecting the need for stable governance.

**Question 3:**

*Correct Answer: B) It builds on the principles outlined in the first passage, offering practical steps for implementation.*

**Explanation:**

The second passage usually builds on the ideals of the first by creating a framework to implement those principles, like how the Constitution builds on the ideals of independence to form a government.

**Question 4:**

*Correct Answer: C) The challenge of balancing liberty and order.*

**Explanation:**

Both passages explore the tension between protecting individual liberties and maintaining social or governmental order, a central theme in both revolutionary documents and governing frameworks.

**Question 5:**

*Correct Answer: B) The first document reflects revolutionary ideals, while the second is focused on governance stability.*

**Explanation:**

The first document may come from a period of upheaval, advocating for revolutionary change, while the second focuses on stabilizing the new government and ensuring long-term governance.

**Question 6:**

*Correct Answer: A) Both use appeals to morality to justify their claims.*

**Explanation:**

Both documents appeal to moral principles to justify their arguments, whether it be the natural rights of individuals or the ethical necessity of a government structure that protects those rights.

**Question 7:**

*Correct Answer: A) The first passage uses more revolutionary language, while the second reflects a desire for institutional stability.*

**Explanation:**

The first passage, dealing with revolutionary ideals, is more charged with language pushing for drastic change. The second, aiming for stability in governance, uses language focused on institutional longevity and order.

**Question 8:**

*Correct Answer: B) Both passages suggest that government must be restrained to protect individual liberties.*

**Explanation:**

Both documents emphasize that government should be limited or checked in power to ensure it protects the liberties of individuals, reflecting a shared concern for preventing tyranny.

**Question 9:**

*Correct Answer: A) It makes the second passage feel more personal and urgent.*

**Explanation:**

The use of first-person perspective in the second passage often makes the speech more personal and engaging, creating a sense of immediacy, compared to the more formal and generalized tone of third-person narrative in the first passage.

**Question 10:**

*Correct Answer: C) Both documents agree that government must be limited by the consent of the governed.*

**Explanation:**

Both passages emphasize the idea that government authority should derive from the consent of the people, a foundational principle in democratic governance.

**Question 11:**

*Correct Answer: D) Both passages argue that rebellion should be avoided unless the government fails to protect fundamental rights.*

**Explanation:**

The documents may agree that rebellion is justified only when the government violates fundamental rights or fails to protect the people, though one passage may emphasize the severity of this last resort more than the other.

**Question 12:**

*Correct Answer: A) The first passage uses religious references to strengthen its moral argument, while the second avoids religious language entirely.*

**Explanation:**

The first passage may appeal to divine authority to justify its claims, while the second avoids invoking religious references, focusing instead on secular governance.

**Question 13:**

*Correct Answer: D) Neither passage directly addresses economic issues.*

**Explanation:**

While both passages focus on political and philosophical concepts such as liberty and governance, they do not focus on economic concerns directly, even if those concerns are implicitly part of the larger debate.

**Question 14:**

*Correct Answer: B) By offering a more detailed and structured approach to governance.*

**Explanation:**

The second passage likely builds on the first by offering a more practical, detailed plan for governance, such as the creation of laws and institutions, in contrast to the more philosophical focus of the first passage.

**Question 15:**

*Correct Answer: B) It provides concrete examples that ground the abstract ideas discussed.*

**Explanation:**

The use of specific historical events in both passages provides real-world context for the abstract principles being debated, helping to ground the arguments in the realities of their time.

**Question 16:**

*Correct Answer: C) Both passages argue that compromise is only acceptable when basic rights are protected.*

**Explanation:**

Both documents may acknowledge the necessity of compromise but also emphasize that certain core rights must remain protected, reflecting the belief that some values are non-negotiable.

**Question 17:**

*Correct Answer: C) Both passages call for greater representation, but differ on how it should be achieved.*

**Explanation:**

Both documents may advocate for the need for representation in government but approach the specifics differently, with one perhaps favoring broader or more direct forms of representation.

**Question 18:**

*Correct Answer: A) Both passages cite historical figures to lend credibility to their arguments.*

**Explanation:**

Both passages may use references to historical figures or precedents to strengthen their arguments by showing that their views align with respected authorities from the past.

**Question 19:**

*Correct Answer: A) The first passage is more optimistic about the future, while the second emphasizes the need for vigilance.*

**Explanation:**

The first passage may express optimism about the potential for change and progress, while the second emphasizes the ongoing need for vigilance to protect what has been achieved.

**Question 20:**
*Correct Answer: A) The first passage emphasizes liberty above all, while the second focuses on justice and equality.*

**Explanation:**
The first document may prioritize liberty as the fundamental principle, while the second focuses on creating a balanced framework where justice and equality are also key concerns.

# Historical Document 3: Understanding Historical Nuances and Author Perspectives

**Question 1:**
*Correct Answer: A) The passage refers to a wartime event that emphasizes the need for national unity.*

**Explanation:**
The passage likely references a significant wartime moment, such as a call to maintain unity during conflict. This event shapes the author's argument by stressing that national unity is essential during times of crisis.

**Question 2:**
*Correct Answer: A) The author's personal experience with war shapes their pro-peace stance.*

**Explanation:**
The author's background, such as having personal experience with war, influences their perspective by making them more inclined toward promoting peace, as they understand the devastating consequences of conflict.

**Question 3:**
*Correct Answer: B) Reflective and cautious.*

**Explanation:**
The tone of the passage is reflective, as the author carefully considers historical events and their implications. The cautious tone indicates a desire to avoid repeating past mistakes.

**Question 4:**
*Correct Answer: A) To remind readers of a past mistake that should not be repeated.*

**Explanation:**
The author references a specific historical event to serve as a warning, urging readers to learn from past errors to avoid similar consequences in the present or future.

**Question 5:**
*Correct Answer: B) By acknowledging their merit but ultimately refuting them.*

**Explanation:**
The author acknowledges opposing viewpoints but refutes them with well-structured arguments, showing respect for alternative opinions while firmly supporting their own stance.

**Question 6:**
*Correct Answer: B) It conveys the gravity of the situation, emphasizing the urgency of action.*

**Explanation:**
The author's word choice highlights the seriousness of the political situation, underscoring the need for immediate action to prevent further deterioration.

**Question 7:**

*Correct Answer: A) The passage highlights the tensions between two political factions of the time.*

**Explanation:**

The passage reflects the broader historical context by focusing on political tensions between factions, illustrating the conflicts that were prevalent during the period in which the document was written.

**Question 8:**

*Correct Answer: B) The author uses logical arguments, presenting clear evidence to support their stance.*

**Explanation:**

The author relies on logical reasoning, using clear evidence and well-organized arguments to persuade the reader of the validity of their position.

**Question 9:**

*Correct Answer: B) The passage builds up to the main argument gradually, laying out context and details first.*

**Explanation:**

The author gradually introduces background information and context, allowing the argument to build momentum before delivering the main point, making the argument more compelling.

**Question 10:**

*Correct Answer: B) The author advocates for gradual change to prevent social disruption.*

**Explanation:**

The author favors gradual change, expressing a cautious approach to reform in order to avoid sudden disruptions to society or established systems.

**Question 11:**

*Correct Answer: B) The author points out past failures to suggest that a different strategy is needed.*

**Explanation:**

The author highlights historical failures as examples of what should be avoided, using these past mistakes as justification for pursuing a new or different strategy.

**Question 12:**

*Correct Answer: A) The emphasis on individual rights and freedoms.*

**Explanation:**

The passage reflects the author's ideology by prioritizing individual rights and freedoms, suggesting that these principles guide their argument and influence their perspective on governance.

**Question 13:**

*Correct Answer: A) The author is hopeful that the situation will improve with time and effort.*

**Explanation:**

The author's tone suggests optimism, expressing hope that, with the right approach and sustained effort, the situation can be improved over time.

**Question 14:**

*Correct Answer: A) It makes complex ideas more relatable by comparing them to everyday concepts.*

**Explanation:**

The use of metaphor or symbolism helps simplify complex concepts, making the argument more accessible by relating abstract ideas to familiar, everyday experiences.

**Question 15:**

*Correct Answer: D) The author views leadership as a form of service that demands self-sacrifice.*

**Explanation:**

The passage suggests that the author sees leadership as a responsibility that requires personal sacrifice, indicating that true leaders must be willing to put the needs of others above their own interests.

# Historical Document 4: Critical Analysis and Evaluation of Historical Arguments

**Question 1:**

*Correct Answer: A) The need for immediate action to address a social injustice.*

**Explanation:**

The author's primary argument is focused on the urgency of addressing a social injustice, calling for immediate reform or action. This is typical of historical speeches or documents advocating for social or political change.

**Question 2:**

*Correct Answer: C) The author refers to historical precedents, giving their argument a sense of legitimacy.*

**Explanation:**

By citing historical examples or precedents, the author lends credibility to their argument. Historical references help to frame the argument within a larger context, showing that the issue has been addressed before, which strengthens the author's point.

**Question 3:**

*Correct Answer: B) By acknowledging their merit but refuting them with stronger evidence.*

**Explanation:**

The author effectively addresses counterarguments by acknowledging that they exist, but then refuting them with stronger evidence. This shows a balanced and well-reasoned approach to building their case.

**Question 4:**

*Correct Answer: A) The author appeals to logic, providing clear and well-reasoned arguments.*

**Explanation:**

The author's rhetorical strategy relies on logical reasoning and evidence. By structuring the argument around facts and clear reasoning, the author persuades the reader with a rational approach.

**Question 5:**

*Correct Answer: A) The author builds the argument progressively, starting with simple ideas and leading to more complex points.*

**Explanation:**

The author starts with basic concepts and gradually introduces more complex ideas, building the argument step by step. This structure allows the reader to follow the argument more easily and understand the logic behind it.

**Question 6:**

*Correct Answer: C) Passionate and urgent, encouraging the reader to take action.*

**Explanation:**

The tone is passionate and urgent, which reflects the author's desire for immediate action. This emotional tone helps to motivate the reader to engage with the issue and consider the need for change.

**Question 7:**

*Correct Answer: A) The passage reflects contemporary social tensions that shaped the author's perspective.*

**Explanation:**

The historical context of the passage plays a key role, as the author's argument is influenced by the social tensions of the time. This shapes the urgency and direction of the author's call for reform or change.

**Question 8:**

*Correct Answer: A) The author assumes the audience agrees with their moral stance, which reinforces their emotional appeals.*

**Explanation:**

The author's argument is shaped by the assumption that the audience already agrees with their moral perspective. This allows the author to use emotional appeals effectively, as they expect the audience to respond positively to these moral arguments.

**Question 9:**

*Correct Answer: B) By diving into the complexities, providing a thorough examination of each aspect.*

**Explanation:**

The author does not shy away from complexity; instead, they address it head-on by thoroughly examining the various facets of the issue. This approach gives the argument depth and demonstrates the author's understanding of the topic.

**Question 10:**

*Correct Answer: A) The use of clear, straightforward language makes the argument accessible and effective.*

**Explanation:**

The author's clear and straightforward language enhances the argument by making it accessible to a broad audience. The simplicity of the language ensures that the message is easily understood and persuasive.

**Question 11:**

*Correct Answer: C) The author argues for balanced governmental powers to ensure fairness.*

**Explanation:**

The author supports a balanced approach to government, advocating for powers that protect individual freedoms while ensuring fairness and social stability. This perspective reflects a desire for a well-structured, fair government.

**Question 12:**

*Correct Answer: A) The author uses examples of past failures to argue for a new approach.*

**Explanation:**

The author draws on historical examples of failure to demonstrate the need for a new approach. This strategy strengthens the argument by showing that previous methods have not worked and change is necessary.

**Question 13:**

*Correct Answer: B) The failure to address key counterarguments that weaken the main point.*

**Explanation:**

The most significant flaw in the author's argument is the failure to fully address some key counterarguments. This oversight leaves gaps in the argument, weakening its overall persuasiveness.

**Question 14:**

*Correct Answer: B) The author's role as a social activist informs their calls for immediate change.*

**Explanation:**

The author's background as a social activist influences the argument, driving the call for immediate and decisive action. This background shapes the urgency and moral foundation of the argument.

**Question 15:**
*Correct Answer: B) The author sees the issue as ongoing, requiring gradual change over time.*

**Explanation:**
The author's long-term vision for the issue suggests that while immediate action is necessary, the issue will require sustained effort and gradual change over time to be fully resolved.

# Variety of Topics: Humanities, Science, History

# Passage 1: Humanities – Exploration of Artistic Movements

**Question 1:**
*Correct Answer: D) Its lasting legacy on societal norms.*

**Explanation:**
The central theme of the passage focuses on how the artistic movement in question left a lasting impact on societal norms, influencing cultural values and standards that persist today. While the movement might have influenced modern art techniques (A) and other aspects, the passage primarily highlights its broad societal effects, making (D) the best choice.

**Question 2:**
*Correct Answer: A) The development of new architectural styles.*

**Explanation:**
The passage provides examples of how the artistic movement influenced various disciplines, with architecture being one of the most concrete and visible examples. The development of new architectural styles illustrates how the movement's aesthetic principles shaped the built environment, making (A) the best answer. The other options, while relevant to broader discussions, are less direct in their influence on disciplines outside art.

**Question 3:**
*Correct Answer: B) The movement still heavily influences contemporary culture.*

**Explanation:**
The author's perspective suggests that the artistic movement continues to play a significant role in shaping contemporary culture. The passage describes how the movement's principles and innovations remain present in modern creative expressions, cultural values, and societal structures. This makes (B) the correct answer, as the other options either underestimate or misrepresent the movement's current influence.

# Passage 2: Science – The Ethical Implications of Gene Editing

**Question 4:**
*Correct Answer: B) The possibility of creating genetic inequality.*

**Explanation:**
The author highlights the potential social consequences of gene editing, particularly how it could lead to genetic inequality, where only certain groups or individuals could afford or access enhancements. This raises concerns about a future where societal divides are reinforced through genetic means. Other concerns, like the potential misuse (A) and irreversibility (D), are relevant but are not presented as the primary issue in this passage.

**Question 5:**

*Correct Answer: B) By suggesting strict regulatory frameworks to mitigate the risks.*

**Explanation:**

The author takes a balanced approach, acknowledging the immense potential benefits of gene editing while also recognizing the significant ethical risks. To address these concerns, the author advocates for strict regulatory frameworks to ensure that gene editing is used responsibly and safely. This makes option (B) the best answer, as the author does not dismiss the risks or suggest halting research entirely.

**Question 6:**

*Correct Answer: D) It will revolutionize both medical and non-medical fields.*

**Explanation:**

The passage implies that gene editing, particularly through CRISPR technology, holds transformative potential not only in the field of medicine but also in areas such as agriculture and biotechnology. This revolutionary impact is emphasized throughout the passage, making option (D) the correct answer. While the technology's future use may be regulated, the author suggests a broad and powerful impact across various sectors.

# Passage 3: History – The Formation of the United Nations

**Question 7:**

*Correct Answer: A) To prevent future global conflicts.*

**Explanation:**

The primary motivation for the creation of the United Nations after World War II was to prevent future global conflicts and maintain international peace and security. The devastation caused by the two World Wars led world leaders to establish an international body dedicated to diplomacy and conflict resolution, aiming to prevent another such catastrophic conflict.

**Question 8:**

*Correct Answer: C) The destruction and chaos following World War II.*

**Explanation:**

The passage discusses the aftermath of World War II as the key driving factor behind the creation of the United Nations. The scale of destruction and human suffering experienced during the war highlighted the need for an international organization that could work to promote peace, stability, and cooperation between nations to avoid similar conflicts in the future

**Question 9:**

*Correct Answer: B) The organization has largely succeeded but faces new challenges.*

**Explanation:**

The author's stance on the effectiveness of the United Nations is nuanced, recognizing the organization's successes in fostering international cooperation and preventing many conflicts. However, the author also acknowledges that the UN faces ongoing challenges, including issues related to enforcement power and adapting to new global threats, such as terrorism, climate change, and shifting political alliances.

# Passage 4: Philosophy – The Debate Between Free Will and Determinism

**Question 10:**

*Correct Answer: A) Human behavior is entirely shaped by biological and environmental factors.*

**Explanation:**

The author's main argument in support of determinism is that human behavior is entirely influenced by factors such as biology, environment, and external forces, which means that people's actions are predetermined rather than a result of free choice. This is a central tenet of determinism, as it asserts that every action is the inevitable result of preceding causes.

**Question 11:**

*Correct Answer: B) By highlighting examples of behavior controlled by external circumstances.*

**Explanation:**

To counter arguments in favor of free will, the author uses examples of human behavior that are clearly influenced by external forces, such as upbringing, social environment, and even genetic predispositions. These examples are meant to show that individual choices are not as free as they may seem, but are instead shaped by factors beyond one's control, undermining the concept of free will.

**Question 12:**

*Correct Answer: A) Scientific studies showing brain activity before conscious decisions.*

**Explanation:**

The author supports their deterministic viewpoint with scientific evidence, particularly studies that demonstrate brain activity occurring before a person is consciously aware of making a decision. This suggests that what we perceive as free choices are actually determined by unconscious processes, providing strong empirical support for the argument that free will is an illusion.

# Passage 5: Environmental Science – Climate Change and Global Policy

**Question 13:**

*Correct Answer: A) International agreements to reduce greenhouse gas emissions.*

**Explanation:**

The passage emphasizes the importance of global political actions in mitigating climate change, specifically highlighting international agreements like the Paris Agreement, which aim to reduce greenhouse gas emissions. These agreements are critical for global cooperation to combat the rise in global temperatures and the adverse effects of climate change. The correct answer reflects the need for nations to work together in reducing emissions.

**Question 14:**

*Correct Answer: A) As a fundamental requirement that remains difficult to achieve.*

**Explanation:**

The author acknowledges that global cooperation is essential to address climate change, but also points out the challenges in achieving it due to differing national interests, economic concerns, and political obstacles. The complexity of coordinating international efforts makes cooperation difficult, though necessary. The correct answer captures this tension between the need for cooperation and the difficulty in achieving it.

**Question 15:**

*Correct Answer: B) That continued political pressure will lead to meaningful change.*

**Explanation:**

The author suggests that while progress in climate change policy has been slow, continued advocacy and political pressure from international organizations, governments, and citizens can eventually lead to meaningful changes in how climate issues are addressed. The author is cautiously optimistic, emphasizing that political will and sustained efforts are key to future success in climate policy.

# Inference and Analysis Exercises
## Section 1: Direct Logical Inferences

**Question 1:**

*Correct Answer: A) She is disappointed but hopeful.*

**Explanation:**

The passage mentions that Sarah "missed her chance" but also notes that "there would be another opportunity tomorrow," indicating she feels some disappointment for missing the train, yet remains hopeful for the next chance. Her emotions reflect both regret and optimism for the future.

**Question 2:**

*Correct Answer: B) He is anxious about managing without the chef.*

**Explanation:**

The passage describes the restaurant owner feeling nervous because the chef hasn't arrived, with customers coming soon. This suggests anxiety about how to handle the situation without the chef present, not that he is unconcerned or considering closing the restaurant.

**Question 3:**

*Correct Answer: A) He is determined to succeed.*

**Explanation:**

Mark knows this is his "last chance" and that "failure was not an option," which implies he is focused and determined to succeed. There is no indication that he is indifferent, confident, or ready to give up.

**Question 4:**

*Correct Answer: B) They are committed to reaching their destination despite the dangers.*

**Explanation:**

The group continues their journey despite knowing the dangers of the storm and the treacherous path, indicating they are committed to reaching their goal and not turning back or believing the storm will pass quickly.

**Question 5:**

*Correct Answer: B) She is distracted by her thoughts.*

**Explanation:**

Maria is repeatedly reading the same paragraph but is preoccupied with thoughts of her argument with her friend. This clearly indicates distraction, rather than focus or enjoyment of the book.

**Question 6:**

*Correct Answer: B) They are doubtful about the politician's promises.*

**Explanation:**

The silent reaction of the crowd, combined with their skeptical expressions, implies that they are not convinced by the politician's promises. There is no indication of confusion or enthusiasm.

**Question 7:**

*Correct Answer: B) She is overwhelmed by her workload.*

**Explanation:**

Despite being exhausted, Alice is aware that she still has hours of work ahead, suggesting that she feels overwhelmed by her workload rather than finished or ready for sleep.

**Question 8:**

*Correct Answer: C) He is content and enjoying the moment.*

**Explanation:**

The old man is smiling as he watches the children, indicating contentment and enjoyment. There is no indication that he feels lonely, angry, or annoyed.

**Question 9:**

*Correct Answer: B) She is empathetic and willing to help.*

**Explanation:**

The manager listens carefully and agrees to "do everything I can to address the issue," which shows empathy and a willingness to help the employee, rather than dismissing or ignoring the concerns.

**Question 10:**

*Correct Answer: C) They are determined to reach the campsite despite the weather.*

**Explanation:**

The hikers are sheltering from the rain but know they still have miles to go. This implies they are determined to continue, not considering turning back or being close to their destination.

**Question 11:**

*Correct Answer: B) She is uncertain about sending the email.*

**Explanation:**

Jen hesitates and is unsure if sending the email is the right decision, indicating uncertainty. There is no suggestion that she has already sent it or feels excited about it.

**Question 12:**

*Correct Answer: B) They are confused and unsure how to respond.*

**Explanation:**

The sudden silence and the exchange of unsure glances suggest confusion and uncertainty in how to respond to the announcement. There is no sign of relief or happiness.

**Question 13:**

*Correct Answer: B) The dog is locked outside and wants to come inside.*

**Explanation:**

The dog is barking at the door, likely wanting to be let inside as the sun is setting and the temperature is dropping. There is no indication that the dog is lost or barking at another animal.

**Question 14:**

*Correct Answer: B) She is nervous about speaking in front of the class.*

**Explanation:**

The student raises her hand timidly and speaks with a trembling voice, suggesting nervousness about speaking in front of others. There is no sign of confidence or anger.

**Question 15:**

*Correct Answer: A) He is in a hurry to get somewhere.*

**Explanation:**

The driver glances repeatedly at the clock and drums his fingers, which implies he is anxious and likely in a hurry. There is no indication of enjoyment or confusion about his destination.

**Question 16:**

*Correct Answer: B) She is worried that something might go wrong.*

**Explanation:**

Despite her excitement, Emily feels that "something was off" and doubt begins to creep in, suggesting worry that things may not go as planned, rather than confidence or indifference.

**Question 17:**

*Correct Answer: B) They are comfortable in each other's company.*

**Explanation:**

Though the friends sit in silence, the passage implies a comfortable and reflective mood between them. There is no indication of anger or preparation for goodbye.

**Question 18:**

*Correct Answer: A) She is pleased with her students' performance.*

**Explanation:**

The teacher's smile and positive statement that "you all did well" suggest she is pleased with her students' performance. However, her comment about "room for improvement" indicates she believes they can still improve.

**Question 19:**

*Correct Answer: A) He is upset about losing his ice cream.*

**Explanation:**

The tears welling up in the child's eyes suggest he is upset about his ice cream melting. There is no indication of happiness or anger toward his mother.

**Question 20:**

*Correct Answer: B) They are uncomfortable with the CEO's message.*

**Explanation:**

The polite clapping and tense atmosphere suggest that the audience is uncomfortable with the CEO's remarks, rather than enthusiastic or eager to leave.

## Section 2: Context-Based Inferences

**Question 1:**

*Correct Answer: B) They are in a delicate political situation with unresolved conflicts.*

**Explanation:**

The diplomats' tense conversation with veiled references to past conflicts suggests an unresolved, delicate political situation. Their interaction is polite, but the tension reveals underlying issues.

**Question 2:**

*Correct Answer: B) The area feels eerie and potentially unsafe.*

**Explanation:**

The deserted streets and the description of people staying indoors with windows shut and curtains drawn suggest an eerie, potentially unsafe atmosphere rather than peacefulness or a festival.

**Question 3:**

*Correct Answer: B) She is distracted, anticipating the arrival of someone.*

**Explanation:**

The hostess is engaging with her guests but repeatedly glances toward the door, indicating she is expecting someone else, which distracts her from the event.

**Question 4:**

*Correct Answer: B) They are nervous and possibly afraid of something.*

**Explanation:**

The villagers' hushed tones, glancing over their shoulders, and the apprehensive atmosphere suggest that they are nervous and potentially afraid, rather than excited or angry.

**Question 5:**

*Correct Answer: B) They are hesitant to speak openly, possibly out of fear or uncertainty.*

**Explanation:**

The students' brief and cautious responses, despite the teacher's encouragement to speak freely, suggest hesitation, possibly due to uncertainty or fear, rather than comfort or disinterest.

**Question 6:**

*Correct Answer: B) It is a somber or uncomfortable gathering.*

**Explanation:**

The slow movement of guests and the long shadows cast by the chandelier imply a somber or uncomfortable mood, rather than a lively or informal event.

**Question 7:**

*Correct Answer: B) He is nervous despite trying to appear confident.*

**Explanation:**

John's steady voice contrasts with his nervous hands and the tremor in his tone, indicating he is trying to appear confident but is actually nervous.

**Question 8:**

*Correct Answer: B) The recipient is deliberately avoiding reading the letters.*

**Explanation:**

The letters piled high and gathering dust suggest that the recipient has intentionally left them unopened, possibly avoiding the messages rather than forgetting them or awaiting more letters.

**Question 9:**

*Correct Answer: B) They are pretending to be happy, but feel indifferent or negative.*

**Explanation:**

The smiles that "never quite reached their eyes" indicate that the guests are pretending to be happy but actually feel indifferent or negative about the situation.

**Question 10:**

*Correct Answer: B) She is unfamiliar with the environment and feels out of place.*

**Explanation:**

The woman moves quietly and seems unnoticed and "out of place" in the busy market, implying unfamiliarity with the environment, rather than being a regular visitor or looking for someone.

**Question 11:**

*Correct Answer: B) He is hesitant or unsure about his departure.*

**Explanation:**

Marcus stands still with his suitcase untouched, suggesting hesitation or uncertainty about leaving, rather than eagerness or waiting for someone.

**Question 12:**

*Correct Answer: B) They are accustomed to such storms and feel safe inside.*

**Explanation:**

The family's calm conversation around the fireplace, despite the storm outside, indicates they are used to such storms and feel safe, rather than frightened or preparing to evacuate.

**Question 13:**

*Correct Answer: B) She is focused on a flaw and dissatisfied with her work.*

**Explanation:**

The artist's fixed gaze on a flaw and her lack of response to compliments suggest dissatisfaction with her painting, rather than pride or excitement.

**Question 14:**

*Correct Answer: B) He is eager to leave the stage.*

**Explanation:**

The performer's strained smile and glances toward the exit indicate that, despite the applause, he is eager to leave the stage, rather than preparing for an encore.

**Question 15:**

*Correct Answer: B) It is peaceful and calm, offering a refuge from the busy city.*

**Explanation:**

The description of the bookstore as a "quiet oasis" with customers moving softly suggests a peaceful and calm atmosphere, in contrast to the bustling city outside.

**Question 16:**

*Correct Answer: B) They are confused or surprised by the outcome.*

**Explanation:**

The audience's murmurs and whispering in disbelief indicate confusion or surprise at the results, rather than satisfaction or indifference.

**Question 17:**

*Correct Answer: B) He believes the vase is a key piece of evidence.*

**Explanation:**

The detective's lingering gaze on the broken vase in an otherwise immaculate room suggests that he considers it a key piece of evidence, rather than something irrelevant.

**Question 18:**

*Correct Answer: A) They are eager to leave the park.*

**Explanation:**

The parents' weary eyes and glances at their watches suggest that they are eager to leave the park, rather than being fully engaged in watching their children or planning to join them.

**Question 19:**

*Correct Answer: B) They are skeptical and are planning to write critically about the speech.*

**Explanation:**

The reporters' knowing glances and scribbling in their notebooks indicate skepticism about the politician's speech, suggesting they may write critically about it.

**Question 20:**

*Correct Answer: B) They are feeling a sense of calm and quiet as the night falls.*

**Explanation:**

The quiet conversations and the growing shadows suggest that the campers are feeling a sense of calm and peacefulness as the evening progresses, rather than becoming more lively.

# Section 3: Inferences About Author's Opinions and Attitudes

**Question 1:**

*Correct Answer: B) The author thinks the industrial revolution had negative consequences for workers.*

**Explanation:**

The author's use of phrases like "at what cost to the working class" implies a critical view of the industrial revolution, focusing on the negative impact on workers rather than its technological advancements.

**Question 2:**

*Correct Answer: B) The author believes social media has a mostly negative impact on personal relationships.*

**Explanation:**

The author contrasts the claim that social media connects people with the "reality" that it drives people apart, indicating a negative stance on its impact on personal relationships.

**Question 3:**

*Correct Answer: B) The author criticizes the decision for favoring corporate interests over the environment.*

**Explanation:**

The phrase "yet another example of short-term gains taking precedence over long-term sustainability" indicates the author's criticism of the politician's decision to prioritize corporate interests over environmental concerns.

**Question 4:**

*Correct Answer: C) The author acknowledges its success but is critical of its shortcomings.*

**Explanation:**

The author recognizes the nostalgia for the 'golden age' of cinema but points out its flaws, particularly in the treatment of minority actors, showing both acknowledgment and critique.

**Question 5:**

*Correct Answer: C) The author sees both positive potential and significant risks in artificial intelligence.*

**Explanation:**

The author describes artificial intelligence as both "exciting and terrifying," suggesting a balanced view that acknowledges both its potential benefits and risks.

**Question 6:**

*Correct Answer: B) The author thinks the policy only helps a small group of people.*

**Explanation:**

The author states that the policy benefits "only a select few," which implies that the author believes the majority of people are left worse off by the new policy.

**Question 7:**

*Correct Answer: C) The author fully supports the scientific consensus on climate change.*

**Explanation:**

The phrase "overwhelming scientific consensus" along with "urgent action" indicates that the author supports the view that climate change is real and requires immediate action.

**Question 8:**

*Correct Answer: B) The author advocates for more compassionate and supportive refugee policies.*

**Explanation:**

The author's use of "emotionally charged language" to highlight the "plight of refugees" suggests a compassionate stance, advocating for policies that address the crisis with care and support.

**Question 9:**

*Correct Answer: B) The author thinks the company's actions contradict its claims of sustainability.*

**Explanation:**

The passage highlights a contradiction between the company's claims and actions, suggesting that the author views the company's environmental practices as hypocritical.

**Question 10:**

*Correct Answer: B) The author thinks the reform is mainly about saving money.*

**Explanation:**

The author's suggestion that the reform is "an attempt to cut costs" rather than improve education indicates skepticism about the true intentions behind the reform.

**Question 11:**

*Correct Answer: B) The author is critical of the historical figure's actions.*

**Explanation:**

The author mentions the "moral complexities" of the historical figure's actions, suggesting a critical stance that acknowledges both innovation and exploitation.

**Question 12:**

*Correct Answer: B) The author acknowledges the artist's talent but is aware of the personal controversies.*

**Explanation:**

The author notes the artist's recognition as a visionary but also highlights the controversy surrounding their personal life, suggesting an awareness of both the artist's talent and flaws.

**Question 13:**

*Correct Answer: B) The author believes that the town's improvements have neglected the poor.*

**Explanation:**

The passage indicates that while the town has improved in infrastructure, the needs of poorer residents have been ignored, implying that the author is critical of the town's neglect of its less fortunate citizens.

**Question 14:**

*Correct Answer: B) The author praises the novel but is concerned about its prejudiced elements.*

**Explanation:**

While the critics have "lauded" the novel's plot, the author is troubled by the "undertones of prejudice," showing both appreciation and concern.

**Question 15:**

*Correct Answer: B) The author is cautious about the long-term impact of the initiative.*

**Explanation:**

The author's statement that "one must wonder if the long-term effects have been fully considered" suggests caution about the potential future consequences of the initiative.

**Question 16:**

*Correct Answer: C) The author presents both sides but does not express a clear opinion.*

**Explanation:**

The author discusses the debate surrounding the museum's decision but does not take a clear stance, suggesting a neutral presentation of both perspectives.

**Question 17:**

*Correct Answer: B) The author questions the validity of the findings due to the absence of peer review.*

**Explanation:**

The lack of peer review raises "serious concerns" for the author, indicating skepticism about the reliability of the researcher's findings.

**Question 18:**

*Correct Answer: C) The author acknowledges the benefits but is critical of the impact on long-time residents.*

**Explanation:**

The author mentions the positive outcomes of gentrification, such as new businesses, but is critical of the displacement felt by long-time residents, showing a balanced perspective.

**Question 19:**

*Correct Answer: B) The author is critical of the lawmaker's inconsistent actions.*

**Explanation:**

The author points out a discrepancy between the lawmaker's claims to fight for equality and their voting record, suggesting a critical view of the lawmaker's actions.

**Question 20:**

*Correct Answer: B) The author appreciates the protagonist's development but finds fault with the ending.*

**Explanation:**

The author finds the protagonist's struggles "poignant" but is critical of the "predictable ending," suggesting both appreciation and disappointment.

## Section 4: Inferences on Missing or Implied Details

**Question 1:**

*Correct Answer: B) The town faces economic challenges in the winter.*

**Explanation:**

The passage contrasts the town's thriving economy in summer with the empty streets and closed shops in winter, implying that the economy struggles during the colder months.

**Question 2:**

*Correct Answer: B) The family has limited financial resources.*

**Explanation:**

Although the house smells of fresh bread, the family goes to bed hungry on some nights, suggesting that they may not have enough resources to consistently afford food.

**Question 3:**

*Correct Answer: B) The politician might be avoiding addressing the issue of budget cuts.*

**Explanation:**

The omission of recent cuts to the school budget, despite discussing education, suggests the politician is avoiding the topic of reduced funding.

**Question 4:**

*Correct Answer: B) The coach is dissatisfied despite the win.*

**Explanation:**

The coach's silence and focus on the game board while the team celebrates implies dissatisfaction or concern about something beyond the win.

**Question 5:**

*Correct Answer: B) The garden was likely being watered regularly.*

**Explanation:**

The lushness of the garden despite a lack of rainfall suggests that it was being maintained with additional watering.

**Question 6:**

*Correct Answer: B) The villagers may be secretly concerned or uneasy about the changes.*

**Explanation:**

The fact that the villagers smile outwardly but whisper behind closed doors suggests unease or concern about the changes.

**Question 7:**

*Correct Answer: B) The dessert menu was not appealing to customers.*

**Explanation:**

Since customers often leave without dessert, it implies that the dessert options may not be as appealing as the restaurant's gourmet dishes.

**Question 8:**

*Correct Answer: B) The man is likely under significant pressure or has important tasks to complete.*

**Explanation:**

His urgency and decision to work late into the night after his colleagues have left indicate that he may have significant responsibilities or deadlines.

**Question 9:**

*Correct Answer: B) The building has fallen into disrepair.*

**Explanation:**

The boarded-up windows and graffiti-covered walls suggest that the once prosperous building is now in a state of disrepair.

**Question 10:**

*Correct Answer: B) She is distracted and preoccupied with her earlier mistake.*

**Explanation:**

Although she smiles and accepts the award, her thoughts about her earlier mistake indicate she is preoccupied and not fully focused on the ceremony.

**Question 11:**

*Correct Answer: B) The employees are likely overworked or under pressure to complete their tasks.*

**Explanation:**

The fact that the office lights are still on hours after sunset and employees are still working suggests a heavy workload or a pressured work environment.

**Question 12:**

*Correct Answer: B) There may be underlying conflict or unresolved issues between them.*

**Explanation:**

The tension between the two, despite their outward friendliness, implies that there may be unresolved issues or conflict in their relationship.

**Question 13:**

*Correct Answer: B) The house likely lacks proper insulation or heating.*

**Explanation:**

The family's realization that the house is colder than expected suggests that the house may not have adequate insulation or heating.

**Question 14:**

*Correct Answer: B) The store is not attracting many customers despite its reputation.*

**Explanation:**

The store is hailed as the best in town, yet the empty parking lot suggests that it is not as popular or successful as its reputation would imply.

**Question 15:**

*Correct Answer: B) The presentation, though well-prepared, may have lacked engagement or impact.*

**Explanation:**

Although the presentation was well-researched, the audience's lackluster reaction suggests it may not have been as engaging or impactful as expected.

# Section 5: Inferences on the Interrelation of Concepts

**Question 1:**

*Correct Answer: B) Rising sea levels are forcing governments to adapt their economic strategies.*

**Explanation:**

The passage links the environmental impact of rising sea levels with the necessity for governments to reconsider their economic planning, suggesting that environmental changes are directly influencing economic policies.

**Question 2:**

*Correct Answer: B) Technology has increased communication speed but reduced in-person communication.*

**Explanation:**

The passage explains that while technology makes communication faster, it has led to a decrease in face-to-face interactions, showing both a positive and a negative impact on social interactions.

**Question 3:**

*Correct Answer: B) Job creation and industrial expansion are linked to greater environmental stress.*

**Explanation:**

The passage describes how policies that promote job creation also lead to environmental degradation due to unchecked industrial expansion, illustrating the trade-off between economic and environmental factors.

**Question 4:**

*Correct Answer: C) Technological innovation creates wealth for some but increases inequality for others.*

**Explanation:**

The passage indicates that technological advancements lead to prosperity for some individuals while leaving others struggling with the consequences, highlighting the uneven distribution of benefits.

**Question 5:**

*Correct Answer: B) The agricultural revolution caused environmental degradation while increasing food production.*

**Explanation:**

While the agricultural revolution boosted food production, it also led to environmental harm, such as land degradation and loss of biodiversity, demonstrating a clear negative consequence alongside the positive outcome.

**Question 6:**

*Correct Answer: B) Urbanization improves economic growth but creates difficulties in housing and transportation.*

**Explanation:**

The passage points out that while urbanization drives economic growth, it also presents challenges in infrastructure, specifically housing and transportation, indicating a mixed impact.

**Question 7:**

*Correct Answer: B) The use of antibiotics has both positive effects (saving lives) and negative effects (resistance).*

**Explanation:**

The passage highlights the dual impact of antibiotics: saving lives but also contributing to the emergence of drug-resistant bacteria, showing both positive and negative consequences.

**Question 8:**

*Correct Answer: B) Educational reform increases access but also raises the risk of higher student debt.*

**Explanation:**

While educational reform has improved access to higher education, it has simultaneously increased student debt, showing a complex relationship between these two outcomes.

**Question 9:**

*Correct Answer: B) Globalization increases international trade while making competition harder for local industries.*

**Explanation:**

The passage illustrates how globalization promotes international trade but intensifies competition for local industries, showing both positive and negative effects.

**Question 10:**

*Correct Answer: B) Conservation efforts and economic development are in conflict, with development threatening habitats.*

**Explanation:**

The passage shows that while conservation efforts help preserve endangered species, economic development projects threaten natural habitats, creating a conflict between environmental and economic goals.

**Question 11:**

*Correct Answer: B) While renewable energy reduces fossil fuel dependence, it presents new challenges in storage and distribution.*

**Explanation:**

The expansion of renewable energy has reduced reliance on fossil fuels but has introduced new challenges in energy storage and distribution, showing both advancements and difficulties.

**Question 12:**

*Correct Answer: B) Artificial intelligence improves efficiency but raises concerns about job loss.*

**Explanation:**

The passage explains that while artificial intelligence enhances workplace efficiency, it also raises concerns about job displacement, showing a complex relationship between technology and employment.

**Question 13:**

*Correct Answer: B) The rise of digital platforms has led to concerns about misinformation as print media declines.*

**Explanation:**

The passage suggests that the decline of traditional print media and the rise of digital platforms have led to increased worries about the accuracy of information, highlighting a potential negative outcome of this transition.

**Question 14:**

*Correct Answer: B) While public transportation reduces traffic, its maintenance creates financial strain for local governments.*

**Explanation:**

The passage explains that investment in public transportation helps alleviate traffic congestion but creates financial burdens for local governments due to the cost of maintaining these systems.

**Question 15:**

*Correct Answer: B) The smartphone revolutionized communication but contributed to social isolation.*

**Explanation:**

The passage describes how smartphones have greatly improved communication but have also led to increased social isolation, indicating a trade-off in the use of technology.

# Section 6: Inferences on Tone and Language

**Question 1:**

*Correct Answer: B) The speaker finds the event disturbing and intense.*

**Explanation:**

The use of "vivid imagery" to depict the scene as "chaotic and overwhelming" suggests that the speaker perceives the event as disturbing and intense rather than exciting or calm.

**Question 2:**

*Correct Answer: B) The author is critical of the policy and suggests it should be replaced.*

**Explanation:**

Words like "outdated" and "ineffective" show the author's critical stance toward the policy, implying it is no longer useful and should be replaced.

**Question 3:**

*Correct Answer: B) He sees the regulation as ineffective and unworthy of serious consideration.*

**Explanation:**

The dismissive tone and the phrase "a laughable attempt" indicate that the speaker views the regulation as unworthy of serious consideration and ineffective.

**Question 4:**

*Correct Answer: B) The author is deeply concerned about the severity of the situation.*

**Explanation:**

Phrases like "monumental failure" and "irreparable harm" reflect the author's deep concern and negative view of the environmental impact, suggesting they see the situation as serious.

**Question 5:**

*Correct Answer: A) The writer believes the changes are unnecessary and sarcastically criticizes them.*

**Explanation:**

The sarcastic tone of the phrase "the perfect solution to a non-existent problem" implies that the writer sees the changes as unnecessary and is mocking them.

**Question 6:**

*Correct Answer: B) The author admires and respects the artist's contributions.*

**Explanation:**

The reverent language, with terms like "genius" and "visionary," indicates the author's admiration and respect for the artist.

**Question 7:**

*Correct Answer: B) The speaker views the past with fondness and longing.*

**Explanation:**

The nostalgic tone and the reference to "the golden days" suggest that the speaker looks back on the past with fondness and longing.

**Question 8:**

*Correct Answer: B) The author is frustrated with the inefficiency of the government plan.*

**Explanation:**

The phrase "yet another bureaucratic mess" indicates the author's frustration with the inefficiency of the government plan.

**Question 9:**

*Correct Answer: B) The author admires the initiative's willingness to take risks.*

**Explanation:**

The use of positive terms like "bold" and "audacious" suggests the author admires the initiative for its risk-taking nature.

**Question 10:**

*Correct Answer: B) She is resigned and somewhat accepting of the situation.*

**Explanation:**

The resigned sigh and the phrase "I suppose this is just how things are now" indicate that the speaker is accepting the situation, though perhaps not happily.

**Question 11:**

*Correct Answer: B) The author sees some potential for improvement amidst the challenges.*

**Explanation:**

The phrase "a glimmer of hope" amidst a "bleak scenario" suggests that the author has a cautiously optimistic outlook on the situation, seeing a potential for improvement.

**Question 12:**

*Correct Answer: B) The speaker is deeply appreciative and thankful for the support.*

**Explanation:**

The celebratory and grateful tone of the passage suggests that the speaker is expressing deep appreciation for the support received.

**Question 13:**

*Correct Answer: B) The author is skeptical and doubtful about the effectiveness of the plan.*

**Explanation:**

The tone of disbelief in the question "Could anyone really believe that such a plan would work?" indicates the author's skepticism and doubt about the plan's success.

**Question 14:**

*Correct Answer: B) The author is disappointed by the unexpected negative consequences.*

**Explanation:**

The shift from hopeful to somber tone as the unforeseen consequences are discussed suggests the author's disappointment with the outcome of the project.

**Question 15:**

*Correct Answer: B) The speaker is excited and enthusiastic about the technological achievement.*

**Explanation:**

The use of an excited tone and the phrase "a groundbreaking achievement in technology" indicates the speaker's enthusiasm and positive attitude toward the new development.

# Section 7: Multiple Inferences from Multiple Sources

**Question 1:**

*Correct Answer: B) The first scientist is more optimistic about the significance of the results than the second scientist.*

**Explanation:**

The first scientist believes the results will revolutionize the field, while the second scientist finds them interesting but not revolutionary. This suggests the first scientist is more optimistic than the second.

**Question 2:**

*Correct Answer: B) The environmentalists prioritize ecological benefits, while opponents focus on economic concerns.*

**Explanation:**

The environmentalists are pleased with the policy's ecological benefits, while opponents are concerned about its economic impact, particularly on the timber industry.

**Question 3:**

*Correct Answer: B) The second passage shows skepticism about the potential risks of the technology.*

**Explanation:**

While the first passage emphasizes the benefits of reduced energy consumption, the second passage expresses concern about the long-term environmental effects, showing skepticism.

**Question 4:**

*Correct Answer: B) The author believes the leader was ultimately successful, while the critic points to negative consequences.*

**Explanation:**

The author praises the leader as a visionary who led to greatness, while the critic argues that the leader's decisions caused harm, suggesting contrasting views of the leader's legacy.

**Question 5:**

*Correct Answer: B) The book received mixed reviews, with some praising its complexity and others criticizing its pacing.*

**Explanation:**

One group praises the book as a masterpiece with complex characters, while others criticize it for slow pacing, indicating mixed reception.

**Question 6:**

*Correct Answer: B) The system was environmentally beneficial, but not all residents had access to its advantages.*

**Explanation:**

The system is praised for its efficiency and reduced carbon footprint, but some residents are frustrated by limited routes and accessibility issues, suggesting its success was not universal.

**Question 7:**

*Correct Answer: B) The policy increased healthcare access but did not solve broader economic issues.*

**Explanation:**

The policy improved healthcare access for rural areas but failed to address economic disparities, indicating partial success in its implementation.

**Question 8:**

*Correct Answer: B) The artist's early work was more innovative than their later projects.*

**Explanation:**

The first excerpt praises the artist's early groundbreaking work, while the second focuses on later, more commercial projects, suggesting a decline in innovation.

**Question 9:**

*Correct Answer: B) The initiative was praised for its environmental impact but criticized for its financial burden.*

**Explanation:**

The initiative was celebrated for its potential environmental benefits but criticized for its high costs, showing a contrast between its ecological and financial impact.

**Question 10:**

*Correct Answer: B) The reforms are aimed at improving access but may not fully address deeper causes of inequality.*

**Explanation:**

While the reforms seek to reduce educational disparities, critics argue they do not tackle the root socioeconomic causes of inequality, suggesting partial success.

**Question 11:**

*Correct Answer: A) The policy improved employment opportunities but did not result in higher wages.*

**Explanation:**

The policy led to increased employment, but wages remained stagnant, indicating that while jobs increased, workers did not benefit financially from higher wages.

**Question 12:**

*Correct Answer: B) The regulations did not fully address the issues of worker safety.*

**Explanation:**

While the new regulations aimed to improve safety, unsafe working conditions and accidents persisted, suggesting the regulations were not completely effective.

**Question 13:**

*Correct Answer: C) Some critics believe the novel's portrayal is both accurate and exaggerated for effect.*

**Explanation:**

The first passage finds the novel accurate and insightful, while critics argue it exaggerates some aspects, suggesting that the novel is both realistic and exaggerated in places.

**Question 14:**

*Correct Answer: B) The program was celebrated for its scientific achievements but criticized for its costs.*

**Explanation:**

While the program is acknowledged for its scientific breakthroughs, its high costs and lack of immediate practical benefits raised concerns, showing mixed perceptions.

**Question 15:**

*Correct Answer: B) Early adopters were enthusiastic, but others found the product's functionality lacking.*

**Explanation:**

Early adopters were excited, but some consumers expressed disappointment in the product's functionality, suggesting that the product had mixed reception.

**Question 16:**

*Correct Answer: B) The initiative struggled to meet its goals despite its good intentions.*

**Explanation:**

Although the initiative aimed to provide affordable homes, it has been slow in delivering on its promises, leaving many families still waiting for housing.

**Question 17:**

*Correct Answer: B) The first passage is supportive of the movement, while the second passage is critical of its tactics.*

**Explanation:**

The first passage supports the environmental movement as a force for change, while the second criticizes its tactics as too extreme, showing differing views on its effectiveness.

**Question 18:**

*Correct Answer: B) There is excitement about its potential, but some experts are cautious about its limitations.*

**Explanation:**

While the first passage is enthusiastic about the technology's potential, the second passage expresses caution about its practical applications, indicating a balance of excitement and skepticism.

**Question 19:**

*Correct Answer: A) The industrial era was marked by both innovation and social challenges.*

**Explanation:**

The first passage highlights the industrial era's innovation and prosperity, while the critic points to inequality and harsh working conditions, indicating a mix of progress and challenges.

**Question 20:**

*Correct Answer: B) The reforms achieved progress but failed to fully resolve some significant challenges.*

**Explanation:**

While the reforms aimed at inclusivity and made some strides, they fell short in addressing major issues like funding disparities, indicating progress with lingering problems.

# Tone and Perspective Interpretation
## Section 1: Identifying Author's Tone

**Exercise 1:**

*Correct Answer: B) Sarcastic*

**Explanation:**

The use of the phrase "yet no consultation with employees was considered necessary" suggests a sarcastic tone, implying the author disapproves of the lack of employee input.

**Exercise 2:**

*Correct Answer: A) Critical*

**Explanation:**

The statement "it remains as flawed and ineffective as ever" indicates the author is critical of the education system's failure to improve despite reforms.

**Exercise 3:**

*Correct Answer: B) Pessimistic*

**Explanation:**

The phrase "such promises rarely come to fruition" reflects a pessimistic view toward political promises and the likelihood of them being fulfilled.

**Exercise 4:**

*Correct Answer: B) Excited*

**Explanation:**

The use of "groundbreaking" and "a completely new perspective" conveys an enthusiastic tone, indicating the author's excitement about the study's results.

**Exercise 5:**

*Correct Answer: A) Disappointed*

**Explanation:**

The phrase "despite numerous warnings" suggests disappointment in the student's continuous disregard for the rules.

**Exercise 6:**

*Correct Answer: A) Cautious*

**Explanation:**

The author acknowledges the excitement about technological advancements but expresses concern about privacy risks, indicating a cautious tone.

**Exercise 7:**

*Correct Answer: B) Skeptical*

**Explanation:**

The phrase "track record suggests otherwise" implies the author doubts the government's promise of reform, indicating skepticism.

**Exercise 8:**

*Correct Answer: C) Ironic*

**Explanation:**

The phrase "entirely pointless" after the chaos and confusion suggests an ironic tone, highlighting the futility of the meeting.

**Exercise 9:**

*Correct Answer: A) Mocking*

**Explanation:**

The contrast between "great fanfare" and "evident lack of innovation" indicates a mocking tone, suggesting the author finds the excitement unjustified.

**Exercise 10:**

*Correct Answer: A) Critical*

**Explanation:**

The author's observation of the "striking resemblance" to previous pieces suggests a critical attitude toward the artwork's originality.

**Exercise 11:**

*Correct Answer: B) Critical*

**Explanation:**

The phrase "failed to meet even the most basic of expectations" shows the author's critical tone toward the project's outcome.

**Exercise 12:**

*Correct Answer: B) Optimistic*

**Explanation:**

The phrase "the future is bright for those willing to adapt" indicates an optimistic tone about the future for adaptable individuals.

**Exercise 13:**

*Correct Answer: B) Sarcastic*

**Explanation:**

The repeated promises and mistakes, combined with the tone, suggest sarcasm, as the author doesn't genuinely expect change.

**Exercise 14:**

*Correct Answer: B) Confident*

**Explanation:**

The phrase "leaving no room for doubt" conveys a confident tone about the thoroughness of the study.

**Exercise 15:**

*Correct Answer: C) Critical*

**Explanation:**

The author notes the decision's failure to account for all factors, indicating a critical stance toward its success.

**Exercise 16:**

*Correct Answer: A) Optimistic*

**Explanation:**

Despite the threat of rain, the festival is celebrated with enthusiasm, suggesting an optimistic tone.

**Exercise 17:**

*Correct Answer: B) Skeptical*

**Explanation:**

The phrase "similarities to previous models were undeniable" reflects a skeptical attitude toward the company's claims of innovation.

**Exercise 18:**

*Correct Answer: A) Critical*

**Explanation:**

The author criticizes the vagueness and frustration caused by the unclear instructions, indicating a critical tone.

**Exercise 19:**

*Correct Answer: A) Sarcastic*

**Explanation:**

The phrase "except those in charge" reflects a sarcastic tone, implying that the solution should have been obvious to those in charge but was not.

**Exercise 20:**

*Correct Answer: B) Ironic*

**Explanation:**

The description of a long-planned event becoming a "complete disaster" conveys an ironic tone, highlighting the contrast between the planning and the outcome.

## Section 2: Recognizing Shifts in Tone

**Exercise 1:**

*Correct Answer: B) From enthusiastic to cautious*

**Explanation:**

The tone initially conveys enthusiasm for the new policy but shifts to caution as the focus turns to its potential downsides.

**Exercise 2:**

*Correct Answer: B) From frustrated to optimistic*

**Explanation:**

The passage begins with frustration over the government's lack of action, but the tone becomes more hopeful as potential solutions are explored.

**Exercise 3:**

*Correct Answer: A) From supportive to critical*

**Explanation:**

The author praises scientific progress at the beginning, but later adopts a more critical tone when questioning the potential costs.

**Exercise 4:**

*Correct Answer: B) From resigned to motivated*

**Explanation:**

The author starts with resignation about the failed project but ends on a determined note, indicating a shift to motivation to try again.

**Exercise 5:**

*Correct Answer: C) From admiring to critical*

**Explanation:**

Initially, the author shows admiration for the historical figure, but later presents a more balanced and critical perspective.

**Exercise 6:**

*Correct Answer: A) From confident to skeptical*

**Explanation:**

The author begins with confidence in the new findings but becomes skeptical as doubts about their validity emerge.

**Exercise 7:**

*Correct Answer: A) From curious to disappointed*

**Explanation:**

The passage starts with curiosity about the topic but ends in disappointment when the results do not meet expectations.

**Exercise 8:**

*Correct Answer: C) From optimistic to cautious*

**Explanation:**

The passage begins with an optimistic tone about technological progress but shifts to caution as ethical concerns are raised.

**Exercise 9:**

*Correct Answer: A) From critical to solution-oriented*

**Explanation:**

The author begins by criticizing past policies but shifts to a more positive, solution-focused tone.

**Exercise 10:**

*Correct Answer: C) From dismissive to supportive*

**Explanation:**

The author initially dismisses the idea but later acknowledges its potential, indicating a supportive shift.

**Exercise 11:**

*Correct Answer: A) From enthusiastic to cautious*

**Explanation:**

The passage starts with excitement about the discovery but shifts to caution as risks are discussed.

**Exercise 12:**

*Correct Answer: B) From skeptical to confident*

**Explanation:**

The author begins with skepticism but becomes more confident as the proposed solution is explained.

**Exercise 13:**

*Correct Answer: A) From critical to supportive*

**Explanation:**

The passage begins by questioning the program's effectiveness but concludes with a positive view of its long-term potential.

**Exercise 14:**

*Correct Answer: A) From neutral to critical*

**Explanation:**

The author starts with a neutral stance on the policy but later becomes more critical of its impact on the community.

**Exercise 15:**

*Correct Answer: A) From critical to supportive*

**Explanation:**

The passage starts with skepticism about the new research but becomes more supportive as additional evidence is presented.

# Section 3: Author's Perspective and Bias

**Exercise 1:**

*Correct Answer: B) The author believes immediate climate action is necessary*

**Explanation:**

The author's critique of the slow response from policymakers and the emphasis on urgency suggest a strong belief in the need for immediate action on climate change.

**Exercise 2:**

*Correct Answer: B) The author shows a bias in favor of innovation over ethics*

**Explanation:**

The author favors technological advancements, disregarding potential ethical concerns, which reflects a bias toward innovation.

**Exercise 3:**

*Correct Answer: C) The author's long-time support for free market policies affects their viewpoint*

**Explanation:**

As a long-time advocate of free market policies, the author's perspective on deregulation is influenced by their ideological background.

**Exercise 4:**

*Correct Answer: D) The author believes recent reforms are not beneficial and prefers traditional methods*

**Explanation:**

The author's critique of recent reforms and preference for traditional education methods reflects opposition to modern reforms.

**Exercise 5:**

*Correct Answer: B) The author shows a clear bias in favor of one side of the conflict*

**Explanation:**

The author's consistent portrayal of one side as justified reveals a bias, as they dismiss the actions of the opposing side.

**Exercise 6:**

*Correct Answer: C) The author's viewpoint is influenced by their profession, leading to a focus on provider benefits*

**Explanation:**

As a practicing physician, the author's argument for reforms that benefit healthcare providers over patients is influenced by their professional background.

**Exercise 7:**

*Correct Answer: B) The author supports renewable energy, focusing on its environmental benefits*

**Explanation:**

The author's emphasis on the environmental benefits of renewable energy while downplaying economic concerns shows a strong support for renewable energy.

**Exercise 8:**

*Correct Answer: C) The author shows bias against government intervention, favoring free markets*

**Explanation:**

The author argues that government intervention leads to inefficiency, showing a preference for free markets and revealing a bias against government involvement.

**Exercise 9:**

*Correct Answer: B) The author's perspective is shaped by a collectivist cultural background*

**Explanation:**

The emphasis on community over individualism is influenced by the author's collectivist cultural background, shaping their perspective.

**Exercise 10:**

*Correct Answer: C) The author is critical of the effects of globalization on small businesses*

**Explanation:**

The author highlights the negative impact of globalization on small local businesses, indicating a critical view of globalization.

**Exercise 11:**

*Correct Answer: B) The author shows bias toward reform, ignoring potential challenges*

**Explanation:**

By emphasizing the benefits of legal reform and ignoring the challenges, the author displays a bias in favor of reform.

**Exercise 12:**

*Correct Answer: C) The author favors lower taxes on corporations to boost economic growth*

**Explanation:**

The author's advocacy for lowering taxes on corporations as a means to stimulate economic growth reflects a bias toward pro-business policies.

**Exercise 13:**

*Correct Answer: B) The author shows bias against mainstream media, accusing it of political bias*

**Explanation:**

The author criticizes mainstream media for being overly sensationalistic and politically biased, reflecting a clear bias against it.

**Exercise 14:**

*Correct Answer: B) The author's perspective is influenced by their experience, resulting in support for free trade*

**Explanation:**

The author's support for free trade policies is influenced by their background as an economist with experience in global markets.

**Exercise 15:**

*Correct Answer: C) The author is biased against environmental regulations, favoring economic growth*

**Explanation:**

By downplaying the importance of environmental regulations and prioritizing economic growth, the author shows a clear bias against environmental protection.

# Section 4: Comparing Perspectives in Two Texts

**Exercise 1:**

*Correct Answer: C) Author A advocates for government action, while Author B trusts technological progress*

**Explanation:**

Author A emphasizes the need for immediate government intervention to combat climate change, while Author B relies on technological advancements to reduce emissions over time, showing a clear difference in their approaches.

**Exercise 2:**

*Correct Answer: B) Author A is more concerned with economic growth, while Author B stresses national security*

**Explanation:**

Author A focuses on the positive economic impact of immigration, while Author B emphasizes the importance of stronger border security and enforcement, indicating different priorities regarding immigration reform.

**Exercise 3:**

*Correct Answer: B) Author A believes local efforts are sufficient, while Author B advocates for national policies*

**Explanation:**

Author A suggests local efforts are essential for climate adaptation, while Author B argues that broader, national-level policies are more effective in addressing climate-related issues.

**Exercise 4:**

*Correct Answer: B) Author A emphasizes taxation, while Author B focuses on education and skills development*

**Explanation:**

Author A believes that taxation is the best way to reduce income inequality, while Author B supports education and skill development as more effective solutions.

**Exercise 5:**

*Correct Answer: B) Author A advocates for government involvement, while Author B relies on market competition*

**Explanation:**

Author A supports government subsidies to promote renewable energy development, while Author B believes that market competition will naturally drive innovation in renewable energy.

**Exercise 6:**

*Correct Answer: C) Author A sees technology as essential, while Author B is cautious about its impact*

**Explanation:**

Author A views technology as a critical tool for education, while Author B warns about the potential over-reliance on digital platforms and its impact on education quality.

**Exercise 7:**

*Correct Answer: C) Author A favors unrestricted free speech, while Author B supports some limits*

**Explanation:**

Author A argues that free speech should have no limitations, while Author B believes that restrictions are necessary to ensure inclusivity and respect on college campuses.

**Exercise 8:**

*Correct Answer: C) Author A promotes government-funded healthcare, while Author B advocates for privatized systems*

**Explanation:**

Author A supports universal healthcare funded by the government, while Author B prefers privatized healthcare options with minimal government intervention.

**Exercise 9:**

*Correct Answer: B) Author A focuses on risks, while Author B emphasizes the benefits of innovation*

**Explanation:**

Author A highlights the potential risks of unchecked innovation, while Author B is more focused on celebrating the benefits of scientific advancements without dwelling on the risks.

**Exercise 10:**

*Correct Answer: B) Author A sees globalization as beneficial to all, while Author B views it as favoring wealthier nations*

**Explanation:**

Author A presents globalization as equally beneficial to all countries, while Author B argues that wealthier nations disproportionately benefit from globalization.

**Exercise 11:**

*Correct Answer: B) Author A supports AI's advancement, while Author B focuses on its ethical concerns*

**Explanation:**

Author A views AI as a tool for societal advancement, while Author B is more concerned about the ethical implications and potential job losses associated with AI.

**Exercise 12:**

*Correct Answer: B) Author A believes social media increases political involvement, while Author B warns about misinformation*

**Explanation:**

Author A argues that social media enhances political participation, while Author B is concerned that it leads to misinformation and political polarization.

**Exercise 13:**

*Correct Answer: B) Author A focuses on glorifying the events, while Author B takes a critical approach*

**Explanation:**

Author A presents a glorified version of historical events, while Author B offers a more critical analysis, pointing out the complexities and challenges of the same events.

**Exercise 14:**

*Correct Answer: B) Author A advocates for universal accessibility, while Author B believes the market should regulate access*

**Explanation:**

Author A supports making medical innovations accessible to all, while Author B argues that access to new technologies should be determined by market competition.

**Exercise 15:**

*Correct Answer: C) Author A is in favor of maintaining traditional methods, while Author B advocates for change*

**Explanation:**

Author A favors preserving traditional educational methods, while Author B supports progressive changes to reform the current educational system.

## Section 5: Analyzing Author's Intent and Purpose

**Exercise 1:**

*Correct Answer: B) To highlight the policy's flaws and suggest alternatives*

**Explanation:**

The author's critical tone towards the government policy indicates their disapproval. The intent is to point out the shortcomings of the policy and possibly offer better solutions.

**Exercise 2:**

*Correct Answer: B) To evoke an emotional response from the reader*

**Explanation:**

By focusing on personal experiences, the author aims to connect emotionally with the reader, making the issue more relatable and highlighting the real-world effects of the healthcare law.

**Exercise 3:**

*Correct Answer: C) To suggest that current struggles mirror those of the past*

**Explanation:**

The author draws on the history of the civil rights movement to highlight the similarities between past and present social justice efforts, reinforcing the ongoing nature of these issues.

**Exercise 4:**

*Correct Answer: B) To undermine the credibility of corporate social responsibility efforts*

**Explanation:**

The author's sarcastic tone casts doubt on the sincerity of companies' social responsibility claims, suggesting they may prioritize profit over true social values.

**Exercise 5:**

*Correct Answer: C) To emphasize the scientific consensus on climate change*

**Explanation:**

By repeatedly referencing scientific studies, the author aims to solidify the argument that climate change is real and supported by a strong scientific consensus, countering denialist arguments.

**Exercise 6:**

*Correct Answer: B) To create an emotional connection with the reader*

**Explanation:**

The narrative format personalizes the abstract concept of income inequality, helping the reader emotionally engage with the issue through relatable stories.

**Exercise 7:**

*Correct Answer: D) To provide a balanced view and foster critical thinking*

**Explanation:**

By comparing two opposing viewpoints on immigration, the author encourages the reader to think critically and understand both sides of the debate, rather than advocating for one specific solution.

**Exercise 8:**

*Correct Answer: C) To evoke a strong emotional response from the reader*

**Explanation:**

The use of vivid imagery serves to make the issue of deforestation more immediate and alarming, engaging the reader's emotions to stress the importance of environmental conservation.

**Exercise 9:**

*Correct Answer: D) To highlight the flaws in the counterargument*

**Explanation:**

By including a counterargument, the author demonstrates an understanding of opposing views but ultimately uses this as an opportunity to refute those arguments and strengthen their own position.

**Exercise 10:**

*Correct Answer: B) To undermine confidence in the policy's effectiveness*

**Explanation:**

The rhetorical questioning of the new education policy's effectiveness suggests doubt and aims to reduce the reader's confidence in the policy's ability to bring about meaningful change.

## Context Meaning Questions

## Section 1: Understanding Word Meaning Through Context

**Exercise 1:**

*Correct Answer: b) Persuasive but empty language*

**Explanation:**

The word "rhetoric" in this context refers to language that is persuasive or designed to influence, but lacks actual substance or meaningful content.

**Exercise 2:**

*Correct Answer: a) Careful and precise*

**Explanation:**

The word "meticulous" means showing great attention to detail, being very careful and precise.

**Exercise 3:**

*Correct Answer: b) Impulsive and unplanned*

**Explanation:**

"Spontaneous" here refers to a decision made impulsively, without prior planning or forethought.

**Exercise 4:**

*Correct Answer: b) Hypothetical and uncertain*

**Explanation:**

The word "speculative" means based on conjecture or guesswork rather than solid evidence, indicating uncertainty.

**Exercise 5:**

*Correct Answer: b) Difficult to find or capture*

**Explanation:**

"Elusive" in this context refers to something that is hard to capture or achieve, like the butterfly in the sentence.

**Exercise 6:**

*Correct Answer: b) Simple and economical*

**Explanation:**

"Frugal" refers to someone who is economical, avoiding waste and extravagance, despite having wealth.

**Exercise 7:**

*Correct Answer: b) Disrespectful and scornful*

**Explanation:**

"Contemptuous" describes an attitude of disdain or disrespect, showing scorn toward the rules.

**Exercise 8:**

*Correct Answer: b) Innovative and groundbreaking*

**Explanation:**

"Revolutionary" means bringing about significant change or innovation, particularly in technology.

**Exercise 9:**

*Correct Answer: b) Places them side by side for comparison*

**Explanation:**

"Juxtaposes" means placing two things next to each other to compare or contrast them, emphasizing their differences.

**Exercise 10:**

*Correct Answer: a) A lack of interest or concern*

**Explanation:**

"Indifference" refers to a lack of interest, concern, or enthusiasm toward something, such as the outcome of the game.

**Exercise 11:**

*Correct Answer: a) Threatening and foreboding*

**Explanation:**

"Ominous" describes something that appears threatening or suggests that something bad is about to happen, like the gathering clouds before a storm.

**Exercise 12:**

*Correct Answer: b) Patronizing and superior*

**Explanation:**

"Condescending" refers to a tone or attitude that makes others feel inferior, often by speaking to them in a patronizing manner.

**Exercise 13:**

*Correct Answer: b) Complicated and difficult to follow*

**Explanation:**

"Convoluted" describes something that is complex or difficult to understand, often due to being overly complicated.

**Exercise 14:**

*Correct Answer: b) Short-lived and fleeting*

**Explanation:**

"Ephemeral" refers to something that is temporary or brief, like the fleeting nature of fame.

**Exercise 15:**

*Correct Answer: b) Sharp and focused*

**Explanation:**

"Incisive" means clear, sharp, and analytical, cutting through unnecessary details to make precise arguments.

# Section 2: Identifying the Function of Words in Sentences

**Exercise 1:**

*Correct Answer: b) As an adjective describing the overview*

**Explanation:**

"Comprehensive" functions as an adjective that describes the extent of the overview provided by the doctor.

**Exercise 2:**

*Correct Answer: b) It is an adjective describing the type of analysis*

**Explanation:**

"Critical" functions as an adjective, specifying the type of analysis conducted by the scientist.

**Exercise 3:**

*Correct Answer: d) As an adverb modifying "effective"*

**Explanation:**

"Remarkably" is an adverb that modifies "effective," describing how effective the speech was.

**Exercise 4:**

*Correct Answer: b) As an adjective describing the nature of the study*

**Explanation:**

"Exploratory" functions as an adjective, modifying the noun "nature" to describe the type of study.

**Exercise 5:**

*Correct Answer: c) As an adjective modifying "comments"*

**Explanation:**

"Brief" is an adjective that describes the comments, indicating their shortness in duration.

**Exercise 6:**

*Correct Answer: b) As an adjective modifying "results"*

**Explanation:**

"Preliminary" functions as an adjective describing the initial results of the study.

**Exercise 7:**

*Correct Answer: a) As an adjective modifying "work"*

**Explanation:**

"Influential" functions as an adjective, modifying "work" to describe its effect on modern design.

**Exercise 8:**

*Correct Answer: c) As an adjective modifying "agreement"*

**Explanation:**

"Tentative" functions as an adjective that describes the nature of the agreement between the two companies.

**Exercise 9:**

*Correct Answer: a) As an adjective modifying "placement"*

**Explanation:**

"Strategic" functions as an adjective, modifying "placement" to explain the careful planning behind the placement.

**Exercise 10:**

*Correct Answer: b) As an adjective modifying "behavior"*

**Explanation:**

"Considerate" is an adjective that describes the quality of the behavior, indicating kindness or thoughtfulness.

# Section 3: Using Surrounding Sentences to Clarify Meaning

**Exercise 1:**

*Correct Answer: 3. Open to multiple interpretations*

**Explanation:**

The preceding sentence indicates that the scientist's argument was unclear, allowing for various interpretations. This suggests that "ambiguous" means "open to multiple interpretations."

**Exercise 2:**

*Correct Answer: 2. Complicated*

**Explanation:**

The sentence describes how the process, initially straightforward, became more challenging and required careful attention to detail. This indicates that "convoluted" means "complicated."

**Exercise 3:**

*Correct Answer: 4. Uncertain*

**Explanation:**

The speech offered no clear solutions, leaving people unsure about future policies. This context suggests that "vague" means "uncertain."

**Exercise 4:**

*Correct Answer: 3. Rejected*

**Explanation:**

The sentence implies that the proposal was not accepted and the committee moved on to the next topic. This suggests that "dismissed" means "rejected."

**Exercise 5:**

*Correct Answer: 2. Variable*

**Explanation:**

The artist's use of color was described as lacking harmony, indicating that it changed in an unpredictable way. This suggests that "inconsistent" means "variable."

**Exercise 6:**

*Correct Answer: 3. Ironic*

**Explanation:**

The sentence mentions that the sarcastic remarks were intended to make the audience reflect on the absurdity of the situation, indicating irony. Thus, "sarcastic" means "ironic."

**Exercise 7:**

*Correct Answer: 2. Believable*

**Explanation:**

The explanation convinced the jury to reconsider, suggesting that the word "plausible" means "believable."

**Exercise 8:**

*Correct Answer: 2. Precise*

**Explanation:**

The lawyer's careful preparation ensured that no detail was missed, implying that "meticulous" means "precise."

**Exercise 9:**

*Correct Answer: 3. Uncertain*

**Explanation:**

The politician's stance frustrated voters because it lacked clarity, indicating that "ambivalent" means "uncertain."

**Exercise 10:**

*Correct Answer: 1. Dull*

**Explanation:**

The performance showed none of the expected energy or enthusiasm, suggesting that "lackluster" means "dull."

## Section 4: Interpreting Figurative Language in Context

**Exercise 1:**

*Correct Answer: 1. She was overwhelmed by her tasks.*

**Explanation:**

The phrase "drowning in a sea of responsibilities" uses the metaphor of drowning to suggest that she is overwhelmed by the number of tasks or responsibilities she has to manage.

**Exercise 2:**

*Correct Answer: 2. A small but significant source of hope.*

**Explanation:**

The phrase "a spark in the darkness" is a metaphor indicating that the idea provided a small but important source of hope or inspiration in an otherwise difficult or uncertain situation.

**Exercise 3:**

*Correct Answer: 3. The project was on the verge of failure.*

**Explanation:**

The metaphor "ticking time bomb" implies that the project is dangerously close to failing due to the ongoing delays, much like a time bomb that could explode at any moment.

**Exercise 4:**

*Correct Answer: 2. It collapsed easily under stress.*

**Explanation:**

The phrase "crumbled like a house of cards" suggests that her confidence was fragile and collapsed easily under the pressure of the interview, just as a house of cards would fall apart with a slight disturbance.

**Exercise 5:**

*Correct Answer: 3. The profits were highly unpredictable.*

**Explanation:**

The metaphor "a rollercoaster ride" implies that the company's profits fluctuated dramatically, just like the ups and downs of a rollercoaster, indicating unpredictability.

**Exercise 6:**

*Correct Answer: 2. The explanation was confusing and unclear.*

**Explanation:**

The phrase "clear as mud" is an ironic expression that actually means the opposite of clear. It implies that the explanation was confusing and did not make sense.

**Exercise 7:**

*Correct Answer: 2. They had both positive and negative effects.*

**Explanation:**

The phrase "double-edged sword" implies that her words had both positive and negative consequences, impacting both sides in the discussion or argument.

**Exercise 8:**

*Correct Answer: 2. The CEO was in a very risky situation.*

**Explanation:**

The phrase "walking on thin ice" is a metaphor that implies the CEO was in a dangerous or precarious position, where one wrong move could lead to serious consequences.

**Exercise 9:**

*Correct Answer: 2. His memory of the event was fading or unclear.*

**Explanation:**

The metaphor "swept away by a strong wind" suggests that his memory was becoming unclear or fading, much like how objects can be swept away by the wind and disappear.

**Exercise 10:**

*Correct Answer: 2. The debate became intense and hostile.*

**Explanation:**

The phrase "turned into a battlefield" implies that the debate escalated into an intense and hostile exchange, with both sides "launching verbal attacks," as if they were engaged in a battle.

# Section 5: Recognizing Multiple Meanings of Words

**Exercise 1:**

*Correct Answer: 4. A false outward appearance.*

**Explanation:**

In the context of the passage, "put up a brave front" means presenting a false appearance of bravery or confidence despite inner turmoil. The word "front" here refers to a façade or outward appearance that doesn't necessarily reflect inner feelings.

**Exercise 2:**

*Correct Answer: 1. A leading position.*

**Explanation:**

In this context, "front" refers to the leading position, as the soldier is at the front of the line. It is used to describe a place of prominence or leadership.

**Exercise 3:**

*Correct Answer: 2. To make a reservation.*

**Explanation:**

Here, the word "book" refers to making a reservation for a hotel room. This meaning of "book" is commonly used in the context of securing appointments or accommodations in advance.

**Exercise 4:**

*Correct Answer: 2. To carry or endure.*

**Explanation:**

In this passage, "bear" means to endure or carry a responsibility. The word is used to describe someone managing or shouldering a heavy duty or burden, often in difficult situations.

**Exercise 5:**

*Correct Answer: 2. To reach an agreement.*

**Explanation:**

The word "strike" in this context means to make or reach an agreement, as in striking a deal with the supplier. It does not imply physical action but rather the act of negotiating a mutual agreement.

# Sentence Correction and Grammar

## Section 1: Sentence Structure and Syntax

**1. Identify the sentence fragment:** *Correct Answer: B. Running through the park and never stopping.*

**Explanation:**

This is a fragment because it lacks a complete thought or subject performing an action. It's missing the main clause that completes the idea.

**2. Which sentence is a run-on?** *Correct Answer: B. The rain stopped, the sun came out, we went outside.*

**Explanation:**

This is a run-on sentence because independent clauses are not properly connected with conjunctions or punctuation.

**3. Choose the sentence that avoids a run-on:** *Correct Answer: C. The cat purred contentedly while lying in the sun.*

**Explanation:**

This sentence has a proper structure, with one independent clause and a dependent clause, avoiding any run-on issues.

**4. Which of the following is a complete sentence?** *Correct Answer: B. The children were playing in the backyard.*

**Explanation:**

This is a complete sentence with a subject and verb, expressing a complete thought.

**5. Identify the sentence that correctly combines the clauses:** *Correct Answer: A. He wanted to go to the beach, but the weather was terrible.*

**Explanation:**

This is a properly combined sentence using a conjunction and a comma to connect two independent clauses.

**6. Which sentence corrects the fragment?** *Correct Answer: B. The baby slept peacefully in the crib.*

**Explanation:**

This is a grammatically complete sentence with both a subject and a predicate.

**7. Choose the grammatically correct sentence:** *Correct Answer: B. The books on the shelf are old and dusty.*

**Explanation:**

This sentence has correct subject-verb agreement, with "books" (plural) and "are."

**8. Select the correct complex sentence structure:** *Correct Answer: B. If you study hard, you will pass the test.*

**Explanation:**

This is a complex sentence with a dependent clause ("If you study hard") and an independent clause ("you will pass the test").

**9. Correct the run-on sentence:** *Correct Answer: B. She read the book, and she wrote the report.*
**Explanation:**
This corrects the run-on sentence by properly using a conjunction and a comma to link the clauses.

**10. Which sentence is a fragment?** *Correct Answer: A. The man who was waiting at the bus stop.*
**Explanation:**
This is a fragment because it lacks a main verb and does not complete a thought.

**11. Choose the sentence that corrects the fragment:** *Correct Answer: B. She was running down the street when she turned the corner.*
**Explanation:**
This sentence is grammatically complete, correcting the fragment by providing a full thought.

**12. Identify the grammatically correct sentence:** *Correct Answer: B. The cake smells delicious; however, it is not ready yet.*
**Explanation:**
This sentence correctly uses a semicolon and a transitional word to combine the clauses.

**13. Which of the following avoids a run-on?** *Correct Answer: D. They went to the store, bought groceries, and then they came home.*
**Explanation:**
This sentence uses commas and conjunctions properly to avoid a run-on.

**14. Choose the correct sentence structure:** *Correct Answer: D. The teacher said to study hard, because the test is going to be difficult.*
**Explanation:**
This sentence has proper punctuation and structure for clarity.

**15. Correct the sentence with a fragment:** *Correct Answer: B. Because she was late to work.*
**Explanation:**
This is a fragment because it does not contain a complete thought or main clause.

**16. Which of these is a grammatically correct sentence?** *Correct Answer: B. Neither of the boys is ready for school.*
**Explanation:**
The subject "Neither" is singular, so "is" must be used.

**17. Identify the sentence fragment:** *Correct Answer: C. While walking to the park.*
**Explanation:**
This is a fragment because it is an incomplete thought without a main clause.

**18. Choose the correctly combined sentence:** *Correct Answer: C. She enjoys reading books, listening to music, and traveling.*
**Explanation:**
This sentence uses parallel structure to list her activities properly.

**19. Which sentence is a fragment?** *Correct Answer: B. Studying hard for the final exams and hoping for the best.*
**Explanation:**
This is a fragment because it lacks a main clause or complete thought.

**20. Identify the correct sentence structure:** *Correct Answer: A. The test was hard; however, I think I did well.*
**Explanation:**
This sentence uses a semicolon properly to connect two independent clauses with a transitional word.

**21. Which sentence is correct?** *Correct Answer: B. The results of the study, which was conducted last year, were surprising.*

**Explanation:**

This sentence uses correct punctuation with the non-restrictive clause "which was conducted last year."

**22. Choose the sentence with no grammatical errors:** *Correct Answer: B. He goes to the gym every day to stay fit.*

**Explanation:**

This sentence is grammatically correct and properly punctuated.

**23. Which sentence is correct?** *Correct Answer: C. The team's winning the championship was a major accomplishment.*

**Explanation:**

This sentence uses correct structure, focusing on "The team's winning."

**24. Which sentence is grammatically correct?** *Correct Answer: B. His decision was both wise and quick.*

**Explanation:**

This sentence uses parallel adjectives "wise and quick" to describe his decision.

**25. Identify the sentence with correct subject-verb agreement:** *Correct Answer: B. The group of students is going to the museum.*

**Explanation:**

The subject "group" is singular, so the verb "is" must be singular to match.

## Section 2: Verb Tense and Agreement

**1. Choose the correct verb tense:** *Correct Answer: A. She runs every morning before work.*

**Explanation:**

"Runs" is in the present tense, which is correct for habitual actions.

**2. Which verb agrees with the subject?** *Correct Answer: B. The dog barks at strangers.*

**Explanation:**

"Barks" agrees with the singular subject "dog."

**3. Select the correct verb tense for the sentence:** *Correct Answer: A. By the time we arrived, the show had already started.*

**Explanation:**

The past perfect tense "had already started" indicates an action that occurred before another past event ("we arrived").

**4. Which sentence uses the correct verb form?** *Correct Answer: A. She was cooking dinner when the phone rang.*

**Explanation:**

This sentence correctly uses the past continuous tense for an ongoing action interrupted by a past event.

**5. Identify the correct subject-verb agreement:** *Correct Answer: B. Each of the students has completed the assignment.*

**Explanation:**

"Each" is singular, so "has" must be used.

**6. Choose the sentence with correct verb tense consistency:** *Correct Answer: A. She was reading when the lights went out.*

**Explanation:**

The past continuous "was reading" is consistent with the past simple "went out."

**7. Which sentence has correct subject-verb agreement?** *Correct Answer: B. The team is planning their next move.*

**Explanation:**
"Team" is a collective noun and takes a singular verb, "is."

**8. Select the correct verb form for the following sentence:** *Correct Answer: C. If I were rich, I would travel the world.*
**Explanation:**
The subjunctive "were" is used for hypothetical situations.

**9. Which sentence has consistent verb tenses?** *Correct Answer: B. He studies hard and takes a break.*
**Explanation:**
The present tense is used consistently here for habitual actions.

**10. Choose the correct verb to complete the sentence:** *Correct Answer: B. They have never seen a play before.*
**Explanation:**
"Have" is the correct auxiliary verb for the subject "they."

**11. Which verb agrees with the subject?** *Correct Answer: B. The books on the shelf are dusty.*
**Explanation:**
"Books" is plural, so "are" is the correct verb.

**12. Select the correct verb form for this conditional sentence:** *Correct Answer: A. If he had known, he would have acted differently.*
**Explanation:**
The past perfect "had known" is used in this third conditional sentence.

**13. Identify the correct verb tense:** *Correct Answer: B. I was going to the store when I saw an old friend.*
**Explanation:**
The past continuous "was going" is used with the past simple "saw."

**14. Choose the correct sentence:** *Correct Answer: B. Neither of the boys is going to the party.*
**Explanation:**
"Neither" is singular, so "is" is the correct verb.

**15. Which sentence has correct verb tense agreement?** *Correct Answer: B. When he arrived, she had been waiting for him.*
**Explanation:**
The past perfect continuous "had been waiting" is used for an action that occurred before "he arrived."

**16. Identify the sentence with the correct subject-verb agreement:** *Correct Answer: B. The group of students was excited for the trip.*
**Explanation:**
"Group" is a singular collective noun, so "was" is correct.

**17. Choose the correct verb form:** *Correct Answer: A. She has been working on the project for hours.*
**Explanation:**
The present perfect continuous "has been working" is correct for an ongoing action.

**18. Select the correct verb for the sentence:** *Correct Answer: B. The children were playing in the park.*
**Explanation:**
"Were" agrees with the plural subject "children."

**19. Which sentence is correct?** *Correct Answer: A. The teacher is speaking to the students about the assignment.*
**Explanation:**
This sentence uses the present continuous tense correctly.

**20. Identify the sentence with proper verb tense consistency:** *Correct Answer: C. After she had studied, she took a break.*

**Explanation:**

The past perfect "had studied" and the past simple "took" are consistent.

**21. Choose the correct verb form:** *Correct Answer: C. He was driving when the car broke down.*

**Explanation:**

The past continuous "was driving" is correctly paired with the past simple "broke down."

**22. Which verb agrees with the subject?** *Correct Answer: B. The bag of apples is on the counter.*

**Explanation:**

"Bag" is singular, so "is" must be used.

**23. Select the correct verb tense:** *Correct Answer: B. They had already left when we arrived.*

**Explanation:**

The past perfect "had already left" is used for the earlier action, and "arrived" is in the past simple.

**24. Identify the sentence with proper subject-verb agreement:** *Correct Answer: B. Everyone in the room is excited about the announcement.*

**Explanation:**

"Everyone" is singular, so "is" must be used.

**25. Choose the correct verb form:** *Correct Answer: B. The flowers in the garden need watering.*

**Explanation:**

"Need" is the correct plural verb for the subject "flowers."

## Section 3: Pronouns and Antecedents

**Question 1: Which pronoun correctly completes the sentence?** *Correct Answer: B) his or her*

**Explanation:**

The pronoun "his or her" is correct because "each" is singular, and "students" refers to both male and female individuals, requiring gender-neutral language.

**Question 2: Identify the correct pronoun to complete the sentence:** *Correct Answer: A) his*

**Explanation:**

The pronoun "his" is correct because "neither" refers to a singular subject, and the subject "John or Mark" is masculine, thus needing a singular, masculine pronoun.

**Question 3: Choose the correct pronoun to match the antecedent:** *Correct Answer: C) he or she*

**Explanation:**

"Anyone" is singular, and to maintain gender neutrality, "he or she" is the appropriate pronoun.

**Question 4: Which sentence uses pronouns correctly?** *Correct Answer: B) "Somebody forgot their umbrella."*

**Explanation:**

While technically "somebody" is singular, modern usage often allows "their" as a singular, gender-neutral pronoun when the gender is unspecified.

**Question 5: Identify the pronoun error in the sentence:** *Correct Answer: B) Replace "they" with "he or she"*

**Explanation:**

The subject is "the teacher or the students," a singular subject. Therefore, "he or she" should be used to match the singular antecedent.

**Question 6: Which pronoun correctly completes the sentence?** *Correct Answer: B) their*

**Explanation:**

"Both" refers to two individuals, requiring the plural pronoun "their."

**Question 7: What is the correct pronoun to agree with the subject in this sentence?** *Correct Answer: A) its*

**Explanation:**

"Committee" is a collective noun and requires the singular pronoun "its."

**Question 8: Which sentence contains a pronoun-antecedent agreement error?** *Correct Answer: C) "Each of the children brought their lunch."*

**Explanation:**

"Each" is singular, so the pronoun should be "his or her" instead of "their."

**Question 9: Correct the pronoun error:** *Correct Answer: C) Replace "they" with "he or she"*

**Explanation:**

"A student" is singular, so the correct pronoun would be "he or she" to agree with the singular antecedent.

**Question 10: Which pronoun correctly completes the sentence?** *Correct Answer: B) its*

**Explanation:**

"Neither" refers to a singular subject, so "its" is the correct pronoun.

**Question 11: Identify the correct pronoun to agree with the antecedent:** *Correct Answer: B) his or her*

**Explanation:**

"A person" is singular, and the correct pronoun to maintain gender neutrality is "his or her."

**Question 12: Which sentence is grammatically correct?** *Correct Answer: B) "The group of students took their seats."*

**Explanation:**

"The group" refers to a collective noun, and "their" is correct since it refers to the students.

**Question 13: Correct the pronoun-antecedent agreement error:** *Correct Answer: B) Replace "their" with "his or her"*

**Explanation:**

"Anyone" is singular, so "his or her" should replace "their" for correct agreement.

**Question 14: Which pronoun correctly completes the sentence?** *Correct Answer: A) his or her*

**Explanation:**

"Each" is singular, requiring the singular pronoun "his or her."

**Question 15: Identify the correct pronoun to match the antecedent:** *Correct Answer: A) its*

**Explanation:**

"Team" is a collective noun and requires the singular pronoun "its."

**Question 16: Which sentence contains a pronoun-antecedent agreement error?** *Correct Answer: C) "Each member of the jury gave their opinion."*

**Explanation:**

"Each" is singular, so the pronoun should be "his or her" instead of "their."

**Question 17: Correct the pronoun usage:** *Correct Answer: B) Replace "their" with "his or her"*

**Explanation:**

"Somebody" is singular, so the pronoun "his or her" is needed instead of "their."

**Question 18: Which pronoun correctly completes the sentence?** *Correct Answer: A) their*

**Explanation:**

"Class" refers to a group of students, so "their" is the correct plural pronoun.

**Question 19: What is the correct pronoun to agree with the subject in this sentence?** *Correct Answer: A) its*

**Explanation:**

"Board of directors" is a collective noun and takes the singular pronoun "its."

**Question 20: Identify the sentence with correct pronoun-antecedent agreement:** *Correct Answer: D)* *"Every student must bring his or her own materials."*

**Explanation:**

"Every student" is singular, requiring "his or her" to agree with the antecedent.

## Section 4: Punctuation and Capitalization

**Question 1: Which punctuation mark correctly completes the sentence?** *Correct Answer: C) :*

**Explanation:**

A colon is used to indicate a time format, such as "9:30."

**Question 2: Where should the comma be placed in the following sentence?** *Correct Answer: B) After* *"bus"*

**Explanation:**

The comma comes after "bus" to separate the introductory clause from the main sentence.

**Question 3: Which sentence uses punctuation correctly?** *Correct Answer: B) "He didn't know how to* *respond, so he stayed silent."*

**Explanation:**

This sentence uses a comma correctly before the coordinating conjunction "so."

**Question 4: Which punctuation mark correctly completes the sentence?** *Correct Answer: A) :*

**Explanation:**

A colon is needed before listing items, such as "bread, milk, and eggs."

**Question 5: Where should the colon be placed in this sentence?** *Correct Answer: A) After "sure"*

**Explanation:**

A colon introduces the following statement or explanation.

**Question 6: Which sentence is punctuated correctly?** *Correct Answer: C) "After the rain stopped, we went* *outside."*

**Explanation:**

The comma separates the dependent clause from the independent clause.

**Question 7: Which punctuation mark is needed to fix the sentence?** *Correct Answer: B) :*

**Explanation:**

A colon introduces a clause that explains or elaborates on the first part of the sentence.

**Question 8: Where does the semicolon belong in this sentence?** *Correct Answer: A) After "home"*

**Explanation:**

A semicolon separates two independent clauses that are closely related in meaning.

**Question 9: Which sentence correctly uses a comma?** *Correct Answer: A) "Although it was raining hard, we* *went for a walk."*

**Explanation:**

A comma is used after an introductory dependent clause.

**Question 10: Which sentence is capitalized correctly?** *Correct Answer: B) "We visited the Grand Canyon in* *Arizona last summer."*

**Explanation:**

"Grand Canyon" and "Arizona" are proper nouns and must be capitalized.

**Question 11: Where should the comma be placed in this sentence?** *Correct Answer: B) After "sets"*
**Explanation:**
The comma separates the dependent clause from the independent clause.

**Question 12: Which punctuation mark is needed in this sentence?** *Correct Answer: B) :*
**Explanation:**
A colon is used to introduce a list.

**Question 13: Which sentence uses semicolons correctly?** *Correct Answer: B) "We went to the park; we played soccer; we ate lunch."*
**Explanation:**
Semicolons are used to separate independent clauses in a list when commas are not sufficient.

**Question 14: Which sentence is capitalized correctly?** *Correct Answer: C) "I saw Professor Smith at the university."*
**Explanation:**
"Professor Smith" is a proper noun and must be capitalized, but "university" is not.

**Question 15: Where should the period be placed in this sentence?** *Correct Answer: A) After "dinner"*
**Explanation:**
The period completes the first independent clause before moving to the second.

**Question 16: Which punctuation mark is needed to fix this sentence?** *Correct Answer: A) ;*
**Explanation:**
The semicolon connects two closely related independent clauses.

**Question 17: Which sentence uses a colon correctly?** *Correct Answer: B) "Here are my favorite subjects: math, science, and history."*
**Explanation:**
A colon introduces the list of subjects after a complete sentence.

**Question 18: Where does the comma belong in this sentence?** *Correct Answer: C) After "traffic"*
**Explanation:**
The comma separates the introductory clause from the main clause.

**Question 19: Which sentence is correctly punctuated?** *Correct Answer: A) "We visited Washington, D.C., last summer; it was great."*
**Explanation:**
The semicolon is used correctly to connect two independent clauses.

**Question 20: Which punctuation mark completes the sentence correctly?** *Correct Answer: B) :*
**Explanation:**
The colon is used to introduce a list following the sentence.

## Section 5: Parallelism

**Question 1: Which sentence maintains proper parallelism?** *Correct Answer: B) "She likes hiking, swimming, and riding a bike."*
**Explanation:**
This sentence is parallel because all the items in the list are in the same form: "hiking," "swimming," and "riding a bike" are all gerunds (verb + ing). This consistency creates balance in the sentence.

**Question 2: Choose the sentence that maintains parallel structure:** *Correct Answer: B) "The job requires you to work quickly, efficiently, and carefully."*

**Explanation:**

This sentence is parallel because the adjectives "quickly," "efficiently," and "carefully" are all adverbs modifying the verb "work" in the same manner, maintaining a consistent structure.

**Question 3: Which option presents the most parallel sentence structure?** *Correct Answer: B) "We spent the day swimming, playing volleyball, and hiking."*

**Explanation:**

This sentence is parallel because "swimming," "playing," and "hiking" are all gerunds, creating a balanced structure for the sentence.

**Question 4: Select the sentence with the correct parallelism:** *Correct Answer: C) "He wanted to run a marathon, to learn Spanish, and to read books."*

**Explanation:**

This sentence is parallel because the infinitive form "to" is used consistently before each verb: "to run," "to learn," and "to read."

**Question 5: Which sentence demonstrates proper parallel structure?** *Correct Answer: A) "The teacher told us to study hard, practice often, and be prepared."*

**Explanation:**

This sentence maintains parallelism by using the base forms of the verbs: "study," "practice," and "be." These verb forms are consistent, creating a balanced sentence.

**Question 6: Which sentence is structured in a parallel way?** *Correct Answer: B) "She enjoys dancing, singing, and writing poetry."*

**Explanation:**

The sentence is parallel because "dancing," "singing," and "writing" are all gerunds, ensuring a consistent structure.

**Question 7: Choose the sentence with correct parallelism:** *Correct Answer: B) "The company values dedication, innovation, and hard work."*

**Explanation:**

This sentence is parallel because "dedication," "innovation," and "hard work" are all nouns, maintaining the same form for all items in the list.

**Question 8: Select the option that maintains parallel structure:** *Correct Answer: B) "The students were advised to read carefully, write clearly, and prepare thoroughly."*

**Explanation:**

This sentence is parallel because the verb phrases "to read," "to write," and "to prepare" are consistent in form, ensuring parallelism.

**Question 9: Which sentence uses parallel structure correctly?** *Correct Answer: A) "The coach told the team to play hard, to stay focused, and finish strong."*

**Explanation:**

This sentence maintains parallelism because "to play," "to stay," and "finish" are in consistent forms, balancing the sentence.

**Question 10: Which sentence maintains parallel structure?** *Correct Answer: B) "To cook well, you need fresh ingredients, patience, and to follow directions carefully."*

**Explanation:**

This sentence maintains parallelism by listing nouns ("fresh ingredients," "patience") and an infinitive phrase ("to follow directions") in a consistent manner.

**Question 11: Which sentence is parallel?** *Correct Answer: B) "I plan to visit museums, attend a concert, and eat at a new restaurant."*

**Explanation:**

This sentence is parallel because "to visit," "attend," and "eat" are all verbs in their base form, maintaining a consistent structure.

**Question 12: Choose the sentence that maintains proper parallelism:** *Correct Answer: D) "The candidate has experience, is qualified, and communicates well."*

**Explanation:**

This sentence maintains parallelism by using the verb phrases "has experience," "is qualified," and "communicates well" consistently.

**Question 13: Which sentence is grammatically correct and maintains parallel structure?** *Correct Answer: B) "For breakfast, I had eggs, toast, and coffee."*

**Explanation:**

This sentence is parallel because "eggs," "toast," and "coffee" are all nouns, maintaining a consistent structure.

**Question 14: Select the option that presents parallel structure:** *Correct Answer: A) "To succeed, you need to work hard, stay focused, and be lucky."*

**Explanation:**

This sentence maintains parallelism because the verb phrases "to work," "stay," and "be" are all in consistent forms, ensuring balance.

**Question 15: Which sentence is parallel?** *Correct Answer: B) "He enjoys playing soccer, reading novels, and cooking."*

**Explanation:**

This sentence is parallel because "playing," "reading," and "cooking" are all gerunds, creating a balanced sentence.

**Question 16: Choose the sentence that maintains parallel structure:** *Correct Answer: C) "The tour included visits to the Eiffel Tower, the Louvre, and the Seine River."*

**Explanation:**

This sentence is parallel because "visits to the Eiffel Tower," "the Louvre," and "the Seine River" are all nouns, maintaining consistency in structure.

**Question 17: Which sentence maintains proper parallelism?** *Correct Answer: D) "The athlete was strong, quick, and had endurance."*

**Explanation:**

This sentence is parallel because "was strong," "quick," and "had endurance" maintain a consistent grammatical form.

**Question 18: Select the option that shows proper parallel structure:** *Correct Answer: B) "She is known for being intelligent, kind, and helpful."*

**Explanation:**

This sentence is parallel because "intelligent," "kind," and "helpful" are all adjectives, maintaining consistency in form.

**Question 19: Which sentence correctly follows parallelism rules?** *Correct Answer: C) "We must decide whether to attend the concert, go to dinner, or stay home."*

**Explanation:**

This sentence is parallel because "to attend," "go," and "stay" are all in the same verb form, ensuring balance.

**Question 20: Which sentence is parallel?** *Correct Answer: B) "Her goals include traveling the world, learning a new language, and writing a book."*

**Explanation:**

This sentence maintains parallelism because "traveling," "learning," and "writing" are all gerunds, creating a consistent structure.

## Section 6: Modifiers and Word Placement

**Question 1: Which sentence correctly places the modifier?**

*Correct Answer: B) "Walking to school, I felt the rain start to fall."*

**Explanation:**

This sentence correctly places the modifier "Walking to school" at the beginning of the sentence, and it logically modifies "I," the subject of the sentence. In option A, the rain is incorrectly doing the walking, which creates confusion.

**Question 2: Choose the sentence where the modifier is correctly placed:**

*Correct Answer: C) "Having finished the book, the students watched the movie."*

**Explanation:**

The modifier "Having finished the book" correctly modifies "the students," who are the ones who completed the book and then watched the movie. Other options wrongly modify "the movie."

**Question 3: Which sentence places the modifier correctly?**

*Correct Answer: C) "The cake, covered in chocolate, was enjoyed by the kids."*

**Explanation:**

This sentence places the modifier "covered in chocolate" next to "the cake," which it describes. In other options, the placement of "covered in chocolate" suggests that the kids were covered in chocolate, which is incorrect.

**Question 4: Select the sentence that correctly places the modifier:**

*Correct Answer: C) "While I was reading the book, the loud noise distracted me."*

**Explanation:**

The modifier "While I was reading the book" is correctly placed, as it clearly refers to the action of the speaker being distracted by the noise. Other options either create confusion or illogical meanings.

**Question 5: Choose the sentence with the modifier in the right position:**

*Correct Answer: C) "To get to school on time, he rode a bike."*

**Explanation:**

This sentence correctly places the modifier "To get to school on time" at the beginning of the sentence, clearly modifying "he," the person who rode the bike. Other options have misplaced modifiers that disrupt clarity.

**Question 6: Which sentence correctly places the modifier?**

*Correct Answer: C) "Tired after the game, he slept easily."*

**Explanation:**

The modifier "Tired after the game" correctly modifies "he," the person who slept. In other options, the modifier is placed in a way that distorts the meaning or creates ambiguity.

**Question 7: Select the sentence where the modifier is correctly positioned:**

*Correct Answer: C) "Running beside her, the dog accompanied her to the store."*

**Explanation:**

The modifier "Running beside her" correctly modifies "the dog," which is the subject of the sentence. Other sentences misplace the modifier, leading to confusion.

**Question 8: Which sentence properly places the modifier?**

*Correct Answer: B) "Hoping to improve the project, the team made changes."*

**Explanation:**

The modifier "Hoping to improve the project" correctly modifies "the team," the group that made the changes. The other sentences place the modifier in positions that distort the meaning.

**Question 9: Which sentence places the modifier correctly?**

*Correct Answer: C) "After finishing the meal, I washed the dishes."*

**Explanation:**

The modifier "After finishing the meal" correctly modifies "I," the person who washed the dishes. Other options either misplace the modifier or make the sentence unclear.

**Question 10: Choose the correct sentence:**

*Correct Answer: B) "Shining brightly, the stars were visible in the sky."*

**Explanation:**

The modifier "Shining brightly" correctly modifies "the stars," which are doing the shining. Other options either misplace the modifier or create confusing meanings.

**Question 11: Select the sentence where the modifier is correctly placed:**

*Correct Answer: B) "Driving home, I saw the beautiful sunset."*

**Explanation:**

The modifier "Driving home" correctly modifies "I," the person who saw the sunset. Other options misplace the modifier, making the sentence unclear or illogical.

**Question 12: Which sentence avoids a misplaced modifier?**

*Correct Answer: C) "The teacher handed the students papers written with a red pen."*

**Explanation:**

This sentence correctly places the modifier "written with a red pen" next to "papers," which it describes. In other options, the modifier placement creates ambiguity.

**Question 13: Which sentence correctly places the modifier?**

*Correct Answer: B) "While I was cooking dinner, the doorbell rang."*

**Explanation:**

The modifier "While I was cooking dinner" correctly modifies the subject, indicating the time when the doorbell rang. Other sentences misplace the modifier, leading to confusing meanings.

**Question 14: Choose the sentence where the modifier is placed correctly:**

*Correct Answer: B) "Exhausted from work, I found the bed inviting."*

**Explanation:**

The modifier "Exhausted from work" correctly modifies "I," the subject. Other options have misplaced modifiers that create illogical meanings.

**Question 15: Which sentence has the modifier in the correct position?**

*Correct Answer: B) "Driving through the countryside, I found the scenery breathtaking."*

**Explanation:**

The modifier "Driving through the countryside" correctly modifies "I," the person who found the scenery breathtaking. In other options, the modifier placement creates confusion.

**Question 16: Select the sentence that correctly places the modifier:**

*Correct Answer: C) "Reading the book, I understood the plot better."*

**Explanation:**

The modifier "Reading the book" correctly modifies "I," the subject of the sentence. Other options misplace the modifier, leading to ambiguous meanings.

**Question 17: Which sentence properly avoids a misplaced modifier?**

*Correct Answer: B) "Looking through the window, I saw the garden full of flowers."*

**Explanation:**

The modifier "Looking through the window" correctly modifies "I," the person doing the looking. Other sentences either misplace the modifier or create unclear meanings.

**Question 18: Choose the sentence with the correct modifier placement:**

*Correct Answer: B) "Taking the exam, I found the questions easier."*

**Explanation:**

The modifier "Taking the exam" correctly modifies "I," the person who found the questions easier. Other options misplace the modifier, leading to confusion.

**Question 19: Which sentence correctly places the modifier?**

*Correct Answer: B) "More data was needed to finish the report."*

**Explanation:**

This sentence correctly places the modifier "to finish the report" at the end, modifying "more data." Other options have misplaced modifiers that disrupt clarity.

**Question 20: Select the sentence where the modifier is correctly placed:**

*Correct Answer: B) "Walking through the park, I thought the trees looked beautiful."*

**Explanation:**

The modifier "Walking through the park" correctly modifies "I," the subject. Other sentences misplace the modifier, leading to confusion or unclear meanings.

# Section 7: Word Choice and Precision

Question 1:

**Answer: B) condescending**

**Explanation:** The word "condescending" means showing an attitude of superiority, which fits the context of the sentence where the speaker's tone prevents the audience from taking her seriously. Words like "joyful" and "casual" do not convey the same negative impression.

Question 2:

**Answer: B) challenging**

**Explanation:** "Challenging" fits best because it implies that the mountain trail is difficult to navigate, which aligns with the idea of needing proper gear. Words like "flat" and "easy" would not match the difficulty implied in the sentence.

Question 3:

**Answer: B) monotonous**

**Explanation:** "Monotonous" means dull and lacking in variety, which explains why the audience lost interest. Other options like "compelling" or "inspiring" would suggest that the speech held the audience's attention, which contradicts the sentence's meaning.

Question 4:

**Answer: B) marred**

**Explanation:** "Marred" means damaged or spoiled, which fits the context of errors negatively affecting the study's results. Words like "boosted" or "complicated" don't imply the same negative impact.

Question 5:

**Answer: B) consensus**

**Explanation:** "Consensus" means a general agreement, which is what the committee reached after debating. Words like "division" and "conflict" indicate disagreement, which does not match the outcome described in the sentence.

Question 6:

**Answer: A) ambiguity**

**Explanation:** "Ambiguity" means uncertainty or being open to multiple interpretations, which aligns with the idea that the artist's work left viewers with more questions than answers. "Clarity" would suggest the opposite.

Question 7:

**Answer: B) tactful**

**Explanation:** "Tactful" means showing sensitivity in handling difficult situations, which is why the manager's actions were praised. Words like "reckless" or "abrasive" would imply poor handling of the crisis.

Question 8:

**Answer: B) applauded**

**Explanation:** "Applauded" means praised or approved, fitting the context of the new legislation being seen positively for environmental protection. Words like "criticized" or "condemned" would imply the opposite reaction.

Question 9:

**Answer: C) lucid**

**Explanation:** "Lucid" means clear and easy to understand, which makes it the best choice for describing how the scientist's explanation was accessible to the general public. Words like "obscure" or "convoluted" would suggest the explanation was hard to understand.

Question 10:

**Answer: C) balanced**

**Explanation:** "Balanced" means presenting all sides fairly, which is the most precise word for describing a view that includes both successes and failures. Words like "biased" or "one-sided" would indicate favoritism, which contradicts the sentence's meaning.

Question 11:

**Answer: B) verbose**

**Explanation:** "Verbose" means using too many words, which explains why the speaker's language made the presentation difficult to follow. "Simplistic" or "concise" would suggest the opposite effect.

Question 12:

**Answer: B) profound**

**Explanation:** "Profound" indicates a deep and significant desire, which fits the motivation for such a major life decision. Words like "casual" or "fleeting" suggest less commitment or seriousness.

Question 13:

**Answer: B) heighten**

**Explanation:** "Heighten" means to increase or intensify, which is what the use of vivid imagery does to the emotional impact of the story. Words like "diminish" or "undermine" would suggest reducing the impact, which is not the intended meaning.

Question 14:

**Answer: B) exponential**

**Explanation:** "Exponential" describes rapid growth, which is appropriate for a company becoming a leader in the industry. "Stagnant" or "negligible" would indicate a lack of growth, which contradicts the sentence.

Question 15:

**Answer: B) collective**

**Explanation:** "Collective" refers to the combined effort of the team, which led to their victory. Words like "halfhearted" or "disorganized" would imply a lack of effort or coordination, which does not fit the context of winning.

Question 16:

**Answer: B) pragmatic**

**Explanation:** "Pragmatic" means practical and focused on results, which fits the description of the speaker's approach. "Theoretical" or "idealistic" would suggest a more abstract or less practical approach.

Question 17:

**Answer: B) insightful**

**Explanation:** "Insightful" means showing deep understanding or knowledge, which matches the description of the speaker's comments. Words like "vague" or "irrelevant" would suggest the opposite.

Question 18:

**Answer: B) coherent**

**Explanation:** "Coherent" means logical and well-organized, which is why the argument was convincing. Words like "weak" or "disorganized" would imply the argument was ineffective, which does not fit the sentence.

Question 19:

**Answer: C) exceptional**

**Explanation:** "Exceptional" means outstanding or remarkable, which explains why the crowd was in awe of the athlete's abilities. Words like "mediocre" or "lackluster" would imply a less impressive performance.

Question 20:

**Answer: B) harsh**

**Explanation:** "Harsh" describes difficult or severe weather conditions, which would make a rescue operation more challenging. "Ideal" or "mild" would suggest favorable conditions, which contradicts the sentence's meaning.

## Section 8: Subject-Verb Agreement and Consistency

Question 1:

**Answer: B) The group of students is planning a field trip.**

**Explanation:** "Group" is a collective noun, and in this context, it is treated as singular. Therefore, the correct verb is "is."

Question 2:

**Answer: B) The results of the experiments were conclusive.**

**Explanation:** "Results" is a plural noun, so it requires the plural verb "were."

Question 3:

**Answer: B) Neither of the options was available at the time.**

Explanation: "Neither" is singular, so the correct verb is "was."

Question 4:

**Answer: B) Each of the members has a unique perspective.**

Explanation: "Each" is singular, requiring the singular verb "has."

Question 5:

**Answer: B) The data show a clear trend in the results.**

Explanation: "Data" is a plural noun, so the plural verb "show" is required.

Question 6:

**Answer: B) Either the manager or the assistants are responsible for the error.**

Explanation: When two subjects are connected by "either...or," the verb agrees with the subject closest to it. In this case, "assistants" is plural, so the verb "are" is correct.

Question 7:

**Answer: A) The team is winning every match this season.**

Explanation: "Team" is treated as singular in American English, so the verb "is" is correct.

Question 8:

**Answer: B) The news about the recent events is disturbing.**

Explanation: "News" is a singular noun, requiring the singular verb "is."

Question 9:

**Answer: B) Everyone in the audience was excited about the performance.**

Explanation: "Everyone" is a singular pronoun, so the singular verb "was" is correct.

Question 10:

**Answer: A) The committee has decided to change its meeting schedule.**

Explanation: "Committee" is a singular collective noun in this context, so the singular verb "has" is correct.

Question 11:

**Answer: B) Either the teacher or the students are responsible for setting up the project.**

Explanation: The verb agrees with the plural subject "students," so "are" is correct.

Question 12:

**Answer: B) The jury is currently deliberating on the case.**

Explanation: In American English, "jury" is treated as singular, so "is" is correct.

Question 13:

**Answer: B) Neither the employees nor the manager was aware of the issue.**

Explanation: The verb agrees with the singular subject "manager," so "was" is correct.

Question 14:

**Answer: B) The pack of wolves was seen near the forest.**

Explanation: "Pack" is singular, so the singular verb "was" is correct.

Question 15:

**Answer: A) Either of the two candidates is a good choice for the position.**

Explanation: "Either" is singular, so the singular verb "is" is correct.

Question 16:

**Answer: B) The number of applicants for the program is increasing.**

Explanation: "The number of" is treated as singular, so the singular verb "is" is correct.

Question 17:

**Answer: B) The herd of deer is moving across the field.**

Explanation: "Herd" is singular, so the singular verb "is" is correct.

Question 18:

**Answer: A) None of the candidates was selected for the position.**

Explanation: "None" can be singular or plural depending on the context. Here it refers to "not one," so the singular verb "was" is correct.

Question 19:

**Answer: A) The police officer, along with her colleagues, is investigating the case.**

Explanation: The subject is "police officer," which is singular, so "is" is correct. The phrase "along with her colleagues" does not affect the verb.

Question 20:

**Answer: B) The fleet of ships was anchored in the harbor.**

Explanation: "Fleet" is singular, so the singular verb "was" is correct.

Question 21:

**Answer: A) The board of directors is meeting to discuss the issue.**

Explanation: "Board" is treated as singular, so the singular verb "is" is correct.

Question 22:

**Answer: A) The group of researchers is presenting their findings.**

Explanation: "Group" is singular, so the singular verb "is" is correct.

Question 23:

**Answer: B) One of the books is missing from the shelf.**

Explanation: The subject "one" is singular, so the singular verb "is" is correct.

Question 24:

**Answer: A) The stack of papers is on the desk.**

Explanation: "Stack" is singular, so the singular verb "is" is correct.

Question 25:

**Answer: A) The crew was ready for the mission.**

Explanation: "Crew" is a collective noun treated as singular in this context, so "was" is correct.

## Section 9: Redundancy and Wordiness

Question 1:

**Answer: C) She left because she was tired.**

Explanation: This option is the most concise and avoids redundancy. "Tired" alone conveys the meaning without the need for "feeling" or "exhausted," which are repetitive.

Question 2:

**Answer: D) The meeting should be postponed until next week.**

Explanation: This sentence is the simplest and avoids the redundancy of "In my opinion" and "I think," which are unnecessary.

Question 3:

**Answer: B) She enjoys reading books in her free time.**

Explanation: This sentence conveys the same meaning as the others but does so in the most concise way, avoiding unnecessary phrases like "a person who."

Question 4:

**Answer: D) The teacher explained clearly.**

**Explanation:** This version is the most direct and concise, removing unnecessary details that are implied by "explained clearly."

Question 5:

**Answer: C) He planned ahead for the event.**

**Explanation:** "Planned ahead" is a concise phrase that avoids the redundancy of "in advance" or "to prepare."

Question 6:

**Answer: C) The train delay caused them to arrive late.**

**Explanation:** This sentence eliminates wordiness by focusing on the cause ("train delay") and the result ("arrive late") without unnecessary phrases.

Question 7:

**Answer: B) The big, energetic dog ran across the yard.**

**Explanation:** This sentence is concise and avoids unnecessary descriptions like "big in size" and "very energetic," which are redundant.

Question 8:

**Answer: B) Success requires hard work and effort.**

**Explanation:** This sentence is the most concise, eliminating the unnecessary phrase "it is necessary to" and redundant wording.

Question 9:

**Answer: B) He gave the presentation live.**

**Explanation:** This version is the most direct, avoiding repetitive phrases like "in person" and "presented live."

Question 10:

**Answer: D) She refused to participate in the competition.**

**Explanation:** This option eliminates the unnecessary intensifiers "absolutely" and "completely," which do not add meaning.

Question 11:

**Answer: B) We are currently reviewing the budget proposal.**

**Explanation:** This sentence is the most straightforward and avoids the wordy phrases like "at this point in time."

Question 12:

**Answer: C) He asked the question to get more details.**

**Explanation:** This sentence is clear and concise, eliminating unnecessary words while conveying the same meaning.

Question 13:

**Answer: C) The schedule for the event will be finalized later.**

**Explanation:** "Later" is sufficient without repeating "in the future," making this the least redundant option.

Question 14:

**Answer: B) She smiled while telling the story.**

**Explanation:** This option eliminates the unnecessary "laughed at the same time," which is redundant.

Question 15:

**Answer: B) The committee has decided to reschedule the meeting.**

**Explanation:** This version is concise, avoiding the redundant "postpone and reschedule."

Question 16:

**Answer: B) The trip was postponed due to unforeseen circumstances.**

**Explanation:** This is the most concise version, avoiding the repetitive "to a later date."

Question 17:

**Answer: C) I hope to meet you in person.**

**Explanation:** This sentence avoids unnecessary words like "the opportunity to" and "with," making it more direct.

Question 18:

**Answer: D) He opened the door and entered the room.**

**Explanation:** "Entered" implies going inside, so "inside the room" is redundant in other options.

Question 19:

**Answer: D) While writing her essay, she made sure to edit it carefully.**

**Explanation:** This version avoids the unnecessary repetition of "edit and revise."

Question 20:

**Answer: B) During the meeting, several important issues were discussed.**

**Explanation:** This option is the most concise, eliminating wordy phrases like "During the course of" and "were addressed."

## Section 10: Idiomatic Expressions and Prepositions

Question 1:

**Answer: B) She is responsible for taking care of her younger siblings.**

**Explanation:** The idiom "responsible for" is the correct phrase to use when indicating someone's duty or obligation to something.

Question 2:

**Answer: C) He is interested in learning new languages.**

**Explanation:** The correct preposition with "interested" is "in," as it expresses involvement or focus on an activity.

Question 3:

**Answer: B) She prefers to focus on her studies.**

**Explanation:** "Focus on" is the appropriate idiomatic phrase to use when discussing concentration on something.

Question 4:

**Answer: B) The book is full of interesting facts.**

**Explanation:** "Full of" is the correct phrase, indicating that something contains a large quantity of something else.

Question 5:

**Answer: B) He is capable of completing the project on time.**

**Explanation:** "Capable of" is the correct phrase to describe someone's ability to do something.

Question 6:

**Answer: C) They are concerned about the environmental damage.**

**Explanation:** "Concerned about" is the appropriate phrase, expressing worry or care regarding something.

Question 7:

**Answer: D) She is excited about the idea of traveling to Europe.**

**Explanation:** "Excited about" is the correct preposition, indicating enthusiasm for something.

Question 8:

**Answer: B) I am familiar with the rules of the game.**

**Explanation:** The idiomatic phrase "familiar with" is used when someone knows or understands something well.

Question 9:

**Answer: A) The manager was impressed by her performance.**

**Explanation:** "Impressed by" is the correct expression, used to indicate admiration for someone or something.

Question 10:

**Answer: B) They are capable of making quick decisions.**

**Explanation:** "Capable of" is the correct expression for describing ability.

Question 11:

**Answer: D) We are looking forward to meeting you.**

**Explanation:** "Looking forward to" is always followed by a gerund ("meeting"), indicating anticipation for an event.

Question 12:

**Answer: C) She is afraid of spiders.**

**Explanation:** "Afraid of" is the correct idiomatic expression to express fear.

Question 13:

**Answer: A) He succeeded in passing the exam.**

**Explanation:** "Succeed in" is the correct phrase, indicating success in doing something.

Question 14:

**Answer: C) The team worked hard at achieving their goal.**

**Explanation:** "Work hard at" is the correct idiomatic phrase used to describe effort directed toward achieving something.

Question 15:

**Answer: B) I am good at cooking Italian food.**

**Explanation:** "Good at" is the correct phrase, indicating skill in a particular activity.

Question 16:

**Answer: B) He is proud of his accomplishments.**

**Explanation:** "Proud of" is the correct idiomatic phrase used to express pride in something.

Question 17:

**Answer: B) She is accustomed to the climate in the area.**

**Explanation:** "Accustomed to" is the correct preposition, indicating familiarity or adaptation to something.

Question 18:

**Answer: B) They are aware of the potential risks.**

**Explanation:** "Aware of" is the correct idiomatic phrase to express awareness or knowledge of something.

Question 19:

**Answer: C) He is interested in the new project.**

**Explanation:** "Interested in" is the correct preposition, indicating involvement or curiosity about something.

Question 20:

**Answer: A) She was involved in the project from the beginning.**

**Explanation:** "Involved in" is the correct idiomatic expression, used to indicate participation or engagement in something.

# Section 11: Combining Sentences

Question 1:

**Answer: B) The artist painted a mural that depicts the city skyline at sunset.**

**Explanation:** This version effectively combines the sentences by using a relative clause ("that depicts"), which maintains clarity and conciseness.

Question 2:

**Answer: A) She studied diligently for the exam because she wanted to improve her score.**

**Explanation:** This option combines the cause and effect clearly, using "because" to show the reason behind her action.

Question 3:

**Answer: C) Even though the concert was sold out, we were lucky to get tickets.**

**Explanation:** This option correctly uses "even though" to contrast the fact that the concert was sold out with their luck in obtaining tickets.

Question 4:

**Answer: B) The report, which took three hours to complete, was finished.**

**Explanation:** The sentence is effectively combined with a non-essential clause ("which took three hours to complete"), making the sentence clear and concise.

Question 5:

**Answer: A) The cat chased the mouse that ran into a small hole.**

**Explanation:** This sentence combines the ideas clearly by using "that" to connect the mouse's action with the chase.

Question 6:

**Answer: C) The book was both interesting and informative.**

**Explanation:** This option efficiently combines the two qualities of the book in a parallel structure ("both... and...").

Question 7:

**Answer: B) I arrived at the meeting early to prepare my presentation in advance.**

**Explanation:** This option expresses purpose clearly by combining the sentences with "to," which shows the reason for arriving early.

Question 8:

**Answer: C) After the car broke down on the highway, we called a tow truck.**

**Explanation:** This version uses a time clause ("after") to show the sequence of events clearly and concisely.

Question 9:

**Answer: B) The player scored the winning goal, ending the game shortly afterward.**

**Explanation:** This option uses the participle "ending" to effectively combine the two ideas into a single, clear sentence.

Question 10:

**Answer: A) The recipe called for eggs and milk, but I had neither ingredient at home.**

**Explanation:** This version combines the sentences using "but" to show contrast between the recipe's requirements and the speaker's lack of ingredients.

Question 11:

**Answer: B) She enjoyed both reading novels and writing short stories.**

**Explanation:** This option uses parallel structure ("both... and...") to combine the two activities she enjoys.

Question 12:

**Answer: B) Since the weather was sunny, we decided to go to the beach.**

**Explanation:** This version clearly shows the cause-and-effect relationship using "since," which links the weather to their decision.

Question 13:

**Answer: C) The movie, although long, had an exciting ending.**

**Explanation:** This option correctly contrasts the length of the movie with its exciting ending using "although."

Question 14:

**Answer: C) Since he missed the bus, he walked to school instead.**

**Explanation:** This version uses "since" to show the reason for his walking, making the relationship between the two events clear.

Question 15:

**Answer: B) Even though I had studied all night, the test was difficult.**

**Explanation:** This option effectively combines the sentences with "even though," showing contrast between preparation and the test's difficulty.

Question 16:

**Answer: B) The children enjoyed learning about history at the museum's many exhibits.**

**Explanation:** This version is clear and concise, combining both the museum's features and the children's enjoyment.

Question 17:

**Answer: B) While I was cooking dinner, the phone rang.**

**Explanation:** This option clearly shows the timing of the events using "while," making the relationship between cooking and the phone ringing clear.

Question 18:

**Answer: A) Her hard work paid off, as she won first place in the competition.**

**Explanation:** This sentence uses "as" to connect the two ideas and show that winning was the result of her hard work.

Question 19:

**Answer: D) He loves to travel and enjoys meeting new people.**

**Explanation:** This option effectively combines the two related activities in a concise and parallel structure.

Question 20:

**Answer: B) Topped with fresh strawberries, the cake was delicious.**

**Explanation:** This sentence combines the two ideas using the participial phrase "topped with fresh strawberries," clearly describing the cake's deliciousness.

## Section 12: Consistency in Tense and Tone

Question 1:

**Answer: A) She was studying for the exam when her friend called to invite her out.**

**Explanation:** The verb tense is consistent with the past continuous ("was studying") and simple past ("called"). This maintains uniformity in tense throughout the sentence.

Question 2:

**Answer: A) The data was collected meticulously, and the analysis of trends was highly insightful.**

**Explanation:** This sentence maintains the formal, analytical tone by using "highly insightful," which is appropriate for academic writing and consistent with the tone of the first part of the sentence.

Question 3:

**Answer: A) He had been preparing for the presentation all week and delivered his speech with confidence.**

**Explanation:** This sentence maintains consistent past perfect ("had been preparing") followed by simple past ("delivered"), aligning with the tense used earlier in the sentence.

Question 4:

**Answer: A) The findings of the study were profound, but the results were remarkably surprising.**

**Explanation:** "Remarkably surprising" is formal and academic, keeping a consistent tone with the earlier part of the sentence, unlike more casual alternatives like "blew my mind."

Question 5:

**Answer: A) The children played outside while their parents watched from the porch.**

**Explanation:** Both verbs are in the past tense ("played" and "watched"), which ensures consistency in verb tense within the sentence.

Question 6:

**Answer: A) The professor explained the complex theory, providing a clear example that was enlightening.**

**Explanation:** "Enlightening" maintains the formal and academic tone of the sentence, fitting better than casual alternatives like "cool" or "pretty neat."

Question 7:

**Answer: D) She is writing the report and submitted her research findings yesterday.**

**Explanation:** This maintains consistency by using the present progressive ("is writing") for an ongoing action and simple past ("submitted") for an action completed in the past.

Question 8:

**Answer: A) The impact of climate change is deeply concerning and must be addressed immediately.**

**Explanation:** "Deeply concerning" fits the reflective and serious tone of the passage, providing a balanced and formal expression.

Question 9:

**Answer: D) The research team gathered data over several months and is now preparing their final report.**

**Explanation:** The sentence maintains consistency by using the simple past ("gathered") for a completed action and the present progressive ("is now preparing") for the ongoing action.

Question 10:

**Answer: A) The experiment yielded significant results, but the entire process was a challenge.**

**Explanation:** "A challenge" keeps the tone formal and professional, consistent with the earlier part of the sentence, avoiding casual expressions like "a hassle" or "a big pain."

# Section 1: Improving Sentence Clarity

1. **Answer: a) After the meeting, Julia told Maria that Maria had made a mistake.**
   **Explanation:** This revision clarifies who made the mistake by explicitly naming both "Julia" and "Maria," eliminating ambiguity caused by the pronouns "she" and "her."

2. **Answer: a) The team was late, so the game had to be postponed.**
   **Explanation:** This version removes wordiness and presents a more direct and concise explanation by using "so" instead of "due to the fact that."

3. **Answer: c) He explained the concept in detail because it was difficult to understand.**
   **Explanation:** This option is clearer because it specifies what was being explained in detail, maintaining a formal and direct tone.

4. **Answer: a) The report stated that the company made a profit.**
   **Explanation:** This sentence is clearer and more direct because it eliminates passive voice and presents the subject "report" as the one making the statement.

5. **Answer: b) Surprisingly, the seminar was attended by only a few people.**
   **Explanation:** This version moves "surprisingly" to the beginning, making the sentence more straightforward and emphasizing the surprising fact.

6. **Answer: b) Every student must complete his or her project by Friday.**
   **Explanation:** This revision clarifies the pronoun usage by specifying "his or her," which makes the sentence more formal and precise.

7. **Answer: b) The manager was responsible for scheduling meetings.**
   **Explanation:** This version is clear and concise, removing unnecessary words and directly stating the manager's responsibility.

8. **Answer: b) After reviewing the plans, the engineer explained that the plans needed more work.**
   **Explanation:** This sentence is clearer because it specifies that "the plans" need more work, making the sentence more specific and eliminating ambiguity.

9. **Answer: b) The students did not complete the assignment because the instructions were confusing.**
   **Explanation:** This revision places the cause ("confusing instructions") directly after "because," making the sentence clearer and more direct.

10. **Answer: a) His dedication was evident in how he always met deadlines.**
    **Explanation:** This version simplifies the sentence while maintaining the clear link between dedication and meeting deadlines, improving clarity.

11. **Answer: d) Despite her efforts, the short deadline prevented her from finishing the project on time.**
    **Explanation:** This option clearly states the relationship between her efforts and the short deadline, emphasizing the difficulty she faced.

12. **Answer: a) He mentioned in his speech that the new policy would be implemented soon.**
**Explanation:** This version places the action of mentioning clearly at the beginning of the sentence, making the meaning more straightforward.

13. **Answer: a) The teacher repeatedly explained the concept to ensure understanding.**
**Explanation:** This revision makes the sentence clearer by focusing on the teacher's repeated explanation and ensuring comprehension.

14. **Answer: d) The new time for the rescheduled meeting was not communicated until later.**
**Explanation:** This version eliminates unnecessary words and presents the information in a clearer and more direct manner.

15. **Answer: b) To apply for the position, applicants must submit a resume with their experience, qualifications, and references.**
**Explanation:** This sentence is clearer and more concise, presenting the requirements in a straightforward order.

16. **Answer: b) Last week, the museum's new exhibit opened and attracted many visitors.**
**Explanation:** This version is clear, concise, and presents the sequence of events in a logical and direct way.

17. **Answer: c) The scientists were surprised by the results of the experiment and were unsure how to interpret them.**
**Explanation:** This version is clear and effectively conveys both the scientists' surprise and uncertainty.

18. **Answer: a) The concert was canceled because of unforeseen circumstances.**
**Explanation:** This sentence is the most direct and eliminates unnecessary wordiness, making it clearer.

19. **Answer: a) The project required teamwork, patience, and effective communication skills.**
**Explanation:** This revision is clearer and more concise, replacing "the ability to communicate well" with "effective communication skills."

20. **Answer: a) Everyone was surprised by the sudden announcement, but we were unsure if it was true.**
**Explanation:** This version presents the information in a clear and concise way, improving readability.

21. **Answer: a) It's important to read the instructions carefully to avoid mistakes.**
**Explanation:** This revision is the clearest and most direct, presenting the information without unnecessary complexity.

22. **Answer: a) The students became excited as soon as the results were announced.**
**Explanation:** This option clearly links the announcement of the results to the students' reaction, making it more straightforward.

23. **Answer: d) The book clearly showed that the main character had a hard time making decisions.**
**Explanation:** This sentence is clearer because it directly connects the book's content with the character's difficulty making decisions.

24. **Answer: c) She requested a favor in her letter but didn't specify what type.**
**Explanation:** This version improves clarity by specifying the action ("requested") and eliminating unnecessary complexity.

25. **Answer: b) No reason was given for their decision to change the schedule.**
    **Explanation:** This revision is clearer and more direct, making the meaning easier to understand.

## Section 2: Logical Flow Between Sentences

1. **Answer: d) Therefore**
   **Explanation:** "Therefore" indicates a logical consequence of the sun setting quickly, leading to the need to hurry and set up the tent.

2. **Answer: a) However**
   **Explanation:** "However" introduces a contrast, showing that despite the concert being nearly sold out, they managed to get tickets.

3. **Answer: c) As a result**
   **Explanation:** "As a result" effectively links his studying for weeks with the confidence he feels for the final exam, showing cause and effect.

4. **Answer: b) Accordingly**
   **Explanation:** "Accordingly" indicates that the decision to reschedule was made in response to the predicted rain, maintaining logical flow.

5. **Answer: c) Nevertheless**
   **Explanation:** "Nevertheless" introduces a contrast, indicating that even though she wasn't feeling well, she still went to work.

6. **Answer: a) Therefore**
   **Explanation:** "Therefore" indicates a cause-and-effect relationship between the traffic accident and the people being late for work.

7. **Answer: c) For this reason**
   **Explanation:** "For this reason" links the success of the first meeting to the expectation of similar success for the rest of the project, showing logical continuity.

8. **Answer: b) As a result**
   **Explanation:** "As a result" indicates the logical progression from her hard work to her plan to submit the final draft.

9. **Answer: d) As a result**
   **Explanation:** "As a result" links the team's daily practice to their confidence going into the championship game, showing cause and effect.

10. **Answer: d) As a result**
    **Explanation:** "As a result" introduces the logical outcome of the company's decreasing profits, leading to cost-saving measures.

11. **Answer: c) Consequently**
    **Explanation:** "Consequently" indicates the cause-and-effect relationship between her diligent studying and earning a scholarship.

12. **Answer: b) As a result**
    **Explanation:** "As a result" logically connects the positive product reviews to the sales exceeding expectations.

13. **Answer: c) Consequently**
    **Explanation:** "Consequently" shows that the sale on winter coats led to the speaker buying a jacket at a great price.

14. **Answer: b) Consequently**
    Explanation: "Consequently" indicates the logical result of the car making strange noises, leading to it breaking down.

15. **Answer: b) However**
    Explanation: "However" introduces a contrast, showing that despite being told the weather would be warm, it was cold and rainy.

16. **Answer: b) As a result**
    Explanation: "As a result" indicates the logical consequence of her strong background in marketing, leading to her promotion.

17. **Answer: d) However**
    Explanation: "However" introduces a contrast, indicating that while the seminar was informative, it was unexpectedly long.

18. **Answer: c) As a result**
    Explanation: "As a result" connects the successful presentation to the positive feedback from the clients.

19. **Answer: b) Therefore**
    Explanation: "Therefore" shows a cause-and-effect relationship between the power outage and the closure of businesses.

20. **Answer: b) Likewise**
    Explanation: "Likewise" indicates that, in addition to the cakes being popular, the bakery's pastries are also well-liked, maintaining logical flow.

## Section 3: Paragraph Coherence

1. **Answer: b) The second sentence**
   Explanation: Moving the second sentence ("As a result, we expect continued success in the coming quarters.") to the end of the paragraph provides a logical conclusion after presenting the data about the company's growth.

2. **Answer: b) The second sentence**
   Explanation: Starting with "The technology sector continues to grow rapidly" provides context for why the company has invested in research and development and launched a new product.

3. **Answer: c) The third sentence**
   Explanation: The sentence about employee satisfaction being tied to workplace policies introduces a new idea that fits better earlier in the paragraph to explain employee reactions.

4. **Answer: d) The fourth sentence**
   Explanation: "It is now ready for release" logically concludes the paragraph, summarizing the outcome of the team's hard work, research, and testing.

5. **Answer: d) The fourth sentence**
   Explanation: Placing "The leadership team has prioritized global growth" last provides a clear link to the strategic focus on international sales and future goals.

6. **Answer: b) The second sentence**
   Explanation: "We anticipate further updates in the coming months" shifts focus away from the current success and disrupts the flow of positive feedback and user numbers.

7. **Answer: c) Between the second and third sentences**
   **Explanation:** Adding the sentence about customer service between positive reviews and ease of use improves coherence by acknowledging the role of the support team.

8. **Answer: d) The fourth sentence**
   **Explanation:** The sentence about employees working remotely introduces a different topic unrelated to productivity and security, disrupting the paragraph's focus.

9. **Answer: c) After the second sentence**
   **Explanation:** Placing the sentence about the correlation between customer satisfaction and product quality after the survey results emphasizes the connection between the two ideas.

10. **Answer: c) The third sentence**
    **Explanation:** Moving "This demographic is increasingly engaged with social media platforms" before discussing the campaign's focus on social media improves the logical flow.

11. **Answer: c) The third sentence**
    **Explanation:** The expansion of office space disrupts the focus on budget cuts and saving money for reinvestment.

12. **Answer: b) After the first sentence**
    **Explanation:** Placing "The team met all of its quarterly goals" after the expectation of continued growth strengthens the paragraph's flow by providing supporting evidence.

13. **Answer: a) The first sentence**
    **Explanation:** The sentence about the sales team exceeding its targets serves as the topic sentence, setting up the paragraph's focus on the company's success.

14. **Answer: c) After the second sentence**
    **Explanation:** Placing the sentence about increasing community engagement after the description of the public works program's focus adds logical progression.

15. **Answer: c) The third sentence**
    **Explanation:** "Environmental responsibility is a key focus for the company" is redundant because the paragraph already discusses sustainability initiatives.

16. **Answer: d) The fourth sentence**
    **Explanation:** "We expect more employees to join as the program progresses" serves as a logical conclusion to the paragraph about the leadership program.

17. **Answer: c) The third sentence**
    **Explanation:** The sentence about customers eagerly awaiting the project's results should come after the sentence about the project's valuable insights.

18. **Answer: b) After the first sentence**
    **Explanation:** Placing "These measures will enhance the company's competitiveness" after mentioning the cost-cutting measures improves the logical flow.

19. **Answer: c) The third sentence**
    **Explanation:** "We introduced the new product last quarter" is redundant, as the paragraph is focused on the current performance of the product line.

20. **Answer: b) Between the first and second sentences**
    **Explanation:** Adding the sentence about mixed employee reactions between the introduction of new policies and their focus on work-life balance makes the paragraph more coherent.

# Section 4: Eliminating Redundant or Irrelevant Information

1. **Answer: b) The second sentence**
   **Explanation:** The second sentence repeats the idea that the product was recently launched, which is already implied by the first sentence. Removing it improves conciseness.

2. **Answer: d) The fourth sentence**
   **Explanation:** The fourth sentence repeats the information from the previous sentences about cost-reduction and saving money, making it redundant.

3. **Answer: d) The fourth sentence**
   **Explanation:** The deadline being fast-approaching is implied by the urgency expressed in the previous sentences. Removing this sentence improves the paragraph's clarity.

4. **Answer: c) The third sentence**
   **Explanation:** The mention of traffic congestion introduces an unrelated topic that disrupts the focus on the environmental policy.

5. **Answer: d) The fourth sentence**
   **Explanation:** The fourth sentence repeats the idea of improved navigation, which is already covered by the third sentence, making it redundant.

6. **Answer: c) The third sentence**
   **Explanation:** The restaurant's location is irrelevant to the focus of the paragraph, which is on the success of the new menu and customer reactions.

7. **Answer: d) The fourth sentence**
   **Explanation:** The CEO mentioning lunch with investors is unrelated to the speech's content and disrupts the paragraph's focus on future plans and strategies.

8. **Answer: d) The fourth sentence**
   **Explanation:** The fourth sentence repeats the same idea about the company's sustainability, which has already been explained in the previous sentences.

9. **Answer: d) The fourth sentence**
   **Explanation:** The sentence about attending an industry conference introduces an unrelated detail that does not contribute to the main topic of the project.

10. **Answer: d) The fourth sentence**
    **Explanation:** The fourth sentence repeats information about social media already covered in the second and third sentences, making it redundant.

11. **Answer: c) The third sentence**
    **Explanation:** The hiring of new staff members is unrelated to the focus on updated procedures and efficiency improvements, disrupting the flow of the paragraph.

12. **Answer: d) The fourth sentence**
    **Explanation:** The fourth sentence repeats the information from the second and third sentences about reviewing financial results, making it redundant.

13. **Answer: d) The fourth sentence**
    **Explanation:** The fourth sentence repeats information already provided about social media, which was mentioned in the second sentence, making it redundant.

14. **Answer: c) The third sentence**
    **Explanation:** The sentence about winning an industry award introduces a topic unrelated to the focus on reducing production costs.

15. **Answer: a) The first sentence**
    **Explanation:** The first sentence is redundant since the rest of the paragraph provides more specific details about the app's success, making it unnecessary.

16. **Answer: c) The third sentence**
    **Explanation:** The meetings held to discuss the policy are irrelevant to the focus on the details of the tax reform, making this sentence unnecessary.

17. **Answer: c) The third sentence**
    **Explanation:** While market trends are important, this sentence disrupts the focus on the team's efforts to meet the deadline and collaborate with other departments.

18. **Answer: c) The third sentence**
    **Explanation:** The mention of the hospital cafeteria's new menu introduces an unrelated topic that disrupts the focus on safety protocols.

19. **Answer: b) The second sentence**
    **Explanation:** The second sentence repeats information already stated in the first and fourth sentences about the company's expansion and demand, making it redundant.

20. **Answer: c) The third sentence**
    **Explanation:** The mention of the new research center introduces an unrelated topic that disrupts the focus on scholarships and student support.

# Section 5: Correcting Ambiguous Pronouns and References

1. **Answer: b) When Sarah told her friend that Sarah was late, the friend didn't understand.**
   **Explanation:** This revision clarifies that Sarah was the one who was late and that her friend didn't understand.

2. **Answer: b) The manager spoke to the employee about the employee's performance, but the employee didn't listen.**
   **Explanation:** This revision clarifies that the manager was talking about the employee's performance and that the employee didn't listen.

3. **Answer: b) The teacher gave the student her notebook, but the student forgot it at home.**
   **Explanation:** This revision clarifies that the student was the one who forgot the notebook at home.

4. **Answer: a) James and Robert went to the store, but Robert forgot his wallet.**
   **Explanation:** This revision makes it clear that Robert forgot his wallet.

5. **Answer: a) Mary handed the report to Lisa, and Lisa reviewed it carefully.**
   **Explanation:** This version clarifies that Lisa reviewed the report.

6. **Answer: b) The dog followed the girl to her house, but the dog ran away before the girl got there.**
   **Explanation:** This revision makes it clear that the dog ran away and that the girl had not arrived at her house yet.

7. **Answer: a) When the firefighter saw the house was on fire, he rushed to put it out.**
   **Explanation:** Using "he" clarifies that the firefighter, not "they" or the house, was the one putting out the fire.

8. **Answer: a) The committee decided that it would change the rules, but the committee took too long to implement them.**

**Explanation:** This version clarifies that the committee would change the rules and implement them.

9. **Answer: c) The doctor told the patient that the patient's blood pressure was high, but the patient didn't seem concerned.**
   **Explanation:** This revision makes it clear that it was the patient's blood pressure that was high and that the patient didn't seem concerned.

10. **Answer: a) The teacher called the student into the teacher's office, but the student didn't show up.**
    **Explanation:** This revision clarifies that the student was the one who didn't show up.

11. **Answer: c) The boy told his friend that the boy was upset.**
    **Explanation:** This revision removes any ambiguity and clarifies that the boy, not the friend, was upset.

12. **Answer: b) The actor spoke to the director about the film, and the director agreed to make changes.**
    **Explanation:** This version clarifies that it was the director who agreed to make changes.

13. **Answer: a) The principal called the teacher into his office, but the teacher was not available.**
    **Explanation:** This version clarifies that the teacher, not the principal, was not available.

14. **Answer: b) Sarah lent her jacket to Susan because Susan was cold.**
    **Explanation:** This revision clarifies that Susan was the one who was cold.

15. **Answer: b) The coach told the player that the player needed to improve.**
    **Explanation:** This version makes it clear that the coach was talking about the player's need to improve.

16. **Answer: a) The student turned in the assignment late, and the teacher was not happy about the lateness.**
    **Explanation:** This revision clarifies that the teacher was unhappy about the late submission of the assignment.

17. **Answer: a) The committee discussed the proposal with the board, and the board decided to make some changes.**
    **Explanation:** This version clarifies that the board was the one that decided to make changes.

18. **Answer: a) The man talked to his brother, but his brother didn't respond.**
    **Explanation:** This version clarifies that the brother was the one who didn't respond.

19. **Answer: b) The dog barked at the neighbor, but the neighbor didn't seem to notice.**
    **Explanation:** This version clarifies that the neighbor didn't notice the dog barking.

20. **Answer: a) The supervisor spoke to the employee, but the employee didn't agree with the decision.**
    **Explanation:** This revision clarifies that the employee didn't agree with the decision made by the supervisor.

## Section 6: Combining Ideas for Clarity

**Question 1 Answer:** C) The scientist conducted an experiment to test the hypothesis.

**Explanation:** This option most effectively combines the two sentences by clearly stating the purpose of the experiment. The first two sentences are combined into a cohesive sentence that avoids redundancy and repetition, making the relationship between the experiment and the hypothesis clear and concise.

**Question 2 Answer:** B) Highlighting the financial crisis, the report also focused on its impact on global markets.

**Explanation:** This option combines the sentences by using a participial phrase ("Highlighting the financial crisis") that leads smoothly into the main action of the second sentence. This structure improves clarity and flow, making the sentence more concise and avoiding unnecessary repetition.

**Question 3 Answer:** D) To finish his project before the deadline, he woke up early.

**Explanation:** This sentence most effectively combines the original ideas by clearly showing the reason for waking up early using the infinitive phrase "To finish his project before the deadline." It directly connects the cause (finishing the project) to the action (waking up early), maintaining the original meaning while improving clarity.

**Question 4 Answer:** C) Because the weather was unpredictable, the picnic was cancelled.

**Explanation:** This option provides the clearest combination by using "Because" to indicate the cause-effect relationship between the unpredictable weather and the cancellation of the picnic. It improves the clarity of the sentence without introducing unnecessary phrases.

**Question 5 Answer:** D) She wanted to study law because her father was a successful lawyer.

**Explanation:** This option effectively combines the sentences by explaining the causal relationship between the father's success and the daughter's desire to study law. It maintains the logical connection and presents it in a direct, clear way.

**Question 6 Answer:** D) After working hard on the project, the team presented it to the board on time.

**Explanation:** This sentence best combines the original ideas by showing the order of events—first the team worked hard, then they presented the project. The phrase "After working hard" establishes the sequence clearly, making the sentence more fluid and cohesive.

**Question 7 Answer:** B) The movie was both long and boring.

**Explanation:** This sentence efficiently combines the original ideas by using the phrase "both long and boring," which eliminates redundancy and repetition while maintaining the clear relationship between the two characteristics of the movie.

**Question 8 Answer:** C) The author wrote an engaging novel that quickly became a bestseller.

**Explanation:** This option best combines the two sentences into a clear, logical structure. The use of "that quickly became a bestseller" provides a smooth transition between the two original ideas, making the sentence more fluid and concise.

**Question 9 Answer:** C) The students followed the clear instructions precisely.

**Explanation:** This sentence is the most concise and effective combination of the two original ideas. It eliminates redundancy by merging the actions into a single, clear statement, while maintaining the original meaning.

**Question 10 Answer:** C) The severe storm caused damage to many homes.

**Explanation:** This sentence combines the two ideas most effectively by emphasizing the direct cause-and-effect relationship between the storm and the damage to homes. It improves clarity by presenting the information in a straightforward manner.

**Question 11 Answer:** A) The company's new product gained immediate popularity after its release.

**Explanation:** This sentence best combines the two ideas by using a clear sequence of events, showing that the release of the product led to its immediate popularity. It is concise and avoids unnecessary repetition.

**Question 12 Answer:** A) After studying for the exam, she felt confident about her performance.
**Explanation:** This option effectively combines the original ideas by indicating the sequence of events. The use of "After studying for the exam" makes the relationship between her preparation and her confidence clear and logical.

**Question 13 Answer:** B) The city council met yesterday to discuss new environmental regulations.
**Explanation:** This option best combines the original sentences by using the infinitive phrase "to discuss," which creates a clear connection between the meeting and its purpose. It is concise and maintains the original meaning.

**Question 14 Answer:** C) Assigning a difficult project, the professor provided extra resources for assistance.
**Explanation:** This sentence combines the original ideas smoothly by using a participial phrase ("Assigning a difficult project"), which leads into the main action. It presents the information clearly and logically.

**Question 15 Answer:** B) After recovering from surgery, the patient began physical therapy the next week.
**Explanation:** This sentence most effectively combines the original ideas by clearly showing the sequence of events. The use of "After recovering from surgery" provides a logical connection between the two actions, making the sentence clear and cohesive.

**Question 16 Answer:** C) The photographer's stunning pictures were featured in a magazine.
**Explanation:** This option best combines the original sentences into a clear and concise statement. It eliminates unnecessary repetition and presents the ideas in a straightforward manner, improving clarity.

**Question 17 Answer:** B) The well-organized event was highly attended.
**Explanation:** This sentence effectively combines the two ideas by placing emphasis on the "well-organized event" while maintaining the connection to the high attendance. It is concise and avoids unnecessary repetition.

**Question 18 Answer:** D) The speaker delivered an inspiring message, which prompted a standing ovation from the audience.
**Explanation:** This sentence best combines the original ideas by using "which prompted" to show the cause-effect relationship between the speaker's message and the audience's reaction. It is clear and maintains the logical flow of the ideas.

**Question 19 Answer:** A) The chef's new recipe became a signature dish at the restaurant.
**Explanation:** This sentence most effectively combines the original ideas by clearly stating the relationship between the new recipe and its status as a signature dish. It is concise and avoids unnecessary phrases.

**Question 20 Answer:** A) Working together on the project, the students successfully completed it ahead of schedule.
**Explanation:** This option effectively combines the two ideas by showing the cause-effect relationship between the students working together and the successful completion of the project. It is clear, concise, and maintains the logical flow of the original meaning.

## Section 7: Enhancing Sentence Variety for Better Flow

**Question 1**
**Answer:** A) The dog barked loudly, and the neighbors heard it.
**Explanation:** This option improves sentence variety by combining the sentences in a clear and concise way. It eliminates unnecessary repetition and creates a smooth flow by using the adverb "loudly" to modify the action of barking, making the sentence more engaging.

**Question 2**

**Answer:** A) After going to the store, she bought some milk and returned home.

**Explanation:** This option provides better sentence variety by using a dependent clause ("After going to the store") to indicate the sequence of events, which improves the overall flow of the sentence and avoids the repetitive structure of short, choppy sentences.

**Question 3**

**Answer:** B) Using bright colors, the artist painted a beautiful landscape.

**Explanation:** This sentence improves variety by employing a participial phrase ("Using bright colors") at the beginning, which allows for a smoother and more engaging sentence structure. It combines the original ideas while maintaining the original meaning.

**Question 4**

**Answer:** D) Studying hard for the exam, she felt confident and prepared to do well.

**Explanation:** This option creates variety by using a participial phrase ("Studying hard for the exam") at the start, which connects the effort to the feeling of confidence in a cohesive and flowing manner. It keeps the original meaning intact while improving readability.

**Question 5**

**Answer:** C) Walking down the street, the man saw a bird that flew away.

**Explanation:** The sentence uses a participial phrase ("Walking down the street") to introduce the action and adds variety to the original structure. It clearly shows the sequence of events in a flowing manner and avoids repetitive sentences.

**Question 6**

**Answer:** D) Preparing the meal, the chef added spices, and the food smelled delicious.

**Explanation:** This sentence improves sentence flow by placing the action of preparing the meal at the beginning as a participial phrase, which leads into the additional actions. It keeps the original meaning while making the sentence smoother and more dynamic.

**Question 7**

**Answer:** C) Climbing the high tree with its thin branches, the cat moved swiftly.

**Explanation:** This sentence improves variety by placing a participial phrase at the beginning ("Climbing the high tree with its thin branches") and uses more descriptive language to improve the flow and clarity of the sentence.

**Question 8**

**Answer:** A) The teacher gave a hard test, making the students nervous.

**Explanation:** This option combines the original ideas by using a participial phrase ("making the students nervous"), which improves the sentence's flow and eliminates the repetition of short sentences while maintaining the original meaning.

**Question 9**

**Answer:** A) The red flowers bloomed in the garden, looking beautiful.

**Explanation:** This option improves sentence flow by combining the ideas into a single, concise sentence that places emphasis on both the appearance of the flowers and the setting. It avoids unnecessary repetition and improves variety.

**Question 10**

**Answer:** A) The car stopped at the red light, its engine idling.

**Explanation:** This option provides better sentence flow by combining the actions in a cohesive way, using the phrase "its engine idling" to add descriptive detail without separating the ideas into multiple short sentences.

## Question 11

**Answer:** A) Opening the book, he started reading and liked the story.

**Explanation:** The use of a participial phrase at the start of the sentence ("Opening the book") improves sentence variety and creates a smoother flow, linking the actions together in a more engaging way while maintaining the original meaning.

## Question 12

**Answer:** D) The storm came quickly, bringing heavy rain and flooding the roads.

**Explanation:** This option improves sentence flow by combining the actions into a single sentence using a participial phrase ("bringing heavy rain and flooding the roads"), which makes the sentence more fluid and engaging while maintaining the original meaning.

## Question 13

**Answer:** A) After making dinner, she set the table and called her family to eat.

**Explanation:** This sentence improves variety by using a dependent clause at the start ("After making dinner") to indicate the sequence of events. It creates a smoother flow and avoids the repetitive short-sentence structure.

## Question 14

**Answer:** C) Performing well, the actor bowed to the cheering audience.

**Explanation:** This option improves variety by starting with a participial phrase ("Performing well"), which provides a more engaging and smooth sentence structure, connecting the performance with the actor's bow and the audience's reaction.

## Question 15

**Answer:** C) The cold, fast-flowing river moved over slippery rocks.

**Explanation:** This sentence improves flow by using a more descriptive structure that combines the original ideas into one cohesive sentence. The use of "cold, fast-flowing" as modifiers improves clarity and engagement.

## Question 16

**Answer:** B) After writing and mailing the letter, she waited for a reply.

**Explanation:** This sentence improves variety by using a dependent clause at the start ("After writing and mailing the letter") to show the sequence of events, making the sentence more engaging and eliminating the repetitive structure of the original sentences.

## Question 17

**Answer:** C) During the long meeting, everyone contributed to the productive discussion.

**Explanation:** This option improves flow by indicating the context first ("During the long meeting"), which sets the stage for the contributions. It avoids choppy sentence structure and improves overall variety.

## Question 18

**Answer:** A) The audience took notes and asked questions during the informative presentation.

**Explanation:** This sentence effectively combines the original ideas by merging the actions of the audience into a single, fluid sentence. It avoids the repetition of short sentences and improves the overall flow.

## Question 19

**Answer:** B) Arriving late, the crowded train let many people off.

**Explanation:** This sentence improves sentence variety by using a participial phrase ("Arriving late") at the beginning, which helps to combine the original ideas in a more fluid and engaging manner.

**Question 20**

**Answer:** C) He finished the race, feeling tired but proud.

**Explanation:** This option improves sentence flow by using a participial phrase ("feeling tired but proud") to combine the two ideas, creating a smoother and more engaging sentence without losing the original meaning.

# Section 8: Maintaining Consistent Tone and Style

**Question 1**

**Answer:** A) The company has been performing exceptionally well with all the recent product releases.

**Explanation:** This revision best maintains a formal tone by replacing the informal phrase "killing it" with "performing exceptionally well." The vocabulary is more professional and suitable for a formal passage.

**Question 2**

**Answer:** A) The professor was somewhat disappointed with the research results.

**Explanation:** The phrase "somewhat disappointed" is more formal and appropriate than the informal "kind of disappointed," preserving the tone of the passage.

**Question 3**

**Answer:** A) The government's initiative was beneficial in aiding the community.

**Explanation:** This revision replaces the informal "cool" with "beneficial," which is more appropriate in maintaining a formal tone and style.

**Question 4**

**Answer:** A) The findings of the study were somewhat unclear and difficult to interpret.

**Explanation:** The revision improves the formal tone by replacing "kind of confusing" with "somewhat unclear" and "not very clear" with "difficult to interpret," which better suit a professional or academic context.

**Question 5**

**Answer:** A) The CEO delivered a speech that was nearly identical to the one given last year.

**Explanation:** The phrase "nearly identical" is a more formal and precise expression compared to "pretty much the same," which is informal.

**Question 6**

**Answer:** A) The experiment was highly successful, and all participants were pleased.

**Explanation:** This revision maintains an academic tone by using formal expressions like "highly successful" instead of the informal "super successful" and "all participants were pleased" instead of "everyone was really happy."

**Question 7**

**Answer:** A) The candidate performed exceptionally well in the debate and impressed the audience.

**Explanation:** The phrase "performed exceptionally well" is formal and professional, maintaining the tone, whereas "totally rocked" is too casual for a formal passage.

**Question 8**

**Answer:** A) The team executed the project effectively and received substantial positive feedback.

**Explanation:** This revision uses formal language like "executed the project effectively" and "substantial positive feedback" to maintain a professional tone, avoiding the informal "nailed it" and "a lot."

**Question 9**

**Answer:** A) The results of the study were quite positive and offered valuable insights.

**Explanation:** The phrase "quite positive" and "offered valuable insights" better suit a formal tone, as opposed to the more casual "pretty good" and "useful."

**Question 10**

**Answer:** A) The company's marketing campaign was highly effective and well-executed.

**Explanation:** The revision improves the tone by replacing the informal "awesome" and "totally worked" with the more formal and appropriate "highly effective" and "well-executed."

**Question 11**

**Answer:** A) The professor informed the students about the upcoming exam.

**Explanation:** The formal verb "informed" is more appropriate in an academic context than the casual phrase "gave a heads-up," maintaining a consistent tone.

**Question 12**

**Answer:** A) The weather during the hike was ideal, and we thoroughly enjoyed the experience.

**Explanation:** This revision uses formal language like "ideal" and "thoroughly enjoyed" to maintain a consistent and professional tone, avoiding the informal "had a blast."

**Question 13**

**Answer:** A) The results of the project were somewhat unexpected, and we are still determining the cause of the issues.

**Explanation:** This option maintains a formal tone by using phrases like "somewhat unexpected" and "determining the cause," replacing the informal "kind of unexpected" and "figuring out."

**Question 14**

**Answer:** A) She performed exceptionally well in the interview and secured the job.

**Explanation:** This revision maintains a formal tone by replacing the informal phrase "totally crushed" with "performed exceptionally well" and "secured the job," which are more appropriate for a formal passage.

**Question 15**

**Answer:** A) The presentation was highly informative and well-executed.

**Explanation:** The phrase "highly informative" and "well-executed" maintain a formal tone, whereas "super informative" and "really well done" are more casual.

**Question 16**

**Answer:** A) The team is currently working on it and should complete the task shortly.

**Explanation:** This revision maintains a formal tone by using "complete the task shortly" instead of the more informal "be done pretty soon."

**Question 17**

**Answer:** A) We are nearing completion and expect to finalize things soon.

**Explanation:** The use of "nearing completion" and "finalize things soon" maintains a professional tone, in contrast to the more casual "wrap things up quickly."

**Question 18**

**Answer:** A) The technology was cutting-edge and highly practical.

**Explanation:** This revision uses formal language like "cutting-edge" and "highly practical," avoiding the more casual "super useful" in order to maintain a consistent tone.

**Question 19**

**Answer:** A) The speaker delivered an excellent presentation that was well-received by the audience.

**Explanation:** The formal phrases "delivered an excellent presentation" and "well-received by the audience" are appropriate for maintaining a professional tone, compared to the more informal "gave a great talk" and "everyone loved it."

**Question 20**

**Answer:** A) The marketing strategy was highly effective and significantly benefited the company.

**Explanation:** This revision maintains a formal tone by using precise, professional language like "highly effective" and "significantly benefited," rather than the informal "on point" and "helped a ton."

# Section 1: Clarifying Ambiguous Sentences

**Question 1**

**Answer:** A) Despite receiving many complaints, the company was slow and unclear in responding to the issues.

**Explanation:** This revision improves clarity by rephrasing the sentence to indicate that the company's response was both slow and unclear. It eliminates ambiguity by directly linking the company's response to the complaints and making the statement more straightforward.

**Question 2**

**Answer:** A) The scientist's hypothesis was more complex than initially thought and confused much of the audience.

**Explanation:** This revision clarifies that the hypothesis was more complicated than originally expected and that this complexity led to confusion. The sentence is more precise and removes any ambiguity about what caused the confusion.

**Question 3**

**Answer:** A) The report listed several recommendations, but none were specific enough to address the main concerns.

**Explanation:** This revision clearly communicates that while the report included recommendations, none of them were sufficiently specific to address the key concerns, improving the directness and clarity of the original sentence.

**Question 4**

**Answer:** A) Some team members did not explain their ideas clearly during the project discussion, leading to misunderstandings.

**Explanation:** This option clearly connects the lack of clarity in explanations to the misunderstandings that occurred. It eliminates ambiguity by specifying that the problem arose during the discussion and was due to the unclear communication of ideas.

**Question 5**

**Answer:** A) Although the environmental impact report was comprehensive, it lacked critical details about the local wildlife.

**Explanation:** This revision makes it clear that while the report was thorough, it did not include important information about local wildlife, thus improving clarity and removing any uncertainty about what details were missing.

**Question 6**

**Answer:** A) Poor organization of the event led to confusion about where people were supposed to go and what they were supposed to do.

**Explanation:** This option clearly states that the event's poor organization caused confusion regarding directions and actions, improving clarity by directly linking the cause (poor organization) to the effect (confusion).

**Question 7**

**Answer:** A) The instructions were unclear, which caused everyone to misunderstand how to operate the new system.

**Explanation:** This revision directly links the unclear instructions to the misunderstanding of how to operate the system, improving clarity by eliminating ambiguity and focusing on the cause-and-effect relationship.

**Question 8**

**Answer:** C) The main point of his presentation wasn't clear because he rushed through it too quickly.

**Explanation:** This revision clarifies the cause of the audience's confusion by stating that the presenter rushed, making it difficult to grasp the main point. It eliminates ambiguity by specifying the problem with the presentation.

**Question 9**

**Answer:** C) The company's new policy, despite being well-intentioned, worsened the problem rather than solving it.

**Explanation:** This revision clearly states that the policy, although created with good intentions, made the problem worse. It improves clarity by removing redundancy and making the cause-effect relationship more direct.

**Question 10**

**Answer:** A) The unclear project timeline made it difficult for team members to know when their tasks were due.

**Explanation:** This revision clearly identifies that the unclear timeline caused confusion about task deadlines, improving clarity by making the sentence more direct and focusing on the cause of the difficulty.

**Question 11**

**Answer:** D) The study's results were intriguing, though some questions remained unanswered and unclear.

**Explanation:** This option improves clarity by specifying that unanswered questions were also unclear. It provides a more direct and precise statement of the issue with the study's results.

**Question 12**

**Answer:** A) The meeting location was changed hastily, and many attendees didn't receive the updated information.

**Explanation:** This revision improves clarity by directly linking the hasty decision to change the meeting location to the lack of communication to the attendees, making the sentence more concise and precise.

**Question 13**

**Answer:** A) The way the proposal was written made the main objective unclear.

**Explanation:** This revision eliminates ambiguity by clearly stating that the wording of the proposal caused the main objective to be unclear, improving the precision of the original sentence.

**Question 14**

**Answer:** C) The explanation included unnecessary details that obscured the speaker's point.

**Explanation:** This option improves clarity by directly linking the unnecessary details to the obscured point, making the cause-effect relationship clear and eliminating any ambiguity in the original sentence.

**Question 15**

**Answer:** A) The politician made ambiguous statements, leaving the audience unclear about his stance on the issue.

**Explanation:** This revision improves clarity by clearly linking the ambiguous statements to the audience's lack of understanding of the politician's stance, eliminating vagueness in the original sentence.

**Question 16**

**Answer:** A) The meeting ended suddenly, leaving the next steps unclear.

**Explanation:** This option clarifies that the abrupt end of the meeting caused confusion about the next steps, improving clarity and directness by making the cause-effect relationship explicit.

**Question 17**

**Answer:** A) The lawyer's confusing argument left the jury unsure of her main point.

**Explanation:** This revision improves clarity by specifying that the lawyer's confusing argument caused the jury's uncertainty, removing any ambiguity and focusing directly on the cause of the misunderstanding.

**Question 18**

**Answer:** A) The team struggled to implement the new system because his explanation lacked important details.

**Explanation:** This option clearly states that the lack of details in the explanation caused the team's difficulty in implementing the system, improving the precision and clarity of the original sentence.

**Question 19**

**Answer:** B) Key information was missing from many documents, making it unclear what decisions were required.

**Explanation:** This revision clarifies that missing information in the documents led to confusion about necessary decisions, improving clarity by directly stating the cause-effect relationship.

**Question 20**

**Answer:** A) The vague instructions she gave on operating the equipment caused the staff to make mistakes.

**Explanation:** This revision improves clarity by directly linking the vague instructions to the mistakes made by the staff, eliminating any ambiguity and focusing on the cause-effect relationship.

## Section 2: Enhancing Logical Flow Between Sentences

**Question 1**

**Answer:** C) Because she studied for hours every night, her final exam performance was exceptional.

**Explanation:** This option best improves the flow between the sentences by clearly establishing a cause-effect relationship. Using "Because" effectively connects her studying to her performance, making the transition between ideas smoother and more logical.

**Question 2**

**Answer:** A) After the experiment failed the first time, the team adjusted some variables and achieved success.

**Explanation:** This revision improves the flow by establishing a chronological order between the failure and subsequent success. The cause-effect relationship is clear, and the sentence transitions naturally from the experiment's failure to the adjustments and eventual success.

**Question 3**

**Answer:** B) The decision to launch the new product in the spring coincided with a period of economic growth.

**Explanation:** This option improves the flow by connecting the company's decision to the external economic conditions. The use of "coincided" creates a logical connection between the timing of the product launch and the economic context.

## Question 4

**Answer:** B) Because the city's infrastructure was in dire need of repairs, several bridges were closed for safety reasons.

**Explanation:** This option improves flow by using "Because" to directly link the need for repairs with the closure of the bridges, creating a clear cause-effect relationship that enhances the logical connection between the two ideas.

## Question 5

**Answer:** A) Students often struggle with time management, leading them to fail to complete their assignments on time.

**Explanation:** This revision improves the flow by clearly linking the cause (struggling with time management) to the effect (failing to complete assignments). The transition is smooth, with a logical progression of ideas.

## Question 6

**Answer:** C) The shift toward electric cars is driven by increasing environmental concerns.

**Explanation:** This option improves the flow by presenting the shift toward electric cars as a response to growing environmental concerns. The sentence is concise and maintains a clear connection between the cause and effect.

## Question 7

**Answer:** A) As the character faces a difficult decision, he also grapples with feelings of guilt and regret.

**Explanation:** This revision improves the flow by linking the character's decision-making process with his emotional struggles. The use of "As" helps to show that these events are happening simultaneously, creating a smoother connection between the two ideas.

## Question 8

**Answer:** B) Because the factory was outdated and inefficient, the company decided to build a new facility.

**Explanation:** This option improves flow by making the causal relationship explicit. The use of "Because" directly links the factory's condition to the company's decision to build a new facility, making the sentence clearer and more logical.

## Question 9

**Answer:** A) Despite the critical acclaim for its direction and cinematography, the movie's box office performance was disappointing.

**Explanation:** This revision improves the flow by using "Despite" to contrast the movie's critical acclaim with its poor box office performance. The transition is smooth, highlighting the surprising outcome of the situation.

## Question 10

**Answer:** A) In addition to making communication faster and more efficient, new technologies have improved access to information.

**Explanation:** This option improves the flow by smoothly transitioning between two related benefits of new technologies. "In addition to" clearly connects the improvements in communication with the increased access to information.

## Question 11

**Answer:** B) In addition to using bold colors, the artist frequently incorporates geometric shapes into her work.

**Explanation:** This revision improves flow by linking two artistic techniques. "In addition to" provides a smooth transition, highlighting both the use of bold colors and geometric shapes in the artist's work.

**Question 12**

**Answer:** B) Despite the setbacks they faced, the team ultimately completed the project on time.

**Explanation:** This option improves flow by clearly showing the contrast between the team's setbacks and their eventual success. The use of "Despite" makes the relationship between the challenges and the outcome more coherent.

**Question 13**

**Answer:** A) Regular exercise not only helps maintain physical fitness but also benefits mental well-being.

**Explanation:** This revision improves flow by linking the benefits of exercise for both physical and mental health. The phrase "not only…but also" creates a balanced and logical connection between the two ideas.

**Question 14**

**Answer:** B) Interest rates are expected to rise, which could affect consumer spending.

**Explanation:** This option improves the flow by using "which" to link the expected rise in interest rates with its potential effect on consumer spending. The sentence clearly shows how one event could influence the other.

**Question 15**

**Answer:** D) She enrolled in a rigorous pre-med program as the first step toward achieving her goal of a medical career.

**Explanation:** This option improves flow by clearly linking her decision to enroll in the pre-med program with her ultimate goal of pursuing a medical career. The sentence logically connects her actions with her aspirations.

## Section 3: Combining and Restructuring Sentences for Coherence

**Question 1**

**Answer:** C) Sitting on the windowsill, the cat looked outside.

**Explanation:** This option combines the sentences by using a participial phrase ("Sitting on the windowsill"), which improves coherence and keeps the original meaning intact. It is concise and clearly shows the relationship between the two actions.

**Question 2**

**Answer:** C) He enjoys reading books and writing stories.

**Explanation:** This sentence is the most efficient way to combine the two ideas. It maintains clarity and simplifies the structure without changing the meaning, improving readability and coherence.

**Question 3**

**Answer:** A) The scientist conducted the experiment and carefully recorded the results.

**Explanation:** This option most effectively combines the sentences by using a simple conjunction ("and") to link the actions. It keeps the meaning clear and the sentence structure straightforward.

**Question 4**

**Answer:** A) The beautiful painting captured the essence of nature.

**Explanation:** This option combines the sentences smoothly by turning "beautiful" into a descriptive adjective and linking it directly with the action of capturing the essence of nature. It improves coherence while keeping the meaning intact.

**Question 5**

**Answer:** A) After finishing her homework, Maria went to the park.

**Explanation:** This option provides a clear sequence of events, improving the flow by using "After" to indicate that finishing the homework came before going to the park. It maintains clarity and the original meaning.

## Question 6

**Answer:** C) The setting sun turned the sky orange.

**Explanation:** This option simplifies the two sentences by combining them into one concise sentence that directly links the setting sun with the change in the sky's color, maintaining the original meaning while improving coherence.

## Question 7

**Answer:** A) He is a talented singer who has won several awards for his performances.

**Explanation:** This option combines the sentences in a clear and logical way by adding a relative clause ("who has won several awards"), improving the flow and keeping the meaning intact.

## Question 8

**Answer:** D) She loves baking cookies, which she then gives to her friends.

**Explanation:** This sentence combines the two ideas effectively by using a relative clause ("which she then gives to her friends"). It maintains the original meaning while improving the sentence's coherence.

## Question 9

**Answer:** B) Studying hard for his exams, John passed with excellent grades.

**Explanation:** This option uses a participial phrase ("Studying hard for his exams") to combine the sentences and clearly shows the cause-effect relationship between John's hard work and his success.

## Question 10

**Answer:** A) The storm damaged many homes and flooded the streets.

**Explanation:** This option most efficiently combines the sentences using "and" to link the two effects of the storm. It maintains the original meaning while keeping the sentence simple and coherent.

## Question 11

**Answer:** A) The captivating novel keeps the reader engaged until the last page.

**Explanation:** This option smoothly combines the sentences by describing the novel as "captivating" and showing how it keeps the reader engaged. It maintains the original meaning while improving flow and coherence.

## Question 12

**Answer:** B) Taking a deep breath, she stepped onto the stage.

**Explanation:** This sentence effectively combines the two actions by using a participial phrase ("Taking a deep breath"). It maintains the original meaning and provides a natural flow between the actions.

## Question 13

**Answer:** A) The bright and colorful flowers in the garden are blooming.

**Explanation:** This option efficiently combines the sentences by integrating the descriptions of the flowers ("bright and colorful") and their action ("blooming") in a clear and concise way.

## Question 14

**Answer:** A) He bought a fuel-efficient, environmentally friendly car.

**Explanation:** This option combines the sentences smoothly by condensing the descriptions of the car ("fuel-efficient" and "environmentally friendly") into a single sentence, maintaining coherence and clarity.

## Question 15

**Answer:** A) The park, with its many beautiful walking trails, is a great place to relax.

**Explanation:** This option combines the sentences by using a prepositional phrase ("with its many beautiful walking trails") to link the park's features with its relaxing nature. It improves flow while keeping the original meaning.

## Section 4: Eliminating Redundancies and Wordiness

**Question 1**

**Answer:** C) We are reviewing the results.

**Explanation:** This option eliminates unnecessary phrases like "At this point in time" and "currently," making the sentence concise and direct. The word "currently" is implied by the present continuous verb form.

**Question 2**

**Answer:** A) She made a brief introduction to start the meeting.

**Explanation:** The word "brief" already means short, so "short" is redundant. This revision removes the unnecessary repetition and retains the clarity of the original meaning.

**Question 3**

**Answer:** C) I believe that the project will succeed.

**Explanation:** "In my personal opinion" and "I believe" convey the same idea, so "personal" and "opinion" are redundant. This revision eliminates the repetition, keeping the sentence clear and concise.

**Question 4**

**Answer:** B) He left the room because he was tired.

**Explanation:** This option removes the redundant phrase "The reason why" and streamlines the sentence by directly stating the cause, improving clarity.

**Question 5**

**Answer:** A) The book she wrote was interesting and captivating.

**Explanation:** "That" is unnecessary here, and the sentence becomes more concise by removing it, while still retaining the meaning.

**Question 6**

**Answer:** A) The outcome of the game was a complete surprise to everyone.

**Explanation:** The word "final" is redundant because "outcome" already implies the end result. This revision eliminates the extra word, making the sentence more focused.

**Question 7**

**Answer:** B) Every student must complete the assignment.

**Explanation:** The phrase "Each and every" is redundant, as "every" alone sufficiently conveys the meaning. This option simplifies the sentence without losing clarity.

**Question 8**

**Answer:** A) She stood up to make an announcement.

**Explanation:** "Stood up" and "rose to her feet" are redundant. This revision keeps the action clear and concise without unnecessary repetition.

**Question 9**

**Answer:** C) We experienced a heatwave in July.

**Explanation:** "Extremely hot" is redundant because a heatwave already implies high temperatures. This option eliminates unnecessary words and improves clarity.

**Question 10**

**Answer:** B) He ran to catch the bus that was about to leave.

**Explanation:** The word "quickly" is redundant because running already implies speed. This revision simplifies the sentence and maintains its original meaning.

**Question 11**

**Answer:** A) They postponed the meeting.

**Explanation:** "Until a later date" is redundant because postponing already implies the meeting will occur later. This revision removes unnecessary words, making the sentence more concise.

**Question 12**

**Answer:** C) He added an extension to the document.

**Explanation:** "Extra" is redundant because an extension already implies something added. This revision eliminates redundancy and improves clarity.

**Question 13**

**Answer:** C) The students gathered in the cafeteria for the announcement.

**Explanation:** The phrase "gathered together" is redundant, as "gathered" alone implies coming together. This revision simplifies the sentence while retaining the original meaning.

**Question 14**

**Answer:** A) She always plans ahead to avoid last-minute rushes.

**Explanation:** "Plans ahead" already implies doing something in advance, so "ahead of time" is redundant. This revision keeps the sentence concise and clear.

**Question 15**

**Answer:** C) He returned home after a long day at work.

**Explanation:** "Returned back" is redundant, as "returned" already means going back. This option eliminates the redundancy while keeping the sentence clear.

## Section 5: Improving Paragraph Coherence

**Question 1**

**Answer:** C) The city is known for its towering skyscrapers and bustling streets, making the park a perfect escape from the noise.

**Explanation:** This sentence shifts the focus from the park to the city, disrupting the coherence of the paragraph, which is about the park as a relaxing space. Removing this sentence improves the overall focus on the park's atmosphere.

**Question 2**

**Answer:** D) The company offers great benefits, including health insurance and paid vacation days.

**Explanation:** This sentence is irrelevant to the topic of the paragraph, which is about the meeting and John being late. Removing this sentence improves the paragraph's focus on the meeting.

**Question 3**

**Answer:** C) The campus library is open 24 hours a day, which provides students with a place to study.

**Explanation:** This sentence does not connect directly to the paragraph's focus on time management during exams. It introduces an unrelated detail, and removing it improves the coherence of the paragraph.

**Question 4**

**Answer:** D) The climate is an important factor to consider when planning a trip.

**Explanation:** While relevant in some contexts, this sentence disrupts the flow of a paragraph focused on the experience of traveling and exploring new places. Removing it improves coherence.

**Question 5**

**Answer:** C) The cafeteria in the office building is being renovated to offer more food options.

**Explanation:** This sentence introduces an unrelated detail about the cafeteria, which does not connect to the discussion of the company's marketing strategy. Removing it improves coherence.

**Question 6**

**Answer:** C) The local museum offers art classes for children.

**Explanation:** This sentence is unrelated to the focus of the paragraph, which is about outdoor summer activities. Removing it keeps the paragraph focused on outdoor activities.

**Question 7**

**Answer:** C) The new shopping mall is expected to open next month.

**Explanation:** This sentence is irrelevant to the paragraph's focus on the benefits of reading. Removing it improves the paragraph's overall coherence.

**Question 8**

**Answer:** D) Many people still enjoy sending handwritten letters.

**Explanation:** This sentence contradicts the theme of the paragraph, which focuses on how technology has transformed communication. Removing it improves the paragraph's coherence.

**Question 9**

**Answer:** C) The park next to the restaurant is a great place to take a walk.

**Explanation:** This sentence shifts focus away from the restaurant and its features. Removing it keeps the paragraph focused on the restaurant and its popularity.

**Question 10**

**Answer:** D) Some students prefer to study in groups, while others study alone.

**Explanation:** This sentence introduces an unrelated topic about study preferences, which disrupts the paragraph's focus on study habits and strategies. Removing it improves coherence.

**Question 11**

**Answer:** C) Cooking healthy meals is another important aspect of maintaining a balanced lifestyle.

**Explanation:** This sentence introduces a new topic unrelated to the focus on exercise and its benefits. Removing it improves the coherence of the paragraph.

**Question 12**

**Answer:** C) The gift shop offers a range of unique souvenirs.

**Explanation:** This sentence is unrelated to the main focus on the museum's exhibits and learning opportunities. Removing it improves the paragraph's focus and coherence.

**Question 13**

**Answer:** C) Eating a balanced diet plays a key role in overall health.

**Explanation:** This sentence introduces a new topic about diet, which is unrelated to the focus on physical activity. Removing it improves the coherence of the paragraph.

**Question 14**

**Answer:** D) It was a great way to spend an afternoon.

**Explanation:** This sentence is too general and shifts the focus away from the movie's specific qualities. Removing it improves the paragraph's focus on the movie itself.

**Question 15**

**Answer:** C) The venue for the conference was beautifully decorated with floral arrangements.

**Explanation:** This sentence introduces an irrelevant detail about the venue's decoration, which does not relate to the paragraph's focus on climate change and environmental initiatives. Removing it improves coherence.

# Section 6: Correcting Punctuation and Grammar Errors

### Question 1

**Answer:** B) The scientist's research, which was groundbreaking, changed the way we understand climate change.

**Explanation:** This option correctly places commas around the non-essential clause "which was groundbreaking," clarifying that this clause adds extra information but is not necessary to the main sentence. This punctuation improves clarity and flow.

### Question 2

**Answer:** A) After finishing the report, Sarah went home to rest.

**Explanation:** A comma is needed after the introductory phrase "After finishing the report" to properly separate it from the main clause. This corrects the punctuation while preserving the sentence's meaning.

### Question 3

**Answer:** C) The company plans to expand into new markets; however, they must first secure more funding.

**Explanation:** The semicolon correctly separates two independent clauses that are connected by the transition "however," ensuring proper punctuation and clarity. The comma after "however" is also necessary.

### Question 4

**Answer:** B) The book is about history, science, and literature.

**Explanation:** This option uses correct punctuation for a list of three items. The comma before "and" (known as the Oxford comma) is optional but often used to avoid ambiguity.

### Question 5

**Answer:** A) He's a great athlete; he won three gold medals at the Olympics.

**Explanation:** A semicolon is required to separate two independent clauses that are closely related in meaning. This revision corrects the run-on sentence.

### Question 6

**Answer:** A) We wanted to go on vacation, but the weather was too bad.

**Explanation:** A comma is needed before "but" to correctly separate the two independent clauses, improving the sentence's clarity and grammatical structure.

### Question 7

**Answer:** A) There were three options available: green, blue, and red.

**Explanation:** This option correctly uses a colon to introduce the list of options, and the commas between items in the list are placed appropriately.

### Question 8

**Answer:** D) While driving to the store, I realized I had left my wallet at home.

**Explanation:** A comma is necessary after the introductory clause "While driving to the store" to improve sentence structure and clarity.

### Question 9

**Answer:** B) My favorite activities include hiking, swimming, and biking.

**Explanation:** This option correctly uses commas to separate items in a list. It eliminates unnecessary colons or extra punctuation, making the sentence clear and correct.

**Question 10**

**Answer:** B) The meeting is scheduled for Monday, April 4th, at 10 a.m.; please arrive on time.

**Explanation:** A semicolon is required to correctly separate the independent clauses. This revision resolves the comma splice and maintains the sentence's clarity.

## Section 7: Replacing Vague Words with Specific Language

**Question 1**

**Answer:** A) The event was a tremendous success, with hundreds of people attending.

**Explanation:** This revision improves the sentence by providing more specific details. "Tremendous success" is more descriptive than "big success," and "hundreds of people" gives a clearer sense of scale than "many people."

**Question 2**

**Answer:** A) He gave a passionate speech during the ceremony.

**Explanation:** "Passionate" is a more specific and evocative term than "nice," improving the clarity and impact of the sentence by conveying the speaker's emotional investment.

**Question 3**

**Answer:** C) The artist's new painting is captivating, featuring vivid colors and bold strokes.

**Explanation:** This option enhances the sentence by providing specific details about what makes the painting captivating. "Vivid colors" and "bold strokes" give concrete imagery that replaces the vague term "good."

**Question 4**

**Answer:** A) She had an informative and engaging experience at the conference.

**Explanation:** This revision replaces the vague term "interesting" with more precise descriptions of the experience ("informative" and "engaging"), making the sentence clearer and more meaningful.

**Question 5**

**Answer:** A) The restaurant offers a variety of dishes, including seafood, pasta, and vegan options.

**Explanation:** By specifying the types of dishes offered (seafood, pasta, vegan), this option improves clarity and provides concrete information, making the sentence more informative than "many dishes."

**Question 6**

**Answer:** B) The company made significant changes to the policy, including adjustments to work hours and vacation benefits.

**Explanation:** This revision replaces the vague "a lot of changes" with "significant changes" and provides specific examples (work hours and vacation benefits), which improves the precision of the sentence.

**Question 7**

**Answer:** A) She had a major problem with the budget for her project.

**Explanation:** This option improves the sentence by specifying the nature of the problem ("budget"), replacing the vague term "big problem" with a more precise and informative description.

**Question 8**

**Answer:** A) The presentation was informative, and the audience was engaged.

**Explanation:** "Informative" and "engaged" are specific terms that describe both the content of the presentation and the audience's reaction, replacing the vague "good" and "liked it" with more meaningful details.

**Question 9**

**Answer:** A) The car sped down the road at 80 miles per hour.

**Explanation:** This revision replaces the vague "fast" with a specific speed ("80 miles per hour"), providing concrete information that enhances clarity and specificity.

**Question 10**

**Answer:** A) He completed the project efficiently and delivered excellent results.

**Explanation:** This option replaces vague terms like "quickly" and "good" with "efficiently" and "excellent," which are more precise and give a clearer sense of the quality of the work.

## Time Management Instructions:

It is crucial for students to manage their time efficiently during each section of the SAT. Encourage students to keep track of the time as they progress through the questions, ensuring that they do not spend too long on any one question. Remind them that pacing is key: spending excessive time on difficult questions can create pressure and reduce performance on easier questions.

Advise students to approach each question with focus but also to recognize when they are stuck. In such cases, they should mark the question, move on, and return to it later if time allows. This strategy helps prevent getting bogged down and ensures they complete the section with enough time to review flagged questions. Developing a time-management routine during practice tests will build their confidence and improve overall performance during the real exam.

**Thank you for choosing this book as part of your SAT preparation journey!** I hope it has empowered you with the skills and confidence you need to achieve your goals. Your success is my greatest reward, and I would be truly grateful if you could share your experience by leaving a review on Amazon. Your feedback not only helps me grow but also assists other students in finding the resources they need. Thank you for your support, and best of luck on your path to success!

Made in the USA
Las Vegas, NV
27 November 2024

12733763R00260